MONASH

THE OUTSIDER WHO WON A WAR

LIEUTENANT GENERAL SIR JOHN MONASH,
COMMANDER OF THE AUSTRALIAN CORPS:

'. . . the only General of creative originality produced in
the First World War . . .'
A.J.P. TAYLOR

'Monash was, according to the testimony of those who knew well his
genius for war and what he accomplished by it, the most resourceful
General in the whole of the British Army.'
LLOYD GEORGE

'He was in some ways an utter contrast to the traditional idea of a
great military commander . . . He, more than anyone, fulfilled the idea
that developed in the war – that the scale and nature of operations
required a "big business" type of commander, a great constructive and
organising brain. He views were as large as his capacity.'
SIR BASIL LIDDELL HART

ALSO BY ROLAND PERRY

The Fifth Man
Hidden Power: The Programming of the President
The Exile: Wilfred Burchett, Reporter of Conflict
Mel Gibson, Actor, Director, Producer
Bradman's Best: Sir Donald Bradman's Selection of the Best Team in
Cricket History
Bradman's Best Ashes Teams
The Don: A Biography of Sir Donald Bradman
Captain Australia: A History of the Celebrated Captains of Australian
Test Cricket
Bold Warnie: Shane Warne and Australia's Rise to Cricket Dominance
Waugh's Way: The Steve Waugh Story: learner, legend, leader
Lethal Hero
Elections Sur Ordinateur
Shane Warne, Master Spinner
Programme for a Puppet (fiction)
Blood is a Stranger (fiction)
Faces in the Rain (fiction)

Documentary Films
The Programming of the President
The Raising of a Galleon's Ghost

MONASH

THE OUTSIDER
WHO WON A WAR

A biography of Australia's greatest
military commander

ROLAND PERRY

RANDOM HOUSE AUSTRALIA

Random House Australia Pty Ltd
20 Alfred Street, Milsons Point, NSW 2061
http://www.randomhouse.com.au

Sydney   New York   Toronto
London   Auckland   Johannesburg

First published in hardback by Random House Australia in 2004
Paperback edition first published 2005

National Library of Australia
Cataloguing-in-Publication Entry

Perry, Roland, 1946–.
Monash: the outsider who won a war.

Bibliography.
Includes index.
ISBN 1 74051 280 4.
ISBN 1 74051 364 9 (pbk.)

1. Monash, John Sir. 1865–1931. 2. Australia. Army –
Officers – Biography. 3. Generals – Australia – Biography.
4. Engineers – Australia – Biography. 5. World War,
1914–1918 – Campaigns. 6. Australia – History – 20th century
I. Title.

355.0092

Cover design by Darian Causby/Highway 51
Maps by Trudi Canavan/The Telltale Art
Index by Frances Paterson/Olive Grove Indexing Services
Author photograph by David Smith
Typeset by Midland Typesetters, Maryborough, Victoria
Printed and bound by Griffin Press, Netley, South Australia

10 9 8 7 6 5 4 3 2 1

To Major Warren Perry
and the memory of Tim Burstall

Front cover image: *The Last Salute:* Monash
on his favourite white charger for the last time
reviewing his diggers as they march on Anzac
Day 1931.

Contents

List of Maps		ix
Introduction	Engineer of Victory: 8 August 1918	xi
1	Going for Gold	1
2	School of Soft Knocks	11
3	The Engineer's Language	32
4	Battle Engagement	53
5	Rebirth	68
6	A Bridge Too Far	92
7	Pipe Dreams Realised	113
8	1914: The Enemy Within	147
9	Thirty Days in Hell	176
10	Gallipoli Breakout	204
11	Goodbye to 4th Brigade	237
12	The King and I	253
13	Western Front 1917: Messines	270
14	Broodseinde Up; Passchendaele Down	288
15	1918: Ludendorff's Lunge	310
16	Commander to the Corps	329
17	Breakthrough at Amiens	354
18	Jugular Days: Mont St Quentin and Péronne	388
19	Operation Hindenburg Line	412
20	Afterglow	444
21	Back to the Future	462

22	Many Causes; Enough Time	486
23	Zenith and End	501
24	Postscript	517
Acknowledgements		532
Notes		535
Bibliography		551
Index		558

List of Maps

Page 177: *Gallipoli.* The Hamilton plan saw a double invasion at Cape Helles by mainly British Forces, and Anzac Cove by mainly Anzac Forces.

Page 182: *Australian Positions Held at Anzac Cove from 26 April 1915.* Anzac forces attained these positions by the second day of the invasion – 26 April. No further territory was taken beyond the arc above Anzac Cove until evacuation eight months later.

Page 217: *The August Offensive 1915: The Battle of Sari Bair: The 'Left Hook' Attempt by Monash's 4th Brigade.* Hamilton and Birdwood decided to break out of the locked-down Anzac Cove by advancing north in a semi-circle heading for Hill 971, held by the Turks.

Page 285: *The Flanders Campaign 1917: Battles of Monash's 3rd Division.* John Monash's 3rd Division in 1917 was part of successful British attacks on German-held Messines and Broodseinde. Haig's insistence in attacking during atrocious conditions in October at Passchendaele ensured defeat.

Page 313: *Advances of Monash's 3rd Division during March, April, May, June & July 1918.* Monash's 3rd Division took a stand against the German advance on 27 March 1918, held the line and gradually pushed the enemy back.

Page 353: *Battle of Hamel: 4 July 1918.* Monash gave new meaning to the expression 'military precision' with his planning to take Hamel. His use of tanks at night, and various tactics such as smoke and noise screens, along with a minimum of casualties, presaged the way he would attempt to win the war for the Allies. He had a deadline. In three months, the 1918–19 winter would set in.

Page 373: *Battle of Amiens on 8 August 1918, Spearheaded by the Australian Corps.* Monash reached the peak of his powers as a battlefield commander with the success of his troops in crashing through the German lines on 8 August 1918.

Page 387: *Battle of Chuignes and Bray, Spearheaded by AIF's 3rd Division, 23 August 1918.* Monash's success on 23 August 1918 in taking Chuignes and Bray convinced him he could obliterate the enemy if given the opportunity.

Page 403: *The Battle for Péronne and Mont St Quentin, 31 August – 3 September 1918 Exclusively by AIF's 2nd, 3rd and 5th Divisions.* Fourth Army Chief Rawlinson scoffed at Monash's conviction that the AIF on its own could take Mont St Quentin and Péronne with remnants of his battle-weary 2nd, 3rd and 5th Divisions. Monash proved correct in the toughest close combat by the Australians in the push to the Hindenburg Line.

Pages 414–415: *The Australian Corps Campaign in France: 4 July – 5 October 1918.* The AIF spearheaded the last three months of battles by the British forces from Amiens to Montbrehain, winning every major battle. This forced the Germans to sue for peace.

Page 425: *Battle for Hargicourt and Hindenburg Outpost Line, 18 September 1918, Spearheaded by AIF's 1st and 4th Divisions.* The AIF's sense of invincibility continued on 18 September with the smashing of the outer shell of the Hindenburg Line – the nine-kilometre-wide, eighty-kilometre-long German defence system. Monash's use of dummy tanks, among his many tricks, caused the quick capitulation of the enemy.

Page 435: *Breaching of the Hindenburg Defences by AIF's 2nd, 3rd and 5th Divisions with the US 27th and 30th Divisions, 29 September – 5 October 1918.* Monash pushed his troops one last time to break the complete Hindenburg fortification with the help (and hindrance) of the American forces. The last battle, by the 2nd Division, to take Montbrehain further east, was an unnecessary fight too far for the AIF ordered by Haig and Rawlinson.

ENGINEER OF VICTORY: 8 AUGUST 1918

Lieutenant General Sir John Monash, the commander of the Australian Corps, paced the 130-metre drive of his HQ, the Château de Bertangles, from its steps to its medieval front gates. It was just after 4 a.m. on 8 August 1918. The night sky was black except for the odd artillery shell. Planes buzzed overhead, drowning the squeal of tanks beginning their crawl forward like giant armadillos. The air was heavy with pungent wafts of fuel, smoke and earlier gas attacks. In less than twenty minutes, the five Australian divisions under his command east of Amiens on the Western Front in France would fight together for the first time in war. They would be the spearhead of the massive Allied offensive against the German Army.

There was more than an edge of anticipation in Monash's step as he glanced at his watch every few minutes. His movement along the path and agility up and down the château steps were those of a man half his fifty-three years. The build-up to this most important battle of the war had seen him shedding weight until his frame was as lean and hard as that of any commander in the field. His face would never betray nerves or fear. Monash had trained himself that way.

This event on 8 August was the most important in Australia's history, next to 25 April 1915, when the Anzacs had landed at Gallipoli. Monash more than anyone else would foster the importance of that day during the disastrous invasion of Turkey, which marked Australia's entry into the war. But his expectations as the man in charge of this attack were greater. Heroic stalemate and honourable retreat would not be enough here. Nothing short of a smashing victory would do.

Monash had unbounded faith in the fighting capacities of his troops, who formed the biggest corps on the entire Western Front. In turn, the soldiers had a growing faith in their commander. He had a reputation, in modern parlance, as a 'winner'. Monash's planning was seen first when he organised the defence of Monash Valley at Gallipoli. Then 40,000 Turks in the hills above had been set against 12,500 Anzacs locked in an arc beyond the beaches below. His approach to preparation was perfection to the point of obsession unmatched in the annals of military history. His concern that his soldiers should not be used in unnecessarily dangerous operations had filtered through to every digger at the front. His attitude was diametrically opposed to the apparent 'men as cannon fodder', bumbling battle philosophy of the British High Command. This approach had seen hundreds of thousand of soldiers sacrificed in the war. The British Army had not had a decisive win until Monash took charge of the Australians in mid-1918.

He was as ruthless as any commander on either side. But it was anathema to him to fight unless he had prepared so meticulously that he was certain of victory. Anticipation of a huge breach of the German defences only minutes away before dawn set him on edge on this cool summer morning. This was his biggest battle so far.

At 4.15 a.m. Monash stood on the steps of the château, ready.

Most of the German Army was catching precious moments of sleep. Enemy sentries were oblivious to what now sent a shiver up the Australian Corps Commander's spine. A hundred thousand of his infantry, spread over twenty kilometres, waited for the signal to start the attack of Amiens. Some were already crawling forward to get within seventy metres of the German line. It was about to be hit by the biggest single artillery barrage of the war.

4.16 a.m. 'All feel to make sure their bayonets are locked,' Monash recounted, 'or to set their steel helmets.' Company and platoon commanders, whistles suspended near their mouths, glanced at their watches. They gave a last look over their command. Their runners were by their sides. The officers detailed to control the direction in which the infantry would move had their compasses set.

'Carrying parties shoulder their burdens, and adjust the straps,' Monash imagined. 'Pioneers grasp their picks and shovels; engineers take up their stores of explosives and primers and fuses . . .'

4.17 a.m. Monash's heart beat faster. His blood pressure would be up as it always was at tense moments. Less than 600 metres from him, his machine and Lewis gunners whispered to their magazine and belt-box carriers to make sure they followed up. The corps' Stokes mortar carriers slung their heavy loads. Their loaders checked to see whether their cartridge haversacks were in reach.

Planes kept buzzing overhead. Tanks clamoured forward.

Monash the battle commander was also Monash the manager. He spared a thought for the 'scores of telegraph operators'. They sat by their equipment at HQ with their 'message forms and registers ready to hand, bracing themselves for the rush of signal traffic'. There would be a torrent within moments.[1]

Dozens of staff officers spread their maps at Bertangles and in the field behind the lines. They would use coloured pencils to record the stream of information.

4.18 a.m. In pits and trenches the last guns were run up, loaded and laid on the opening lines of fire.

4.19 a.m. Scores of sergeants checked the range. Layers stood silently, lanyards in hand. The section officers, watches on wrists, counted the last seconds. Thirty seconds. Twenty seconds. Ten seconds.

'FIRE.'

More than a thousand guns began Monash's beloved 'symphony . . . a great illumination lights up the Eastern horizon; the whole complex organisation, extending far back to areas almost beyond earshot of the guns, begins to move forward'.

Out in the field, Gunner J.R. Armitage recalled: 'All hell broke loose and we heard nothing more. The world was enveloped in sound and flame, and our ears just couldn't cope. The ground shook.'[2]

Lieutenant Colonel Arthur Wilson of the 7th Field Ambulance, who controlled more than 400 men, twenty-nine vehicles and seventeen horsed ambulances, noted in his diary: 'At 4.20 a.m., zero hour, the barrage opened with a terrific crash. Fortunately the retaliatory bombardment was non-existent.'

The attack had come as a complete surprise to the Germans. Reflecting the concerns of his vital part of the operation, Wilson added: '. . . the one thing of which we had the greatest fear, i.e. an intensive Gas [mainly mustard gas] bombardment as the men formed up on the "jumping off" tape, did not eventuate.'[3]

One of Monash's staff, Major Walter Berry, said: 'Sir, this is a most wonderful day for you.'

Monash put his hand on his shoulder and replied: 'No, Berry. It is a wonderful day for Australia. History will bear this out.' Monash entered his office. His chief of staff, Brigadier General Blamey, was there, smoking a cigar, his feet up on the desk.

'I have nothing to do,' Blamey said, 'so we can wait while they count thousands of prisoners.'

Monash was not ready to relax and reach for his beloved Havelock tobacco and pipe. Instead he had a cigarette. This was more a signal of nerves and concentration for him, as he stood at a window watching his concert from Hades. He was thrilled to appreciate that 'every man, every unit, every vehicle and every tank' advanced as the early summer dawn began to break. The commander was perhaps carried away with creative and theatrical analogies when he noted that the deafening artillery blast 'surely surpasses in dynamic splendour any other manifestation of collective effort'.[4]

Not for the German Army, rudely awoken. It was Armageddon. The barrage rained on them. Those who had collected their senses scrambled for their helmets and weapons amidst the air-splitting sounds of exploding shells. They faced the menacing sight of those brutal tanks emerging from the mist. Within minutes vision was lost, except for flashes. A cloak of dust, smoke and spume blinded the stunned soldiers. The German Army did what any force would do under the same fierce attack: it retreated. Many soldiers left their guns, big and small. Some – the foolhardy and the frozen – braced themselves and returned fire. But the Germans were overrun.

Every tentacle of this mighty Australian octopus was coordinating well in the first hour.

Arthur Wilson noted at 5.20 a.m., one hour into the battle:

All the cars and wagons [ambulances] moved forward to their stations . . . as arranged and on time, although some considerable difficulty was experienced in getting the horses past the heavy guns and 18 pounders. A thick fog made it impossible to see more than 20 or 30 yards ahead . . . things were going well as droves of German prisoners were coming back along the main road. They were equipped with stretchers, and were carrying out wounded (both Australian and German).[5]

The Australian Corps had already penetrated the enemy lines to the designed imaginary 'green line' – the first phase objective. It carried the attacking divisions more than three kilometres. The return artillery died, as if the enemy was running out of shells. He wasn't. The artillery was being captured, which Monash had demanded be done in the first phase of the operation. The harm done to the attacking forces was minimised.

The enemy's garrisons were mostly destroyed or captured. The Australians kept coming, swooping into the second and third phases in a 'walkover'. The 2nd and 3rd Divisions, which had spearheaded the assault, came to a halt, their job done.

The Battle of Amiens had been going 150 minutes.

Monash kept updated his two immediate superiors, Field Marshal Douglas Haig, leader of the British forces in France, and the British Fourth Army Commander, Sir Henry Rawlinson, at Fourth Army HQ.

At 7 a.m. he telegraphed: 'Gailly Village and Accroche Wood captured. Enemy artillery has ceased along my whole front. Flank Corps [British and Canadians] apparently doing well.'[6]

The pea-soup fog helped the attack forces, but hindered the planes that Monash had requested for intelligence work at the front. Still the phone and telegraph were used, as were pigeons.

By 8 a.m. the fog veil had lifted to reveal a stunning view of the Somme Valley. The mid-summer sun filtered through the haze over the steep wooded slopes and folds of the northern riverside, Chipilly Spur. Monash feared this forbidding ridge would give him trouble. Rawlinson had refused him control of the assault on it, leaving it in the hands of an inexperienced British corps. Less worrying since they were already under Australian command were the flatter grass and wheat spurs on the southern approach. They seemed colourful and even serene. Scattered parties of Australian infantry were on the long, flat top of the finger east of the 'Long Gully' from Lamont to Cerisy, and across the summit of the Villers-Bretonneux plateau. Some were still digging; others were looking out from their newly dug trenches. More still strolled or stood in groups. Some smoked. They might have appeared nonchalant to the untrained eye. But these hardened Australian troops from the 2nd and 3rd Divisions were letting tension drain from them. They had finished their fighting for the moment at the 3500-yard (three-kilometre) 'green line' – the first objective. Soldiers from 4th and 5th Divisions leap-frogged them as planned in pursuit of the scattered enemy. Mobile artillery was more active as it was pushed forward. Pioneers and engineers were clearing and repairing roads.

Tanks in their hundreds dotted the landscape. Only a few had been immobilised. Two sizzled in meltdowns from direct artillery hits. Smoke spiralled from them. Most were operational, staying more or less in line with the troops. Monash's tactic of using them at night had been employed just once before: by him at the Battle of Hamel on 4 July 1918. Scepticism about their use in combat had now evaporated, along with the enemy's confidence in facing them. The Australian troops, ahead of any others, had grown to love these cumbersome yet brutal machines-in-arms.

With visibility now good, planes dotted the horizon skies and seemed to be dive-bombing close to the ground. They were swooping lower than 150 metres so that observers could scribble notes or mark maps to show how the Australian and German front lines were changing by the quarter hour. They would then be piloted back to fields near Bertangles. Maps and notes were wrapped in weighted, multicoloured streamers and dropped. Cyclists seemed in constant motion, bumping across fields to collect the intelligence, which was whisked back to a staff office at Bertangles. This further Monash innovation meant that messages were reaching him and his staff from the front line in just ten minutes.

By 8.30 a.m. he was able to tell Haig and Rawlinson that the 'green line' was almost confirmed as captured along the whole corps front. Major conquests in Australian hands included Accroche Wood, Gailly, Warfusee, Lamotte villages and the entire Cerisy Valley. Thousands of German soldiers – heads down, in shock or fatigued – were marching or straggling back behind the Australian lines to be locked into huge 'cages'. The first spoils of this battle – artillery pieces – some with huge bores that had pulverised Amiens for months, were being hauled away.

Maestro Monash continued to be pleased with the mellifluous sounds coming from his military orchestra. Performers not involved in the actual fighting were also blending in. The field ambulance units had already evacuated the wounded of the 2nd and 3rd Divisions. They turned their attention to soldiers of the 4th and 5th as they began engaging the enemy in the so-called 'open warfare' stage.

Arthur Wilson noted that the engineers were working efficiently at mending shell-damaged roads. 'It was soon possible to bring the large [ambulance] cars through to the advanced dressing stations being set up behind the advancing 5th Division.'[7]

The red and blue lines were now the next targets. The aimed-for eight kilometres of fresh territory was almost in Australian hands across its entire front, except for the extreme left north of the river at Chipilly Spur.

Monash's fears and expectations had materialised. The English troops – composed of poorly trained youths and middle-aged men of the 58th Division III Corps – had fought bravely in attempts to dislodge the Germans from their fortified positions on the ridge. But it might have been a case of 'lions led by donkeys'. Poor leadership and organisation had seen the English troops beaten back, leaving Australia's left flank vulnerable to German artillery barrages.

The Australians forged forward on the other side of the Somme. At 10.55 a.m. Monash could report that Cerisy, opposite the difficult Chipilly, had been captured and 300 prisoners rounded up. A quarter of an hour later the advancing troops had taken Morcourt, about a kilometre southeast of Cerisy. The Somme opposite Morcourt flowed in a horseshoe around the troublesome Chipilly Spur. Monash soon could add the town of Bayonvillers positioned about four kilometres southwest of Morcourt in a clean sweep south of the Somme.

'We are nearing our second objective [the red line] and have reached it in places,' Monash telegraphed. Haig was excited when he learned that the Cavalry Brigade, which he had been keen for Monash to push into action, had passed the red line. The whole corps operation was now moving on to the final objective of the blue line.[8]

Just after noon, Major General Hobbs' 5th Division took the railway line town of Harbonnières another kilometre further southeast of Bayonvillers. It had reached the blue line, the operation's southernmost objective.

At 1.15 p.m. Monash had enormous pride and delight in telling Haig and Rawlinson: 'Australian flag hoisted over Harbonnières at midday today. Should be glad if Chief [Haig] would cable this to our Governor-General on behalf of the Australian Corps.'[9]

Germany's Commander-in-Chief, General Ludendorff, acknowledged that 8 August was the worst day for his army in the entire war. It was more than a turning point. Germany would never again in this conflict contemplate victory. It could only hope to defend.

Monash had achieved much at Hamel. But this moment was the finest of his military career, and more. It was the pinnacle of his life. King George V travelled to the battlefield to knight him on 12 August – the first time a king had knighted a commander on the battlefield in 200 years.

The comprehensive breach of German defences of the Battle of Amiens on 8 August was followed by a series of victories commanded by Monash until the end of the war. They established him as an outstanding general. Some experts ranked him as the finest on the Allied side. Among them was Sir Basil Liddell Hart, the leading English military commentator and historian of the time. He said Monash might well have replaced Haig as Commander-in-Chief of the British forces had the war continued into 1919. Liddell Hart was a believer in technological advances changing the face of conflict, something at which Monash excelled. 'He was in some ways an utter contrast to the traditional idea of a great military commander,' Hart said. 'He, more than anyone, fulfilled the idea that developed in the war – that the scale and nature of operations required a "big business" type of commander, a great constructive and organising brain. His views were as large as his capacity.'[10]

This was Monash to the letter. He had made his name in business before the war as a construction engineer. British Prime Minister Lloyd George, who had been thrashing around in 1918 for a Haig replacement, came to the same conclusion, too late to do anything about it. 'Monash would . . . have risen to the height of it [Commander-in-Chief],' Lloyd George wrote, 'but the greatness of his abilities were not brought to the attention of the [British War] Cabinet in any of the dispatches . . . Monash was, according to the testimony of those who knew well his genius for war and what he accomplished by it, the most resourceful General in the whole of the British Army.'[11]

These views were supported by a long list of experts for decades after the war. They included British historian A. J. P. Taylor. He portrayed Monash as 'the only General of creative originality produced in the First World War'. Sir Anthony Eden, who saw combat in the 1914–18 war and went on to be British Prime Minister in the mid-1950s, said much the same thing. So too did the outstanding World War II commander, Field Marshal Bernard Law Montgomery (of Alamein).[12]

Liddell Hart had done his homework on Monash far beyond his combat duties. He observed that the strongest testimony to Monash's capacity was 'the distance he went in spite of a tremendous compound handicap of prejudice'.[13] The historian was considering four admitted huge handicaps of birth (in a far-flung colony), race (Jewish), background (German descent) and the fact that he was from the militia, not the regular army.

How and why did John Monash, the classic outsider, overcome these obstacles and reach a position that allowed him to play a major role in winning World War I? How did such a gentle individual, regarded as a Renaissance man, with his philosophical outlook and love of music, theatre and literature, develop one of the toughest minds of the war?

For answers we must begin with his roots in central Europe.

GOING FOR GOLD

Monash's father Louis was the most adventurous of his family, who had come from Prussia (now Poland). Whereas two of his nine siblings had gone to the USA, Louis in 1853 took the dangerous sixteen-week boat trip halfway around the world to the British colonies in Australia. Like several of his family, he was driven away by the lack of prospects in a Jewish cultural centre, Krotoschin (now Krotoszyn near Poznan in Poland's West) – an unfortunate part of Europe where Prussian (German) and Russian interests clashed. His father Baer-Loebel, a bookbinder turned printer and publisher, had run a successful business, which at its height had thirty-six employees. He specialised in religious books in German and Hebrew and an outstanding Jewish scientific journal.[1] Yet in the forty years he ran it, the operation was always under pressure of collapsing. Many of the Jewish inhabitants left the area. The market for his printing and publishing diminished.

There were several rabbis in the Monasch ancestry, and Baer-Loebel wanted his five sons to be Jewish scholars (he and wife Mathilde Wiener also had five daughters). Louis, the third-born male and the brightest, was, like his father, more business-minded than scholarly. He wished to break from the family traditions and make his own way in the wider world. Louis found work as a clerk in a Berlin trading house. Yet he was restless. He had seen his father build a sizeable business but struggle because of a lack of funds. In 1853, aged twenty-two, he read about the gold rush in Victoria. Louis resolved to visit the colony, make his fortune and return home after five years with funds to help his father and set up his own business.

Louis left on the *Julius Caesar* in early October 1853 with 2000 Marks worth of the trading company's 'wholesale fancy goods and toys', which showed his intention not to join the diggers for gold at Ballarat or Bendigo. Louis had read about the tens of millions of pounds worth of the precious metal being found. Melbourne, which had a population of 23,000 when Victoria became a separate colony from New South Wales in 1851, had attracted another 100,000 inhabitants since the discovery of gold. There were opportunities for merchants to sell to the newly enriched and expanding market.

Louis spent most of the arduous boat trip improving his limited English. When he arrived in Melbourne early in 1854, he was disappointed to learn the city was suffering from a depression. But any foolhardy thoughts about changing his mind and trying his luck in the goldfields were quashed when he was told that the tough conditions had caused discontent among miners. The colonial rulers – dominated by conservative landowners – were demanding mining licence fees. The police on the goldfields were brutal in their collection methods.

Louis found that many English merchants were already selling goods similar to the ones he had brought. Competition had already driven prices down. Louis decided to stay in Melbourne. He liked its frontier spirit with tens of thousands of immigrants flooding in, primarily from Britain, and he saw more opportunities than at home. Within months he formed a partnership with Louis Martin, also from Prussia. They opened Martin & Monash, Soft Goods Importers, trading as commission agents and general merchants in Flinders Lane West in the heart of Melbourne. They began importing wholesale goods from Nuremberg and Frankfurt, including combs, brushes, paper and envelopes, Bohemian glassware, cutlery, concertinas, flutinas, Berlin embroideries, tobacco pipes, snuffboxes, playing cards and beads. Their market was the burgeoning middle class in a city that was fast becoming one of the richest in the world. Monasch became Monash, dropping the 'c' to fit in with the predominantly Anglo-Celtic population.

After a little more than two years he was naturalised as a subject of Queen Victoria in front of Mr Justice Sir Redmond Barry 'to establish himself for life' in the colony. Yet Louis was never at 'home' in his new land and with its English-speaking inhabitants. It was not easy for a 'foreigner', especially if you had a thick German accent, to fit in. He yearned for the culture he had left. In 1858, in order to have some link with his roots, he became secretary of the local German Association, where he could mix with the city's German speakers. It was his only real social life. Louis was lonely.

In the same year, the firm moved to 19 Little Collins Street West. It was struggling. Louis and Martin had no choice but to live on the premises. But Louis had decided to stay longer than the five years he mentioned to his father. He still thought his prospects were better in Australia. By 1860 Victoria's population was 500,000, nearly half the Australian total. If you were going to be in this raw land, Louis informed his father, this was the place to be.

'My son Louis has not returned from Australia,' Baer-Loebel wrote in his diary on 19 April 1860. 'In an early letter he promised me five hundred Marks towards the marriage of my third daughter, Charlotte. But he has sent me no assistance.'[2]

Trade picked up for Martin & Monash. In 1861 Louis wrote to his father asking if he could send his younger brother Max (Baer-Loebel's fourth son), aged sixteen, to help him. The father was sad to see another child move away, especially as it was now eight years since he had seen Louis, the favourite. But Baer-Loebel relented. 'Louis sent forty pounds Sterling for his travelling expenses,' he recorded, 'and I added one hundred Marks to fit him out and to accompany him to Hamburg.'[3]

Max made the long journey with Albert Behrend, Baer-Loebel's grandson (the son of his first-born, Julia) and they arrived in Melbourne on New Year's Day 1862. It prompted Louis to rent a villa in St Kilda for the four of them, including Martin. Business continued to improve. A year later Louis decided to return to Europe to buy goods and perhaps even meet a woman to bring home as his wife. He was thirty-two and feeling it was past the time he should marry.

'One great joy accompanied the misery of the year [1863],' Baer-Loebel wrote at a time when he had to pay off the debts of his sons Isidor and Julius. 'Louis from Melbourne arrived in Krotoschin on the eve of Passover and spent a fortnight with us. His arrival seemed like a ray of hope that I might be able to live my last years happily and free of worry. I have always kept my worries to myself and never wanted to confide them to anyone except Louis.'[4]

He took his son to the cemetery to visit the graves of Louis' grandparents and his sister Hanchen. Baer-Loebel poured out his woes to Louis, explaining how, while helping everyone else in the family, he had fallen into debt himself. Louis was indignant that his father had not written to him much earlier when he could have prevented him falling into a debt spiral. The family had stopped him from writing, he explained. Louis said he would pay off all the debts and send him an annual allowance of at least 1000 Thalers a year.

'My heavy heart danced with joy,' Baer-Loebel recorded, 'to have such a good son.'

Louis travelled to Stettin (Szczecin) in northern Prussia (northwest Poland) to buy goods and to meet Bertha Manesse, the sister of the wife of his brother Julius. He had heard good reports about her. Bertha, who was twenty-one and handsome rather than beautiful with a superb figure, captured Louis's lonely heart on their first meeting. Her large dark eyes enchanted him. Louis wrote back to Max telling him that he had 'fallen in love'. She was his 'black-eyed Xanthippe (shrew)'.[5] She played the piano 'like an angel'. But she was not quite his yet. There were complications.[6]

Her father, Jacob Manesse, was a successful merchant. He had no desire for his daughter to disappear to the ends of the earth. Manesse and the family had drifted from their orthodox Jewish roots. Their town, Dramburg, a few kilometres from Stettin, had only a small Jewish population and no synagogue. Jacob and his wife, Charlotte Benjamin, had assimilated into non-Jewish society. They had no wish to let any family member slip again into the religious culture they had abandoned. They also felt Bertha would be marrying down if she united with this 'Australian'.

Jacob refused Bertha permission to marry or even to communicate with Louis. But that 'feeling of twinned helplessness', as the poet Robert Graves called love at first sight, was powerful. Bertha, like her suitor, was a strong character. She wanted the dashing, worldly Louis, who sent her charming letters via his siblings while on his travels to buy stock for Melbourne. The responses he received boosted his confidence that he should fight for her.

'You may feel quite sure of her,' his sister Ulrike informed him. 'She commissioned me to send you a multitude of greetings and kisses.'[7]

Bertha fought her parents with every emotional trick she could pull, from interminable crying to self-induced illness. But then the wilful, love-struck woman claimed that she was prepared to break with her family and elope to Australia. It was said with such force that her mother knew she meant it. Charlotte persuaded Jacob to relent. Better to have a daughter in the far-off wilderness than no daughter at all. They let the two lovers meet in the hope that familiarity would breed enough contempt to dissuade her from going so far. Less than subtle comments were made about Australia being a desert inhabited by 'savages that might eat her for dinner'. Louis gently and amusingly assured her in letters that there were no 'savages' in Australia. The 'natives', he instructed her, were 'noble hunter-gatherers', not headhunters. Bertha became even more confident of her well-travelled man of the world.[8]

Louis asked for her hand again. This time, Jacob granted it, albeit begrudgingly, with the promises that there would be a civil marriage in Stettin and that Bertha would return to Prussia within five years. To appease both families, they had a civil marriage and a Jewish wedding at Stettin on 15 November 1863. Baer-Loebel travelled from Krotoschin, but without his wife Mathilde Wiener, who was ill. '. . . the young couple came to Krotoschin a week after the nuptials to pay a visit,' a proud Baer-Loebel wrote. 'Before his departure, Louis repeated his promises [of financial support] to me.'[9]

Louis was happy to leave Prussia. War between it and Denmark was brewing, and he wished to be well away. They honeymooned in Paris for a week, then London for just a few days, before taking the boat from Liverpool on 11 February 1864. In his rush to depart, Louis had booked the wrong clipper, taking the rotting *Empire of Peace* instead of the *Star of Peace*. They found themselves with only eight other cabin passengers. The other 259 in steerage included a fair proportion of 'rogues, thieves and drunks'. Many, the experienced Louis reckoned, were on the run from the law. Bertha felt under siege and handicapped by her lack of English, which brought derision from some of their rougher fellow travellers. Instead of fretting in her cabin, she resolved to improve her command of the language.

They could not wait to be on land after a hard trip that lasted eighteen weeks – a month longer than it would have taken on the right clipper. Louis had arranged for Max and Albert to come to the *Empire* as soon as it anchored at Port Melbourne. They rowed over and called out their names, much to the mirth of the abusive English immigrants. Louis and Bertha were lowered with their considerable baggage into the boat.

It was a testing beginning for Bertha. Yet she was resolute. Louis was more than proud of her and his own decision to make her his wife.

✕

Bertha and Louis moved into the St Kilda villa with Max, Albert and Louis Martin. The living quarters were cramped. A setback followed within weeks when Martin had a stroke and left for Prussia where he felt medical care would be better than in the fledgling colony. Martin & Monash was dissolved, although Louis kept trading. The newly-weds moved to a bigger place, Richhill Terrace in Dudley Street, West Melbourne, on the north side of the Flagstaff Gardens.

Unbeknown to Louis, his father had further financial troubles not long after bailing out his first son Julius from bad debts. Julius had misled his father into making loans to him that only fuelled his debt. Baer-Loebel wrote in his diary: 'Louis' visit, and the rumours that he was very rich, and had made great purchases of goods in Europe for export to Australia, had the effect that I lost all my credit. People were convinced that my son had left me a lot of money . . . I found that I could no longer cover my old debts with new bills of exchange.'[10]

He was forced to sell the family home to pay off debts. Even with this sacrifice Baer-Loebel's credit rating was diminished. The pressure seemed too much for his wife Mathilde. She died in April 1864.

Two months after her death, Louis, was unaware of it. But he knew the family was struggling. He wrote and implored his father to let the youngest girl in the family, Ulrike, migrate to Melbourne. 'He hoped to marry her well,' Baer-Loebel noted. 'He promised to provide travelling expenses and a trousseau.' Ulrike was thrilled. Her father was sad, but agreed to her leaving. Her disgraced eldest brother, Julius, who was escaping mounting debt, decided to go with her.

John Monash was born while Baer-Loebel accompanied Ulrike to Berlin, the first leg of her trip to Melbourne. The date was 23 June 1865, according to the birth certificate. All other records filled in by his family and Monash himself put the date as 27 June. Another mistake on the birth certificate makes the date on it unreliable. His birthplace is given as Rachel Terrace when it was Richhill. The most likely explanation is that Louis' strong accent caused the registrar to make the link to the popular Jewish female name.

Naming him 'John' seemed a suitable compromise between its biblical origin and another acknowledgement that he would be brought up a British subject. Calling him after his grandfather would have been a throwback to an older branch of the family. Giving him a first name like Bruce or Douglas would have seemed incongruous.

He grew up cared for by loving, doting parents with plenty of attention from the extended family including Uncle Max, Cousin Albert, Uncle Julius and Aunt ('Tante') Ulrike. He heard and picked up German as quickly as English in a cultured atmosphere dominated by Bertha's expertise at the piano. The Jewish and German links were kept. John would learn Hebrew and all the children would attend the synagogue, but neither Louis nor Bertha was a strong member of their local Jewish communities. Bertha particularly was keen on continuing her family's experience of assimilation. The main aim was to keep options in all walks of life open for the children (John, Mathilde, born in 1869, and Louise, born in 1873) in a new, promising land.

There were no specific signs of genius or any special gifts in young John's early years. Yet at two, Tante Ulrike noticed that he drew railway engines, and he kept sketching well as he grew older. At six in 1871 he started his education at St Stephen's Church of England School in Richmond near his new five-room home, which Louis had bought in Clifton Street. It was in Richmond Hill, an area growing in popularity because of its proximity to the city. Louis named it Germania Cottage. Bertha began teaching John piano and took him to concerts, which he enjoyed.

In 1873 John was showing ability in all subjects at school. He was a quiet, diligent student, whom his headmaster thought industrious, intelligent and promising, at least in his future schooling. He now had a gift for drawing caricatures, and he amused his friends with sketches of them. Louis wrote to his father about the boy's progress, which included a school prize in his second year.

Baer-Loebel, now seventy-two, retired, free of debt and comfortable thanks to Louis' monthly allowance, wrote to John on his eighth birthday: 'I am glad to hear that you are doing well at school; if you go on like that, you will become a great, good and famous man.'

John kept the letter as a little piece of inspiration from a man he had heard good things about all his short life, but would never meet.

Louis had struggled ever since the enforced split with Martin. He had never managed to make profits from his buying spree in Europe and was in debt. In 1873 there were no prospects of a worthwhile cash flow from selling goods that were no longer a novelty in prosperous Melbourne. His brothers, Max and Julius, also without any trade or profession, tried their hands as storekeepers in country New South Wales at Narrandera and Wanganella. Louis had little choice but to attempt rural shopkeeping, too. In 1874 he moved to Jerilderie in the Riverina area of southern New South Wales and opened a general store. Bertha was unhappy about moving to the country. She enjoyed the cultural opportunities of Melbourne and disliked the idea of isolation in the bush. Reluctantly, she, John, now nine, Mathilde, five, and Louise, one, joined Louis at the beginning of 1875.

Jerilderie was a frontier town with just 250 people living in about fifty wooden homes at crossroads near Billabong Creek. Louis' risk and hope was that his little corner business would grow and prosper with the town's development. But he had misgivings as a prolonged drought reduced the prosperity of cattle- and sheep-farming and kept the town population down. The through traffic on the flat plains from nearby towns, such as Max's Narrandera, was limited in the days before motor vehicles were common.

Louis and Bertha, the only 'foreigners' in the town, threw themselves into communal activities and were soon popular. They were both concerned that the children, particularly John, would get a reasonable education and a chance to develop. Education was in the hands of one man, William Elliott, then twenty-three, who was in charge of the seventy children in the local state school, which was just a year old.

Elliott's specialty was mathematics, although he was not university trained. He spotted John's aptitude in the subject from the first day. Elliott passed on all he could. John absorbed it and was hungry for more. The teacher obtained advanced textbooks and taught his star pupil beyond the school curriculum as well as setting him practical puzzles and problems in geometry. John began tutoring many of the other children in maths in his first year at the school. His gentle manner with those less gifted allowed him a minor status in a working-class farming community. His classmates were sons and daughters of battling farmers, miners, farmhands, shearers, itinerants and road workers. Mathilde, who adored her brother and often tagged along with him, received special tuition in all subjects. Monash's patience, attention to detail, clear thinking and articulateness made him a natural teacher.

After school, when his schoolmates played with makeshift footballs in the winter and cricket bats in the summer, John went home. He didn't care for sports and was happy to amuse himself playing the piano or working out word and maths puzzles found in the back of the *Australasian* and

Town and Country Journal. (Monash later thought that the maths puzzles in particular formed an important part of his education.) Yet young John was as active on the local properties and along the bends of the creek as any of the local kids. It was an idyllic bush setting in which to grow up. He became familiar with everything from life on a sheep property and the local Aborigines to the goats and kangaroos.

Like many children in the district, he loved goat-herding at milking time in the evening. 'We copied the drivers of bullock-teams, swimming our charges across the waist-deep river,' Monash told a Melbourne *Sun* interviewer in 1926, half a century after the vivid experience. 'We rejoiced over the births of any kids to the flock. We organised boat races. And sometimes, we made goat-carts, decking the harnessed goats with red ribbons.'

In the evenings he learnt to ride on a little bay mare with his mother, who had a tall chestnut. He would never be an accomplished horseman, but he was comfortable in the saddle and loved horses.

After a year, Bertha was unhappy with living in the bush. She felt that both she and her children were being deprived. She fought with Louis, who, although discontented with his lot, had little choice but to stay in Jerilderie and little inclination to try again in Melbourne. After months of bickering, Bertha took the children back to Melbourne early in 1876 in time for the new school year. John was enrolled at the South Yarra College, where he made an immediate impression on all the teachers. But then news came from Krotoschin that Baer-Loebel had died, aged seventy-five. The compassionate Bertha returned with the children to Jerilderie to be with the grieving Louis.

She remained disgruntled with country life, just managing to endure the rest of 1876. Bertha paid close attention to John's development and chatted often with Elliott, who spoke in glowing terms of the boy's potential. Yet he worried that Bertha was pushing him too hard. John was studying German, French, Hebrew and music at home on top of his school subjects, primarily English, history, geography and maths. Then there was the extracurricular load that Elliott was giving his star pupil. In 1877 he wondered how the eleven-year-old boy's health would hold-up. Yet the teacher underestimated John's self-discipline and organisational ability. He would draw up a schedule each evening when he arrived home from school and would more often than not achieve it. Any spill-over would be incorporated into the next day or the weekend. This way John coped with his study load, a nagging father and an encouraging yet demanding mother.

A few months after John's eleventh birthday, Elliott told Bertha that he was reaching a point where he couldn't teach John anything new. His outstanding intellect needed professional tuition that only the best schools in Melbourne could provide. He suggested finding an institution that would incorporate all the major subjects, including those that Bertha and Louis were teaching him at home.

Bertha discussed it with Louis and urged him to try again in Melbourne. Louis refused. They considered the cost of a private school. Bertha suggested that the £3 a month he used to send to Baer-Loebel could be put towards the education of John and his sisters. After further dispute, unselfish Louis agreed to let his wife and children return to Melbourne indefinitely.

John said goodbye to his friends and Elliott. He assured them that he would be back in the holidays to visit his father. Elliott asked him to write. John spent many hours writing letters to uncles and aunts in Europe whom he would never meet, and found it a chore. But keeping contact with Elliott would be a pleasure. Their bond would last a lifetime.

Bertha and the children returned to Germania Cottage in late September 1877. She began her search for the most appropriate school. She spoke to friends and on their advice visited Scotch College, Wesley College and Melbourne Grammar.

Scotch College was the choice. It even taught Hebrew.

SCHOOL OF SOFT KNOCKS

Bertha was most impressed by Scotch's headmaster, Dr Alexander Morrison, the tall, vigorous forty-eight-year-old classicist from the University of Aberdeen. The bearded Scot had run the school for twenty years with not the proverbial iron rod but the leather strap. It was the biggest private school in the country. Morrison had built it into one of the most innovative, competitive and successful institutions in Australia. Although the Scottish Presbyterian Free Church had controlled the school since it began in 1851, Morrison's achievements allowed him a semi-autocracy in its development. Despite being a disciplinarian, he was a humanitarian who strove for academic excellence.

There was method in Morrison's ways. The Church, perhaps driven by its own standards of frugality, let Morrison control all income and expenditure. He could keep the surplus after annual expenses. If he were canny and enterprising, he could become a wealthy man by setting high fees to match the school's teaching standards. He could also increase the number of pupils. This background developed a degree of liberalism and open-mindedness that the Church itself eschewed. Morrison's Scotch adhered to the Church's directions concerning religion but was open to all denominations. Even atheists were welcome if they could manage the fees.

Bertha might well have expressed concern about the Church's attitudes and intolerance. The Rev. John Ewing, for instance, often harangued his Toorak Presbyterian congregation with anti-Semitic sentiments. Unscrupulous greed, he told them, was 'the evil characteristic of the . . . needy-looking little Jew'.[1]

But she was pleased to learn that Jews were welcomed at the school and even chased by Morrison and his staff. When Bertha first wrote to him, enclosing John's school reports, he insisted that she and John come to see him. She would have been charmed if she could understand his still broad, staccato accent. He introduced her to Hebrew teacher Morris Myers, who would be leaving at the end of the year, and the orthodox Moses Moses (a Master of Arts and a law graduate), who took post-matriculation classes and could turn his mind to teaching any discipline with equal facility. Morrison had started Hebrew at the school, and now it had a class of thirty, when the school had about 340 pupils. No pupil had to take religious instruction with which his faith didn't agree. John could join Old Testament studies but was excused from prayers. Morrison would have been eager to tell Bertha about his recent trip abroad in which he visited the best and most advanced English schools. As a result, German would be taught. He had also introduced weekly tests to keep the students working hard and steadily.[2]

Bertha thought John would be forced to sit out the rest of 1877 at home and that she would have to teach him beyond the usual subjects he studied. Morrison suggested he should not waste the last three months of the year. Bertha then enrolled him to begin on 9 October.

Monash, now an effetely handsome, dark-featured twelve-year-old, began a morning routine that he stuck with most of his first two years at Scotch. He rose at 7 a.m., did piano practice or homework until 8 a.m. and left for school at 8.30 a.m. after breakfast. He took twenty minutes to make the 2.2-kilometre walk. His path from Clifton Street, Richmond, was along lanes to Punt Road, through the park above the Melbourne Cricket Ground (already a notable sporting arena), across Wellington Parade to Fitzroy Gardens and the bluestone buildings of the school on Lansdowne Street, East Melbourne. There was a ninety-minute break for lunch, the main meal of the day. Monash would usually walk home for it but sometimes stayed at school for a leisurely time in the uncultivated Gardens opposite. Classes finished at 4 p.m. After school it was a mixture of choir practice, extra German lessons, preparation from the Reverend Isadore Myers for Monash's bar mitzvah and homework. There was synagogue every Saturday, choir on Sunday morning and piano lessons on Sunday afternoons. Saturday afternoons and nights were his time off.

Morrison himself taught Monash in geography and history. His brother Robert (an MA from Edinburgh University) took him in mathematics and science, the latter being part of the school's educational innovation. Morrison was not hidebound by the traditional English system that pervaded other schools. Scotch was the first Australian institution to teach English literature and to introduce a science laboratory.

Otto Mueller had him for German and French, while Edmund Augustus Samson, from King's College, London, taught him English and elocution. Samson attempted to iron out Monash's guttural vowels, caused by his speaking German at home, but was not entirely successful. The teacher did, however, help Monash over a slight shyness in speaking to the class. His experience at reading to his mother such books as *Tales of the Arabian Nights* or *The World of Wonders* at least once a week soon saw him gain self-confidence. In the days before microphones, boys were taught how to breathe correctly when speaking in public and how to enunciate – skills that were to prove useful for Monash for the rest of his life.

Frank Shew, a Yorkshire-born Master of Arts, taught classics as did J. B. Moran, an Irishman with a Bachelor of Arts, while John Nelson took Monash for drawing lessons. He was encouraged to sketch caricatures, which were fashionable in all papers and magazines.

The mix of qualified teachers with a wide variety of backgrounds was exactly what William Elliott had envisaged for his star pupil. Monash enjoyed all his studies except for Latin. He also did much to avoid gymnastics class and all sports, which were not compulsory. Scotch had strong first XIs and XVIIIs, but Morrison was thirstier for top academic results. Sports were peripheral to his vision of how his lads should develop.

The headmaster did see some value in military drills. He employed Sergeant-Major Whitehead, who began army cadet training at the school earlier in 1877. Monash never missed a session. He concurred with Major General Sir Julius Bruche (a Scotch graduate in 1890, later Chief of the Australian General Staff), who said Whitehead was his 'military father . . . He was a lovable character and a very fine man.'[3]

Whitehead was an unsung initiator of the colony's military defence. He began his career in 1861 when the local rulers passed legislation to allow voluntary units in the city and country. In 1870, when the British garrison troops packed up and went home for good, Victoria became the first colony to open a Defence Department. The minister had nothing to do but worry about protecting its boundaries from attack or invasion.

Whitehead became part of a small permanent force supported by volunteers organised into cavalry, infantry, artillery, engineers, torpedo and signal units. This force grew to about 4000 in the 1870s in the wake of the growing armaments race in Europe. There was further anxiety over Asian immigration. European concern began during the gold rush with the number of Chinese coming into the country, and it extended with the rise of Japan. There was further nervousness over what the French were doing in the New Hebrides.

Whitehead was on loan part time to the school from the military to give pep talks and to instruct the boys on drill. He was also a history buff, who lectured the boys on major wars, ancient or more recent. He regaled them with tales about key leaders from Alexander the Great to Napoleon. Whitehead could relate set-piece battle actions, especially from more recent conflicts such as the American Civil War and the Crimean War, which had stimulated the Colonial Government to set up its defences. He often urged pupils to consider a military career. Monash was one among several students who took it seriously, although his preoccupation at school was to achieve the best possible results in subjects that would lead to other professions.[4]

No particular career path had settled in his mind yet. But Morrison's methods of pinpointing a student's skills and deficiencies were going to sort him out. The school had a merit system in the four key departments: English, mathematics, classics and modern languages. If a boy was bright in one subject he would find himself in an 'upper' class in that discipline and perhaps a 'lower' class, if he was less proficient, in another.

Morrison and his staff did their assessment of Monash in the remaining weeks of 1877, examining him in every subject.

Monash returned to Jerilderie to stay with his father in January 1878, and kept in contact through regular letters. Louis was struggling to keep his corner store business going and was always looking for ways to cut costs. The main means of transport was the horse, and he was in the market for one early in the year. Horse-traders were common. Dealers, usually from over the border in Victoria, would drift through the town and region. One such dealer was the twenty-three-year-old outlaw Ned Kelly, who had been stealing and trading horses since his early teens. Kelly and his gang of bushrangers would seek out the German immigrants in the area, some of whom they regarded as similar to them in their anti-British sentiment. A noted example was William Baumgarten, who owned a property on the Victorian border. (Later in 1878 he would be charged with dealing in horses stolen by the Kelly gang and sent to jail for four years.) As Ned Kelly noted later in his famous 'Jerilderie letter', there were good Germans and bad ones. The Kelly gang knew that some Germans were open to dealing without questions being asked about where and how the horses had been 'acquired'. Louis was one of them.

Early in the first week of February, the gang made a fleeting visit to Jerilderie. They came to the Monash property, and Louis bought a horse from Ned Kelly. Louis would later boast that he had outdone Kelly in the cash deal. But as the horses cost the gang nothing, any payment, even if discounted from market value, was accepted. The Kellys were on the run and needed the money. The gang was at the property for at least an hour. An awe-struck John Monash had the courage to approach Ned. According to Monash, they chatted for a while. Kelly gave him a shilling to mind his horse.

'He gave me some good advice,' Monash said, without specifying what these words of wisdom were. The attraction of the Kelly gang as outlaws captured public imagination, and boys of Monash's age are impressionable. He ranked that meeting as a highlight of his life. (Even after the war of 1914–18 he spoke of the encounter in the same breath as his exploits as a commander. Monash seemed more impressed by the gang's horsemanship than anything else. Later he would muse on what great soldiers they would have made.)[5]

When Monash returned for his first full year at Scotch a few days later he didn't even let his close friends know about the encounter. It wasn't prudent to speak of fraternising with bushrangers, especially when his father could be jailed for dealing with them. (It wasn't until the mid-1920s that Monash spoke about the Kelly incident. By then Kelly stories – approaching half a century after his hanging – were becoming fashionable.)

Monash found himself in the 'lower fourth', 'upper fourth' and 'lower fifth' in three departments. Most of his classmates were from one two years older. He was being fast-tracked to match his mind and potential.

Monash was disappointed to learn that Louis was too busy to travel from Jerilderie to Melbourne for his bar mitzvah a few days after his thirteenth birthday in June 1878. Monash wrote to tell him how thrilled he was with the gifts. They reflected the interests of a budding modern renaissance man. There was a microscope from his parents and a volume of Shakespeare's plays from a friend of the family. Uncle Max had given him a gold watch. Aunt Ulrike had matched that with gold studs. His cousin Albert had imported a chemistry set from Prussia. Perhaps the most prized gift was from his Uncle Graetz (married to his father's eldest sister Julie), who sent him a signed copy of his renowned *History of the Jews* in French. There were also more conventional presents, such as a penknife and a stamp album.[6]

Louis's response to Monash's letter was unimaginative. There were barely congratulations before he launched into a harangue about his duty to his parents, who had sacrificed so much. It would have disappointed Monash, who was well aware of the efforts his parents had made on his behalf and the privileges he had been given. He had hardly wasted them. Morrison thought his conduct was impeccable. Other letters from relatives were also full of moral imperatives about the way he should behave. Monash found them boring, repetitive and, ambiguously, 'without wit'.[7]

On his visits to Jerilderie, he had more joy in seeing Elliott than his father, who was increasingly distant and preoccupied with his business worries. Elliott told him he was thinking of giving up teaching. He wanted one day to be a journalist. He was considering a job on the local *Jerilderie Gazette*.

Monash wished he had witnessed an incident in Jerilderie that would make the town part of Australian folklore. Almost a year to the day since he had met Ned Kelly, the gang returned to hold up the entire town over the weekend of 7–10 February 1879.

Elliott, the prospective newspaperman, found himself in the middle of the scoop of his life when he walked into the Bank of New South Wales to make a deposit during his Monday lunch-break from the school. He was bailed up by the gang and forced to help fill a sugar bag with money. Elliott was later taken prisoner with thirty others and held at the Royal Mail Hotel for most of day. He witnessed a dramatic confrontation in the bar between an unarmed local policeman, Constable Richards, and Ned Kelly.

Elliott wrote to Monash and later recorded in articles his assessment of the Kelly gang and the extraordinary day. He thought Ned himself was a bluffer. 'In appearance and gait,' Elliott said, 'he resembled a military man . . . he would seemingly have liked to have been at the head of a hundred followers or so to upset the existing government or bring it to terms.' In Ned he saw a 'lot of Don Quixote'. He was also 'a bit of a fanatic, or rather, a dreamer in his own way'.[8]

Monash, back at school on 11 February after the summer holidays, was thrilled to read of the newspaper accounts of the Jerilderie hold up. He knew all the names that came up, from the local police to the hotel staff and the people at the bank.

Monash's progress at Scotch pushed him at fourteen into the Matriculation Class – 'Upper Fifth' – in 1879. He was enjoying the school and the challenges, and had developed friendships with boys from a variety of backgrounds, despite his lack of interest in any team sports. His closest friend was a tough character, George Farlow, a scholarship winner from a poor background. Monash was not physical. Nor was he bullied. Most boys steered clear of confrontations with him because he could make them look foolish with his sharp tongue or his arguing skills. If that failed, Farlow would be there to back him up.

Despite Monash's accent and looks, which were different from those of the predominantly Anglo-Celtic boys, he said he experienced no racism.[9]

He sat the matriculation and civil service exam, passing all nine subjects: arithmetic, algebra, Euclid (geometry), English, Latin, French, German, history and geography. He shone in the mathematics subjects and was one of only five students (three from Scotch) to obtain passes in all nine subjects. In internal assessments in the Upper Fifth, he was top in German, fourth in mathematics and seventh in French.

Monash felt he enjoyed the descriptive subjects more and was tilting towards studying arts at university. He flirted with being a writer and toyed with the idea of doing a book set in the Civil War in England. He managed two pages of an unfinished play.

In 1880 he was in a post-matriculation class at Scotch studying mathematics and logic (second in the form), French (fifth) and Latin (sixth), as well as Greek and German. His main rival was James Whiteside McCay, a Presbyterian minister's son, seven months his senior, who pipped him in all subjects and was dux of the school. It was the beginning of a strong rivalry and friendship. Monash was runner-up for the Sir James McCulloch prize for English composition. His stylish, padded, hagiographic 4000-word essay was on 'The Life and Times of John Milton', the great seventeenth-century English poet, historian, pamphleteer and civil servant. Monash was disciplined enough to rethink and rewrite. His archive has three drafts in longhand before his final submission.[10]

Although still only fifteen and a half, Monash thought he was going on to university in 1881, but Morrison enticed him back to Scotch for one more year and a tilt at the exhibition prizes – money awards that could pay for his first university year.

After a relaxing holiday with Aunt Ulrike and his cousins at Sorrento early in 1881, Monash saddled up for his fourth full year at Scotch. He took mathematics, French, German and logic, dropping Greek and Latin for a year. Morrison was keen for a select few boys to do well so that Scotch could outshine Wesley College, which had become its main rival for results. Moses Moses, for whom Monash had high regard, took him for mathematics. Otto Mueller sharpened up his German one on one; A. C. Aucher did the same with his French. Monash set himself a rigid study timetable, often working from after his evening meal for five hours until midnight on as many as five nights a week.

This rigorous dedication paid off. He had a brilliant year, coming top in maths, logic, French and German in the school exams, which placed him equal dux with James S. Thomson (who went on to be a physician). This gave him a book voucher prize of five guineas. He bought himself sets of Froude's *History of England*, Gibbon's *Decline and Fall of the Roman Empire* and Scott's Waverley novels. Monash won another five guineas for this time winning the school essay, moving from Milton to the set essay on Shakespeare's *Macbeth*. His excellent effort was on display at the school for several years. It began with a quote from Byron: 'A man must serve his time to every trade,/save censure – critics all are ready made.'

Perhaps the young Monash, burning with ambition, and now flush with achievement, was showing a measure of perspicacity concerning his own career, whatever that might be.[11]

Morrison's faith in Monash's capacity for application and hard work were rewarded when he sat the external (public) exams and won the exhibition in mathematics with a first-class honour (1881 being the first year honours were registered). He also gained firsts in French and German. This effort helped Morrison to achieve his aim of maintaining Scotch as the number-one academic institution in the colony.

Monash, now sixteen, relaxed first at his aunt's again in Sorrento, then for three weeks in Narrandera (125 kilometres northeast of Jerilderie), where Louis had taken over his brother Max's store after struggling for six years with the Jerilderie business.

Inspired by his own success, Monash began writing a diary early in 1882 – a discipline he would keep for most of his life. His writing skills were apparent early. They accentuated clear, layered thinking and logic. Yet he displayed imagination and was a lateral thinker, someone likely to come up with a different perspective. Like many a bright young scribbler, he dreamt of becoming a Dickens or a Milton, or even a Shakespeare.

The Exhibition Prize was worth £25, enough for Monash to finance his first year at Melbourne University, the colony's only major tertiary institution. It was in a state of flux and, at times, disorganised. The council, student body and professorial board couldn't agree on such matters as funding for colleges and battles for the chancellorship. There were religious disputes. The university was dominated by the medical faculty, which attracted about 150 of the 450 students enrolled. Women had been admitted only a year earlier. In 1882 changes were taking place. The university was expanding. New chairs were established in Natural Philosophy (Physics), Chemistry, Engineering, English, French and German.

Monash enrolled in arts. He added to his income by coaching a few matriculation students in French, German and mathematics. He had enjoyed his school days despite its rigour, rules and regulations, which were meant to give boys a sense of discipline. But now he was a free agent, without the threat of the strap (Monash himself never received it) or detention for not turning up to school or class on time. There was no headmaster or teacher marking his weekly progress, or parents to admonish him to do better. There were many distractions such as theatre, drinking and parties. He seemed determined to embrace them with the apparent motto of 'Nothing in moderation'.

The rush of 'freedom' was sometimes too much for a sixteen-year-old, despite its being the average age for an 1882 university entrant. Monash rebelled against his parents and was a little short with his sister Mathilde when tutoring her. He was approaching manhood fast. Gone were the gentle, sensitive looks of the pre-pubescent. Instead there was a lean youth with intelligent dark looks that were more refined than those of his parents.

Monash became disillusioned with the arts course and most of his lecturers. None inspired him as Moses Moses, Otto Mueller and the Morrison brothers had. He had dreamt of doing the course. Now he was in it there was a big disappointment. After the first few weeks he hardly turned up for a lecture. If he did, he was rarely at the university before mid-morning. Monash overcame the letdown by creating his own parallel course, which he found much more stimulating. He camped at the public library reading literature and history as recommended by anyone whose opinion he respected. Monash also began keeping journals that recorded his thoughts and memorable sayings, axioms and aphorisms. He began attending the Wesley Church Improvement Society after joining it the year before. At meetings he would get up and read everything from his celebrated *Macbeth* essay to Koran translations. There were other readings and speaking at the Scots Church Literary Society and the Victoria Parade Young Men's Association. He was keen to gain control of himself and the audience, a tough task considering his age. When extemporising on one occasion he 'froze'. Monash was mortified by the experience and was very hard on himself, although honest. He decided, prematurely, that he would never be a notable orator.

There were moments when he thought it prudent to study his arts subjects, but picking up on the big contemporary topics in the newspapers sidetracked these bursts – this week federalism, next week Australia's lack of military defences. His mother's cultivation of German, Jewish and English migrants and cultural (the concert and the theatre) links had developed a wide circle of friends. Their opinions on the major topics of the day sparked evenings of vital discourse at Germania Cottage. Among their friends with English backgrounds were the Hodgson, Huntsman and Deakin families. Alfred Deakin, aged twenty-five (a member of the Victorian Government and future Prime Minister of Australia), his young wife Pattie and his sister Katherine were frequent guests. Deakin, who had taken a law degree in 1877, showed particular interest in Monash and was impressed by his precocious intellect and talent for playing Chopin. Among the German and Jewish families were the Wischers, Puttmanns, Sanders and Meiers.

Bertha's aim was to make her children feel less like outsiders. There would always be some cultural and ethnic divide, yet she was succeeding. She also wished her son especially to be 'informed'.

Monash was interested in the activities of Deakin and the others, who were pushing for reforms in the Colonial Government and electorate. Yet he wasn't radical in his views or sparked by local politics. His mind was swamped by deeper intellectual issues, and overriding these was his passion for writing. He was keeping it alive in a practical way (for additional pocket money) by attempting to place articles in country papers. He sent many of these to William Elliott, who had himself realised his dream of becoming a journalist. He was now owner and editor of the *Jerilderie Herald*, successor to the *Jerilderie Gazette*.

Monash was attempting to grapple with the major ideas of religion and philosophy. His rational, logical mind came fast to a sense of agnosticism, defying his Jewish heritage and that of his education in a Christian school. A sense of intellectual superiority came through in his diaries but yet still did not show arrogance. Through the lather of words and thought explorations, Monash showed integrity and intellectual toughness in his search for 'truth'. Underneath it all was a deeper search for self. He was unashamedly ambitious. Yet he wasn't sure for what or why.

Monash wrote in his diary a couple of months after turning seventeen in 1882 that he had an 'overmastering desire . . . a fitful, self-expiring eagerness in the pursuit of "fame." Is not life one great longing, yearning, hoping, desiring? . . . I have read, heard and seen enough to know that there is no true happiness in life, and the sole thing that bears up my failing spirits is this ambition . . .'[12]

This perpetual probe was linked, unwittingly at the time, to his strong sense of nationalism. Monash was connected to Germany culturally but not politically. He was not born there. 'Germany' had been united as such only since 1871. He made this clear in letters to his cousin Leo Monash in the USA, who was clinging to his German affiliations above links in America. Monash admonished him for this.

To what country and people do I owe most? [he asked rhetorically.] To that which I have never seen, with which I have no connection, but that it is the home of some of my relatives? Or to that in which and among whom I was born, have grown up, where I have learned all that I know, to which I owe all the happiness that I have experienced? . . . Shall I in return for this look upon it as a foreign land, to be deserted at the first convenient opportunity?

No, it is my native land; I have contracted from it a heavy debt, *and it will ever be to me a prominent object, in some measure to repay that debt.*[13]

Australia, not yet officially a nation, was his home and first love. He wanted to support its birth and cheer for anything that was identifiably Australian. And since he was from an immigrant family that had no affiliation to Great Britain, he did not crave that attachment. He would rather see it formed independently of a mother country, especially one that was not his.

In late August 1882 he cheered more loudly than most colonials did when Australia won a Test match against England in England for the first time. Monash, who had no time for cricket before this, was enthralled with the newspaper reports of how the 'Demon' bowler Fred Spofforth ripped through England at the Oval in London, taking seven for 44 in the last innings of the match. Australia won a nail-biter Test by just seven runs. It was the first time ever that an entity called Australia had competed abroad and won anything. The result inflamed nationalism. It sparked further talk of the six colonies uniting as a federation in much the same way as the United States. The colonials had shaken the seat of the mighty British Empire in sport, something not done in any sphere of competition or conflict since Napoleon.

Monash put two clippings on the event into his cuttings book. He even walked his sisters over to the nearby MCG to watch a torchlight procession to welcome the victorious team. Then he wrote an account of it for the *Jerilderie Herald,* noting that illustrious Australian captain, Will Murdoch, had won the 'championship of the world in the manliest of British Games'. It even inspired him to plan to see the big match between New South Wales and Victoria at the MCG at Christmas.

In September he learned that Louis was at last coming back to Melbourne in a few weeks time. He was selling the Narrandera store and planned to build a new family home. Louis was going into a money-lending business with his brother-in-law Max Roth (from Berlin, who was married to Ulrike), who had also been running a store in the Riverina – at Deniliquin. Knowing that his father would pressure him, Monash was motivated into studying for his first-year exams. But it was a bit late. He shocked everyone by failing Latin, Greek and upper mathematics while passing lower mathematics, logic and the combined subject of chemistry, mineralogy and botany.

Louis and Bertha made his humiliation worse by their despair at his performances. 'There was a great mourning,' Monash wrote in anguish, 'and I soon felt fit to drown myself.'[14]

He blamed his downfall on the theatre, which he attended even when his parents believed he was studying. But in his heart he knew he simply had not done enough work. Bright as he was, there was no way he could pass everything without sustained exam preparation. Monash had a second chance to study for supplementary exams in the failed subjects in February 1883. He was unsettled by the tensions surrounding his father's return. Louis was stricter than his more indulgent mother. Yet still Monash allowed himself to be distracted. He was compelled to report a railway collision for the *Jerilderie Herald*, not to mention the writing of a short fiction story on love and murder. When Monash should have been studying, he was playing the piano, sketching and reading literary works – Victor Hugo, Lord Tennyson, George Eliot, Sir Walter Scott, Bulwer Lytton among them. He was in search of romantic literature and enchanted with his discoveries. Religion had been thumped into him at school and in the synagogue. Monash was turning his back on it and beginning to ponder the moral strictures that underpinned it.

Monash was starting friendships with girls and was conflicted, like many a youth fore and since, over his own natural urges. He was enjoying his reading, which was a sweet veneer for his growing secret desires, and was disappointed if he didn't get through a book in a couple of days.

His lack of application in studying the less enchanting set subjects caused him to consult the Morrison brothers and other old masters at Scotch. They were sympathetic but blunt. He was advised to 'put all books asunder' until the 'supps' were over. Yet still he kept ploughing into weighty tomes, sneaking off to the theatre and also working out in a city gymnasium. Monash had reached his full height of 175 centimetres but thought he was too thin. He began using dumbbells to put muscle on his arms, shoulders and chest.

Louis' decision to build a new brick home near the Hawthorn station (four kilometres east of Germania Cottage in Richmond) was yet another excuse for not concentrating on the looming exams. Monash made his 'first venture into engineering' by suggesting revisions to the architect and builder and eyeing the final contract. He loved it and resolved to acquire more practical experience.

Monash jammed in his exam preparation in January and passed five subjects. But he failed Latin, messing up prose he had to translate. This caused him to fail the entire 1882 year. It crushed and humiliated him. His ego was dented and his self-esteem shattered. No amount of telling himself that he had used his time well by his wide reading would salve his depressed feelings.

✕

Monash unhappily began the drudgery in 1883 of repeating most of the subjects he had already passed, but tilted his studies towards getting a double degree in arts and engineering. The latter, introduced as a 'certificate' in 1882, was now a degree course that suited his current program. The first three years of the course was made up of arts subjects with 'majors' in mathematics and physics. Monash added physics to his study list. It meant that with the setback of the first-year failure, he could still obtain his arts degree by the end of 1885 and an engineering degree by the end of 1886. Tutoring gave him some pocket money.

He was soon not turning up for lectures in subjects he had already passed but was enjoying physics under Professor Henry Martyn Andrew, the first lecturer he admired since school days. Before long, he was back to his own literary reading program, taking painting lessons, sketching and sneaking off to the theatre again. His diaries were kept up, but he was stunned and hurt to learn that his parents were reading them. He mastered shorthand to record his most intimate thoughts and hid them. Monash had progressed to becoming secretary of the Wesley Church Improvement Society but was becoming bored with it.

Once more, he left his run at final-year exams too late, and this time he did not even attempt to do the Latin exam. The language of the ancient Romans had been his *bête noir*, and he was glad to avoid it. But Monash would be haunted by the knowledge that he had to pass it to obtain his degree. At some point he couldn't decline his declensions. He would have to face the beast.

He had attained only passes and a third class in the subsequent honours exams. It was enough for him to move on to second year in arts/engineering, but in an unhappy mood. He still had a strong self-belief, but he was not putting the scores on the university results boards for everyone to see. His ego remained dented.

✕

Two extracurricular activities taken up in 1884 boosted Monash's confidence and helped motivate him to continue university life. The first was when he augmented his meagre income a fraction by joining the University (or D) Company of the 4th Battalion, Victorian Rifles, commanded by Lieutenant Colonel John Aitken.

An era of military reform had begun in the colony at the end of 1883. It was boosting and reorganising its defence in response to perceived possible threats. The volunteer force, which had grown over the thirteen years since the British garrison left, was disbanded and replaced by a corps of paid militia – or part-time soldiers. In 1883 some British officers were invited back to fill the senior command positions. This was partly owing to the British needing to protect their interests over much of the world in response to the strengthening of Germany and France, who were both keen and recidivist colonisers. Colonial governments in Australia felt the pressure from time to time to fly the flag for Great Britain, or be prepared to do so if the 'mother country' requested it.

The officers were put in charge of the reorganisation and the new training programs. As one of the colony's borders was ocean, the navy was made bigger. If any foreign gunboats wished to attack or take Melbourne, they would have to pass through the Heads – the cliffs at the opening of horseshoe-shaped Port Phillip Bay. Forts with heavy guns were built.

Four infantry battalions of the Victorian Rifles were part of the new 1883 militia force. D Company of the 4th Battalion was housed at Melbourne University. Monash was invited to join it by its new company commander, Captain (Professor) Andrew, whom he admired so much. He became a recruit and was keen to extend the experience under Sergeant Major Whitehead at school. He took all activities seriously and enjoyed them, even the daily drills taken by Sergeant Sullivan, who had been active in New Zealand's Maori Wars (when British colonisers used force to put down indigenous uprisings) in the 1860s. Sullivan was tough and uncompromising. Monash, who was strong from his walking all over Melbourne and gymnasium work, looked on it as another fitness routine. Andrews, Aitken and others lectured and set exams. Monash passed with a 'special mention' and became a corporal in October. He was a perfectionist, if he felt the subject was worthwhile. Monash saw this non-degree pastime as a sort of public service to the fledgling colony.

The second major new activity beyond his formal studies was the formation of a University Union and a journal, the *Melbourne University Review*. A mood of reform was sweeping through colonial politics. The students, sensitive to issues, wanted representation within the campus set up. Monash, aware of the successful unions at the Universities of Cambridge and Oxford, was a prime mover in creating an organisation to improve the spirit and say of the student body. Debating and public speaking were to be the centrepiece of activity, along with 'socials'. Monash, now nineteen and never without a knotted walking cane, enjoyed 'advertising' himself, the feelings of worth that went with being 'one of the fountain heads' of the Union movement and 'the mainstay and practical conductor of the first genuine Students paper'. He was more concerned with being at the centre of activity and pushing through the 'tiers of society stratas' than any bloated undergraduate sense of power and influence. Acquaintances did not regard him as pushy. They either respected or admired his energy, capacity for hard work and ability to get things done.[15]

Monash's main joy was the *Review*, which he published with C. J. Zichy-Woinarski (a law student who would become a judge) and Jim Lewis (an arts student who had been at Scotch with Monash). Running, editing and writing this publication seemed a natural progression from his massive literary immersion over the past six years. Apart from his formal writing, such as the acclaimed *Macbeth* essay, at school and university, there was his mountain of reading, his own output in attempts at plays, short stories and journalism, not to mention copious diaries. The sheer weight of thought in the latter, and his attempts at clear expression, had developed at least the base for a writing career of some sort.

Monash wanted to test the business of writing through the journal. It was the culmination of his lingering desire to become an author. More than dabbling in the hard work of editing and writing with many other budding scribblers would make or break his secret passion. He had become a stern critic of even the more accomplished professional writers after reading so much so early. Now was the chance to test himself and others with a critical campus audience.

As ever, Monash's studies suffered. He crammed in October 1884 for his second year arts/engineering exams, and gained passes in advanced mathematics, natural philosophy (physics) II, practical chemistry,

French and German. In the honours exams that followed he gained second class, and was placed a disappointing fourteenth in a group of about thirty. It was a blow. Students had to pay (about £3) to sit for honours, which brought awards for the best – money that would finance further study.

Despite many commiserations from friends who expected him to shine, Monash was now more philosophical about his failures to attain academic heights. He recognised that his urges to acquit himself militarily and in political and literary campus activities would mean that he had limited time for the sort of disciplined application to study he had shown in his narrower life at Scotch College.

His involvement in so much was beginning to sort out in his mind where his strengths were and where his future might lie. Although he loved literature, his culminating experience on the *Review* was making him realise that a career as an author or journalist was unlikely. Again showing a characteristic honesty with himself, Monash, while dwelling on his future direction in his diaries, wrote of the impact of mathematics teaching by Professors Andrew, E. J. Nanson and W. C. Kernot.

'I am essentially a mathematical student,' he said. 'Anyone who devotes himself for three or four years to mathematics undergoes a complete mental reconstruction.'[16]

This 'reconstruction' could have taken place in literature too because of his devotion to it over a longer period. But by continual self-examination (the diaries made him his own best psychoanalyst) he was coming around to facing where he might better focus his mind for the future.

Early in January 1885 Monash was issued with the vivid red uniform of his 4th Battalion. Displaying his usual verve, and a certain showy eccentricity, he often wore it in public. The admiration from girlfriends outweighed the mirth it brought some strangers. By late in the month, the 'fun' feelings associated with wearing it evaporated with the news that British General Charles Gordon had been killed defending Khartoum in the Sudan against rebels. Gordon was a great man of the empire, especially for his exploits in the Crimean War and in wars against the Chinese when the British occupied Beijing and Shanghai (1860–65). The reaction of the colonial rulers and opinion-makers was to rush to the aid of the British in the Sudan. Troops were offered. Not everyone agreed.

'. . . our [the 4th Battalion members in uniform] lives have been made a burden to us,' Monash noted in his diary. 'Our appearance in the streets in uniform seems to be the signal for the display of all the wit of which unwashed Melbourne seems possessed.'[17]

Monash would not have been a willing participant in any military expeditionary force to a British occupation halfway around the world. He thought Australian governments should build a national army rather than support their colonial rulers.

Overzealous offers of troops by the colonies were rejected, except for the later offer of a contingent from New South Wales (which thus became the first Australian military unit to serve overseas). Militia activity intensified nevertheless. Many weekends were now taken up with camps and bivouacs. Battles between different companies of 4th Battalion were set up. Monash found himself camping in hills around Melbourne and taking part in mock fights. One company would defend a position, usually at night, and be challenged by an attacking force. He didn't mind roughing it, but he was in the minority who took the exercises seriously. Most used it for an excuse for a drunken weekend with their mates. Monash disliked the lack of control by officers, whom he criticised for their slack drilling.

'It was a rough and vulgar time,' he reflected, 'a paragon of mismanagement.'[18]

✕

In late February 1885 Monash was shocked to learn that his mother had abdominal cancer. An operation was unsuccessful. She had only a few months to live. Monash, Mathilde and Louise took it in turns to nurse Bertha, who suffered great pain. Monash played her favourite composers – Mendelssohn, Weber, Beethoven and Chopin – on the piano every day. His practice intensified in this period, and he threw himself into public performances at university union socials. The hurt of knowing that he would soon be losing the most important person in his life caused him to play her most requested pieces – Chopin's 'Polonaise' and 'Poet and Peasant' – with passion. He performed without nervousness or concern for the audience's reaction. Monash was well received, but he didn't care. His mind was elsewhere.

His studies were neglected more than at any time before in his fitful periods of application. Instead he occupied himself with anything but the subjects that would have given him his coveted, yet prolonged degrees.

Girls, too, began to enter the equation more than ever. He might have been preparing himself for the loss of the woman who had dominated his life and the directions it took. In Monash's mind, replacing his mother would be tough, maybe impossible. Yet there was no shortage of willing partners, without any reaching far beyond the platonic, which is probably just as well. In mid-1885 he built relationships with the four Blashki sisters, the daughters of a city watchmaker and jeweller.

Monash wrote them poetry, read to them and enthralled them with his piano rendition of Mendelssohn's Piano Concerto No. 1 in G Minor. He loved the opera, theatre and concerts. He could dance too, and promised himself the 'necessary evil' of learning to waltz (which he did, the following year). He even made himself popular with card and conjuring tricks he had been taught on those testing military excursions. In short, Monash was a cultural young romantic with flair and charm, an asset in an era when charm meant something beyond a shallow smile. Women liked his looks, strength, style, manners, cultivated demeanour and intellect.

Monash liked being the centre of attention. Again, he was quite happy about 'advertising' himself (as he called it). It was his way of standing out as well as fitting in.

Sometimes he underestimated his impact. The Blashki girls, Minnie, Jeanette, Rose and Eva, all at some point wanted to marry him. His correspondence with them would have filled a book. It revealed the stages in the assumed courtships: flirtation, serious overtures, questioning, rejection and scorn. Louis wisely let Mrs Blashki know that his John had no intention of marrying for years yet. One reason not mentioned was the fact that he had no money, an important factor in the marriage stakes in middle-class Victorian Melbourne.

The girls, it seemed, would have put up even with his impecunious state. But when it became clear that Monash was not serious, they examined his letters more closely on the vital matter of religious belief. He had grappled with this big issue and had rejected the concept of 'God' since his first year as an undergraduate. Now his pontificating on the subject in countless letters, not only to the girls but also to friends, relatives and teachers, had a refined yet fed-up ring to it. In a letter to Eva, the youngest, he said: 'Shall I then throw aside my birthright of enlightenment, ignore my privilege of free thought, do my reason violence, and lower myself to the moral standpoint of the people of thirty centuries ago? Emphatically NO.' Sounding himself like a hellfire preacher or rabbi, he added: 'The ancient conception of God I will and do cast aside once and for all. Am I then without faith, without belief in the Supreme? Still more emphatically NO.'[19]

This denunciation of fundamental historical beliefs (fashionable and brought on by Charles Darwin's theories of evolution without a deity) at first thrilled the girls. It was bold, daring and romantic. When they discovered he was not a marriage prospect, it was a useful excuse not to become involved with such a threat to their religion's authority. He could be dismissed and scorned as some sort of heretic, and an impoverished one at that.

Through all these relationships, not just with the Blashkis but also scores of other encounters, an underlying sexual tension developed. No self-respecting middle-class Melbourne girl would go further than cuddling, kissing and perhaps some sensual touching. If she did so and built a 'reputation', she risked ruining her chances for marriage, especially with a young prospect like Monash with his long checklist of what was required to be his life partner. Words such as 'character', 'bright', 'fairly read', 'warm-hearted', 'sympathetic', 'demeanour', 'mental constitution', 'comportment', 'good background' and 'family wealth' came up in his diaries. 'Good-lover' or 'hot in bed' were not on the list. But Monash continued to seduce women emotionally. He danced around and teased them. When they came under the Monash microscope, they were found lacking because, deep down, that was what he wanted. He was far from ready. He would need to distance himself from his mother's perceived perfections before he could accept a substitute.

Breaks in relationships were often heated. Monash expressed guilt over them. He was not comfortable with a trail of broken hearts. Over the years he was affected by pent-up frustrations he could not quite understand.

Monash needed diversions from diversions. He threw himself into university union activity, raising contentious issues in the *Review* while being a moderate voice in commenting on them. He was always organising: a debate this week; a concert in a fortnight; a social in a month; a series of lectures over the winter. Monash often came up with the concept, planned it, managed it on the day, cleaned up afterwards and then reviewed it in the union magazine.

He was indefatigable too in his battalion work. He was promoted to colour sergeant, which was, if anything, colourless. It meant he was senior sergeant in the company and responsible to his captain for boring chores that no one else would take on, such as administration, preparation of food rations and duty rosters. On parade he was subject to snide remarks and some sniggering as he called the roll, fixed bayonets, opened the ranks and reported to the company commander. His conscientiousness earned him the derisive nickname 'Corporal Potash'. Yet apart from a few remarks in his dairies about the 'childish misbehaviour' and 'schoolboy impulses' of his fellow soldiers, Monash remained unperturbed. The military drew out a maturity that sometimes made him appear born at forty. It was an activity he took more seriously than any other. It stemmed from his need to achieve in anything he took on. He was also acutely aware that someone had to take responsibility for building a defence tradition in a country that had none.

It led to Monash being the first in the company to sit for an exam for promotion to sergeant soon after his twentieth birthday. He was thrilled when he passed and was awarded a certificate of proficiency in flag-signalling. Monash was proud of his rise. He hung the decoration on the wall above his bed. 'With so much accomplished in one direction, and so much gained,' he wrote, 'I feel encouraged and instigated to a fresh start in the race for a position in the world.'[20]

The frantic need for diversions ended on 18 October when Bertha died, aged forty-four. It was a tremendous blow to Monash and the family. The girls were no less devastated. Louis was heart-broken. 'I have lost the dearest and most sympathetic friend I ever had,' Monash wrote to a girlfriend. 'My mother was far more than that – and now I feel utterly, utterly alone.'[21]

THE ENGINEER'S LANGUAGE

Bertha's death caused some big changes in the Monash family. Louis' money-lending business with Roth was struggling. Their funds had not been large to start with. There was strong competition, and their contacts were limited to the Jewish–German community. Louis' income was fitful and limited. At fifty-four, the spirit of risk-taking and adventure had left him. He was suddenly, irreversibly 'old'. Mathilde had shone at her school, the Presbyterian Ladies College (Scotch's sister school), gaining two first-class honours in her matriculation exams. She would go on to be dux of the school, but her chances of doing a university course or having a career were diminished by the family's poor financial situation. Mathilde would have to look after sister Louise and the household.

Monash took stock. He had not done enough preparation to sit his final exams and was in no mental state to attempt them at the end of 1885 or the following February. His dilettante days were over. He had to earn money, but not from work that didn't inspire him or would lead nowhere. He could always step up his tutoring. He was a good, patient teacher, but he didn't see a future in it. Instead Monash came to terms with his real strength – in mathematics. Years later when giving out the school prizes at Scotch College, he would tell the mathematics prize winner (Archibald Glenn, later a leading industrialist) who didn't know which career path to take: 'What are you waiting for? Mathematics is the language of the engineer.'[1]

Monash's own proficiency in the 'language' determined his direction. He began looking for work on engineering projects in public works and private development brought on by Melbourne's second boom, this time in building, a generation after the gold boom. Plans had been drawn up for Princes Bridge over the Yarra River, which would link St Kilda Road to Swanston Street in the heart of Melbourne. Monash's friend Jim Lewis, also a budding engineer, recommended him to the contractor and machinery manufacturer, David Munro, who had the biggest engineering workshop in Australia, employing 5000 men. Monash was offered a paltry thirty shillings a week, less than he could earn tutoring. But he took it. He was unqualified and needed the experience. The bridge was an important construction for Melbourne. It was a design of class, style and size, being ten metres wide.

Monash was thrilled to be working on such a project, but also nervous. He was a novice, pestering Lewis for information. His first job was to draw up the specifications for the masonry. Monash left nothing to chance, asking about every detail he didn't understand. Bigger tasks came his way, such as the mathematical calculations and drawings for the abutments, piers and retaining walls. The senior engineers began setting Monash the tougher, sometimes more dangerous tasks. But the dirtier, more demanding the job, the more he revelled in it. Those rough winter weekends in the mud and slush on army camps and exercises prepared him well.

Monash was disappointed in mid-1886 when the University Company of 4th Battalion was disbanded. Too many of his fellow part-time soldiers had been frivolous and ill-disciplined. Often they made feeble excuses for not turning up for drills and exercises. Monash was at first fed up, but a few weeks after the break-up, he couldn't resist pursuing his desire to advance in the military, although he struggled to understand why he wanted to do so beyond the 'gorgeous' uniforms and pomp.

He applied to join the North Melbourne Battery of the Militia Garrison Artillery, whose fixed guns defended Victorian ports. There wasn't a suitable vacancy. Two of his friends had been quicker in moving. Monash made submissions to the commanding officer, Major Jacob Goldstein, the forty-eight-year-old son of a Polish Jew. But there was no favouritism. Monash had to wait.

After working the better part of a year on Princes Bridge, he asked Munro for a wage increase, and received a useful 33.3 per cent increment to forty shillings (i.e. £2) a week. It was not nearly in line with his growing responsibilities, yet it was recognition that he was needed. Monash was given a lift when the *Age* reported his name as one of the four 'competent and able engineers' employed on bridge construction.

In September 1886 his confidence had returned enough for him to make a belated bid for his third year at arts. This time he studied advanced and mixed mathematics, natural philosophy III, and a combined subject, geology and palaeontology. (Rocks became an interest when he was directed to open granite and bluestone quarries outside Melbourne. They would provide the materials for work on the bridge.) Yet cramming now had to be done after work, and although distractions were fewer, he would often come home exhausted. His study was intermittent. He passed the mathematic subjects but failed the other two. Monash decided to dump physics and audaciously tried political economy, a new subject, in a bid to pass all the supps in February 1887. He borrowed a friend's lecture notes for the year and spent less than four weeks in preparation. It was once more too little too late. He misjudged the difficulty of grasping the ideas of Adam Smith, John Stuart Mill, Herbert Spencer and other early econo-mists, and failed. The dryness of rock studies (and the lecturers), as with Latin, did not inspire him as much as he thought it would when he worked at Munro's Malmsbury quarry extracting bluestone for the bridge. He missed again in geology, which meant he had failed third year. The arts degree still eluded him. Monash was shattered once more, but now aware that he couldn't expect to sail through his degree after a token study effort, especially if he took on new subjects, no matter how full his friends' lecture notes were. He resolved to make a bigger effort in 1887.

Weeks after this setback, he received a compensatory boost in confidence when Major Goldstein admitted him to the North Melbourne Battery in early March. He sat an exam, passed with distinction and was rewarded with an appointment as a probationary lieutenant in early April. He was excited by the achievement and being able to put on the officer regalia. Monash made an exuberant entry in his diary: '. . . a combination of military and engineering professions is a possibility that is before me.'[2] This remark is a reflection of his current occupations rather than being a demonstration of a remarkable prescience. Yet his approach to detail – indeed everything he could learn about both the work at the battery and the bridge – were indi-cators that at the age of twenty-one Monash had found possible career paths. How he would run them concurrently – in 'combination' – was not predictable. Yet their similar appeals were manifesting. He liked order. He felt comfortable with controlling men in some form of disciplined structure. To get things done in these worlds, you had to learn how to plan, organise and direct. An obsession with the minutia was an asset for both.

Engineering and the military, too, were complementary in his life. Building bridges, railways and dams would bring steady work, he assumed, in a boom without end in vibrant Melbourne, Victoria and perhaps Australia. In turn, this would create wealth, which, in the parochial world of a provincial city, brought a measure of status. The military, Monash expected, would bring rank and prestige and further status. Wealth, rank, prestige and status, he hoped, would help him rise above the perceived handicaps of his birth. Still beyond these not insignificant superficialities were the drives to build and achieve impressive useful structures and what Monash saw as his 'duty' to continue with his military training. It was simple logic to him that the coming nation would not last if it was not prepared to defend itself. Monash viewed defence as vital to Australia's destiny in the Asia–Pacific region rather than helping the British Empire maintain its power in every trouble spot.

Monash had his first taste of 'defending the [coming] nation' at a six-day Easter Camp in April 1887, when the North Melbourne Battery manned the fort at Port Nepean on Port Phillip Heads. The big guns were grouped in twos or fours for coastal artillery practice. Monash had to plan the firing and make sure everything and everyone performed efficiently. He demonstrated, as ever, that he had command of the detail of gun drills, their construction and maintenance and the use of sighting scales. Monash loved the whole exercise but hated the disorganisation, inefficiency and lethargy around him. His goal was to change all that.

The learning process intensified as Monash made the most of full-time life on the bridge project for the rest of 1887. He pushed, eased and cajoled himself into each stage of the construction. Having done the drawings and set the specifications for the masonry, he oversaw the carving of it. After organising the quarry there was supervision of the setting of the granite columns. The bluestone from Malmsbury had to be laid. Monash directed the building of the cofferdam (a watertight enclosure used for work on the bridge below the waterline). It collapsed, took in water and had to be rebuilt. It was difficult to pump the water out, and Monash had to work out how to do it along with the workers on the spot. He tested it himself and became submerged in 'mud and calculations'. After much trial and error, it was ready for the masonry.

It was all a learning curve. He took notes, not just for the sake of knowledge. He could get that in lectures. Monash wished to comprehend everything, and that could only be achieved hands on.

There were errors – not surprising since a twenty-two-year-old was doing most of the tougher jobs for the first time on a big construction. He made a mistake on measuring, which could have led to a column collapse, but other engineers picked it up in the mandatory crosscheck on figures. It upset Monash. He was also shaken by deaths on the site. A diary entry noted: 'Yesterday another unfortunate fellow was mangled by a stone. I took him to the hospital and the business has considerably affected me.'[3]

He was in just as much danger as the men under him. He was injured a few times, and once ended up in hospital with a gashed leg. But he was determined to be back at the site early the next morning, feeling himself 'indispensable'. Munro would have found it hard to replace such a hard worker on his meagre salary. At times his restless energy and drive irritated co-engineers and superiors. His persistent probing tested their own endeavours and capabilities.

Monash as ever was the social administrator. He volunteered to organise the employees' picnic for the hundreds of men on the project and their families, and other socials. Monash was made treasurer for these functions. He was compelled to create the right team atmosphere, whether at the university, the battery, the German Club (which he was using as a social venue) or in this ensemble of workers on the bridge project. Whenever Monash was involved the organisation had more of a sense of purpose. He wrote that there was sometimes a mixed reaction to him among his growing range of friends, acquaintances and contacts. After his school days they came from university, engineering, the opera, theatre and concert worlds, and the German, Jewish and Anglo-Celtic communities. Monash told his diary that he wasn't always popular or appreciated. Yet it never seemed to upset or deter him.

In September 1887 he prepared for a longer run at the end-of-year exams, this time swapping geology, which had never fired his imagination beyond the quarries, for jurisprudence. He paused in late October from his after-work studies to prepare for the military exam for full lieutenant, which he passed. It gave him satisfaction and inspired him to work harder to attain that still-elusive third year of arts, which would have been completed three years earlier had he applied himself. This time around he at last passed five subjects. It meant he had passed physics and the two maths subjects three times. When the results were out in January he wallowed in the achievement, especially after his success in the military exam. Monash got drunk on whisky with some battery engineers (with whom he was proud he could now hold his own in liquor consumption), then again at the City Club Hotel the following night.

It was a heady time, yet Monash managed to keep working on Princes Bridge until it was finished. There were prospects for jobs on other projects. Emboldened by his exam success, he asked for and received another ten shillings a week from Munro. His salary of £2 10s was still ordinary, but he could now afford his busy social life. With his confidence running high, he decided to sit in February 1888 for honours in maths, which would have given him a Master of Arts. Yet his enthusiasm was dampened by the knowledge that he still had to pass that old monster Latin for his BA (and later geology, applied mechanics and civil engineering for his engineering degree).

Monash shaped up to the subject again and felt he was getting on top by mid-February, when his battery visited the Williamstown Rifle Range on a Saturday. The bleak place always depressed him, and his being a poor marksman with either rifle or handgun didn't help his feelings.

Another bad shooter in the ranks hit one of the range's staff, who was marking the score during target practice. He was taken to hospital but died. Monash, who was left in charge of the range activity by the battery's captain, John Stanley, was elsewhere supervising other drills when the accident happened. A sergeant was in control of target practice. Stanley sidestepped responsibility. Monash, as the ranking officer in charge on the range, seemed likely to be made a scapegoat. The incident, coming a week before his Latin exam, distracted him so much that he did not sit for it. That arts degree had become a phantom once more. Instead he was compelled to gather evidence for a coronial investigation. When called to the witness box, Monash was well prepared for his defence. The coroner seemed aware that the conscientious lieutenant was in no way to blame. He did not grill the witness. Instead he found there had been misadventure.

Monash took a positive lesson from this harrowing experience. He thought newspaper coverage was useful to him. At the least it taught him the meaning of the cynical axiom 'Any publicity is good publicity'. He also decided to make a special effort to overcome his bad marksmanship and to direct other inaccurate shots to improve their aim. He never wanted such an accident to occur again under his command.

Monash kept working for Munro, planning the masonry for Queen's Bridge over the Yarra. Then it was on to other projects in Melbourne's busy west. Work kept him busy and, according to his diary, saved him from 'much misery and wretchedness'. In fact, he was a workaholic. His only breaks for up to a week from the military and engineering were his bush walks with long-term friend from school George Farlow, who was a part-time law student and member of the North Melbourne Battery. They drifted through Gippsland performing (Monash on piano, Farlow singing) in pubs and at homesteads. They slept rough. Both were well trained in survival techniques, and Monash loved this as much as he did his hectic social life. He was developing as a young man of contrasting interests rather than contradictions. One day he might disappear into the bush; the next he might be at the Melbourne Cup (the one sporting activity he continued as a spectator) in a top hat.

The only common accessory was his walking stick.

One evening in March 1888 at the German Club, Monash told his friend Jim Lewis he was dissatisfied with the small jobs that Munro had been giving him. Monash wanted a substantial challenge, similar to – even bigger than – Princes Bridge. He believed he was ready to take charge of a major project.

'Why don't you try for the Outer Circle Railway?' Lewis replied in jest.[4] This was a huge project that involved building an eighteen-kilometre railway line through Melbourne's eastern suburbs from Oakleigh through Camberwell to Fairfield. Monash thought it was worth a try. He was well aware of the lack of qualified engineers for the glut of building projects. He applied with an impressive CV, which included his school education and his two near-degrees, listing the broad range of subjects he had studied. The Princes Bridge engineering work included a letter of recommendation from Lewis.

Monash had two interviews and was in no doubt that his employers, the big railway contractors Graham & Wadick, were also impressed by his military rank. He waited, impatiently and anxiously, a month for a decision. It went his way. He was thrilled. It was the biggest appointment attained by any of the young engineers in Melbourne at that time. Monash worried that he might be out of his depth. His new employers gave him three months probation, which would expand to twelve months if he satisfied them. The salary was nearly three times that at Munro, but there were catches. He had to employ a clerk at his own expense and supply his own instruments. This would bring his net remuneration down to less than £4 10s, not quite £2 more than he was getting at Munro.

Instead of walking away from Munro graciously, Monash, now twenty-two, showed his inexperience with a pointed letter of resignation, in which he said that he was leaving because there seemed no chance of doing better where he was. Munro thought him ungrateful and fired him. But Monash was already on his way. He pushed aside for the moment any thoughts of finishing his degrees or, as his professors had urged, studying further. He was more academic and intellectual than the average student, yet his urge to get on and produce was far stronger. Any future study would have a practical end.

Monash's first decision was to hire a clerical assistant, twenty-four-year-old Fred Gabriel. He rented a five-room house in Hartwell, in Melbourne's eastern suburbs, where he lived with his wife, twenty-two-year-old Annie, and two-year-old son Gordon. It was easier for Monash to come to Gabriel because of the house's proximity to the proposed railway. Monash decided to use one of the rooms as an office.

He was drawn to Annie. She was attractive rather than beautiful and had a superb figure. There was also a quiet, womanly allure to her, in contrast to the sometimes flirtatious, sexually insecure virgins with whom he had dallied. At first he set out to befriend Annie, a natural aim given that he would be in her home, often into the night, clearing the endless paperwork with Gabriel. Petite, auburn-haired Annie responded to his charm and good manners, which were in contrast to her husband, who was frequently drunk. Their friendship grew. Monash began displaying his romantic side, bringing her books of poetry and prose, which they discussed during work breaks, over meals or when Gabriel was snoring after his nightly binge.

Monash was used to the social 'game' with single women. He would charm them, they would respond, become enchanted, but not dare go further than to accept his kisses. Occasionally, there would be some foreplay, but either the girl or Monash would pull back from the full experience. He was used to the ritual of brinkmanship. But he had not before encountered a married woman in this sensual dance. Annie was less inhibited than the more than fifty young women mentioned in his diaries and prepared to submit to his romantic overtures. She also saw to his every comfort. He found her warm as well as courageous in the way she handled Gabriel's brusqueness and bullying.

Their daily closeness turned the Hartwell home into a hothouse. In May they began exchanging notes without Gabriel knowing, then kisses. Monash wrestled with his conscience over where this was heading. He faced what he saw as his glaring weaknesses, and resolved to address them. 'My absurd vanity and brutal self-assertion give me growing cause for anxiety,' Monash wrote. 'I must check . . . manifestations which make me ashamed and disgusted with myself.' He wanted to give his best characteristics a chance for 'emphatic development'.[5]

By June he had given in to his pent-up impulses. He and Annie were having sex whenever Gabriel was asleep or out. Monash was ecstatic about losing his virginity, and enraptured by his lover, especially after the frustrating years of countless unfulfilled dalliances. But he was also touched by a sense of guilt. He had broken a commandment: thou shall not commit adultery. No matter how much he had rejected the concept of God reaching down from on high to deliver strict guidelines for wholesome living, he could not overcome a sense of doing wrong. Nor would his self-honesty accept the argument that Gabriel was a just a brute and Annie was a damsel in distress. His interest had been primarily carnal. Yet Annie, perhaps shrewdly, extracted from him expressions of love ('a declaration which evidently made her happy'), which, in his euphoric state, he gave gladly. It assuaged any guilty feelings.[6] Monash was steeped in the literature of romance. He reasoned that if he were truly in love with her and she him, didn't that go some way to excusing their feverish, clandestine activity?

✕

Monash didn't let these nightly distractions interfere with working hard in his probation period to impress his employers. He had to start organising the digging and removal of massive earthworks, the laying of the railway and the start of the twenty-five kilometres of roadworks. Despite his early concern about the size of the project, when he broke down the items, there was nothing he didn't feel confident about getting done after the Princes Bridge experience. The construction of a 175-metre, four-span steel viaduct over the Yarra at Fairfield was the biggest challenge. But the building of sixteen iron and timber bridges and scores of culverts, drains and sewers were easy for him. It was a matter of organisation and manpower management, and these held no terrors after what now amounted to four years of military training. Monash believed in strict delegation. The engineer supervised the foremen. They controlled the workers.

His innate planning skills came to the fore and submerged any pre-project nerves. Monash thrived on the control of hundreds of men, the huge budget of £170,000 and the variety of operations that he had to organise. He was relieved and pleased to find that the government engineer-inspector need not be feared. His employers mainly left him to his own devices, and he had no problem in building their confidence in him.

Graham & Wadick told him in mid-June that he had the job for the next year.

The confirmation of his position buoyed Monash and contributed to his boldness in the affair with Annie. 'Annie and I have had some pleasant passages,' Monash told his diary, 'and she led me on in her simple way.'[7]

It was difficult to carry it on while Gabriel was there, so the lovers planned secret meetings. Gabriel became suspicious and followed her to a place on the Yarra about a kilometre from Monash's home at Hawthorn. Gabriel caught them on the riverbank. Monash claimed they were going to discuss a book he was carrying in his satchel. Gabriel wouldn't accept the explanation. There was a cooling between the two men at night when they met to sift through the mounting paperwork. Annie was always there, ready to fix them food or cups of tea. Gabriel remained suspicious, forcing Monash to communicate with Annie via cryptic notes.

In August there was still the odd moment when Gabriel drank himself into a stupor, and they could make love. But their opportunities were limited. The notes grew into passionate love letters. Gabriel got to the mail first and noticed Monash's handwriting on a letter. He opened it and for the first time became fully aware of the affair.

Annie was bullied. Gabriel threatened to throw her out of the home without her little son. Monash was quick to make a grovelling apology to protect Annie. Gabriel, mindful of his position as Monash's employee, said he would accept his apology and not throw Annie out if he agreed to share the expense of running the Hartwell house. Monash had little choice but to agree. If he said no and fired Gabriel, Annie would suffer. But it was not a major concession. He wanted to use the house as his headquarters anyway, now that the contractors had confirmed his work for a year. Realising this, Gabriel requested that the paddock at the back of the house be rented out for agistment. He also wanted to run poultry for market. Both these enterprises would help defray the cost of the house's rent and bring in some extra cash. Monash happily agreed.

After that, their relationship improved, but Gabriel didn't trust his wife. His contempt led to physical abuse. Annie was prepared to run and live with her parents near Allendale in gold-mining country. Fearing she would be lost to him, Monash wrote her a heartfelt letter, suggesting that it was possible that one day they could be together. 'I . . . expressed determinations which I would not be surprised if I shall keep. For I have won from her all that I ever desire in my life.'[8] He was now smitten in his first love and feeling obligated to commit himself.

Annie responded by not running away. Soon after this mini-crisis Monash suggested that Gabriel travel to Ballarat to purchase poultry on a weekend, and he agreed. When he was away, Monash and Annie had a chance to indulge their passion over three days and nights. '. . . the last three days absence of Gabriel in Ballarat,' he wrote, '. . . the most remarkable and pleasant experience I have yet had.'[9] But Gabriel returned early. 'Unexpected return of Gabriel [on 1 July],' Monash's diary noted cryptically, 'and an explosion on both sides.'[10]

There were other consequences from the affair. Annie missed her period. She told Monash that she might be pregnant. He was relieved when it was found to be a false alarm. The scare did not deter either of them. 'This little romance has strengthened me much,' he justified to his diary, 'and has strengthened my trust and reliance in myself.'[11]

In October 1888 Gabriel went to Sydney with the prospect of purchasing horses. This time he was away a week, and the two lovers had their most sustained period together. Monash was now able to show off his full military regalia when he took her by tram to dine in Brunswick. In these brief moments, Monash was living out what he thought a romantic relationship should be with a loving partner. The trouble was that she was officially someone else's partner.

On returning from Sydney, Gabriel was suspicious of Annie's demeanour. He accused her of continuing the affair. She admitted it was true, perhaps willing to precipitate a crisis. Gabriel hit her again. He threatened to beat up Monash. Annie became ill and went to live with her parents. Monash thought it prudent not to visit her, but he couldn't resist writing. As the weeks drifted by his letters became more and more lovesick. 'What have I to live for if your love is gone?' he wrote. 'Night after night, I have lain awake thinking, thinking – calling up one by one all the moments of happiness you have brought me – speaking to you again in thought – hearing the sound of your voice, feeling the touch of your lips – the thrill of your deep and loving looks . . .'[12] Annie's absence was making Monash's heart grow fonder and his pen flow.

The continuing six-month affair had no impact on Monash's work. By November, he was certain that he had found his profession. The more he had to organise and manage, the more he felt comfortable. He loved his capacities being stretched to the limit. Hard work calmed him, and brought 'a state of mental balance and goodness of spirits' that made him happier than ever.

'I feel a new sense of dignity and importance as a tangible factor in the production of wealth,' he told his diary. His reading of the eighteenth-century Scottish philosopher and economist Adam Smith was giving clarity to his sense of self. Monash was a natural free-enterprise man. He agreed with Smith's famous exposition, in *The Wealth of Nations*, of the 'invisible hand' of competition as guiding an economic system based on individual self-interest. Monash had no time for an opposing theory, put by Prussian Jewish political theorist, Karl Marx, whose book *Das Kapital* had recently been republished posthumously. It, along with his *Communist Manifesto*, was inspiring workers in industrialised nations to strike for better wages and conditions.[13]

Navvies – workers – on Monash's project struck for higher pay in November 1888. It annoyed him. It disturbed his orderly planning and cut into the thin margins of Graham & Wadick. It created tensions. Monash was caught in the middle between the employers and the workers. He measured both sides by his own attitude to and capacity for 'work'. Monash noted that the contractors' capital had been made by their hard work and self-denial. By contrast, he was not enamoured of the attitude of the navvies. He regarded a lot of them as lazy drunks, having seen daily evidence of laziness and drunkenness on the various project sites. Considering the demand for employment at the time, Monash thought wages should be lower, not higher. Graham & Wadick agreed.

After some delay the strike was called off.

Annie went back to Gabriel in mid-December 1888, and her return triggered another round of furtive assignations between her and Monash, although never now at the Hartwell house. He kept the homage to his first love coming in an outpouring of letters but there seemed now to be more words than action. The two lovers talked about divorce and where they might live, for the scandal would probably mean that they could not live in Melbourne. Sydney was talked about, as were places in country Victoria, such as Jerilderie, yet nothing was set in concrete.

Gabriel followed his wife on several occasions. She managed to slip away from him. In mid-March 1889 she thought she had evaded him and met Monash in Studley Park, Kew. They were embracing when Gabriel surprised them, knocked Monash to the ground and dragged off the protesting Annie. Monash thought it best not to get into a brawl, which would only exacerbate the situation.

Annie and Monash remained out of touch for a few days before he received a letter from her father imploring him – at Gabriel's demand – to leave his daughter alone.

Annie decided to stay with her parents again. Monash wrote to Annie, saying she had to divorce Gabriel. It was the only rational course if they were going to end up together. In the meantime, Gabriel realised his work for Monash was untenable, and he left the job. Soon afterwards he wrote to the ailing Louis, demanding money to leave Victoria, without Annie. Monash ignored the offer. There was no mention of Gordon, and Annie would never abandon her son. Monash could not trust Gabriel, whom he judged was not above blackmail. Also Monash had yet to come to terms with Annie, despite the plethora of letters declaring his undying commitment. There were still many questions for both in this rough course of true love. Could the whole affair end in scandal? Could she fit into the ambitious Monash's world? How would young Gordon Gabriel fare if the parents lived in separate colonies? New divorce legislation was about to be written in Victoria, but what would apply in South Australia or New South Wales?

Annie, as much as Monash, was wavering and worried.

After six weeks of not seeing each other, Monash took the train to Ballarat in late April where Annie met him. They travelled to the country town of Buninyong and spent the day there. May passed without another meeting. They both wondered whether the affair was waning.

The long breaks and the part-time nature of the affair meant that, despite its episodic dramas, Monash followed the main paths of his career and life without major interruption. In June he passed the captain's exam with a high mark and was encouraged to think of further promotion. Just twenty-four in mid-1889, he had already developed a huge grasp of every aspect of the military. He was making several areas his specialties, including drilling and weaponry – particularly artillery. He wanted more drilling such as he experienced each Easter: under simulated war conditions in the forts facing Melbourne's ports, rather than in drill halls at night. He lobbied to dump arcane musketry practice and to replace it with greater expertise for gunners. The authorities should have to pay incentives to encourage them to achieve first-class status. He lectured on artillery.

Monash was in the precision arm of the military, which relied on science more than the infantry and cavalry, where physical endurance was a key prerequisite. The artillery needed accurate computations to make sure it hit targets, whether they were invading ships, landing infantry or stationary objects. Monash revelled in this discipline. The cavalry was on the way out and infantry developments were limited, yet there were no limitations on the growth of scientific applications to warfare. By chance, Monash had stumbled into the one military area where he would never become bored. His training as an engineer was perfect for comprehending new weaponry and devices.

Monash proved it by developing a breech-loading gun for practice drilling after consulting a mechanic and a fitter. It became known as the 'Stanley-Monash gun'. Captain Stanley had commissioned Monash to create it, but it was solely Monash's design. The colony's Defence Department at first refused to pay him the £100 he estimated was needed for the simulated gun's development. Months after it was ready he was paid £140 costs. Unfortunately for him, there were no legal mechanisms for patenting such devices, especially for someone in the indirect employ of the Victorian Government.

The gun was capable of popping up over a parapet and forts, similar to those that would guard Melbourne ports and the bay's Heads. It could fire and then recoil under cover, which was more than useful for fighting an enemy coming ashore. The press reported on the gun when it proved successful and, later, indispensable. Monash gained credit. Ministerial approval was given for the gun for the Harbour Trust, Port Fairy, Portland and Warrnambool batteries.

Major General Sir Julius Bruche recalled seeing it at the time when he took over command of the senior cadet company of the North Melbourne Battery Garrison at Toorak. 'The first thing that struck me there was a model gun,' Bruche recalled. 'The barrel was made of wood, but all the rest was a proper gun as at Queenscliff . . . it enabled the men to drill in the drill-room and use the correct ammunition and mechanism. When they went to Queenscliff they were very efficient.'[14]

Just to make his military commitment complete, Monash worked hard on his poor marksmanship for twelve months as he promised himself he would do after the accidental death at the Williamstown range. He faced his lack of hand/eye coordination, something that bedevilled all his attempts at ball sports, and made a study of what was required to be a good shot, especially with a handgun. Monash began by taking one apart, as he had done with the breech-loading weapon, and examining each part of the mechanism. Then he took lessons from experts. When satisfied that he fully comprehended it, he spent twice as much time at the Williamstown range as in any other year practising. After seventeen months of application he was, by any measure within range for a handgun, an excellent marksman. No one in the North Melbourne Battery was better.

Monash's reputation as a remarkable young military man was now much wider than the drill hall confines of the North Melbourne Battery. The time he was making a contribution to the military, and his wide expertise meant he was operating and learning beyond anyone in the militia (the part-time 'citizen' force) or the regular armed forces. Apart from those who had experienced war, there was no more expert young military officer in Australia.

Monash's successful rise through the ranks saw another side of him emerge: the Peacock. He never missed an opportunity to attend balls in full regalia. He loved the effect uniform had on women, who gravitated to him.

Because of the unresolved, uncertain nature of the affair with Annie, Monash had never given up seeing others, although all were platonic relationships.

In the middle of a nine-week lull – the longest break for him and Annie since their first meeting – Monash went to a dance at the German Club on 22 July 1889. A twenty-two-year-old dark-haired Jewish beauty, Vic (Victoria or 'Victory') Moss, caught his attention. She was tallish with a good figure, large, black–brown eyes and nice bone structure. Vic, unlike Annie, listened to Monash 'disclose' himself without offering much about herself. She was cool, if not cold, whereas, he noted, Annie was warm. Vic seemed unimpressed by his achievements as an engineer or in the military, whereas Annie expressed her admiration at every turn. Vic was anything but submissive in her manner. By contrast, Annie would do his bidding.

While he chatted with Vic, in full view of the customary chaperone, Monash checked any remark about Annie for the first time he could remember in anyone's company, male or female. He was touched by something he couldn't quite comprehend. She was an orphan. Her English-born parents, Moton Moss, a merchant and hotelier, and mother, Rebecca Alexander, had died in 1879 and 1882. Her sisters had brought her up. Yet there was nothing pitiable or waif-like about this straight-backed young woman. 'She is a woman far beyond her years,' he wrote, trying to fathom his experience soon after meeting, 'and has a disposition startlingly akin to my own.'[15] Monash was intrigued. His passion for Annie remained, but he couldn't get Vic out of his mind.

Annie returned early to Melbourne in July 1889. The affair, with all the secret assignations, was on again. It was nearly over by misadventure. Monash was supervising the lifting of heavy stones on the first arch of the Fairfield viaduct when a roped snapped. Someone yelled a warning. Monash looked up. The terror of the stones coming at him caused him to freeze. Had he moved he might have been killed. One stone missed his head by centimetres. A mason close by was not so fortunate. His hand was crushed. After taking some time to stop the bleeding, Monash took him to hospital.

A letter to Annie about his 'frightening escape' showed Monash in a fateful mood. He had seen his life 'flash in front of him'. The time had now come for major decisions. In the back of his mind was a looming second option with another woman. He wasn't quite sure whom at that point. Yet at twenty-four – above the average age for marriage in the 1880 and 1890s – he wanted to marry, have a family and get on with life. Vic was there as a vague option. But he kept comparing her and others to Annie.

Two months after meeting Vic, he thought, perhaps in youthful arrogance or just optimism, she was in love with him. But she wasn't as 'soft' and 'womanly' as Annie, and he wasn't sure about her inner character.[16] Still, he began, in his own verbose, humourless yet romantic style, to write to Vic, after going through the protocol of gaining permission from her elder sisters. He and his sister Mathilde were invited to the Moss home. Monash amused the little party with his old card tricks. Vic remained unmoved. It wasn't until he sat at the piano and played the Polonaise that he saw a flicker in the eyes of his graceful hostess. Vic, too, was an accomplished pianist. Here there seemed some common ground between them. Despite telling his diary that he seemed to puzzle her, the reverse was the case. He couldn't grasp her character, predict her thoughts or impress her. Vic, after two months and a few formal, rather stiff meetings, was still a mystery.

Monash began to feel the impediment of his affair with Annie. The social set they moved in had heard rumours. It was a hot topic among the day's social elite. Now Monash was beginning to see it as inhibitive. He would have to either do some explaining to any other prospective marriage option, including Vic, or reach a resolution with Annie.

In August 1889 the pressure mounted. His family, particular strong-willed Mathilde, urged him to do more than just consider Vic. She was an excellent prospect, he was told. She was a capable hostess, cultured at least in her musical tastes, and beautiful. She was even a bit of a socialite who promenaded 'the Block' at the 'Paris End' of Collins Street in the city. What more could he want?

'Annie Gabriel' was his plaintive response. He felt now he was being railroaded into marriage with someone he admired and respected in a dim way, but didn't love. He was miserable and confused. In desperation, he wrote to Annie pleading with her to elope. He was shocked when she wrote back agreeing to do it. His first reaction was to recoil.

The consequences of running away – they would have to move to another colony – came into focus. Monash would need to abandon his military career in Melbourne. His commission would stand, but he was entrenched in the politics of the North Melbourne Battery. Chances for advancement were dependent on his rise through its ranks. Starting again would throw away the five years he had spent setting up a rise to the top. He also knew it would mean the end of his finishing off his degrees in arts and engineering. Monash's experience in engineering would give him a chance of work, but Melbourne is where he had 'networked' against what he saw as the handicaps of his background. Starting again in Adelaide or Sydney would be tough.

Now the vague image of Vic as a wife refined itself. He wrote in his diary of 23 August: '. . . since meeting Vic – who fulfils . . . all the requirements of a suitable wife to me – dim visions of a home life, and a finality to all my present struggles have been assuming a prominent place in my thoughts.' The choice between the passion he felt for Annie and the possible suitability of Vic as a wife caused him 'harmful mental agony'.[17]

It seemed as if Vic was aware of his dilemma, and she might well have been. His parents had read his diaries. It is possible that Mathilde, aware of a pending crisis for the brother she loved, was now doing so and encouraging Vic without informing her about the more than serious competition.

Monash received a telegram from her on the 24th. This method of communication was reserved for a special occasion or something urgent. Monash replied by telegram, inviting her to his home on the 25th. Vic arrived, again observing etiquette, with her elder sister Belle. The moment she left, Monash went straight to his confessional – the diary – and faced what was bothering him most about Vic.

He was disappointed in her. He didn't think she could 'subjugate herself to me sufficiently to suit' his temperament.[18] Neither did Vic touch him at all emotionally. As ever, he compared her to Annie. A key was Vic's lack of compliance. She would not bend to his will as Annie was prepared to do. Monash believed in order at the battery, in the workplace and in the home. He was the master engineer, the officer in charge. The wife would be the subaltern or the forewoman. The children would be the privates or navvies. A woman who challenged him or his authority – other than intellectually – would be a distraction from his career endeavours.

If Monash had then considered Vic a better prospect, he would have dumped the messy situation with Annie. But a combination of his honour, his ego and the fact that he was in his first intimate sexual relationship was keeping him loyal to a situation that he was well aware could spell disaster for him. 'There comes to me the choice,' he wrote to a friend, 'Annie and infamy or "reputable home of my own".'[19]

A danger wish in him caused him to commit himself to Annie, although he was less than full-hearted about it. He imagined that if he couched it in uncertain terms, she might back off. Instead she made the stakes higher by telling him that she was pregnant to Gabriel, without saying her relationship with Monash should end. She knew her paramour. Her desperate situation drew out a chivalry in Monash. Taking the cue from her that she wanted a way out, he rushed to her 'armed with drugs and money' to arrange an abortion. But in the back of his mind, he hoped this startling development would be an excuse to end the relationship. He stopped short of the Gabriel home, now in inner-suburban Abbotsford. Gabriel would not allow her to leave and was on sentry duty for any sighting of Monash.

That was on the evening of 29 August. Monash returned home to Hawthorn and thought better of his intended action. Realising that he would be aiding and abetting the termination of a life, which would look monstrous if ever brought up in divorce proceedings, he rejected that idea. Monash wrestled with the problem, went to bed and found difficulty sleeping. He got up in the early hours and planned in a note to Annie a course that was honour-bound: 'This is the crisis of our lives,' he wrote, with melodrama, yet possible veracity, 'if you are prepared to trust yourself and your child to me for the rest of your life, come now *at once* to Hawthorn.'[20]

The vigilant Gabriel foiled Monash by tracking down their secret methods of exchanging letters and notes. He intercepted the letter containing the directive and reacted by taking Annie to a hotel in South Yarra. When Monash learned this, he used another mutual friend to deliver his letters to her. He now repeated his suggestion that she leave with him, but added a little 'out clause'. He was leaving the decision, he wrote, entirely to her. If she did come to him he would elope with her to Adelaide.

Having despatched this challenge, Monash then turned to his diary and wrote something that would have seen Annie reject his offer if he had made the remark to her: 'And deliberately I will for her sake go to my ruin.'[21] This was hardly an attitude that would lead to a viable – let alone happy – future together. If it was going to be that bad, logic would suggest, there was no point in going through with it. But Monash appeared to have lost his sense of perspective in the crisis.

As if still reaching for an alternative, he dated Vic on Saturday night, 7 September. They went to the theatre in the city. She was cold and unresponsive, perhaps because she had an inkling of his mindset. She even dropped calling him 'Jack', which his intimate friends used.

Vic didn't measure up. He focused more on Annie.

She hadn't responded after several days. Monash waited and worried. He made a long action list regarding banking arrangements, lodgings and travel to Adelaide, and set them in train. On 12 September Annie returned with Gabriel to Abbotsford. She managed to sneak a note to Monash. She promised to come to him the next day, Friday 13 September.

Monash could not turn back. He spent all Friday visiting his bank, lawyer and friends, making final arrangements for his furtive, desperate departure with a married woman. Was it illegal to abscond with another man's wife, no matter how willing she was? Monash didn't care. He had made a decision he didn't really want and didn't believe would have ever eventuated.

Late in the afternoon, he packed a suitcase full of essentials, with directions for a reluctant Mathilde to forward more effects. Then, after dark, he took a train to Abbotsford and waited at a prearranged spot a few blocks from the Gabriel home. Annie, carrying a suitcase and a hatbox, managed to slip away to meet her lover. They embraced, then hurried by train to a home in South Yarra where a friend met them with young Gordon, now aged five. Monash, Annie and Gordon then hustled back to South Yarra station in a hansom cab. They dismounted in Toorak Road and began to cross it.

Gabriel, who had tailed them, rushed at Monash, cracking him in the head with a walking stick and then thumping him with a fist to the face. Monash fell to the ground, momentarily unconscious. Bloodied, he got to his feet and stumbled towards a cab, in which Gabriel had bundled Annie and Gordon.

'All will be right, Annie,' a groggy Monash called, 'you know what to do.'

'Yes, Jack!' she cried, frightened and ashen-faced.[22]

A solicitous small crowd gathered, then dispersed. Monash was concussed. He staggered towards Punt Road, then back to the station. He took a cab home and went straight to bed. He awoke mid-morning with a splitting headache and a closed black eye. He did not rise until after lunch. Rosie Blashki, his closest friend among the four sisters, consoled him in a walk to the riverbank nearest his home. Monash was depressed. They strolled back to find several friends had turned up to be with him at a critical moment. He was buoyed. No one knew, or was letting on, where Annie had been taken. Monash learned on Monday 16 September that Gabriel had taken Annie and Gordon to Sydney.

By Tuesday Monash's mind was clear. The nightmare has passed, he wrote in his diary. He felt an enormous relief. He claimed that he didn't care if he ever saw her again, which was untrue but his way of attempting to come to terms with the dramatic events. Monash had been living out a misguided and dangerous, yet duty-bound affair. Now it was over.

BATTLE
ENGAGEMENT

Monash mourned his lost lover for a week before he brought himself back into social circulation by going to the wedding of Eva, another of the Blashki sisters. Vic Moss was there, and she looked ravishing. He had not seen her for twenty-five days, and had left her wondering what was happening. He made excuses about 'working all hours' and that important battery operations were taking up his spare time. Monash needed to repair his self-esteem and image among friends and enemies. After getting over the inevitable questions about his black eye, he warmed to moving on Vic with all his old charm. For better or worse, the affair with Annie Gabriel had given him an extra dimension. Monash, the calculating engineer and military expert, was now a man with sex appeal. Despite the 'shock/horror' rumours of the affair, about which the girls on 'the Block' had gossiped, there was something more alluring about a man with experience.

Monash found himself on the rebound at the Blashki wedding. It caused his behaviour to run ahead of his deeper thoughts. He considered the checklist concerning his increased interest in Vic. The more the points in similarity of religion, culture and class, he was told by family members and some close friends, the better chance the marriage had of success. Even by the end of the wedding, Monash was half-convinced that Vic was the logical choice. He told himself that he liked to make decisions based on the head, not the heart. This was even after sexy, submissive Annie had drawn out passions he had denied in himself.

Monash weighed up the list for and against Vic. He concluded that she seemed more like 'the one' than ever before. In his diary he urged himself to forget the past and move on – at a pace. The next night Monash was at Vic's home playing a piano duet of Haydn's symphonies with her. He enjoyed that evening more than any other so far with her. A sense of harmony was running through them for the first time. He was encouraged. He asked her to come with him to see Henrik Ibsen's play *The Doll House*. It had caused controversy since first performed in Europe a decade earlier. In it, Ibsen exposed the individual's loss of freedom and expression as he or she conformed to society's conventions. The main convention in this case was marriage, a topic swamping the thoughts of Monash and Vic. The play demonstrated how a husband brought about – unwittingly – his wife's intellectual and financial enslavement. The London production a few months earlier had sparked a vehement debate about 'Ibsenism'. The Melbourne production had caused a similar literary storm. Some critics in London and locally saw it as scandalous.

Monash expected he might have an interesting discussion with Vic over supper after the play. But she proffered nothing. Either she couldn't grasp the significance for her possible position as a wife or she didn't care. He found the play stimulating, but tiptoed round the main theme. Perhaps with the experience of marriage itself, they might have had a hot debate. But at this point they were in the first throes of love, making them if not blind, then oblivious to anything that would distract them from their path.[1]

Monash kept running. He went to another play one night and on the next delivered a lecture on weaponry – 'Death of the Musket' – to several hundred soldiers from all the metropolitan batteries. The emphasis was on how technology was changing warfare. A useful example was his own Stanley-Monash gun. He was well received, and there was some publicity in the morning papers. Monash could draw a good crowd. He enjoyed the acclamation, especially at this moment of ego repair.

In mid-October 1889, he and Vic were walking along the riverbank near his home, without a chaperone. It was warm spring night. They were talking about how much they felt for each other when Monash proposed. Vic accepted with a simple, dignified, gentle: 'Yes, Jack darling, yes.'[2]

He was happy, although even at that moment he had to push away intrusive thoughts about Annie. The news was not made public. Only family and close friends were informed of this impulsive decision. There was an enthusiastic response, perhaps out of relief more than anything.

Mathilde, his closest relative and fiercest critic, was angry about how fickle he had been. She knew this was a rebound decision based on the hurt of not succeeding with Annie. Mathilde felt he was rushing things and told him he should keep the engagement a secret for at least a year. She did not expect the new relationship to work.

But in Monash's mind, committing himself to another was the cleanest possible way to cut off any residual thoughts about reviving the affair with Annie. He had been making inquiries about her. Monash knew where she was and had sent letters to her, telling her that he could arrange for her to leave Gabriel if her situation became intolerable. He just couldn't bring himself to break off all contact with his first true love. But the geographic near-impossibility of Annie being in Sydney (always under Gabriel's fierce guard) and now this ultimate act of commitment to another was as much as Monash could do to distance himself from the affair.

Monash went into self-analysis, at once trying to understand his decision and work out why he felt the way he did about Vic. Part of this therapy was to write to his new fiancée about it. He told her she was different from the others. Then he confessed that he had dedicated his life so far to the 'gallantry' of women, which was a euphemism for the flirting with, charming, impressing, romanticising and, more recently, seduction of them. 'But there is something about you,' he wrote, perhaps with a love song coming on, 'that banishes from my manner the least attempt at artificiality, and I only appear to you as my own clumsy self.'[3]

Just being bumbling old Jack with her around would not have been the line that Vic would have hoped for. It was a signal that now she was betrothed to him, he could get on with his grand schemes in the military and in business. Chivalry, courtliness, politeness or even romance towards his partner were features of the chase and therefore past. Vic might not have been as educated, intellectually developed or ambitious as he was, but she was not dim. After receiving this deadening declaration, she reacted in a way that puzzled him.

On a Saturday, they took the train to Flinders Street where he guided her over Princes Bridge. Vic didn't utter a word of praise. She seemed bored. Not one question emerged from her sensual lips about the design or the stonework. Monash was deflated. How could she not be stimulated by his work of art? They walked on in silence to South Yarra. Then she rounded on him and accused him of having secret lovers. Monash protested, guessing that someone in their circle had told her about Annie. He stuck to the line that there were no other women of importance in his life. It was true, but misleading. If Vic had accused him of someone in the recent past, then he would have been in a sweat. But she did not. Events had moved so fast that someone knowing of his affair might have warned Vic, unaware that it was over with Annie. Vic wanted to believe him. So she claimed she did. When they reached her front gate and he told her how much he wanted her, Vic's mood swung again. Now she was tender, touching him lovingly and exciting him, but not yet in a powerful sexual sense. Not the way Annie had.

Monash went home feeling relieved that the atmosphere in which they parted was good. But when he went to his diary, he reflected. She was on to him and sharper than he thought. He was critical of his fiancée. Did she have any 'refined sense of high motives or purposes'? Or was she just clever and small-minded?[4] He was preparing himself for disappointments or even another broken romance.

The next night they went to a German Club ball. Monash was made to feel vulnerable when Vic flirted with a male admirer, who kept wanting to dance with her. It put Monash on edge. He had no hold on Vic as he had Annie. Vic might have been flirtatious by nature, but she was testing Monash. Aware of those persistent rumours about a 'concealed armour', she was unsure herself. She remained icy.

'Vic showed little emotion of any kind,' Monash told his diary. 'Her frigidity laid chains to my tongue, and I felt full of all kinds of doubts and misgivings.'[5]

She kept up this attitude until the first Tuesday in November – Melbourne Cup Day. They both had a bet and Vic won. Her demeanour changed. She was loving, although she resisted his advances to sleep with him. Vic was keeping that ace well in hand. He would have to wait, she told him, until the wedding night.

It was a long way off. It made him more than keen to make love with her.

They decided on an eighteen-month engagement, with plans to marry in April 1891. In the meantime the relationship was bumpy, with Monash expressing his misery, doubts and regrets. In June 1890 – ten months from the wedding date – Monash was so frustrated and disappointed that he suggested calling off the engagement. He had become disenchanted by not being able to educate her. Vic was not one for reading widely or learning about art and architecture. Nor did she utter any word of admiration for Monash or his work, ideas or writings. She was not inspirational. Vic began to berate him, perhaps in reaction to his elitist attitudes and attempts to change her 'lack of thirst for light [i.e. intellectual enlightenment]'. She pointed out his faults and weaknesses so much that it distressed him.

In August 1890, ten months after he had renounced his gallantry towards her, he made another gaffe that would have raised Vic's hackles. 'I cannot reconcile my thoughts of you to a quiet home life at my fireside,' he wrote in an offer to end the engagement. Once more, it was not what a strong-willed, fun-loving virgin in her early twenties wanted to hear. She was not excited about bringing slippers to any master of the house, now or in the future.

Further correspondence between them led Vic to calling his bluff. She offered to break it off. Monash was quick to reconcile. Vic now had the upper hand. She insisted that he 'didn't assert any rights or claims' against her. Nor could he place any restrictions on her 'conduct, actions or words'. Monash wrote that he 'could not help admiring her calm dignity and firmness'. But this seemed about all. He was upset to learn that she had been out with another man. She was the subject of gossip on the Block and at dinner parties. But he had to either take it or leave it.

'You have conquered, Vic,' he wrote to her. 'Make of me what you wish.'[6]

After a year of their relationship, he was beginning to understand what a marriage to such a strong character would be like. Vic would stand up to him. He would have to learn the art of compromise more than he imagined. Yet she did succumb to his persistent advances and made love to him. But she resisted making it a regular feature of their premarital relationship.

Monash refused to see her not bending to him as a positive. In fact the only thing about their partnership that he saw as other than negative was his desire to study again. The engagement had stopped him chasing women. He had more time to finish his degrees that had been dangling in a way that offended his sense of order.

He saw Professor Kernot at a recent address on Monash's two major projects – Princes Bridge and the Outer Circle Railway – to the Engineering Students' Society. Kernot urged him to complete the course. In September, he asked his friend Jim Lewis and others to dig out their old lecture notes for him. He again crammed for exams in civil engineering and applied mechanics, which he enjoyed, and geology, which still bored him. After nine years he passed all the required subjects. He could at last frame and hang up his engineering degree. Inspired, he decided to go for honours in February 1891.

By mid-January he was again wondering if he had taken on too much alongside his military and engineering work. The Outer Circle Railway project was finished, but there were months of cost calculations yet to be done with railway officials. In a black period, in which he had misgivings about his forthcoming marriage, he wrote in his diary: 'Vic . . . not only does not seek opportunities for happy love-making, but even resists my attempts to do so . . . More than ever she shows her irritating tendency to disagree with every suggestion I make, in things great and small.'[7] This plus the strain of his poor finances, and Louis' lingering illnesses, told on him. But he was notified on 24 March that he had come top, scoring a high second-class honour and winning the *Argus* scholarship. Monash was buoyant on 4 April at the degree ceremony.

It came at a propitious time – just four days before his wedding – as he continued to be miserable about the prospect of marrying Vic. Realising this, she wrote a tender note to him the night before they were to take their vows. She urged him to forget the past. Their wedding day should be a new beginning for both of them. Monash's diary on his wedding day – 8 April 1891 – was not encouraging. 'I have been dull and unhappy,' he wrote. 'Today I marry Vic. So I close the record of my past life.'[8]

This morbid mindset might have been a case of pre-ceremony nerves rather than anything else. The day went well enough. Rabbi Williams married them at the Freemasons' Hall, Collins Street East, before more than 400 guests from several sections of society, reflecting Monash's wide network of contacts. About a hundred were Jewish, a handful were German, and there were many from school, the military, university and engineering. They partied afterwards and spent their first married night at the Federal Hotel. The next afternoon they took the overnight train to Sydney for their honeymoon.

They were lucky enough to have a carriage of their own on the first leg to Albury, arriving at midnight. For the Sydney leg in the early hours of

10 April, Vic stayed in a sleeping car, and Monash joined one fellow travel-ler – a Victorian Railways engineer – in the smoking car. 'We passed the night in the carriage talking and dozing,' Monash noted. 'Breakfast at Moss Vale. Vic joined us. Arrived Sydney at 11 a.m.'

When they were walking up the platform at Sydney's Central Station Monash noticed Fred Gabriel standing in the distance. Monash was 'astonished' but pretended not to see him, and said nothing to Vic. He did not wish to ruin their honeymoon. Instead he glanced back a couple of times to see whether Gabriel was following. Then he realised he was unlikely to tail them to the Grosvenor Hotel, where they would stay. Gabriel had probably read recent letters to Annie in which Monash had told her of the honeymoon plans, and that he would try to catch up if there was an opportunity.[9]

He and Vic spent six days in Sydney and made the usual tourist excur-sions on trams and ferries to the Art Gallery, the Bondi Aquarium and the Cyclorama. They went to the theatre three times and a concert, thus indulging the main two interests that they had in common. Monash's spirits were high. He reported in a letter to Mathilde how proud he was to be seen out with his 'beautiful wife'. He made no effort to see Annie. There was little time and less inclination to do so.

After Sydney they spent a week in the Blue Mountains and at the Jenolan Caves, where the autumn weather was perfect. As they arrived at Sydney's Central Station for the return journey home, Monash and Vic agreed that they had enjoyed every day of their two-week break. Not even a second sighting of Gabriel, who must have been making sure Monash left when he said he would, could dampen his spirits.

The marriage had started well. Monash and his new bride were in a state of uncommon bliss.

✕

Back in Melbourne, the reverie of the honeymoon was forgotten as he began the tough search for a job. Monash was aware before most of the colony's professionals that the 1880s building spree, which led to the speculative boom, had crashed by the middle of 1891. He had been disappointed that he didn't have capital to invest. Yet it could have been a blessing. He might have been saved from the ruin experienced by many of those in his circles who had money with which to play the markets. The crash was aggravated by a sharp fall in the prices of Victoria's main exports of wheat and wool. Finance societies and land banks began to go belly up.

In the second half of 1891, few new projects were being started. Engineers in established government bodies were being retrenched. Monash was one of hundreds looking for work as unemployment began to climb. He used every part of his considerable network to help him seek employment and experienced the cold hand of rejection many times over most of the year.

There were short assignments in this period that gave him hope. Monash gained a strong sense of achievement by designing the first ever swing-bridge in Victoria – over the Maribyrnong River. There was other dreary short-term work at Victoria Dock designing roads and drainage systems and the odd transit shed. He saw it all as good experience, but he wanted something with at least potential for longer-term security.

Professor Kernot told him of a vacancy at the Harbour Trust. Monash started work there in November on about £5 a week, which was less than the salary he ended on at the Outer Circle Railway. Unlike that project, which gave him a free reign, he found office work in a government department stultifying. Initiative was not encouraged, nor was hard work. But he had no choice. Times were tough and becoming tougher.

Government expenditure dropped, and the battery's funds were reduced. Monash turned his mind more to lecturing – on weapons, artillery and explosives. He studied the most up-to-date literature on the modern military, with particular interest in how new scientific developments would affect warfare. Illustrations, including lantern-slides projected on the wall, added to his lecturing skills, which were already first-rate. Monash could talk on a subject as dry as elementary artillery for up to an hour and captivate an audience with style, delivery and enthusiasm. His historical perspective gave him an edge over others. Military personnel, used to taking instruction and not thinking for themselves, found Monash refreshing.

✕

The struggle to find work and the frugal times put pressure on the Monash marriage. They rented a modest house in Clifton Street, Richmond, which promised relief from family pressures at least. Mathilde had to look after ailing Louis more, but he still burdened Monash, who every now and again had to pay off a debt from the failed money-lending business. At one point, there were court threats to seize all Louis' resaleable goods, such as two leather chairs. Monash was forced to find £100 to settle the debt.

The mood of the idyllic honeymoon in New South Wales was not sustained. Monash detested Vic's insistence on the freedom to go out with friends of both sexes. It created more rumours and humiliated him. His attempts to awaken an intellectual spark in Vic annoyed her. She was irked by his need to mould her into something she could never be. He began to conclude that she was too much of a lightweight, materialistic socialite for his liking. She found him demanding and intellectually pompous. Monash continued to bemoan her lack of support and praise for him. Vic resented his need to be the focus of attention.

Vic's reading of his diaries made both their attitudes worsen. She knew what he was thinking about her. His words reduced her self-confidence and her confidence in their relationship as she learned how disappointed and dispirited he was by her. It made the defiant Vic dig in more against his will. Monash was mortified to think that she was invading his privacy just as his parents had a decade earlier.

There were splits and breaks, with Vic disappearing to the homes of relatives and friends – once because she was tubercular, other times after fights. The turmoil saw Monash recoil further into his intellectual pursuits. If he wasn't researching matters military, he was at the university in his spare time where his studies were his hobbies. While many of the educated class of his age group were in a quandary about what to do, Monash was investing harder than ever in his own development. In August 1891 he went for the tough municipal surveyors' exam, set over three days at six hours a day, and passed.

Next, the law attracted him. His friendship with lawyer Alfred Deakin, who had been joint leader of the colony's coalition government, was helpful in considering what to study. On his advice, Monash enrolled as a student at the colony's Supreme Court. Two months later, in early 1892, he began preparing for the water supply engineers' exam, coached by a recent Irish immigrant and engineer from Dublin, J. T. Noble Anderson, with whom Monash had struck up a friendship. Monash liked his style. Anderson surveyed all the exam papers over a decade and provided his pupil with almost every question for the four-part exam. Not surprisingly, Monash managed a near perfect score.

At this time he identified a speciality skill, which needed qualification in law and engineering. He experienced plenty of disputes on the Outer

Circle Railway project between contractors and government departments. Many went to arbitration. Monash learned first hand how valuable a knowledge of contract law could be. There were several such specialists – legal engineers – in the UK, and Monash had been researching all the published cases in which they had acted.

His experience and interest paid off in April 1892 when his old employer on the railway project, Graham & Wadick, asked him to represent them against the railway department in the Arbitration Court. The contractors had been unhappy with the railways' offer on their claims. Monash charged five guineas a day as well as his lost pay while on leave from the Harbour Trust.

He was nervous about performing in court. Most of the bewigged players were twice his age (then twenty-six), and there were jibes in the press about his youth. He was under such stress on one occasion that he asked the court for an adjournment, saying he needed more time to research an aspect of the case. Instead he went for a long walk to a secluded spot on the river at South Yarra, where he composed himself. Once over his anxiety, he returned to the courtroom.

Over the three months of the case, his confidence grew. His advocacy won a decision for Graham & Wadick. It was a spur for him to carry on with law, even though the course had been made much tougher than ever before. The result brought him positive press. The Harbour Trust responded by ending his month-by-month employment and appointed him as senior draftsman at £260 annually. Monash didn't receive a raise, but regular work was assured at time when the colony was slipping further towards an economic abyss. The security allowed Monash to concentrate on his studies.

He had a break from them to deliver a lecture to the University Science Club in August called 'Fighting Machinery'. In it he explained how science had been applied to the military more than any other area, a trend that has continued ever since. An enthralled audience of students and graduates sat through a lecture on how new chemicals were used in creating explosions. Monash showed them how physics was used in plotting the trajectory of shells and other early 'missiles'. Then he moved on to the virtues of his own 'baby', the breech-loading weapon. This was followed by new obsessions since he had become such a brilliant shot with a pistol: developments in small arms.

Towards the end of 1892 he tackled and passed property, obligations, Roman law, and constitutional and legal history.

His diary in early January 1893 saw him in a more positive mood over the vicissitudes of marriage. He was proud of Vic and reckoned they were right for each other. A few weeks later, on 22 January, their only child, Bertha, was born. Inspired, a month later Monash took his masters in engineering. He felt he was on an academic achievement roll and performing the way he should have in his teenage years at university. This success lifted his confidence. Monash decided to stamp his authority on the battery, which he commanded a few weeks later at Easter. Its lack of discipline and slack behaviour in public had rankled with him for years. He was in the mood to speak his mind. Battery members had to project a better image. Eating, drinking and singing were forbidden on railway stations and when they arrived at the Queenscliff camp. There would be no skylarking in the town. Men had to retire early and not be rowdy as they did so. There was some grumbling in the ranks about these directives from the twenty-seven-year-old lieutenant. But most agreed with Monash that the militia had to shed any loutish image and gain respect from a sceptical public and press. There was a practical reason for his attitude. If the battery was to secure increased funds from the government in stringent times, they had to be worthy of them in deed and appearance.

More of an inkling of the Monash style was seen in internal staff directives. He wanted strict adherence to the chain of command. This method delegated more authority at each level down the chain. In turn, this increased the self-importance of his officers, who were reminded that they were competent to solve problems, with which they did not need to bother the commander. At first glance, Monash would be aloof from officers and all ranks. But their respect for him and themselves was boosted. Through this development, Monash did not lose the common touch. He made a point of remaining informed about all the sensitive issues in the battery.

On 1 May 1893 all Victorians were stunned to learn that most banks had suspended payment. It caused panic in the city. Angry crowds milled around banks, demanding access to their accounts. Melbourne was in turmoil. Monash learned that the institutions in which he had accounts were not paying out. But because there was very little in them, he was not affected directly, although nothing financial in his life – or that of any

other Victorian – was secure. Monash went to work at the Harbour Trust and his nine-to-five job as usual, but received a shock when told that he might have to be retrenched. He had a drink that night after work with Jim Lewis in the city and learned that he was out of work. His long-term friend had earned the enviable salary of £14 a week – three times Monash's pay – on Princes Bridge. Monash was able to arrange a couple of quids worth of work for him at the Trust.

But Lewis was not alone. Most engineers had no hope of finding jobs as public works slowed down. A few years earlier Melbourne had been thriving and outpacing in development all other Australian cities and most overseas. Now the construction industry was dead. There was a ghostly atmosphere on building sites, which had begun work but were now left abandoned. Melbourne, once Australia's development jewel, was the country's basket case. Victoria had ridden on booms since the Gold Rush forty years earlier. Now it was experiencing something new, which future economists would call a depression.

Monash, without a fortune to lose, was rational in his analysis. His study of economics and history made him aware of other boom/bust periods in the USA and Europe. The way out of the depression was to do away with the colony's protectionist policies (until now advocated by his mentor and friend Deakin), which pushed up prices and restricted imports of cheaper goods. Monash advocated government support to boost mining and farming, which would soak up unemployment and earn increased export income.

He still believed in the theories of John Stuart Mill and the development of the individual will. The idea was to spark the individual to gain 'personal support and enrichment'. This would lead to the colony and Australia progressing once more. By contrast, Monash's experience working for the Harbour Trust had seen him lose all faith in 'the State' and socialism, which had growing support, particularly in Victoria, where unfettered free enterprise had seen plenty of exploitation. Monash hated the 'dead level inaction of departmental service'.[10] More and greater government, in growth and control, was anathema to his thinking. Yet so also were the excesses of 'artificial and speculative enterprises'. He advocated government support for individuals and businesses working hard to develop the abundant wealth in and on the land.

Despite his sentiment concerning the Harbour Trust, he was most grateful to learn a few days after the threat on 1 May that he was not, for the time being, one of the employees to be retrenched. His salary was left intact, while others were cut. Yet the warnings that he could soon be out of work were clear.

The Harbour Trust, under constant press attacks for extravagance, was quite happy to give him leave without pay for a few days in mid-1893 to allow him again to perform in a court case, this time as an expert witness. Deakin, who had once been employed by the *Age*'s editor and owner David Syme as a politics and literature features writer, approached Monash about a case he was working on. Richard Speight, former Chief Commissioner of Railways, was suing Syme. The *Age*, the most radical and opinionated paper in the country, had attacked Speight in a series of articles for being profligate with public funds in running the railways. Speight lost his job. He sued Syme and the *Age* for libel.

Deakin did not think that the paper's attacks on Speight were backed by sufficient evidence to win the case. Could Monash provide something more substantial?

Monash's politics were closer to those of the conservative *Argus* newspaper, for which he had written on occasions under the pseudonym 'Equity'. The court case was billed as a battle between the left, increasingly represented by the *Age*, and right-leaning forces of the government. Monash thought Speight had been hard done by before he spoke to Deakin. He was convinced of it once he examined the research behind the attacks, telling friends in letters that he was on the case between 'Speight and Slime'. But still he took on the job at £20 for his court appearance on Syme's behalf. He needed the money, especially as the Harbour Trust's guillotine was hanging over him.

Monash knew from his years on the Outer Circle Railway that there had been much waste in construction of cuttings, embankments, stations, ballast and fencing. He used his favourite physical hobby – walking – to trudge the Glen Iris and Outer Circle lines. Clipboard and pencil in hand, he made his calculations as he went. Monash added it all up and concluded that there had been 127,000 cubic yards of excess earthworks on the Outer Circle line. Twenty-eight per cent of the cost – running to tens of thousands of pounds – had been unnecessary.

Deakin rehearsed him well. In court Monash presented clear, damning figures and photos. A tough cross-examination could not shake him or the importance of his discoveries. Both the left- and right-wing press, including the *Argus*, gave him favourable 'reviews' for his presentation. Again he had to weather jokes in court about his age and youthful appearance. His lack of girth, in a court of overweight advocates and reporters, promised to produce some satire. Monash was mindful of cynical comment in the case for Graham & Wadick. He knew his lack of apparent *gravitas* in manner and look might tell against him getting further advocacy or expert witness work. He had no trouble from the *Age* reporters, who did not wish to damage Syme's case. But his occasional part-time employer the *Argus*, which would like to see its rival pay heavily in court in both financial and political terms, had to be persuaded not to include cartoons depicting Monash as a child.

The case had to be reheard. Monash collected another £20 for his second appearance, in which he had more facts and figures about waste on the line. Syme won. Monash looked forward to further employment in this area.

The court appearance inspired him to finish his law degree at the end of 1893, which meant sitting exams in wrongs and equity, procedures, and international law. He added his old nemesis Latin to the list, in an attempt also to nail his wayward arts degree. Although the stress brought him nightmares, Monash at twenty-eight was better settled than he had been since he was dux of Scotch. With some input from Lewis, encouragement from Anderson and Deakin, and the £10 entrance fee loaned by Farlow, Monash rushed so hard at his part-time studies in October 1893 that he made himself ill. A long-term friend, teacher Will Steele, eased the pressure by transcribing exam papers and organising State Library contacts to supply lecture notes.

At the end of 1893 Monash went into the exams with mixed feelings but passed everything. This gave him the two degrees in arts and law to hang next his masters in engineering. His supreme three-year part-time effort had been rewarded. But his joy was short-lived.

In March 1894, a few weeks after learning of his dual success, he heard a whisper that he was about to be retrenched from the Harbour Trust. So much for the years of solid study. They mean nothing to Monash at that moment. He was desperate. He appealed to anyone who might have the pull to keep him employed, even the Trust's Jewish commissioner, E. L. Zox. Monash wrote to him pleading support for 'the only Jewish engineer in good practice in Victoria'.[11]

It didn't help. He was fired on 13 April. Monash then began the demeaning business of looking for employment when vacancies in positions for which he was vaguely qualified came up. But for every job there were hundreds of competitors. His searching came to nothing.

Monash's mood was not helped by his experience at the 1894 annual Queenscliff Easter Camp. He thought the highest-ranking permanent officer, Major General Sir A. B. Tulloch, was wasteful and out of touch with modern weapons development when he insisted on placing an obsolete gun at Nepean. Monash also thought another regular, Colonel Dean-Pitt, was an incompetent fool for trying to combine all the forts as a single fighting system. Distances and different firing and fighting agendas made it impossible. Monash believed the chaotic breakdown of the Easter exercises made the six days a waste of time. They also demonstrated that 'none of the present VA [Victorian Army] officers have the necessary largeness of intelligence, skill of administration, or general scientific knowledge to grapple with the large and critical questions on which our success depends'.

A bitter and frustrated Monash wrote in his diary: 'Their little minds are devoted to gun drills and petty routine.' He wondered whether such matters as a planned fighting strategy or the tactical study of a location had ever been touched on.

Monash's major complaint was that the permanent officers were unable to grasp how science could be applied to the military. His immediate goal at the battery would to be address this problem.

REBIRTH 5

Eighteen ninety-four promised to be the toughest year in Monash's life to that point. He was fired from his job, his father became seriously ill, his wife wanted a permanent separation, the battery was underfunded and disorganised, and his career in the militia seemed stalled without chance of promotion. In the depths of this *annus horribilus*, Monash, with nowhere to turn for work, joined forces with Joshua Anderson, who had tutored him so well for the water supply engineers' exams. They opened up at 49 Elizabeth Street, Melbourne, as Monash & Anderson, civil, mining and mechanical engineers. They added the title 'Patent Agents', which would combine their knowledge of law and new inventions and designs in a creative era for the engineering industry.

Anderson, at thirty, a year older than Monash, had tried to woo him into a business relationship for two years. Since first meeting in 1891 they had become good friends with plenty in common. They were outstanding mathematicians and had both heard 'the music of the spheres', as the saying goes for those inspired by abstract numbers and calculations. They respected and admired each other's intellect. Monash saw Anderson as 'brilliant'. Anderson was in awe of Monash's creativity and lateral thinking skills, and had known no one with anything like his capacity for hard work. It helped that their wives, Vic and Ellen, got on very well, too. The four often socialised together.

Anderson, like Monash, was a charmer, who loved to entertain and be the centre of attention. Anderson was more flamboyant. He was a bigger drinker and had more time for partying that Monash. People took to his lively style even quicker than they did Monash, who himself was no slouch as an impressionable character and networker. Most importantly, they trusted each other.

Anderson was a good salesman useful at opening up contacts and doors for business. But he was not one to follow through with project submissions and the detailed solid application that secured a deal. He tended to be sloppy. Within a month, Monash, the planner and detail man, had worked out how the two men complemented each other. He would do the bookkeeping and painstaking detail in tracking accounts. Anderson, more often than Monash, would be the front man sent to glad-hand potential new business. Then Monash would combine with him to secure a contract and hold on to it.

Their advertising gimmick was clever. Their introductory letters claimed that between them they had been responsible for works worth more than a million pounds. Yet they didn't begin by charging like millionaires. Their rock-bottom fees were two guineas a day for either or both of them in the city and another guinea for projects in the country. In a time of drastic cost-cutting they set out to undercut the competition within and outside any organisation that employed engineers. Every shire in Melbourne had visits from the new firm as they tried to persuade mayors and councillors that they could save much by employing them as consultants rather than by taking on full-time engineers.

Monash found the innumerable rejections in the city dispiriting. They began to shift their marketing push more towards South Gippsland, where coal and gold companies were busy constructing mines and treatment plants. Every miner met them, but just one, the Coal Creek Pty Co., used them on a trial basis as consultants. It happened to be the biggest and best company operating. It and other coal-miners were under threat from a group that had formed a ring to buy in cheaper coal from overseas and other colonies.

The local owners were more than interested in Monash's idea of lobbying government through the press. His successful representation of David Syme and the *Age* meant that the paper responded well to his ideas about supporting the local coal industry. It fitted with Syme's long-term push for protectionism. Such policy offended Monash's *laissez-faire* attitude to free enterprise. Now he was forced to be a firm propagandist for nurturing Victorian businesses. He called for government subsidies to help the locals, and urged the banning of the undercutting buying ring.

Monash & Anderson found itself in competition so tough that sometimes they waived the small fees and worked just for expenses. The hope was that they would impress enough to snare future work. Others with less to offer were working for nothing to gain experience that would make their CVs look better. The two battling engineers had to be flexible. They supervised open-cut mining operations, and worked out whether the Barwon River at Geelong could be used to transport coal. They even presented themselves as marine engineers to join a syndicate that was raising a sunken ship off Victoria's coast.

There were ups and downs in the business's income. Monash secured a lucrative engagement as an advocate in a mine lift accident, but some companies insisted on paying them in partly paid shares. One had the cheek to make a call payment on their shares. Monash & Anderson paid up only to see the share price collapse.

The pressure to keep the firm afloat caused problems with their wives, who were unhappy about their husbands' many long breaks for work in South Gippsland. Vic complained often. It didn't help the relationship when Monash arrived home at night to find her out socialising with other men while little Bertha was left with a babysitter. It went the other way, too. When he arrived home late, which was not uncommon, Vic would express her feelings. Once she attempted to strike him. Their trouble reached a head. Vic left the house with Bertha and saw lawyers about a separation in early September 1894. The child now became the centre of their battle. Monash was quick to put in writing that Vic had no legal position against him and could not expect to keep Bertha from seeing him.

He took his ailing father to see Bertha while she and Vic were staying with friends. Monash and Louis kidnapped Bertha, taking her to the Hawthorn home. His sisters Mathilde and Louise, with a nurse, looked after the twenty-month-old toddler.

During these domestic dramas, Monash tried to present the best face possible in public, at the battery and among friends. He delivered a lecture to the United Services Institution of Victoria on 4 October, accompanied by Mathilde in the hope of avoiding any questions about his absent wife. He saw it as an important event in his career. It was a chance to educate the permanent staff and the militia on the importance of military science. The audience included the Victorian Commandant, Tulloch, and a further twenty colonels and majors.

Monash was articulating a vision that was in advance of anything being said anywhere in the military world. Technology was changing the nature of warfare. Machines were going to play a more important role in supporting people in battle than ever before. Brute force of numbers would no longer be enough to win a major conflict. Monash's engineering and organisational skills were in evidence when he concluded that 'success in a great modern war will only be achieved by the perfect unity and accord between the forces on land and those at sea acting together as a machine'.

Anyone from the cavalry would have squirmed at this confident – even brash – young officer's pronouncements. Fine horsemanship would have no place in this prediction of machine-like precision. Naval and infantry officers would also have been uncomfortable with such concepts. Their independence was threatened. Whether members of the audience were frightened, sceptical or appreciative, one thing was certain. They all respected this precocious young officer's comprehension of the art and science of war. He knew more than all of them combined about how wars would soon be fought. Monash sensed more approval than scorn for his well-honed ideas. He wished that his wife could have been by his side to experience the moment and allay any rumours about the state of their marriage.

The day after this triumph, Monash arranged for Vic to see her daughter. He implored his wife to return, but she was defiant. The strain was telling on her. Her brother, David Moss, thought she needed an indefinite break. He arranged for her to go with him and their sister Belle to England. They sailed on 10 December.

Monash was stunned. He sent a desperate telegram to her when the boat docked at Adelaide, then at Albany in Western Australia. His tone was hectoring and demanding. He berated her for being a 'selfish, jealous, truthless, neglectful' wife and mother. It was not the kind of message that would make the disillusioned Vic jump on the next ship back to Melbourne. She did not reply to his attempts at marital authority. The silence made him reflect that he should have been 'the master' but while making requests in a 'gentle, more pleasant way'.[1]

It was too late. He was left holding their baby, the most important vestige of his connection with Vic. It seemed one slim chance for later reconciliation.

✕

Monash was still grieving at the breakdown of his marriage three days later when his father's health deteriorated. Louis had been fretting for a year over his finances. His properties in Melbourne and the country were heavily mortgaged. Many of his debtors – the clients to whom he had lent money – had not been making interest payments. The consequences of the speculative boom collapse in 1891 and the bank crash of May 1893 were working through all sections of Melbourne's economy. Sixty-three-year-old Louis, weak and dying, did not have the strength to do anything about his growing insolvency. And even if he had been fit, there was little he could do but face ruin, like thousands of other business people, in the wake of the economic malaise.

Monash took him to the doctor, who gave him a complete physical. His heart was weak and his blood pressure high. Nothing could be prescribed except complete rest. Louis was ordered to avoid business problems that caused him stress. Two days later, Monash came home to find him unconscious. He rushed to get a doctor, but when they returned, Louis was dead.

The same pressures that plagued his father Baer-Loebel for most of his life had been too much for Louis. His brave decision to leave the Old World and his heritage for the unknown, wild southern land had not quite worked the way he had wished. The transition had brought huge sacrifices and difficulties. Louis was an outsider in his chosen land because of his background, religion and struggles with the language. He was always viewed as a 'foreigner' in the predominantly Anglo-Celtic colony. Yet he had paved the way for his children and grandchildren to have a better life in a young country. He offered them love and other gifts that might well have been denied them in Prussia and Germany, such as security, education and democratic freedoms.

No matter what the extent of the financial mess he left for his son to clean up, Monash never reproached his father for it. He was always mindful that Louis's determination, courage and drive had given him his chance. Despite the guilty feeling that his own dramatic woes with family and Annie Gabriel had contributed to his father's demise, Monash knew that Louis was proud of his son's endeavours and achievements.

Although Louis had eschewed too much involvement with his religion, he was a respected member of the Jewish fraternity, and not forgotten. Hebrew Congregation rabbis administered last rites. Prayers were said in the family home for four days, and Monash went to the synagogue for the first time in years, apart from attending weddings.

He had the tough task of sifting through Louis' finances. The book assets of £4300 made Louis seem like a moderately wealthy man. But with all his properties mortgaged and only a few of the loan money assets realisable, Monash soon became aware that his father's estate was bankrupt. Banks and other creditors moved on the various properties in Melbourne and the country where he had run retail businesses. Two in Melbourne and one at Jerilderie were to be sold later, but the family home at Yarra Street, Hawthorn, had to go when the bank foreclosed the mortgage early in 1895. Monash had to pay off the debts and was forced to borrow against his own assets, including nearly all of a life insurance policy.

During this wretched time, Monash drank more than at any stage in his life. He went to his clubs – the Yorick, Naval and Military, and Old Scotch Collegians – often, frequented the theatre and came to terms, approaching thirty, with being a single male again. He dated women, but did not take up with any of them seriously. In the back of his mind was the hope that Vic would come back. It was inevitable that she would return, if only to see little Bertha. But if she left it too long, Monash might well be involved elsewhere.

By mid-1895, he wrote in his diary, perhaps deluding himself, that he was 'almost content' without Vic. Yet he knew that if she offered any token of peace between them, he would take it. After all the squabbling, he still kept the door open. Their moments of making up were passionate, he admitted to himself, and more than rivalled the fading memories he had of the hot affair with Annie Gabriel.

To his surprise, he received on 13 July a letter saying that she was on her way back to Melbourne. Her words were matter of fact, not contrite. She made no hint of reconciliation. The letter beat her by only twelve days.

Vic arrived on 25 July and visited Monash at their rented house on that day and the next, spending most of the time with her daughter. When she and Monash were alone and had a chance to discuss the situation, he recorded in his diary that he asked why she returned.

'I am willing to confess that I have more regard for you than I thought,' she conceded.[2] Monash admired her pluck, but distrusted her. He asked for a guarantee that she would not leave him again. Vic scoffed at this. Monash's fears flooded back. He said a second split might be bad for his career. Vic still baulked at any commitment. She was uncertain. 'The child [Bertha] is happy and does not want me,' Vic said. 'You no longer love me and I am sorry I have again come into your life. I will go out of it again.'[3]

Monash was 'deeply moved' by her, and felt love and pity in equal measure. He let her go, but straightaway wrote to her asking for a third meeting. His letter showed tenderness and understanding. He didn't go to work but waited for her to appear again at 2 p.m. on 27 July. They chatted once more. This time Monash didn't make demands, but asked if she would make a special effort to make the marriage work. This meant, from Monash's perspective, more attention to her duties as a wife and mother. He wanted less socialising without him. In turn, Vic suggested that he should not keep such long hours. If he could curtail his out-of-town projects, it would help. This encounter ended more amicably and with some hope, although Monash still doubted her staying power when it came to marital commitments.

Vic returned on the 28th and was far more tender and affectionate towards him. They went for a long riverbank walk, and returned to the house as mid-winter darkness fell. They made love with all the passion of their other numerous reconciliations.

On 29 July Monash wrote a poem in his musings notebook that ended with:

> I am kissing you over and over
> I am holding you close to my heart
> As of old, we'll be lover and lover
> And live in a world apart.[4]

The unintended ambiguity in the last line was perhaps portentous. Monash still had his misgivings and fears about Vic and their relationship. But he was prepared to give their marriage another chance. He rented a four-bedroom house in Hawthorn for £5 a week near the former family home. Mathilde, Louise and a maid moved in with them. Monash made sure to squire his wife around with him at the battery, the theatre and the clubs where possible, in the hope of stopping the whispers about the state of their marriage.

The full house put pressures on their renewed efforts. It was difficult for Vic, who had tenuous relationships with Monash's sisters. Within weeks the marriage was under stress again for much the same reasons as it had been before. It started with argument and Vic refusing his authority. She responded by spending beyond his set budget and fighting with Mathilde. Then she went to the theatre, concerts and the races without asking permission. It was her way of resisting his dominance. Instead of accepting it, Monash tried to further assert his authority. He was running the household within what he saw as the normal conventions of marriage, but tended to behave as if he were at the battery.

There his authority was at last recognised at a higher level in October 1895 when he was made captain. Monash was comfortable with the formal, hierarchical structure, where everyone acknowledged authority up and down the chain of command. At thirty, he now had twelve years of military experience behind him, and had made the right impressions where it counted. His military mentor was Lieutenant Colonel Hall, a state school headmaster by day, who ran the Metropolitan Brigade, which included three batteries: the North Melbourne, Williamstown and Harbour Trust. This and the Geelong-based Western District Brigade made up Victoria's part-time soldier contingent known as the Militia Garrison Artillery (Coastal). Hall recognised Monash as the most gifted young officer of a thousand or so men in the seven forts of the Coastal Artillery under his command, and was drawing out his capacities.

Monash wanted to sit the exams for major straight after being made captain, but his superior at the battery, Major F. L. Outtrim, a senior manager at the Office of Posts and Telegraphs, advised him against pushing too quickly for the higher rank. Outtrim was a gentle battler, who was uncomfortable giving orders or enforcing discipline and was therefore unsuited to running the battery. He was supportive of Monash and grateful to him for helping out with the combat exercises at Easter and on some weekends. The exercises often slipped out of control through lack of management. He let Monash do the replanning. Outtrim told Monash he would pass on the leadership of the Battery to him at the most propitious moment.

Monash & Anderson continued to struggle through 1895 and into 1896. They had to diversify to keep the firm running. Sometimes they took on projects where there were no or few precedents, such as the design and building of an aerial tramway to transport quartz for a miner, Landys Dream Gold Mining Co., in Walhalla, Gippsland. The contract was for £1201, which included some shares in the company. The design was good and workable. The problem was in dealing with suppliers and the company itself, which was inefficient. Parts such as special ropes had to come from England. Both men spent time living in bark huts on the Aberfeldy River's bank during the many delays. The contract, which was the biggest for the firm yet, began to seem like a losing operation. Monash and Anderson stayed with it, but had to borrow from their bank to keep going.

They also took advantage of what they were learning while at the mine. They sold and bought their shares in Landys on inside knowledge about gold discoveries as prices on the share market were run up and down. The income derived for the firm helped counter the effect of contracts lost because of the prolonged project.

Monash and Anderson began to experiment with the tramway and were confident it was about to operate after ten months. But in mid-May 1896 Landys decided to rescind the contract. The firm took them to court. Monash's expertise at organising evidence won the case for the firm. The court awarded it £320 in December 1895. Landys appealed the case, but Monash settled out of court by accepting a smaller payment of £130. Further delays and court preparation would have taken up time better spent working on other contracts. Monash calculated that a ten per cent profit was a fair result for the firm given the cost overruns, problems and time consumption.

The two men battled on as consultants in everything from irrigation schemes and mines to tramway designs and court cases involving the railways. By mid-1896, after two years in operation, the firm was finding it difficult to keep ahead of the bills and the debt collectors.

Despite the struggle, Monash was coping. At home, the pressures had eased with his sisters finding their own accommodation. Vic was happier, more settled and preoccupied with Bertha, who was now three and a half. He was boosted by Outtrim stepping aside at the battery to allow Monash to become its acting commander. He grumbled about the mess he had been left, but revelled in reorganising his command his way.

Monash emphasised from day one of his control that officers and NCOs should never do drills by rote. They had to understand 'the nature of all machinery appliances used and the reasons for every operation'. He wanted every single soldier under him to comprehend what he was doing and why, from dismantling a weapon to cleaning his kit. Monash was treading on novel ground in the military in a subtle, practically intelligent way. He was showing fighting men how to think.

Monash had long ago ruminated on how he would reorganise the battery. He split it in two, with each section under a subaltern. Each section was then divided into three subsections. In turn, each of the six subsections had a sergeant, who could more easily monitor training. The six-way split also led to a more even distribution of responsibility. A sergeant now had to act more like his superior, rather than fade into a lesser role. It was all in the interests of Monash's obsession with order. He could stand astride the two sections and more easily control the battery's functioning.

Monash went further. He insisted that all instruction on everything from weapons use to parade should be delivered as close to perfect as possible. To ensure this and to keep every officer on his toes, he would randomly send them individually to a subsection to explain the use of sighting scales on artillery, or a gun drill, or to direct a gunnery course. This meant that every officer was ready for every situation in a routine operation or a crisis.

It didn't stop there. If a soldier were reported as a poor rifle shot, or incompetent at weapons constructions, he would be instructed until there was improvement. Monash was his own best example. From the weakest marksman in the battery without a shred of confidence when he aimed a pistol at a target, he had become the best.

Order allowed Monash to work towards his concept of a perfectly operating fighting machine. Chaos was his mortal enemy. He had hated it in his marriage, which, when rampant, had reduced him to an emotional wreck. He detested disorder and slackness in the battery, which was now his child. Monash would rest easily at night only if it were running efficiently, very much in his own image.

George Farlow, now under him at the battery, witnessed his methods first hand: 'He never buzzed around the tents of his men to see if they were properly provided for.' Instead he planned in advance, then sent his officers 'to work out the details and report to him as to their satisfactory development'. Farlow also gave an insight to the maturity of Monash in getting his way: '. . . Monash would approve the officer's scheme and then make what appeared to be a casual suggestion.' This would 'enable the officer to achieve his project fully to the CO's satisfaction. The officer was probably unaware that the smooth working came about 1/10 from him and 9/10 from Monash's suggestion.'

There was no hint of the dictator. It would never work with Australians, who had a pathological hate of strutting chiefs and any form of authority. Monash had a fair instinct, as yet unrefined, on how to squeeze the most out his men. He had also learned in five years of a rocky marriage the art of apparent compromise with Vic, the one person close to him whose will he could not bend. If he were to obtain his way at the battery or in the home, he had learned to go beyond bald, harsh demands.

In December 1896 he prepared for the major's exam. Starting from his first full year at Scotch College in 1878, Monash was about sit his hundredth examination in nineteen years. He still felt nervous at the thought as he crammed yet again and had his usual bouts of pre-test hypochondria, haemorrhoids, colds and lassitude. Once his mind was on the study, his now powerful sense of logic and layered exposition began to flow. Monash long ago told himself with his brutal self-honesty that he was not a genius. Yet the cross-fertilisation of study and application across so many disciplines had developed a formidable and creative intellect.

The exams for promotion to major were not expected to be a pushover. Monash prepared for questions on all three arms: infantry, cavalry and artillery. He had to demonstrate he knew all about the formation and movement of a battalion and a cavalry squadron. There would be probes on everything there was to know about a brigade. Demanding queries would be thrown at him about how he would juggle the three arms in the four phases of operations: attack, defence, advance and withdrawal.

Monash began to enjoy learning about his non-specialties of infantry and cavalry, and the tactical and running problems peculiar to them. What fascinated him as ever was how the three had to be organised to make the military a well-oiled machine. It thrilled him. It gave him a sense of what it would be like to be faced with an all-encompassing command.

This deeper interest motivated Monash. He sailed through the written tests and achieved near-perfect results in drill, coast artillery tactics and regimental duties. He was mortified by his failure in the riding exam. He had never been a good horseman, which he put down to a clumsiness that he said 'comes naturally to me'.[5] But he hoped he could do better, with serious and prolonged application, just as he had with handling a revolver.

Finding the time for riding was a less practical issue. He planned to do more of it. Yet failing horse drills didn't matter. His other results were so outstanding that he passed overall.

In April 1897 he was officially gazetted as a major and confirmed as Commander of the North Melbourne Battery, Garrison Artillery. At thirty-one, he had realised a long-held ambition. It gave him the greatest satisfaction so far in his triple career in the military, engineering and law.

In 1897 the Monash & Anderson firm was in its third year and was still struggling to do more than survive. Monash was carrying his effervescent partner and generating seventy-five per cent of the firm's revenue, and sometimes more. But their relationship was solid and trusting. They had each other's measure. Anderson accepted Monash's rigorous style, and Monash coped with Anderson's sometimes slack work. They counterbalanced and still needed each other. Monash was in demand now as a 'witness' in complex cases concerning engineering issues, and this took him away from their Melbourne base. He could rely on Anderson to carry on seeking business, as long as he made moves after consultation with Monash. Once, Anderson put in such a low bid for a big job that Monash reckoned it could have bankrupted the firm if they had won the contract as submitted. Monash had to redo the bid. After that, they both made a habit of checking each other's proposals.

Monash would have preferred to be contracted on big engineering works. They generated substantial income. Yet his time was becoming increasingly consumed by his expertise in court cases. His daily retainer rate was now the firm's bread and butter. Win or lose, income was derived from the cases, and bonuses were possible in big disputes.

In May 1897 Monash was retained in Portland for a week by Austral Otis Engineering Co. against the Portland Freezing Co. He was pleased to be able to use his skills as an advocate. He demolished the arguments put forward by the Portland Co.'s expert witness who sat squirming in the witness box. Monash bamboozled his target, who kept appealing to the case's arbitrator. He intervened, but not enough to prevent Monash making a fool of the witness, who became angry. Monash kept on cornering him. At one point the witness was left speechless. In the silence that followed, Monash thought the man was going to become violent.[6]

Monash and Austral Otis Engineering representatives were certain at the end of the week in court that the decision would go their way. On judgement day, the decision went to the local company. There was no hope of a bonus for Monash. He learned later that there had been corruption in the case. The witness had paid off the arbitrator.

Monash lived in hope of the huge bonus. A chance emerged a few weeks after the Portland fiasco when contractors Baxter & Saddler wanted to use him in a case against the Queensland Government. Their final claims for building a section of railway from Gladstone to Bundaberg had been rejected. Monash's experience with Graham & Wadick won him the work. He took a ballast engine ride to the contractor's camp where he worked through every bit of the contract with the contractors, their engineers and foremen. Then he travelled the line himself in a first-class cabin enjoying the sights of the coast from Bundaberg and Harvey Bay north to Gladstone.

Monash was inspired. He worked up twenty claims of about £25,000. Not for the first time he saw it 'as a chance of a lifetime'. He wrote to Vic: 'If I win a success it will be the biggest thing I ever done, and my name will be made.'[7]

After five years of marriage and struggle, he was always looking for the chance to tell Vic, who loved a bet at the races, that this or that contract would be the jackpot. They would be wealthy and secure, he hoped. His letters were optimistic and impatient for this elusive 'success'. Monash believed that hard work, which he revelled in, and his unusual skills, born of two decades of study and experience, should be rewarded. It irritated him that it didn't happen fast.

Any reward, however, for Monash in his life so far, had been not in the lucky Melbourne Cup Double but the detail.

He absorbed everything on new technology in obscure building journals, as much in German and French as in English.

He had read about the invention of Joseph Monier from St-Quentin-la-Poterie north of Nîmes, in France. Monier was a keen gardener, who started a modest business making pots for plants. Customers returning his broken goods exasperated him. The containers would collapse under the weight of earth added to them. He fiddled for years with experiments to make his pots stronger. At first he formed iron frames and moulded coarse mortar around them. That didn't work. Pots disintegrated just as easily as if the iron was not supporting the mortar. Then in 1867 he hit on using a grid of small-diameter iron bars running through the mortar. Monier added inordinate amounts of stones and dirt to his pots. They stood firm. He let them slip off benches. They remained intact. Then he experimented with rocks dropped on them. They withstood this serious brutality. Monier realised that the iron took the tensile strains while the mortar or concrete withstood the compressive strains. The combination brought great strength and elasticity to the pots.

After a few months of no returns from customers, he realised he was on to something. Monier quietly patented his design, and left sleepy St-Quentin-la-Poterie for Paris. His business grew. His pots were sold in the French capital and all over the country. Through the next decade, Monier extended the technique and patent to cover everything involving mortar from buildings and aqueducts to arch bridges and dams.

Monash, always fascinated by examples that employed his two jobs – patency expertise and engineering – read about a German engineer, G. A. Wyass, taking out a number of licences for building small arched bridges using the Monier method. It was spreading but regarded as nothing more than a vague technique – of passing interest to most engineers in Germany and France. The method was untried in England or Australia by the early 1890s. Its innocuous beginnings in pots did not impress ambitious, tough-minded engineers wanting to build massive buildings and bridges with impressive spans. But a few were willing to consider something different.

Engineer W. J. Baltzer, an enterprising German immigrant working for the New South Wales Public Works Department, followed developments in Germany and obtained Monier licences for the Australian colonies. Baltzer linked up with engineering contractors Carter Gummow & Co. They did some trials on tiny arched bridges over streams. Satisfied, they won contracts to build two arched sewerage aqueducts over Johnstone's and White's creeks in the Sydney suburb of Annandale. They were constructed in 1896. Both were given overvigorous tests with heavy rollers.

Carter Gummow knew a good operator if they saw one. It hired Baltzer as their chief engineer.[8]

Baltzer began using every forum he could to push the Monier method in the hope of big contracts for his new employer and to help sell his licences in other colonies, particularly Victoria. Despite the crash of

1891, it was still the most important market in the country. It was unlikely to return to the glorious growth of the 1880s, yet it was slowly being re-established.

Early in 1897 Baltzer delivered an enthusiastic lecture in Sydney with wall-projected diagrams to the Engineering Association of New South Wales. Again, hard-bitten engineers, used to their own tried and tested ways, were not fulsome in their response. In May, Carter & Gummow featured their arched aqueducts at Annandale in an enlarged array of photographs and diagrams in a stand at the Engineering and Electrical Exhibition in Sydney. Never had the movement of sewerage been made so exciting. Still the New South Wales engineering world was sceptical. It wasn't until the respected industry magazine, *Building, Mining and Engineering Journal,* gave it a positive write-up in July that more professionals take notice.

Even academics became interested. Monash's old mentor and confidant Professor Kernot planned an exhibition – with Baltzer's assistance – at Melbourne University. Monash, back for a few weeks in July from the Baxter & Saddler case, lunched with Kernot before travelling to Jerilderie for another expert witness case. The magazine article and the upcoming exhibition would have been a prominent topic between them. Monash would not have missed such a show, especially with Kernot now involved. Monash was well aware of the Monier concept's potential impact on the engineering industry. If he couldn't attend himself because of his out-of-Melbourne assignments, then Anderson would represent the firm.

Monash returned to Jerilderie twenty years after he had last lived there in 1877. At first glance the town seemed not to have changed. There were 350 inhabitants and about seventy houses, still with a ramshackle look, but the main street seemed brighter. The Royal Mail Hotel and Bank of New South Wales, raided by the Kelly Gang on the infamous weekend of February 1879, appeared to have had a fresh coat of paint – in reaction to the growing number of curious visitors. William Elliott, now forty-six and the experienced editor of the *Jerilderie Herald,* greeted him. Elliott interviewed Monash about the hot topic in the town that had brought him there.

Pastoralists, farmers and town representatives had pooled funds to hire him as a consultant in their battle with David and Samuel McCaughey, who owned substantial properties in the area. They were diverting water from the Billabong and Columbo creeks, arteries of the southern Riverina, and damming them to irrigate their land. Members of the groups complaining were all affected by water shortages. Monash was briefed, did a tour of the creeks, and attended the beginning of the hearing before the local New South Wales Land Board at Urana.

Early in August 1897 the peripatetic advocate returned for six weeks to Brisbane and the Darling Downs between Bundaberg and Gladstone. Monash was back in Melbourne about the time of Kernot's exhibition on the Monier process in late September but was too busy to attend. Spurred by Kernot's enthusiasm, Monash empowered Anderson to negotiate for their firm being Gummow's exclusive representative in Victoria. The paperwork was sent to Monash in Jerilderie, where he continued working on that dispute, for his perusal. He made contract agreement changes and approved the Monier deal. Within weeks, he gave Anderson the green light to start negotiations over the firm's part in a link with Gummow over the building of a Monier-style bridge over the Yarra at Anderson Street (a coincidence) in South Yarra.

The firm had stolen a march on other Victorian engineers. It expected this bridge to be the first of many Monier constructions. But although the significance of their deal was not lost on Monash and Anderson, the firm still had to create base revenue to keep it solvent. Monash's advocacies remained the mainstay of the firm's income.

The constant travel through 1897 was beginning to affect his health. Despite a strong constitution and a love of the outdoors, he had not stopped now for months, zipping north to Queensland and into New South Wales to Jerilderie. No mode of transport then available missed his attention from the horseback or horse and trap to the train and coach. Monash hated the sweat of the tropical north, where his haemorrhoids flared and diarrhoea kept him running. But he loved the cool spring of the Riverina, where his illnesses subsided.

In October he told the aggrieved Jerilderie townspeople that the New South Wales Land Board's ruling 'compromise' between the parties was nothing more than a cave-in to the rich McCaugheys' interests. He advised them to sue, then took control of the wording and instruction in the writs served against the McCaugheys for 'damages'. It was becoming a complex issue. He did more work surveying the creeks and creeping around the McCaughey dams, sometimes at night, while camping out. During the day there was work to do in court.

In early November 1897 Monash took the train to Sydney for more court preparation concerning the McCaughey cases before going on to Brisbane for Baxter & Saddler. He was disappointed to miss the Melbourne Cup. Yet surprised to see how popular the race was in Sydney. It was not a public holiday in Sydney, but the city stopped for the event. Monash went for his usual constitutional walk and followed a crowd of people who ended up in a warehouse basement near Haymarket. It was a betting shop. Behind a counter were 'seven young men, coatless and collar-less, hoarse and perspiring, crying the odds and gathering coin by the shovelful'. Monash watched for half an hour as 'old men, clerks, out-at-elbow vagrants, factory girls, women, bell-toppered men and little boys swept past' to take a punt. He was not tempted. Vic would be putting a quid on a horse for him at the race itself.

At 3.50 p.m., race time, he left his hotel and joined a surging mass at King Street opposite the Telegraph Office, where the winner's name would be posted in the front window, seconds after the race was over. In eerie contrast to the tumult he knew would accompany the actual event at home, 'a deathly hush' fell on the big Sydney crowd as the post office clock began to chime. It was the signal that the Cup was over. 'Out flashed the name GAULUS . . . it was instantly repeated by thousands of throats. Many hats went up, and there were not a few curses. Slowly the crowd dispersed, but the business of the day was done.'[9] Monash caught the train to Brisbane that night satisfied that he had had his 'Cup day fun after all' in scenes he would recall later in life with as much clarity as any Cup he witnessed.

In Brisbane he resumed his work for Baxter & Saddler on five guineas a day, which was more than he received in a week for Graham & Wadick seven years earlier. Then he was a raw engineer, now he was doing the work of a solicitor and barrister in organising evidence, witnesses, company employees and railway officials for examination in court. He was up against an experienced foe in Sir Arthur Rutledge, leader of the Queens-land Bar. Monash held his own, sometimes forcing Rutledge to bypass cross-examination.

✕

He began to daydream again about the bonus he would receive and how it would lead to his commanding high fees in the future. In December 1897 he was consumed with this and the Jerilderie case, juggling the firm's new Monier work with Anderson and trying to justify all the rushing about to a disgruntled Vic at home with Bertha. On the 23rd he bounced up to Sydney again to give evidence before the Land Appeal Court. It ruled in his favour (that is, the Jerilderie residents) against the McCaugheys, who were told to reduce their damning.

The winning of a small battle put a smile on Monash's face as he stayed, without enough relaxation, in Melbourne over Christmas and the New Year. He had just enough time to reflect, a luxury he rarely afforded himself now. He even found a private moment on New Year's Day 1898 to write in his intimate dairy. The words, here and there, were those of an exhausted man sounding sixty-two rather than thirty-two. Yet he was finding his way in life, even if it were not quite via the route he dreamed of as a youth. Monash had not touched this diary for five years – almost the duration of his desperate thrashing about to make ends meet and build his fledgling business with Anderson.

'Five turbulent, struggling not very happy years,' he wrote, 'except latterly. For at last I seem to have smooth waters.' He reckoned he was successful 'but a long way short of his early ambitions'. Monash saw no way around further success being based on 'hard work' and 'rigid method in all my affairs'. This did not indicate that Anderson, Vic or his subordinates at the battery were in for a gentler time from Monash's disciplined, driven ways. Yet home life was on the up: 'I am happy in my domestic sphere and I try to do my duty to my dear wife and darling daughter, and I feel they love me.'

Monash's long absences, it seemed, had made both his and Vic's hearts grow fonder. This, their own maturity together and a sense that Monash's endeavours would not only pay the bills but also provide luxuries (Vic had recently spent £55 on a second-hand, good-quality piano) all combined to make the marriage work after a relatively poor and loveless start. His diary also noted that Mathilde and Louise were cared for. 'I feel now that my position and future are assured,' he wrote, '. . . I fear I am as self-conscious as ever, yet I have grown sober – more contended, and single of purpose.'[10]

Monash believed he had fewer friends now that he was 'successful' because success did not 'foster' friendships. In other words, his business life, which consumed most of his waking time, did not leave him leisure hours as it once had done. And business, he knew, was ruthless. In the depression years of the 1890s there was a 'take no prisoners mentality' in Melbourne among those striving to make their way. It was not an atmosphere conducive to making new mates as found at a tennis club or a charity fund-raising society. Yet through all that, Monash's diary seemed credible when he said he was not motivated by the need to acquire material things and that he felt 'worldly prosperity is less than nothing'. He looked forward to 'less feverish striving'. He had other motivations as yet undefined beyond family needs, ego and a vague sense of purpose. Pushed further back in his mind now was the youthful belief or faith that he would some day, somehow be famous.

By mid-January 1898 he was shaken from this rare moment of rumination by donning his Assam silk suit and porous cellular shirt for the final address for Baxter & Saddler in Brisbane. It took four days. Monash walked away happy and at last believed that his long sought-after 'reputation' would be made, win or lose. He was wrong. Baxter & Saddler was awarded £7722 – about half what was expected. Costs soaked up most of that. Monash's hoped-for fat bonus remained elusive. He put away the pith helmet and returned crestfallen to Melbourne.

There was little time to feel sorry for himself. He had abandoned the long-running intimate diary that registered his deeper feelings over failures, triumphs, loves and hates. Perhaps it drained him too much. But it was more likely that he would keep up only his normal diary as opposed to a more intimate one. Monash was a young man in a hurry with little time, and less inclination, to look back. The tougher realities of life's challenges were catching up with him.

He concentrated on preparing for the upcoming Supreme Court battles in Sydney in *Blackwood v McCaughey*, the first of three cases for damages against the McCaugheys. Monash was advising the urbane Sydney barrister Sir Julian Salomons, who manoeuvred him with gentle finesse through the evidence he had gathered around the soggy banks of Billabong Creek. Monash, who was better primed on all aspects of the case than any lawyer or witness, waited expectantly to be called by the McCaugheys' nifty interrogator, J. H. Want, QC. But the defence was clever. It avoided the star witness and did not attempt to interrogate him. Instead, Want appealed to the parochialism of the jury by referring to Monash several times in final address as 'this gentleman of Victoria': 'Now this gentleman of Victoria says that the cubic feet of water damned is such and such. How did he measure it? How do we know that his measuring technique is accurate? We have only this gentleman of Victoria's word for it . . . why, we wonder, does the New South Wales plaintiff employ this gentleman of Victoria . . .?'

The inference was that there was something suspicious about a Victorian being involved in a New South Wales case. Monash was furious with the 'damnable iteration'. In the lunch break he confronted Want. What was he up to with this constant repetition? Monash asked indignantly.

'It's all in the game,' the old stager Want told him with a smile. 'Come and have a drink.'[11]

The case was over but for the court's decision, so Monash obliged. Want's confidence was high. He thought he had delivered by baulking an adversarial encounter with Monash. They filed back into court after several convivial drinks. To the McCaugheys' dismay and the Jerilderie group's elation, £2000 damages were awarded.

Monash chatted with jury members after the decision. They were embarrassed by the references to the 'gentleman of Victoria', which one referred to as 'a fool of an address'. The experienced Want had miscalculated so badly that the McCaugheys could not win the remaining cases on the precedent of the first. Want advised them to settle the remaining actions, which were much larger, for a total of £27,000 costs. Want threw in a guarantee that the McCaugheys would stop grabbing more than their fair share of water for damming.

Monash had made a big impression. Even one of the opposition litigants, Samuel McCaughey, approached him, asking for help in solving the general problem of irrigation. Monash believed the solution lay in damming the Murrumbidgee without making it and other rivers unnavigable.

Monash's clients did not share his tendency to think he had failed if he didn't make big wins for them. Baxter & Saddler knew he was the best witness they could secure in these complex cases involving both engineering and the law. Monash was one of just two operators so qualified in Australia. They snapped him up again for another big railway case similar to that in Queensland, this time in Western Australia. The contractors were making claims against the colony's government for the final stage of the 320-kilometre Mullewa–Cue section of the railway from Geraldton to the Murchison goldfield.

With little prospect of such remunerative work elsewhere, Monash accepted the fee of four guineas a day with the promise of a big staff of nine and a personal secretary, who took dictation. Monash looked forward to this time-saving luxury, which was a concession to his busy lifestyle. He believed it would be for five weeks only and was able to persuade Vic that the money was worth it. She was unhappy but placated by his genuine sadness about leaving Melbourne and the family for more prolonged travel.

From the first two weeks Monash knew that the job was going to take far longer than five weeks. He was partially seduced by the largesse and rich lifestyle of the two principals, Baxter and Saddler. They introduced him to the cream of Perth's social circle, where Monash was a hit. It appealed to his need to feel accepted at the top in the fledgling colony, which, because of its own recent gold rush, looked something like Melbourne a generation before. A spirit of endeavour and the prospect of quick riches permeated the social elite. Monash's correspondence to a despondent Vic reflected his renewed enthusiasm. There was talk of relocating there, but like his father he was too late to cash in on gold discoveries, which began after the government geologist detected the precious metal in 1885. The discovery began a rush to Hall's Creek until 1887. That was more than a decade ago, but there was optimism in Perth that huge untapped stores of gold and other precious minerals would be discovered in Western Australia's vast outback.

In this fresh atmosphere Monash's desire for the jackpot seemed even stronger than ever after the gloom of Melbourne's depression. He was also keen to find a way of moving on from the need to tramp remote creeks and railway lines to gather information for his work as an expert witness. Perth hustlers were everywhere looking for investors, and they were quick to entice Monash. He was approached soon after he arrived to consider investing in a quarry producing road metal. Monash was interested. He knew about excavations and rocks, having organised digging and super-vised stone selection for bridges. The study of geology, a compulsory subject in his engineering degree, had given him another level of knowl-edge, although he found the subject uninspiring. It was ironic to him that he could now see an investment in a quarry, which might provide a new direction for his drive for a fortune.

Monash was shown over the excavation site outside Perth by its owner, W. B. Shaw, a friend from his days on the Outer Circle Railway. He reminded Monash that the westernmost colony was in a development stage, a point reinforced by the need to travel along dirt tracks to reach most destinations. The region would need huge infrastructure, including plenty of roads. Shaw told him £1000 was needed. Monash was enthusiastic. He decided to invest £200 of his own money and wrote to Anderson urging him to invest. Anderson refused. Monash suggested they commit the firm's money. His partner was reluctant. Monash pushed hard. He was generating most of its capital, and this put pressure on Anderson, who was reluctant to back what he saw as a speculative venture. There was some angry, yet never acrimonious correspondence. Monash was upset by not being able to persuade his partner that his judgement was sound. Anderson came halfway and agreed they commit £100 from the firm.

Monash was then able to invest £300 towards the venture – a thirty per cent interest. Shaw and his partner staked most of the rest. Monash was told that the total investment of £1000 could generate up to £1700 a year. This meant the commitment from him and the firm would return £500 a year – about half his income for a full year's work, and more than Monash and Anderson were making together as annual profit from their firm.[12] It was a delicious prospect, especially as the investment would change him from a well-paid, over-travelled worker into a part-time capitalist. He would let his money do the work.

The manager hired to run the quarry upset his dreams once more and absconded with most of the funds. He was never caught. Monash was despondent. His judgement might well have been accurate about the possibilities. But Anderson's caution in a time conducive to con men and charlatans was correct.

The stay in Perth dragged on. Monash had to tighten up to make up the loss, which would take more than seven weeks to cover, if he didn't touch any of his daily wage. He rejected overtures to come out and spend and instead joined a local lending library and took up the piano again, playing in an amateur orchestra.

In the breaks from the railway work, he made three trips to Kalgoorlie, advising investors who were considering mining there. Monash compensated for this lonely travel and the drudgery of his expertise by writing a vivid account of the isolation of Australia's outback. But the drift of this elongated work for Baxter & Saddler made him yearn for Vic's companionship. He arranged for her and Bertha to join him in Perth in December 1898. The move was important for their marriage.

Vic proved a success. Her beauty, grace, charm and fine dress sense allowed her to ease into impressionable Perth society, which still looked to Melbourne as the country's style and fashion capital. She was soon as social, even flirtatious, as ever. But now the thirty-four-year-old Monash didn't mind. He trusted her and accepted her need for flattery from male admirers, which not so long ago he had seen as a threat to his authority in the relationship.

Monash was worried about being away so long from his beloved North Melbourne Battery. There had been rumblings about his long periods on official leave. But his immediate superior, Lieutenant Colonel Hall, covered for and supported him. George Farlow sent him detailed accounts of battery operations, doings, changes and gossip. Monash didn't miss the sniping from the permanent forces and its use of 'spies' to monitor the militia operations. But he was conscious of his duties as a major and concerned about the well-being of his men. A year earlier one officer had been on a fraud charge involving forgery. Monash had defended him, and had him acquitted. But while Monash was in Perth the officer's military conduct had slipped, and he had been dismissed. In an unrelated incident another officer suicided. Monash couldn't help thinking that if he had been in Melbourne more, he might have been able to help the man.

Monash felt helpless at such a distance, and was anxious to return for the annual Queenscliff Easter Camp in 1899. He was surprised by the state of his command. It was bigger at 186 men. Standards that Monash had built up in his first couple of years in control had been maintained. He was impressed by the battery's shooting prowess. The two companies in the battery were now classed under British regular service regulations as 'First Class' at artillery shooting. Monash was proud of the results of the toughest test, where a target at two kilometres was towed at twelve knots and attacked by artillery fire. The target was hit twelve times from sixteen shots. According to a regular officer observing the shooting, it matched or was better than anything in the British regular service. Monash had been the driving force behind improving standards, especially where technical applications, such as calculating trajectories and firing calibrations, were vital.

Thanks to Farlow, the standards had not slipped. It made Monash keener than ever to return to Melbourne. He pushed for the final reconciliation of Baxter & Saddler's forty-six claims, which totalled £150,000.

Monash prepared the contractors' brief while urging a settlement out of court. Baxter & Saddler would have been content with a payout of £50,000. They had not expected Monash's high figure, which was based on his thorough research. Yet that was why they had hired him.

Monash's detailed investigation and resulting demands did not please the local arbitrator, C. Y. O'Connor, the colony's engineer-in-chief. O'Connor had scant regard for contractors, especially those whom he thought were scrounging money from the local government. He let the government know that he thought it was in its interests that claims be set before him and fought over, not settled out of court.

The showdown came in May 1899 when Monash and a top barrister, Walter James, faced Septimus Burt, a renowned barrister and politician.

O'Connor carried out the arbitration as if he was in a rush, sometimes cutting off Monash and James in full flow. It was disconcerting as he abruptly handed down low settlement figures on claim after claim. After forty-two claims had been settled for just £15,000, Monash called a halt and urged Baxter & Saddler to appeal the last four claims in the colony's Supreme Court. Delays, perhaps orchestrated, irritated Monash as he attempted to settle out of court. After a month the government settled for a further £30,000, making a total of £45,000 for the forty-six claims.

Monash's assignment had taken exactly a year. He had again expected a bonus, but it was not forthcoming. He had to be content with the £800 that he had cleared in the Perth stay after accounting for the £300 loss over the failed quarry misadventure. He returned to Melbourne with Vic and Bertha on 4 July 1899 wondering just how he was going to earn that sort of money again and whether he could keep his firm afloat.

A BRIDGE TOO FAR

Monash was among the large crowd in South Yarra on 20 July 1899 as a massive fifteen-ton roller was hauled to the beginning of the Anderson Street Bridge over the Yarra River. Would the three slender, thirty-metre arches take the strain along with the very heavy dead weight? Much hinged on the result. Some engineers were sceptical of the Monier application in the arches, with its cement mortar containing a grid of iron rods. Many professionals and the press were ready to condemn the method if cracks appeared or the bridge collapsed. Monash would then be loath to continue attempting to obtain more contracts beyond the three already secured by Anderson, who stood near the bridge with Monash as the roller began to move.

Anderson was just as concerned. He had designed two other bridges, also in conjunction with Gummow. One was a four-arched bridge for Fyansford, near Geelong, and the other was at Wheeler's Creek, not far from Creswick. It was not that either engineer was among the sceptics looking on. It was more that redesigns and reconstructions added to big costs and delays in payments from tardy shire councillors.

As the roller edged to the centre of the bridge, both men looked to the foot of the nearest arch as council workers in a boat prepared to record readings with 'extensometers'. They would determine how much the bridge had stretched under the extreme weight and whether there were cracks. There were no immediate signs of concern from the measurements. The tests went on. The bridge stood firm. Monash later examined all the data and was more than satisfied with the Monier process. The big attraction was the much lower cost when compared to straight iron or steel works. The aesthetics could be better, too. The new construction method could be shaped in a way that would inspire designers and architects.

Monash immersed himself in all there was to learn about it, mainly from Baltzer. Monash now sniffed considerable prospects, not just in bridges but also in the production of Monier pipes. The same process applied with iron rods forming a grid in the pipe's cement. He contacted David Mitchell (father of Dame Nellie Melba), the big contractor and cement maker, who had built Scots Church in Collins Street. They reached an agreement. The firm could use land next to Mitchell's cement works in Burnley if the pipe factory used his cement.

Monash then assigned himself to the two other Gummow–Anderson designs. He loved the hands-on approach to construction as much as, if not more than the design stage. In his mind, the only way to learn about Monier's pluses and minuses was to be involved and in charge of every stage. In September he began the Monier work on the Wheeler's Creek bridge.

Despite the obvious promise of this breakthrough, the firm was unlikely to reap quick dividends. Monash still had to be alert for piecemeal work, such as arbitration, engineering and building jobs, to keep the firm afloat. He was still generating most of its revenue, but was prepared to carry Anderson and to remain loyal to a friend in hard times.

Monash was trying to find long-term solutions to the firm's continual cash crisis. It needed capital injection. Saddler was invited to invest with the promise of a share in the profits. So were other wealthy contacts as Monash touted the virtues of Monier. Saddler was sympathetic, but not a believer in what he saw as a still unproven, radical process. He arranged a bank to loan the firm £500, but would go no further. It was not a time for investment in new processes that required substantial funding.

Monash and all the Australian military read with great interest about the growing crisis in South Africa. The republic, made up of primarily Boer (Afrikaner) farmers with a Dutch background, under President Paul Kruger refused political rights to English miners. The British responded by reinforcing its South African garrison. This action led to the South African War, which began on 11 October 1899. The British built the garrison's troop numbers towards an eventual 500,000.

Some Australians were keen to fly the flag for Britain. A militia officer began raising a unit to join the fight. Monash thought about whether he should rush off with it. He was tempted. It offered an opportunity to gain experience in the one thing he lacked in his sixteen-year military career: war. He was thirty-four. The chance of being involved in any conflict seemed slim. It was not quite a case of 'now or never' for Monash, who dreamt of higher promotion and testing his great knowledge under battle conditions. It was rather a 'now or when?' situation. Would he ever see conflict?

Monash was again unsettled, as he had been over the war in the Sudan in 1885, by the thought of not pursuing the ultimate act for an officer: engagement in a war. Yet once more Monash had an even greater feeling of unease about joining a conflict that had nothing to do with Australia and did not threaten it. His rationale and background did not cause him to blindly follow Great Britain in maintaining its empire.

A young lieutenant in his battery, Dave Bevan, wrote to him asking whether Monash thought he should join the volunteer, unofficial 'Australian' force. 'This is certainly not an occasion where patriotism demands the making of any personal sacrifices,' Monash wrote. He added that if anyone wanted military experience and he could afford to go (like this single young man), the South African War offered a chance.[1] His response reflected his own internal conflict. It would be tough for him to justify sailing across the ocean and leaving his family and the firm, which was in a precarious position. If he did go, it would collapse. Then Vic, Bertha and Mathilde among several others would be left destitute. The struggle over eight years would amount to nothing. Monash helped resist the temptation by learning that neither the British War Office nor the Australian officer raising a unit wanted artillery – least of all garrison artillery. They sought infantry first and then cavalry. The war would be fought over rugged terrain, not at coastal ports.

Yet still Monash was touched by the considerable sentiment and support in Victoria for the volunteers when he helped arrange their send-off.

Any pricking of his conscience about not going was soon overridden by the firm's growing problems. Anderson was having trouble over the Fyansford Bridge. The shires and engineers involved were either slow in their payments or negligent. This in turn put pressure on the firm, which had to make excuses to its licensor, Gummow, and to banks for late payments.

The bridge itself had no major problems, but the politics behind it had presaged trouble.

Before building even began the *Geelong Advertiser* reported a special meeting of the Corio Shire Council in which a Councillor Taylor failed to see why the shire should 'undertake the erection of a Monier bridge, which was not only a large work but an experiment in river structures'.

Nevertheless it was built by late October and ready for testing by November. Tensions and disgruntlement from Taylor and other councillors continued, but Monash and Anderson had the upper hand. They refused to test it and thereby stopped its opening unless due payments were made. An arbitrator was called in. After a compromise and promises by the shires to pay, a date was set for an eighteen-ton roller to run across it early in the New Year.

Monash had a harrowing time, hardly enjoying the New Year celebrations that heralded 1900. On top of the business problems, Vic and he were fighting again in response to Monash's 'general retrenchment' at home and at the office. This meant demands for Vic to cut back on her extravagant buying of fashionable clothes. Monash had showered her with affection and gifts from Perth to help compensate for his absence. But back in Melbourne with the firm's costs mounting, he was tightening belts, or at least making do with last year's model rather than a new one for the Cup.

He went to the Fyansford test on 16 February in front of a big crowd. These roller events were like a sporting contest, with the outside chance of witnessing a bridge collapse. Monash was most relieved when it passed. He now decided to tackle the Corio and Bannockburn shires, which claimed that they were not responsible for extra work agreed to by their engineers. Cost overruns in such constructions were normal, and the firm was denied about £1500. Monash tried negotiation but failed. He sued, knowing that the case might take a year to be heard. Matters were made worse when Anderson went down with typhoid.

In March, the test for the Wheeler's Creek bridge also succeeded. With three bridges now operating, Monash led the drive to secure contracts to build eight Monier bridges in Bendigo. The local council wanted to control flooding and silting in the Bendigo Creek by building a concrete-lined channel through the city. It would need bridges over it. The City Engineer, J. R. Richardson, had drawn up the designs for these using conventional techniques that had dominated bridge-building for decades. They had timber decks with steel girders resting on masonry supports.

Monash and Anderson put their Monier concept to Richardson, and at least managed to have him consider their 'radical' proposal. He called for tenders for the eight bridges, including one – the King's Bridge on the main route north through Bendigo – which had to be built at an extreme angle (or 'skew').

Monash thought the firm had an even money chance of winning the other seven bridge contracts, but this more difficult construction was another matter. There was heavy opposition to the firm. A concerted campaign against the use of concrete by contractors and unions saw Monash putting in much time lobbying the Bendigo Council and Richardson from May through August. He was sidetracked by events that, if made public, would have sabotaged that contract.

Monash had to rush to Creswick to examine the Wheeler's Creek bridge. Cracks had appeared. It was monitored. By August Monash judged it was in danger of collapse. The Monier work was fine. The problem was inferior cement in some of the supports. Instead of fighting the shire, he agreed to carry out repairs at the firm's cost. A court fight at the moment they were struggling to win a political battle in Bendigo would have seen the firm lose that contract and the cash injection it would bring. Monash & Anderson were now operating more precariously than ever on 'letters of intent' from the Bendigo Council and others, which the partners passed under the noses of their bank managers as debts mounted and more credit was required.

Problems multiplied. They won another contract for a big timber bridge over the Tambo River at Bruthen, 320 kilometres east of Melbourne. But the firm's perpetual dread – government inspectors from the Public Works Department – caused trouble. Monash had to spend far more time than he would have liked travelling there by train and horse to defend the construction. The main problem centred on the quality of the timber. Monash had to demonstrate that no better wood could be obtained from inside Victoria. He did so, showing tact and diplomacy. Some inspectors had to justify their jobs. Monash now had plenty of experience with bureaucrats and egos, and managed to smooth matters after eight trips and much cost.

The Tambo River Bridge was a sound construction, but the firm would not see much profit from it.

The firm's survival now depended on securing seven of those eight Bendigo contracts. The lobbying against it reached a head in late August when there was a special conference at Trades Hall. Ironworkers, bricklayers, iron founders, builders and contractors protested against the City Council giving the contracts to Monash & Anderson. On 9 September 1900 the *Geelong Advertiser* published a letter from a local contractor. 'It would be a serious matter for the workers of Bendigo,' it said, 'if the council accepts a tender for foreign material instead of local production.'

Monash pointed out that concrete was wrongly branded as 'foreign'. All the materials were local. If anything, he reiterated, the new method was cheaper and arguably superior in resilience, strength and design. The Bendigo councillors had several acrimonious meetings and were split over which designs – something conventional or the Monier process – to choose. Had the other three Monier bridges not been operating the firm would have had no chance of winning the contracts.

An unexpected opportunity arose when Richardson set a figure of £1200 to design the problematic King's Bridge. No conventional contractor had managed to submit any proposals cheaper than £1600. Learning this, Monash did the figures and moved fast. He offered to include all eight bridges in a deal worth £7000, which slotted the King's Bridge in at £1200 to meet Richardson's budget. This overall figure was up to 25 per cent less than that of any other contractor. Monash kept pushing and lobbying, using photographs of the other three bridges. Apart from the functionality of these constructions, he maintained, the council and Richardson could realise dreams that would make their mark on the city's history and development. Eight bridges of impressive design would have many benefits for the city's transport and aesthetics well into the twentieth century.

Going on Richardson's recommendation, a final council meeting in early October saw it sign the deal. Work on the bridges would begin in 1901. The firm would use cement from two of its main creditors, Mitchell's Melbourne works and Taylor's at Fyansford.

Monash and a recovered Anderson broke open the champagne. The firm was viable, for the moment.[2]

Monash was too busy in the last half of the 1890s to be other than a well-informed, interested onlooker as Australia moved towards nationhood. He knew all the ins and outs of the political bargaining from discussions with his friend and former mentor, Alfred Deakin. He and New South Wales barrister and politician Edmund Barton were the two biggest players in pushing for Federation. They led politicians around the country who, in a spirit of altruism, mostly supported Federation.

Monash's vested interest in what was developing centred on the military and the formation of one national defence force. There had been a vague, sometimes hysterical reaction to foreign invasion ever since the Crimean War of 1853–56. That was mainly a squabble fought on the Crimean Peninsula of the Black Sea between the Russians on one side and the British, French and Turks on the other. It could not have been more distant from Australia, but British involvement in it made headlines and fuelled concern about threats to the British Empire from an ill-defined European enemy empire. Such concern focused towards the end of the nineteenth century on Germany after it was federated in 1871. The colonies also feared being overrun by Asians, or 'Yellow Hordes' as the influential *Bulletin* called them. This worry was created by the influx of Chinese during the Victorian Gold Rush and stewed up into paranoia in Queensland, which was closer to Asian nations.

The Queensland colony became the trendsetter in concern over invasion from Germany when early in 1883 it seized the southeastern part of Papua New Guinea. The British, although embarrassed by this brazen act, were forced to tag along in 1884 and annexed the southeast, albeit reluctantly. This prompted the Germans, through the German New Guinea Company, to take over the northeastern section.

There was some rational basis to concerns about Britain's far-off battles to maintain its many conquests, gathered over 400 years. History taught that territory was sometimes swapped, stolen or bargained for with no more decorum than that found in a Turkish bazaar. Hence the trigger-happy desire from the Australian colonies to support the status quo in terms of who ruled what among the warring empires. Monash's contribution was to emphasise and articulate to Deakin at every chance the importance of Australia having a unified defence force controlled by the new Federal Government.

There were no surprises when the first government, instituted on 1 January 1901 and led by the nation's first Prime Minister, Edmund Barton, formed a defence department, along with the machinery for the High Court of Australia and a Commonwealth public service. Barton, who doubled as Minister for External Affairs, calmed fears of invasion by carrying the 'white Australia' Immigration Restriction Act, which was supported by both conservatives and labour. In theory, the drawbridge was shut to European and Asian conquests. If they did try to storm Fortress Australia some sort of unified force would be ready for them. It was all part of the important jingoistic sense of nationhood. Being thought desirable for takeover was good for a new nation's sense of relevance and importance.

The death of Queen Victoria on 22 January 1901 after a sixty-four-year reign created a feeling of unease even in her distant Dominions. Monash noted the importance of the event and the political analysis afterwards. She had been the most powerful and stable influence in Europe. In theory, Victoria had experienced the first decline of a British sovereign's power. Academics, historians and political commentators spoke often of the concept of a 'constitutional monarchy' during her reign. The Queen's role was seen to be 'above' political parties and foreign affairs. In reality she had, in many ways, as much power as any previous monarch, for two reasons. First, her influence was great outside the United Kingdom because of the marriages of most of her nine children into the royal families of Europe. They in turn had influence with governments and rulers. Second, despite the alleged diminution of her power, Victoria had huge prestige, presiding as she did over an empire covering a quarter of the world on which, it was said, the sun never set. Coupled with her determination at times to master political detail, her influence was subtle but strong and far-reaching. Victoria had been in favour of peace and reconciliation in foreign affairs, despite the scores of small wars fought in her empire during her long reign. She was more often than not a calming influence on empires and their rulers, dictators and elected officials.

Monash's reflective notes highlighted how in 1864 she had urged her ministers not to intervene in the Prussia–Austria–Denmark War. Victoria's letter to the German Emperor (whose son had married her daughter in 1875) helped avert a second Franco-German war. Her shrewd view on Britain's policy towards the declining Turkish Empire in the 1870s held sway. Victoria thought there should be reforms, but that Britain ought to uphold Turkish domination as a bulwark of stability against Russia. She pushed for bipartisanship on the issue that could have involved Britain in taking sides and entering the conflict.

Monash wondered how her fifty-nine-year-old son, Edward VII, would cope with her legacy of enormous responsibility, power, influence and diplomacy. What would be the impact on the German, French and Russian empires with their acquisitive tendencies?

The new Commonwealth Government took control of defence forces around Australia on 1 March 1901. Monash's battery became known as No. 3 Victorian Company, Australian Garrison Artillery. This sort of change in concept and name would keep the new federal and state bureaucracies busy for years. But while the influential politicians congratulated themselves and got on with running the new country, the tyranny of geographic distances between the states, and their mixed history, kept a staunchly parochial mentality in the various regions. Victorians were still Victorians. They couldn't feel closer to New South Welshman and their convict background. A sentiment of dislike rather than hate, based on ignorance, was mutual. Attitudes about the 'deep North' of Queensland remained for anyone south of Brisbane. Those in the West still regarded anyone from 'back east' with suspicion. Tasmania couldn't be towed closer to the mainland. It remained remote. The majority of people from one far-off region rarely encountered those from another.

The country had officially become a nation. Deakin, a sort of Gough Whitlam reformer of his day, with a sense of fiscal responsibility, in particular had a grand vision for a better nation. He recognised the importance of the profit incentive and the driven individual in the private sector, such as his friend Monash. But in modern economic jargon, he also believed in a 'safety net' for every Australian and primarily the battlers – the workers and their families. Yet he differed from the economic rationalists of 1900 by his insistence on legislating for a structure over and around the net. It centred on protection of Australian manufacturers by the slapping of duties (tariffs) on imported goods. There was to be an arbitrated flow-on in increased wages to workers. This was 'trickle-down' theory (whereby a booming economy would mean rewards would reach employees by osmosis) with a government tap to make sure there was a steady stream.

Deakin saw this new legislation as 'the beginning of a new civilisation'. One observer called him a 'rich man's Friedrich Engels'. He was at least setting the stage for his new civilisation. The structure would be in place, but the new nation needed a soul. These promising, practical ideals aside, it was still a dispirited bunch of former colonies, running themselves less now there was a Federal Government, yet getting on with their lives as they had for decades.

The fact that there was now an Australian high court, parliament, public service, defence force and a policy that kept non-whites out of the country could not contrive a true sense of nationhood. Australia was not yet a nation in spirit.

Monash was in Sydney in January 1901 and joined in the celebrations with Frank Gummow as the Commonwealth was inaugurated. The Bendigo contract success had emboldened him to the point where he offered Gummow £400 for the sale of the exclusive rights to the Monier process in Victoria. Gummow, himself overextended, asked for £500, and an agreement was reached. Monash couldn't lay his hands on that size of funds. Instead he offered Gummow a royalty from bridge contract revenue until the £500 was paid off. The Sydney contractor agreed. However, the agreements over all works stood as they were until the firm owned the Monier rights in Victoria. In other words, Gummow, Forest & Co. still had final say on all technical matters. Gummow, through its chief engineer designer Baltzer, and the firm would often do parallel engineering calculations on bridge works. They would differ from time to time. When they did, Baltzer's numbers would be used unless Monash or Anderson made a good case for a change.

Monash had now put himself under even more pressure. Every bridge had to be successful. He worried about the difficult King's Bridge. Baltzer's design, sent from Sydney, came up with a fifty-three-degree skew. Monash thought it was too much. The strains on the bridge's parts, particularly its lateral support structures (or abutments), might be dangerous. He took his concerns to Richardson, who insisted on his right to control the project's development. Monash argued that a smaller tilt would make the construction easier, reduce the bridge's span and the forces against the supports. Richardson agreed to reduce the skew to fifty degrees.

On 14 May Richardson, thirty council employees and Monash joined the usual throng of spectators for the bridge's test. Workers moved into the channel below to attach the extensometers under the bridge. Richardson directed the council roller driver to compact the newly-laid road surface. The roller was driven back and forth twelve times. It and a traction engine were then both driven on so that Monash could take pictures. Richardson then ordered the test begin. Workers made their way under the bridge to read the extensometers. A long, fine crack was noticed on the undersurface (or soffit). There were signs of distress on other points. The extensometers showed some permanent give or stretch.

Richardson, Monash and several other engineers went under the bridge to have a look. All cracks were judged as superficial. They all knew the history of Monier constructions. It took three times the load after similar signs to cause serious cracking or collapse. Richardson would not put anything like triple the roller weight of about twenty-five tonnes on this one. In fact, he, Monash and the others believed the bridge would never again have such a load on it.

Richardson and Monash returned to the top of the bridge. The tests started up again. The roller and the traction engine were brought within a few metres of each other in the middle of the bridge. Richardson asked for readings from the workers underneath. There was no substantial change. He ordered the two vehicles off the bridge, then on again. He called for readings once more. Again the figures were static. The original stretch (or deflection) remained as it was.

Richardson was not satisfied that the test had been tough enough. He ordered the traction engine leave the bridge, turn around and return to the middle of the bridge so that its back axle was as close as possible to the roller's. This meant that a thirty-tonne load was concentrated mid-span.

Council workers this time didn't wait for Richardson's requests for measurements. They began shouting that deflection was increasing and wouldn't stop. Mortar from the bridge's undersurface began dropping into the channel. Workers ran, scrambled or threw themselves clear. Seconds later those on top became aware that one of the three strips of the span was ripping away. The three-man crew on the traction engine jumped out of the vehicle, but went down with the arch strip, as did Richardson and several others. A split second later, the engine slipped off sideways taking an onlooker, A. E. Boldt, with it. He was crushed to death.

Monash was standing next to the roller on the centre strip, which held for a few seconds before rods connected to it began ripping free. This left the roller precariously balanced. Monash and the roller driver rushed to the one intact strip, then the channel underneath.

In the last decade, Monash had been close to death and severe injury on the Princes Bridge, the Outer Circle Railway project and the Williamstown Rifle Range. But this was the most traumatic moment so far in his career. Yet within a minute of the collapse, Monash was in control of himself and the situation. He organised every able body to help those caught in the mess of concrete, bricks, rods and coping blocks. By a miracle, Boldt, a business associate of the traction engine owner, was the only major casualty. The injured were ferried to hospital.

When the dust settled two days later, Anderson joined Monash in a meeting with the lucky Richardson, who apart from bruising and battered pride after his ride down to the channel with the wayward bridge strip, was in fair shape. After the shock had subsided they were all baffled by the collapse. They, Gummow, Baltzer and four other experienced engineers had made the calculations on how the bridge should be constructed. The numbers and methods had not varied. Only Monash's suggestion of the skew reduction had changed the original numbers. In hindsight that seemed a correct move. Everyone had been satisfied with the workmanship and materials.

Monash moved fast. Slow reaction or no reaction might well have been the ruin of the firm. He agreed to rebuild the bridge at the firm's cost, which was estimated at £1000. He promised to put forward a new design. The profit from the eight bridges would be reduced, but Monash was banking, literally, on the cash flow from the eight Bendigo constructions, if they all went ahead. Opposition in the council now had ammunition.

In the weeks that followed the test failure, other alleged 'experts', often with indirect connections to the project, had opinions, which were often aired in the press. Some observers, especially engineers, who preferred masonry bridges, reckoned that the arch might have been too flat. One experienced tradesman said that the bridge's tilt was impossible to build. Then there were the inevitable attacks on the Monier process itself. The firm had to counter criticisms, all of which came from those who had vested interests – primarily certain engineers, councillors in their pockets and unions – in seeing it discredited.

A counter-tactic by Monash was to contribute to the industry news-paper, *Building, Engineering and Mining Journal*. It probed the demise of the King's Bridge and editorialised that the Monier process was not to blame.

An official inquiry into the collapse was held in Bendigo before a judge and jury. In the crisis, Monash turned to his friend Professor Kernot, one of the people who had influenced him to use the Monier process, as an expert witness. Kernot's investigation covered whether the accepted way of analysing skew arches was correct. This was a radical step in engineering circles. The master of British engineering theory, W. J. M. Rankine, had endorsed the method used, which was regarded as conventional. But Kernot couldn't find one mathematician who could work out the mechanics on the skew arch, a point that he sagely made public at the inquiry. Engineering was a tried and accepted science, but this was a rare example for the time of where it was not exact. After making the case for uncertainty and inexactitude, Kernot, armed with chalk and a blackboard, proceeded to baffle the court with evidence provided by trials with small-scale models in cement, plaster and even soap. He came up with possibilities: there was not enough cement in the abutment concrete; the abutment might have been embedded in foundation material that was too soft; a sharp projecting corner in one abutment might have been unable to withstand the thrust caused by the test.

Kernot, however, deflected the court's mind away from the failure of material, arches, abutments and foundations by returning to his main suggestion that all the textbooks on the subject of bridges built on extreme angles could well be wrong. If a design engineer followed the conventional method, which had the esteemed Professor Rankine's imprimatur, then he could, in the case of extremely skewed constructions, come to grief.

In the face of all the testimony to the high quality of the workmanship and materials used on the bridge, this was a telling argument. It took the inquiry even further away from any suggestion that the Monier process was in any way inadequate. The jury was reminded that if a design engineer used accepted unchallenged theory and it didn't work in practice, then he had a strong defence in law if ever charged with negligence.

Kernot's evidence swayed the jury. It decided that the designers and builders had 'acted reasonably and could not be expected to foresee the problem'. The verdict was that the hapless Mr Boldt had met his death accidentally. '. . . no blame could be attached to anyone.'

After months of anxiety, Monash could now turn his mind to a new design. The arch would not be rebuilt like the original. He suggested keeping the original abutments and building a new support in mid-stream. The bridge would now be essentially made up of two arches each with a 13.2-metre span rather the original of 28.5 metres. This would reduce the thrust on the abutments to about a quarter of that for the single arch. The firm was confident that the bridge could stand a test twice as tough as before and not collapse.[3]

✕

Before the next bridge test, Monash had to contend with the settlement mess with the Corio and Bannockburn shires over the Fyansford construction. Led by the recalcitrant Councillor Taylor, who had caused trouble when the bridge was on the drawing board, the shires, through their lawyers, had managed to filibuster the court case. It was June 1901, sixteen months after the bridge was up and tested. Monash was thankful for his legal expertise. If he had not been qualified and experienced, the firm would have been out of business long before now. One of the innumerable points he had learned was to document every detail of a project, including agreements that were originally made verbally. The documentation on what the engineers for the shires had commissioned beyond the original plans, and the agreed costs, was watertight.

The judge hearing the case let the shires see the detail Monash had gathered. The shire and their lawyers panicked when they realised they were certain to lose with the defence prepared. In desperation, they changed their position and claimed that the firm had been fraudulent in manipulating the measurement of quantities.

Monash was at first offended. He soon realised that the shires had been transparent in their attempt to corrupt the case. The judge wrapped up proceedings by awarding the firm £1900: £1500 for the original claim and £400 on top as a penalty of sorts. He put on the record that the claim of fraud was 'scandalous' and admonished the shires and their lawyers.

The penalty didn't seem harsh enough. The shires still refused to pay. They responded to the court demands with a move that compounded the scandal. A special levy was imposed on their ratepayers. The shires also sold land they controlled. This was not in order to pay the £1900. The money raised would be used to appeal to Victoria's Full Court and retain two of the best barristers in the state.

The firm tried to scare the shires into settling out of court by using their legal rights to seize council furniture and auction it. This realised a fraction of the money owed and did not have the desired effect.

The bitter battle would go on.

A few months later, in October 1901, Monash prepared for the next harrowing moment in his career with bridges: a test on the first of the seven conventional structures across the channel in Bendigo. He had been warned that if this one collapsed the council would cancel the contracts for the remaining six. This construction was smaller than the King's Bridge, but Monash was forced to demonstrate his faith in the Monier method by an extreme check of thirty tonnes. A failure would have seen the firm slip further into the mire of costs, inquiries and law suits. Monash revelled in the legal battles, but another failure would be a bridge too far. The firm would be bankrupt.

With these thoughts heavy on his mind, he took control of the test under the watchful eye of councillors and engineers. To his considerable relief, the extensometers hardly budged at any moment in the build-up and final test.

The firm was still afloat. Monash returned to Melbourne, his way clear to expanding the firm's operations. He was prepared to back his belief in the process and its eventual profitability. He and David Mitchell had discussed beginning the Monier Pipe Company. Now they could go ahead. The firm and Mitchell each held forty per cent. The remaining twenty per cent went to the company's management in a shrewd move to encourage its officers to work hard.

Monash ended a year living on the edge by taking a holiday at Strahan in western Tasmania where, just before Christmas, he was to advise on an arbitration case. Over the vacation into the New Year, 1902, he went bush at Hell's Gates, Macquarie Harbour. Monash had been inspired to visit locations in the classic novel, *For the Term of His Natural Life*, by Marcus Clarke, which depicted 'the dismal condition of a felon during his term of transportation'. Hiking through these remote locations was a refresher course in the ruggedness of Australia's geography, which Monash loved exploring. It was also his way of clearing his thoughts about his business worries.

He returned home ready for the challenges and stresses that would confront him, beginning with a mid-January test for the redesigned King's Bridge. A crowd of about a thousand, including plenty of pressmen from Melbourne and locally, lined the channel to watch Monash conduct the test, with every Bendigo councillor looking on. The two-arch reconstruction lived up to expectations and passed.

Monash walked away with his faith in Monier vindicated. It would never fail him, but tardy council payers would. After the test, he began the now-mandatory round of arguments about monies owed. These were underway when Monash at last entered Melbourne's Full Court to contest the appeal over the Fyansford case.

The firm retained Leo Cussen, a forceful barrister, who would work in tandem with Monash, against the shires' two expensive representatives. One was the cunning barrister Edward Mitchell. The other was the formidable Isaac Isaacs. The son of a Jewish tailor, the forty-six-year-old Isaacs, like Monash, defied his relatively poor 'outsider' background to develop into one the nation's finest legal brains. He had been a Victorian politician, twice serving in the 1890s as Attorney-General. Isaacs had impressed Monash when he demonstrated an unrivalled knowledge of constitutional law during the convention between the colonies in 1897–98 to prepare for Federation. He had been a surprise exclusion from the committee drafting the laws that would underpin the form and powers of the new Federal Government. His friends, particularly in the liberal press, called him too 'ambitious and forthright' to work with such a committee. His enemies branded him 'pushy and devious'.

With these descriptions in mind, Monash was uneasy about a contest against him. At stake now was not the unpaid £1900 but £4000, the cost of the appeal to Victoria's Full Court. The case seemed to proceed smoothly enough for the firm. The three judges presiding deferred judgement without setting a date.

The firm's finances remained delicately balanced. So much so that Anderson decided to leave it. He knew Monash had carried him since the firm's inception in 1894. His early handling of the Fyansford contract had, in part, led to the later problems. His departure was carried out with mixed feelings on both sides. Bailing out now left Monash with all the debt payments, but this was balanced by his having sole control over the Monier rights. In mid-1902, even with them, Anderson didn't think the firm had a viable future. The legal struggles seemed to take up more time than engineering projects.

The two men remained on good terms when Anderson took up a post in Dunedin, New Zealand, in charge of the sewerage works. After observing the corruption in the Fyansford case he wrote to Monash saying he was 'dealing in the same environment as those corrupt shires'.[4]

The firm waited until August 1902 for the Fyansford verdict. It was shocked to learn that the judges – Holroyd, Hodges and a'Beckett – had awarded them a paltry £800.

Cussen and Monash pored over the judgement and concluded that the judges had somehow overlooked or forgotten key arguments. Cussen was so incensed that he asked the Full Court to justify its decision. It admitted overlooking important points. He branded the judges privately as either dim-witted or corrupt, and was prompted to appeal to the Privy Council in England, the last recourse in law. Monash's backers – Mitchell and Saddler – were prepared to take it that far. But Monash had the final call. He looked at the downside. If the firm lost it would be a costly disaster. If it won, the award would probably not cover costs. Under the bluff that they would go to the Privy Council, the firm squeezed a settlement of £1000 out of the shires.[5]

This was £3000 short of Monash's expectations and the firm's needs. Yet he remained optimistic. Any other attitude would have seen him embracing insolvency. He calculated that even if the new pipe-making business did not live up to hopes, then he would be able to pay off everyone by 1905.

The economic stringency in Monash's life continued into 1903 as the family moved into a modest boarding house in East Melbourne. He kept up appearances by taking Vic to the theatre, concerts and balls. He had to keep networking, although the need irked him. He also remained the Godfather of his extended Jewish family. When his sister Louise needed support to marry in England, he provided it. He never missed a weekly payment, increased to £3, to his beloved sister Mathilde, even when they were fighting. It allowed her to survive modestly without working. When his cousin Karl (one of widowed aunt Ulrike's three sons) ended up a beggar in New South Wales after illness and his pharmacy business failed, Monash sent him money. After another cousin, Karl's brother Louis, looked like being jailed for embezzlement, Monash paid for his defence and set him up on the other side of the continent. The only one whom the Godfather did not favour was the third brother, Herman, who worked for the firm and siphoned off funds. Monash fired him and banished him from the family.

The older generation turned to him. When Ulrike was distressed by the way her three sons had let the family down, Monash arranged for Mathilde to live with her. He paid her rates and mortgage. Even Albert Behrend, his much older cousin, who had joined Monash's father in Melbourne in 1862, was helped out after failing to make a life with his family back in Europe.

Somehow, Monash, himself strapped for cash, always found more than a few quid for an unfortunate member of the family or a friend, especially

Serious young man: John Monash, aged nine, in 1874. Not long after this image was captured, he and his family moved to Jerilderie in southern New South Wales.

Talented teenager: Monash, aged 16, in 1881, was dux of Scotch College, Melbourne, the year before entering the University of Melbourne.

Militia beginnings: Colour-sergeant John Monash (left, rear) in 1886 just before his 21st birthday. This photograph marked the disbanding of the University Company, 4th Battalion. Less than a year later, he joined the North Melbourne Battery.

Surveying a future: Monash (at right), aged 22, in 1888 in his role as engineer-in-charge of the Melbourne Outer Circle Railway from Fairfield to Oakleigh. This was his second major job, after being one of four engineers to build the Princes Bridge, Melbourne.

An affair to remember: Annie Gabriel in 1888, the year she began an affair with Monash. She called him 'the love of my life'. It was certainly a romantic and sensual relationship. They remained close until her death in 1929.

Opposites attract: Monash, aged 25, with Hannah Victoria (Vic) Moss, 21, whom he married in April 1891. The relationship was tempestuous in its early years.

Annus horribilus: Monash, aged 29, with daughter Bertha, aged 20 months, and his father, Louis. In 1894, a hard year for Monash, he was estranged from Vic.

Rapprochement: Monash, aged 33, in 1898 with his family. He and Vic were separated for a year but reunited in 1895. Three years on, Monash was making painstaking headway as an engineer and lawyer as the Depression lingered.

Those nerve-racking tests: Monash in 1899 in attendance with 1000 spectators at a test with a heavy roller for one of his firm's reinforced concrete showpieces – the Morrell (now Anderson Street) Bridge at South Yarra. This style of construction led to Monash making his fortune before World War I.

The peacock: Monash in regalia in 1900, aged 35. Throughout his military career, he enjoyed looking smart in uniform.

A sign of success: In 1911, Monash bought his favourite house, Iona, in St George's Road, Toorak, for £4750. He lived at Iona for the last twenty years of his life, except for the years abroad in 1915–1919.

Cataloguing an exceptional mind: In the library at Iona, Monash had 5000 books, along with his record and art collection, which were all catalogued. The home's long hallway was lined with war memorabilia, from guns and swords to shrapnel from Gallipoli and the Red Baron's propeller from the Western Front.

Colonel at the crossroads: Monash, aged 48, early in 1914 when he was in charge of the 13th Infantry Brigade. At this time, Sir Ian Hamilton observed Monash commanding a mock battle exercise in the extreme heat at Lilydale outside Melbourne, and then wrote a glowing report about him for the British High Command.

Challenging command: Colonel John Monash (centre, in profile) in October 1914 inspecting the 13th battalion for the first time at Liverpool, Sydney. A few weeks earlier, Monash had been appointed commander of the new 4th Brigade. It was a tough assignment. The 13th and 14th Battalions came from New South Wales and Victoria, respectively. Two more (the 15th and 16th) would be drawn from the other States. (Australian War Memorial Negative No. H00520)

Two small pyramids: Monash (left) and his Chief of Staff Major J.P. McGlinn in Egypt at the foot of the Sphinx in early 1915. The two heavyweights in charge of 4th Brigade, dubbed Tweedledee and Tweedledum by rivals in the AIF, were preparing for an invasion of Turkey.

A most vulnerable command post: Monash in May 1915 (seated, without head-gear) at his command post near the head of Monash Valley, Gallipoli. Courtney's Post was 20 metres up the scrubby slope. Just 10 metres beyond the post marked the beginning of the Turkish trenches, harbouring 40,000 enemy Muslim soldiers, prepared to die for Allah and country. (Australian War Memorial Negative No. G01187)

if they were battlers who had fallen on hard times. Monash, the realist, was fully aware that others (such as Saddler and Mitchell) found a way to lend to him when he was struggling. The only difference was that Monash had to pay off his loans. The money that helped the family would never be returned. Nor did he expect it.

After the eight Bendigo contracts, Monash found bridge-building work slow through 1903. He did manage to construct small Monier bridges at Kyneton, Ballarat, Mansfield and the Upper Coliban. But there were thin profit margins in them. The pipe factory was barely ticking over. This forced him to whittle away at his small mountain of debt with court witness work in engineering and patent cases. The latter frustrated him. He despaired that patentees never received royalties. He thought patent agents were swindlers, who, like fortune-tellers, told tales about bright futures, which were never realised.

His attitude and experience caused everyone who worked with him, and even those against him, to recognise that he was the best professional 'witness' – effectively a special investigator – in the country. Leo Cussen went further. 'Any solicitor who failed to retain John Monash as an expert on any patent matter,' he said, 'was prima facie guilty of negligence.'[6]

Cussen backed up his words by hiring Monash in a case where a resident of his old suburb, Hawthorn, had sued the council for not providing a drainage system for river and rain flooding, which affected his property. Cussen and Monash represented the resident, a Mr Kannaluik, against the City of Hawthorn, represented by Isaac Isaacs. It was the first time that Monash and Isaacs had faced each other in court since the Fyansford case, which would rankle with Monash for a long time yet. He was more than keen to win, and as usual did his due diligence in researching the case with care. He came up with a digestible summary for the judge and a one-liner that stuck: 'A small payment of £150 by the Council to a reputable water engineer will allow the construction of an adequate drainage system and settle the matter.'

This was a slap at Isaacs for not advising his client to pay up. The judge concurred. Sitting for days discussing floods, the depths of mud and how to engineer a drain did not inspire him. His irritation led to caustic remarks to Isaacs and the council. Perhaps he was bored and would rather have been pottering in his own properly watered Toorak garden. He found against the council and ordered it to pay costs.

Showing the sort of arrogance (or cunning) that had annoyed many in legal and political circles, Isaacs advised that the case should go to the Full Court. The council obliged. It lost again. Isaacs knew he was on a 'nice big earner' with a profligate group of councillors, who would make their counterparts in Corio and Bannockburn look frugal by comparison. He urged the Hawthorn councillors to go further and make history by taking the case to the Privy Council. They did.

It is not recorded what the illustrious lords in London really thought about having to sit in judgement over the fate of a soggy backyard in a Melbourne suburb. But they barely warmed their seats before sweeping away the appeal and supporting the Victorian Full Court's decision in favour of the aggrieved gumboot-wearing Hawthorn resident.

Monash's notebook was the key exhibit. Because it travelled as far as the House of Lords, presumably so that the Privy Councillors might sit around on the Woolsack thumbing through it, *Kannaluik v. City of Hawthorn* became Monash's most celebrated case. No longer would ratepayers be left knee deep in mud with nowhere to turn because negligent councils had failed to provide drains, run-offs and river barriers. It set the standard for court conflicts concerning the liabilities of municipalities in disputes over draining and flooding of properties.

Monash enjoyed victory over Isaacs. There was some feeling between them after two drawn-out and (at times) acrimonious cases, especially as the losses from Fyansford nearly ruined the firm and forced lingering debt on it. Yet still Monash could not help harbouring great respect for Isaacs, who possessed one of the finest minds in the country. The feeling was mutual. In early 1904, not long after the Kannaluik case was resolved, Isaacs paid him for advice on a problem he was having with a neighbour over who owned the rights to water from a creek at his country home at Mount Macedon.

After that Monash was invited to stay with him there. They talked about Isaacs' work in the first Commonwealth parliament, disagreed on protectionism (Monash was against it philosophically despite once fighting to protect local coal producers) and agreed about the importance of the USA's successful democracy. According to Monash's notes, they also discussed religion and had similar convictions, or lack of them.[7] Isaacs, a left-leaning liberal with essentially pacifist views, argued with Monash about Australia's need for a strong defence force. Isaacs thought the new nation's isolation would protect it from invaders. Monash didn't trust the expansionist aims of empires. He thought that Australia's size and great potential mineral wealth would make it attractive to foreign powers in the future. He suggested the fledging nation had to be vigilant.

They were both outstanding intellectuals, who were multilingual and well versed in the arts and sciences. Although an unpopular figure, Isaacs proved his skills in constitutional law and as a federal Attorney-General. (He would later add to his record on the High Court in 1906, the Privy Council in 1924, as chief justice in 1930 and as the first Australian-born Governor-General from 1931 to 1936.) Monash's career diverged here. After more than a decade of tertiary study on three degrees and gaining military rank, most of his energies were now thrust into using all his accumulated knowledge for producing and building. It was almost as if he had exercised his mind enough on academic pursuits. Now he wished to be hands on and create structures, while still using his brain pragmatically in his work and litigation.

There were differences, too, in their attitude to wealth creation. Monash, a businessman, engineer and contractor now for thirteen years, had employed thousands of workers in construction. He believed in the force of the individual. As a result of his experience in working for government bodies and in trials against them and shires, Monash had developed a contempt for their attitudes, waste, work practices, lack of productivity and corruption. Isaacs by contrast put much time into pushing for the extension of Federal Government powers and progressive reform. He was also a shrewd operator for government bodies and shires in his legal work. He had little time for or understanding of business.

Monash twice demonstrated in court that he was at least Isaacs' intellectual equal. His record as an investigator and witness showed he was more of a problem-solver and pragmatist. His two relaxed days with Isaacs gave them a better understanding of each other. This plus their mutual respect meant, after an early rivalry, that a friendship might develop.

By early 1904 Monash was covering all bets in his effort to build and make his company profitable. Bridge-building had slowed. Substantial pipe sales remained a dream. He tendered now for construction jobs using reinforced concrete. This third Monier arm began modestly: a flat roof for a ballroom here, a porch portico there. Then, in mid-1904, Monash put this product to the test in a big tender for a reinforced concrete interior in a seven-storey office block. Other tenderers told the government's Building Surveyor's Department that the new block wouldn't cope with a fire if Monash's product were used. He had to conduct several tests to show that reinforced concrete was fireproof. The publicity generated by the battle with the department ended up being positive. Monash won the contract, and then another to build a big storage facility for a financier in inner-city Kensington.

True to his prediction, he was pulling the company around to profitability. He had a juggling act to keep his operations going. Monash was keen to plough back profits and keep David Mitchell, his main backer with forty per cent, from becoming impatient and disgruntled that he was not seeing a dividend. To keep the peace, he distributed a small return to the investors in late 1904. Meanwhile, he continued to urge Gummow to give him sole patent rights for Monier use in South Australia and Western Australia. The verdict was not yet in on how the process would go in the long term in Melbourne. No other engineers in Adelaide or Perth had even bothered to make inquiries about it. Gummow itself was struggling in Sydney. In the end, after eighteen months of discussions, Gummow decided it had nothing to lose by letting Monash loose on the two new markets.

Monash was becoming tired of his expert witness work, which he always regarded as a stopgap income earner. After five years of using the Monier process, it was time to formalise his drive for it in deed, word and image. Early in 1905, he formed a new company, the Reinforced Concrete and Monier Pipe Construction Co. – RCMPCC. It was a mouthful but also a statement. He was nearly forty – a critical birthday in his mind, given that his mother had been just forty-four when she died. Monash felt compelled to follow his educated instincts on what he thought was the best and quickest route to making his name and fortune.

PIPE DREAMS
REALISED

The life John Monash was leading had etched itself into his appearance. Long gone was the soft, lean look of the idealist and permanent under-graduate. At forty, his hair was thinner. The jowls – in fact all his features – were heavier. A thick black moustache added to an image bordering on lugubrious. He remained handsome but in a mature way. Women were still attracted to him for his dark looks (a rarity in Anglo-Celtic Melbourne), ever-present charm and a powerful sense of purpose in life. His brown eyes, described variously as forlorn, sensitive and serious, were a key to where he was and what he had been through. Those who encoun-tered him at that time said they never left you or blinked. It was, his closest friend George Farlow, said, 'un-nerving if you didn't know him'.[1] That unwavering glare, it seemed, verified his 'sorry maxim for humanity': 'Assume every man is a rogue till he is proved honest.'[2]

Petty extortionists, harassing debt-collectors, corrupt councillors, unprincipled patent agents, suborned judges, fraudulent relatives, embezz-ling mine managers, merchants of tease and promise. They had all taken their toll. Yet his depressing homily came from a string of business experi-ences during the worst period of the long depression of the 1890s. Monash also had a lifetime habit of taking people other than businessmen at face value. He looked for the best in people. When his trust and respect was gained, Monash's warmth came through. When a friend was in trouble, the compassion was there, too, lurking and quick to emerge.

A journalist for the 'soldier's paper' *Smith's Weekly* in 1933, looking back three decades later, gave another dimension to that intense expression:

'. . . in a few hours of ferocious concentration, smoking furiously and incessantly all the while, he would produce a solution to a problem that had baffled his contemporaries [engineers] for months.'[3]

Monash's politics, unshaped in his early idealistic student years, headed further towards the conservative through two decades. Scotch College and Melbourne University did not embrace socialism or communism other than as a comparative study in his days there. His father Louis' interpretation and denunciation of the Karl Marx inspired 'revolution' in Prussia in 1848 had lightly coloured Monash's early thoughts. Louis said the ensuing destabilisation in Prussia was a reason for his leaving Europe.

Monash's dealings with budding socialist unions allowed him to make his own political judgements. They were confirmed by his militia experiences. Politics in general, and radical politics in particular, were scorned, ignored or seen as potentially subversive to the system that they were trained to defend. A tongue-in-check diary remark about his audience at Port Melbourne when he lectured on artillery demonstrated an attitude. He was in 'a den of ill-bred, ungrammatical socialists'. Presumably, he would have preferred well-mannered, well-spoken conservatives.

Yet, as is often the case with a brilliant, dynamic intellect, he had developed into a character of contradictions. Monash was brutally honest with himself. He searched always for the integrity of an issue or situation regardless of whether it fitted his preconceptions. As mentioned, he was for free trade as a principle but could be persuaded to help protect an industry from foreign domination. Monash favoured the conservative *Argus* over the radical *Age* but read them both. He would never vote other than for conservatives and actively supported right-wing politicians. Yet he was happy to build at least a solid acquaintanceship with Isaacs and remained close to Alfred Deakin.

Monash once said that 'physical deprivations are the least of human sufferings by a long shot'. But he never failed to help those in poverty who came in contact with him, whether friends, family or even strangers.

Monash was an elitist. Yet one of the most common phrases describing him as he matured was that he had the common touch. He would not much modify his demeanour for a king or a commander, a navvy or an NCO. Nor did he talk down to people. Monash's support for the lowliest battler in his battery, even if charged with a crime, was a feature that endeared him to the ranks. Here was a leader who looked after his men. Because Monash was now officer rank, he was not going to get drunk with them as he often did in the past. Yet to a man, the militia he led respected him. They would go far for him.

✕

Monash had laboured gloomily under the impression that life ended rather than began at forty. It affected his look and manner as he struggled through his late thirties. But to his delight and relieved astonishment, in 1906 his business began to capitalise on an economic revival. He had endured fifteen years since the Crash of 1891, which occurred as he was beginning his working career. Its horrors and dog-eat-dog business competition had toughened and shaped him. Having survived, Monash was more ready and fit than he supposed he would be to ride a boom.

He gave up nearly all private engineering and law court work to concentrate on RCMPCC's expansion. The contracts rolled in at an exhilarating rate, and required Monier properties. Suddenly there were more bridges than he could handle, especially in the country. There was a bewildering demand for tanks needing concrete, underground channels and siphon systems of all kinds that required piping. Sometimes there were tenders. But such was the reputation of Monash and RCMPCC that half the time he was simply offered an exclusive contract.

Monash took on graduate assistant engineers and clerks. An agent was hired to sort out the flood of business. In came the orders for university and government buildings, banks, bush post offices, warehouses, abattoirs and reservoirs. Everything that held water, housed something or needed piping, it seemed, was being supplied by RCMPCC. And not only in Victoria. His courageous, risky, far-sighted move to gain the Monier rights for South Australia paid off when, with patent protection, he opened up the market in that state. Wars with the building trade – the brick contractors and unions – were as tough as ever, and Monash won some (notably the Preston Reservoir) and lost some (the dome at the public library). Losing always hurt, and he felt being defeated over the library more for the prestige than anything else. In the past a major loss would mean his retiring to the courts for his daily rate, or doing patent jobs, which he disdained. Now there was so much work he didn't need to do that any more.

Before 1906 was over, he had paid off all his debts and was sending fat dividends to Mitchell, who had stuck with him. Monash sent a £250 'cheque of gratitude' to John Gibson, the dashing Scot who managed the

Mitchell cement operation. In 1907 his income was £2000, ten times what he had cleared less than a decade earlier. It was increasing exponentially with RCMPCC's revenue as he picked up five per cent of every contract's value.

No one could tell Monash that prosperity and an ever-increasing workload was bad for his health. At forty-two, he felt more alive than ever. His energy levels were rising to match his swelling bank account. He was happy to wave goodbye to his youthful exuberance and embrace maturity. 'I can enjoy the fruits of a first rank position fairly won,' he noted, 'doubtless by much hard work, but then work which I have keenly enjoyed.'[4]

The 'fruits' were modest. Monash could at last keep Vic, whose health was sometimes poor, in the manner to which they both hoped she would become accustomed. She could buy more clothes, and they could take annual holidays. Bertha, now a teenager, attended the Presbyterian Ladies College. They still boarded in East Melbourne, although Monash could now buy a property if he wished. The guesthouse-style living, with its meal and domestic services, suited Vic for the moment. At times she wasn't well enough to prepare meals and do housework. When she was, she still preferred someone else to do it. The only drawback for them was the boarding house's unsuitability for proper home entertaining.

The marriage, now fifteen years mature, had steadied. Monash always strove to please Vic, although the opposite was not always true. They had developed at different paces, yet each had grown tolerant of the other's foibles. After he showed her the Princes Bridge when they first courted, and she had been unimpressed, Monash had tried and failed to engender her interest in his work in engineering, the law or the military. He had long ago given up any hope that she might be a sympathetic or supportive, let alone an inspiring partner. His discussions with male friends made him realise that such qualities did not always go with the marriage package. But every now and then he saw them in other couples, and it rankled with him. Monash was also irritated by Vic's occasional suspicions that he was playing up outside the marriage on his long trips. Their emotions over such matters had reversed. Vic's sensitivities had been simmering ever since she sneaked a read of his diaries and learned about his torrid affair with Annie Gabriel. She was miffed that they still corresponded. Vic's actions and reactions had been a factor in Monash writing less personal reflections in his notes. The diaries, as such, were now almost nonexistent. In their place were notebooks with no free expression in them.

Monash would always remain loyal to at least a friendship with Annie. He would always be a charmer. He wanted women to admire him. The intensity and alertness of his expression was attractive to many. He was not the life of the party any more, and had long ago put away his conjuring tricks. Yet he could still play Chopin with élan and dazzle with his knowledge and views on every buzzing issue.

The main thing that drew Monash and his wife together as a couple was a love of the theatre and concerts. It was a constant they enjoyed even in the tough times when any such event was a luxury. Monash, not Vic, could do without the balls and galas. They bored him. But a fine piece of opera, a good orchestra, or a topical play would allow him to escape and dream.

Parallel with his good fortune was a much-needed change in his military career. By early 1907 he had given nearly a quarter-century of service, with a few frustrating breaks, first to his university regiment, then the North Melbourne Battery, and had gone just about as far as he could go. He knew all there was to know about garrison artillery. He had developed a flair for leadership. Monash had put in as much time as the average officer from the permanent force.

Salvation came in the form of an old school acquaintance and rival, Colonel James Whiteside McCay, who had beaten him to the dux of Scotch College award in 1880. He was a lawyer who had served as Defence Minister and was in command of the 8th Infantry Regiment. McCay had a reputation for not suffering fools and slack soldiers of any rank. This didn't always endear him to his superiors, particularly the Military Board, which had been instituted by the first Federal Government to run the armed forces. He had an uncompromising moral sense, engendered by his preacher father. McCay's manner could be abrasive. But not with Monash. He was the one person in the military or the militia whom he regarded as at least his equal.

McCay, on behalf of the chief of intelligence, Colonel W. T. Bridges, approached him about a position in the newly formed Intelligence Corps. It had been set up by Bridges, a member of the Military Board. The new corps was to have a staff of sixty militia officers organised state by state. Bridges had been stung into action after press reports had been scathing about Australia's lack of experienced spies. There was no data-collection system to speak of. Despite press bleating about the potential dangers to Australia from various hordes and barbarians of different hues in Europe and Asia, no one had done any serious analysis of who might be a serious threat or why. Not even such fundamental matters as professional mapping of the states had been carried out. If the fledgling nation was ever attacked, there was a chance that it wouldn't know who the enemy was or what sort of terrain he had entered. Australia would be uncertain about its own transport routes and water supplies.

Would Monash like to take on the new challenge of commanding the Victorian section of the Australian Intelligence Corp (AIC), with its mixture of intrigue, investigation and prosaic duties?

Monash reminded McCay that he had been a major for twelve years. Would promotion come with the new post? McCay offered him the rank of lieutenant colonel.

Early in 1908, Monash agreed to take up the challenge.

This was Monash's first chance to build a staff from scratch. His firm had grown into a company, but he was limited in the Monier business as to how many people he could take on. Most had to be engineers, who worked on a contract by contract basis as assistants. Monash prided himself on being a good manager of people, and those who worked with him on projects were loyal and inspired by his precision and brilliance. All found that Monash would reverse roles to help out, guide and even educate. He would become the assistant and was generous with his time for those who wanted the knowledge. Monash knew all there was to know about smashed cofferdams, snapped bridges, burst pipes and how to avoid them and myriad other engineering or building problems. His drive and zest were balanced by a fair and caring attitude. His common touch was neither indulgent nor contrived.

Monash applied it to his choice of staff of fifteen specialists in the Intelligence Corps. He made no secret of the fact that he wanted educated men. But he wanted staff in his own image. They had to be courteous, disciplined and prepared to get their hands dirty, literally.

The brief for state units was at first vague and open-ended, although tight budgets limited their scope. The broad duties included collection of data about the military resources of Australia, countries in the region, especially the Pacific, and any potential enemy. There was to be a smaller, more secret continuous operation to monitor 'foreigners' and potential subversives. It was an area Monash would keep a tight lid on. He was sensitive about his German background and did not want unnecessary surveillance to infringe on the liberty of citizens.

Looming far larger than anything else in the collective mind of the Military Board was the embarrassing fact that no one in the army could lay their hands on a good standard topographic map of Australia itself, or any major neighbour from Tahiti to the Solomon Islands. This lack had to be addressed without delay. The home front had to be a priority. Monash's men would have to 'go bush' in their spare time to map strategic areas of Victoria. Another early assignment for the corps would be to test the efficiency of Australia's warning system against an invasion or raid. It was a task sure to create despair and frustration, given the nation's size.

Monash created a grid of disciplines he wanted among his part-time officers that would offer a variety of experiences and allow the unit to run efficiently. He assessed candidates and began hiring the best for his aims and the brief. All were aged thirty-nine to forty-one, close to Monash's forty-three years. He had a command and was running officers, but there was a collegiate atmosphere in the unit. It was nothing like his control of the battery, where strict regimentation of young officers was necessary.

It was no surprise that four of the first half-dozen he chose were university-graduated engineers, whose expertise covered all areas of the science from water to construction. Monash also took on an accountant, skilled at handling cashbooks, ledgers and expense accounts. A journalist was also essential. He had to be adept at editing reports and organising everyone to produce corps publications, a monthly intelligence diary and military handbooks. The unit couldn't function without a librarian for the all-important filing and indexing. A business manager would run the office. There was also a survey draftsman, who prepared maps, a stationmaster who ran transport, and an architect.

Monash's second-in-command, Major J. M. Semmens, was a secretary for the Department of Ports and Harbours, a more than useful character for monitoring shipping and its loads. Seven of his choices had solid military backgrounds ranging from four to twenty-six years in the militia. The staff had strong qualifications in everything from infantry, artillery and engineering to transport, weaponry and topography.[5]

Monash had delineated Germany and, in the aftermath of the 1904–05 Russo-Japanese War, an increasingly militant Japan as the most likely threats to Australia. He was not much concerned with biblical axioms, but one was important to him: 'Know thine Enemy.'

He made sure there was a good budget for the less thrilling but necessary business of scouring local and foreign technical periodicals. The Germans were prolific at producing magazines, books and papers on military strategies, tactics and their history. He wrote in German (under a pseudonym as a private citizen pursuing a 'hobby', not as an intelligence operative) to specialist publishers and book retailers in Germany asking for any publication on these aspects, military science in general, and weapons development in particular. He also sought information in the public domain on the topography of Germany, along with detail on transport and supply.

Monash was on the look out for clues to German designs on Papua New Guinea, where it already had a presence, or other territories. Any profile on military figures, no matter how thin, in obscure magazines or popular German daily papers, was cut and filed. Monash devoured the lot. He was pleased to exercise his rusty linguistic skills wading through the driest of volumes such as the journals *Kavalleristiche Monätschfte*, *Militär Wochenblatt* and *Deutsche Kolonial Zeitung*.[6]

There were early teething problems. The mapping became an impossible time-consumer, with almost all staff out wandering parts of Victoria. Some even went by bicycle, which showed an impressive dedication to the task. But results would be painfully slow. Monash could see his unit being swamped by topographic assignments and not achieving his aims. He complained to McCay, who agreed it was impractical. He set up a group of cartographers from the permanent force. It was to take directives from Monash, who was most concerned that fine, accurate maps be produced.

No one was better at mapping. The skill was vital to the way Monash saw himself functioning as a battle commander. His decades of experience in the bush as an engineer, bushwalker and military man had developed a knack for visualising any area by examining it on an accurate map. For military purposes, Monash was interested in one thing above all others. When he rolled a map open, did it depict the true shape or form of the area and the different levels? If it were a flat piece of ground between hills, for instance, Monash wanted to know the height and gradient of the hills. Once he had the picture in his mind, he could make decisions on transport, troops and firepower to attack, or what was the best means of organising a defence or retreat.

In the war games that he devised for his battery, or when his Intelligence Corps was attached to them, it was one of the most important simulations that would be almost the same in an actual battle. If he had a good map, he could make quick decisions on manoeuvres. Without one, he was lost.

Long after Monash had honed this capacity by experience and instinct, he learned that some of the greatest military commanders in history, from Julius Caesar to Napoleon, had it. This knowledge caused him to improve it even further. Where other officers might be content to use maps for simply pinpointing a location, Monash was obsessed with the cartographer's artistic endeavours. Maps were an essential part of Monash's kit, more vital to him than his revolver. He felt naked without them.

Monash threw himself into all the unit's work, which was often fused with the duties of 'operational staff activities'. He had pushed for his officers to be attached to field forces to help with organisation and to observe simulated battles. The permanent officer Major Julius Bruche, another Old Scotch Collegian, had helped him. He was also a lawyer with a German background (although non-Jewish), who was fast becoming a close friend of Monash. He saw the importance of developing a strong intelligence force, which he felt must be kept in touch with the soldiers in the field and the logistics of the build-up to combat. Bruche encouraged Monash's enthusiasm for every aspect of administration or the organising of war, which, to even the most diligent clerk, could at times lead to utter boredom. Like Bruche, Monash saw the big picture. When he referred to 'operations' he was more likely alluding to the whole gambit of the build-up to conflict than the conflict itself, which was just one feature.

Monash, in a speech at the time, said: 'Marches, movements by rail and water, laying down lines of communication or supply, selecting and occupying a bivouac, billeting in a town – are all operations of war.'[7] He was at pains to explain that training of officers was as much about management, administration and organisation than about teaching them ways to kill the enemy – if not more so. Monash was emphatic that all the features of fighting at which he excelled – tactics, rifle shooting, gunnery and leadership – were useless if the machinery behind them seized up because of poor organisation.

Monash's philosophy was an extension of the adage that an army marches on its stomach. If water supply and food didn't turn up for troops resting between fierce engagements, it wouldn't be long before they were rendered useless. A company of Victoria Cross winners would be ineffective if they ran out of ammunition. Water, food and ammunition, and all the other accoutrements of battle, had to be transported, preserved and supplied.

The logistics of war were huge. Monash always likened them to an engineering project such as a bridge. He knew only too well what happened if the calculations in design were out, even just a degree or two. Added to that were all the other elements in construction, such as supply of the right strength cement and correct specifications of the spans and the abutments. They were all as important in assemblage as the actual erection of the structure. If precision preparation were not done, then the bridge would collapse. Similarly, if a force on the battlefield was not well equipped and informed, it would lose.

With that grand vision in mind, Monash took a keen interest in every problem of 'operations', from the dull business of troop transport right down to how staff officers communicated with each other.

He was a gladiator in the war against ambiguity. Once when asked to comment on a draft exam paper for promotion to lieutenant colonel, he objected to the description 'the heights of East Frimley'. Monash pointed out that the map, which he noted was poor, showed no distinct heights there. He suggested that the paper could refer to either 'about a half mile from Frimley' or even just 'at Frimley'.[8] This was not simply a matter of pedantry or fussy attention to detail. If a battalion was ordered to head for the hills east of Frimley and they were ten kilometres east of the town across flat terrain, then the soldiers could well be vulnerable to an attack. Such an error in a directive could sway a small engagement. Twenty such mistakes could lose a battle.

Monash was gaining enormous experience beyond the limitations of the garrison artillery, and within six months he realised he had made a timely career move. He wasn't alone. He recommended five of his officers for promotion. Monash was most impressed by those who could analyse critically and articulately (on paper and verbally) the manoeuvres to which they were assigned.

He led the way. Monash was often employed as an umpire, who would create the exercises to be played out at camps. He became proficient on tactics up to infantry brigade level, and often stood in judgement on fellow militia officers. He revelled in testing theory he knew against actual events in the field. Anyone out for a lazy week wandering around the countryside was in for a rude shock with umpire Monash. His first big project in 1908 was at Langwarrin in country Victoria. He wrote the 'narrative' of the encounter between competing brigades, then reported on all aspects of manoeuvres covering transport, supply, signalling, medical back-up, and troop protection and security.

Monash was concerned right from the start of his experiences in the field with how troops on an exercise were protected. He looked to the flanks of one brigade in the advance phase of the exercise and found them lamentably vulnerable. He observed ahead of the troops and found them deployed in full view of the enemy. One way or the other, he noted, this brigade would be wiped out. Protection of the advancing soldiers was high on his list of imperatives. Any commander who ignored this point would incur his written wrath in reports and would be marked down.

Another of his bugbears was lack of communication throughout the force. Monash was brutal in his assessment of command staff who sent out orders that, because of lack of force or clarity, did not reach the appropriate recipients. Senior officers who did not have maps would not receive high marks. If they didn't know the meaning of a brigade's tactical and strategic operations, they and their commanders were given low grades.

A third Monash pet hate was poor cleanliness and sanitation. The captain who did not cover latrines in the winter or prepare food hygienically would be in trouble. The soldiers themselves were never blamed for such lapses. Monash spared no one, from commanders to NCOs, his stinging judgements. Nothing, it seemed, from the biggest blunder to the smallest administrative detail escaped his eagle eye.

He was happy when the next big exercise – at the Easter Camp of 1909 – came around. This was again at Langwarrin. Monash had full control for the first time over the narrative of the combat exercise to be played out by two competing brigades. He retired to his tent on the first afternoon of the camp and came out four hours later with his war game. Langwarrin itself was the centre of the simulated battle to be defended by one and attacked by the other. After an exhausting four days of mock combat, Monash's plans were so well thought through that neither side could be declared the winner. The competing colonels both claimed it was the most exacting yet challenging assignment they had ever had.

Monash's knowledge of battle strategies, tactics and manoeuvres was deepening. In October 1909 he attended a fortnight-long War Course given by Colonel H. J. Foster, the director of Sydney University's military science department. Foster used the Franco-Prussian War of 1870–71, won by Prussian forces, as his model. Monash knew every aspect of the conflict and was an expert on every skirmish of it. But that was as a reader on the outside. Foster, a brilliant lecturer, took him and the other student-officers inside by simulating what Prussian brigade staff faced in their bunker. How did they repel landings? How did they handle advances and retreats? What was the best method of transport for ferrying troops to the front line? What problems were encountered in billeting tens of thousands of men on the march? How did they keep up the troops' morale? How did the staff organise the trains to carry troops vast distances?

Monash and other 'students' were asked to take the place of Prussian staff officers, do their assessments of a problem and give orders. Monash revelled in the opportunity. He was faced with the question of how to attack troops of superior numbers embarking on a train at the French city of La Perouse. Monash planned to take the ground in front of the embarkation area and then hit it with artillery, rather than try to take the enemy head-on. His solution, which had to be made fast once he was apprised of the situation aided by maps, highlighted Monash's approaches to battle. He would not, if possible, waste his troops fighting against difficult odds, no matter what the prowess of his men. At every chance he would use his firepower – the artillery – to soften the enemy and swing the odds the other way before pushing his troops forward.[9]

Here Monash realised that he had to become the cold commander in making decisions. In modern war, he would rarely be at the front line directing officers and even leading the fight himself. That style of warfare was becoming old-fashioned. With the increased hardware of war and the size of battles, it was far more important for the new commander to stay in his bunker and act as the cool brain. Dead heroic leaders could give no orders to switch an attack or retreat.

Monash now appreciated that in this war game, during field simulation exercises or actual combat, the conditions for the best running of a show were the same. 'Troops are just as non-existent as they are at exercise,' Monash wrote in his 'solutions and notes' on the War Course. This remark might have sounded callous. But war was a callous business. Monash reckoned that if he was to be an effective leader, he had to be as dispassionate as possible in his decision-making. Today, the war room, not the front line or the heat of battle, was going to be the place where he did most of his assessment and decision-making.

For the first time, too, Monash at this War Course began to think more in another dimension like his heroes Napoleon, Julius Caesar and – his favourite of all – Stonewall Jackson. Monash was adept at visualising terrain by studying his trusty maps. But now here in the bunker, he developed further the extended skill of 'seeing' the position of his troops and those of the enemy, and how a particular order would affect either side.

Foster noted Monash's enthusiasm. He encouraged him to work on this capability, reminding him that it was a 'supremely important' feature, which would sort out the good commander from the not so good. Monash's painstaking love of all things topographical now had a new, vital layer.

A few months after that exhilarating experience in Sydney, Bruche made sure Monash joined him and two other permanent officers in planning the exercises for the most important camp yet held in Australia. It would be at Seymour, north of Melbourne, between 10 and 16 January 1910. It was to be attended by the most celebrated officer in the British Army, Lord Kitchener.

Horatio Kitchener was not in the best of moods when he arrived in Australia late in 1909 for a whirlwind visit. He had been based in India as commander-in-chief since 1902 and had recently been informed that he wouldn't be made viceroy. It was a bitter blow. Kitchener, then a few months short of sixty, would have been happy to see out his years running the Indians. He loved the heat and didn't mind the flies. Most of all he wanted to distance himself from the intrigues of Whitehall and the vicinity of his political masters, for whom he had, on the whole, contempt. Kitchener, who made his reputation in the Sudan beating off rebels, and nearly lost it in the way he ran the war against South Africa using concentration camps (from 1900 to 1902), could have avoided all that as a benevolent despot, languishing in style in the last and biggest jewel of the British Empire. But he had missed out on the top job. This short visit to Australia was a consolation prize before he returned to England and an uncertain future.

Kitchener had to report on the state and efficiency of the local force. He would also lobby the government about the concept of conscription.

Rumblings in Europe indicated that war with Germany was inevitable. The British command was checking just what standard and size of forces it could muster from the reaches of its far-flung empire.

The more public Kitchener was also in Australia to drum up support for the compulsory military training of youths, which would be a nice lead-up to a conscripted army. Alfred Deakin's government had passed the youth training policy into law, but the mechanics had not been worked out. Kitchener arrived with a plan. Teenage boys would be trained in school cadet corps. After their schooling was complete, they would attend an annual camp for another seven years. This scheme would be used to phase out the old militia. It would make way for a better organised citizen army.

The British were shrewd and diligent about protecting all the territory they had annexed over the centuries. Australia might have become a nation running itself, but the mother country was still capable of directing it to protect British interests.

Kitchener was a strong advertisement for them. He had a manufactured charisma augmented by myth and was portrayed in press photos as good-looking. Journalists gave him excellent coverage. He appeared to make an impression at every function he attended. Men were in awe of his war record. Women allegedly loved his charm and style, or was it the myth working overtime? They fantasised over his being single and, technically, 'available'. Vic, who never met him, had a typical reaction. 'He looks (in press photos) just lovely,' she wrote to Monash at Seymour. 'How some woman has not stolen, drugged and married him, I don't know.'[10] Vic wasn't to know that Kitchener was not interested in women. His sexual instincts, a biographer noted, 'were wholly sublimated like those of a Catholic priest'.[11]

Author J. B. Priestley, who met him a few years later, was not so impressed. 'I had a close view,' he wrote, 'finding him older and greyer than the familiar pictures of him. The image I retained was of a rather bloated purplish face and glaring but somehow jellied eyes.'[12]

In the days before television, image could be massaged into myth and manipulated more easily for public consumption. Kitchener's face would soon become famous in a UK poster featuring an artist's impression of him, when the government began its push to recruit volunteers for the armed forces. The poster, headed 'Britons', had him, his big moustache bristling, as secretary for war, pointing and saying, 'Join your country's army!'

Prime Minister Herbert Asquith, who appointed him, said: 'He is not a great man; he is a great poster.' Sir Arthur Conan Doyle concurred. 'Kitchener grew very arrogant,' he wrote. 'He had flashes of genius but was usually stupid . . . But he was a great force in recruiting.'[13]

His presence at Seymour in early 1910 gave an extra edge to a momentous week for Monash. He would himself be reporting on the biggest operation he had witnessed. It would go to the Victorian commandant, who would incorporate it into his own report to Kitchener.

Part of the exercises was a war game where a division (in this case 12,000 men) attacked a target. The logistical support was far bigger than anything with which Monash had been involved before. He immersed himself in finding the usual faults in communication right through the lines. Junior ranks had little or no idea of what was happening. Officers seemed 'compartmentalised' – yet another constant irritation for Monash. His previous reports had implored that officers in different sections communicate with, rather than remain remote from, each other. But from the outcome at Seymour it seemed that few officers were talking, listening or reading.

Monash had strong words for the divisional commander who ignored his brigadiers and tried to control the brigades directly. It led to confusion. Officers did not even know the direction in which they were supposed to go.

Monash had worked for three weeks solid on his maps depicting the terrain around Seymour and Avenel, where the divisional action took place. He was determined to show them to Kitchener. There was not an opportunity for a prolonged one-on-one meeting between the two men. Monash's relatively junior status at the time saw him well down the list of those fêting the famous Irish-born Briton.

But if they ever had a deep discussion, Monash might have been disappointed. The scope of Kitchener's mind was not impressive. His education – at the Royal Military Academy, Woolwich –had been narrow and limited. Kitchener's energy and thoroughness were impressive, but his attitude to warfare remained rooted in the methods of the previous century. Conan Doyle noted that Kitchener 'could not see any use in munitions. He was against tanks.'[14] Lord Northcliffe, publisher of the UK *Daily Mail*, wrote that Kitchener had not moved on from the explosives technology and methods of fighting used in the war against South Africa. Science was rapidly changing approaches. But Kitchener would not embrace it. This attitude would not have made him appreciative of

Monash's enthusiasm for change and his study of science applied to the military.[15]

Yet given that they did not have any revealing talks, Monash would have remained impressed for a key reason: Kitchener's leadership record in actual battle. He had been there and was perceived as a 'winner', albeit in small colonial wars. Until Monash had the chance to prove himself, he would remain deferential to such a figure, especially as Kitchener would soon be the most powerful Briton prosecuting war.

After the Seymour experience, Monash spent much of the next two months preparing for his first overseas trip, which was scheduled from March until November 1910. RCMPCC's prosperity meant that at forty-four he could undertake a trip he had long dreamed about. He was the company's engineer taking five per cent for every contract. John Gibson managed the show, and this gave Monash the chance to escape with Vic and Bertha (now sixteen and finished school) for eight months. The trip would be mostly for pleasure, but Monash being Monash would treat much of it as an education. There was also the little matter of his being an officer in an intelligence corps. The most likely enemy was accepted now as being Germany. Any conflict would cover territory from Germany's eastern borders into Russia and its western borders across France and Belgium to the narrow English Channel. The portly (now 100-kilogram) German-speaking Australian travelling with his family would be no ordinary tourist. He would be gathering as much information as was prudent concerning war preparedness in Europe. It would help shape his decisions on his next career moves.

Monash planned the trip with his usual near-manic obsession for detail, itemising everything, right down to the toothpicks in their luggage. He prepared to note all expenditure, including any extra toothpicks acquired en route. (He listed one acquired at Maxim's in Paris.) It is difficult to imagine enjoying such a tour if every purchase was categorised and written down. Yet Monash did it not out of meanness but to satisfy his highly organised mind. Even when sitting in a café on Paris's Boulevard Montparnasse, Monash scribbled down the cost of the coffee, croissant, newspapers – French, German and English – bought at a kiosk, and the tip given to the waiter.

He had a remarkable capacity for compartmentalising his interests.

Doing a flow chart of expenses took him about fifteen minutes a day and fascinated him as much as examining a bridge, visiting an art gallery, going to the theatre or meeting new people. Whereas such fiscal diligence would irk anyone but an accountant, for him it was just a small part of the intellectual stimulation of the trip.

They planned eight weeks in England, twelve in Europe and two in the USA, and travelled first class on the Australian liner, the *Otranto*. First stop was four days in Rome, followed by similar periods in Florence, Venice and Paris. Monash squeezed in every cultural attraction possible, keeping up a furious pace that sometimes left Vic and Bertha at the hotel or sitting in a café watching the passing parade. Monash took time for that too, but never stopped photographing or taking notes. No new underground train system, building or construction of style missed his attention.

He did the same thing in London, but found it a letdown after the continent. At first glance it was not as beautiful as the European cities, and it seemed dirtier. The food was abominable, and the people were not as friendly. It didn't help that the country was in mourning after the death of affable, popular Edward VII on 6 May 1910. The Victorian agent-general gave them tickets to watch the funeral from a makeshift stand in Horse Guards Parade, along with a couple of thousand other dignitaries, and countless more Londoners lining the streets.

The former debauched, playboy prince, 'Edward the Caresser', who modified his behaviour as monarch, had provided a near-decade fresh breeze after the austerity of his mother Queen Victoria's reign. He was succeeded by his second son, George V, who was then very much an unknown quantity in terms of how he would handle the reduced power of the monarch and the prospect of war. Now two of Victoria's grandchildren, George and the German emperor, Wilhelm II, were on their respective thrones as relations between the British and German empires deteriorated. Without even a vague inkling of how much the new king would influence his life, Monash had only a passing interest in what the press was saying and any informed gossip about him.

Monash was pleased to see his sister Louise and brother-in-law Walter Rosenhain, whom he had grown to respect through their correspondence. Monash had even asked him to do some secret 'research' on the development of the airplane industry and how it would affect the military. The Rosenhains were part of a little Jewish circle of Australian expatriates that included an old friend from Melbourne, the vivacious Lizette Bentwitch.

After her tobacconist father had died, she inherited enough money to leave Australia and set up in London in 1900. She moved in a social circle and led the life of a happy dilettante. Lizette had circulated in the same set as the upwardly mobile Monashes in Melbourne in the 1890s. She had liked Monash then, but there had been no spark between them. Now, two decades on, he was a man of means and a distinguished, strong-looking military officer. The padding around his midriff was viewed as no more than a sign of prosperity, which in his case it was. There was more than a glimmer of attraction towards him. Her mild flirtation now ignited him, and he was charming towards her, but nothing more. Monash was aware of Vic's sensitivities and would not have done anything to inflame any feelings or jealousies, especially with Bertha in attendance.

Vic was unaware of Lizette's increased interest. She had always been single, loquacious and flighty, and never as attractive as Vic. Lizette Bentwitch would never have been seen as a threat under normal circumstances.

The family was happy to leave London for the continent again. Three days more in Paris then Brussels were followed a long sweep around Germany and Austria with planned stops at Cologne, Berlin, Dresden, Breslau, Vienna and Munich. Monash noted the industry: the movement of all forms of transport vehicles from cars and lorries to those drawn by horses everywhere in Germany. The activity seemed far greater than in England, France and Belgium, and made Australia seem somnolent by comparison.

After a few days in Berlin, they made the 120-kilometre train trip north to Stettin (Szczecin), about thirty kilometres south of the Baltic Sea coast. None of the immediate Manesse family was alive, but Monash was able to find the graves of his maternal grandparents, Jacob and Charlotte Manesse at the village of Dramburg. He thought about his mother and the romantic dramas that went on forty-seven years earlier; how his brave father had initiated the move to a far away country, different in language, culture, beliefs, history, hope and future; how fortunate he himself had been to be the recipient of such endeavour and sacrifice. He knew the story well. Yet the visit gave him another perspective of mixed emotions. He was both saddened and inspired.

The family returned to Berlin for the night, then caught a train 250 kilometres southwest to Breslau (now Wroclaw, Poland). Monash left Vic and Bertha at a hotel there and took another train 140 kilometres north to Krotoschin for a fleeting visit to see the home of his grandfather

Baer-Loebel and grandmother Mathilde. Monash met his surviving great-uncles and aunt in the impoverished town, which was still a backwater. They took him to his paternal grandparents' graves, in the cemetery where Baer-Loebel had walked with Louis on his return from Australia in 1863. Monash took pictures. Then he picked up leaves from his grandparents' graves and pocketed them. They were itemised and added to the growing list of souvenirs.

Monash was then taken to the printing shop where his grandfather's firm still operated. The current owners were proud to show him the hand-press and type fonts that had been used since 1835 to produce countless prayer books and scientific journals. The firm was in its seventy-fifth and final year. Monash was given a couple more souvenirs.

On the trip back to Breslau he reflected on the note he had received on his eighth birthday from Baer-Loebel congratulating him on winning a school prize. 'If you go on like that,' his grandfather had written, 'you will become a great, good and famous man.' Monash felt he hadn't lived up to the great and the famous. At his age, there wasn't much chance of either now. But he was sure his grandfather would be proud of his more than modest achievements and recent prosperity.

The family travelled on to Vienna, then the Alps for four weeks, six in England and Scotland, and a final two in the USA and Canada. The USA impressed Monash even more than the other countries he had visited. He loved New York, particularly its advanced architecture and skyscrapers, and the modern designs such as Pennsylvania Station. To build skywards in the Manhattan's limited space seemed logical to him. Reinforced concrete was dominant, and this thrilled him. Monash had the engineer's eye for the impact of electricity on everything from hotel lifts and domestic heating to radio and railways. He dared not think of what he would have done with his life had Louis taken off for the USA instead of Australia.

After returning by boat via Honolulu, Suva and Brisbane, it took him a few days to adjust to Australia, which he now saw as 'a little, provincial place'.

Monash wrote to Walter Rosenhain in London urging him to visit the USA. 'You can discard the accepted impression about America and her people as confidently as you can discard the average Englishman's impression of the Germans,' Monash wrote. What struck him was the 'new and vigorous, and arresting attitude of mind towards life in all its activities'.[16]

Back in his sleepy province, Monash set out to accumulate £10,000 by 1914 by working harder than ever. That money would allow him to retire and be comfortable while looking after his extended family. He was so uplifted by the travel that he planned another trip in 1914.

Monash took a deep breath and set out on his quest knowing that the RCMPCC patents had run out. His agreements with Gummow were over. Other engineers would include the Monier process in their choice of building methods. The brick industry had never gone away and would be bigger than ever. The competition would be tougher.

Early pessimism after his long break was based on those grinding years of depression from 1891 to 1905. The up-turn, now five years old, although not the boom of the 1880s, was steady and strong. Monash and his company could not coast. Yet they were well placed to flow with the prosperity. Surprise contracts that came in during 1911 were seen as 'good luck', whereas in fact he had created the conditions for a continued change in fortunes.

Monash kept bound copies of all his business correspondence, and the letters are testimony to a bewildering amount of activity in this period.[17] The focus was in and around Melbourne as he left the continued Monier–Monash imprint on banks, bridges, arcades, cool-rooms and railways. The work included the occasional prestige project, such as extensions to the Town Hall and the building of Collins House at the top end of town, where the moneyed elite had their offices and practices. When it was built Monash would be joining them in his own plush suite of offices. His style, intellect, cultural interests, achievements, 'clubbing' and sudden affluence gave him more upward mobility than a six by Victor Trumper.

The elitist Melbourne Club at the salubrious end of Collins Street was not yet ready to accept a Jew, no matter how brilliant and accomplished. But many of his friends lounged in its plush leather chairs, hobnobbed at its bar and dined there on roast beef with Yorkshire pudding and spotted dick for dessert.

Other trappings of his success were there or on the way. Monash bought himself his first car for his forty-sixth birthday. The eight-seater twenty-horsepower Berliet cost £575. It had fashionable painted vertical black and dark-green stripes, along with an ostentatious monogram 'JM' on the tonneau door. Monash gave up trying to drive, but it motivated

Bertha to go for her licence. Vic was almost embarrassed to turn up at the races in it, but soon overcame that feeling. Monash hired a chauffeur – a near-mandatory accessory for Melbourne's rich – and began looking for a home to buy. He paid £4750 for a property (to be called 'Iona') in St George's Road, Toorak, Melbourne's plushest suburb.

After twenty years of marriage, Vic was living the life which Monash had provided. The cost of new outfits each year for the Melbourne Cup, Nellie Melba's Grand Opera season and dress-circle seats for a J. C. Williamson Company play were now not of concern. They were both dining too, well. Monash was fit enough, but his constant rushing about for the army and the company was not enough to offset a spreading waist-line. He tried cutting down on bread and sugar and eating more fish, but wasn't prepared to give up his beloved soothing glass or two of Dewar's whisky each night after his usual demanding day. He joked that it was for 'medicinal purposes'. But it didn't help his battle of the bulge.

Vic's problem was the opposite. Her intermittent illnesses, asthma and 'nervous condition' – a euphemism for neurosis or depression or both – left her underweight. Monash was always pleased when she put on weight, even up to seventy kilograms. Vic needed plenty of holidays to recuperate. She insisted on solo stays in Adelaide or Sydney to compensate for Monash's many weeks away on 'army business'. She wrote to him during one break: 'I have come to this conclusion that there is no man alive, or at least that I have met, that can compare with you in any way . . . You want to go away from your hubby to realise how much you think of him.'[18] Monash had longed to hear this direct from her lips. He might have wondered why she had to go away to appreciate him. But he would be settle for this written endorsement, which had taken two decades to be given to him.

Having received this declaration of adoration, which arrived with the trappings of wealth, Monash was working as hard as ever to maintain his status, but with assistants and secretarial help. He managed his time to the half-minute and began to put his energies into even more activities beyond his long working day. They were never far from his core pursuits. He lobbied the government for university funds, moved on to its building and finance committees, joined its council, linked up with the Victorian Institute of Engineers, and was active in managing the Boy Scouts. He liked the idea of lads being able to camp out and tie knots. It was good preparedness for later army training.

✕

Military exercises were taking up more of his time, partly on his own volition and partly because he was carried along by the push for war readiness. He threw himself into the January 1911 camp at Seymour, wrote the narrative for exercises at the Kilmore Easter Camp, and in October enjoyed every moment of his second fortnight of War Courses conducted by Colonel Foster in Sydney.

Monash was now stepping up his study of military history and had developed a fine, catalogued library. Two years earlier he and McKay had set down the reading of Stonewall Jackson and the American Civil War by G. F. R. Henderson for intelligence officers to study and be examined on. Now it was the Russo-Japanese War of 1904–05. Monash and McCay prescribed a wide reading list of thirty books and articles from Ellis Ashmead-Bartlett's *Port Arthur: The Siege and the Capitulation* to Count Gustav Wrangel's *Cavalry in the Russo-Japanese War*.

There was no substitute for actual battle, but Monash recognised early that it was essential to be well versed in the strategies and tactics of previous conflicts. His photographic memory allowed him to take mental snapshots of the terrain covered in exercises and then write the narrative for the mock combats. He imagined how Napoleon or Jackson would handle such a conflict, on the basis of their recorded manoeuvres in similar situations. By 1912 Monash had memorised all the major battles since the late 1790s and the classic wars of ancient military history. He was often seen with pencil and paper explaining how confederate General Robert E. Lee had used Jackson to outflank federal General Joseph Hooker in the woods of Chancellorsville in the American Civil War, or how Napoleon gained the ascendency at Austerlitz against Russia and Austria in 1805. If not, it would be how Prussia's Helmuth von Moltke had been the architect of victories over Denmark in 1864, Austria in 1866 and France in 1871.

He demonstrated his knowledge further in early 1912 by winning the inaugural Gold Medal Essay competition on the subject, 'The Lessons of the Wilderness Campaign – 1864'. The idea was to explain how this turning point in the American Civil War – set in wild and tangled woodland – provided instruction for the defence of Australia. The bloody battle in northern Virginia was between the federal Union Army led by Ulysses S. Grant and the confederates led by Lee. Grant's forces had superior artillery and cavalry and twice the number of men. Lee hoped the heavy underbrush would aid his cause. The fighting was brutal, the casualties massive.

Monash knew the story inside out, but it was another matter finding lessons in it for Australia. He studied it with the determination and flair he had applied to the *Macbeth* essay at school thirty years earlier, citing eleven books in the bibliography from Henderson's *Science of War* to Colonel Foster's new publication, *Organisation*. He showed enterprise by including the recently published *Photographic History of the War* as a source. Not content with coming first, Monash studied the judges' appraisals and noted the criticisms.

He saw parallels between Australia and the USA. He thought the military training was similar and that the character of the troops was alike. Monash also reckoned that the rough landscape was at least analogous to that found in Australia in various forms from the jungles of the north to the rugged bushland in Tasmania. This meant the tactics in tackling it and an opposing army would be comparable. Monash's bias towards the militia came through when he noted that both countries produced citizen armies, which were 'well-skilled in bushcraft and horsemanship'. The citizen soldiers of both countries were 'bred in an atmosphere of personal liberty and independence, and were well qualified physically'. He noted that the most successful US commanders were West Point graduates with war experience, but who were often also professionals in areas other than the military.

Monash had an amateur's attitude to the military, but was just as professional as any regular soldier in the country. He thought that permanent soldiering 'limited a man's scope'. He likened it to working as a government engineer where there was a limited stimulus compared to working in private enterprise. Militiamen had to put in a hard day's work at their craft or profession, which made them sharper than the full-timer. It was the same for the lowliest soldier to the most exulted general.

A biographer of Field Marshal Douglas Haig described his day about the time Monash wrote his 'Wilderness' essay:

> The day passed evenly. The early hours of the morning he spent on horseback, supervising the training of the units under his command; when the inspection was over, he would indulge in a sharp gallop across country . . . At 11 o'clock he reached his office at Army Headquarters and worked there until lunch-time. From lunch to tea was play time – either golf or tennis . . . or sometimes he preferred the role of onlooker and watched the game of some

sections of his command. After tea two hours were devoted to [army business] reading and this brought the day to a close.[19]

This was his routine day in, day out for years. There was no comparison with Monash's days. They were never the same. He was faced continuously with different mental and sometimes physical challenges. When multiplied by years and decades the divergence between the two experiences was staggering. It shaped the mentality, imagination and will of each man.

The breadth of Monash's articulation in the essay was seen by his strong conclusion that commanders must be allowed a free reign by politicians to conduct a war the way they saw fit. This was based on General Grant's unfettered support from politicians. Monash highlighted that this had been a factor in his success in seeking out and destroying the enemy. Grant's policy of taking his time to wear down Confederate forces had been unpopular early.

The essay was published in the obscure *Commonwealth Military Journal* of April 1912. If it had been picked up by the mainstream press there would have been a controversy. Ill-informed public opinion, Monash implied, was a weakness of democracy. Politicians must not be influenced by it (in say, stopping the funding of a war) or interfere in how commanders conducted war. Monash's contention was that if ignorant politicians started giving orders in this specialised area, then they could endanger soldiers' lives and perhaps help lose a war. If weak-kneed politicians stepped in when a commander's strategy was halfway to completion and looked shaky to the ill-informed observer, then this could be disastrous for the conduct of the war.

This conclusion could have been construed differently. Monash's views were little short of advocating that military dictators should run countries during wartime. It was not something that his good friend Alfred Deakin or any other politician in the fledgling democracy of Australia would countenance. They would always want power over the military. If public opinion threatened their position of power then they had to be in a position to appease it.

His essay proved more instructive about how Monash would behave than about lessons for Australia's defence. By instinct, he was someone who would attack in preference to defending. By nature, he was a confident future commander who wished to follow his thorough plans through to victorious completion. He would be uncomfortable about anyone, including military superiors, not allowing him to finish off the job. It demonstrated not so much an ego as Monash's obsessively well-organised mind. He wanted all the loose ends to be tied up, every strategy to be played out. So much did he believe in his own control over every aspect of a battle, on the basis of exhaustive preparation and planning of tactics, that he wanted nothing to stop it, not even a large number of casualties.

This attitude also exposed a ruthless element deep in his character. The great battle commanders of history also had it.

Monash received a blow in 1912 when the Intelligence Corps looked like being dissolved and absorbed into the Victorian District Military Command. McCay, his superior, was at such odds with the Military Board that he could not stop it. He was too fond of taking on authority and was in a strange position. Having been a federal minister with pull and clout made it tough for him to be subordinate to the board, and often he was not. He went overseas on leave. Moves were then made towards terminating the corps.

Monash asked for a meeting with the District Military Command's Major Cyril White. The genial major, aged thirty-seven, had never quite known how to handle Monash. Although he tried, he couldn't quite pigeonhole him. The diligent White was the quintessential self-made Australian. The son of a bankrupt Queensland farmer, he left school at fifteen to work as a bank clerk before he joined the army as a young man. His steadiness as an administrator was rewarded with a term at the Staff College in England, then three years in the War Office, where he lectured and trained regular troops. White gained a reputation as a first-rate organiser. His horizons didn't stretch to leading in the field. This might have been where he and Monash could not quite reach a deep understanding or appreciation. Monash was born to organise, but he was ambitious to achieve as a battle commander, if the opportunity arose. It was another dimension in a person's nature: a need to prove himself under enormous stress and pressure, both physical and mental. White would always be the consummate staff officer. Dogged, reliable, intelligent. He was content with this important role, and less driven. Monash, by contrast, despite all his achievements in academia and business, was unfulfilled in the hobby that was becoming his profession.

That rendezvous between the two began uncertainly and turned frosty.

Monash was disappointed to learn that White was ignorant of the Intelligence Corps operations past, present and planned.

'It seems to me, Major,' Monash said in his customary direct manner, 'that, under the proposed organisation, you are not going to have any suitable place or duty for a senior lieutenant colonel like myself.'

'No,' White replied coolly, 'I do not suppose we will.'[20]

Monash felt as if he had been cut adrift. By the end of the year he was an officer without a home or force. He considered retiring from all duties. But the feeling was fleeting. He began assessing options. Perhaps the only well-placed person Monash couldn't rely on was the inflexible Colonel Bridges, whom even official war correspondent and later official historian Charles Bean tried and failed to humanise. ('He could not, by a kindly word or a tactful hint, help another out of difficulty,' Bean wrote.[21])

McCay, as ever, was supportive. White, although not a friend, recognised Monash's abilities, despite not knowing what he had been doing in intelligence. Colonel Foster was willing to testify to his capacities. Even Stanley from his early artillery days would recommend him. Bruche fought for him, asserting to the Military Board, perhaps prematurely, that Monash was 'a genius'. The board, which had none among its ranks, would not have been impressed. Geniuses were for ivory towers at universities, not on the battlefields leading men. Could he command? Artillery was not infantry. Furthermore, the board had little or no comprehension of his work in intelligence.

Despite some objections among staff officers, who had found Monash a little too assertive and direct in his assessment of commanders in mock battles, he was appointed commander of the 13th Infantry Brigade. Monash was delighted, but disappointed that it had not made him a full colonel so that he would be higher in rank than all his battalion commanders. He would be put on probation until the next camp, which was to be at Easter 1914. Monash complained. The Military Board relented. He was made a full colonel on 12 August 1913, backdated to 1 July.

Monash had coveted this rank since he first joined the North Melbourne Battery in 1887. Twenty-six years was a long time to wait. But, as with many of his ambitions, such as his prosperity, he had to be patient. The appointment gave him just as sweet a feeling as it would have twenty years earlier, but in a different way. He had dreamed of such a position being his in his twenties, but knew in his heart that unless he proved himself on the battlefield it was not attainable then, or even due to him.

Now, at forty-seven, Monash did feel he had earned it. He was equipped to face the responsibilities and challenges of handling a brigade of 4000 to 5000 men. The artillery experience among the rank and file for more than twenty years, topped off by his four years staff experience with the Intelligence Corps, was a strong preparation. He had seen both sides of the military story and knew their importance.

The brigade comprised the 49th, 51st and 52nd Battalions, along with the soon-to-be attached 46th and 48th, which were regarded as reliable and conscientious. All came from the southern suburbs. Monash said, perhaps hopefully, that it was the 'pick of the commands'. If it wasn't, he would set out to make it that.

He soon learned that there had been friction between the brigade and regimental commanders. He invited them all to dinner at Iona to sort it out. He called a conference of his battalion commanders to give them a taste of the Monash style. He wanted them to 'weld' together into an efficient machine. He would invoke healthy rivalry between the battalions, but they had to be sympathetic to each other. There was to be no bitching outside the brigade to those at other commands or the press. Monash told them that he would encourage individual enterprise and leadership. But he would step in and on toes to get things done his way, which would be the correct way. Monash spoke about such things as 'discipline', which they had heard since schooldays without any sense of what it meant beyond punishment for breaking rules. Monash enunciated a clear idea. He wanted every man to bend to his superior officer's will.

He went to the trouble of writing his thoughts down in a pamphlet, *100 Hints for Company Commanders*. It was a creed for life and behaviour rather than the narrow, stilted kind of document associated with the military. If there had been any bullyboys, cowards and braggarts among his men, they would have been uncomfortable with his strictures about how they might improve their characters by cultivating 'self-control and self-confidence'. They would have cringed at his directives for 'good temper', 'self-sacrifice', 'dignity towards subordinates' and 'coolness under stress'. Monash, as ever, underlined the importance of communication up and down the ranks. It was the most frustrating point of weakness in military operations. He had seen it at the battery for years. When in the Intelligence Corps, he was convinced that the failure in communication he witnessed in mock conflicts would have led to carnage and defeat in actual battle.

He had been a thinking person in an intellectually stagnant military environment now for thirty years, and he was determined to open the minds of his officers and anyone who aspired to be one. He had done it at the Intelligence Corps, but there he had been able to handpick bright men who would be receptive. Now he had a tougher job. He asked his officers to study textbooks and manuals. There were a few complaints about how boring they were, but these dwindled as he took them on to military history and they began applying the theory to the great battles of the past. With his 'Wilderness' essay still etched in his mind, he used the American Civil War to show that brute force and superior numbers could be overcome by thinking commanders using smart tactics. If you could fool the enemy by a smokescreen or a feigned action or a false document, do it. Monash would ask, why make a frontal attack when a flanking movement might achieve the same result? He was inculcating new methods, which involved cleverness and innovation.

Monash, who had developed into a fine, occasional lecturer in engineering, combined the verve of the much-missed Professor Kernot (who died in 1909) with the creativity of Colonel Foster in making history live for the officers. They were asked to write précis and sit written tests. Monash stressed clarity and simplicity. He was determined to get them from the most sluggish of his command.

All the time, he was reassessing and expanding his own comprehension of how his command might tick over better. During this period, one salient point came through. He might have just become a colonel in charge of a brigade for the first time, but he was thinking like a general.

Monash at first found his brigade not so much infantry but a sloppy mix of several military sections. He began restructuring and shaping it until the end of 1913 when he felt it was a complete, cohesive body of dedicated soldiers. The 13th had five infantry battalions, two artillery batteries, a survey company, an Army Service Corps unit and an ambulance. After four months with Monash in charge, the brigade was a small, almost self-contained little army in his own image.

In November 1913 Monash was both excited and nervous about the news that British General Sir Ian Hamilton, Inspector-General of British overseas forces (including military operations in its former colonies), would be coming to Australia. Like Kitchener, he would report back to the

War Office. Unlike Kitchener, he would put much thought into his assessments. Monash's brigade would be the first in the country to present manoeuvres to this very VIP. That is where Monash's nerves set in. He would have been in charge for half a year by the time sixty-year-old Hamilton was due to watch the 13th hold its tactical exercises at Lilydale outside Melbourne in February 1914. Was it enough time? Would they look better than the divisional operations Kitchener had seen three years earlier? Monash was also thrilled about the visit. He had had enormous respect for Hamilton ever since reading the two volumes of his *Staff Officer's Scrap Book During the Russo-Japanese War*. He had set it as mandatory reading in 1911 for his Intelligence Corps and had done the same thing for his brigade commanders. Monash considered Hamilton the best author he had come across on matters military. The flow and cadence of his sentences were uplifting compared with most writing, let alone the turgid prose found commonly in texts on war.

Monash pointed out to his men that Hamilton had been attached to the Japanese Army as an observer of the major land battles of the Russo-Japanese conflict at Yula, Liaoyong and Mukden; the bloodbath siege of Port Arthur; and the climactic destruction of the Russian fleet at Tsushima. He had recorded the impact of the machine-gun and barbed wire on the battlefield. Now Hamilton would be fixing his binoculars on 2500 part-time Australians at scorching Lilydale. It was not quite the same as real war at Port Arthur and the Yalu River. But Monash didn't think that would affect the lively, penetrating prose of Hamilton's observations.

More than instinct was telling him that he had to put on a terrific show. With this in mind, Monash pushed his officers through tactical exercises without troops at Lilydale for a day in late December, in much the same manner Colonel Foster had taught him. But there was a difference. Monash took his officers to the practice battlefield to conduct their bunker operations rather than sitting them in an underground lecture theatre.

In the lead-up to the February manoeuvres, Monash had a chance to meet Hamilton twice at the Naval and Military Club and a couple of times at District Command HQ. Photos Monash had seen of Hamilton portrayed him as not quite the typical member of the British ruling class. There was a high forehead and lifted chin, but also a softness in the eyes, a sensitivity in the face. In person, Monash was impressed but not fooled by the frail-looking, partly war-crippled old soldier's humility, charm and warmth. Here was a courageous, battle-hardened warrior, who had twice been recommended for the Victoria Cross in the course of forty years service that included tours of Afghanistan, Burma, India, the Sudan and South Africa.

Over the dinner table with a dozen other officers, there were moments when Monash realised that Hamilton was a multilinguist like himself. It was not in the pretentious use of a phrase but in the way the name of the German cavalry journal – *Kavalleristische Monatschäfte* – rolled off his tongue or the manner in which he spoke of a French town.

Monash noticed that when speaking about Germany, Hamilton didn't express a dollop of animosity. Hamilton knew like everyone else that it was very likely to be England's mortal 'enemy' at any moment. Yet he was too much of an Edwardian gent, who had seen more of life and death and war than anyone in the British forces, to lower himself to vilifying the opposition.

Hamilton always seemed to skip the conversation away from probes by others into his fighting experiences. He looked to the literary allusion or the poetic metaphor for diversion, which endeared him to Monash even more. He thought they had a rapport. It was comforting, but would mean nothing if the brigade didn't perform.

Monash wrote the scenario for the pretend battle, making it as tight as possible. It would be difficult for one battalion commander to overcome the other. It would also be physically demanding. Monash had picked the best two battalions of his command, with the emphasis on youthful soldiers who could stand the heat. He had even gone to the trouble of seeking medical advice on how far young men could march in the lead-up to a pitched battle. Monash then put the brigade through a full-dress rehearsal on the day before.

On the day of the exercise, Monash met Hamilton and his entourage of British and Australian permanent force officers at dawn at the camp near the dusty Lilydale hills. The sun was already hot. The forecast was for 100 degrees (thirty-eight degrees Centigrade) as a cruel northerly wind created the worst conditions imaginable for any outdoor activity except bathing. Bushfires partly ringed the area. Some officers wondered whether the exercise should be modified or even called off by late morning. Monash wanted to go on with the full day. Hamilton agreed with him.

At 8 a.m. journalists arrived. Then the Governor-General, Sir Ronald

Munro Ferguson, turned up to meet Hamilton and inspect the troops with him. Ferguson was not a mere figurehead. Since arriving in Australia in the previous May, he had been, effectively, Kitchener's main war propagandist and recruiter for the coming conflict with Germany. He was also pushing the Federal Government over the issue of conscription. If that were to happen in Australia, Kitchener could be more sure of the numbers available for the British cause. Ferguson, an urbane, wealthy Scot, would be writing to the Minister for War and other key people in the UK Government about Australia's capacities for fighting and aiding the British cause. But he was no spy. His purpose was overt and transparent enough. He knew, and every minister in the Australian Federal Government was aware, that the British still treated its 'Dominion' as if it were a colony, albeit a self-governing one. Ferguson was the King's representative in Australia and that of the government in London. He had more than intrinsic political clout.

He hadn't got up at 6 a.m. to be in time for morning tea and hobnob with other dignitaries at Lilydale. Ferguson wished to see his good friend Hamilton and judge for himself, as a former Grenadier guardsman, how much Australia could contribute to the British Empire's cause.

Hamilton and Ferguson were both impressed, but more taken with Monash as a potential field commander. Hamilton told him that his lads looked as good as, if not better than, regular brigades he had inspected.

Monash gave the signal for the exercise to begin. Through the morning he monitored the condition of his men, making sure they had plenty of water and adequate breaks. A march of fourteen kilometres in full battle gear and then the rush of combat would be a test. Monash had faith. He urged his commanders on.

A halt was called at 12.30 a.m. for a VIP lunch under a gum tree. Hamilton asked for a conference. Monash addressed his officers.

'I was prepared for intelligent criticisms,' Hamilton recalled, 'but I thought they would be so wrapped up in the cotton wool of politeness that no one would be very much impressed. On the contrary, he stated his opinions in the most direct, blunt way.'[22]

Monash let each battalion and company commander know what he thought. He spared no one, and spoke of the consequences of their actions, reactions and sometimes lack of either, in a real battle. Some officers were chastened, no one was humiliated. All were inspired to finish the day better than they had performed in the morning.

At the end of the long day, the companies marched back to camp covered in dust and grime. They looked sunburnt and parched but strong. Hamilton took the salute. He and all the onlooking regulars were touched by the determination and enthusiasm of these citizen soldiers.

When the parade was over, Monash moved among the companies, talking to the troops. They seemed cheerful. When he asked how they were, no one complained. They had beaten the conditions. Some even claimed that they could go with another exercise after half an hour's rest.

Hamilton congratulated Monash on his handling of the brigade and the exercises.

After he had made other inspections, Hamilton wrote a comprehensive report to the War Office, which was different in tone and emphasis from the press coverage. The *Age* was critical. Over the next six weeks it attacked Monash, who was portrayed as too tough and uncompromising. The military was upbraided for allowing citizen forces to be treated so harshly. The paper editorialised that 'it was too high a price to pay for efficiency if only one man is overtrained'.

The negative publicity caused a stir for the Military Board. Monash defended himself. He told Bruche: 'I shall adhere to my policy of training for war and not for picnics.' How else, he asked, should he prepare for real conflict? Armies had to march, sometimes in terrible conditions. Armies had to fight. There were no comfortable conditions for that.

Meanwhile, Hamilton's report on his weeks in Australia circulated in the British War Office. He singled out Monash for praise. The colonel was 'a man of outstanding force and character'. He had the makings of an excellent commander. Hamilton noted one other characteristic that he himself was said to lack. It was that ruthless streak. Yet the author's capacity to craft a brilliant assessment meant that this description would be between the lines. It would be understood.[22]

A month after the Lilydale exercise an issue developed that would be a far greater threat to Monash than his forceful nature. 'Home Rule' in Ireland – allowing limited autonomy from British government – had been a festering problem for forty years. By March 1914 it looked set to become law and apply to the six counties of Ulster (Northern Ireland), where the Catholics would be in a minority. It was unpopular with both Ulster Unionists and predominantly Catholic republicans in Ireland.

The president of Melbourne's Celtic Club, Major McInerney (a South African War veteran), was reported in the *Argus* attacking the Home Rule concept and one of its supporters, the 1st Earl Roberts, who had been an outstanding combat leader in the Second Afghan War (1878–80) and the South African War. McInerney was critical of Roberts' leadership. His attack was a breach of military etiquette. An officer should never criticise a fellow officer in public. The Naval and Military Club was not happy. McInerney was asked, in writing, to withdraw his remarks about Roberts' military capacities, not his comments about Home Rule, which were accepted as 'personal views'. McInerney refused to rescind his attack. Other appeals were made to him, but he remained unmoved, even by the threat of possible expulsion from the club. It called for a special meeting and a vote on whether McInerney should be thrown out. He was given a chance to defend himself, but was expelled on the motion put by its vice-presidents, one of whom was Monash.

McInerney made a public statement that he had been thrown out of the club because of his political views. Monash wrote to the *Argus* and the *Age* explaining that he had not been removed for his political views but for the breach of etiquette. In perhaps an exposition too far, he added that the minority who wanted him to stay in the club only voted that way to prevent McInerney setting himself up as a political martyr. The article implied that he was cowardly and disloyal to his fellow officers.

Monash's direct, articulate, yet layered style as ever left no room for subtlety or ambiguity. McInerney was incensed. He had close contacts within an Irish Catholic–Labor Party circle and would use them in attempted acts of retribution. First, on 27 May he used a Melbourne contact in the federal Labor Party, who asked the relevant minister in parliament if Colonels James Burston (president of the Naval and Military Club), Monash and F. G. Hughes (the other vice president) had volunteered for the South African War. The answer came back that they had not. This was meant somehow to lead to the conclusion that they were cowards and unworthy of their current status in the club. Monash was not asked to explain why he had not enlisted for war. The excuse he had articulated to relatives – that Britain's defence of its empire had little or nothing to do with Australian interests – would have created doubts about him. To most Anglo-Celts, even some of Irish Catholic background like McInerney, British Empire and Australian interests were one and the same. Monash's rationale could have been made to look even thinner in the light of the fact that Australia was not even a nation as such but a group of British colonies for most of the South African War.

McInerney's supporters, including four federal Labor men, arranged a dinner for him on 3 July and invited the *Argus*. It reported next day that Dr William Maloney attacked Burston, Monash and Hughes. 'Are we going to allow these lickspittle little puppies to interfere with our freedom?' he asked. McInerney remarked he thought that 'centuries of persecution would have seared tolerance into the heart of the Jew'.[23]

Monash, it appeared, had created a new and tenacious enemy.

1914–15: ENEMIES WITHIN

On 28 June 1914 Archduke Franz Ferdinand, heir to the Hapsburgs, the Austrian imperial family, and his wife were gunned down by a young Bosnian Serb assassin. The crude aim was to free Bosnia from Austria so that it could be integrated with Serbia. The shots triggered a chain reaction of political and military manoeuvring. The blood-related royals from several countries did some frenetic letter-writing. George V (who was married to a German, formerly Princess Mary of Teck) and Wilhelm II, communicated but, unlike their grandmother, neither had the will or the clout to keep the peace. There was talk of a conference of the royals, but there was never the determination to organise it. The powers of monarchs were in decline anyway. Any major war promised to all but end their major influences and, in some cases, their positions as well.

Even if a dominant peace-keeping royal had emerged, there was no time to stop the political and military fission. It took thirty-seven days after the assassination for Europe to be engulfed in war. Russia and France aligned against Germany, Austria and Turkey. The UK was dragged in, and it declared war on Germany on 4 August. All England's Dominions, including Australia, were expected to take part in the conflict.

There were two likely outcomes. If Britain and her allies won, Europe would in some way be realigned. Democracy in the British Dominions would remain intact. If Germany won and forced British capitulation, its intentions were clear. It would extend its empire as much as it could. Before war began, it tried to keep Britain out of the conflict by promising not to touch French territory, only its colonies. If Germany won and advanced as far as the English Channel, it might not demand UK territory, only its Dominions.[1]

That threat, even more than a desire to fight for the British in another remote conflict, was motivation enough for Monash. Unlike the Sudan upheaval and the Boer War, Australia was almost certain to be affected by the outcome of this one. It had 'to help the Empire to crush a peril which may mean the end of Australia as a free country', Monash wrote to a relative.[2]

He had been clear in his mind on the two previous occasions, and expressed why the previous conflicts in 1885 when he was nineteen, and 1899 when he was thirty-four, had not attracted him. When he was both times more or less of military age, Monash had stood firm. There was no moral imperative or incentive for him to rush off. This attitude distinguished him from the thousands who could not wait to have any excuse to fight for the glory of the British Empire. Their motives were more personal. War gave their profession as soldiers some reason and rationale. Monash's decisions not to travel abroad on both occasions brought some scorn and comment, particularly concerning his staying put during the Boer War. But now, aged forty-nine, when most professionals faced being too old for battle, and with an unequivocal logic again clear in his mind, Monash was going to war. His main reason was that it was in Australia's interests. Other motives would begin to take shape. Monash was more than a student of war and the great battle commanders. There was a fair possibility now that he would be given the chance to test himself in the field of battle. His attention to detail made him ideal for war administration, yet Monash did not see his own potential as a back-room brigadier. He had progressive ideas about the prosecution of battle, some of them too advanced, it seemed in 1914, for the senior generals of the British Army, who would be his superiors. Yet Monash had been studying, lecturing and practising in the field so many aspects of war that he might well have thought that providence was allowing him a chance to exploit his obsession with all matters military on the battlefield itself.

Despite his success with the 13th Brigade, he was not sure where he stood in the pecking order of commanders and what the government's plans were. On 9 August he received answers to these questions in part when McCay rang asking him if he would take over his job as Deputy Chief Censor in the Chief of the General Staff's Department. McCay had been chosen to command a brigade of the Australian Imperial Force's 1st

Division under Colonel Bridges' control. They would sail to the Middle East in October with a volunteer force already being put together. Australia, in perhaps months, would be involved in war.

Monash gave himself a day to consider the offer. He would be giving up the 13th Brigade, which he had led for less than a year. But he was satisfied that he had completed his aims for it. Its militia soldiers were as proficient as any professional unit. The men took pride in their activity. Monash agreed to take on the job as long it didn't limit his chances of being offered his own brigade. McCay assured him it was only a temporary position. It would not damage his opportunities. On the contrary, he would be closer to the Chief of the General Staff, Colonel J. G. Legge. It would help Monash's cause.

Monash was in a good position. He was financially secure, and his business would tick over – with sound management – in his absence. He took on the censor job eight days later. Local action against Germany had already begun. The German steamer *Pfalz* was stopped from escaping through Melbourne's Port Phillip Heads by a shot across its bows from one of big guns that Monash had often fired for the North Melbourne Battery. Troops had been despatched to Rabaul, German New Guinea and a few close Pacific islands to take control of German possessions. The ensuing fighting saw the first Australian casualties of the war, and the first prisoners-of-war were captured. Japan took over Germany's island possessions north of the equator: the Marshalls, the Marianas and the Carolines. After these incidents, there was renewed wariness about the Japanese. Anything German had a frightening stigma.

Sydney newspapers reported on a twenty-five-year-old who wanted to volunteer. The enlisting officer asked where his parents were born. The man, whose profile fitted Monash's, replied that his parents had been born in Germany but had settled in Australia.

'All our interests and our home are here,' the volunteer said.

The officer refused to sign him up.

'But I demand to be enrolled,' the volunteer said. 'I want to defend what we've got.'[3]

The officer relented and initialled his papers.

In this frenzied atmosphere, Monash began his censorship work and hated it from day one. McCay, not for the first time, had left a mess to be cleaned up. Much of the work caused anxiety. The British War Office had laid down strict rules. Any communication with Germany, or even any other potential enemies, had to be stopped. His main aim was to prevent any information going to Germany on troop or shipping movements. There could be no wireless traffic. German businesses were shut down. The press had to be pulled into line. It wasn't allowed to publish any battle reports that were not confirmed by the government. No articles that could give comfort to enemy nations were to be printed.

Monash felt the pressure. He ordered all his family not to write to his relatives. Aunt Ulrike was told not to speak German in public. He had to stop subscriptions to German magazines. His allegiances were never in doubt in his own mind. Thirty years earlier he made it clear in writing to relatives that he was Australian, and therefore British, not German. But pain came from being the person in the government in charge of severing all vestiges of links with his roots. It was made all the more unpleasant by the internment of some Germans. Among them were a group of academic scientists whom Monash had enticed to Australia for conferences as guests of the Association for the Advancement of Science. They had turned up, only to be turned in.

His main problems came from the press. There had never been any such censorship in Australia. He found that papers in some states accepted the rule but others in other states didn't. Monash tried to treat them uniformly, but ran into trouble with difficult editors and publishers. Newspapers protested against the 'fog of war'. There were complaints that 'scarcely a whisper reaches Australia'. At first the *Sydney Morning Herald* didn't care. It reckoned that as long as Britain's mighty fleet was undefeated 'there is probably no nation that feels this struggle less'.[4] Perhaps the fog had blinded the paper's vision.

After three weeks experience with this terrible tangle of red tape and bureaucracy, Monash still had not been appointed to any command. There were rumours of a second division being formed. The effort to enlist volunteers had been successful. A fourth brigade was being put together.

Colonel J. G. Legge, Chief of the General Staff, had been sent Ian Hamilton's appraisal of Monash. This, plus McCay's influence, caused him to ask Monash to notify the Military Board that he was available to serve. Monash obliged on 10 September. Legge then recommended him to the Minister for Defence, E. D. Millen, who considered the candidates as one of his last acts before being replaced by George Pearce. On 15 September a relieved Monash happily quit his stressful censorship position and was appointed to lead the 4th Brigade.

He had to put together his force inside fifty days. The task was made tougher by the fact that the brigade was to be a truly national unit. Two battalions were to come from Victoria and New South Wales (the 13th and 14th). Another two (the 15th and 16th) were to be concocted from the other states. Monash as ever took the positive view. He would make it a cohesive force. He chased Bruche as his first appointment, but he was prevented from joining the brigade by a technicality. Monash was content with his second and third choices, Lieutenant Colonel J. P. McGlinn, from New South Wales, and Captain C. H. Jess from Victoria. They met at Iona to plan the brigade's quick creation.

Within two weeks of his appointment, hysteria over Monash's origins became a serious problem. Over the decades he had endured jibes and remarks about his Jewish background, which at times were particularly personal. Even the Governor-General, Munro Ferguson, who had watched the Lilydale mock battle, later wrote to Hamilton about Monash being 'an able Jew'.[5] It's unlikely that this remark helped Hamilton, who had observed Monash. He knew Monash was not disabled and didn't care about his ethnicity. Hamilton was only concerned that he was pro-British and a resourceful leader.

Others went further. There was a craving to describe Monash anatomically, as if his background rendered him as somehow alien. The satirical magazine *Punch*, which was allowed some licence, was still malicious and gratuitous in its remarks in an article damning him with faint praise. It said Monash was 'neither romantic in appearance or in style'. He was 'stout and ruddy with the typical Hebrew mouth and typical Hebrew eye'. A biographer noted that his 'face suggested both strength and sensitivity. He had a prominent Jewish nose . . .' White, whose inferiority complex towards him was growing, noted that 'Monash's brain, like that of so many of his race, was quick to grasp and quick to learn; even if the knowledge was without depth'.[6]

About the only area not described, it seemed, were his private parts. But Charles Bean, perhaps looking for something else that was un-British with which to alienate Monash, remarked later: 'We do not want Australia represented by men mainly because of their ability, *natural and inborn in Jews, to push themselves.* Monash and [Major General Sir C.] Rosenthal have both the quality, though Monash does not use it shamelessly.

Rosenthal does.'[7] Bean had been blinded by the name. Rosenthal – also a noted architect of Sydney churches and an accomplished musician – was not Jewish. Yet the journalist's attitude was more typical than not of the ignorance that abounded and shaped images. Many more assessments of Monash expressed the same racist sentiment. He was Jewish, therefore 'different'. He was 'not one of us', and therefore not to be trusted.

As isolating as this was, such crude sentiments were fashionable at a time when people, particularly the major seats of 'empires', in France, Germany and Britain, were proudly, openly racist. Propaganda on all sides espoused racial superiority. Anyone not of your race was inferior. The English took this attitude to everyone, especially the Irish; the Germans about 'Slavs'; the French about Belgians, and any nation that didn't have French as its first language. The Jews had been on the receiving end for a millennium or two anywhere the culture prospered. Yet in Monash's case most of the comments were written in confidence or whispered. It was something that he could take as long as the racism was not too blatant. But now another aspect of his background was a far bigger threat. Far more disconcerting than being Jewish, for the moment at least, were his German roots.

The unforgiving Major McInerney was livid when he learnt that Monash had taken command of the new 4th Brigade. He began a campaign to bring Monash down. He and several contacts wrote anonymous letters to G. F. Pearce, the Minister for Defence, and to Kitchener at the War Office. All contained bald facts mixed with mischievous errors. Each one dwelt on something in Monash's background. He had dropped the 'c' from his name (he hadn't – his father had done so). His family had lived in Germania Cottage. He and his children (he had only one child) had been born and educated in Germany (wrong on both counts). They had all been active members of the German Club. His father had been hostile to British interests. Monash had trouble even speaking English correctly (wrong again). How could he be expected to lead Australians against his true home country?

A petition was created to protest Monash's appointment, although none of the names on it were prominent people. McInerney kept in the background. Pearce felt the pressure but held firm. He had the views of Legge, McCay, Hamilton and a score of other reputable people in positions to judge Monash. They all supported him. Kitchener passed all the letters over to Pearce and the Military Board to handle.

McInerney's next move was to have about fifty letters written and published in the *Argus* towards the end of October. They spoke a little too concertedly of the 'alien danger'. Monash was a target. But writers eased the pressure on him by their inanity. Vic Monash had become the sister of Pearce's wife. That's how Monash got the job. There were stupid threats, too. When taken prisoner in war, German-born naturalised Australians would be treated as deserters from the German military and as a result would face a firing squad.

Monash had cold comfort from knowing that he was not the only target. Bruche, Rosenthal, Jess and many others in the forces with suspect names and backgrounds were checked and, in some cases, investigated.

'If I had listened to all the gossip and slander, as I was urged to do,' Pearce remarked later, 'Monash would never have gone to the War.' Some, such as Bruche, suffered. He was forced to remain at home as Western Australian commandant for two years when, like Monash, he wanted to be a leader in the field. (A year later in 1915, the Military Board would cease to commission officers born outside Australia.)[8]

Monash didn't let the furore distract him from his main task. He knew he had support where it counted. One friend, Melbourne University vice-chancellor J. H. McFarland, commented after Monash had seen off the attacks: 'God has given you a very strong nervous system. I hope it wears well.'[9]

The first contingent of the Australian Imperial Force (AIF) – the 1st Division, consisting of about 18,000 men, and a 1st Light Horse Brigade – was very much the creation of Bridges, the division commander, and Cyril White, his chief of staff. Bridges, a South African War veteran, wanted a separate body of soldiers – preferably at least a division – to march under an Australian flag. Given the spirit of nationalism and transition to Federation when he fought the Boers in 1900 and 1901, it was disappointing for volunteer Australians to be shoved into British companies and brigades without any sense of their new identity.

Colonels H. N. MacLaurin, McCay and E. G. Sinclair-MacLagan would lead the 1st, 2nd and 3rd Brigades. Bridges and White went after what they thought were the best staff officers in Australia. Monash was not considered. White felt intimidated by him and did not want to be outshone in a staff environment. But it didn't matter to Monash. He wanted to be a battle commander in the field in charge of his own brigade. This was his chance.

The first contingent took off in October for a secret destination – Egypt – and not the Western Front, as was hoped and expected by the soldiers and Bridges.

On 29 October, a few weeks after the departure, Turkey entered the war on Germany's side. Not much was known at the War Office about its capacity. In the recent Balkan Wars (1912–13) between the members of the Balkan League – Serbia, Bulgaria, Greece and Montenegro – and the Ottoman Empire (predominantly the Turks) on almost its last legs, the league had won. The empire lost almost all its European territory, and the Turks didn't appear to distinguish themselves, although they did recover part of Thrace in the second conflict. Political change led to a German Military Mission being 'invited' to train the Turks, more by Germany's cajolery than their host's desire. The Turks had an ancient, ruthless military tradition. Their strengths, according to experts, were in long marching, planning and entrenching a position, and in stubbornness in holding it. They had good artillerymen. But in recent times their army had been poorly equipped and behind the times in its capacity to invade and take foreign territory.

Those now in control of Turkey still had something to prove in this department.

While Germany and Turkey were expediently accommodating each other, the second contingent in Australia was still being constructed. It would be made up of four Brigades: Monash's 4th (the biggest), the 1st Australian Light Horse led by regular officer Lieutenant Colonel Harry Chauvel, the New Zealand Infantry led by Colonel F. E. Johnston, and New Zealand's Mounted Rifles.

Monash and the other brigade leaders wanted a certain type of volunteer. It was preferable that he be of strong physique and a good horseman and marksman. This shifted the emphasis towards country lads. But the contingents catered for a balance of city men, many of whom would be professionals and craftsmen, such as harness-makers, saddlers and boot-makers. There would also be electricians and a range of engineers.

One of the engineer volunteers for his 4th Brigade was twenty-eight-year-old Gordon Gabriel, the son of Annie. She and Monash had stayed in contact over the decades by correspondence and with the occasional assignation when he was in Sydney. Since her husband Fred's recent death, Annie had decided to move back to Melbourne. Now her son would be under Monash's command in wartime. He and Monash had developed a rapport. On his advice, Gordon had become a mining engineer. Now he wanted to follow him into combat. Annie sought assurances from Monash that he would look after her son. Gordon joined the mud-splattered final camp in the Melbourne suburb of Broadmeadows in late November.

Battalions were ordered to do forty-kilometre route marches to the city and back in the heat. Monash would like to have had more time, but by mid-December his national brigade at least looked as good as his former 13th. He clamped down on long hair and slovenliness. The camp's emphasis was on flag work, including a Monash-designed new scheme, bayonet fighting and a strenuous set of exercises to toughen his troops. Monash had suggested some of the muscle-strengthening routines, which he wished he had adhered to himself. At forty-nine, he admitted he had lost his 'war against obesity' after his desk job as censor and the months of planning the new brigade. It left him with a faintly comical look, especially when next to his portly chief of staff, McGlinn, who was about the same height as Monash. Both men weighed 100 kilograms. Their big belts sat over protruding stomachs and pushed out their tunic jackets so that they flapped like an elephantine ballerina's tutu when they walked.

White dubbed them Tweedledum and Tweedledee.[10] There was a deal of inter-divisional rivalry in the characterisation. White reckoned he was in the First Eleven. He had helped pick it. Monash and the Irishman McGlinn had not been selected. They were leading the Second Eleven. It was expected that the 1st Division would be first to land abroad, first to fight, first to gain glory for Australia.

Monash knew, but had to keep secret, that his destination would be Egypt. He didn't expect the war to last long – perhaps six months at the outside – and he comforted Vic and Bertha (and Annie, whom he saw just before leaving) with his assurances that he would be back by winter. Even if it were longer, he expected that the Australian and New Zealand contingent would be left to garrison Egypt until the end of the war. If in the unlikely event that the conflict in Europe dragged on until past that expected half-year, then Monash thought he might be on the Western Front. It seemed a remote prospect.

As the commander of the biggest brigade, he was in charge of the nineteen-ship convoy of Australian and New Zealand vessels. He couldn't sit back on the *Ulysses* and sun himself on the deck as he had done on his last trip abroad four years earlier. The long ride began with a test of his patience, organisational and people skills. There was a three-day pause at Albany where everything that could go wrong did. Every single ship had either some of the wrong stores or the wrong personnel on board. Communication between the ships was near impossible. Local tug masters, who had only once before ever dealt with such a huge convoy (the first contingent) refused to guide some ships to moorings after dark. They were in dispute with the navy and went on strike. Monash found that the naval officers either ignored or countermanded his orders. Rather than cause a row that might have jeopardised the entire trip, Monash preferred to complain in writing to Legge back at Military HQ, should the farce of the Albany docking reach his attention.

Monash's love/hate affair with chaos continued. On the one hand, it disturbed him to face any organisational mess. He would fret, write down his concerns and loose sleep over them. On the other hand, he was born to organise his way from disorder to order. Long before the chaos theory to define how the universe began, Monash treated any disorganisation problem as something that could be handled with scientific analysis. He would engineer his way out of it, as long as there was time and space to do so. Without time and space he was lost and life was miserable. A sense of serenity came from solving chaotic puzzles or, even better, having completed preparation well enough to avoid them altogether.

The Albany debacle frustrated him, but once the convoy sailed for Egypt, escorted by just one fully armed submarine, Monash felt becalmed. At first it was a thirty-six-kilometre snake and he couldn't see the tail. Monash gave orders. The convoy responded to every signal 'as to course, speed, distance and interval'. Within hours he could see the 'whole fleet spread out in regular formation'. This measured control over the ships, spread over an area four kilometres wide by ten kilometres long, was a serene experience. He could write and plan. He could sit down with his commanders and set up on-board training and leisure schemes.

Two days out of Albany every vessel, especially the flagship *Ulysses*, was a blend of Monash's planning. On the saloon deck he would lecture officers on reconnaissance. There would be drilling and weapons classes. Semaphore practice could be heard as a sergeant signalled and his class called out the alphabet letters. French and German lessons for officers would be in progress, giving a broad hint to where everyone thought the final destination would be. On another side of the saloon there might be football or cricket with the shouts of appeal and applause for shot or catch. In a leisure area, there could be a chess competition or even a two-up school. Bands seemed never to stop. One would be practising aft. Forward, operatic selections were popular. In a 'smoking room' an investigation into a soldier's behaviour or even a court martial might be going on. The wireless operating room, like the band, seemed to be always in operation.

Men not on duty were 'allowed to dress pretty well as they like,' Monash wrote, 'and the variety of design and fashions would do credit to the resources of the Rue de la Paix.' Monash encouraged recreational activity. He had learnt long ago that idle soldiers needed physical outlets for excess testosterone and energy. Boxing and wrestling were mandatory. While watching a match between two blindfolded boxers, the guide for one of the contestants directed a hit wide of the mark. It landed in Monash's mid-rift, much to the mirth of spectators. If it hurt, he didn't react. Instead, he later presented his unwitting assailant with a trophy, a strong handshake and a smile.

Monash was still an unknown quantity with most of the rank and file. He was neither aloof nor arrogant, yet he wasn't one to linger long with the troops. There was always planning, directing or lecturing to his officers to be done. He was strict on discipline but reasonable. The officers were moulded to his designs. There was more directing and advising than bullying. He was friends with the *Argus* journalist on board, C. P. Smith, who wrote glowing reports about his 'powerful personality and powerful sense of justice'. But claims that every man on the convoy would follow Monash 'to the ends of the earth' to fight were premature.[11] Nevertheless, his officers had growing confidence in him. It would filter down.

Despite Monash's good intentions, the trip could not be quite as smooth and harmonious as he would have liked. Illness and death travelled with the convoy as stealthily as the sub beneath it. There was an outbreak of measles, which was overlayed with pneumonia. Typhoid struck twice. There were burials at sea. Doctors worked overtime to inoculate the men. Monash regretted not having nurses on board. There were HQ concerns about having any women on the trip, but Monash would have argued harder had he foreseen the suffering of ill men, who needed comfort and support. He made a note to insist on nurses in the future.

Most of the soldiers were going abroad for the first time. They saw it as a paid vacation. At first they planned to 'see the sights of Europe' and dreamt of Paris and clichés about French girls. Now on board and aware that Egypt was the destination, the talk was of the pyramids and what the Cairo bars and bazaars might offer. Despite the screening that allowed the volunteers into the force, no one could be certain how they would be behave en route and on disembarking.

While the convoy cruised north across the Indian Ocean, events were developing in London that would decide the Australian and New Zealand contingents' engagement in the war. They had begun on New Year's Day 1915 when the Chancellor of the Exchequer, Lloyd George – a member of the War Council – circulated a classified memorandum suggesting that the Russians needed assistance in the Balkans. This was in accord with the attitude of forty-year-old Winston Churchill – another War Council member and the man in charge of the Admiralty. On 2 January Secretary of State for War Kitchener received a telegram from Russia's Tsar Nicholas II. The Russian army was struggling in the Caucasus – the mountain range in its southwest – against the Bulgarians and Turks. Nicholas wanted the British to create a 'demonstration' that would draw Turkish reserves away and so ease the pressure on Russian troops.

The telegram was passed to Churchill. In an afternoon, he drew up more than the Tsar requested. The proposal he sent to Kitchener was to attack Turkey's Gallipoli Peninsula. It was grand in concept but thin on detail. Kitchener didn't say no, but made it clear that he could not spare one infantry division from the swathe of fronts on which he was now fighting the Germans. Churchill didn't care. He reckoned his navy could blow the Turkish defences away without help and sail on up the Dardanelles, the sixty-one-kilometre narrow strait between the Gallipoli Peninsula in Europe and the mainland of Asia Minor. Churchill's ultimate aim was to take the Turkish capital of Constantinople.

In the weeks that followed, the original need for a distraction to help Russia was rendered unnecessary by the folly of Enver Pasha, one the triumvirate of revolutionaries running Turkey and what was left of the tottering Ottoman Empire. Enver boldly led 90,000 men into southern Russia on 4 January and met Russian troops head-on at the Battle of Sarikamish. Enver might have seen himself as Napoleon, but he hadn't read his Napoleonic history. It was a bad winter, and the Turks suffered. Only about 10,000 would ever come back. But intelligence filtering back to London was thin. Nobody – perhaps deliberately – informed the over-worked Kitchener. As far as he knew, the Turks still needed to be distracted in order to assist Russia.

But that skimpy Churchill proposal had now assumed a life of its own. On 12 January the British War Cabinet approved the preparation of a naval expedition for February to 'bombard and take the Gallipoli Penin-sula with Constantinople as its objective'. The idea was to show great largesse to their ally the Russians by handing over Constantinople to them. It would mean that half their exports, which went through the Dard-anelles, would be protected. No one explained just how the navy would 'take' a peninsula. If anyone asked Churchill he would say that the fleet could use its own reserves and marines. No intelligence or research was submitted on what sort of defence the Turks would put up.

Monash's convoy anchored at Colombo, Ceylon (now Sri Lanka), a few hundred metres from the shore early on 13 January 1915. Monash went through several formalities, including an inspection by the British commander of Ceylonese forces and lunch with the Governor.

The next afternoon about forty small boats were bobbing near the ships, with locals calling out about the bars and women. More than 500 men – mostly 'young and untrained' – slid through hatches and portholes and down anchor chains from two vessels. Monash sent three officers and fifty men in a fast launch to herd them back. The launch reached the pier before some of the fugitive boats, but the small force could only apprehend about half the culprits. The rest absconded and headed all over town, including to Colombo hotels. Monash sent a force after them. All but twenty men were rounded up by nightfall and taken back to the 'clinks' on the convoy.

The contingent sailed away from Ceylon at daybreak on 15 January with a 0.01 per cent attrition rate when deserters and deaths were counted. It worried Monash. He felt his responsibility for every single soldier. Ceylon's military commandant sent an exaggerated report to Australian HQ about drunken brawling in some bars and the convoy's 'poor security'. Monash would be later answerable for it.

As the convoy slipped on, two divisions of Turks were being assembled with nine batteries of field artillery and another of howitzers (short guns for high-angle firing of shells at low velocity) at Beersheba (located in southern Israel). The commander was the wild-eyed Djemal Pasha, Minister of Marine, another of the triumvirate ruling Turkey. A Bavarian colonel, Kress von Kressenstein, was the strategist behind him. They planned to invade Egypt as a counter-measure to the build-up of British and French forces. Their approach march was by the tracks from Beersheba to Ismailia, a very arduous route across 300 kilometres of the Sinai Desert, made worse by the need to carry pontoons with them for crossing the Suez Canal. The scheme was to avoid the Royal Navy and military stationed north of Ismailia.

On 29 January 1915 Monash's convoy reached the Suez Canal, via the Indian Ocean and the Red Sea. It went single file into the southern part of the canal, which was guarded by a 'huge British cruiser'. Its troops came to attention. Buglers met the Australian and New Zealand contingent, and the flags were dipped. As the convoy passed, the 'blue-jackets' on the cruiser cheered. Monash's men responded. It was an exhilarating moment for him – 'a revelation of Empire' – which extended for an uplifting eight hours as the convoy wound its way eighty kilometres towards the canal's halfway point at Ismailia. More cheering came from French, Egyptian and British forces – including King's Own Scottish Borderers, New Zealanders, Lancashire Territorials, Sikhs, Bengal Lancers and Gurkhas. Through this inspirational haze, Monash had his first real sense of war.

'Both banks are fully entrenched and held by infantry,' he wrote. 'Every half-mile or so is a huge redoubt or field fortification, bristling with rifles, guns and machine-guns. On the Western (Cairo) side, every few miles there is a huge camp tucked away in the palms, with long convoys of packs, animals and wagons travelling with supplies in every direction.'

On the eastern or Arabian side were long stretches of wire entanglements and trenches. Beyond these Monash could see desert patrols to the horizon. The convoy dropped anchor at Ismailia for the night. 'It is a beautiful scene,' Monash noted, 'and it is difficult to realise that we are in the midst of war. A considerable Turkish and Arab army is within a few miles of us, led by German officers.'[12]

He was still in the thrall of the power of 'Empire' the next day as they sailed on to Alexandria. There was increased activity on the Arab bank. Soldiers called out that 'the Turks were five miles away . . . everybody expects a big fight tomorrow.' Still there seemed no threat to this elongated display of military might.

On 31 January Monash's 4th Brigade marched to the New Zealand 'Aerodrome' Camp at Heliopolis, eight kilometres outside Cairo and twelve kilometres from Bridges' 1st Division. The second contingent was to be led by the British commander, Sir Alexander Godley, who had impressed, first by not making the contingent march a long way to camp, and second, by making a car and driver available to Monash. The two gestures caused Monash to be well disposed to this patrician-looking, thin-lipped superior whom he had met before in Melbourne. His height (195 centimetres) and elegance of dress and bearing made him a more imposing figure than Colonel Bridges, his counterpart running the first contingent. So did his charm. Monash wanted to like and admire the man with the cold stare who would have a large say in his destiny and that of another 13,000 men in the second contingent. In those early days he described the tall, languid Godley as 'genial and expansive'. Perhaps Godley was trying to be imposing. But soon after lengthier meetings Monash was modifying his views of him.

'His strength lies rather in his magnetic and stimulating personality than in high technical ability,' Monash wrote.[13] This was code – a diplomatic way of saying that Godley was of the old military school. He was not innovative and lacked the skills needed to run a division in a modern war.

Godley, who rarely wasted his charm on people other than his superiors, had a convivial dinner with Monash and let slip a fraction of his background. He had been to Sandhurst and had come from a socially well-connected middle-upper class family. After serving in the Boer War, Godley had taken up a post in New Zealand in 1910 to run the army there and introduce compulsory military training. This demonstrated to Monash that Godley was not a man of means or inherited wealth. Unlike many of his fellow officers, he had to work to keep up with their expensive tastes, and he was not thrilled by such an imposition on an otherwise privileged existence. After four years, he was pleased that he could get out of New Zealand and into the eye of the British High Command again.

Monash might have expected such an important officer to be educated other than at soldiering, or he might have hoped for another Hamilton to converse with and be inspired by. Godley mentioned Trumper, Hobbs and the fact that he knew W. G. Grace. He loved shooting, fishing and riding to the hounds. The two men made a connection over the Melbourne Cup, which Godley was quick to tell him he had seen from the Victorian Governor's box. But Monash remained mute over polo, social connections and perpetual name-dropping on a scale the Australian couldn't match even if he cared to. He walked away from those early meetings feeling let down. The two men knew without saying so that they could never be close. Monash would never have great respect for Godley, but he would support him and do nothing to undermine him. This was all that counted to Godley. He viewed Monash as 'a very energetic and capable commander, and [I] believe that he will do well in the field. He is always very ready to act upon all suggestions and orders . . . an excellent officer.'[14]

Reading between the lines, Godley would be happy with him as long as Monash did what he was told and never, ever upstaged him. This was emphasised at an early review of a big divisional manoeuvre. The brigade's artillery commander asked Godley why he had put the right-hand battery so far to the east. It had thrown Monash's whole brigade 1000 metres further to the east than intended. Godley replied 'with a most charming smile' that it was the best position from which to shoot. That smile evaporated as he added that he wanted his orders to be carried out 'even if you think it is impossible'.

His comments about the 4th Brigade's effort in the mock battle was, as Monash was learning fast, pure Godley: '. . . they fell into place, and did what they were ordered to do with a punctuality, precision, steadiness and thoroughness, which make further comment unnecessary.'[15]

Monash was satisfied. He was further at ease with his circumstances when compared to his counterparts in Bridges' contingent. Its battalion commanders were bitching about the administration staff in a way that Monash believed his leaders would 'never dream of doing'. He found his good friend McCay agitated.[16] It made Monash think he was lucky to be in Godley's division.

In the long run, the relationship with Godley might not mean as much as his connection with the man who would run the two antipodean contingents, known collectively as the Australian and New Zealand Army Corps – Anzac. This was Lieutenant General Sir William Birdwood, with whom Monash dined in Cairo.

Monash wrote privately of his first impressions. Where Godley was well named at least for his looks, height and image, Birdwood ('Birdie' to the troops) too seemed aptly named: 'A small, thin man, nothing striking or soldierly about him.' He even spoke with a stammer and was 'nervy' and 'unquiet'. That was the outward appearance, but Monash was a better judge of character than that. He added: 'There is no mistaking his perfectly wonderful grasp of the whole business of soldiering.'[17]

On 2 February Monash wrote more to Vic about Birdwood, saying he was 'a fine, dapper little chap, with whom I am sure I shall get on very well . . . the weather is quite cold today, but yesterday there was a violent sandstorm and it was very uncomfortable. No chance of moving here for a month at the very least.' In a passing reference to the nearby Turks, Monash added: 'The Canal Campaign seems to have fizzled out for the present.'[16]

Not quite. The next night at 3 a.m. Djemal, von Kressenstein and their fatigued Turkish force, which had endured the heart of the sandstorm, launched their pontoons from the Suez Canal's east bank south of Tussum. The British forces had spotted their long march and were waiting for them. A garrison on the west bank opened fire and destroyed all but three pontoons. The soldiers on them made it to the bank but were rounded up. A second Turkish assault was made at dawn with a similar result.

This spectacular miscalculation saw Djemal and von Kressenstein withdraw their force at noon pursued by just two companies of Gurkhas for a short distance. The fiasco cost the Turks 2000 men. More than 700 were captured. The easy victory made everyone, from company commanders upwards, believe that the Turks would be a pushover.

The Anzacs took notice of the battle, but soon resumed their preparation for joining the war in Europe. In the first weeks, Monash watched and learned from the way Birdwood handled his men. Birdwood too observed Monash in a letter to Australia's Governor-General: 'An exceptionally able man on paper, observant – and with knowledge but I am doubtful about his being able to apply his knowledge in the field, partly because he does not seem to possess enough physical activity on horse back.'[17]

Birdwood's 'able man on paper' comment was pertinent. Both were forty-nine, but had vastly different backgrounds and approaches to war. Birdwood was another Sandhurst-educated cavalry officer who had been on Kitchener's staff in the South African War. He didn't much like staff work. Planning, strategy and the new methods of warfare were not his strengths. He believed in moving among the men on any line, especially the front. He preferred the stimulation of being where the action was, and preferably on horseback.

As Monash observed in Egypt: '. . . I have been around him for hours and heard him talking to privates, buglers, drivers, gunners, colonels, signallers and generals and every time he has left the man with a better knowledge of his business than he had before. He appeals to me most thoroughly.'[18]

'Birdie' was uncomfortable about making concessions to the new ways, in spite of the long-range rifles and powerful artillery that could destroy targets such as men on horseback at up to twenty kilometres. He found it difficult to acknowledge that the real action in this war took place at the big guns where artillery men would pore over trigonometric tables to calculate a hit correctly at long distances from their targets. Monash's attitude embraced the new methods. He saw the job of command as being centred on planning, strategy and tactics. You stayed at a central point directing orders to meet the dynamics of modern war.

But Monash got the hint from Birdwood in Egypt. He left the car to please his Anzac commander and jumped on his favourite horse, the 'gentle, well-mannered and strong' Tom. '[He] . . . answers to the slightest hint,' Monash wrote affectionately, 'both as to pace and direction.' Yet Monash, who was atop Tom sometimes ten hours on end, was still conscious of his need to think and plan. '[Tom] stands perfectly still when told,' he said, 'still enough for me to write orders in the saddle.'[19]

More worrying concerns about Monash than his apparent disinclination for equestrian displays flitted in and out of Birdwood's mind. 'Lord Kitchener recently sent me a certain amount of nasty correspondence about him from Australia with reference to his alleged German proclivities,' he informed the Governor-General. 'But I told him [Kitchener] I am not prepared to take any action in the matter which I understand was fully enquired into in Australia.'[20]

Monash was unaware he was still fighting the McInerney clique. But by mid-February his integrity and skill were becoming evident. Birdwood and Godley were beginning to appreciate him and compare him favourably to the troubled 1st Division under Bridges, whose lack of experience in leading troops was also emerging. Godley told Monash: 'General Birdwood and I have been closely watching the work of your Brigade for the past ten days [7–17 February], and we have quite made up our minds that yours is the best Australian Brigade in Egypt.'[23] Monash was informed that he could abandon elementary training and precede to advanced operations, such as a night manoeuvre in the desert near Suez, which involved Godley's complete division.

This caused some tensions in the less efficient 1st Division. It had been in Egypt two months longer but had yet to be considered ready for a full division workout. On top of this embarrassment, some of Bridges' men had seen enough of the pyramids and the other sights in their recreational time and were frequenting Cairo whore-houses. Venereal disease was a growing problem. Bridges was looking at all the black marks that could see men sent home. Contracting venereal disease was one. Major J. G. Gellibrand – a Sandhurst graduate and Tasmanian orchardist, who had served in the British Army – thought being foreign-born should be another. Bridges disagreed. He showed Gellibrand the letters about Monash, which Birdwood had given him, and remarked pointedly: 'Then charge Monash as an alien Jew with suspicion and his wife with open disloyalty. Would you recommend his discharge?'

'Yes,' Gellibrand replied feebly, 'if his men distrust him he should go.'[22]

Even if Bridges, feeling the competitive pressure, had been stupid enough to attempt sending Monash home, it would have not happened. First, Monash was born in Australia. Second, much to Bridges' chagrin, he had no jurisdiction over 4th Brigade. It and Monash were answerable to the Military Board.

Monash's quick, positive impression even saw *Sydney Morning Herald* reporter Charles Bean take some notice of 4th Brigade for the first time. He was Australia's official war correspondent, having narrowly beaten Keith Murdoch to the honour in a vote by the Australian Journalists' Association. Bean, aged thirty-five, had attached himself to Bridges' division even before it left Australia. He had developed friendships with men of his own generation including Gellibrand, Bridges' staff officer, Major Thomas Blamey, a thirty-one-year-old schoolteacher, and particularly Cyril White, with whom he seemed infatuated. White's battler-made-good image appealed to Bean, who saw him as 'the ideal staff officer'.

White was either a good listener or he had his eye to his place in history, or even useful publicity that would help in any promotion. He clearly paid a lot of attention to whatever wisdom Bean was dispensing in their chats in Australia, on board the convoy to the Middle East and in Egypt. 'He never forgets anything,' Bean gushed. 'He is the only man I know to whom there is never any necessity to mention anything twice.'[23]

Lanky, redheaded and bow-legged Bean had been born in Australia, but spent most of his first twenty-five years in England, where he graduated in classics and law at Oxford. He returned to Australia in 1904, became bored with the law and decided in 1908 to become a journalist with the *Sydney Morning Herald*. One of his early assignments was a series of articles on the wool industry of western New South Wales. There he focused on rugged, muscular types: shearers, farmhands, stockmen and pastoralists. He considered that they represented the quintessential Aussie male, whom he idealised as the rock of the fledgling nation. He was following them now into war, which again was part of his conscious search for the 'true' Australian character. He was looking forward to reporting deeds of dash and derring-do in the true British tradition of how wars had been won in the past, with cavalry charges and fixed bayonets.

Bean made the trip to Godley's second contingent to see Monash and McGlinn for the first time. There was a polite meeting, but not much rapport beyond the niceties. Bean in his report on the meeting didn't even check the spelling of McGlinn's name, calling him 'McGlynn'. Perhaps these two Australians didn't quite fit the war historian's image of fighting Anglo-Celtic commanders (despite McGlinn fitting at least Bean's ethnic standards) as much as those in Bridges' division.[24]

Yet if he had studied Monash as he had White, he would have found a character closer to his ideal:

> The bush sets the standards of personal efficiency even in the Australian cities [Bean wrote in his official history of the war]. The bushman is the hero of the Australian boy; the arts of the bush are his ambition; his most cherished holidays are those spent with country relatives or in camping out. He learns something of half the arts of the soldier by the time he is ten years old – to sleep comfortably in any shelter, to cook meat or bake flour, to catch a horse, to find his way across country by day or by night, to ride, or, at the worst, to 'stick on' . . .[25]

Monash, more than any other officer, had this 'city boy-loves-the-bush' background but not just in his youth. Despite moving to luxurious circumstances in his forties, he was still a frequent bush operator through his bridge-building, work with the militia, bushwalking and mountain-climbing vacations in remote areas. Maybe that paunch of recent good living had fooled the journalist into believing the brigade commander was 'soft' and purely a city slicker. Yet the bush 'smarts' would never leave Monash.

That night in Heliopolis with him and McGlinn was not destined to bring deeper mutual appreciation. Bean threw up after dining with them.

Churchill's proposal of early January came to part-fruition on 19 February 1915 when the British Fleet used powerful fifteen-inch guns to bombard the outer forts of Kum Kale and Sedd-el-Bahr on the tip of the Gallipoli Peninsula. A German naval officer was killed. The fleet repeated this attack on 25 February. Parties of marines landed and went about destroying what was left of the guns at the forts. There wasn't a Turk in sight. But a few resisters, even a battalion of them, would not have been the main concern. The Turks had mined the entrance to the Dardanelles. No matter how much Churchill pushed the fleet's officers, there was no way around mines. They had to be swept up, but even that was fraught with dangers. The fixed guns of the outer forts had been accounted for. But the hidden mobile guns of the intermediate defences had not. Unprotected minesweepers were under fire and had to contend with a difficult current. A vicious circle developed and caused a stalemate. Those deadly mines remained.

Churchill and Kitchener became impatient. If the fleet couldn't force its way through, there had to be a Plan B. That would include a land invasion and therefore infantry.

On 12 March Ian Hamilton was summoned to Kitchener's office and told: 'We are sending a military force to support the fleet now in the Dardanelles, and you are to have command.'[28]

Hamilton was not completely taken aback. Churchill had told him he would be recommending him to Kitchener for the job. Hamilton's force was to include the British regular army's 29th Division, the two divisions of Australian and New Zealand troops stationed in Egypt, the Royal Naval Division and a French contingent. It was a force of about 75,000 men, which was bigger than anything Hamilton had been in charge of before. Kitchener made the enterprise of conquering Turkey sound as if it were a formality.

Hamilton was both honoured and concerned. He had no knowledge of the Dardanelles or the strength of the Turks. There wasn't much point in asking Kitchener. He wouldn't know any more than Hamilton. His old boss handed him two small travel guidebooks for Turkey and a textbook on the Turkish Army. They were useless. There was hardly any reference to the Gallipoli Peninsula. Its ugly ridges and valleys were rugged and barely habitable. It was populated by just a few villages of shepherds and fishermen. No tourist would bother travelling the 300 kilometres from Constantinople. No one had bothered to survey the area.

The great expedition would have to go ahead without maps. Churchill's brainstorming, superficial proposal of 2 January about smashing the Turks and handing Constantinople to Tsar Nicholas and the Russians had become an official directive from the Minister for War.

On 23 March the order became urgent as the allied British and French fleet at the mouth of the Dardanelles was routed. Seven hundred sailors were killed and nine ships disabled, including three battleships sunk. Hamilton was now more aware of the task he had so perfunctorily been given. His force would have to control the Gallipoli Peninsula before any fleet could reach that narrow strait and sail on to Constantinople. This was the only way around the vicious circle of mines, battery attacks and sunken ships at the mouth of the Dardanelles.

The peninsula would be armed with howitzers and batteries along two coastlines. One faced the Aegean Sea and one faced the straits. Hamilton would have to devise a sophisticated coordinated attack on the peninsula. He began to wonder whether he had enough men to achieve a victory. Kitchener had a begrudging attitude to the whole exercise. It had seemed like a wonderful idea to distract the Turks and win a victory while things looked grim on the Western Front – a nice morale booster for the Allies. But when he actually ordered the operation to go ahead, he was going to be mean with men, weapons, equipment and supplies. They had priority on the Western Front, not a sideshow in the Aegean.

Although the War Council had kept the operation secret, its lack of planning killed any element of surprise.

The Turks had their spies everywhere. They had seen the shipping jamming the Suez Canal, the build-up of military camps outside Cairo and the activity in the Aegean. They were aware that the attempts by the

British Fleet to sail the Dardanelles were not for the annual regatta in the Marmara Sea. Enver Pasha, recovered from his chastening experience in southern Russia, faced his inability to fulfil his Napoleonic complexes. It was one thing being a leader with ambitions. It was another to face a huge, disciplined and armed imperial invader. He needed to bow to the experience of another equally powerful imperial force opposed to the invader. The Turks had no love for the Germans and vice versa. But they had mutual needs now.

The Turks were a chess piece in a big game plan. They were begrudgingly prepared to be that Knight, if it meant survival. Enver swallowed his pride and asked the new, recently arrived head of the German Military Mission, Otto Liman von Sanders, to organise the defence of the Dardanelles. After that disaster in southern Russia and the bungled attempt to invade Egypt, the triumvirate of terrorists was more interested in defence than invasions and attacks, for the time being.

Von Sanders was no great strategist, but he was efficient and thorough. He moved into the former French consul's home in the Gallipoli township on the east coast and set about garrisoning the peninsula by digging, wiring and preparing gun emplacements above the most likely landing points. This experienced German military technician intended to build the troop numbers there to 60,000, with access to another 60,000 stationed nearby. Most of them would be in six divisions set up within a few kilometres of the most obvious and accessible point on the coastlines. Flexibility would be the von Sanders hallmark. The peninsula's size (varying from about three kilometres wide in the south to about eighteen kilometres in the north, and about sixty-one kilometres long) meant that divisions placed up the central part of the peninsula's spine could be moved with reasonable speed. Von Sanders had 'security detachments' and lookouts scattered all round the peninsula. They would alert the divisions that would move to the key trouble spots in force.

The German had no idea when the invasion would take place. But after the attempted forcing of the Dardanelles on 23 March, every hour's preparation counted.

By 23 March Monash and the Anzac divisions were becoming fidgety. Their war training was finished, and they were waiting for orders to

move. Like everyone from the generals down, he was looking for clues on what was happening. He was about as informed as the Turkish triumvirate and their German advisers. But one clue that the enemy didn't have occurred on 29 March, when Hamilton arrived at Heliopolis and reviewed the troops.

> When I rode alongside of Ian Hamilton yesterday during the March Past [Monash wrote to Vic], he cocked his head on one side in the funny little way he has and said: 'Well, Monash, when we sat under the gum tree twelve months ago [at Lilydale], we didn't think, either of us, we should meet again so soon.' What a tremendous responsibility that man must have on his shoulders, as it looks as if he is going to command the operation of the Allies at this end of the show.[27]

Still the divisions waited and filled in their time, sometimes usefully, sometimes not. Monash seemed to be a multi-denominational magnet. He was surprised to receive a deputation of Jews headed by the Grand Rabbi of Cairo, who asked him to gather Jewish officers for the Purim service. On St Patrick's Day, McGlinn and all the Catholics in his brigade took him to a Greek church service at Heliopolis. On a Sunday, the Anglicans asked him to attend a service.

Monash began visiting museums and had a weekend trip among the ancient, 200-metre deep tombs of Luxor. 'By far the most wonderful and impressive sight I have seen anywhere,' Monash wrote. He marvelled at the beautifully preserved galleries, chambers, hieroglyphics, sarcophagus, and 'in it the absolutely perfect mummy of Amenhotep II, the great Pharaoh of Joseph's time . . . undisturbed over 4000 years, with all his history and that of his time carved in the stone all around.' As one writer observed, 'one can be pretty certain that the engineer in him was busy with calculations of strains and stresses, quantities and labour costs'.[28]

Monash kept up his correspondence, especially with Vic, who was forming a branch of the Purple Cross Service for wounded horses and working for Belgian Flag Day. She had struck up an acquaintance with the federal Attorney-General, W. M. (Billy) Hughes, and his wife while on a vacation at Clifton Springs, north of Melbourne. Vic thought that Hughes was 'a dear'. It was a such a pity he was hard of hearing, she said. Hughes gave Bertha a copy of his book, *Case for Labor*!

Earlier on in his stay in Egypt Monash had been homesick on paper, but that had been replaced by the anticipation of what was ahead. Yet a little sentimentality was still evident in his mood. He asked Vic and Bertha (who was working as a nursing aide through the war) for miniature photographs of them in a locket that would serve as an identity disc.

Not all the troops handled the frustrating waiting-time so well. There were drunkenness, subordination, desertion and attacks on locals, mainly perpetrated by members of the troubled 1st Division. Bridges sent the 300 worst cases home, which was the ultimate humiliation for most.

On Good Friday, a dozen drunken Australians and New Zealanders tore up a whorehouse in the Haret el Wasser, the notorious Cairo street of brothels. Then they torched it. They had been angered over weeks by the price of the prostitutes and the adulterated beer, not to mention the venereal diseases that some of them and their mates had picked up. There had also been robberies of wallets, watches and jewellery. The disturbance caused about 2000 troops to congregate near the burning brothel. Several similar houses were then set alight.

Military police arrived but were chased off. The Lancashire Territorials were called. They had trouble quelling the rioters. Their commander ordered them to fix bayonets and advance on the crowd. The troops thought better of taking on the 'chooms' and dispersed. The main offenders were arrested.

The Australians called the incident the First Battle of Wozzer (Wasser). Monash, because of his legal training and experience in court cases, was called to act on a court of inquiry early in April. He disliked the task, not the least reason being that he would be standing in judgement on many in Bridges' division. Fifty witnesses, including some Syrian women, were examined. The court 'judges' inspected the partly destroyed street of brothels. Prostitutes hurled abuse, which wasn't surprising. The Australians had been big spenders at the rat-infested houses of ill repute. Now many of the prostitutes were left with nothing other than their reputations, a few thousand fewer soldiers to rip off and no place to ply their trade.

The court sat for several days and produced an inconclusive report. No ringleaders were sent home.

Monash and his fellow officers were hoping more than ever for the directive to go to war.

The order came on 10 April. Monash's brigade left their Heliopolis camp and bonfires to destroy rubbish the next night amid scenes of 'indescribable enthusiasm'. The brigade then took the train to Alexandria and on 13 April was on a ship headed for the Greek island of Lemnos in the Aegean, where a combined British–French armada was assembling. Monash was able to tell his officers and troops that the mission was 'a forced landing on the Gallipoli Peninsula and an invasion of Turkish territory'. He didn't know when the attack would take place, but he knew Hamilton's grand scheme for the 'Mediterranean Expeditionary Force'.

Either Monash was erring on the side of caution or he was showing exceptional perspicacity when he addressed his assembled troops: 'You may be faced with privation and hardship, sometimes hunger, often tired and miserable. That is what soldiering amounts to . . . I call on you with confidence to do your level best for the sake of your manhood, for the sake of Australia and for the sake of the British Empire.'[29]

The commander had studied his charges. He knew it would have been futile to mention just the British Empire. His men wanted to forge a reputation in battle as Australians. But he appealed first to their manhood – to show courage. If most of them responded, as he expected they would under any circumstances, then at the very least his command would acquit itself well.

On 14 April Monash mused on the news that the Ottoman Empire was the target, not Germany. This had ramifications beyond taking Constantinople. 'One probable result of the war,' he wrote, 'will be freeing of Jerusalem and Palestine from the Turkish yoke.' By 21 April he knew dates and enough details to write his first operational order, 'without a tremor and with as little excitement as if it were merely all pretence like our peace manoeuvres'.[30]

The Anzac Corps would make a landing on a wide, 1800-metre beach on the west coast of the peninsula, just north of Gaba Tepe ('Rough Hill') before dawn on 25 April. Reconnaissance from the sea determined that the best place to land was opposite gentle hills and valleys. It seemed suitable for a successful assault and thrust inland. Godley's division would begin landing later in the day a little further north. The New Zealand Brigade would hit the beach first in the afternoon, followed by Monash's 4th Brigade.

Simultaneously, a British division (the 29th) would make a forced landing on five beaches at Cape Helles at the peninsula's southern tip. The

French would land on the Asiatic side of the Dardanelles. The British Marine Division and Naval Brigade would land just inside the straits, on the European side. At the same time, the plan was for the British fleet to enter the straits led by a squadron of trawlers to sweep up the mines. Once the narrow waters were cleared, the fleet would head for Constantinople. If the fleet couldn't get through, the Anzac and British divisions were meant to 'dispose of all the Turkish Army' south of Gaba Tepe. They would then sweep across the southern half of the peninsula and storm the forts that were giving the fleet such a tough time.

'The whole operation is the greatest feat of arms ever attempted,' Monash wrote to Vic on 23 April, 'even putting in the shade Port Arthur.' He thought it was 'a tremendous compliment to Australia to choose us to carry out so important a share in the enterprise'.[31]

This was the sort of upbeat, profound tone he was expected to express. Yet had he been in Birdwood's position as Corps Commander, he would have wanted the answers to a thousand questions. They would have started with queries about the strength of the enemy and how much fortifying von Sanders had been able to do in the last few weeks. Monash would wish to know about the terrain they would be in. He hated being without detailed maps. But he was still a humble brigade commander, who was expected to follow orders, not to query them. Besides, he had faith in Ian Hamilton. His engaging manner and romantic sense of history captivated his officers. They were reminded that the Narrows, twenty kilometres from the mouth of the Dardanelles, was where Xerxes, the Persian king, had built a bridge of boats for 360,000 of his army. This was to cross from Asia (where the French in Hamilton's campaign were supposed to be coming from in far more modest numbers) to Europe in 480 BC. Xerxes was en route to conquer the Greeks. Alexander the Great crossed from the European side on his way to conquer Asia Minor in the winter of 334–333 BC.

Yet there was no mention of the more pertinent history concerning similar amphibious landings the British Army had made. One was in 1762 during the Seven Years War against the Spanish when the fleet had landed at Havana, Cuba, and had taken the city after a bloody battle. The other was in late 1814 at New Orleans, which the British invaded from the Gulf of Mexico. The army was slow in its planning to take the city. This gave the US's General Andrew Jackson a chance to gather an army of frontiersmen and volunteers to fortify and defend the city. The Americans were victorious on 8 January 1815.

Hamilton would have known of these failures. But at this point he would not be dwelling on them. He would want to appear confident.

Monash kept his penultimate letter to Vic breezy as he noted: 'It is astonishing how light-hearted everybody is, whistling, singing and cracking jokes, and indulging in all sorts of horse-play and fun. Yesterday we bought four donkeys (for £9) to carry our spare kit and spare food, and these have caused no end of fun, both bringing them on board and on deck.' Less 'fun' was Godley's mood. He was 'irritable and cross' while holding a conference to discuss the kit that the soldiers would carry and the landing plans. Monash had become disillusioned with his commander.[32]

On the same day, letters arrived from Vic and Bertha. He wrote farewell replies to them, saying with some feeling that he hoped he had been a good husband and father, and how much he loved them. He acknowledged the possibility that he would die and said that his main regret was the grief it would bring them.

Monash was remarkably calm. At nearly fifty, he had lived a full and active life. Rationalising his situation, he suggested that he had 'only a few years of vigour left. Then would come decay and the chill of old age and perhaps lingering illness.'[33] The reality that he wasn't about to embark on the kind of peace manoeuvre he had been doing for thirty years was sinking in.

✕

On 25 April at 9.30 a.m. the 4th Brigade sailed for Gallipoli in sunny weather, aware that hours earlier Bridges' 1st Division had hit the beaches, but unaware of its fate. About noon, they heard the muffled coughs of big naval guns, although they still could not see land.

Monash, on the deck, was still writing. It would be his last letter before engagement. He had the 'keenest expectation, the thought of the world stirring drama in which we are taking part overshadowing every other feeling'.[34]

He was ready. In the afternoon he managed to scribble in his diary: 'At 2 p.m. we passed the entrance to the Dardanelles, and witnessed the furious bombardment of Achi Baba [by the British Fleet at the mouth to the straits], and the enemy's shelling the beach at Cape Helles [where the British 29th Division had landed].' These two observations were in line with Monash's expectations.

At about 4 p.m. his boat came opposite Gaba Tepe and Anzac Cove, just north of it. '[We] commenced to hear musketry and saw enemy shrapnel on the ridges.'[35] Monash's first experience of war had begun.

THIRTY DAYS
IN HELL

Action greeted Monash that sunny Sunday afternoon of 25 April 1915. He could see it on the beach, in those brutal, jagged cliffs and in the air above them now stiff with shrapnel. It was in the crackle of communication between commanders. He had tried to make some sense of events on shore from garbled messages from Godley and disjointed responses from some of the wounded.

The landing began the day the way it ended – in confusion. The English had named the intended point 'Brighton Beach'. It was attractive, and the slope up into those uninviting hills and ridges was manageable. The first small boats drifted, for a reason never established, nearly two kilometres further north. That brought the 1st Division's 3rd Brigade – the first soldiers to hit the beach – in front of a scrubby-faced cliff.

The Turks believed (and still do, to this day) that the landing point was intentional. It avoided the exposed areas and allowed the force to land unhindered as about fifty soldiers, under sporadic fire from a limited defence force, scrambled up the cliff to the top of a ridge. Contrary to myth, no one was killed on the beach itself. The Turks, on another ridge looking down on them, were running away. No one had expected the invasion to take place where it did. In that limited respect, the initial moment of invasion, when the Anzac legend was born, was successful.

The Australians pushed on up the steep terrain towards the high ground for several hours until they were close to the crest of Chunuk Bair (Hill). Beyond it was the higher ground. The Turks were in retreat. The Australians halted their advance on the western slopes of the hill. In that

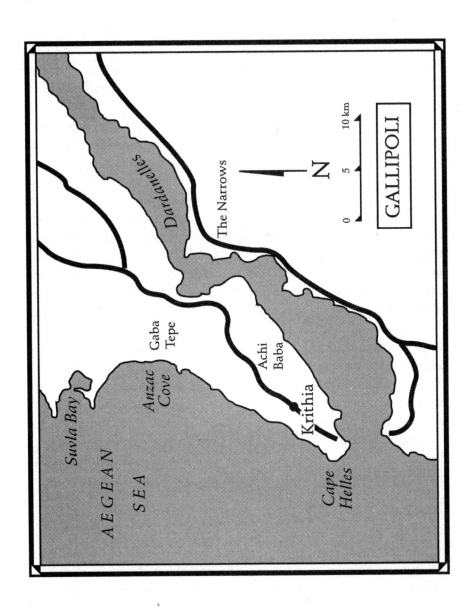

vital lull, the Turks regrouped and counter-attacked. Lieutenant Mustafa Kemal, the commander of one of the six Turkish divisions on the peninsula, had led the counter-offensive, ordering regiments not to run but to stand and fight, then rush the Anzacs. Acting on the instinct of a natural battle leader, Kemal took a great risk in the first place by sending his men to the high ground and not to the beach landing area. He had not been able to reach his German commander and had made decisions that, if wrong, would have seen him shot by a firing squad. Kemal's instincts proved right.

The slopes of Chunuk Bair saw the first battle of the invasion. Australians from 1st Division poured into the area in support of the men under assault.

In the late morning, the New Zealand Brigade of Second Division had landed under fire from Turkish artillery placed above Gaba Tepe, south of the 1000-metre-long invasion beach now known as Anzac Cove. There was no question about the intentions of the Turkish artillery and small defence. There might have been only about 200 of them, but they were prepared to scrap to the last man to defend against the invaders until Kemal could organise a major counter-attack. He realised – and soon the triumvirate running the Ottoman Empire would know – that it could be the last stand.

The pandemonium in the hills and on the beach added to the confusion from the Anzac commanders, who were sending mixed signals to Monash on his ship – *Seeangchoon* – and eager to come ashore. Godley and Bridges wanted to evacuate their divisions. They had taken heavy losses and reckoned it was hopeless to reach the set objectives of sweeping across the peninsula's spine. The steep rugged terrain put the Anzacs at a huge disadvantage to the Turks, who were now concentrating on the high ground and picking the invaders off with rifles, machine-guns, artillery fire and grenades.

Hamilton, who would make the final decision on whether to go on or withdraw, had had the toughest day of his life. He had established himself and his HQ in the conning tower of the battleship *Queen Elizabeth*, where he hoped for a good view of the two battles he had directed. He ordered General Hunter-Weston, in charge of the British 29th Division's invasion at the tip of the peninsula, and Birdwood off Anzac Cove, to remain in their ships. It was the best way, he thought, to remain in radio communication with them. But this failed. The navy needed the radio for its own use. If Hamilton were sitting on it, there would be no way that accurate, safe artillery support could be given to the soldiers on the shore. Hamilton couldn't hear himself speak when he was allowed brief interludes at the radio. He could only learn piecemeal how bogged down the two forces were at different points on the peninsula. His task of coordinating two separate attacks using the army and the navy was ambitious. Hamilton realised too late why amphibious invasions, even on much lesser scales, had been few and far between. Many of the 29th Division had been cut down by machine-gun. The Anzacs had been stopped in their aimless tracks. The pathetic reconnaissance done from sea had misrepresented the battleground with its hidden ravines, dead-end escarpments and treacherous ridges.

It might have flashed across the engaging Hamilton's mind that he would have been more suited to an ivory tower teaching poetry and history rather than a battleship conning tower controlling two major war engagements.

Reinforcements were needed for the Anzacs. Godley was uncertain about whether to use fresh men for relief or to push harder for a withdrawal. While he dithered, Monash managed to get part of his 15th Battalion and all of his 16th ashore. But the rest of 4th Brigade had to sit tight as yet another small convoy of wounded were brought on board the *Seeangchoon*. At this moment the activity on Monash's ship was at its height as one side of the ship hoisted the wounded on board while boats were lowered from the other.

After several hours delay and indecision, Birdwood came ashore after 9 p.m. and consulted Godley and Bridges. Then he sat down and scribbled a request to evacuate the Anzacs. It too reflected uncertainty: 'Both my divisional generals and brigadiers have represented to me that they fear their men are thoroughly demoralised by shrapnel fire to which they had been subjected all day after exhaustion and gallant work in morning. Numbers have dribbled back from the firing line and cannot be collected in this difficult country. Even New Zealand Brigade which only recently engaged lost heavily and is to some extent demoralised.'

This was not accurate. Monash had not been consulted. He had been ordered by Godley to remain on his ship. He was getting around the directive by pushing his brigade out to the shore piecemeal. He wanted to continue. More pertinent was the attitude of the leader of the New

Zealand Brigade, General Harold Walker (commanding in the place of the ill Colonel Francis Johnston). He didn't want to evacuate, full stop.

Birdwood's disjointed missive to Hamilton continued: 'If troops are subjected to shell fire again tomorrow morning there is likely to be fiasco [*sic*] as I have no fresh troops with which to replace those in the firing line.' Birdwood rounded off, saying: 'I know my representation is most serious but if we are to re-embark it must be done at once.'[1] Birdwood was fence-sitting with his hints that he was opposed to evacuation while all his key officers were for it. But the mere fact that he was putting the withdrawal plea to Hamilton meant he had his doubts.

The English journalist Ellis Ashmead-Bartlett, a friend of Hamilton with whom he had covered the Russo-Japanese War, took the note to the expedition leader at about 10.30 p.m. Hamilton spoke with his staff, none of whom had been ashore. They weren't helpful. He then called a meeting with the admirals who would have to organise the proposed evacuation. While they were all in conference at about 11 p.m., a destroyer came alongside Monash's ship and yelled orders to 'lower all boats' ready for sending ashore in case 'the Admiral decided to re-embark the whole force'.[2] At 11.30 p.m., Hamilton, his staff and the admirals worked their way to the decisive point. Evacuation from Anzac Cove would take three days. The Turks were already surrounding the troops and firing down on them. If they sniffed an evacuation it might induce a massacre.

Weighing more heavily on Hamilton than the welfare of his troops was the reaction from his boss Kitchener and his friend Churchill. The Allies would see evacuation as a huge failure. Hamilton's reputation as a commander would be destroyed. Just before midnight, he wrote his response to the ambivalent Birdwood:

> Your news is indeed serious. But there is nothing for it but to dig yourselves in and stick it out . . . Hunter-Weston despite his heavy losses, will be advancing tomorrow which should divert pressure from you. Make a personal appeal to your men and Godley's to make a supreme effort to hold their ground. PS. You have got through the difficult business, now you only have to dig, dig, dig until you are safe.[3]

The view looked better from the *Queen Elizabeth* than it did from in front of the ugly, yellow-scratched cliff faces at Anzac Cove and the bloody beaches of Cape Helles. Hunter-Weston's troops were just as courageous as anyone else. But he was unlikely to relieve the Anzacs. Survival would be the 29th's key mission.

Although some of the Anzac commanders wanted evacuation, and Hamilton was intent on holding ground, Turkish historians with some hindsight felt that the Anzacs should have pushed on, especially on 26 April, when Turkish reinforcements had not yet arrived. The entrenchment directive might not have been the best one.

Monash, unaware of Hamilton's decision, took advantage of his lowered boats and released the rest of his 15th Battalion and his 13th to go ashore. He had to wait on board with his 14th Battalion and HQ staff until the next morning. With crowding on the beach, another thousand men would only add to the problems in the dark.

At 2 a.m. Birdwood received Hamilton's note. Soon afterwards, Monash was informed that there would be no evacuation. He managed to get to his bunk but in 'a dreadful night' had little sleep.

It was the end of 25 April 1915, a harrowing day, which began well and ended in indecision. Hundreds of Australians, New Zealanders and British were wounded. Many were dead. It would not be a memorable day for them.

Monash went ashore at 8.05 a.m. on 26 April with his HQ and 14th Battalion, which came under heavy shelling. They were directed to a bivouac on the beach, which was bound at the northern end by the dominating outcrop called the Sphinx, and crowded with soldiers from the cliff face to the water's edge.

Monash's first aim was to gather his brigade. It was another test for his 'nervous system', so admired by friends. But this examination promised to be far more demanding and prolonged. He had scrappy information about their fate and positions. One strong rumour was that up to 150 soldiers of his 15th Battalion, which had been put ashore after dark, had been cut down while coming ashore.

From where he first stood on the beach at Anzac Cove, his men were scattered from Russell's Top, a craggy point forty-five degrees and 750 metres left, to 400 Plateau, which ran to the right at sixty degrees and was about 600 metres away.

Monash steeled himself to show leadership. He and McGlinn scrambled their way up from the right of the cove at Shrapnel Gully surrounded

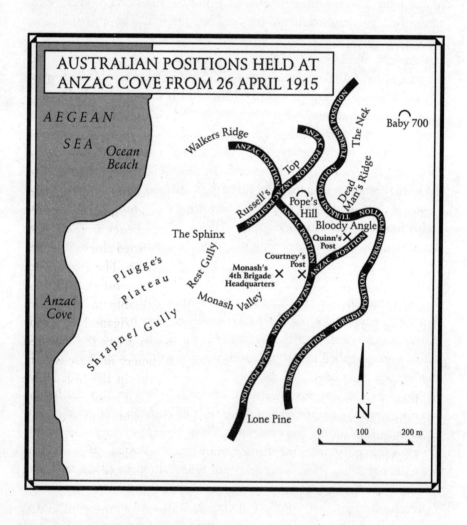

AUSTRALIAN POSITIONS HELD AT
ANZAC COVE FROM 26 APRIL 1915

AEGEAN

SEA

Ocean
Beach

Walkers Ridge

ANZAC POSITION

ANZAC POSITION

ANZAC POSITION

TURKISH POSITION

The Nek

Baby 700

Russell's
Top

Pope's
Hill

Dead
Man's Ridge

TURKISH POSITION

Bloody Angle

The Sphinx

Plugge's

Plateau

Rest Gully

Quinn's
Post ✕

Courtney's
Post

Monash's
4th Brigade
Headquarters ✕

✕

ANZAC POSITION

TURKISH POSITION

Anzac
Cove

Monash Valley

Shrapnel Gully

ANZAC POSITION

TURKISH POSITION

TURKISH POSITION

Lone Pine

N

0   100   200 m

by a 'bodyguard' detail from the 14th Battalion. These two corpulent men were nimble enough in leading the pace as they soon realised why the route was so named. Despite Monash's weight, he had continued bush-walking since his youth and was now pleased he had done so. 'The everlasting tramping about,' he wrote to Bertha, 'mile upon mile, up and down those steep hills – my own Wallaby [bush-walking club] walks have proved an excellent training.'[4] But the remote parts of Tasmania and Western Australia were never subject to a hail of shrapnel. The bullet-filled projectiles burst above them and sent their contents whistling and zinging in every direction. One spent pellet clattered into him. He picked it up and pocketed the souvenir, which was intended for the long hallway of memorabilia at Iona.

Monash led his men into an 800-metre narrow cleft (to be known from that point as Monash Valley), its high walls baked yellow and free of vegetation. The debris of war, including dead mules with their packs scattered, marked the passage. Coming the other way was another chilling reminder that the enemy was pressing and oppressive. A steady trickle of the wounded was being stretchered or led back to the beach. Quick conversations with Ambulance Corps established clues to the hot spots and where members of his brigade might be. The path taken through thick scrub curved round the hills to the most exposed and treacherous part of the valley, which was vulnerable to snipers in vantage points. Monash chose a place for his 4th Brigade HQ to the right of the valley no more than twenty metres from the elevated Courtney's Post. Monash had to weigh up the danger in the position, which was semi-exposed, depending on how close in the hills above Turkish marksmen could reach. Sandbags and the dugout, which ate into the valley wall a fraction, would provide protection, if the HQ staff were ultra-cautious.

To Monash's left as he faced inland were the New Zealanders at Walker's Ridge and to the north of Russell's Top. To his right were brigades run by MacLaurin and McCay of Bridges' 1st Division.

The main aim was to 'dig, dig, dig', as Hamilton had instructed, and to defend. The Turks commanded the high ground. The Anzacs were stuck in a labyrinth of gullies and ravines within a half-circle from Anzac Cove with a radius of roughly 750 metres covering 400 acres. The Turks were breath-takingly close, sometimes in trenches just fifteen metres from their invading foe. The Anzacs wouldn't be able to break out without massive

losses and reinforcements to replace the casualties and relieve the beleaguered soldiers. Nor could the 29th help out as Hamilton had hoped.

On day two at Gallipoli, Monash was struggling to get his bearings.
The whole Hamilton venture seemed uncertain. The moment to attack,
attack, attack rather than dig, dig, dig had been lost.

Along with the indiscriminate danger from shrapnel, there was a constant
threat from snipers. They occupied the high ground at deadly positions
such as Baby 700, the Chessboard (a network of trenches in front of
Pope's), the Nek, the Bloody Angle and the most treacherous of all, the
aptly named Dead Man's Ridge. Marksmen from there had already struck
down a score of Anzacs. Other snipers could slip behind the lines and pick
off targets. All Turkish sharp-shooters on the high ground could hit, from
in front and behind, defence trenches at the head of Monash Valley known
as Quinn's, Courtney's and Steele's Posts. The better shots could also hit
targets in many spots in the valley itself.

The trenches were positioned at the top of slopes twenty to thirty
metres above the valley. They could only be accessed by climbing ropes.
Ammunition, food and water were hauled up at night.

Another defensive entrenchment at Pope's Hill at the head of Monash
Valley, about 200 metres left of Quinn's, was isolated from it by Dead
Man's Ridge and the Bloody Angle. In the rush of 25 April, the 4th
Brigade's companies from 13th and 15th Battalions had found themselves
at Pope's grimly hanging on and separated.

Monash's early task was to reorganise the defence units while continuing to pull his scattered battalions under his command. His 4th Brigade
had the most vital mission of all the Anzacs. It had to hold the line at the
head of Monash Valley. If it were forced back to the beach there would be
a retreat, a frantic evacuation to the ships and mass slaughter.

By day three, 27 April, Mustafa Kemal's forces had assembled in their thousands. He ordered his men to attack ferociously. It caused a stir on the beach,
where Monash had spent the night at the bivouac. At 8.30 a.m. he took his
14th Battalion, under fire, to the valley and detached two companies for
MacLaurin's sector. Then, under severe sniping, he hurried north with the rest
of the battalion. They climbed up the valley wall to reinforce Quinn's. Two

companies were digging in when a machine-gun fired into them. Two hundred men, including twelve officers, were mowed down in a massacre.

'Among those killed was Captain Hoggart who won my shield at Williamstown two years ago – which you presented to him,' Monash wrote to his wife. 'Among those hit was Gordon Hanby. He was struck through the chest while tying to drag a wounded soldier to safety.'[5]

What Monash didn't tell Vic was that there was some doubt about whether the attack had come from 'friendly fire', that euphemistic oxymoron for slaughtering your own soldiers. Some in the 14th thought the fire had come from close range. Others believed it came from the direction of Courtney's Post about seventy-five metres away, which was being manned by the 4th Brigade's 15th Battalion. Captain B. H. Perry, speaking for the majority of the 14th involved, told Monash that he was adamant the fire had not come from the 15th but from the Turks.

Monash was satisfied after investigating the incident that Perry was correct. The Turkish onslaught from the dawn had caused confusion. It continued through midday and didn't give Monash a moment to dwell on the disaster at Quinn's.

The 27th was shaping as a day that no one in the valley could forget, although they might try to.

No one could rest from snipers. Even the most vigilant could be hit. Simply moving positions in a trench could lead to death. Everyone from Birdwood to the lowliest private was unsafe. Leon Gellert penned a poignant poem, 'The Jester in the Trenches', that touched on the fear of assassination by unseen riflemen in the hills:

> 'That just reminds me of a yarn,' he said;
> And everybody turned to hear his tale.
> He had a thousand yarns inside his head.
> They waited for him, ready with their mirth
> And creeping smiles, – then suddenly turned pale,
> Grew still, and gazed upon the earth.
> They heard no tale. No further word was said.
> And with his untold fun,
> Half leaning on his gun,
> They left him – dead.[6]

At 1 p.m. Monash attended a conference in the valley below Steele's Post with Harold Walker (New Zealand Brigade), Sinclair-MacLagan commanding 3rd Brigade, Colonel MacLaurin commanding 1st Brigade, his brigade major F. D. Irvine and Bridges, to sort out the boundaries between their sectors. Sinclair-MacLagan, exhausted and under stress, handed over his sector to MacLaurin and Irvine, a British regular, who both seemed upbeat and jaunty. Just after Monash left the conference, Irvine scrambled up the slope to Steele's Post to survey the area. He wished to pinpoint where the snipers were most active. Irvine stood up in the trench.

'Get down!' a man near him called, followed by others, almost in chorus.

Irvine ignored him.

'Down, sir – you'll be sniped for certain,' another warned.

'It's my business to be sniped,' Irvine snapped back.[7]

A few seconds later, a Turkish marksman on a southern slope from Russell's Top, which looked into the back of the posts, had more time than usual to steady his aim and fire from about 150 metres. Irvine fell dead, his business finished.

Ten minutes later, MacLaurin stood up on a ridge just south of Steele's Post and in the same line of fire that had struck down Irvine. A sniper on Russell's Top, perhaps the same one, killed him too.

Monash, who had rushed to Steele's Post when he heard of Irvine's demise, was appalled at the stupid waste of leadership. It was one thing to demonstrate indifference to danger. It was another to be killed doing so when it was an unnecessary show of bravado. The attrition rate was bad enough without foolhardy, reckless acts adding to it.

'It [the deaths were] undoubtedly avoidable,' Monash remarked. He was still reeling from the realisation that his own brigade, which began at more than 4000, now amounted to fewer than 2300 men. 'Such unnecessary exposure does no possible good, but seriously impairs morale.'[8]

Yet Monash too was subject to perhaps unavoidable lapses in his carefulness. The day after MacLaurin's death, Monash's HQ was temporarily in the open and exposed. It was being fortified with sandbags when the phone rang. Monash was waiting for a call from Godley. His brigade clerk answered it.

'Colonel Monash,' the clerk called, 'it's for you, sir.'

Monash was crouched ten paces away next to sandbags having a cigarette. He stood up. A split-second later the clerk fell dead, hit by a sniper.

Monash helped a stretcher-bearer gather the clerk's body while a staff sergeant picked up the phone. He too was hit by a sniper and wounded in the arm. As he was taken away, Monash reached for the phone. One of his staff pushed him clear as another bullet hummed into the exposed bunker and pierced a sandbag.[9]

In this incident among many, Monash was not consciously trying to be brave or even set an example. He was simply caught in the moment, intent on doing his job, as were the clerk and sergeant. In the intensity of the work, most men, including Monash, felt that bullets and shrapnel were not meant for them, until they were hit. Even then many returned to the fray if they could or were allowed. Others had their spirits broken, as well as their bodies.

Spirit, in fact, was a commodity in short supply in the first few days, which had seen Murphy's Law – everything that could go wrong, will go wrong – in triplicate. The conditions in this battle zone of just 400 acres might well have been the worst of any encounter in the entire war.

Apart from the ever-present threat of snipers, the noise of shrapnel, bullets and explosions was incessant and preyed on men's nerves. Monash, ensconced in his vulnerable HQ dugout just below Courtney's from the night of 27 April, counted ten seconds as the biggest lull at any time of day or night.[10] He could distinguish the different sounds. The bullet that passed within five metres, such as the one that killed his clerk, purred, 'like a low caressing whistle, long drawn out'. Those that passed high above from a distance cracked like a whip and felt closer than they were. Enemy rifle and machine-gun fire seemed like cracker packets going off overhead even though they were coming from up to 600 metres away. The Anzac rifle fire from where he was sounded like 'a low rumble and growl'. The Turks' shrapnel seemed 'like a gust of wind in a wintry gale and ending in a loud bang, and a cloud of smoke when the shell burst'. But the noisiest of all was the Anzac artillery. The discharge of the guns and the shell burst were 'ear-splitting', with an echo that reverberated for thirty seconds. Many soldiers would be made deaf or partly so by the experience.[11]

Amidst this, the Turks kept pressing. Quinn's Post took the biggest barrage on 28 April. It was the gateway to the triangular valley, the beach and the Anzacs' definite defeat. Replacement troops at Quinn's heard unbelievable horror stories concerning gunfire and fire itself that turned out to be true. It was at times literally too hot in the trenches, especially when the Turks made their intermittent forays, which ended in their repulsion by the use of bayonets. Being sent up to Quinn's was just about the biggest adrenalin-pumping moment for soldiers, especially when Captain Quinn himself would whisper as the first-timers entered the trenches: 'Don't talk too loudly or they'll hear what you say.' Anyone disbelieving this would feel a tingle in the spine when they heard a Turk less than thirty metres away mimic Quinn by screaming: 'Come on, you kangaroo shooting bastards!'[12]

Most of the Turkish forces were locked up holding the Anzacs. Hamilton decided to reinforce his 29th Division with the French, who had been sitting on the southern or Asia Minor side of the Dardanelles, and attack on the southern tip of the peninsula. The move was made on 28 April, but the 'First Battle of Krithia' (named after a deserted village eight kilometres northwest of Cape Helles) was a dismal failure. It left the 29th in disarray and short of the target, Achi Baba. Hamilton now faced the prospect of a costly stalemate or even major defeat on the peninsula, unless the Anzacs could break out.

The next day, 29 April, Monash relieved the pressure on Quinn's to the extent that rushing it became suicidal – not always a deterrent for some of Mustafa Kemal's Muslim forces. Bean, who doled out a little credit here and there for Monash, noted that his defence organisation was 'an object lesson in covering fire'.[13]

Monash managed to have machine-guns placed at Pope's and on Courtney's Post. Their fire overlapped in front of the post. Higher still on the northern part of Russell's Top and close by at Steele's Post, machine-guns protected the front of 4th Brigade and the head of the valley. Its length was being barricaded by sandbags two or three deep. Yet movement along the path was still perilous in several spots.

April 29 and 30 were less brutal at Anzac after the all-out Turkish assault of the previous two days. Monash snatched the moment to have a conference with his commanding officers. It was overdue. He also wanted the chance to boost everyone's confidence. He was in his element now as he began to engineer order out of the previous five days mental disorganisation. His agenda had sixteen headings, including attention to regular alternation in the front line so that each company and group could have a breather on the beach; placement of machine-guns; digging and construction of concealed trenches approaching fortifications (sapping); links between the posts (a tunnel would be built between Quinn's and Courtney's running about seventy-five metres. Consideration would be given to another more ambitious tunnel all the way to Pope's); open encampment areas; keeping the roads clear; sanitation; the monitoring of casualties and the movement of all his men. Even now, one and a half of his four battalions still were not under his control.

'It needed a lot of nerve to keep cool enough,' he said, writing to Vic about this period, 'to reinforce at the critical points, to hold the proper reserves of men at the proper times and in the proper places, to organise the ammunition supply, and the food and the water supply.' Monash was mindful of his own demeanour. Not only did he have to show courage. He also had 'to keep everybody cheerful and hopeful, and to make exhausted men do just that little bit more that turned the scale'.[14]

He had just finished his quick conference when he heard that British marines positioned near Courtney's were being overrun. He despatched soldiers from his 13th Battalion to counter-attack. They held the line. They had to. Meanwhile, Quinn's was hit repeatedly. Messages were rushed to Monash. The men didn't want to retreat. They pleaded for periscopes (being scrambled together on the beach) with which to pinpoint the attacks. They also wanted grenades, even crude imitations.

On 30 April Hamilton was looking for a quick success at Anzac after the flop in the south. He and Birdwood discussed an attack on the high ground, and the order was passed on to the division chiefs, Bridges and Godley. Bridges was ambivalent about such a move, but Godley thought it was a good idea. Brigade leaders were approached. Monash didn't like the plan put to him. He agreed with the concept of taking the high ground, particularly Baby 700, a hill behind the Chessboard, the Nek and Dead Man's Ridge. He had been saying it from the moment he assessed the area on 26 April. But Godley's strategy was sketchy. General Harold Walker, who had taken over the 1st Brigade after MacLaurin's death, was against it, too. He refused the directive. He was a regular, who knew Godley well and how unprepared he was. Walker complained to Bridges,

who deferred to Walker's professionalism and also refused to endorse Godley's plan.

That left the 1st Division out of the scheme and Monash's 4th Brigade and Johnston's New Zealand Brigade in it.

Monash argued with Godley, demanding that one of his staff come up and have a look at the problems faced. He submitted a different plan based on his own reconnaissance of the terrain to be attacked. But Godley and Birdwood, who had not seen or been over the ground themselves, rejected it. Monash told Godley to his face that the plan was weak and could not be sustained with the limited troops available. But Godley wanted to bumble on. Monash's intervention served only to put off the advance by a day.

He was given the final plan at 2.15 p.m. on 2 May and had just five hours to prepare his commanders and their troops. He was most unhappy with what he believed was an overambitious scheme that lacked vital detail. Godley wanted to capture Baby 700, the Turkish positions over-looking Monash Valley and Mortar Ridge behind them. Monash had to obey orders and put aside his misgivings. There was no point in lowering the morale of his brigade by complaining about how poor the preparation was. Monash had to fire them up with serious enthusiasm. It didn't take much. The men were fed up with the hazards of defence. They wanted to go forward.

At nightfall they would be making the first attack across a front from Quinn's to the main target, Baby 700. New Zealand's Otago and Canterbury Battalions, who would be advancing left of Monash's force, would follow them into the fight. A battalion of British marines had been seconded by Godley to push in behind the 4th Brigade's move.

The attack began with the batteries in Anzac Cove aiming artillery fire over the top of Monash Valley and into the region of Dead Man's Ridge and Bloody Angle. Shells fell short and uncomfortably close to Monash's dugout HQ below Courtney's. This meant that the Turks were alerted rather than alarmed. They were ready. They began bombarding the head of the valley as the 4th Brigade's 16th Battalion made its charge. Monash heard the cheers then, to his pride and astonishment, his men singing 'It's a Long Way to Tipperary' and – their favourite since the 2nd Division had left Australia – 'Australia Will be There'.

They dug in 100 metres ahead. But where were the New Zealanders? Johnston had been tardy in getting his men up Monash Valley to a point on a ridge from where they were meant to attack, hitting the Turks from the left. Instead, the Turks began shelling. When the New Zealanders were in position – ninety minutes late – and charging over the crest of the ridge, they were hammered with star shells and machine-gun fire. Half the Otago Battalion was cut down in a bigger massacre than the one experienced by Monash's 14th Battalion five days earlier.

Godley, a leader who planned on the basis of assumptions rather than clear information, expected the Otago soldiers to have reached at least the base of Baby 700. But the several hundred left in action were just holding a position beyond the crest at which they had started. Making the wrong assumption that they had reached their objective, he sent in the Canter-burys to take the Nek. But it was still well held by the Turks, who once more battered their opponents. Godley then ordered the British marines in to support Monash's 16th Battalion. They were hanging on grimly until stray 'friendly fire' from the battery on the beach destroyed a vital eighty metres of the trenches that the 16th had built. Its line broke, and left the marines vulnerable.

Dawn began breaking, making it impossible for the Anzac and supporting marine forces to regroup and attack. The Turks could now see their targets across the fifteen- to fifty-metre divide and could pinpoint the attackers. The medley of sharp cracks heralded the enemy machine-guns. The sound was persistent, signalling that the counter-attack was hitting targets. They were answered by Anzac machine-guns, sounding from Monash's HQ like kettledrums. But they were not nearly as incessant. The Otagos were forced to withdraw, leaving Monash's 13th Battalion, which had come into the battle to the left of the Otagos, clinging on to their position well short of the Nek.

Only three days earlier, Monash had rejoiced inwardly over being able to address the disorder. Now once more he faced his nemesis. It was even worse than that encountered on 26 April. Information about casualties began to trickle to his little bunker. He wondered how many precious fighters he would have left. He was distressed at what he saw as the futility of Godley's attitude of 'bumbling through'. It was not the way Monash had been trained. He still couldn't think like a professional such as Godley, nor would he ever want to. The mind of the British regular was more conditioned to rationalising any failures on the battlefield to his superiors. Soldiers were expendable.

It offended Monash's sense of logic. You didn't go into battle, he thought, unless you had a pretty fair chance of victory. That happened only if you had given yourself time to plan every imaginable detail and contingency. The logic came from preserving your men. If sloppy planning led to unnecessary mass killings, then your strength and morale would be diminished.

Monash was already doing the calculations on the morning of 3 May. By his count, his brigade might be down to fewer than 1800 men. This was his first offensive manoeuvre. Any more like it would see him in command of a battalion-sized force rather than a brigade.

He ventured out of his HQ in an attempt to assess the damage. Anzacs were dead and dying from the head of the valley to well into it. Marines, who had blundered into the wrong places, were looking for someone to command them. Mid-morning on that depressing Sunday, Monash ordered the 16th and the marines to withdraw. They did so by 1 p.m. The 13th was given the same directive, and they managed to retreat by 3 p.m. There were still companies in vulnerable spots. Monash ordered them to withdraw after nightfall when they could.

In mid-afternoon Bean came to see Monash. The commander would love to have told the journalist what he really thought. But that would be imprudent. Rage would also be inappropriate. He could only present a dispirited demeanour.

'Monash seemed to me a little shaken,' Bean wrote. 'He was talking of disaster and said our men would certainly have to retire from the part of the new ground which they now held.' Monash also said that 'they've tried to put the work of an Army Corps on to me'.[15]

This was the extent to which he could bring himself to complain about his superiors, Hamilton, Birdwood and Godley. Because of the 1st Division's decision not to take part, Monash had shouldered the main responsibility of the physical side of the offensive, especially with Johnston's failure to turn up on time. The result was a thousand casualties, and in essence ground had been given up. The Turks would now be able to add the abandoned Anzac trenches to the Chessboard, which would enhance their capacity to hold, even control, the head of the valley.

Monash was highly critical of the 2–3 May operation. He put his assessments on the record, as commanders were meant to do in reviewing operations. They centred on the paucity of numbers and the poor strategy and tactics. Godley read his comments, but they had no impact. As long as

Monash took orders and didn't go behind his back with complaints, that was fine by him. Besides, Godley knew he had a strong commander in Monash, on whom he could rely to keep the troops together and inspired in the face of such death and disaster. He praised him in a letter to Australia's Defence Minister, G. F. Pearce: 'Colonel Monash had a very heavy responsibility, a most anxious time – without sleep or rest of any kind for about a week, and has done admirably.'[16]

Despite the dead and dying that scattered the area and the beach, Godley sketched a positive portrait of events, reminiscent of the scene from *Monty Python and the Holy Grail* in which a beleaguered knight remains optimistic despite being dismembered. Godley's motto could well have been: 'Don't spend too much time on planning, don't look back, don't review, don't learn from mistakes. Move on.'

Bean was unaware of most of the night's horrors and the hideous blunders created by Godley's poor, rushed planning and communication. He saw only Monash's despair in contrast to the detached Godley's positive disposition. At that moment, in Bean's mind, Monash paled in comparison to Bridges, White and Walker, who were on the beach waiting to hear the full result of the disaster that they had managed to avoid.

After the debacle, Monash urged Godley to replace most of 4th Brigade and its leadership. Godley didn't reply until the following morning. His message said he was hopeful that Monash, his battered staff and what was left of the shredded brigade were 'somewhat rested'. Monash sent back a terse response to Godley on the beach that was delivered as if through clenched teeth: 'Thank you for your kind enquiries.'[17]

Any favourable impressions about Godley from that first meeting at Heliopolis thirteen weeks earlier had evaporated. Even Birdwood, one removed from this strained relationship and further removed from the impact of the battle itself, didn't seem to grasp the devastation. When Monash told him that the efficiency of the brigade was badly impaired and that he was down from 4500 to 1750 men, Birdwood responded with: 'I have told Monash that I cannot accept this and that he must produce more [men].'[18]

Monash was not amused. He was now fully aware of the British regular leadership's attitude to the soldiers at the front. They were machine-gun fodder that was expendable. The answer always to the request for replacements was to find them in the British tradition of the last 400 years as the world's dominant military power.

This was driven home a week later on 9 May when Godley called for a meeting with Monash and his four battalion commanders. Godley claimed he had intelligence that the Turks had switched the bulk of their force to Helles to defend renewed attacks by the British and French there. Turks had been taken from the main positions in front of Quinn's and from their dominating positions above the valley, Monash was informed. Godley wanted another big offensive.

Monash didn't submit an alternative plan this time. He did what Walker had done and refused his directive, which was not even a plan but a vague idea about a fresh attack.

Godley tried another tack. He appeared to compromise by asking for a night 'patrol' to determine how much the Turkish defences had been weakened in front of Quinn's by the rush to the Helles front in the south. If a line of trenches was found to be vulnerable, the force was to take and hold it. These were really two directives that should have been one. It was reconnaissance and securing forward trenches by force, if the trenches were found to be obtainable.

Monash was uneasy, although relieved that a showdown between them had not been forced over the original order for one of Godley's mindless big offensives.

At 10.45 p.m. Monash arranged for his men at Pope's to sustain machine-gun fire to cover the noise and movement of 300 men in three companies who moved over the crest of the Valley and forward of Quinn's. Monash stationed another 500 men from his 16th Battalion in positions ready to support the companies. The target was achieved quickly. The companies seized the trenches and began digging furiously in the direction of Quinn's. This went on for several hours until 3.45 a.m. when Turks lying in trenches between Pope's and Quinn's began hurling grenades and bomb at both Anzac positions. This pinned down the three companies, who could not dig further. The 16th Battalion attacked but was driven back.

At 4.50 a.m. the fickle fingers of dawn began to creep over the area, leaving the newly entrenched men vulnerable. The Turks opened up with unrelenting machine-gun fire as the companies tried to withdraw. The companies were decimated. In the aftermath of yet another shocking operation ordered by Godley, 207 casualties were counted.

The battalion was shattered physically and in terms of morale. Any shred of confidence Monash might have had in Godley was stripped away late in the morning. Godley told him that he knew all along that the

Turkish forces at Anzac had not been depleted to replenish those at Helles.[19] This was a new military concept for Monash. Until now he had believed that you were meant to deceive the enemy only.

Monash and his brigade had taken the brunt of the Anzac fighting for ten days. On 12 May, half of the 4th and the British marines were replaced by Colonel Harry Chauvel's 1st Australian Light Horse Brigade, which would act as infantry. Chauvel replaced him as commander of the section, but Monash stayed on in the valley to make it easier. The new leader was anxious about taking over the most brutal area in the conflict, especially with the nerve-racking proximity to the action, which could spill into the HQ dugout below Courtney's. It was made worse by the fear that unhelpful Godley was likely to order another hare-brained scheme at any moment.

Monash and Chauvel were reminded hourly of their perpetual vulnerability. On 14 May, Birdwood climbed up to Quinn's to have a look at the Turkish positions for himself. It took gut-wrenching courage just to be there. Yet now at least the need to stand up to assess the area, as Irvine and MacLaurin had done on 27 April, was alleviated by periscopes. They were attached to rifles, which allowed a soldier to aim and shoot without raising his head above the parapet.

Birdwood used a rifle this way to view the area. A sniper shattered the mirror as it appeared. A bullet fragment hit the top of his head. Birdwood slumped back, bleeding from the scalp. He collapsed but recovered after a minute. He was helped down into the valley, stretchered off, stitched up and relieved. Luck would see him operating as normal within a day.

On 15 May Bridges, who been displaying the unnerving (for his staff) tendency to stand in exposed spots, moved from the beach up the valley to below Steele's Post to see Chauvel and Monash. Bridges stopped behind a sandbag barrier two metres thick to have a cigarette and chat with a medical officer.

Bridges, with cigarette in hand, moved a few paces to the valley path side of the barrier, which left him exposed yet again. A sniper on Dead Man's Ridge took his chance and struck. Bridges was hit in the thigh, his femoral artery and vein split open. He was taken to a hospital ship, where he died three days later.

It was a chilling reminder for Chauvel that those in command bunkers were nearly as vulnerable as those on the front lines. Both a corps and a division commander had been struck down in the three days he had been in charge of the sector. Twelve of Monash's HQ staff had become casualties, some of them killed or wounded (by snipers or shrapnel) close by him. McCay and all his 2nd Brigade staff had been wounded while taking part in the attack at Cape Helles on 8 May when helping out the British forces attempting to advance again.

Bridges' demise was unsettling. It was a needless waste of another leader when they were in short supply. There was a thin line between bravery and bravado. They were cousins at Anzac but different. Bravado such as that displayed by Bridges was more closely related to foolhardiness – even stupidity – which, when revealed in death demoralised the troops. In contrast, bravery as exemplified by John Simpson (Kirkpatrick) of the 3rd Field Ambulance inspired everyone. Monash wrote to Vic:

This man has been working in this [Monash] valley since 26th April, in collecting the wounded, and carrying them to the dressing-stations. He had a small donkey, which he used to carry all cases unable to walk. Private Simpson and his little beast earned the admiration of everyone at the upper end of the valley [in the war zone] . . . Simpson knew no fear. He moved unconcernedly amid shrapnel and rifle-fire, steadily carrying out his self-imposed task day by day. He frequently earned the applause of the personnel for his many fearless rescues of wounded men from areas subject to rifle and shrapnel-fire.

Simpson and his donkey were killed by a shrapnel shell [on 19 May, the day after Bridges died].[20]

It was learned after his death that Simpson, from the north of England, had not belonged to any of the ambulance units of Monash's brigade. He had been separated from his own unit, although no one seemed to know which one. This helped create a myth. The cheerful, smiling Simpson became a kind of rough angel, who was there to assist and comfort the wounded and dying. More than that, he was a symbol of selflessness, mateship and courage at Gallipoli.

Monash had found his own level of steel. He was determined never to show fear. It was an essential part of his desire to demonstrate leadership in all situations. Now he had to. He conditioned himself from his first tramp up Monash Valley to ignore the shelling and bullets. After that first day, he coped and managed to carry on with sensible caution, but without shirking the need to be seen at the forward posts. Monash let necessity dictate the moment. If he had to go up to Quinn's to formulate a plan, he would, making sure he used the cover available. But he wasn't going to attempt to impress his men for its own sake by taking a rope up the steep slope from the valley to stand up in the trenches – the equivalent of playing Russian roulette.

On the other hand, Monash's ruthless streak – a necessity in the brutal, close encounter with the enemy at Gallipoli – would not countenance cowardice among his officers. He was scathing in private communication with two of them, who had lost their nerve. He was amused by a superior who would not take the rope up to Courtney's Post for some reconnaissance when he was planning an attack. Monash had calculated the balance between the level of intestinal fortitude needed for leadership and the caution required for at least a chance at self-preservation. He would not go beyond it either way and expected nothing more or less from those under him or superior to him.

The legendary Simpson and his donkey had died during a heavy artillery bombardment by the Turks that preceded a huge offensive directed by von Sanders early on the morning of 19 May. Almost 40,000 Turks were massed against 12,500 Anzacs, but the odds were not as uneven as those numbers suggest. The Anzacs were well entrenched. In the ten days since their attack on the Turks, Monash, with Chauvel looking on, had fortified the head of the valley, especially with the positioning of machine-guns from Pope's to Courtney's. Now the 14th (including twenty-two-year-old Private Albert Jacka and his companions from Bendigo) and 15th Battalions were able to hold firm. When the dawn crept over the killing fields between the opposing trenches this time, it was the staccato sound of Anzac machine-guns that raked over the enemy. But as with the Anzacs in the previous encounters, the Turks kept coming from the first onslaught at 4.20 a.m. But they were not supported by artillery. The Anzacs were able to climb on to the parapets of their trenches and blast the oncomers without being fearful of shells. Wave after wave of Turks, in a long line from in front of Russell's to Bolton's Ridge, inspired by a band playing military dirges and shouting their love of Allah, came at the Anzacs.

On one occasion, about twelve Turks broke into the line at Courtney's, threatening to run over the top and down into the 4th Brigade's HQ just below in the valley, where Monash and Chauvel were prepared for the worst outcome, their revolvers close by. The attackers hurled bombs, reaching a firing trench in which they took cover. They were pinned down from in front and behind by members of the defending 14th Battalion. The one behind them was Albert Jacka. The Turks would charge on any second, aiming for an empty communications trench. If some Turks made it, they could career down the valley and open the way for scores of their comrades in a massive haemorrhage into the Anzac lines. The moment called for a decisive response. Lieutenant K. G. W. Crabbe yelled to Jacka, the fiercest fighter he knew: 'Bert, can you make the C Trench?'

'Yeah, sure!'

'If I get you support can you charge 'em?'

'Yeah! I want two or three!'

Crabbe ordered four soldiers into the communications trench, just as Jacka jumped in beside them. They hesitated only for the time it took to fix bayonets. Then they straddled the parapet and charged the firing trench. Two of the five Australians were wounded in the fight. Jacka dashed back behind the Turks. Two others scrambled back to the communications trench, leaving the two wounded men lying in the open.

Crabbe yelled plan B, all of one minute later. He and the two unwounded Australians would climb on to their communications trench parapet, firing in an effort to distract them. Jacka would attack from behind again.

Crabbe and the others did their bit. The Turks responded, their backs to the cool, yet demonic Jacka. He charged and was in the trench next to them before they realised it. He bayoneted two and shot another five. The other five panicked, scrambled out and ran for their lines. Jacka's 'two or three' had turned out to be seven. His desperate feats, motived by the death of mates, had done most to hold the line. Action such as this lifted everyone in sight and those who would hear about it in the following hours.

Crabbe soon afterwards congratulated Jacka, telling him he would be 'recommended' for the highest bravery award in the British Army: the Victoria Cross.[21]

Over a gruelling eight-hour period, a scythe of Anzac rifle and machine-gun fire cut down 10,000 Turks until midday, when they stopped coming. Three thousand were killed, another 7000 wounded. It was 'better than a wallaby drive [hunt]', one lieutenant from the bush observed.[22] The result was most evident opposite Courtney's where the bodies of the fearless Turks were piled in their hundreds. By contrast the Anzacs had 600 casualties, including 160 killed.

A weary Monash found a moment in the dugout to write in his diary: 'Everybody exhausted with want of sleep and mental strain.'[23]

The number of bodies, running to thousands, now created an assault on the men's olfactory senses. The stench of decaying flesh, scattered between all the trenches, was vomit-making. It would make the attendant smell of thyme a stomach churner for the rest of the Anzacs' lives.

'You can almost fancy that you are chewing it [decaying flesh and thyme] every time one breathes,' a lieutenant told Bean. 'It is so thick.'[24]

The threat of disease was as near as the bodies. Maggots, not content with the dead, ambitiously wriggled their way into the trenches, which had to be swept out every few hours. Their parents – the flies – had arrived early in the late spring with the prospect of thousands of exposed corpses. Not content with crowding the dead, these bluish, bloated pests, retarded by their overfeasting, were irritating the living, settling on every possible area of exposed skin, especially orifices. Australians who frequented beaches or the outback at home at the height of summer could not recall anything like this plague. It motivated poet–soldier A. P. Herbert to pen an 'Ode to Flies':

> The flies! Oh, God, the flies
> That soiled the sacred dead.
> To see them swarm from dead men's eyes
> And share the soldiers' bread.
> Nor think I can forget
> The filth and stench of war,
> The Corpses on the parapet,
> The maggots on the floor.[25]

The soldiers could hardly bear this, but the *coup de grâce* that made some of them wish for a bullet to end the misery was the accompanying dysentery. Eighty per cent of the troops would get the Anzac trots. Monash was one of the few who missed out. He boiled all the water he had and was careful with his food. He did suffer from interminable colds. It was a condition that everyone of his brigade would have swapped for the dysentery pain in the gut that would cause soldier' knees to bang together and buckle.

There had to be a truce to clean up the rotting bodies, some of which had been in no man's land between the trenches for weeks. On 24 May, after certain armistice protocols had been observed, the Turks and Anzacs emerged from the trenches to collect and bury the dead. Most of the fallen Anzacs were behind the lines. It was an opportunity for the Turks, who seemed just as interested in picking up valuable rifles as their fallen comrades.

Monash was not happy about the two sides becoming too chummy. Later in lecture notes he would tell his commanders that such a gathering 'destroys the will to kill. And we must discourage, and rightly put down, everything in the way of attempting to fraternise with the enemy. Never encourage. Suppress it. Give the men to understand that they are dealing with some human vermin they are going to eradicate.'[26] Perhaps this was necessary propaganda in theory, but in reality, up in front of Quinn's and Courtney's, the exchange of a few cigarettes and tins of bully beef was hardly going to soften the attitude to the enemy. This was time out in hell. Sanity and humanity were never going to prevail for more than a few hours as both sides removed the bodies and some of the stench, and marginally eased the threat of disease.

During the truce, Monash noted: 'The Turks observed all the rules punctiliously, even better than we did.' Up on Pope's Hill with Godley he noticed a Turk about a hundred metres away trying to repair a loophole in a Turkish trench. Monash signalled this violation to a Turkish officer, 'who ran over to the man and gave him a sound belting with a stick'. The officer returned to Monash and Godley and expressed his regrets at the soldier's folly. 'He then very politely intimated that he would esteem it a favour if we refrained from using our field glasses, because this would give us an unfair advantage.' That Turkish officer would never know how unfair. Monash hated being without maps more than any other officer. He was forced to make do with these quick reconnoitres and to rely on his photographic memory for terrain. His finely honed survey skills would be translated into a tactic.

The burying went on all day. At 5 p.m. 'we were at it again hammer and tongs'.[27]

Two days later, Monash accepted Hamilton's invitation to join him aboard his HQ base on the battleship *Arcadian* at Imbros Harbour for a couple of days and nights break. The tension in his demeanour was evident when he was asked to climb a ladder to get aboard. Despite the deprivations on Gallipoli, he had not lost much weight.

'I've come for a rest, not to do gymnastics!' Monash snapped.

A gangplank was lowered for him.

He was able to have a proper bath and rest from the 'mental strain and responsibility' after thirty days of constant pressure. Hamilton later claimed that the break saved Monash's life. The expedition leader, himself sixty-eight, appreciated that Monash, forty-nine, needed to be recharged, inspired and praised. Hamilton was just the leader for that. They dined together on the night of the 26th. The conversation was swamped early by comment about a German sub's torpedoing of the British battleship, the *Triumph*, off Anzac the day before. It had dumbfounded the watching Anzacs in the hills. They also talked of the continuing battle onshore, its distant cacophonous symphony punctuating any pauses in the chat.

There weren't many. Hamilton asked about Vic and Bertha, remembering their names and those of other people they both knew in Australia. He reminisced again about that hot day at Lilydale, which had left an impression of Monash that had been vindicated by his leadership over the past horrific month. Hamilton, a bon vivant and true clubman, mentioned Melbourne's Naval and Military Club where they had lunched and dined.

He told Monash that 'the attention of the whole world' was focused on 'Anzac and Helles to a far greater degree than on Flanders or Galicia [Poland]'. Monash accepted this limelighting, which was a subtle way of pushing him on. He had been cut off from the rest of the planet now for a month. Even newspapers they received in the valley and on the beach were a month old. They didn't mention the peninsula. Monash also accepted Hamilton's reminder that this British force was 'the only one in occupation of enemy territory . . . Australian troops were the first of the Empire to set foot on any part of the enemy's territory.'[28] It was Hamilton's way of justifying the bogged-down position. It was meant to make his commanders feel that they were important in their holding of a small chunk of all but uninhabitable land not fit for grazing even the smallest goats.

Hamilton flattered and praised, talked about the 'splendid [a hackneyed adjective, used by all officers] work' of the Anzac troops. Like many

British of his background he had a certain fascination with the laconic, iconoclastic digger and his anti-authority, anti-discipline attitudes. The myth of his capacities as a fighter was now found to be true. They spoke of that nerveless assassin Albert Jacka and his already legendary exploits. Hamilton wanted to know all about this hard-as-nails labourer's son, who kept a useful diary and an ice-cool head.

They agreed he should get the VC. There were other stories, which would become myths, such as Simpson and his donkey, and how Bridges had behaved so bravely after being fatally wounded. Hamilton told the tale of how an officer – 'a rather superior type' – had asked a group of Australian soldiers if they had heard that the powers-that-be had given General Bridges a posthumous knighthood.

'Have they?' one of the soldiers had replied. 'Well, that won't do him much good where he is now, will it, mate?'

That cynical style, born of Australia's disregard for authority and developed by the extremes on Gallipoli, somehow, in a perverse way, appealed to the British. It said much about life and death, and the mind-numbing reality of what they were experiencing, without even the chance for a warm bath, let alone a leisurely hour or two to savour a favourite beverage. That soldier might have added, with his ultra-dry tone, that he knew plenty of men alive and dead who deserved such a high decoration more for their valour in the thick of the action. He would have been allowed such a riposte, too. The Anzacs had respect. They were tough. They could fight, better than the Turks, Monash was certain, and with more brutal efficiency than the other British troops on the peninsula.

Monash was being fêted in this modest way after his 'job splendidly done' because he was a special commodity on Gallipoli. He knew just how to handle these uncouth men and how to keep his brigade going and motivated against huge odds. There were secrets to handling the Anzacs, Monash told Hamilton. It was not the powers of discipline that he could wield, 'but the healthy public spirit of the men themselves, who would not allow a slacker to live among them'.

His job was to keep those spirits high. They had to be fed, rested, rotated and given everything he could garner to support their murderous intent. He was a facilitator of that Anzac spirit as much as a leader. Hamilton understood this. Monash was his kind of officer for this capacity alone. The fact that this atypical Australian was also well read, cerebral, urbane, educated, mannerly and yet still hard added to his attraction. He was a sort of antipodean strongman's Disraeli (the former British Prime Minister), Hamilton would tell Churchill, to whom he would appeal also.

In that brief, convivial respite, Monash was opposite the first leader who was not threatened by him in any way; someone who appreciated him on several levels; someone with enormous influence, no matter what the outcome on Gallipoli. The experience of getting on so well with Hamilton buoyed his own spirits and lifted his hopes and aspirations. Dining with the chief was the only golden moment in those first thirty days of murder, blood and mayhem. The experience would keep him going.

On 27 May, Monash's brief R&R on the *Arcadian* was soured by another torpedo sinking – this time of the British battleship *Majestic* off the peninsula's southern tip. Hamilton, never one to avoid eloquent imagery even at critical moments, likened the second sinking to a hunter picking a royal stag out of a harem of does. The next day, when Monash was leaving the *Arcadian*, many of the fleet were moving to safer realms of the Aegean. The does had been frightened away by the unseen hunter.

Yet nothing on 28 May could dampen Monash's lifted spirits. He was told he had been 'mentioned in despatches'. Promotion would come sooner rather than later, despite the Australian Government's cringing reluctance to grant advances to him and his fellow officers. Officials from the PM down could not grasp that an Australian volunteer could be a better leader than a British regular.

Monash had lived for two days in an unreal world of baths, rest, decent food and elegant company. Now, as he was rowed ashore, he prepared for what had become his real existence of deafening, rhythmless noise, stomach-turning smells, of hard beds in precarious shelters, of flies with everything he ate and did. Not to forget more than 35,000 hostile Turks close and pressing with howitzers, machine-guns, grenades and plenty of nasty surprises. A factor that would keep him ticking over, after being recharged, was the constant need to organise and direct in the battle that had become a siege at Anzac. The constant requirement that he make decisions distracted Monash from that ghostly lady who accompanied everyone, even Albert Jacka, at Anzac: fear.

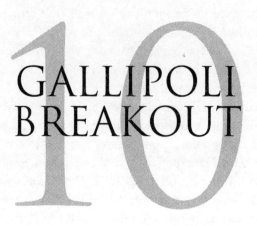

GALLIPOLI
BREAKOUT

Hamilton, 'that bloody poet', as the ingenuous Kitchener called him, was under pressure in June 1915 to try something that would turn the war on the peninsula. Allied attacks at Helles were not breaking through. No matter how many Battles of Krithia on the nail of this ungainly thumb of hostile land were planned and fought, they were not going to crash past the Turkish defences. German torpedos had scattered the Allied fleet, and there was no talk of forcing the Dardanelles now. The Anzacs were hemmed in and in stalemate.

The uncomfortable spotlight had fallen on Hamilton and his capacities as a commander. His friends, more than his enemies, were directing the illumination. Ellis Ashmead-Bartlett, that gifted war chronicler, who had been with him a decade earlier watching the Japanese humiliate the Russians, had, it seemed to Hamilton, turned against him. Ashmead-Bartlett's dilemma was a clash between his respect and liking for the so-civilised expeditionary director and the unpalatable truth, which he felt honour-bound to pass on to the War Council. The superficial brainchild of Churchill was not working, he told the thin-skinned Winston himself. The lean campaign leader might not be up to it.

Hamilton had been forced to abandon the dangerous low seas, leave the *Arcadian* in Imbros Harbour and camp on the Greek island. He was feeling the pinch.

What a change since the war office sent us packing with a bagful of hallucinations [he wrote a touch sorrowfully in his *Gallipoli Diary*].

Naval guns sweeping the Turks off the Peninsula, the Ottoman army legging it from a British submarine waving the Union Jack; Russian help at hand; Greek help on the *tapis*. Now it is our own fleet which has to leg it from the German submarine; there is no ammunition for the guns; no [conscription] drafts to keep my divisions up to strength; my Russians have gone to Galicia [Poland] and the Greeks are lying lower than ever.

Hamilton was trying to convince himself that the campaign was a lousy idea in the first place, which was a limp-wristed slap at Churchill. He was reminding himself also that once the concept was executed he never received the back up of men and supplies that he needed, which was gentle poke in the eye for his boss Kitchener.

He was right, as were those now pointing the finger at him as not the right commander for such a complicated exercise, which had been made more complex by incompetence at various levels of command. Hamilton was no fool and didn't live in the past. The present was too challenging. But at heart, this likeable, brilliant Scot preferred the simplicity of the cavalry charge. This Dardanelles-sized campaign, at least the way it had panned out, required attention to detail he didn't care for. He had never had the temerity to push his boss, nor the confrontational style to bully his subordinates. Hamilton, in short, was a little too nice for this kind of prolonged war, although he would never admit it.

His diary in June read like self-pity, which was the way a lot of war diaries read when scripted alone and at night. But Hamilton was made of sterner stuff. He would have another go at winning this wretched sideshow.

He consulted his most trusted Corps Commander, Birdwood. Was there a workable option to this confusing maze of blocked paths? Birdwood was as usual cheerful and optimistic. What's more, he had maps of the entire peninsula. They had been rifled from Turks since the last big wave of attacks at Anzac on 19 May. They seemed comprehensive. Birdwood was confident that they were enough, at last, to plan a few moves to turn the conflict. The maps were a step forward, and even a chimpanzee could have been trained to calculate the next move. With the sea to the west, Krithia blocked in the south and reluctance to use the Dardanelles to the east, the remote territory to the north had to be a route for making a fresh attempt at a breakthrough. Yet again, as so many times in this war, mistakes of the past seemed destined to be repeated. No one had yet done a reconnaissance of the peninsula's north.

It was even tougher terrain than on Anzac.

✕

While the War Council become grumpy over the campaign after reading confidential reports from Ashmead-Bartlett, and Hamilton thrashed around on Imbros looking for a solution, Monash was finding the summer months less tense than his first thirty days. Those on the front lines had to be vigilant. At times they were threatened, but in the main Kemal and his Turks seemed to have temporarily lost the capacity or urge to push the stolid invaders back into the sea.

The 4th had been relieved from Quinn's and Courtney's by 1 June, a few days after Monash had returned from Imbros. The brigade was mainly rested in Reserve Gully, a large open area jammed between the sandy cliffs of Walker's Ridge and the Sphinx. Monash relaxed the dress code and allowed khakis to be cut down as shorts, which started an Australian fashion that would carry into the next millennium. Some companies were allowed a 'holiday' on Imbros. Games and activities were encouraged. Monash made time for church parades and chess with anyone who could play. He read newspapers and completed mathematical puzzles like those he tackled ever since he was a young boy at Jerilderie. He wrote letters to everyone from the family and friends, to Lizette and Annie Gabriel, who had been an excellent 'correspondent' ever since they had been entwined.

Monash saw Bean on 2 June. Bean had stayed close to the 1st Division. He had not witnessed any of the 4th Brigade's exploits since the failed offensive of 2 and 3 May, and had not appeared near HQ under Courtney's until 24 May, well after the last major Turkish counter-attack on 19 May when the brigade's defence was at its most magnificent. He had hardly mentioned the 4th in his articles, having linked it in his head more with New Zealand activity than Australian.

Monash took the opportunity to complain that the 4th was not getting its due in press coverage. He grew heated when Bean demonstrated that he knew very little of the brigade's hard work. The brave journalist, the most conscientious reporter on Anzac, was offended. He worked harder at ferreting out the facts than anyone, and prided himself on being meticulous and accurate. He was not as concerned with his style as Ashmead-Bartlett, who would never jam facts into his story at the expense of the entertaining metaphor or the dry analogy. Bean was very conscious as his role as official war correspondent, and Monash's inference that he was ignoring, or ignorant of, an important part of the Anzac endeavour was unsettling.

The relationship that had begun over a bad meal in Heliopolis was now broken perhaps beyond repair. Bean was professional, yet also human. Negatives about Monash would creep into his thinking, link with others' complaints and join with a little (common) racial prejudice to shape an assessment unfavourable in comparison to Bean's heroes in 1st Division. The correspondent's written and verbal appreciation of Monash would be sparing, even begrudging. Monash understood the value of publicity, but not the way the mind of professional journalists operated. He saw them more or less as a vehicle for reporting the exploits of his command. He didn't allow for their being inherently thin-skinned when it came to criticism. Nor did he comprehend their power. Even if he had, Monash would have handled Bean the same way.

After the meeting, the journalist only managed to scribble in his diary of 2 June that the 4th was 'a fine brigade, rather easier and freer with their officers and not so neat or rigid as our division'.[1] Compared to Bean's capacity for superlatives with the 1st, describing the 4th as 'free and easy' with officers was not complimentary in his eyes. Not being 'neat and rigid' was code for sloppiness. The reference to 'our division', which was the 1st, said much about Bean's sentiment. Monash (and his crew) wasn't even one of us.

After this confrontation, Monash set aside time in an attempt to gain favourable publicity for his brigade by asking Vic and friends to send material, such as a 'thank you' speech by Godley to it on 1 June, to the press. But the mention of names was censored.

Just before dawn on 27 June, a minor Turkish attack occurred on Walker's Ridge above the Reserve Gully amphitheatre. The New Zealanders repulsed it, but the din woke Monash. It was his fiftieth birthday. He received congratulations and makeshift presents throughout the day. His unofficial 'bodyguard', 14th battalion, sent collective greetings with caricatures that he would treasure. Officers from every company on Anzac wandered into the gully to shake his hand during the day. Boxes of cigars, bottles of everything from Greek retsina to French champagne, and other gifts flowed into his tent.

At 5 p.m. he shared champagne with his staff. At 5.30 a cake sent by the imperious Lady Godley in Alexandria was decked with fifty matches acting as candles and presented to Monash. His deputy McGlinn, whom he admired for his courage, hard work and friendship, made a little speech. Then Monash sat down on a kerosene tin to enjoy a delicious four-course meal prepared by the brigade cook.

Monash was touched by the attention and gestures of warmth, friendship and respect. He knew at times he had been tougher than he should have been with some of his command. He worried on occasions if he had pushed them too much. But the response on a day that he took seriously for its significance in his life touched and lifted him even more than his golden moment with Hamilton in Imbros Harbour.

Life, for just one day, was happily memorable and not at all like Hades.

Monash received a cablegram of 10 July from Vic: 'Congratulations on promotion to brigadier-general well love.'

It was the first he had heard of it. The Australian Government, unappreciative of what had gone on at Gallipoli, had not been supportive. There were also the lingering rumours about his German links, which should have been rendered invalid by his valour on the peninsula. Kitchener had stepped in to pressure Pearce. The promotion had been gazetted in Australia without Monash being informed.

Vic's news was confirmed soon afterwards, and he enjoyed being called 'General'. It gave him satisfaction to know it would stun his enemies. They had been reactive in Australia. Was the 'McInerney clique' at it again? Monash was too far away to investigate. The German 'background' problem was evident once more.

Rumours were vicious and hurtful for Vic and Bertha. One said he had been shot as a German spy and traitor. There were returned servicemen who swore that they were at his execution in Egypt, on Anzac and in the Aegean. One regular army representative even visited Iona with the sad news that Monash had faltered under the strain of command. He had resigned and was on his way home. Still another official, apparently also believing his information to be true, had informed the family that Monash had broken down. He was in hospital. He would soon be on a ship homeward-bound.

Frail Vic fell ill herself with such reports. Bertha, younger and stronger, would have none of it. She was closer to her father and felt she knew him.

That 'strong nervous system' would not crack, she was sure of it. She was right, but even the most faithful could never know how any man would stand up at Gallipoli. There were many instances of men being sent home for misdemeanours, nervous breakdowns, insanity and plain cowardice. Vic, in the end, just wished him back in Melbourne, whatever the reason. But Monash's 'promise' to be back before the (southern) winter of 1915 was not going to be kept.

Bertha could not see him returning to Australia without fulfilling long-held ambitions to reach the top of the military tree, whatever it took and wherever it took him.

Birdwood's plan for the Gallipoli breakout built during July. Hamilton thought it was a good one. His reputation and place in history would ride with it. Monash wasn't yet privy to enough detail to judge. Godley had created mystery and expectation by telling Monash to sharpen up his bushwalking and compass skills. Then he spoke about a 'left hook' and demonstrated the proposed action with a wide sweep of his left arm and a punch.

Monash was not a pugilist, but he understood. He took a couple of staff officers on a secret trek north to survey the region of the Sari Bair range. He couldn't go far. The terrain made Anzac seem like his back garden at Iona by comparison. Someone called it insane. Another reckoned it must been created by a very angry god. Perhaps the observer had in mind Mars in a mad moment. It was not fit for anything, not even war. 'Watercourses changed direction,' one observer wrote. 'Seemingly gentle slopes conceal a precipitous and treacherous surface under the scrub; there is no method in anything.'[2] Confusion was not just likely; it was certain. Ridges looked the same. If a hiker scaled a ridge in search of a summit to act as a guide, then scaled another ridge, he would find himself further away from the summit, not closer as intended. Monash assumed the final maps used would be explicit and clear; otherwise he would be forced again into Godley's muddle-through mentality.

The next day he and three of his battalion commanders jumped on a battleship and cruised north up the coast. There was much pointing and consideration of maps as they made a reconnaissance of spurs. They couldn't always agree on what height was what. Notes were scribbled and binoculars used. The sporadically placed Turkish artillery in the hills was fired in a half-hearted way as if to let the floating enemy know they were watching.

This did not indicate that the Turks were unaware of the Australian plans. Mustafa Kemal, now proving a master strategist, had predicted that the British would attempt to sweep out of Anzac with a move north, then a semicircular march right and an attempted knockout blow – Godley's telegraphed left hook – at Hill 971. It was the gateway to the high ground of Chunuk Bair, the place the Anzacs had been stopped on the first day of the invasion. Kemal and von Sanders had divisions placed ready for the next British attempt to win control of the peninsula.

Monash's brigade was in no condition for long left hooks or even short jabs. The remnants of the brigade that had survived since 25 April had suffered dysentery, gastric problems, bronchial infections, rapid pulses, heart dilation and loss of weight. The reinforcements that brought it up to strength were under-trained, and they too had serious health problems, having endured the conditions on Anzac through the hot, dry, flyblown summer months of June and July. Monash himself was fit. The brigadier general was not the Colonel Blimp he had been when he left Australia. He had at last lost weight but not through illness, and was closer to ninety kilograms than 100. It made him optimistic, especially when he handled the hills and reconnoitring better than staff twenty years younger. He tended to judge his men by his own strong, lucky constitution.

Perhaps also he wasn't allowing enough for the fact that the rump of soldiers left from the horrific stress of the first thirty days was shell-shocked. The physical deprivations brought on by disease made matters worse.

Monash had made an amateur study of medicine over the years, and would have loved to have gone back to Melbourne University to do a course, had he not been there for eleven years doing his other three degrees. He could always converse at an intelligent level – down to the esoteric phraseology – with doctors. He knew more about fitness levels and military exertion than just about anyone. This caused him to show some concern in the summer about the condition of his brigade.

He had four doctors run their stethoscopes over every man in it during July. Three of the examiners were adamant. These men were not fit to shovel trenches or anything else. Just one doctor reckoned they were in condition to march for half a day over unforgiving terrain, as long as they had adequate water, food and rest. This meant all doctors agreed that the brigade's overall fitness couldn't be guaranteed in any concentrated effort to take the heights.

Monash's tough side emerged again. He didn't wish to capitulate to the conditions before a battle had been fought and won. His optimism as much as his ruthless streak saw him opt for the minority medical report, even though most of the brigade should have been resting in hospitals rather than undertaking strenuous activity – in armed conflict.

The knowledge that a strong contingent of men would be coming in to back them up buoyed everyone and lulled Monash and his staff further into believing that the sick brigade would rise to the exciting occasion. Indeed, Hamilton's repeated requests to Kitchener for a bigger force saw him receive 25,000 more men who would land at Suvla Bay north of Anzac Cove. Another 30,000 would back up the Anzac force.

The thought of such a reinforcement boosted the 4th's morale and confidence, as did the news on 30 July that Jacka had become the first of the entire corps on Gallipoli to win the VC.

The prospect of a massive victory that would be wrapped up in a couple of days bolstered physically weak men for a venture for which they were really not prepared. There was another motivation. The men were keen to move out of Reserve Gully with its stinking, swelling latrines and sun, and strike out in 'clean' country.

Birdwood's final plan for the battle of Sari Bair would begin with feints at Helles and Lone Pine, three kilometres southeast of Anzac Cove. These were meant to distract and tie up Turkish divisions while the main thrust went for Hill 971 and Chunuk Bair. At night Monash's 4th Brigade would move out on the widest sweep, along with the New Zealand Brigade and the newly arrived 29th Indian Brigade, consisting of three battalions of Gurkhas and one of Sikhs. Sweeping inside these three brigades would be the New Zealand Mounted Rifles on foot.

Hamilton had brought in a fifty-five-year-old Indian Army veteran, Major General H. V. Cox, under Godley. Monash's description of the new man in charge indicated he had less than mixed feelings about the choice: 'He is one of those crotchety, livery old Indian officers, whom the climate had dried and shrivelled up into a bag of nerves . . . Cox hampered me greatly, as I had to constantly to refer to him and defer to his views.' Cox seemed an odd choice, given that he had suffered a nervous breakdown after the shattering impact of failures at Helles. From Monash's appraisal, Cox was in no shape for a gruelling march into the unknown and perhaps further prolonged engagements.[3]

On the morning of 6 August, Cox and Godley addressed the officers and NCOs of 4th Brigade. Godley invited Monash to speak. As usual his capacity to absorb detail and then regurgitate it clearly came to the fore. His enunciation of the 4th Brigade's role was far better than that of its author, Cox, who stood with Godley nodding at Monash's words.

Bean was there to listen. He was in no mood to praise Monash then, but sixteen years later he remarked on the speech: 'As a clear logical exposition of a scheme of operations, it surpassed any that I had ever listened to . . . It was a masterful piece of lucid explanation.'[4]

Mid-stream, the Turks used this propitious moment to shell the gully over Walker's Ridge. But they could not stop Monash's flow, even though several men were hit while sitting in their dugouts on the ground and pigeonholes in the cliffs. He managed to keep his voice steady and 'an uninterrupted thread to one's remarks'.[5]

Everything looked, or was made to look, very promising for the Battle of Sari Bair – on paper.

On the afternoon of 6 August, the first distraction at Helles was meant to tie down five Turkish divisions in front of the much-sought-after Krithia, but the feint turned into two actual attacks. The British VIII Corps incurred more than 4000 casualties. Worse, von Sanders had calculated that the real assault would come out of Anzac. While the British forces were being slaughtered needlessly (if the directive for a 'feint' was taken as it was meant originally by Birdwood), the Australian 1st Brigade became embroiled at 5.30 p.m. in another full-scale battle at Lone Pine. It lost 2000 casualties in a vicious clash with the Turks, who lost 7000. It was a clear victory for the invaders, a rare event on the peninsula, but at a horrible cost.

Oblivious of the scale of this slaughter earlier in the day and its implications, the battle for Sari Bair was kept on schedule, at least to start. The territory dictated that the force would have to move in columns – sometimes one man behind the other. Cox was out of Reserve Gully heading north at 9.30 p.m. on 6 August with a column consisting of Monash's 4th Brigade, the 29th Indian Brigade, a mountain battery and a company of New Zealand engineers. Monash had estimated that the 4th would reach its first target at 1.40 a.m. on 8 August – in just four hours and ten minutes. This seemed fair for an eight-kilometre trek when the terrain was viewed from that battleship three weeks earlier.

The Turks were waiting for them. They greeted the column with an artillery attack.

'It was like walking out on a stormy winter's night from a warm cosy home into a hail, thunder and lightning storm,' Monash wrote. 'We had not gone a kilometre when the black tangle of hills between the beach road and the main mountain range became alive with flashes of musketry, and the bursting of shrapnel and star shell.'[6]

After three kilometres, the column approached Walden Point on the beach road. Major Percy Overton, the New Zealand scout at the column, decided, on the advice of a Greek guide, to take a short cut inland through a narrow gorge (Taylor's Gap). The men were forced to go single file and were impeded by prickly gorse and dwarf oak, which engineers had to hack their way through. Turk sharpshooters in the hills began peppering them.

The short cut had not only slowed the march to an upright crawl; it had also exposed the column to the Turks they were supposed to scout around. The single file stretched right back to Reserve Gully and made communication, early in the offensive, almost impossible. On top of that, it was a blacker night than usual. The men could not see ten metres in front of them.

The 600-metre gorge took three and a half hours to negotiate. It was 2 a.m. when the head of the column squeezed into the valley (Aghyl Dere), which was supposed to lead them on to the major destination ridge, Abdel Rahman Spur.

Cox had insisted that Monash walk in the middle of the brigade, which had irritated him. How could he make decisions if he didn't know what was happening at the head of the column? But crusty, insecure Cox stayed with his original decision, until the column halted and volleys of shots were heard ahead. Monash pressed Cox again. He wanted to go forward. Cox let him send a staff officer. He didn't return inside twenty minutes.

The word passed along the line that the officer had tripped in the thickets and impaled himself on a bayonet.

The firing by snipers in the ridges at the entrance to the gully continued. Monash sent his staffers Lieutenant Locke and Captain Eastwood forward, with orders for several of the best fighters in the 13th Battalion to climb to the ridges and counter-attack the shooters. This seemed to work, but the column was still not moving. Tension mounted. A frustrated Monash demanded that he go forward himself. Cox relented. Monash scrambled to the front.

Their actual location was not in dispute when it should have been. If Overton were wrong it would jeopardise the main objective of reaching Hill 971 on the heights. Eastwood and Locke assumed, in the true Godley tradition, that Overton knew where he was. When Monash reached them, the debate was not about their position but which way they should go from there. Everyone, including the Greek guide and the commander of the 13th Battalion, Lieutenant Colonel Tilney, was arguing. Tilney wanted to take Cox's designated route via the Aghyl Valley. Overton thought there was a better way.

'What damned nonsense,' Monash yelled. 'Get a move on, quick!'[7]

But they couldn't. Monash conferred and made a decision to ignore Overton, whose earlier deference to the Greek guide had slowed them. Instead he went with a variation of Cox's plan to go across the Aghyl Valley. He began deploying companies. The force spread out over nearly two kilometres. The 13th and 14th Battalions moved northeast over Aghyl Valley into a wild cornfield about a thousand metres long (which would become known as Australia Valley). The 15th and 16th swept more east or right along Aghyl Valley.

At this point, around 2.45 a.m., the brigade was split in two. Although they were moving roughly in the same direction, there was a danger of dislocation in the rugged, deceptive terrain with its sharp, tight ridges, unseen precipices and blackness.

The 15th Battalion on the far right of the line came across a strong Turkish attack. The New Zealand brigade had been making its own left hook on a smaller arc. It had driven the Turks off a hill – Bauchop's, south of Aghyl Valley – and into the advancing Australians. The battle intensified as they moved forward across rough country for less than two kilometres. The darkness made the fighting more precarious as the Australians used the bayonet more than the bullet. It was an exhausting encounter for men who were struggling after a six-hour march of several kilometres, which was the equivalent in this country of marching a half marathon of forty kilometres.

With dawn approaching at 4.30 a.m., Monash set up his HQ 500 metres east of Taylor's Gap. He wrote that the 4th Brigade was 'on a line of ridges overlooking Asma Dere', the valley that had to be crossed before he reached the precipitous Abdel Rahman. Because of Overton's critical error about their location when they left Taylor's Gap, they were 650 metres west of where they thought they were. Monash was not overlooking Asma Valley but Kaiajik Valley. The 4th's battalions would have to cross Kaiajik Valley and Asma Valley before they could tackle the formidable spurs of Abdel Rahman. In short, Monash was lost and didn't know it. His temporary HQ was an exposed location, but he weighed that against his position, which kept him in range of both halves of his brigade.

The 15th and 16th battalions overran a Turkish base. Monash was just in the process of setting up some of the loot – a captured copper tub and fold-up bed – in his own HQ when he heard noise in the scrub near him. He pulled out his revolver, then took a few steps forward.

'Who goes there?' he challenged.

Two Turks crawled out. They stood up, hands held high in surrender. Monash ordered his staff to send them to the growing prisoner 'camp'. He holstered his weapon and went on with his HQ construction, chuffed that he had made his first ever personal captures.[8]

At first light, Monash checked the battle area and conferred with the 15th's commander, Colonel James Cannan, and the 16th's Pope. They had incurred 300 casualties. 'I counted 500 Turkish dead and wounded,' Monash said in his war letters. 'We made over 600 prisoners, including many officers. [We also captured] stores, rifle and gun ammunition, immense quantities of equipment, several fine chargers, telephone and camp equipment.'[9]

This was spin for posterity. The men of the 15th and 16th had just about collapsed on their feet. Monash ordered his commanders to dig in and rest. The commanders reported by phone (cut in an attack and restored) that they didn't have the energy for it. Not even another shot of rum, which had bucked them up earlier, would help.

Monash had not had any rest when English Major Cecil Allanson from the 29th Indian Brigade arrived with a small detail at Monash's HQ. Allanson was under Cox's orders to support the 4th. Allanson wished to know what the plan was. When would it be moving forward? He would bring his battalion of Gurkhas up if assistance were needed.

Monash was tired. He wanted to cooperate with Allanson, but there was nothing he could do at that moment. It was what the major wished to hear. 'I found the 4th Brigade engaged with a large body of Turks,' Allanson would tell the UK Dardanelles Commission two years later. 'There was an apparent precipice in front. I saw no hope of ever getting to the top of the hill [even] if I supported them.' It was too 'hot' for Allanson and his battalion of Gurkhas. 'I think they [4th Brigade] got into an impossible country,' he added. 'I think my battalion had tremendous luck in striking good country.'

Allanson wanted to keep his fortunes running by departing this nasty territory and away from Turkish fire as fast as possible. He rushed a message to Cox, which seemed to have been 'embroidered'. Cox, who had been wounded by shrapnel, hurried forward to confront Monash about an hour later.[10]

Cox wanted Monash to push on to Abdel Rahman Range and Hill 971. Monash was adamant. His brigade would not be going anywhere. He only had to gesture at some of his men nearby. Many lay where they had dropped after the night of fatigue. Cox had no choice but to allow Monash to entrench, especially with artillery and snipers encroaching on them from the right.

It had not been a terrific day at the office for any of Monash's superiors: Hamilton, Birdwood, Godley and Cox. The whole Gallipoli campaign was at a turning point. After the costly victory by the Australians at Lone Pine and the further setback at Helles, 7 August was a watershed. The back-up 29th Indian Brigade had made some progress, but not enough to have any major influence. The New Zealanders on that short left hook, and to the right of 4th Brigade, had done good work on a more direct mission. But they had not overcome the Turks on the heights. The New Zealanders' commander, Brigadier General Francis Johnston, drunk in the morning, had dithered while waiting for reinforcements – the Canterburys – that didn't arrive on time.

On the assumption that these forces would come over Battleship Hill, on the approach to Chunk Bair between it and the Nek, Chauvel's Australian Light Horse Brigade, acting as infantry, would charge up the Nek at 4.30 a.m. on the morning of 7 August. This plan was to box up the

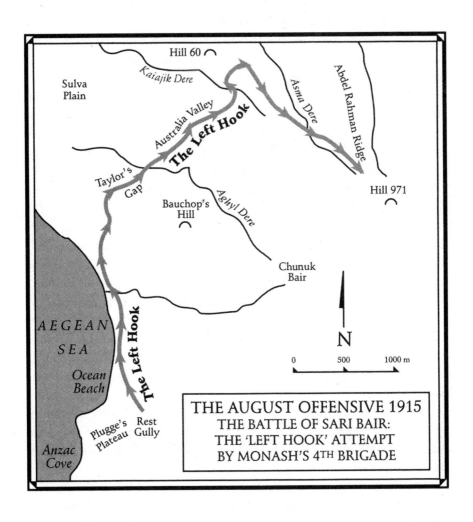

Hill 60

Kaiajik Dere

Sulva
Plain

Australia Valley

Asma Dere

Abdel Rahman Ridge

The Left Hook

Taylor's
Gap

Bauchop's
Hill

Aghyl Dere

Hill 971

Chunuk
Bair

N

AEGEAN

SEA

The Left Hook

Ocean
Beach

0   500   1000 m

Plugge's   Rest
Plateau   Gully

Anzac
Cove

THE AUGUST OFFENSIVE 1915
THE BATTLE OF SARI BAIR:
THE 'LEFT HOOK' ATTEMPT
BY MONASH'S 4TH BRIGADE

eight lines of Turkish trenches looking down on the Nek, a narrow saddle running east–west between the ridgeline of Russell's Top and Baby 700 (sitting between Battleship Hill and the Nek). The Turkish trenches were twenty to sixty metres from the Australians. But the New Zealanders were 450 metres short of their objective. The Australians charged and were cut down by machine-gun fire strong enough to sheer off limbs. The brigade had 372 casualties, including 234 killed.

Other disasters beset the Royal Welch Fusiliers scrambling up the steep walls of Monash Valley between Russell's Top and Pope's, with the aim of taking the Chessboard network of Turkish trenches. But their efforts depended on the Australians being successful on the Nek. The chain reaction of misadventures, caused again by the poor planning of Birdwood and the careless Godley, assured that the Fusiliers, too, never made it. They lost sixty men before their commander called off the assault.

Assumptions, suppositions, hopes and mindless inflexibility from Godley on autopilot had done much to propel the campaign towards failure.

As these horrific mishaps were unfolding, the 4th's 15th and 16th Battalions dug in all through a very hot day. It was a miserable exercise for the men, who on occasions had to lie flat to dig. The snipers were even more active now that they could see their targets. Some in the 4th even ventured the wish to be back in the stink and heat of Reserve Gully.

At 5.30 p.m. on 7 August Cox gave the new plan to Monash. It must have seemed now like a pipe dream. He had to 'attack with such troops as I could up Abdel Rahman Spur, so as to draw the enemy down the spur from attacks the other way'.[11]

Hill 971 was now a target too far for 4th Brigade. Cox's operation, which included the New Zealand Brigade, appeared to place the main emphasis on the southern crests of the Abdel Rahman Range – at Chunuk Bair and Q Hill.

The 4th had already been held up by fatigue, the terrain and the actual fighting with the Turks. Any combat had seen the men rise above their deplorable condition and acquit themselves with the courage and ability displayed on Anzac. But they were never going to beat the territory. Especially not when that navigational error meant coming out of Taylor's Gap they had twice as much 'impossible' ground to cover.

Monash protested to Cox that the 4th could not go on. Cox refused to let them retire. Monash then demanded reinforcements from the British IXth Army, which had landed on 6 August. Cox agreed. Monash was given a New Army unit, the 6th King's Own Royal Lancasters. It would be used to hold the present 4th Brigade line with the 13th Battalion. This would release the 14th, 15th and 16th Battalions for the 'dash' under fierce fire across the two valleys to the big ridge, which was, everyone agreed, the most forbidding on the entire Gallipoli Peninsula.

Then came the most incongruous decision of Monash's Anzac experience. He put Pope in charge of the three battalions that were to attack. Monash would stay back on the line already held by the 13th. He would remain in telephone contact with Pope. It seems almost certain that Cox, who wanted to stay in close contact with Monash, and therefore in command of the operation, ordered him to stay put. It was consistent with Cox's earlier blunder in placing Monash in the middle of the column marching to Aghyl Valley, which left the brigade in confusion until Monash sorted it out.

At 6 p.m. Godley sent Monash orders to attack at 3 a.m. the next morning, 8 August. Monash spent ninety minutes on reconnoitring, and had a conference with his commanders at 8.30 p.m. After that he went to bed for four hours – from 10 p.m. to 2 a.m. It was his first 'rest' for two days.

At 2.30 a.m. on 8 August Monash was up on a high knoll above his HQ position directing his troops. At 4 a.m. the 15th Battalion led by Pope marched off towards Kaiajik Valley with the 14th and 16th behind it. They were hit by an 'inferno' coming from their right. It began with an incessant blast of machine-gun fire. Shelling followed. The moment that it abated, the Turks, with heavy reinforcements, attacked.

Monash's telephone lines were sabotaged in the clever Turkish counter-attack. The Cox decision to hold him on the entrenchment line had backfired within a half-hour of the 4th's move. Now Pope was in charge of his own battalion, and he was the de facto brigade battle commander. It was an impossible demand under such trying conditions of terrain and against a now sustained, fierce opposition.

When the lines had been restored by about 7 a.m., Pope and the 16th's commander, Cannan, reported the hopeless situation. They were desperate to withdraw. The troops were bogged down and in trouble. There was no hope of going forward. With two such proven fighting commanders in accord, Monash put three options to the difficult, twitchy Cox. They could entrench, or they could advance. In the latter case, Monash wanted two back-up battalions. The third option was withdrawal. Cox realised (as Monash knew) that entrenchment would mean many more men would be butchered. There was no time for reinforcements. Cox had no choice now but to agree to a withdrawal. Monash, who had been against the advance, was once more displeased with his superiors' poor judgement. Cox's thoughtless leadership had matched Godley's bumbling and cold-bloodedness.

Monash ordered his powerful machine-gun unit into position. The 4th began its retreat. The Turks came out from cover in the full light of the early morning and were chopped up by the gunners. By 8.30 a.m. on 8 August, the 14th, 15th and 16th were back at the 4th's line. The mission was over, unaccomplished.

The four-hour 'attack' had incurred 700 casualties, mainly among the 15th Battalion in the lead. The decision not to have Monash closer to the front line made no difference to the outcome, but was wrong on at least two counts. One was the burden on Pope. The other was the uncontrolled bickering between the 14th and 15th Battalion commanders during the withdrawal. This was a hangover from the suspicion that the 15th had accidentally fired on the 14th at Quinn's. Monash's presence would have prevented any discord.

Another mishap became apparent in the retreat. The ambulance units had not been informed of the attacks. The result was an uncoordinated, slow evacuation of the wounded, who struggled or were carried back to the 4th's line. Some casualties were still lying there eight hours later in mid-afternoon before stretchers arrived.

It was a depressing part of the engagement for the 4th. But it didn't end there. On 9 August the Turkish counter-attack continued and intensified. Only strong resistance by the 13th Battalion, supported by the battered 15th, which the indefatigable Pope continued to inspire, managed to hold its section of the British line. The 16th had to relieve a British battalion that had been hammered.

On 10 August Cox was trying to plug holes as the Turks threatened penetration while pushing back the British line. He turned every time not to the fresh New Army arrivals but Monash's men. Even if only 100 of the 14th and 200 of the 15th could be spared, Cox directed them to the trouble spots.

For these testing days, the 4th was behaving as if it were back at the head of Monash Valley holding the line. They were depleted, without water, good ammunition supplies or adequate provisions. They were resting without covering and were in need of a complete break. Bronchitis was beginning to run through the battalions as fast as dysentery. Yet their spirit, buoyed by Monash, and defensive fighting with rifle, bayonet and machine-gun, was near unbreakable. It was a matter of hardness and sheer will, prepared well in Egypt, and shaped and honed at Anzac. They were always going to do far better than the inexperienced relieving British troops, who were in awe of the enemy, the terrain and the Anzacs.

It was not surprising that Cox wrote home to his wife at this time raving about the 4th Brigade and wishing that he had more Australians. But unless the British command had a couple more fit divisions of them that had also been toughened by an Anzac type of experience, they would be struggling for victory. As the days unfolded and the British forces could not make inroads, it was becoming clear that the leaders, strategists and planners were not competent enough for such a challenging campaign.[12]

The 4th's failure was one of a litany of unfulfilled missions. On 9 August Allanson's battalion of Gurkhas from the 29th Indian Brigade had fought well to take Hill Q, but were driven off it by 'friendly' artillery fire from ships off Anzac Cove and fierce shelling from the Turks. On 10 August the dogged New Zealanders had dug in on Chunuk Bair, but had to be relieved after an exhausting effort. Their replacements from two New Army battalions were driven from the crest by a Turkish counter-attack, and butchered.

Meanwhile incompetence of a high order reigned at Suvla Bay long after the landing of the 25,000 soldiers of IX Corps. Lieutenant Sir Frederick Stopford, a retired sixty-one-year-old 'elderly English gentleman', who had never commanded in battle before, was supposed to lead this force forward with objectives to take certain of the high ground above the bay. The dithering by him, his staff and commanders on the beach for two days allowed von Sanders and the resourceful Kemal to bring in four battalions (4000 men) to control the heights just as they had at Anzac and Helles. But there was a notable difference. They were able to render an entire corps useless and create a third siege without a serious fight.

Monash was scathing about the IX Corps:

. . . while there was an open road to the Dardanelles, and no opposition worth talking about, a whole army corps sat down on the
beach while its leaders were quarrelling about questions of seniority
and precedence; and it was just that delay of 48 hours which
enabled the Turks to bring up their last strategic reserve from Bulair
and render futile the whole purpose of landing. That was to protect
the left flank of the Anzac advance. The failure to do this held up
our further advance.[13]

On 10 August Birdwood and Godley had a cheery lunch with Hamilton
on Anzac. Birdwood, who had been conspicuous by his invisibility during
the week of the offensive, reported that things had not gone quite according to plan anywhere – except at Lone Pine, and even that was meant to be
a feint more than a fight. The promise by Birdwood and Godley that they
would deliver those several left hooks and then a knockout blow had not
yet been fulfilled. But they did not dare say that the Gallipoli Peninsula
might not ever be presented to Hamilton now.

Despite his unrealistic optimism, in his heart Hamilton must have had
a fair inkling of this. He had been at Suvla Bay and witnessed for himself
the disorganisation of Stopford's corps, owing not to the Turks but to a
lack of will to direct and engage. Yet Hamilton was still very much in
denial. By 16 August he took steps belatedly to keep his hopes alive. He
sacked Stopford and his generals.

Gallipoli wasn't over for the battered remnants of 4th Brigade, which was
down from 3350 to 1400 men. It was involved in another grand plan,
whereby the Suvla forces, under allegedly more inspired command, were
meant to link with Godley's mixed bag of forces to 'attack Hill 60', an
unprepossessing knoll with a sixty-metre slope that Monash's HQ had
been near on 7 August. Now it was in Turkish hands. It had to be retaken.

There was no further talk of sweeping left hooks to take the heights and
crashing across the peninsula. The collective genius of the campaign's
command was being poured into a scramble for a bit of territory on low
country a few kilometres from the beach between Suvla Bay and Anzac
Cove. The ubiquitous Kemal, who had been leading his men in key
defences and attacks on the heights, didn't fear these moves. As long as the
battles were confined closer to the sea and he commanded the high

ground, then common sense said he could not lose. The invaders, sooner or later, would have to step up their numbers yet again or get out.

For the first time, Birdwood and Godley came forward to the combat zone to be taken over the 4th's lines by Monash. They were impressed by the positioning, 'excellent trenchwork' and obvious resourcefulness of the men. So much so that 500 of the best and halfway fit fighters from the 13th and 14th Brigades were plucked out by Cox to form a right flank, which would be connected to the IX Corps linking up from Suvla.

Cox, who had written to his wife so enthusiastically about the Australians ten days earlier, was not going to risk any of the more recently arrived British forces, no matter how much fresher they were. He had been holding back the Turkish surges with Monash's men. Now he would use them to attack along with a further composite force. It was made up of 400 of the New Zealand Mounted Rifles under Brigadier General Andrew Russell, several hundred from an also depleted Indian brigade, and 330 from the unreliable New Army battalions.

The idea – concocted by Birdwood, Godley and Cox – was to direct the 500 from the 4th on the right flank to charge across 180 metres of open ground in two initial waves in broad daylight, supported by the New Zealanders. In theory it was not a suicide mission. There would be an artillery barrage before the rush.

The battle was timed for 3.30 p.m. Much to Monash's horror, orders were changed at the last minute. The artillery was not in place and ready at the appointed time. 'It was altogether a mis-timed, mis-calculated, and mis-directed operation,' he wrote later. Right at the moment of attack 'everybody got rattled'.[14]

The artillery began. Poor planning made it feeble. It served only to warn the Turks waiting on Hill 60. They aimed their machine-guns, rifles and grenades, and redirected their artillery. The first wave of 150 men from the 13th Battalion charged from Kaiajik Valley. It was shredded. Only forty were not killed or wounded.

The British artillery tried again. This time they succeeded only in starting a brush fire. Again there was more warning to the enemy than protection. In the second wave, the 14th sent out 150 men. Only fifty would survive.

After the battle, Monash could see the carnage. He knew it would be impossible to save the wounded if there were no reinforcements. He had to go over Cox's head to Godley, who was back at Anzac. He sent a runner.

An embittered Monash asked for help for the 'survivors' on the battlefield. Godley turned pedant. He was affronted by the use of the word 'survivors'. He wished, ever so politely, that Monash would talk in terms of the 'exact number of casualties'. Godley would be most appreciative if Monash was to refrain from exaggeration. It could lower morale.[15]

Godley's ungodly reaction was reminiscent of a conversation he had with Temperley, brigade major of the New Zealand Infantry Brigade. In an urgent request for reinforcements, Temperley was telling him of casualties at Chunuk Bair suffered by the brigade in its assault days earlier. In a double demonstration of his attitude to his men as dispensable numbers, he was using binoculars to watch a despatch rider from Suvla dodging bullets in an attempt to reach his HQ. Godley could have been a caller at a steeplechase, or a fox hunt: 'Don't talk like a bloody fool!' he told Temperley. 'By God . . . I think this fellow [rider] will get away with it after all! . . . A man who's been in action always comes out with some cock-and-bull story about the thousands of casualties . . . Christ! Did you see him duck that time? By God! Look! *Look!* They've got him at last! By God they have! That was a bloody fine shot! . . . When's the next one coming along?'[16]

While Godley played with words like a semantic fetishist, the wounded soldiers in front of Hill 60 lay frying in the burning scrub. Others died from exploding ammunition pouches. The help was not sent.

When the firing fell away after dark, the attacking force had a toehold at the beginning of the mound's gentle slope. Cox now stepped in. He asked Godley for reinforcements without mentioning 'survivors' or even 'casualties'. The force 'numbers' were down. He reckoned he could take this excuse for a hill if he had more men. Godley fumed but agreed. He sent him the 18th Battalion from the 2nd Australian Division, which had arrived three days earlier at crowded Anzac Cove.

The fresh-faced, straight-backed youths couldn't wait to go to the aid of their Aussie compatriots. They were fit and ready but had never been in combat.

At dawn on 22 August, 750 of them lined up 200 metres west of Hill 60. They were ordered to charge with bayonets only. In forty-five minutes, 190 were dead and another 193 were wounded. Some of the rest – the survivors – would live to tell the tale of how their battalion had been massacred by the Turks and Cox's poor planning. They had no artillery support. They had no grenades or 'bombs'. An attack at night would have seen more of them survive what turned out to be a suicide attack for thirty per cent of them. It was their first and last hour on a battlefield fighting for their fallen Australian comrades.

Welcome to Anzac, the gaunt, broken 4th Brigade remnants would have said.

Monash counted his upright men. It was a brigade in name only. He now commanded a battalion-size force of just 968. For the second time at Anzac, his numbers had been slashed. Decimation, it seemed, would be the consequence of the crash-through thinking of Birdwood, Godley and Cox. They decided on another assault on Hill 60 on 27 August. Two hundred and fifty weary members of the 4th were detailed for the attack, which was scratched up from nine battalions.

Monash, supported by Russell, who would lead the assault, protested against attacking again in daylight. Monash and Cox had a heated exchange. Cox would not relent. The attack had to go ahead at dawn. Once more the artillery support was weak.

The assault this time was more successful. They took Turkish trenches. But they encircled only half the lower slopes. The Turks still held the summit. One journalist, whose uncle fought at Hill 60, observed: 'For connoisseurs of military futility, valour, incompetence and determination, the attacks on Hill 60 are in a class of their own.'[17]

More of Monash's officers, including Pope, couldn't carry on and had to be rested. His own constitution was holding up. Because he lacked overall command, he had to accept what was happening, control his own despair and steel himself for any contingency. Otherwise Monash would crack like so many others, and he knew it.

'There is the definite tactical objective,' he noted, 'and that is all important – to capture a hill, or seize a road or a well or a ravine. The great point is to do it, and having done it, to reorganise ready for the next move. If one stops to count the cost, or worry about the loss of friends, or the grief and sorrow of the people at home, one simply cannot carry on for an hour.'

Monash was still feisty and fighting for the rights of his enfeebled force. He had another steamy encounter with Cox, telling him that without officers – all of them had been killed, wounded or broken down – the brigade had to be rested. Cox, defending his multitude of failed directives, began a digressive argument about the state of one of the 4th's trenches, which he claimed had not been linked to others after he had ordered it. This was a week after he had moved through the lines with Birdwood and Godley complimenting Monash on the 'excellent trenchwork'.[18]

Monash protested to Godley about Cox's 'bullying'. He was disgusted with the Hill 60 mission, calling it 'a rotten, badly organised show'. He blamed the near extinguishing of his brigade on the trio of planners. But he confined his remarks to his war letters and diaries. Any such public denunciation would have seen him sacked and decommissioned.[19]

After the debacles at Hill 60, 4th Brigade was at last put out to the less hazardous pastures of the line on Bauchop's Hill. After four months, Monash's force, in its present structure, was spent.

Further botched leadership in a concurrent huge losing battle in the same sector at Scimitar Hill meant that the route to the heights was still denied to the invaders, as was the ultimate control of the Dardanelles. Hamilton's written promise to the King, Prime Minister Asquith and Kitchener – that he would deliver the Gallipoli Peninsula to the empire – was now unrealistic. His writing showed that he was living in cuckoo land: 'As a result of the battles of August 1915, we had gained elbow room and inflicted enormous losses on the enemy . . . but we had not succeeded in our main aim . . . the spirit of the Turks had, however, been broken, and they had been thrown entirely on the defensive.'[20]

Kemal would have been smiling from his lofty throne in the heights. Hamilton was deluding himself, and many in British high places were aware of it. Some of his own staff officers were beginning to think of ways to engineer his dismissal. Hamilton had lost more than 40,000 men for the gain of ground a few kilometres from the beaches that now amounted to 600 acres.

It meant nothing in terms of the original campaign objective.

Monash was able to resume his correspondence, which had dropped off because of his constant battle engagements in August. On 5 September, while resting on Bauchop's Hill, he wrote a reflective letter to Vic summing up the campaign's failure. He said it 'tended to overshadow the many minor successes and brilliant achievements' of the Anzacs.

'It is the old story,' he wrote, 'insufficient troops, inadequate munitions, attempting more than was possible with the means available.' He had a slap at the British, saying: 'Much fault lay in the leadership; the officers do not mix with the men as we do, but keep aloof. Some senior officers appeared chiefly concerned in looking after themselves and making themselves comfortable. It only shows how hard it is to make an army after a war has started.'[21]

He was also scathing about the British troops themselves. Coming from Monash, this was not simply 'Pommy bashing'. It was heartfelt and sincere criticism. He had two New Army battalions under him for a short time.

'Over and over again they have allowed themselves to be driven out of positions which have been hardly won by Anzac troops,' he noted with feeling for his men who had fallen fighting for ground quickly lost.

> They have no grit, no stamina, no endurance, poor physique, no gumption. They muddle along and allow themselves to be shot down because they don't even know how to take cover. Over and over again I have had to mix up a few platoons of Australians among them to keep them steady and teach them how to dig trenches; how to prepare their bivouacs; how to cook their food; how to take cover; how to fight, and how to stand their ground. They have a willing enough spirit, and plenty of dull, stupid courage, but they simply don't know enough to come in out of the wet. Much of the fault lies in the leadership.

On 13 September he was writing from Lemnos, along with the 1st, 2nd, 4th, New Zealand Infantry and New Zealand Mounted Rifles Brigades – the five that had done most of the heavy fighting on Anzac. Monash revelled in his generalship, something in which his own Australian troops had shown little interest. To the Anzacs, an officer was an officer, big deal. Most of them didn't know most of the key commanders by sight, name or rank. But here on the idyllic island over eighty kilometres from Gallipoli, Monash found this new rank was more than useful in getting things done.

'It is that bit of gold gimp on the gorget patches that does the trick,' he said. 'There is always a special picket boat, and a special gangway lowered and special privileges all along the line.'

Ever since joining the militia at Melbourne University thirty-three years earlier, Monash had enjoyed standing out in a special uniform. The peacock in him had always liked the colour and the splendour. Now he was mature and had impressive rank, it was more about status and prestige. He noted that British soldiers and sailors seemed to have a 'special veneration for generals'.

After the bloody fog on the peninsula, where the niceties of rank were observed as a necessity rather than anything special, Monash basked in some modest non-combat respect. But just as he was wallowing in a little glory, with a French naval commander-in-chief who was ingratiating towards 'Monsieur le General Monash', he was brought back to reality with an attack of (his 'old friend') lumbago, along with an assault of acute dysentery.[22] The microbe that his fitness and cautious had helped him baulk at Gallipoli had cornered him.

In mid-September a thirty-year-old Australian journalist, Keith Murdoch, provided the vehicle that Hamilton's enemies had been searching for to get rid of him. Murdoch was acting as the editor of a cable service supplying the Sydney *Sun* and the Melbourne *Herald* from the *Times* building in London. He had missed out on becoming Australia's official war correspondent. He was not as professional as Bean or expressive as Ashmead-Bartlett, yet he was more ambitious for power than both. This made him craftier. Murdoch was always on his way to being something more substantial than a mere wordsmith.

When he visited Gallipoli for four days, he had no hope on his own of grasping what was happening. He needed to have been on the peninsula for four months like the diligent Bean or the creative Ashmead-Bartlett. So he did what all journalists do in such circumstances. He sought out other journalists who knew what was what. Ashmead-Bartlett hit home with his incisive views on what had transpired on the peninsula. Murdoch was stunned at the Englishman's view that the August offensive 'was the most ghastly and costly fiasco in our history since the battle of Bannockburn . . . the muddles and mismanagement beat anything that has ever occurred in our military history . . . my views are shared by the large majority of the army . . .'

Murdoch loved such lavish insights. They were headlines. Murdoch was a cable editor. He thought in headlines. He believed he might achieve something here. But he was cool enough to know that it would be better if Ashmead-Bartlett wrote a letter to Asquith with all his views in it.

Murdoch would be the courier. He dashed off with the letter, was inter-cepted in Marseilles and had it taken off him. He went on to London, and saw his main chance. He wrote his own account of the Gallipoli debacle, based on what Ashmead-Bartlett had told him, for Australian PM Billy Hughes. But he embellished it with his own flourish and slant. Murdoch, the tabloid writer, made it pro-Australian and anti-British. Murdoch, the 'creative' journalist, gilded it with on-the-spot observations, some that he had not made. Murdoch, the would-be power monger, structured it so that governments might sit up.

He was surprised how much they did.

His office at *The Times* had easy access to its editor, Geoffrey Dawson – the kind of newspaperman that Murdoch aspired to be. Dawson knew the King and mixed with the influential figures in government. He put these connections ahead of his independence as a newspaperman or the business of reporting. When Murdoch mentioned his letter, Dawson asked to see it. He wanted it for his own influence. He knew that the snipers in high places were out to get Hamilton, the key figure in maintaining a British force on Gallipoli. This 'independent' report could help Dawson's personal influence with these elevated political assassins.

Dawson took Murdoch to meet the then Minister of Munitions, Lloyd George, whose unconventional methods were making some headway in the constipated English production of the right, modern weapons of war. Murdoch's claims about the lack of the right artillery, grenades and other explosives were of keen interest to Lloyd George, who had been battling Kitchener about supplies. Lloyd George suggested that Murdoch send his now important letter to Prime Minister Asquith, who was at the head of the anti-Gallipoli faction in his own government. Seizing the chance to make Hamilton's position untenable, Asquith took the surprising step of printing the Murdoch letter as a state paper. It was circulated where it mattered. Kitchener felt compelled to fire Hamilton on 15 October.

Murdoch had achieved far more influence than he expected. The opportunist's sheer cheek, courage and intelligence would cause him to go down in Australian history as the journalist who broke the 'story' that told the truth, essentially, about Gallipoli. His reputation was made.

✕

Hamilton's dismissal came at a woeful time for the Allied cause. The year 1915 was shaping up badly. On the eastern front the Russian armies were being hurled backwards. They had lost half a million men and more than 3000 guns in several significant defeats to the Austro-German army. In the Balkans, Bulgaria had been staying out of the major conflict, sniffing the wind to see which team would be best to support. They were likely now to side with Germany. It looked very much like a winner. On the Italian front a strong allied offensive had been repulsed. In France, General Joseph Jacques Césaire Joffre had cajoled Kitchener into another huge autumn offensive. He was in despair over how to meet such demands. Kitchener was looking now at all options to cut losses. With Hamilton out of the way, the Gallipoli campaign was one of them.

Monash wondered where Hamilton's replacement, Sir Charles Munro, would head it. Monash was in the first week of a break with his officers in Egypt when he heard the news about Hamilton's removal. He was not pleased. Despite the peninsula debacle, Monash thought highly of Hamilton. That was part of the problem. Everybody did. He was too nice, too much of a gentleman to run a major British military performance, even if it was viewed from GHQ as a 'sideshow' in the context of the broader conflict.

But life and leadership would go on. Monash's morale was lifted on 18 October when he received a telegram from Birdwood congratulating him on 'being created' a Companion of the Order of the Bath, 'for distin-guished service in the field'. There were now many more 'Baths' than ever before on grubby Gallipoli. Monash's four battalion commanders also received the high order, as did Lieutenant-Generals Walker and McCay. The only higher award to the Anzacs went to New Zealand's Major General Russell. He was knighted. Once more, the New Zealand Govern-ment had shown more enterprise than its Australian counterpart in recognising the huge efforts and sacrifices made at Gallipoli. There was much pride and no cringe in its reaction.

Monash was pleased to pick up his 'new ribbon – a bright magenta'. He celebrated by heading for the Cairo markets to buy Vic three pieces of silk. It was fun for him to visit a shop, 'sit on a divan, sip Turkish coffee and smoke a hookah', while the owner showed his wares. Monash enjoyed the haggle. 'I don't know whether I've been had or not, and don't care,' he wrote to his wife, 'so long as you are a little pleased.'[23]

By 8 November Monash was back on Bauchop's Hill with his brigade. The Turks were entrenched 270 metres away, which was real breathing space

compared to Monash Valley. It was comparatively safe and not expected to flair up. Yet there was always the danger of a stray bullet, an accurate bomb or even an onslaught.

Five days later, he received a mysterious demand, complete with dress code, to meet Birdwood at Mule Gully on the beach before noon. Monash came alone for the last couple of kilometres of the six-kilometre 'tramp'. The other brigadiers and divisional commanders were there. Right on noon, they all turned and gazed out to sea. They could see a tiny picket boat. It weaved its way through lighters, barges, punts, destroyers and submarines in Anzac Cove.

Birdwood walked to the end of a little jetty to meet the visitors. First out of the boat was 'a very tall officer in plain service khaki', Monash wrote. 'It was the great Field-Marshall Earl Kitchener of Khartoum himself.'

He headed a small group including one French and one British general. Kitchener came to shake hands with the Anzac commanders. Monash was the first man to whom he spoke. 'I have brought you all a personal message from the King,' Kitchener said. 'He wants me to tell you how much he admires the splendid things that you have done here.'[24]

That was the extent of the sombre leader's remarks. Thanks for what has been done, past tense. There was no inspirational message or even a platitude about 'carrying on the brilliant work' or 'going for a magnificent victory'. None of the astute commanders picked up on this. They were too thrilled that the great man had come so far to say so little. There was a reason for Kitchener's reticence. Now that Hamilton was out of the way, he and the War Council had decided to evacuate.

When Hamilton was in charge evacuation was never mentioned. Not long before the Murdoch letter incident and Hamilton's dismissal he had made the chilling request for another 90,500 men. Hamilton had been thinking of doubling the invasion, not shrinking it or giving up. It meant that even a month after he had been sacked the military mind-set on Gallipoli was to carry on and prepare for a rotten, freezing winter.

Monash was getting ready. He had used his engineering skills to create all the infrastructure of a small town with tunnelling and constructing underground HQs, chambers, galleries, storage facilities, vents and drains. There were no guarantees that it would withstand a harsh winter and the howitzers with better ammunition that the Germans had promised the Turks, along with fresh supplies of grenades and other bombs. But the 4th Brigade would have the best subterranean village ever built on a battlefield.

He was also doing his best to augment five months monotony of bully beef, hard biscuits, a little bacon, jam and boring tea (the only authorised drink) with other food. Monash pushed for cigarette paper and tobacco, and encouraged facilities for games – playing cards, dominoes, lotto games and, for some, chess. He pushed for mouth organs, concertinas, Jew's harps and plenty of reading matter. Anzac could never be a holiday camp, but Monash was doing everything he could to make the conditions bearable. Yet he didn't know what horrors a severe wet winter would bring.

Monash was never to know. On 12 December he learned it was all over. He wrote in his diary: 'Like a thunderbolt from a clear blue sky has come the stupendous and paralysing news that, after all, the Allied War Council has decided that the best and wisest course to take is to evacuate.'[25]

You could hear Monash's teeth grinding over the word. It was a shock. He didn't agree with it. The decision offended his tidy sensibilities about planning, carrying out an objective and winning. But he and the other commanders could not dwell on the what-might-have-beens. They had to create a strategy to tiptoe off the peninsula. It had to be far more of a secret than the landing. Otherwise there would be wholesale slaughter on the beaches.

The commanders had first to fool their own men. The bluff was that because of the winter conditions, rest camps would be set up at Imbros for battalions and brigades that would be rotated there. The secret plan was in three stages. First, two-thirds would be taken from the peninsula. Second, the last third would patrol the Allied areas. Third, the remaining men would 'make make a bolt for the beaches' in the dead of night where boats would be waiting for them.

Monash feared the enemy reaction if it realised the ruse. But he was just as worried about his own men's reaction. 'I am almost frightened to contemplate the howl of rage and disappointment there will be when the men find out what is afoot,' he wrote. 'I am wondering what Australia will think at the desertion of her 6000 dead and her 20,000 other casualties.'[26]

Monash observed, fascinated, as the war machine unwound. The postal service was disbanded. Supplies of fresh food ended. The military police withdrew, taking defaulters back to their units as they did so. The mule trains stopped. Supplies had to be carried by hand. Several thousand horses had to be led to barges. The hospitals were packed up. Cooking stopped. The city that was Anzac was floating off into the mist.

The next night, the 15th Battalion disappeared at two hours notice. The rumours began in the next few days. The soldiers thrived on the grapevine of innuendo, guesses and speculation. By Friday 16 December the departure was an open secret. Monash told his staff and commanding officers. Then there was a final divisional conference. It was a moment to savour. Men who had been through the toughest challenge and most demanding experience of their entire lives together said their farewells.

Birdwood came from Imbros. He shook hands with all the officers of 4th Brigade. 'I hope you all come through this alive,' he said.[27]

There were no guarantees. The requirement now was brilliant planning by 1st Division's Cyril White and Captain Cecil Aspinall, who devised the evacuation scheme. There were now 20,000 left of the 45,000 on Anzac, and about 20,000 still on the Cape Helles battlefield, down from 35,000.

So far there had no discernible reaction from the Turks. A significant advantage for the British forces was the absence of Mustafa Kemal, the most effective commander of either side during the Gallipoli battles. Exhaustion had led to malaria. He himself had been evacuated to Constantinople to recover. Kemal, with his sixth sense about opposition moves, his comprehension of the land, sea and weather conditions, and his coastal spies, might well have determined the stealthy British departure. But he was not there. The Turks and the German command were fatigued like him. They had a quarter of a million casualties, including more than 86,000 dead – in the defence. The British and French forces had more than 140,000 casualties with more than 43,000 dead. Not surprisingly, after such carnage, any force would not be quite as alert as at the beginning of a conflict. This allowed one of the biggest bluffs in military history a chance of success.

The Turks were conned by the 'quiet' tactic. The British at the two battlefields did not fire their guns for long stretches. The Turks moved forward into dangerous no man's land to see what was happening. Planes buzzed overhead. British soldiers in the trenches were under orders not to look up, so that they would not present a 'sea of white faces' to the intelligence gatherers. The silence drew some intrepid Turks out of their trenches to check out the front. Perhaps the British had gone. When they were met by what sounded like the usual barrage they retreated. Future silences would be treated more cautiously. Perhaps the British were running out of ammunition, the Turkish and German commanders speculated.

Blizzards, rough seas, fogs and long winter nights helped screen the ghostly departure.

On Saturday 17 December McGlinn slipped away with 800 more men. By now all the rank and file knew what was happening to them. They were not on rotation but a one-way ride out of there. On Sunday 18 December, Monash had just 825 men to get off the beach. There were still dangers. One of his staff was shot in the leg while talking to him outside the brigade 'office'.

The amazing conjuring trick went on. A hundred and seventy thousand Turks in nine divisions still thought they had 80,000 British forces under permanent siege in two major locations. By the next morning there would be just a few thousand foreigners – now no longer invaders – left, if the plan worked.

Monash, who loved magic tricks as a young man, revelled in this massive illusion. 'We have a clever device for firing off a rifle automatically at any predetermined time after the device is started,' Monash wrote. 'It is done by allowing a tin to fill slowly with water until it overbalances, falls and jerks a string, which fires a rifle.'[28] Monash had ten rifles rigged up. They would be started as the last men left and would fire five, ten, fifteen and twenty minutes afterwards. The plan was that Turks would think the Anzacs were still in their trenches.

At midnight, Monash and 654 men from the 4th Brigade – along with another 19,000 men at Suvla and Anzac – began leaving with plenty of noise cover from rifle fire, explosives and one or two intrepid soldiers trying out a new (Mills bomb) grenade.

Similar plans were made all over Anzac. Monash recorded:

Down dozens of little gullies leading back from the front lines came little groups of six or a dozen men, the last (in every case an officer) closing the gully with a prepared frame of barbed wire, or lighting a fuse which an hour later would fire a mine for the wrecking of a sap or a tunnel by which the enemy could follow. All these little columns of men kept joining up like so many rivulets, which flow into the main stream. At last they coalesced into four continuous lines: one from the south, two from the east, and one (the 4th Brigade) from the north.[29]

Everything was timed. The men, with loads, walked at three miles an hour. They all arrived at the correct moment at four jetties. A floor of sandbags deadened the sound of marching feet. The men eased into motor barges – beetles – holding 400. The only sound was the 'throb, throb' of the beetles' engines. At the last moment before boarding, Monash scooped some sand from the beach into a jar. It was destined for a prominent place in his private museum in the hallway at Iona.

Just 170 men from the brigade were left. Monash had given each one a card indicating what they had to carry off (machine-guns, and other weapons and stores) and the exact route they had to take to the beach.

At 1 a.m. on 19 December the last patrol of the 4th Brigade heard Turks digging and putting in barbed wire about 200 metres from the Australian trench network near Bauchop's Hill. They were creeping forward, but still unaware of the nearly empty Anzac positions.

By 1.55 a.m. Monash wrote that 'my last man vacated his foremost position, leaving only the automatic devices working'.[30]

Those automatic rifles began firing. At about 2.45 a.m. mines under the Nek were exploded by engineers and created two huge craters. Seventy Turks were blown up and 200 were injured. The Turks responded with rifles and machine-guns at the phantom enemy.

'Thus, dramatically,' Monash wrote on a transport ship, '. . . with bullets whistling overhead, we drew off in the light of the full moon, mercifully screened by a thin mist – and so ended the story of the Anzacs on Gallipoli . . .'[31]

It was the greatest escape of the war.

There was a mixed reaction from the men to leaving, not the 'howls' that Monash expected. The soldiers realised that they had to go. Most of them were relieved. Those who knew in advance had made time for a final visit to the rough graves of their mates and comrades, saying a last word to Mick, Pete, Bob, Walt, Bill and all the other young diggers, who would stay on Gallipoli for eternity.

Some of the departees laid crude wreaths. Others straightened crosses. One of the living Anzacs asked the dead to forgive them for going. They were under orders. Some, long into their twilight years, felt guilt. They were grateful they had been spared, but sorry they had to leave Gallipoli without avenging the fallen (including 8709 Australians and

2701 New Zealanders). Just the thought of their youthful mates, who missed full lives, brought tears to their fading eyes.

The unbreakable loyalty and bond between all Anzacs, including the living and the dead, became a considerable part of the definition of mateship. It had developed in nineteenth-century Australia and matured in a brutal, concentrated way on that godforsaken small jut of land in the Aegean. The soldiers were prepared to die for their mates. When they made the ultimate sacrifice, it hurt survivors to have lived with their memory.

The experience would shape the bedrock of the Australian character. Understanding Gallipoli meant comprehension of key national values.

In the glib analysis of the continuing war, the peninsula campaign was an unmitigated disaster for the British. The empire would prefer to forget it. But Monash, although a pragmatist, would never view it that way. Perhaps more than anyone, he was determined to articulate and foster the essence of the meaning of Anzac. He had unfinished business.

Proud of his gold gimp: Monash, at 50, in Cairo, October 1915, soon after being promoted to Major General and created a Companion of the Order of the Bath following five months at Gallipoli. Monash's strong constitution and nerve had seen him survive, disease-free – better than most.

(Australian War Memorial Negative No. A01241)

'Splendid' deception: Monash (third from left) waiting at Anzac Cove for a secret visit by Lord Kitchener on 13 November 1915. Kitchener carried a message from the King mentioning the 'splendid things that had been done' at Gallipoli. No hint about evacuation (which came a month later) was given.

(Australian War Memorial Negative No. G01325)

If we win? Monash (at left, in slouch hat) with King George V reviewing 27,000 soldiers of Monash's 3rd Division on 27 September 1916 at Salisbury Plain. It was this two-and-a-half-hour discussion that greatly impressed the King. After this, George V recommended Monash to the Chief of British Forces, Field Marshal Haig. (Australian War Memorial Negative No. P00997.019)

Corps commander in waiting: Monash, 52, on 25 May 1918, at his 3rd Division HQ at Gilsy in the Villers-Bretonneux sector of France. Two weeks earlier, he had been informed that he would become AIF Commander. By now, the knives were out in an attempt to stop him taking command. (Australian War Memorial Negative No. E02350)

Tension between titans: A lean John Monash with Australian Prime Minister Billy Hughes, just before the 4 July 1918 battle of Hamel on the Western Front, France. Hughes was under pressure from journalists Keith Murdoch and Charles Bean to dump Monash as leader of the Australian Corps.

French appreciation: France's Premier, M. Georges Clemenceau (first on left), visited the battlefield three days after Australia had won the 4 July 1918 Battle of Hamel and congratulated AIF Corps Commander Lieutenant General Monash (third from left). It was not a huge battle, but its speed (accomplished in 93 minutes) and decisiveness was an inspiration to the Allies and brought Monash's skills to the attention of political and military leaders. The commander of the 4th Division, Major General Sinclair-MacLagan, is second from left. (Australian War Memorial Negative No. E02527)

A special pleasure: Monash on 20 July 1918 at Querrieu, France, took great pleasure in handing out decorations for courage at the Battle of Hamel to members of the 4th Infantry Brigade, his old outfit from Gallipoli.
(Australian War Memorial Negative No. E02758)

Showing off the booty: Monash on 13 July 1918 at Camon, France, addressing his 2nd Division. Some of the war trophies from the Battle of Hamel, including guns and periscopes, are pictured on the left. (Australian War Memorial Negative No. E02732)

Rewards of Hamel: AIF Corps Commander John Monash (third from left, facing camera) on 13 July 1918 at Camon, France, after Hamel. He presented the Victoria Cross to Second Lieutenant W. Ruthven of 2nd Division. Removing the obstacle of the hamlet paved the way for Monash to plan the most important Australian (British) victory of the war. (Australian War Memorial Negative No. E02730)

Waiting in anticipation: Monash (seated) in the grounds of his Corps HQ, Bertangles Chateau, just north of Amiens, France, on 22 July 1918, with his senior staff officers. His plan for the Battle of Amiens, set to begin on 8 August, had just been accepted by Chief of British Forces Haig and 4th Army Chief Rawlinson. Left to right: C.H. Foott, R.A. Carruthers, T.A. Blamey, L.D. Fraser and W.A. Coxen.
(Australian War Memorial Negative No. E02750)

Staying close: Monash (seated) with aides, 22 July 1918. Left to right (behind him): Captain A.M. Moss, ADC, Major W.W. Berry, camp commandant, and Captain P.W. Simonson, ADC.

(Australian War Memorial Negative No. E03186)

Fit for a King: King George V arrives at Bertangles on 12 August 1918 for the investiture of Monash with the KCB (Knight Commander Order of the Bath) and is greeted by a 600-strong guard of honour. (Australian War Memorial Negative No. E03895)

Arise Sir John: King George V knights Monash on 12 August 1918 soon after the first of a series of massive victories over the Germans that ended the war. The King was pleased to give Monash honours, especially after recommending him to Haig.

Honed and handsome: Monash, aged 52, approaching the peak of his military powers in May 1918, just after being made Australian Corps Commander. He was as fit as any of his field commanders, having dropped 30 kg in weight since the war began.

The Alsatian and the bantam cock: Monash with Prime Minister Billy Hughes on 14 September 1918. Monash's body language reflects the power play between them at that moment. Hughes wanted the AIF to cease all fighting by early October 1918. Monash, now the most successful battle commander on the Western Front, preferred his options were left intact. (Australian War Memorial Negative No. E03300)

The cabal: Journalist Keith Murdoch and Prime Minister Billy Hughes on the Western Front in September 1918. After Murdoch and fellow journalist Charles Bean had conspired to convince Hughes that Monash should not command the AIF and had failed, the trio attempted to undermine Monash's command.

GOODBYE TO 4TH BRIGADE

The break on Lemnos was a relaxing interlude for Monash after the stress of the last seventeen days on Gallipoli. He was able to wallow in a bag of Christmas mail and answer it at his leisure, a luxury he had not expected while entrenched on the peninsula. He made the most of the rest. On New Year's Eve, Monash commanded a liner that took the 4th Brigade to Ismailia and an acute sense of *déjà vu*. It was now nearly a year since he had arrived in Egypt expecting to fight on the Western Front. There was still an air of uncertainty about that. Would they go, or wouldn't they? And if that was not to be the destination, then what was?

There was a rumour that the Turks after Gallipoli were going to invade Egypt. It had been around since the aborted attempt to cross the Suez in late January 1915 just as Monash sailed up the Suez for the first time. After Gallipoli it had greater currency. Kitchener was concerned that now 250,000 men were available for another march from Beersheba across the Sinai. But Kitchener's little foray along the jetty at Anzac didn't qualify him to comprehend the hammering the Turks had taken defending their country. Monash was not worried. The Turks were unlikely to be regrouping for any adventures in Egypt or anywhere for a little while. It was one thing to defend as fiercely as von Sanders had planned and Kemal had inspired. It was another to attempt foreign conquests with a force that was exhausted and depleted after eight months of the closest, toughest fighting imaginable. The Turks would crusade abroad again, but after a respite.

The 4th arrived in Ismailia on New Year's Day. Many were in good spirits for the first time since abandoning Anzac. They realised that they would not have to spend winter in deadly conditions. More importantly, they were alive.

✕

Monash settled in early January 1916 into a laborious routine of refitting his brigade with recruits and equipment. This, plus the perpetual wondering about what was in store for him – promotion, the front or another long stint in Egypt – created an ennui that made way for nostalgia. 'This beastly war is getting to be rather a bore,' he wrote to a long-term female friend, 'and not nearly as much fun as building bridges, or touring round the world, or tending roses in my garden.'[1]

But these thoughts were superseded by anxiety on 19 January when John Gibson cabled him from Melbourne to tell him that Vic was ill. Monash's consent was needed for an operation. Her doctors were unanimous. It was serious, perhaps a matter of life or death. Monash agreed to the surgery without knowing the exact nature of the problem. A few days later Vic had the operation. Monash cabled furiously. He consulted Birdwood and Godley, asking permission to go back to Australia on compassionate grounds if Vic's situation deteriorated. They were firm. There was a war on. Such humane niceties were not allowed.

Monash persisted. All he received as a final comment on the crisis was that the War Office would not let him go. If he left, there would be 'a sacrifice of honour'. In other words, he would let the AIF down. Monash was prepared to do it. He would go on the surgeon's advice. If Vic were dying, Monash would return even if he had to desert to do so.

Cable communication continued for ten days after the operation until 1 February, when the surgeon notified him the operation was successful and that Vic's prognosis was fair. Letters followed with more detail. Monash was further shocked to learn that Vic had had cancer of the uterus. He continued to monitor her progress.

✕

With that crisis averted, Monash could give his full attention to the vexing issue of the expansion of the AIF. It and the Australian Government were even keener after Gallipoli to avoid the force being sent to the Western Front and tacked on, in battalions or smaller units, to British divisions. A way of bringing waves of new recruits up to the required standard more quickly was to split the battalions of each existing brigade in half and to add new men to each half. This way the battle-hardened Gallipoli veterans could help train the recruits.

The 4th Brigade was bisected. One half formed the nucleus of the new 4th, with Monash still in charge. After some nifty negotiation, he managed to hold on to his entire HQ staff, his machine-gunners and signals (who were the most difficult to train up to a high standard from scratch). His shrewdest move was to retain his battalion commanders. Men such as Pope and Cannan, who had proved themselves in the cauldron of battle time and time again on Gallipoli, were as near to irreplaceable as leaders could be.

The other half, the less powerful 'rump' of the 4th, formed the new 12th Brigade. It, the 4th Brigade and the new 13th Brigade changed into the new 4th Division. There were the five Australian divisions, the 1st, the 2nd, the 4th, the 5th (which had come late into the Gallipoli campaign), and the 3rd. It was then being cobbled together in Australia.

The New Zealanders had taken the same road to expansion and national unity by forming their own division. This meant that the original 2nd Division – the one true Anzac Division – of Australians and New Zealanders ceased to exist after Gallipoli. It was a memorable moment for the brigades in the composite division that had fought so well in unison while retaining their national identity. They dissolved in a night of exchanged tributes; Monash attended a dinner, Maori campfire and haka. The New Zealanders came to a concert in their honour. It was a fitting finale to a magnificent force that would be immortalised for their impact at Gallipoli. The Anzac spirit would carry on now as an even bigger and more powerful force as Australian and New Zealand divisions.

Monash and his brigade were in the 4th Division in a new Army Corps run by Godley. Monash had mixed feelings. He thought Godley had treated him fairly but his brigade badly. His 'just do it' approach to ill-prepared attack missions, in the worst British Army tradition of the past four centuries, had seen unnecessary slaughter of Anzacs on several occasions on Gallipoli. It had led to ill feeling towards Godley, especially by the New Zealanders.

The haphazard approach to battle, which offended Monash's sensibilities concerning detail, planning, tactics and strategies, was not helped by Godley's manner and methods. He was a stickler for discipline, the chain of command and a 'treat 'em mean, keep 'em keen' sort of British Regular Army approach. The determination to stay aloof fostered anger in him in keeping with his doctrine.

'Godley has a violent temper,' Monash noted. 'He is also very pernickety . . . and selfish.' He lacked 'urbanity and tact'.[2]

Yet Monash, like all the Anzacs, had to accept the British approach. They were in charge. It was their war. The best that he could hope for was advance up the chain of command with the help of commanders like him. His movement up was dependent on a confluence of positive opinion from his immediate superiors, Birdwood and Godley. Monash would have to hope that Godley might put in a good word for him. If so, he just might be chosen to run the 4th Division, mainly because of his Gallipoli record. He had not missed a day's duty. He had thrice been mentioned in dispatches, along with the recommendation for 'special distinction' over his part in the evacuation.

Prime Minister Hughes (who had taken over from Fisher in October 1915) seemed to have unformed or ambivalent feelings towards Monash, and his ministers might have been squeamish about promotion, but they were concerned that Australian soldiers be commanded by Australians. Pressure was expected from the Federal Government to push for the elevation of White and Chauvel (both regulars) to divisional commands. Monash and Brigadier General W. Holmes, who had temporarily run 2nd Division on the peninsula, were not regulars, yet their records suggested they were capable of higher responsibilities.

White seemed the front-runner. He was now using his middle name Brudenell alongside White, in keeping with his growing status and universally admired abilities. Brigadier General Brudenell White, now on Birdwood's staff, sounded far more impressive than plain Cyril White. This seemed just right for a British regular staff man, perhaps with connections to 'the families of Lord Lucan and Lord Cardigan', as one English writer observed. (There was none.)[3]

Monash thought White 'far and away the ablest' soldier in the force for his meticulous planning and execution of the Gallipoli evacuation. But it was just this area of brilliance that caused Birdwood to retain him on his staff. White was seen as a better administrator than a commander, and he appeared happy with this judgement and occupation. Yet still, had he been available, White would have been chosen for a divisional command ahead of Monash.[4]

Monash was confident in himself and his strong record and experience at Gallipoli. Still, doubts lingered about such a lofty promotion. He knew that opposition to him at home had lingered. He was insecure about the anti-German background clique, who questioned his loyalty. It was of far more concern than the anti-Jewish sentiment, which was more of a second strike against him in the minds of those with strong prejudices. Monash wrote home to warn family members again not to draw attention to the German connection. Those who spoke the language were ordered not to flaunt their cultural background or, for that matter, to fraternise with Vic and Bertha.

These worries caused him to ask Vic, who had made a remarkable recovery, to lobby the PM. 'Do all you can to cultivate Hughes,' he directed. 'He is one of the Wallabies [the walking club] and I like him very much. It may help me for you to be chummy with Mrs Prime Minister.'[5] Monash could not be sure whether his expressed feelings were reciprocated. He was aware of the haranguing Hughes' reputation as a political shark. Monash also asked Vic to push for some useful press coverage for the 4th Brigade.

It was soon announced that the regular staffer, Lieutenant General Legge, who came late in the Gallipoli campaign and was found wanting as a temporary commander, would now be permanent head of the 2nd Division. Another regular, Brigadier General Walker, who had for a time run the Australian and New Zealand Division on Gallipoli, took control of 1st Division, while McCay was handed 5th Division. Monash's oldest rival had beaten him again. That left 4th Division, which Monash wanted. Third Division was still a long way from formation and would not be overseas before mid-year.

His main worry was that he would be overlooked for another regular soldier, despite his performance on Gallipoli being as good as anything a permanent could have done under the trying circumstances. He knew Godley and Birdwood favoured regulars. McCay's promotion came as much from his good record as it did from his strong support in Australia's political circles and his Anglo-Celtic background. He was worthy, but no more or less than Monash.

Monash wondered how much the PM and Pearce supported him. They would have as much clout as the combined views of Godley and Birdwood. He didn't count on negative comment from Legge. He influenced the vacillating Birdwood, who at times seemed swayed by the last strong opinion put to him.

Legge reminded Birdwood of Monash's German links. There was still much feeling about the issue in Australia. Better not to give him such a high-profile command. Birdwood's assessment of him had not changed since their first encounter in Egypt. He was concerned that Monash didn't get about enough with the troops at the preparatory camp or on the battlefield. He needed to chat with those on the front line more often. This was Birdwood's method of leadership, rooted in his nineteenth-century experience, which was being rendered ineffective as the war on the Western Front progressed by the use of machine-guns, better rifles, howitzers, better ammunition, armoured cars and tanks, and an air corps.

An effective divisional commander in the modern age had to be on top of the technology and how to deploy it on the battlefield. Birdwood refused to acknowledge this. Change was taking place too fast for him to assess or adapt it. The horse was still his favourite mode of transport in war, and even as a vehicle for attack. Gallipoli had done nothing to change his mind.

Even if he were to appreciate Monash as the coming style of commander, Birdwood demonstrated how out of touch he was with the truth that had been in front of him for eight months at Gallipoli. 'There is, I believe, among a considerable number of the force,' Birdwood said, 'a great feeling against him on account of what they consider his German extraction.'[6]

If this questioning of his loyalty were to be examined, it would have been seen as illogical. Monash, like every man on Gallipoli, risked his life daily. But the rumour mill continued. He was a German spy who sent reports to von Sanders and Kemal. Birdwood's words ignored the glaring fact that Monash had been commanding forces that were killing the enemy in their thousands. It would take a masochistic spy to pass back intelligence that would lead to direct attacks on himself. This shallow thinking said much about such people as Birdwood and Legge, who had no glaring prejudices but were perpetuating such inanities. But even if this attitude had been exposed for what it was, there was a mindless fall-back argument. The Turks were not Germans. Fighting the dreaded Hun would be the acid test for someone with Monash's background.

And if all arguments against him were found to be fallacious, there was always another factor. Monash wasn't a regular. He was not in the club. Eight months experience commanding in battle was reduced to naught.

He was an amateur soldier. But he might have been a professional military espionage agent.

With these undercurrents swirling around the decision-making, odd bedfellows in the British regular faction and the McInerney-inspired clique defeated McCay and a cautious Australian Prime Minister. Monash's old superior Cox got the job of running the 4th Division. This irked Monash. They had clashed on several occasions. Monash had not been overwhelmed by Cox's capacities, yet once more he would have to defer to the 'peppery' former Indian Army man.

Birdwood took his corps – the 1st, 2nd and the New Zealand Divisions – off to the Western Front over February 1915 while Godley's Corps of 40,000 – the 4th and 5th Divisions – remained at Tel el Kebir, 120 kilometres from Cairo and fifty kilometres west of the canal.

There was a whiff of irony early in March when Cox was ill and Monash took command of the entire Division for nearly a week. By mid-March, having had a taste of running such a big contingent, he was back in charge of the more easily managed 5000 in his brigade, just as Birdwood brought the Prince of Wales (the future King Edward VIII) to see him. The Prince was on the staff of the new Commander-in-Chief, Middle East, General Sir Archibald Murray. The King had wanted his son to see his inheritance at work in war. But Kitchener did not want him and his titled staff members parked with British forces in France.

'You'll be better off with General Murray,' the Prince was told. He was not happy. The limited nightlife in Paris was always preferable to that of Cairo or Alexandria.

'But if anything happens to me,' the indignant Prince told Kitchener, 'I have four brothers.'

'I don't care if you are killed,' Kitchener told him. 'But I don't wish to face the prospect of you being taken prisoner.'[7]

After that unflattering remark, Tel el Kebir would not have salved his spirits. The Prince was accompanied by his staff, a small 'retinue of noble lords, marquis and earls', Monash wrote a touch sardonically, 'who were kids just like himself'. Murray had to play 'daddy' to the Prince all the time.

His Royal Highness rode around seeing the troops at work and shaking hands with commanders. Monash, who would have been curious to meet such an esteemed royal, seemed unimpressed. 'He was not very talkative,'

Monash wrote. 'But he made quite a long speech to me, to the envy of a number of others. What he said to me was, "Mmmmmm." '

The Prince, one of the empire's notable playboys, would rather have been elsewhere. He was still smarting from Kitchener's slight. While the Prince did his duties, he often had an air of undisguised boredom, especially in such a remote desert location, although not in front of this war-hardened Australian Gallipoli commander with the lugubrious features.

Monash observed that 'the youngster was completely bewildered, and most evidently ill-at-ease'.[8]

Perhaps that dark, gun-barrel-straight gaze latched on to the Prince a little too much for comfort.

Monash's loyal and proficient deputy McGlinn moved to join McCay's 5th Division. He was replaced by Major J. M. A. Durrant, who with Monash worked out the detail of a seventy-two-kilometre march to Serapeum for the brigade. It (along with the rest of 4th and 5th Divisions) was replacing the 1st and 2nd Divisions in the local defence of Egypt and the canal. The trek was a success for some and a failure for others. The 13th Battalion managed the three days well. But the 14th Battalion struggled. In the last five kilometres, stragglers were rounded up and helped in by the New Zealanders. They succumbed to dust, biting insects, soft sand and the heat.

Monash rode along the route. He told some that their sisters could do as well. He was cursed for the first time by his troops. Monash didn't charge anyone with insubordination as Cox and Godley would have done. He ignored them and rode on to the canal, where a group of the 15th Battalion had decided to stop short of the destination for a swim in the canal. Monash blasted them. They complained about their boots and the other impediments of the journey. Monash would not accept their excuses. They began to count him out, another first for him. Again, he knew his men. He had made his point. Monash simply galloped off.

The matter didn't end there. Sections of the 4th and 5th Divisions were disgruntled about the toughness of the march. The 14th Brigade of 5th Division went as far as demonstrating against its commander, Brigadier General G. G. H. Irving, in front of the Prince of Wales, who reviewed the men the next day in Serapeum. The men reckoned Irving had been brutal. He had to go.

Their fierce public complaint worked. McCay dumped him. Much to Monash's chagrin, Pope, for whom he had the highest regard, was lured across to the 5th Division to replace the unpopular Irving as the 14th's commander. McCay's poaching of McGlinn and Pope would have tested the strong, three-decade bond between them.

The brigade's next assignment was over the canal and in the Sinai, just in case the persistent rumours about a Turkish attack proved true. Monash hated the experience at 'the end of the world'. The heat and flies were even worse than anything on Anzac. But the worst of it was the dust storms. They left every man gasping with lung, nasal and throat problems or with severe headaches.

The key moment at Tel el Kebir occurred on 25 April 1916. Only a severe storm or a full-scale attack by the Turks would have stopped Monash commemorating what he wished to make the most important day of the Australian calendar. He turned out the whole brigade at 6.45 a.m. Every man who had served on Gallipoli wore a blue ribbon on the right breast. Those, such as Monash, who also took part in the initial landing were allowed to wear a red ribbon as well.

'How few of us are left,' he noted, 'who are entitled to wear both.'[9]

There was a short service in keeping with the solemn occasion to remember the fallen comrades. Monash wanted the day to be memorable as well as enjoyable. He organised a festival of sorts. There were cricket matches in the morning. Then the 15,000 soldier spectators went for a collective dip in the canal, where an aquatic carnival was held. There was even a skit on the Gallipoli landing just to lighten up the occasion. Murray, Godley and the Prince of Wales attended. The Prince this time was more relaxed as he accompanied Monash and enjoyed the fun atmosphere. April 25 finished with lavish mess dinners and band concerts.

'We wished each other the opportunity of enjoying many happy returns of this famous day,' Monash wrote, 'our day.'[10]

Whatever the overall impression, in the usual audience with the King at Buckingham Palace after his travels, the Prince would mention the frolics in the canal, the special celebration and meeting key Gallipoli veterans, including Monash.

News that Godley's corps would soon follow Birdwood's out of the much-loathed desert and on to the Western Front gave Monash a new incentive.

He put aside his differences with Cox and worked in harmony with him to bring his brigade and the rest of 4th Division into battle-ready order. On 29 April, Cox addressed all the division's officers and then invited Monash to speak. The invitation marked a new level in their relationship, which had deteriorated on Gallipoli. Those differences were buried. Cox now had a high opinion of Monash's abilities and began to lean on him. Cox saw his own success in running a division full of 'colonials' depended very much on such people as Monash. There were now 20,000 Australians under his direct command, and there were different ways of teasing the best out of them, which varied from methods used by the English, Indians and others.

For a start, simply dictating to Australians did not achieve the required responses. Stark points of discipline were not enough. Fostering the right atmosphere – or, as Monash called it, 'a sound and healthy public opinion' – in each unit was the better route. It meant creating the conditions in which the diggers felt they were getting 'a fair go' with everything from food to leisure time. The camp couldn't become too regimented or laborious. This approach meant that officers had to work from the grass roots up to achieve results, something unknown in the English military tradition. But Cox was willing to learn about his new command, and this was where a rapport was built with Monash. He did not fail to notice the reports on how well Monash had run the 4th Division in his absence on two occasions.

Cox was prepared to listen and learn. He never missed a chance to hear Monash talk with his battalion commanders, 'simply for the educational value and the pleasure of hearing him speak'.[11] The mutual respect between Monash and his men was a key. Bullying, talking down and not listening were discouraged, although Monash himself was guilty of being tough on his officers, if he felt it would achieve results.

But try as he did, the new divisional commander could not quite rid himself of traditional methods learned with other armies. On 30 April, Cox dressed down the much-respected Lieutenant Colonel Tilney of the 13th battalion, whom Monash regarded as the brigade's best commander next to Cannan now that Pope had left. Cox had made a futile attempt to humiliate Tilney in front of his men over battlefield tactics. Tilney took the matter to Monash, who agreed that Cox had been out of order. Tilney was prepared to complain to Godley. Monash smoothed the matter over with Tilney before it was taken higher. Cox, realising that he had a weak case and had lapsed, was most grateful to Monash.

A week later, there was another more fundamental incident that went to the root differences in tradition and attitude between not just the Australian and British forces but also the cultures of the countries themselves. Monash informed Cox that he wanted a certain sergeant to be commissioned. Cox's first reaction was to veto it. None of the lower ranks ever became officers, he said. Monash replied that the man concerned was a born leader. He had proved himself on Gallipoli as a fighter. He was responsible, popular and strong. He wanted to lead, make decisions and inspire. That's how it was done in the Australian force. It improved efficiency. The men became sorted into leaders and followers according to their abilities, skill and desires.

Cox was angered. He maintained that you couldn't have working-class men leading businessmen and those with university degrees. Monash disagreed. He said it had worked well in the Australian army and always would. 'Men of humble origin,' he said, 'rose during the war, from privates to command battalions.' He told Cox that the major difference was that Australia didn't have a caste system.

'There was no social distinction in the whole force,' Monash explained. 'Officers had to dress like the men, to live among them in the trenches, to share their hardships and privations.' If officers came from among the lower ranks, it was easier to do it. If they looked after their own comfort with, say, food and living quarters before the men, the word would get around. The men would lose respect. Cooperation between the officer and his subordinates would diminish.

Cox stopped fuming. Monash pointed out that it was fine for British army officers to pretend they were superior and to keep a divide between them and the soldiers. But it invited disaster in dealing with Australians. 'Artificial distinctions irked them badly,' Monash told him.[12] Running an Australian force with distinction meant a man needed to understand these fundamentals and promulgate them down through the ranks of officers and non-commissioned leaders. This was one way to get the best out of them. Cox respected Monash so much that he absorbed the hot argument that became a lecture. The sergeant who started it received his commission.

Cox now resolved to help Monash gain control of 3rd Division, which was on its way to England, for two main reasons. First, Cox recognised that Monash was equipped to handle it. Second, while Monash was still in the 4th Division, he would always be the de facto commander of it. The commanders would look to him as the senior, as Tilney did, on critical occasions. Now that Monash had shown him how Australians should be directed, it was better to let him go. On 3 May, he wrote to Birdwood:

> If it is desirable to put in a local product, I should like to say that I am prepared to recommend Monash be given a trial. He is a very able man and now has long experience of training and of war. He is very tactful and his judgment is reliable.
>
> Any little weaknesses which appeared when he was in command of the Brigade at Anzac would not count so much in a Divisional command. He seems to me to have 'come on' very much. This is, of course, entirely off my own bat. He has never said a word about it.[13]

It was not a ringing endorsement, but an endorsement nonetheless. Birdwood preferred the less problematic Chauvel, but he was wanted for the Mounted Division for any military ventures in the Middle East. Birdwood consulted Godley, who agreed that Monash could handle the 3rd Division, but was still dogmatic about him not being in the club. 'One cannot pretend,' Godley wrote, 'that he is as well qualified to command a division as a trained regular officer, but he is a capable, sensible and reliable man and now has had eighteen months of troops in the field and has done it well.'[14]

Birdwood then showed his flexibility by writing to Pearce, and the man to whom he would have to justify a recommendation, the Governor-General, Munro Ferguson: 'I hear that he has carried on excellently with what to all intents and purposes has been a new brigade . . . and I feel therefore it is only right that he should be given the chance.'[15]

In an amazing step forward in Monash's military career, he was about to overcome – temporarily at least – five major hurdles to advancement that would have been unimaginable less than a year earlier. He was a Jew with a German background; he was not from the regular forces; he was from a Dominion; and there were fears about his being an enemy spy. It was not hard to imagine more than a few club members from Melbourne to London choking on their evening Scotches over this possibility. Yet they would have been those with blind prejudices or who had not been in contact with him or aware of his performances in and out of battle.

✕

Monash was aware that he had a chance of taking over 3rd Division, but he left Egypt for France early in June with the 4th Brigade with no official word of his 'promotion'.

'We followed a tortuous course to dodge the submarines,' Monash wrote, 'but had not a single scare.'[16] It was a poignant remark. On 5 June, while at sea they had wireless news of the loss by drowning of Lord Kitchener. His boat, the cruiser HMS *Hampshire*, was sunk by a mine off the coast of Scotland in the North Sea while he was en route to advise the Russian armies. It was a massive blow for the morale of the British forces and people. His public image generated an aura of invincibility. Now he was gone. Kitchener had been the most prominent British person in the conduct of the war. But he was still only one man and had long been regarded by his War Council colleagues as ineffectual. The war would go on.

The solemn mood his death caused was alleviated when the 4th Brigade's boat, the *Transylvania*, docked at Marseilles coast on 7 June. Monash was most appreciative of the change of country. France in June was pleasant and cool. There were no flies, the countryside was lush, and anything, especially lovely French villages, was a relief after visions of endless desert.

Monash and Durrant squeezed in two days in Paris, which was not the rollicking city experienced in 1910. They managed to visit the usual tourist spots but found the Eiffel Tower closed. One night they took in a revue at the Folies Bergère, but were disappointed to find that drinks stopped at 9.30 p.m. everywhere. Nightlife was non-existent. By 11 p.m. the streets of the most exciting city in Europe were deserted.

After Paris, it was on to Brigade HQ in the town of Erquinghem near Armentières on the Belgian border. On 11 June, Monash dined with Birdwood, White, Legge and Russell at 4th Division HQ at nearby Merris in a reunion of Anzac leaders. They all agreed that it was a more amenable setting than Anzac Cove where they had last dined together. But the boom of big guns just seven kilometres away on Merris's eastern outskirts reminded them that they were still close to the front. The conditions might have been better, but the tense atmosphere was familiar.

'When our guns are not making a noise,' Monash wrote of his first impressions, 'we can hear the Boche guns quite plainly. Aeroplanes, both ours and the enemy's, often fly overhead.'[17]

Monash was interested in the influence of air power on the conflict. It was a new arm of war. He would use it, if given the chance, like all the other growing technology, which had been speeded by the necessity to gain the upper hand. On 12 June he witnessed his first dogfight, and was fascinated to record 'an inconclusive' battle overhead.

✕

The British forces under General Douglas Haig planned a major offensive on the Somme for 1 July led by General Rawlinson and his Fourth Army. Raids were to be carried out along the entire front to distract, tie up, wear down and mislead German divisions as to when and where the strongest attack by the Fourth Army would be. Monash's 4th Brigade was seconded to Australia's 2nd Division for it. He nominated 14th Battalion – 'Jacka's mob' – for the mission. He knew it would make a strong first impression. Monash planned the incursion with Lieutenant Colonel G. H. F. Jackson, a British specialist in raids who served with the 2nd Division. On 19 June, Monash went on a reconnoitre with him. The night raid was set for twenty-four hours after the offensive.

On 24 June, Monash heard rumours that he was to 'get 3rd Division'. 'Today I am told by a highly placed officer in Army Corps Staff that the rumour . . . is quite reliable.' The appointment, it was claimed, had been 'received in Australia'.[18] This meant that Hughes, Pearce and Munro Ferguson were in accord with Birdwood. The latter informed Monash on 26 June that it was true. He would command 3rd Division. It was a great moment for him. But Monash could not stop to celebrate as the final plans for the night raid were set.

He prepared by spending four days simulating the raid behind Anzac lines. Then he took his men to nearby La Rolanderie Farm for a full dress rehearsal. On the day of the advance, 1 July, Monash's machine-gunners were still working on much-needed practice while British troops of Rawlinson's Fourth Army attacked over the length of the front.

Oblivious of the impact, and the fact that the Germans were now fully alerted, Monash led his party of eighty-nine men, including six officers, into the night at La Houssoie on the right of the 14th Battalion's sector. The plan was to move through the barbed wire defences in a maximum of ten minutes after they had been broken up by a trench mortar barrage. The raiders were to spend another ten minutes in the German trenches. The aim was to gather information and to inflict as many casualties on the enemy as possible.

A raid, by definition, had to be a quick, concentrated affair. When

Monash gave the signal, the mortar attack began. It wiped out an enemy firing party of ten men. Then Monash and his men, armed with revolvers and coshes, moved across no man's land to the wire barriers. They were spread over sixty metres. The men stopped. The wire had not been destroyed by the mortar barrage. The raiders now had to cut their own way through.

They had not gone sixteen metres before there was counter-fire. There had been ten such raids in the last week along the Anzac line. The German artillery and machine-gunners were ready. They opened up, causing many casualties among the party scrambling to hack through the thick wire. Once through, the reduced raiding party rushed the trenches. They were nearly empty. The attackers clubbed five Germans. A few grenades were hurled into the dugouts. The Germans kept up the counter-attack. Monash's men did some damage to three trenches, but his runners were soon yelling 'Out! Out!' on both raiders' flanks. The pre-planned cry swept through the raiders, who began to run for their lines. For those who didn't hear it, Monash had three green Very lights fired up. The retreat was retarded by a sustained counter-attack. In the confusion, Monash lost contact with his leaders.

In the hours after the mission, he counted his men as they reported in. There were thirty-eight casualties, an attrition rate of more than forty per cent.

The next night the Germans counterattacked through the area where Monash's raiders had opened a path in the wire. In a second night without sleep, he rallied the 14th Battalion to hold their position. They did so, but with further heavy casualties, bringing its losses to nearly 300 in holding a three-kilometre front. The 4th Brigade, like all the others arriving from Anzac via Egypt, were finding battles and survival just as tough as at Gallipoli.

The loss of Monash's men was somewhere near the rate experienced along the whole front on those disastrous first two days in July 1916. More than 60,000 British troops were cut down.

The year was being marred by battle planning based on trench warfare and methods that leaders of both sides had relied on for a century. Massive losses of men in the mud of the Somme and its surrounds were the result, making it unlikely that either side would force victory. A chance of that elusive goal could come from the side that made a breakthrough with some new weapon. Yet so far any innovation had been countered by a similar development by the other side. The force that produced commanders who were imaginative, experienced and able to plan and integrate all the new war technology would give it the edge. Leadership was still the most important weapon.

THE KING AND I

Monash had some regrets about leaving 4th Brigade. It would mean his parting from his own creation, which he had constructed and reconstructed for almost two years. Yet any misgivings were swamped as he began to consider the huge challenge of constructing and conditioning not 5000 men, but 20,000, with his subtle and proven methods.

His first resolution was to get himself into shape, which was a daunting prospect. Monash was aged fifty-one and weighed ninety-five kilograms when he began a regime that said much about his discipline and determination. His aim was to hit the scales at seventy-seven kilograms, which meant shedding about twenty per cent of his body weight. Monash cut out alcohol – except for an occasional beloved red wine – and avoided sugar, fat and carbohydrates. He reduced the size of his meals, eating half-portions every meal. Plates piled high with potatoes were out. Traditional British meals, which he faced for the several months, were avoided, as were rich desserts. The regime did not include giving away smoking.

His sister Louise Rosenhain and her husband, Walter, were surprised by his discipline when he spent ten days with them in Surrey. Not only was he on a strict diet. He was also exercising harder than a man of his age should contemplate without long preparation. His exercise routine centred on a rigorous daily hour's march over the roughest country he could find, along with a tough regime of heavy dumbbell exercises for chest, arms, stomach and legs.

On top of this he found time for a daily romp with his three young nieces, who adored their now-famous uncle, the fighting general. It made him think nostalgically about Vic and Bertha, whom he had not seen now for twenty months. But with resolution of the spreading war not in sight, he could see at least another twenty months of service in front of him. He discouraged his family from making the long trip by boat from Australia to see him. It was too dangerous because of submarines and mines, he told them. Besides, he could be called to the front at any time.

Monash kept his mind sharp too during this short vacation. He played the piano and read for three hours daily. He had further mental stimulation working on a winning roulette system in which the bright Walter found a flaw. He also puzzled over intricate jigsaws that Walter made harder and harder, pushing Monash.

He didn't relax his workout and food disciplines on a short visit to London, which he found dreary because of the blackouts against Zeppelin raids. Nightlife there too was limited. But he did find time for taking out Vic's friend Lizzie Bentwitch, with whom he had built a rapport in 1910. Now she seemed an even more attractive partner and less inhibited without Vic's presence. She went out of her way to entertain him, arranging a restaurant dinner and three visits to the theatre, which she knew he loved. Despite the settled nature of his marriage, Monash had never felt adored by Vic. He enjoyed being pampered and admired by women, something that had not been part of his life for decades. Lizzie fulfilled this need during a period of forced separation from Vic, and when his focus was off family life for one of the few times in twenty-six years. Any relationship could only be fitful. He would be on active duty most of the time. His new job would see to that.

It began on 25 July 1916 at Larkhill, 145 kilometres southwest of London, where several tiny villages and hamlets were tucked away in the green valley of the River Avon. It was located close to Stonehenge, fifteen kilometres north of Salisbury. Monash was eager to meet his staff and then assess the rank and file. Birdwood, with White assisting, made sure he had a strong staff, a vital factor in running such a large body of men. It also had a distinctive Australian flavour. His chief staff officer was Lieutenant Colonel Jackson, the English raiding expert and soldier trainer, who had already worked well with him in France. He had experience with Australians in the same position at 2nd Division. There was Major George Wootten, a graduate from Royal Military College Duntroon who knew

Monash well, and the Australian-born Victoria Cross winner, Major G. G. E. Wylly, who had been an Indian Army officer. The other British officer was Lieutenant Colonel H. Mynors Farmar, who came from an old military family. Even this veteran had a common bond with Monash. He had served well in Gallipoli. Monash lived with him and his family in their comfortable manor a few kilometres from his HQ.

There were an additional eighty clerks, grooms, batmen, police and a squadron of cavalry (Light Horse). They were backed up by the engineers and the divisional Signal Company, which ran telegraphs, telephones and wireless in four sections – one for HQ and one for each brigade. As aides Monash retained two of his nephews, the popular, efficient Paul Simonson and the tough-minded, unpopular Aubrey Moss, who had been sergeants with him at Gallipoli and in Egypt. Both had moustaches and were known as 'Mo' and 'Arf a Mo'.

The total command had more than 20,000 troops, 7000 horses, sixty-four guns, 192 machine-guns, eighteen motorcars, eighty-two motor lorries and 1100 other vehicles.

The brigadiers were W. R. McNicoll, A. Jobson and Cannan (whom Monash plucked out of 4th Brigade and put in the place of a drunken commander) in charge of the 9th from northern New South Wales, the 10th from rural Victoria and the 11th from the other states. The Artillery Brigade was to be run by H. W. Grimwade.

On his first day, Monash jumped on a horse and, with Jackson, trotted around inspecting all the units from twelve battalions – the 33rd to the 44th – and associated troops. He was pleased with what he saw. They looked like a strong lot, who at least had the physique that characterised the divisions on Gallipoli. On closer inspection, he was even happier with the make-up of the men.

'Most of them are men of standing – a great many master tradesmen, owner farmers, miners, professional men, and several members of parliament,' Monash wrote, with no cynicism about the latter. His style of discipline would be easier to apply to such men, who in theory would need less of it anyway. 'They were out for business,' Monash noted, which meant they were in Europe to fight. He was confident this group would not harbour crooks who were into shonky deals and rackets – in such things as army supplies and used tyres – that had plagued other divisions.

So much for the good raw material. There was an enormous amount to do to bring the men up to good fighting order. For a start, not many of them knew each other. Monash had to foster goodwill between and inside brigades and develop camaraderie.

The men had no rifles or bayonets. When Monash inspected men using the latter he shook his head and ordered that every member of the division be retrained. Anything learned in Australia about bayonets had to be unlearned. On one trot around a brigade he watched in amazement as men tried to dig a trench. Monash dismounted and made a token show of how it had to be done. 'The men had never seen a Mills bomb, or a Vickers or Lewis machine-gun, or a Stokes Mortar, or [even] handled their transport,' Monash wrote. 'The gunners had never seen an 18 [pounder] or a Howitzer. All they had learned to do was stand up straight in rows and behave themselves.'[1]

Monash still thought he could bring the division up to standard inside two months. He began his eighteen-hour days with this in mind, but was soon battling an attempt to cannibalise his creation and some nefarious politics behind it. The need to send men to the front had arisen because of the huge casualties that had been suffered by the other four Australian divisions. Monash was calm and in control, but this prospect made him furious.

The original call for men from his new construction came from the War Council. Its motive was to put pressure on the Australian Government to push hard for conscription in Australia in order to produce another 70,000 recruits. This way the 3rd could be kept intact, Prime Minister Hughes and his cabinet were informed through the back channels of the Governor-General's office. In other words, if Australia wished to see its identity remain intact as distinct divisions it had to send more men for the British cause.

Monash wanted to know why the men could not be drawn from the 25,000 other Australians in training camps in England, France and Egypt. Why wreck his efforts to build a force that would have a real impact on the front line? His other concern could be termed the 'mateship' factor, still not understood or appreciated in the War Council hierarchy. Monash wanted to keep together men who had teamed up from different parts of Australia. Breaking those bonds weakened the grass-roots strength of the force. At first, his anger seemed to get him nowhere. On 9 September, six weeks into his new commission, 2800 men were marched out of the Larkhill camp.

Monash now embarked on a definite strategy to save his division from dismemberment and softening. He asked his good friend Julius Bruche to send him the best possible replacements, and then wrote poignant letters to Birdwood. He received no definitive response, but the message was understood. Birdwood had seen Monash and his men on Gallipoli. He knew how they fought together and would die for each other and how this perhaps unique Anzac feature bound them as fighters and defenders. Birdwood saw Haig personally and asked him to intervene, explaining that when Monash's force reached the front line it would be a strong and refreshing contributor to the Allied cause. Haig, never a good listener and not so far impressed by reports on the four divisions' efforts on the front line, surprised by responding favourably. Unless there was a serious excuse for breaking up Monash's 3rd Division, it would be left intact to complete its training and development.

Early on, Monash sent off hundreds of his men for specialist training in everything from modern bayonet fighting to bombs and sharpshooting that could then be passed on to the rest of the division. He wanted to prepare for war all units down to platoons in simultaneous progressive stages. No one unit leapt ahead of another. The division developed uniformly.

Monash supervised everything he could. Julius Bruche recalled an instance where the division was practising attacking and creating craters with their artillery. 'After it was over,' Bruche said, 'there was a great assemblage of divisional officers and a number of British officers. John Monash got up on a heap of rubble and for a quarter of an hour explained exactly what the scheme was, what had been done and the faults that had occurred.' Afterwards a querulous British officer, who demanded to know about Monash's background, approached Bruche. When Bruche informed him, the officer said he didn't know of any British officer who could stand up for a quarter of an hour and give an idea of the operation and criticise it in such a lucid manner.[2]

Monash was being noticed at the top of the heap. He didn't miss anything on the upward curve to readiness. He even included aircraft with some well-planned exercises, linking his infantry with planes and artillery. About the only weapon he didn't use was the tank, although he was reading everything about its early teething problems. When it was available, Monash would push for its inclusion in his growing armoury.

By mid-September, after six weeks of intense training, Monash was confident his men were ready for the front. He was relaxing more at night and socialising. The well-connected Farmars had dinner parties at which Monash found himself mixing with members of the country's ruling elite. He, in turn, found himself being invited to dine at Government House, Salisbury, with his immediate superior, Lieutenant General Sir Henry Sclater of Southern Command, and his wife.

Monash was isolated from his peers for the first time. He was appreciated for his intellect, education and experience as an engineer, lawyer and businessman as well as for his military achievements. There was none of the usual caution, jealousies and insecurities about dealing with such an accomplished all-rounder in the narrow confines of the military. Instead, the British were happy to make his acquaintance, fraternise with him, appreciate his skills and draw him out. He found himself relaxed in such company. There was not a person with whom he could not hold his own if they talked about the law, engineering, business, the war, the opera, the theatre, literature and any number of topics his eclectic mind had tackled or enjoyed. There was even the odd German or French speaker who would drop a phrase or a comment to which he could respond without being seen as a foreign spy.

Monash had been familiar with the mentality of the British ruling class and those who aped them since he was a youngster at Scotch College. His teachers there – the Morrison brothers, Edmund Augustus Samson, Frank Shew and J. B. Moran and others – had been drawn from an elite education system covering England, Scotland and Ireland, as had many of his lecturers at Melbourne University. The same applied to his military experience. Many of his instructors had come from the higher ranks of the British Army. It all allowed him to be comfortable meeting an Ian Hamilton or a Godley. Now his ease among this greater concentration of the British upper-class breed had subtle benefits. The ruling elite received and passed on much about a person by word of mouth. And the word about the Australian General Sir John Monash was more than favourable. In the next three months he would be passed around by the local gentry like a valuable curio. Invitations to dinners at stately homes and to go pheasant- and partridge-shooting came in. Monash enjoyed the socialising, especially as it might be a means to a satisfying end.

Soon he was accepting inspections of his force from the high and mighty of the land, all wanting to meet this impressive Australian, who had fought 'gallantly' and 'splendidly' at Gallipoli. Field Marshal Lord French, Commander-in-Chief of Home Forces, came down to Salisbury to review the 3rd Division. 'I thought he looked old and worn and lifeless,' Monash wrote, 'and no wonder, after what he had been through in early days [of the war] in France. The Field Marshal said he was very pleased with all I had to show him. He praised the training, physique and bearing of the men.' French's endorsement was genuine. He was impressed enough to say he would ask the King to have a look at the division 'before the weather got too cold'. Word-of-mouth about Monash and his men could not go any higher than this. Instinct told him that it was vital he put on a tremendous show for the King.

Monash began rehearsing the division. A few days later, he received the news that the King would come to Salisbury to review the 3rd Division on 27 September. Monash secured the additional participation of 7000 Anzac depot and training battalion personnel, making a total parade of 27,000 men.

✕

The men began starting for the parade ground – Bulford Field – at 7.15 a.m. on the 27th, which began as a dull, overcast day. The division was in position by 11.15 a.m. when the King on a sleek, black Australian horse arrived with his small retinue, which included Sir Henry Sclater. The King was in khaki and wearing on his shoulders the badges of a field marshal, and below them two small crowns with the royal ciphers E.R. and V.R. for the two sovereigns under whom he had served.

As the King rode up alone to the flagstaff, the royal standard was broken and fluttered in the breeze. Monash was on horseback, now looking every inch the mature military commander. Inside three months he had dropped an astounding eighteen kilograms to reach his target of seventy-seven kilograms. His body was hard and muscled from the walks and weight training, and he felt better than he had since his early thirties. For the first time in his senior career, he neatly filled his also plain khaki uniform. Monash was no more the figure who made his horse groan at the prospect of his mounting it. One result of this sudden body hardening was a more solemn look in the leaner face. He now appeared the part of a commander in charge of a small army, which in effect the 3rd Division was.

Monash's mounted retinue included Jackson, Farmar and a two-metre-tall Australian military police standard bearer. Monash gave the order to

'Present Arms'. Twenty-seven thousand bayonets flashed as the sun made a cameo appearance. Sixteen massed bands played six bars of the national anthem. The King remained with his hand at the salute. Monash then gave the order: 'The Parade will slope and order arms, and stand-at-ease.'

The King's hand dropped to his side. Then he trotted towards Monash. It was a great moment in more ways than just the ceremonial in the life of the studious boy from Richmond Hill as he too trotted towards the King, who smiled and extended his hand as they drew near.

'How do you do, General,' he said. 'I am so very glad to be able to come down to see you all. It is the first time I have been able to see Australian troops in England. Shall we go up to the right of the line?'

They began to move to where the artillery was drawn up. The King was in full charm mode. He had done his homework. He mentioned 4th Brigade and how well it had done and was doing on the Western Front. The King spoke of Monash's action on Gallipoli. He then glanced at Monash's ribbons.

'I'm sorry I haven't had a chance of giving you your Order [of the Bath],' he remarked. 'Won't you come up to Windsor some day to lunch and I'll give it to you? See Wigram [his military equerry] about it, won't you, and fix a day to suit yourself, when you can get away.'

The King kept up this breezy chat, starting with information about his own horse, which he had bought in India, 'just a common Australian waler.' Clearly he didn't put Monash in the same category. His Majesty worried about the troops having overcoats. As they approached the artillery, 'he asked a lot of questions about the supply of horses, guns and wagons, sights and harness'.

After inspecting the Artillery Brigade, they rode at walking pace down the long line of troops nearly four kilometres long. Monash told him where each battalion or battery was raised. The King 'was always ready with an appropriate comment'.

'You're sure you have enough overcoats?' the King asked again.

'Yes, Your Majesty, and they have waterproof capes as well.'

'Good, good . . . What part of Australia are you from, General?'

'Melbourne.'

'Oh, a fine city! I've been there twice. Did I meet you there?'

'No.'

'I recall quite well the Marquis of Linlithgow's reception there.'

The King paused to pay closer attention to the battalion he was passing. The conversation fell back to an apparent obsession with warm clothing, which would have pleased Australia's woolgrowers. It suggested he might well have had some unpleasant experience in France without his royal woollies.

'Have you got plenty of warm clothes for yourself?' the King asked.

'I hope so, Your Majesty.'

'Take my advice, and make sure you get the best of woollen warm clothing. It's really very cold in France in the winter.'

When they came to the end of the 3rd Division, the King turned to Monash and congratulated him, saying: 'It's a very fine division. I don't know that I've ever seen a finer one.'

They continued along the line past the additional depot and training battalions. At the end of the line, the King said he would see the parade march past. He and Monash trotted to the flagstaff saluting point. Then Monash and his staff went at full gallop across the front of the parade to head up the huge column in front of the Artillery Brigade. He gave the signal to advance. The 384-member band started playing. The troops began a two-hour march past. After passing the saluting point Monash wheeled around and drew up alongside the King.

Their conversation continued in between saluting. Monash was given a heaven-sent opportunity to chat with the most powerful individual in the empire.

It didn't matter that the conversation seemed trivial more often than not, such as when the King commented: 'Listen to those beautiful bands. How their instruments shine, too!' The mere fact that the King felt disposed to make any small talk at all worked in Monash's favour. All he had to do was be himself. They seemed to have a natural rapport. There were things in common. They were both born in the same month in the same year. Had they extended their one-on-one meeting to a lunch or dinner, they might well have even spoken a little German to each other. Both had a Prussian or German background. The King's grandmother (Queen Victoria), grandfather (Prince Albert), father (King Edward VII) and wife (the German Princess Mary of Teck) all had the connection. There would be no concerns about anyone being an espionage agent on this occasion. Instead of working against Monash as it did in his provincial homeland, the German link might well have been an unspoken under-current working in his favour with the King.

Another factor binding them was their love of the military. The King had been in the navy for a decade until 1892 when his elder brother, Prince Albert Victor, died. The future King, then twenty-seven, needed to undertake specialist training as the eventual heir to the throne.

'His interest in each body of troops, as they passed, was intimate and sustained,' Monash wrote. 'He did not take his eyes off the troops. He asked hundreds of questions and criticized dozens of small details, such as the quality of the artillery horses; the relative utility of leather or web equipment; the rifles; the clothing; the hats; the platoon commanders and their training, and so on.'

The King talked nearly all the time, jumping from subject to subject, every now and then breaking off to mutter: 'Splendid, splendid!'

This near-monologue on his passion in itself would have been a test of sorts for Monash. His responses, kept short by the King's meandering, would not have been lost on him. Over the two hours, the King would have been left very aware that he had been talking with a military expert's expert. Monash's painstaking attention to detail and encyclopaedic knowledge of it garnered over more than three decades was having its most elaborate examination and perhaps a pay-off, even if he were not aware of it.

The King told Monash he had reviewed 1,500,000 men since the war began, adding: 'Isn't it perfectly wonderful?' With a touch of sadness in his voice, he added: 'No man could have done it but Lord K. People kept saying he was going to work in the wrong way, but he knew better. He was right after all.' Not everyone agreed with the King on this one. But he had liked and wanted Kitchener in charge. Like Douglas Haig, he was the monarch's choice. He got whom he wanted.

Changing the subject, the King asked Monash if he had met his son in Egypt, when he probably knew he had. Monash's response was laconic and diplomatic: 'Yes,' he replied, 'I did have that pleasure.'

'He wrote and told me how good all you Australians had been to him.' Moments later, the King began a remark with, 'If we win this war . . .'

Monash, breaking protocol, interrupted him with a smile and said: 'If we win?'

The King threw back his head, laughed and said: 'Oh yes! We'll win right enough; nobody need make any mistake about that.'

Monash's interjection seemed to have touched a nerve. Any royal bloodline ties were swiftly submerged.

'The Germans started out to smash the British Empire!' the King said with real feeling, '– smash it to pieces – and look, just look! He swept his arm up and down the marching columns. 'See what they've really done. They've made an Empire of us.'

The long march past continued. The King was in full flight. Monash listened, gleaning titbits about the war from one of the best-informed individuals in or outside the War Council. He had Monash's full attention, particularly in what he had to say about the introduction of tanks on the front and what the French thought of them. The King also mentioned the recent 'successes' in the conflict and praised the British Dominions.

'Think of it,' he told Monash. 'Six hundred thousand men, marvellous, marvellous! We can beat the German troops, man to man. And make no mistake, they are good troops and hard to beat.'

The King enthused more as the long column came to an end. Monash then presented him to his brigadiers and battery and battalion commanders. They then rode together to the Bulford railway station about two kilometres from the parade ground. Monash's flair for the big occasion reached a climax as he had his troops drawn up, a hundred deep on the sloping field adjoining the road. Each unit 'broke into a deafening cheer' as the King rode by, 'raising hats aloft on bayonets'.

They trotted on, the King with his head down and solemn until they had passed the last of the troops. He was touched.

'It makes a lump come in my throat,' he said, 'to think of all these splendid fellows coming many thousands of miles; and what they have come for.'

The loquacious monarch remained silent for the rest of the ride to the station. He dismounted, gave his horse a lump of sugar and had a quick chat to his equerry Wigram. Monash in typical fashion had timed the whole affair down to the minute. Another of his fetishes – punctuality – was impressive to the King and his entourage, who were also ruled by the chronometer. 'The General couldn't have timed it more beautifully,' the King remarked to Wigram, 'could he?'[3] He shook hands with Monash, reminded him to 'come and see' him and boarded the royal train. It pulled away.

Rain sheeted down. Monash was soaked on the ride back to camp. But he didn't care. It had not rained on his parade that day. On the contrary, for a man obsessed with planning, everything seemed to have come off. Unless the King was a consummate actor, he seemed to have been moved and inspired by the machine-like turn-out of military might.

For all his bristling intellect, Monash was a man of acute instinct. He felt comfortable in the King's presence. There was no sense of attempted dominance, rivalry or prejudice in George V, which was the beauty of his lofty position. He could be above all that and judge people for what they were, or were not.

Having dealt with the British at close quarters for some time now Monash was becoming aware of where intrinsic, sometimes hidden power lay in the complexity of their system. Despite the seat of empire's democratic institutions, the reigning monarch still had enormous influence as the key figure in the ruling elite. If he didn't favour a 'subject', he could have the person removed from his or her position or blocked from advance. If he made it clear he liked someone, that person could rise to almost any position without any discernible trace of how or why. In essence, it was still his empire. It was in the King's interests to influence matters that affected its power and dominance. As the empire was now embroiled in the biggest war in history, the result of the conflict would affect his position and territorial possessions in a profound way. For a start, a loss would see him dethroned, at the very least. This thought from time to time compelled George V to make comments and suggestions about issues and individuals concerning the conduct of the war. Those at whom they were directed rarely failed to act on them.

Monash was more than satisfied with the outcome from the very least perspective of the publicity the King's visit generated. The Australian papers, particularly the *Age*, which had a reporter at the event, played it up. Monash imagined the envy and hate it would have caused among his enemies as his status grew, although it remained to be seen whether they would be silenced. He stole a few more days break in London early in October, meeting with Lizette again and going to the theatre every night. He also caught up with the Rosenhains in Richmond Park, being careful to keep his companionship with Lizette secret from the family. After the King's repeated comments about the cold winters in France, Monash went hunting for warm underclothes and bought himself a chamois vest and underpants.

Back at Larkhill a few days later he had a visit, at the King's specific request, from Lieutenant General Sir John Cowan, a member of the Army Council and the British Army's quartermaster general. The King wanted to make sure Monash had all the warm clothing needed for the 3rd Division. Knowing the monarch's obsession, Monash saw his chance. 'I got him

[Cowan] to promise me a special issue of 20,000 leather vests,' he wrote. The King could rest easy in the knowledge that regardless of the 3rd Division's performance on the Western Front, it would be the warmest fighting outfit. In return, Monash acted on several of the King's criticisms concerning some of the men's long hair and the dirty transport vehicles. As the days rolled by, Monash stepped up general discipline as pride in the division built up and the slackers within the ranks became more and more isolated.

✕

The conscription issue was reaching a peak as Australia prepared to vote in a referendum at the end of October. The 'anti' campaign was gaining momentum. Prime Minister Hughes, who had been influenced by the Governor-General, Munro Ferguson, was pushing hard for it, with the spurious propaganda line that a vote against conscription meant that the voter wanted Germany to win the war. The AIF was organised to vote first on 16 October in the hope that a big 'yes' vote from it would influence the public.

Sensing his side was slipping, Hughes, using his agent Keith Murdoch, asked Birdwood to make a statement in favour of the 'yes' vote. Birdwood was most reluctant to be dragged into the politics, but he agreed. The voting in the AIF had started in France and England when he asked for it to be postponed until after he had issued a statement. The count was stopped and rescheduled among the AIF troops in France, but Monash defied the order and allowed the vote to go ahead at Larkhill before Birdwood's statement was made.

Monash was ambivalent about conscription. He, like all in the five divisions, was proud of being a volunteer, yet he realised the need for recruits. Then again, he disliked Hughes' heavy-handedness and thought he had mismanaged the campaign.

On 21 October Monash took the train to London for his investiture as a Companion of the Order of the Bath at Buckingham Palace. The King was as friendly and chatty as he had been at the parade. He even apologised for not having time for lunch with him. '. . . his [the King's] uncle [the Duke of Connaught] has just arrived,' an equerry told Monash, 'and the family are lunching privately today.'[4]

The AIF voted narrowly in support of conscription, but it had no influence on the national result after the vote on 28 October, which saw the referendum fail. Hughes suffered a political setback, the War Council received a shock and Munro Ferguson was furious. His *raison d'être* in Australia amounted to little. Democracy in the country was effective.

The ramifications for Monash's 3rd Division were dire. The 20,000 troops that Hughes had promised from conscription would not be forthcoming. The PM now suggested that the 3rd Division be used to replenish the others at the front, showing that he had no appreciation of what Monash was doing on Salisbury Plain.

But events were moving faster than Hughes anticipated. The War Office, which had once wanted to cannibalise the 3rd, now understood the importance of keeping it intact as a fighting force. It ordered that it must proceed to France on 21 November.

The division was given an extra six weeks training beyond what most experts, including Monash, thought was necessary. But the extra time – especially the final three weeks – allowed it to be fine-tuned to the point where most knowledgeable observers, including those in the War Office, reckoned it was the best prepared division of all.

Monash used the time to reiterate his creed for officers, which was based on his long experience in the militia, on Gallipoli and on the Western Front. He was fervent about officers taking time to prepare orders on the basis of accurate information and making sure they were understood. Time and time again, he had seen disasters in training exercises or war because orders were rushed, misunderstood, based on wrong information or never received. Monash's ruthless streak was demonstrated when he told his officers that the fighting soldier should be looked after as well as possible, especially with food, rest and comfort, but not for humane reasons. Monash wanted to keep him as part of a 'fighting machine'. When these cogs in the war machine became casualties, Monash wanted his officers in 'a callous state of mind'.

'A commander who worries is not worth a damn,' he told them, a little callously, and with his experience on Gallipoli in mind. 'Hypnotise yourself into a state of complete indifference over losses.' An officer who claimed he had a certain percentage of losses and could not carry on would not be tolerated. A unit could fight with reduced numbers, he told them, 'even if fifty per cent losses' had been suffered.

There was also what could be called the Prozac directive. Officers should be 'optimistic' at all times, now matter how they felt. They had to keep the soldiers cheerful no matter how bad the situation. This might have been good material for a Monty Python sketch, had there not been method in Monash's psychology.

'We are going to face winter conditions [on the front],' he wrote, 'but we are going to have the greatest time of our lives.' Perhaps this was so for some, but a more accurate prediction might have been that they were going to have the 'most memorable' time of their lives. For survivors, recall would often not be pleasant, especially if they were to reflect on their own fears, shocks and the fallen.[5]

Monash concluded by reiterating his trinity: unity of purpose, unity of principle and unity of policy. The engineer in him wanted an efficient fighting machine with all parts in mechanical good order, and with him at the controls.

Yet the perfectionist in Monash was never satisfied. After a last twenty-four-kilometre march on 13 November he reported to Sclater, his immediate boss, on the faults, battalion by battalion. But it wasn't all dissatisfaction. Monash had instigated the wearing of the letter 'A' on the colour patches of sleeves of all those entitled to be called 'Anzacs', and he was pleased to see them paraded. He had ordered the turning down of the soldiers' slouch hat brim to distinguish it from the other divisions, which were turned up. This brought a mixed reaction from the grass roots. Monash was gambling on the idea catching on as the division developed its own identity.

On 21 November 1916, glitches and all, the division began taking eighty-seven trains to Southampton – not a day too soon for the cheering soldiers, who had been itching to leave the camp and join the fight on the front. Monash managed to slip away for a break in London during this long exercise, which had many of the problems of moving a small town from one country to another. It would take six days for every man, weapon, vehicle and horse to reach Rouen via the French port of Le Havre. There was time for the commander to dine with Lizette, who was becoming his closest companion, and to see Walter Rosenhain.

On 24 November Monash turned up at his new HQ, the château of Steenwerck, about a hundred kilometres from the Belgian coast and eight kilometres northwest of Armentières. It was the sector in West Flanders,

Belgium, where the 3rd would be taking over from a British division. It was part of the blimpish Field Marshal Plumer's Second British Army and, within that, Godley's II Anzac Corp. The latter included the New Zealand division and a British division.

Monash was fortunate enough to be attached to the white-haired Plumer's army. The attitudes and thinking there concerning how a force should be run and treated were the nearest to his own in the entire British services. Another key character was Plumer's Chief of Staff, Major General C. H. 'Tim' Harington. He, along with Plumer, made a point of telling officers that they were there to help the rank and file, not to bully or harass them. They were also strong on communication down the line being clear and precise. They both believed in using all the technology available in fighting battles. Monash might have been more comprehensive in his approach to harnessing science, but they were in accord with him. Harmony between Plumer, Harington and Monash was established fast. The culture in this army was something the 3rd Division could slip into without the problems that had plagued the other four divisions in the Fifth Army under General Sir Hubert Gough. It augured well for Monash's ambitions.

Everything seemed to be running well. Even his château was better than expected. It was 'modern' with electric light, a hot-water service and big grounds with stables and garages. Monash had enlarged photos of Iona put up in his bedroom and office, in an attempt to make him feel at home. He found himself in full command of five per cent of the 150-kilometre British line. He had jurisdiction over fifty square kilometres, which included two towns, a dozen smaller villages and hundreds of hamlets, and control over the civil population.

After a few days, Haig, the Commander-in-chief of all British forces, paid the 3rd Division a visit. Monash could only turn out a reserve brigade and detachments from all other units. Still, all his men were now used to inspections and ready to make a good impression. Haig, for his part, was keen to meet Monash and see the much-vaunted new division.

Haig had been more than impressed by Monash ever since his close friend George V had recommended him after a meeting on Salisbury Plain in 1916. The tall Scottish Haig, a graduate of the Royal Military College at Sandhurst, was an establishment man of Empire. He fought in the Sudan in 1898, aged twenty-seven, and in the South African War of 1899–1902. He held administrative posts in India. He would act on any suggestion from the monarch, not just because of his royal position. Haig owed his job to the King, who favoured him when David Lloyd George, Prime Minister from December 1916, did not. It was Haig, as Commander-in-chief of the British Expeditionary Force in France from July to November 1916, who committed masses of troops to an unsuccessful offensive on the Somme River. It cost 420,000 British casualties. Lloyd George, the Welsh son of an elementary school headmaster, feared a political backlash from Haig's policy of attrition, which had been summarised as 'Kill more Germans'. The PM had nothing in common with Haig and wanted him out. The King, by contrast, knew his family well. Haig's wife had been a Maid of Honour to Queen Alexandra, the King's mother. He wanted Haig to stay and, to make the point, promoted him to Field Marshal. Because it was George V's empire, not Lloyd George's, Haig remained.

The brilliant impression that Monash had made at Salisbury Plain was passed on by an enthusiastic monarch at a time when Haig was being told that the Australian Government wished to see a homogeneous Australian force – with all five divisions under one leader – similar to the Canadian Corps. If there were a suitable home-grown corps commander it would help. But Haig had not been impressed by what he had seen of the leaders of the other divisions. He would resist any pressures to have an Australian corps commander for as long as possible.

He and Monash, both mounted, rode around inspecting the soldiers in pouring rain, much to the chagrin of the men. At the end, Haig drew his horse close and threw an arm over Monash's shoulder. 'You have a very fine division,' Haig commented. 'I wish you all sorts of good luck, old man.'[6]

Monash, like other observers, was surprised at this show of affection and appreciation. Haig, like Godley, was not given to displaying emotion – except anger – in public or anywhere else. Haig had next to no knowledge of Monash's background. More curious still was the fact that Monash was not a member of the club. He had not come from the regular forces. A Dominion militia was not the source from which British generals were expected to be called for the very important business of running a corps of 200,000 men, the biggest corps in the war.

Haig's reaction to Monash could mean only one thing. The King had spoken about him in more than just glowing terms. In that tight circle of power, the nod from the supreme commander of all British armed forces and the empire was better than a wink. It was a recommendation, the most important a commander could have.

WESTERN FRONT 1917: MESSINES

Major General Monash's command of a division and the fact that he was known to be favoured by the King meant that he was now moving in an elite circle of power in the British military system. This was reflected by the kind of social invitations he was receiving. Late in December 1916, when the war was in a comparative lull, he was asked to a party thrown by Birdwood at the Château de la Motte, which used to be his HQ. The guests included the Third Army leader General Sir Edmund Allenby, Major General Chichester, one of Plumer's key staff, and old acquaintances Godley, Major General Andrew Russell, commanding the New Zealand Division, and White, Chief of the General Staff of 1st Anzac Division. Co-hosts were the attractive French owner of the château, the Baronne de la Grange, who had moved back in when Birdwood and his staff moved out, and her beautiful daughter, the Princess Bouly. Other notables were the vivacious Countess van der Steen, a Belgian peeress who did selfless good works in a hospital at Poperinghe, the Prince de Croy-Lobu, the young brother of the King of the Belgians, and a highly decorated 'fine old [French] warrior' General J. Eydon, who turned out to be the 'life of the party' with his ripping yarns.

Monash was in his element. He could mix with the most urbane military types while also flirting with charming women, a skill that the decades had not corroded. He could even practise his rusty French. He was hesitant at first, but as the party warmed up and everybody 'talked across and to the whole table . . . in English and French' his confidence built and he became fluent enough, if not always grammatical.[1]

It was a calm, almost too relaxed start to his war on the Western Front. It could not have been a bigger contrast to the way he had begun on the narrow beaches of Gallipoli, where he was under threat of death and not in control of his environment from the moment he jumped into the boat that took him to Anzac Cove. In France he was experiencing an easier, more methodical build-up to battle engagement.

In a January 1917 shake-up, Major General Holmes took Cox's job at the 4th Division and Australia's best gunner officer, Talbot Hobbs, replaced McCay at the 5th. Hobbs, an architect and artilleryman, had a similar background to Monash, whom he had known since his days in Perth twenty years earlier. The strain on McCay had made him ill. He had experienced a tough time at the front in 1916 and was exhausted. He took on a less exacting role commanding AIF bases and depots at Salisbury Plain. Brigadier General N. M. Smyth VC, a British Army regular, took over at the 2nd from Legge, who, like McCay, had had enough. Legge went home. The other British regular, Brigadier General Walker, Birdwood's former chief of staff, still commanded the 1st Division. (Harry Chauvel was commanding the Light Horse Division – the 6th – in the Middle East.)

The musical chairs among the five Australian divisions in France saw Monash move through to be the leading Australian commander on the front (and only second to Walker in seniority), although he had yet to see sustained action in Europe.

In the early months of 1917, the 3rd Division carried out raids. The biggest, on 27 February, used 854 men. It was driven and created by Monash, who worked on it for six weeks and used an original conjuring trick that was more effective than anything he displayed at parties as a teenager. In the three days before the raid, the artillery fired out 'flavoured' (coloured) smoke and gas. It caused the Germans to put on their gas masks whenever they saw smoke. On the day of the raid, Monash ordered high explosives and smoke to be fired at the German trenches, but not gas. The enemy saw the smoke, thought gas was coming, and scrambled to put on their masks. The 3rd's men attacked without cumbersome masks and had a big advantage over the Germans.

Monash was able to report a major success to Birdwood. Monash believed in the importance of raids. They kept his men tuned rather than lying idle or just preparing for bigger missions. They also unsettled the enemy. The 3rd was almost continually raiding and losing about 400 casualties a month with them.

Yet still soldiers from the other four divisions disdained the 3rd. Such sobriquets as 'the Larkhill Lancers' and 'the Neutrals' stung the 3rd's men, who had been eager to fight. Monash steadied them, saying they would get their chance. The war was expected to continue through 1917 at least. The attrition and exhaustion at the front would see them there in the near future.

What he couldn't tell the men was that the next great series of battles would begin at the end of the winter, maybe as late as the summer. In the meantime they would be well tested by the pressing Germans, who were taking their turn to raid the Allies in this relatively quiet area. Until it was time for the bigger challenges, he would get on with the more mundane business of being virtually the mayor of a medium-sized Australian town dumped in Europe. There were around 20,000 mouths (animals excluded) to feed and bodies to house, wash and clothe with fresh underpants, socks and boots as the fighting units were rotated at the front. He was also his own secretary, answering any mail addressed to him from worried relatives.

It was all time-consuming yet well within Monash's organising capacities. He had time to reflect and write. His mind drifted, as it had since the break at Gallipoli, to worries about his business. Vic, thoughtlessly, had passed on misinformation concerning its health after falling out with Gibson. Monash never doubted his integrity, but from a distance he could not help dwelling on his helplessness. Correspondence between the two partners reaffirmed the business's steadiness.

He was nostalgic also for Iona and its garden. He told Vic in letters how much he wanted to be home, and how much he envied people like Legge, who had returned. He wrote of his 'hate' for 'the business of war and soldiering with a loathing . . . the awful horror of it, the waste the destruction and inefficiency. Many a time I could have wished that wounds or sickness, or a breakdown of health would have enabled me to retire honourably from the field of action.' Monash was stopped from backing out of service, he claimed, by his honour and duty to his 20,000 men.[2]

This was all true to a point. Yet in his heart, he knew he was appeasing his wife and daughter, whom he had not seen now for more than two years. He had risen to his current position against all odds and obstacles. He had survived Gallipoli and was for the first time in his military career able to test his real skills on the battlefield. His opportunities were arising under conditions, that would allow him to demonstrate, one way or the other, his true worth as a commander.

The first opportunity was disclosed to him alone on 7 March, sixteen days before the other four divisional commanders, by Plumer, Harington and Godley. II Anzac Corps – the 3rd, New Zealand and 25th British Divisions – would be the main force in an attempt to gain the first big British victory of the war on the Western Front. The IX and X British Corps would support it. The overall plan was to eliminate the German hold on an area south of Ypres, a battered Flanders town twenty-five kilometres due north of where the 3rd Division now defended Armentières.

Monash was used to seeing once proud and beautiful cities and villages reduced to rubble. But there was something about Ypres that made it seem like a tomb. It had the misfortune to stand in the way of the German advance to the Channel ports. The British occupation meant that it became a symbol of sacrifice and defence. It was the hub of the British sector of the Western Front. The main feature of the former fourteenth-century centre for cloth-making was the square known as Grand Place. Every way to it was through an avenue of collapsed houses and buildings.

The poet Laurence Binyon in one verse captured its past, present and future with his 'Ypres':

> There was a city of patience; of proud name.
> Dimmed by neglected time of beauty and loss;
> Of acquiescence in the creeping moss.
> But on a sudden fierce destruction came
> Tigerishly pouncing: thunderbolt and flame
> Showered on her streets to shatter them and toss
> Her ancient towers to ashes. Riven across,
> She rose, dead, into never-dying fame.

The whiff of plaster was strong, but even this was swamped with the fragrance of war familiar to the troops: an uneven mix of chemicals, petrol, chloride and smoke, sometimes acrid, often pungent. On the square were the remains of the once majestic Cloth Hall. Only its tower was standing defiantly against the aggressor. It was a beacon in a sea of bricks, eerie white masonry and stones spilling into the cobbled square.

The main road leading east out to war through this wrecker's paradise was via the Menin Gate, which was a mere breach in the ramparts where a bridge crossed a moat. Two stone lions – symbols of Flanders – guarded the gate optimistically,. They stood either side of the Menin road, which led to the battlefront and by a miracle had remained through the concentrated shelling by the Germans round the clock. The enemy was keen to retard the supplies flowing along the road to the British front.

The living had been often less fortunate than the lions. The bridge over the moat, one soldier noted, was 'a solid mass of stonework supplemented, indeed cemented, by the remains of smashed vehicles and the fragmented bodies of horses and men'.[3]

The Germans would have loved to occupy this diminished piece of European real estate. They lurked in their stronghold five kilometres south of Ypres on the ugly fifty-metre-high Messines Ridge.

When asked what was 'the greatest strategical and tactical objective on the 2nd Army Front', Plumer simply pointed to the ridge. It was his *bête noir*. He had been pointing out its features, such as the burnt-out village discernible on the southern end of the ridge, to visitors for the better part of two years. The symbol of the conflict that had gone on before was the skeleton of the village's church. It was a ghostly representation of the conflict, and for deeper, perhaps darker, reasons it fascinated an obscure German corporal named Hitler. He had plenty of time during the occupation of the ridge to paint third-rate watercolours of it.

Plumer's plan was to make a full-scale army attack on the ridge early in June. This gave Monash plenty of lead-time in which to put his mind to a plan for 3rd Division to take the ridge's southern spur. After his high-level briefing, Godley told Monash to take a fortnight's leave to refresh himself before the build-up to the big offensive. Godley had been more indulgent with Monash in the past few months since Haig had shown exceptional interest in him. Godley had changed from being fair but rarely complimentary to almost showing deference to his 'non-regular' subordinate. After one Monash lecture to officers on forms of attack, Godley effused that it was 'the best lecture he had ever heard'. Monash was earning his respect. Haig (and the King) was helping it along.[4]

✕

Monash was fast developing the 3rd's reputation. It was seen as proficient. It had the lowest crime and sickness rates of all the divisions. Its performances in raids and countering them on the front were bringing praise from

Plumer, Harington and Godley. Monash's painstaking, patient, well-planned construction of a fighting force was paying off after nearly eight months solid work.

Phase 1, the development, was over. Phase 2, full-scale engagement, was ahead. In the meantime, Monash would accept breaks in Paris and Menton on the Riviera, relax and enjoy them. He knew, from long experience, that all the while he was seeing the sights, his fertile brain would be churning over how he would attack that ridge. Even when he dined in Paris at various restaurants, including his favourite, Café de la Paix near the Place de l'Opéra, he carried a notebook for ideas.

He had a chance to observe Parisian life.

What impressed me was the entire absence of 'side' [pretension] [he wrote]. There is absolutely no difference in the manners and style of the waiter, or the French officer of high rank, or the patrician dame, or the girl who checks your tickets in the Metro, or the taxi-driver or the poilu [French soldier]. There is a wonderful camaraderie and egalité, yet withal a marvellous politeness. The politeness of the French to each other and to strangers is remarkable . . . these characteristics of human comradeship and gentle amiability are what appeal to me so much with the French.

The French would have very reassured to hear what he felt about them. He was about to embark on campaigns that would result in either preserving their way of life or seeing it destroyed. For now he would enjoy the best of their cuisine – still within the confines of a diet that was keeping him lean, fit and happy in himself. After seeing a revue at the Casino de Paris, he made a twenty-four-hour rough train journey about 1100 kilometres to the Riviera. Once there, he took in 'disappointing' Monaco, redeemed by a performance of *The Barber of Seville*.

Despite the relaxation, the Riviera being 'alive with French officers and soldiers' brought Monash's mind back to his immediate job. 'Both black and white,' he wrote, 'the majority are magnificent-looking men, smart and soldierly; no one need have any doubt of their élan or fighting qualities.'

The trip seemed to be a refresher not just for his body and mind, but also for putting his situation in context and for inspiration. The army – British, Australian, Canadian and French – was united 'such as there never has been in all history, and is something to have lived for', he wrote to Vic. Holding 'a high command in such an army' was 'something to remember' for the rest of his life.[5]

There was much feeling in Monash's words, penned at a Menton café in the thin afternoon sun of early spring as he watched the crowd promenading. It said much for his state of mind. He was ready for whatever lay ahead. Vic, receiving such sentiment in Melbourne, would have realised that despite his protestations about war and how much he wished to live the quiet life in Toorak, there was little chance that her husband would be returning in the near future.

On 26 March, the day after Monash returned to Armentières, his line was extended to twelve kilometres. He began working long hours on the battle plan for his division that had been percolating while he wandered around Monte Carlo and climbed a mountain.

He was distracted from his main task by a little political subterfuge from PM Hughes and his agent, Keith Murdoch, who was wielding the increased influence he had gained since his Gallipoli 'coup'. Using his official status on behalf of the PM, Murdoch asked Monash to supply him with a confidential appraisal of the 3rd Division's quartermaster-sergeant, A. T. Ozanne, aged forty, who happened to the Labor member for Corio. The election of April 1917 was coming up. Corio was a swinging seat. Hughes was after 'dirt' on Ozanne that he could use in the campaign. Monash supplied it. His report suggested that Ozanne, who claimed a medical problem, had never intended to go from Salisbury Plain with the rest of the division to the front. This implied he was a deserter, who could have been arrested as such and tried in France. Ozanne was instead back in Geelong contesting Corio.

There was an unwritten rule in parliament that members serving in the forces would not be opposed at elections. But Hughes needed Corio if he was to maintain power. (After the Labor Party expelled him over the conscription issue, Hughes had united with the conservative opposition to form the Nationalist Party.) He published Monash's signed report, without his consent or knowledge. The press played up the 'General says Corio Member a Deserter' story. Ozanne lost the seat. His reputation was impugned. Hughes remained Prime Minister.

Monash was incensed at having been used this way. For a few days he was slandered by a Labor member, Dr William Maloney, as 'that cowardly German General'. Maloney later recanted after learning how the confidential report had been manipulated.

Monash's reputation was damaged, which didn't bother Hughes. But it taught Monash a quick lesson. He had to finesse Hughes for support. But he was a powerful politician, who would do almost anything to maintain his base. Monash would have to be more circumspect in dealing with him, and with Murdoch, who was in essence more a power-player than a journalist.

That sideshow 20,000 kilometres away didn't stop Monash focusing on his battle plan. He gave it the modest name 'Magnum Opus'. Under shellfire, early in April he carried out 'big picture' reconnaissance from a ruined castle that overlooked the southern end of Messines Ridge. It would be the subject of his attack – in tandem with the New Zealand Division on his left – that would hit the ridge directly. Monash's mind was wandering over several options that could end German control and allow II Anzac Corps to manage the high ground. Monash made notes on farms, ruins and a river, all of which would be objectives in his schemes. Back at his HQ, he studied aerial photographs of the German defences, notating every strong-point, wire entanglement, mortar emplacement, gun-pit, signal station, machine-gun, dump, buried cable, tramway and enemy trench. He then worked out intricate timetables for their destruction or capture.

On 15 April he gave the Opus to his brigadiers and invited comment and discussion with the battalion commanders who would be in the action. Once he absorbed all their ideas, he wrote detailed objectives and procedures for each battalion, right down to those for platoons and sections.

Harington, who fancied himself as a scholar, was amazed at the layered work put in. He had never seen an Opus of this magnitude in the British Library let alone in the military. It was fifteen centimetres thick. 'Wonderful detail, but not his [Monash's] job,' he commented. But he was wrong. No one in the British military running a division had gone this far or had the mind to do it. Monash, as commander, made it his job.

Bean could not rid himself of prejudices against Monash, but he was an intelligent observer beginning to grasp the scope of the major general's mind. 'Never had a big British operation been prepared in such detail,' he noted. 'In the 3rd Division in particular, Monash issued 36 successive circulars, one of them in seven parts. Points to be bombarded by artillery were carefully listed; 2nd Army staff designed an immense creeping barrage of artillery and machine-gun fire, nearly half a mile deep, ahead of the infantry.'

There would be heavy use of firepower to pave the way for better protected infantry. Plumer was thinking the way Monash was. The accord from Monash's point of view was more than satisfying. Especially in preparation.

'Huge models of the ground [to be covered and fought for] were built and studied by the troops,' Bean noted, 'especially in Monash's division.'[6]

Plumer had been waiting for this moment. There had been plenty of false starts, prevarication and procrastination. Haig and circumstances had put off a massive attack, but now the 2nd Army was ready to tackle what Plumer acknowledged as his fixation.

The army in early 1916 engaged Canadian and English miners, particularly Cornishmen used to working with clay, to lay twenty mines in two deep galleries under the ridge. Then, from November 1916, the 1st Australian Tunnelling Company drove in a third gallery at a rate of five metres daily. A big part of its work was to keep the Germans from learning about the three galleries now stuffed with a million pounds worth of explosives and huge charges: 50,000 and 70,000 pounds of ammonal. This meant fighting underground and exploding tunnels away from their secret spadework.

The enemy, itself building tunnels under the ridge, had no idea about the nearby Allies' time bomb.

The Allies began 1917 with plans for three stages of attacks to repulse the Germans in Belgium and France along a wide front, beginning with the British at Arras in France, fifty-five kilometres south of Armentières, the French in the south, and then at Messines in Flanders by the British 2nd Army, including II Anzac Corps. I Anzac and the British 62nd Division, from General Sir Hubert Gough's Fifth Army, kicked off the offensives at Bullecourt on the old Somme battlefield south of Bapaume. The plan was for the infantry to be covered by a sizeable artillery barrage and then protected in their assault on the objective by tanks.

The Germans had earlier made a tactical withdrawal from the Somme in France. This made their fallback position – along the Hindenburg Line – the target. It was broken successfully, but then events went awry. The artillery work was inadequate. Every single one of the eleven tanks broke down before they even reached the battleground. I Anzac attacked unprotected in a snowstorm and lost 10,000 men. Soon after, the French under General Robert Nivelle, aided by the British, in the south had been crushed by 16 April. The French Army had almost been hit out of the war. The British assumed the role of senior partner after General Pétain replaced Nivelle on 15 May after a series of mutinies in the French Army. They continued for five weeks. They were covered up. Pétain's role was to nurse his force back to full confidence. This kept the French out of all action, even limited offensives, and Haig filled the vacuum in taking the initiative on the Western Front.

A victory in the third planned offensive, at Messines, was now imperative for Allied survival and morale. The Germans were waiting. A spy had informed them that the British offensive would take place a fortnight after finishing the Arras attack.

Haig visited the 2nd Army on 24 May, wishing to inspect the 3rd Division. A few things went wrong in the very early morning preparation, including an accident when a portly Jewish officer was thrown from his horse and slightly injured. Haig seemed distracted during the later inspection, and it was not considered a success for the division. The officers mess that night had an air of gloom. Monash stood up to read the nightly weather report.

'A heavy dew fell this morning . . .' Monash said and then began laughing, as did others, including the fallen officer. It broke the tension and the mood was restored.

Yet Haig's visited kept various pressures on. He avoided Plumer, whom he detested, it was claimed by Harington. Haig had maintained a rivalry ever since Plumer, as an outside examiner at Staff College more than thirty years earlier, had given Haig low marks. Instead he attended a Monash 3rd Division conference and left it full of praise.

'Monash is a clear-headed, determined Commander,' he wrote. 'Every detail has been thought of. His Brigadiers were equally thorough. I was struck with their whole arrangements. Every suggestion I made was carefully noted for consideration.'7

The fact that even an intelligent suggestion from an NCO was given equal consideration didn't matter. Haig was now not mentioning anything about Monash not being in the club. Nor was Godley. Perhaps this militia chap from the colonies had earned an honorary membership.

Plumer appreciated Monash from the start regardless of his background.

✕

Monash concentrated on his split-second timetable in the countdown to 7 June. He worked hard at conferences on coordination with his left flank. He did not want his division to be caught not knowing what its Anzac partner had been doing. Too often on Gallipoli, weak, rushed preparation by Godley at divisional level had seen pathetic or no coordination, which caused the deaths of countless Anzacs. Now Monash had control he took it upon himself to do Godley's job and know, down to the minute, what the New Zealanders and the 25th Division on their left were doing. He also took up his right to know the whole plan right across the attacking front. He trod on toes, mostly Harington's. But Monash didn't mind if he bruised a few egos. It was better than losing a soldier. Or many. The same applied to the opening artillery barrage and mine explosions. Monash did not want to see his formation left stranded and mowed down because of inept firepower and timing as he had on Gallipoli.

For the last three weeks, he again turned into an engineer in charge of a huge construction site. His division made roads, built railways and tramways, formed ammunition dumps, made camouflaged gun emplacements, prepared brigade and battalion battle HQs, and laid a complex system of underground cables. It fixed positions for machine-guns, field guns, heavy guns and howitzers. Further field engineering work was for large dugouts, approach avenues, assembly and jumping off trenches.

Monash also attended to the never-ending verbiage necessary to manage 20,000 men and animals. The orders covered feeding, transport and ammunition supply. Additional directives for the actual offensive strategy began before a single soldier went over the top. They covered the initial artillery bombardment and the blowing up of the mines.

In the last ten days, Monash sent strong raiding parties out to upset the Germans while beginning the final preparation for his 12,000 infantry. Part of this was to delve into the psychology of how to inspire his troops. Monash kept it simple, looking for issues that touched emotions in his military world. He had experimented with morale by the simple dictate over the brim of the slouch hat, but some within the division had not appreciated this. Yet Monash argued that once the untried soldiers of the 3rd had proved themselves, then they might wish to be more distinctive.

'It is because we do not consider psychology enough that we are taking so long to win the war,' he wrote. 'I have always found that it pays to consider the psychology not only of the enemy but also of my own troops, and to study the factors that affect his actions and reactions.'[8]

Again, he experimented just before his men were to engage the enemy by circulating reports about the maltreatment of some Australian prisoners held by the Germans after Bullecourt. This was meant to increase the image of 'the Hun' as evil, brutal vermin that had to be eradicated, and to fire up his troops with thoughts of revenge. There was perhaps another element at work here, which was more about the psychology of Monash than his troops. Only a few weeks earlier during the unfortunate Ozanne incident, he had been described as a 'German General'. The insult to his integrity, patriotism and loyalty had been maintained for almost three years since he had first volunteered to fight. Even after his efforts on Gallipoli, it was pointed out that Turks were not Germans. How would the 'German General' perform when he had to fight his 'own kind'? By pushing out the propaganda about the 'Boche', he was sending a message to everyone about himself and how prepared he was to obliterate Germans.

The last-minute circulars on the treatment of Bullecourt prisoners had a mixed reaction. Some responded with quiet contempt. Others spoke of retribution. Monash's attitude was that if the propaganda worked or didn't work, it was better than not attempting to fire up his men at all.

He did receive more positive feedback for his inspirational messages to fight 'for yourself, Australia and the British Empire'. Most of the men in slouch hats reckoned the priority was about right. If you didn't perform for yourself you had a higher probability of failing. And doing it for Australia meant more than British Empire maintenance. Yet the latter was still appreciated as an important add-on to the reasons they were putting their lives on the line.

✕

At 12.15 a.m. on 7 June, eight attack battalions of 3rd Division began their five-kilometre approach through Ploegsteert Wood in the battle for Messines Ridge. The eerie whine of phosgene gas shells could be heard overhead. The soldiers scrambled for their respirators and most kept moving. As they advanced, more than 500 soldiers were overcome. The other 11,000 reached the start line by 2.20 a.m. as planned. The enemy, still unaware, was just 200 metres away. On the 3rd's left was the New Zealand Division and on its left was the British 25th. Further left (or north) were another five divisions of the IXth and Xth Corps of Plumer's Second Army. About 100,000 men were lined up ready and waiting for the signal along a twelve-kilometre front of attack.

At 3.10 a.m. the artillery opened up in a rowdy exhibition along with machine-guns, but even that noise was submerged in the next sound. Twenty-three mines were blown up in an explosion that was felt across the Channel. While that was still reverberating, the 3rd went over the top into the dust, smoke and flame. It was tough work avoiding the craters in the dark. But the battalions were well drilled. They regrouped and made their assault on the Messines southern spur. The Germans were over-whelmed. Resistance was sporadic, except for that encountered by the 33rd Battalion, which had a serious fight. Before 4 a.m. the 3rd had control of its target.

It had taken Monash's men forty-five minutes to be in a strong position for winning their first major battle.

The 3rd Division now waited for the New Zealanders, who hit the ridge with a job made easier by the softening up and the 3rd's success. At 5 a.m. in daylight the 9th and 10th Brigades were also at their allotted line.

The 3rd's role now was to consolidate. Monash ordered out the wire entanglements and readjusted his artillery. Then he made sure Vickers and Lewis guns and trench mortars were in place. He commenced 'reorganis-ing units in depth, so as to get rid of the heavy congestion of the men in the forward lines'. This reduced casualties from shellfire. By nightfall he felt 'my position was absolutely secure on my new lines'.[9]

By midday the main heights had been taken along most of the battle-front. Only the Xth Corps in the extreme north, near Ypres itself, were in serious, continuing conflict. In the afternoon the Australian 4th Division, in reserve, swept through the front taken by 25th Division and the New Zealanders and were joined by the 3rd Division's 37th Battalion on its extreme left flank. Farther north a similar operation occurred as fresh

British troops moved through the front reached by IXth and Xth Corps.

Late in the day, the 37th Battalion ran into trouble. Blockages happened here and there and called for some different measures in order to achieve a breakthrough. An example was a pillbox that was machine-gunning the advancing Australians. Captain R. C. Grieve volunteered to attempt to counter it. He launched grenades ahead of him and, with a thin covering fire ran forward, hurling more grenades as he went. The smoke from explosions in front of the pillbox allowed him a second or two of cover and surprise. Grieve single-handedly captured the Germans inside it. (Monash recommended him for the VC, which Grieve received.)

The 3rd's victory in essence was scored before dawn. It dug in by evening, helping to give Plumer's Second Army a huge success right along its elongated front. It was described as the 'most perfect attack with limited objective in the war' so far.

Monash made sure all the men in the forward trenches received hot meals by 7 p.m., something that had not been done at Sari Bair on Gallipoli. Throughout the day the wounded were evacuated. Again, if Monash could help it, there would be no repeats of the disasters at Sari Bair when poor divisional leadership left the fallen far too long without help.

He had remained at his HQ through the first twenty-four hours, coordinating every aspect of the battle, giving orders, passing on reports to Godley and making decisions. He bullied his brigadiers when necessary and could be ruthless. If an indecisive report came through on the taking of an objective, he would demand to know: 'Is it ours – or not? Yes or no?' On perhaps just one occasion in the entire day, and in the five days following, his not being on the spot on the front line caused a problem. But weighed against the hundreds of other decisions he made that were just as important, his style of being the 'central brain' of his division's operation proved successful.

Messines was the first major battle victory for any Australian division in the war. No longer would the 3rd receive jibes about their lack of fighting. Monash and his soldiers were now held in esteem. A winning record in battle now fulfilled all the promises about the division and how it appeared to the King, Haig, Plumer and Godley.

The British High Command, short on wins, now had something to boast about. Haig, looking less haggard than of late, visited Armentières on 9 June and kept up his praise for Monash, describing him now as 'a most practical and capable commander' and saying that he had 'done well'. (There is no record of his praising Plumer, but somewhere he must have choked on a 'well done' for him too.)[10]

Soon after the victory, Monash sent a fulsome message of praise to the entire division. Then he wrote a letter to Vic:

> A great victory [Messines], thoroughly defeated the 4th Bavarian Division (under Prince Franz) and the 3rd Bavarian Division, my old antagonists east of Armentières. These Divisions were practically blotted out, as far as infantry is concerned, both opposite my sector.
>
> On my left the New Zealanders had Saxons and Württembergers, who also got a bad beating. Farther north, Prussians [also were defeated].[11]

Monash's evaluation of the battle was tempered by about 600 deaths out of 4000 casualties, a third of the troops employed. But most of the casualties were gas-related, and many of the men rejoined their units after treatment. (There were 12,000 Anzac casualties in a total of 26,000 British in all.)

Ever the perfectionist, he measured the operation by its failures rather than by its obvious successes. There were a few weaknesses, which would have to be addressed. One was the number of casualties when they had reached their target and were consolidating, even though Monash did all he could to thin out the front. He hated with a passion the waste of his men's lives. His conclusion was that if possible penetration should be deep enough to capture enemy artillery. This was more than a limited objective. But it would eradicate the problem caused by enemy firepower.

Apart from this, there were 'astonishingly few' disappointments. Monash was not happy with the 37th Battalion's commanding officer, who was interrogated then fired.

He also did not think much of Bean's battle report. But this time Monash didn't confront him as he had on Gallipoli. Instead he reserved his criticism for a letter to a friend. Bean's report was 'the apotheosis of banality', he wrote. 'Not only is the language silly tosh, but his facts are, for the most part, quite wrong.'[12]

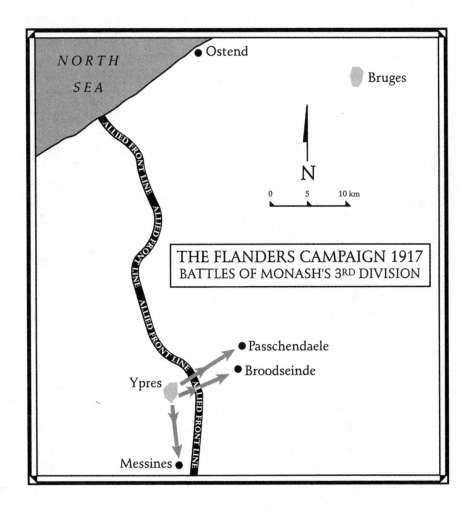

THE FLANDERS CAMPAIGN 1917
BATTLES OF MONASH'S 3RD DIVISION

3rd Division was relieved on 12 June and Monash's HQ was pushed further back from the front at Bailleul. He did not stop reviewing the Messines exercise and kept addressing officers and units. But there wasn't much rest in reserve. The Germans hit the nearby town of Nieppe with artillery fire. Monash took up all the cars, lorries and wagons available. He arranged for some of his men to evacuate 1400 elderly people, children and invalids, while others were detailed to put out the fires in the town's factories. Nieppe's mayor wrote a grateful letter to Monash. It was nice to receive recognition. It had been lacking in the war itself.

The timing of his move from 4th Brigade to the 3rd Division and his five-month stay in England had seen him left out of mentions in despatches before Messines. Monash was also being ignored because he was not part of the main Australian force, I Anzac Corps, which was receiving well-deserved recognition. Unusual clerical errors and inadvertent omissions had caused his name to go missing when he deserved mentions in despatches. As the commander of an Australian division in the British Second Army, he was viewed as neither fish nor fowl. Monash saw himself as 'nobody's child'. Both Birdwood and White were sympathetic and urged him to write to Godley about it.

Monash's lifelong concerns about being an outsider having to fight for recognition surfaced. It crossed his mind that his 'heritage and background' were against him yet again. As ever he felt compelled to look after his interests, since it seemed that nobody else would. On 20 June, with the euphoria over Messines still high, Monash wrote to Godley asking him to give Defence Minister Pearce his impression of the 3rd Division since it had been in II Anzac Corps of the Second Army. In the same breath, he asked for a 'few words' about himself, arguing that it might help counteract 'the bad impression which has doubtless been created in Australia, owing to the pointed omissions of my name from the last two despatches'.

Godley responded that he hadn't had any mentions either. 'But it doesn't worry me,' he added blithely, 'especially that we have now really done something [at Messines] worth being mentioned about.'[13]

These words were cold comfort to Monash, whose expanding experience in dealing with the press, politicians and the military hierarchy told him that recognition in the way of despatches, gongs and any other award going counted in the battle for promotion. But his sense of insecurity had caused him to discount two factors. His success in raising a division that had proved itself now worked in his favour. More important still, Haig was making no secret of the fact that he admired him.

Monash was left to reflect on his achievements. If he never did another thing, he had commanded a major battle victory. It had been a dream for most of his life. But he wanted to achieve much more and was hungry for any advantage that would give him the edge in battle. One weapon that had been judged badly by some observers was the tank. The British Corps in Second Army had already used it with mixed success. Monash, always willing to delve into new technology, wanted to see for himself.

On 24 June, he visited a tank battalion in IX Corps. The commander invited him to take a ride, and Monash accepted, although he would not tackle the controls. He had enough trouble with cars, let alone tanks. Monash was more concerned to understand how it worked and to gauge its advantages. The value of these 'very wonderful and very terrible machines' was not lost on him. He probed the commander and his men with questions. He watched the tanks manoeuvre in formation and out of it. He timed them, interrogated the operators again and took copious notes. After the battle of Bullecourt, when Australians had been left stranded and vulnerable because of the tanks' failures, there had been no confidence in them. But Monash walked away convinced that this weapon should be part of his divisional armoury. He resolved to push for its inclusion in his battle plans.

BROODSEINDE UP; PASSCHENDAELE DOWN

On 30 June 1917 Monash arrived in London for eleven days' leave. He took in the opera, a musical, a revue and two plays. He also had a discreet, late celebration of his fifty-second birthday with Lizette at a Chelsea restaurant close to the Thames. After several meetings since mid-1916, they had become lovers. He was enjoying her attention and companionship. Their intermittent assignations kept a romantic edge to the affair, and Monash was still careful to keep it secret from Louise and Walter.

While he played at night, he had chores, obligations and work interests during the day, including three afternoons at AIF HQ in Horseferry Road, and press interviews. He took a trip to Larkhill to see McCay, inspect three battalion reinforcements and settle 'a lot of outstanding questions'.

On 7 July there was a big air raid, which Monash saw from his suite at the Prince's Hotel, Piccadilly. It took three minutes. He was not impressed. 'By far the greater part of the noise and excitement was made afterwards in the newspapers,' he wrote to Vic and added a line to discourage any new thoughts she might have had about coming to visit him. 'You will gather that London is not just now one of the pleasantest places in the world to live in.'[1]

While Monash was in England, the King visited the front. He wanted to catch up with Monash again. When it was discovered he was on leave, the King, accompanied by Haig, asked to see the 3rd Division's brigadiers. He was effusive about their success at Messines and passed on his congratulations to Monash through them. It was confirmation of the King's attitude and his subtle way of reminding Haig and Godley that his impression of

Monash at Salisbury Plain had been well founded. He had picked a winner. Godley understood. He took leave when Monash returned and left him as acting Corps Commander of II Anzac. For three weeks, he was in control of three divisions, another 20,000 troops from artillery, cavalry, railway and labour companies, motor transport, two air squadrons and two wireless companies. It was only a short stint, but it gave Monash a taste of running this higher command.

It was demanding work, but he was in his element and more informed than he had ever been as the war reached a new phase. Losing battles and then mutinies in the ranks had plagued the French. They were rendering their army ineffective. The Americans had entered the war officially, but no one knew when they would turn up in Europe or how useful they would be. More important was the turmoil in Russia, with the overthrow of the Tsar in March and the creation of a revolutionary government by Russian lawyer and politician Alexander Kerensky. Russia was out of the war for the moment, but could be cajoled back into it. Aware of this, the Germans had not yet begun to withdraw their troops from the Russian front. If they did, they would provide a huge reinforcement of perhaps a million soldiers for the Western Front.

Haig felt that July–August 1917 was the time for the British to force home advantages. Any territorial gains or repulsions of the enemy would be vital. Messines had provided the breakthrough. The Commander-in-Chief wanted that victory to be the first of several offensive gains, later known as the Third Battle of Ypres. One aim was to secure the rail junction at Roulers, only twenty kilometres from the British front. Haig wished also to see the Channel coast cleared. His strategy was to wear down the struggling German Army before it could be bolstered.

For the time being, Haig was happy to pay lip service to Plumer's limited objective approach, whereby troops would move forward under heavy artillery support. Once a target line was reached, the artillery would be brought up for another barrage before the soldiers moved forward again. But Haig's level of commitment to it was sure to be tested when they secured a limited objective and there was a temptation to go on.

Monash let it be known that he was 'the greatest possible believer' in the strategy. 'So long as we hold and retain the initiative [read: reach a point, dig in and maintain the position],' he wrote, 'we can in this way inflict the maximum loss [on the enemy] when and where we like.'[2]

The Plumer philosophy suited Monash's approach of selecting a goal and achieving it with maximum technological support (artillery, machine-guns and mortars, and, if possible in the future, aircraft and tanks) for an advancing infantry. The difference with Haig, Godley and the Fifth Army's Gough, who had been in charge of II Anzac Corps, was that protection of infantry was never a priority. These three and others in the British High Command were of the old school whose methods were rooted in the nineteenth century. They believed in taking risks at their soldiers' expense in the interests of the possibility of making a big breakthrough. They didn't care much for detailed plans that took a minimum of risks and led to a step-by-step advance to that breakthrough.

Two other huge differences from them were entrenched in Monash's mind and, as yet, released so far only on the Messines Ridge. First, you did not make an offensive unless you had a good chance of success, which could not be further from the British High Command's experience and thinking. Second, if you reached that objective and there was a clear, risk-free chance to advance to another line, you took it.

The Haig–Godley–Gough mentality was offensive to Monash. It caused obscene waste of life, and on every occasion it led to failure. Haig's history in the war should have alerted all the limited objective supporters. He had always been a crash-through merchant. The plans he oversaw in July 1917 were dangerous and revealing, even in their ambiguity. His secret aim was to sweep the ridge of Germans after Messines. A big problem was that sections of it were twelve kilometres apart. But that wasn't the end of it. Haig couldn't resist the big thinking approach. He also wanted the Fourth Army to attack along the coast. In turn, Gough's Fifth Army would advance 4000 metres to capture the third German line on the ridge. All this was to be achieved on day one. It could go further if there was a chance. In other words, the bash-through mentality could go on until resistance stopped it going further.

Some of Haig's staff were concerned. It seemed to be a long way from the limited objective doctrine. Even hard-man Gough objected. He needed a month to prepare and plan his strategy. Yet he was from Haig's hammer and hope class. He came around. Plumer was uncertain but agreed. He had been asked to provide a scheme that would fool the German commanders in Flanders into thinking the British were going to make a big assault on the French city of Lille, which was thirty kilometres southeast of Ypres. This appeared to be more or less in keeping with the limited objective.

He in turn approached Monash for ideas. In keeping with his aware-
ness of any new technological development, he came up with the concept
of smoke. A screen was not to come from all his men lighting up at once,
but from an ingenious idea suggested by one of his young subalterns, Lieutenant A. S. Varley. He had been toying with smoke bombs being fired
from a Stokes mortar. Monash, who loved inventions and engineering
creativity, encouraged him. He had used the smoke and gas trick at
Messines. Now he decided to use Varley's innovation. It would both
conceal movement and confuse the Germans. Monash backed his man,
and demonstrated the smoke and mortar firing to commanders. Army
HQ adopted it. Mindful of the lack of returns received in the militia for
his breach-loading 'Stanley-Monash Gun', Monash guided Varley on how
to patent his development. He received an initial tidy payment of £300
and the promise of royalties.

Monash also suggested an attack on the strongly held Windmill Ridge
– the site in August 1916 of a furious attack by (then Lieutenant) Albert
Jacka – and the Warneton railway line and station, three kilometres west of
Messines, as part of the Second Army feint. He saw Plumer twice to be
sure of what was required. When he was clear on the 3rd's very limited
objective compared to Messines, he saw Haig. The C-in-C confirmed the
requirement, while at the same time assuring him that his division would
be brought into the thick of the action later.

Haig was again effusive, treating Monash with deference while still
obscuring his own, more furtive aims.

The C-in-C was receiving plenty of reminders of the interest of his
ultimate benefactor – the King – in Monash. A week before the Third
Battle of Ypres was to begin, on George V's recommendation, the King of
the Belgians turned up to meet Monash. A few days later, George's uncle,
the Duke of Connaught, recently Governor-General of Canada, also
visited his Bailleul HQ, again because the King had advised him to do so.
Mindful of the apparent impact of his big parade at Larkhill nearly a year
earlier, Monash 'formed up a Corps representative parade in the Square at
Bailleul'.[3]

Someone, perhaps Haig, had advised Monash that kings liked to see
the spoils of battle, in the tradition of all monarchs going back to when the
booty became theirs. Monash obliged by showing the Duke 'our collection
of trophies from the Messines battle'. They included weapons of all kinds,
including howitzers, machine-guns and some vehicles. Royalty in bygone

centuries might have expected some more glittering treasures, such as gold bullion, but the Duke seemed pleased enough. No doubt he would report back to his nephew about that splendid Australian general.

Monash had by now recognised that this unusual favouritism, this special royal patronage, had some value. Whether it would become tangible remained to be seen.

✕

A heavy bombardment across the entire Ypres front began on 15 July. On 31 July a grand assault was launched. Haig secretly wished to push on to the town of Passchendaele, twelve kilometres northeast of Ypres. Monash turned to the aptly named Cannan and his 11th Brigade for the attack on Windmill Ridge. One of his many instructions was to take as many prisoners as possible.

Monash was smoking furiously and poring over maps and photographs at his HQ mid-battle when an officer interrupted him. He beckoned the commander outside. There was a young private from the 11th Brigade with two blindfolded German prisoners.

'Mr Monash?'

'Yes . . .'

'You wanted some Fritzies,' the private said, very pleased with himself. 'Well, I've brought you two.'

'So I see,' Monash said admiringly. 'Very well done, Private.' He arranged for officers to take the captured men to the prison. 'Where did you pick them up?'

'Near Windmill Ridge.'

Monash requested a car and driver, and rode back the few kilometres to the front with the young private.[4]

Monash was amused by the young man taking Cannan's directive – 'General Monash wants to see plenty of prisoners' – literally. But he was also thrilled by his enthusiasm. It augured well for the modest operation. It had surprised the Germans, and the ridge was taken. The Germans regrouped and counter-attacked. The 11th Brigade eventually took control but not before suffering 550 casualties.

Monash and Plumer thought this was too high a price, and Monash spent nearly as much time in review as the actual battle itself had taken. Out of it came his belief in 'air observation': reconnaissance and intelligence-gathering by plane. It was the quickest and best way to learn enemy positions. Like the possibility of tanks coming under his control, Monash would always rely on planes, with contingencies if the weather was too bad for flying.

✕

On 9 August Monash handed over his sector to 4th Division, now run by Sinclair-MacLagan, who replaced Major General Holmes. A stray shell at 'Hyde Park Corner' – a road intersection in what was considered a safe place – had killed him.

It rained five times the average in August and turned the flatland clay in front of Ypres into slush and then a bog. Haig's push for Third Ypres – using the 5th Army and General Antoine's First French Army – was halted. It had advanced a kilometre when Haig was hoping and expecting more like ten kilometres. During this struggle forward, there were 100,000 casualties. Ill feeling built. There were threats of mutiny (later realised) in some sections of the Fifth Army, whose men had to attack in such atrocious conditions over open marshland while being shelled and picked off.

By 26 August, Haig did what army commanders do when things don't go well: he pulled out the hapless Gough and replaced him with Plumer in charge of the Fifth and Second British Armies. One English observer saw it in quaint cricket terms. 'Young' (forty-six-year-old) Gough was the rugged, blast-through fast bowler who had not found the wet wicket to his liking. Plumer, the mature (sixty-year-old), wily Hedley Verity–like spinner with a bag of tricks, was brought on. Accordingly, the weather changed. The mud and slush dried out and was replaced by choking dust that the soldiers detested more than the bog. Plumer, who preferred to use guile and cunning, would not provide the smash through that Haig wanted. Yet he was methodical, just as determined and more likely to succeed, provided the weather didn't intervene again. It was back to the step-by-step approach.

Attempts to achieve several limited objectives were planned to begin on 20 September.[5]

✕

In the meantime, the 3rd Division was being brought back to battle strength at Boulogne on the coast, seventy-five kilometres west of Ypres, recuperating, recruiting, refitting and retraining. The stunning, green rolling countryside was a refreshing change from the front flats, and the men enjoyed the late summer sunshine. Monash had returned his Corps Commander duties to Godley and was back supervising the division's revival, making sure that the soldiers recovered with activities, especially sporting competitions, when not drilling or on duty. Cricket, horse shows, athletics, boxing, rugby and Aussie Rules kept most of the men happy.

The division might have been well away from the front, but Monash and the Germans hadn't forgotten each other. His HQ – at the beautiful Château Hervarre near Blequin – was bombed from the air. He collected bomb fragments for his growing exhibition of war souvenirs.

It wasn't all work. He struck up a friendship with the smooth Baron de Gail, his French liaison officer, and his wife. *Le Baron* read *le General* well. He made sure that Monash was amused in his time off, in the company of women. If it was not meeting the charming Duchess of Westminster and the stunning young Marquise d'Armaille at a horse show, it was entertaining Melbourne nurses of the 25th General Hospital in his battle-scarred château. The Baron knew how to throw a good party, and Monash enjoyed the company as the distant sounds of conflict continued unabated day and night.

The rarefied atmosphere didn't allow Monash's mind to drift far from the killing grounds to his east. He took up vantage positions close to watch bombardments during the Third Ypres battle, and began working on Plumer's directive for the 3rd Division. It was to attack Broodseinde on the Roulers–Ypres railway line, eleven kilometres northeast of Ypres, and about two kilometres south of Haig's ultimate prize, the Passchendaele Ridge.

On 19 September Monash attended a corps commanders' conference and began to assert himself, questioning not Godley's authority but his methods and tactics. Monash wanted two fundamental and vital decisions changed. First, Godley thought the maximum depth captured by the first four battalions should be 1350 metres. Monash argued for 1100 metres using three battalions, keeping one in reserve. This would give the artillery a less difficult task in moving up behind and in protecting a smaller area and number of troops. Second, Godley chose a road running to the southern spur of the main ridge to be assaulted as the boundary line between Monash's 3rd Division and Russell's New Zealand Division on the left. Monash pointed out that the British and German barrages would destroy the road. There would be confusion between the advancing divisions. Anzac soldiers would end up being killed by friendly fire. Monash wanted only the enemy in front of his troops. Russell saw the merit in this, but what would be the boundary line? Monash proposed that one man from each front platoon would use a luminous prismatic compass to keep the right direction for the divisions. This would do away with the need to follow roads or look for landmarks.

Godley, to save face, would not agree to the changes at the conference itself. But soon after it Monash's more thorough ideas were adopted.

The next day, the new push by the Second and Fifth Armies (ten divisions) now run by Plumer, began. The 1st and 2nd Divisions of I Anzac Corps were to fight side by side for the first time. It caused elation among the troops. They distinguished themselves in the early battles at Menin Road – a mud track lined with blackened tree-trunks – running due east from Ypres towards the front line.

Menin Road battles saw 5000 casualties owing mainly to heavy German artillery fire. After those encounters, Australia's 4th and 5th Divisions relieved I Anzac Corps. They too fought strongly and further demoralised the battered Germans in the battle of Polygon Wood, about eight kilometres east of Ypres and just north of Menin Road. The wood was a small plateau, which had been a rifle range in peacetime. The Germans nested there, controlling the ground around it with machine-guns. The 14th Battalion, which had distinguished itself at the head of Monash Valley, was chosen to take the plateau. The experience at Gallipoli had put all challenges in a different perspective. Nothing was impossible. The attack ran into trouble as much from the Germans as from shells of their own artillery, and looked like failing until cool Albert Jacka steadied them.

While the 14th recovered, the 31st Battalion's Private Patrick Bugden led a small party against the damaging machine-gun posts. Bugden almost single-handedly changed the outcome of the battle of Polygon Wood, leading several successful attacks with grenades and bayonet. He also emulated Simpson on Gallipoli, risking his life to save wounded soldiers. Like Simpson, his fortune didn't last. There were just so many times a brave man could gamble with his life in the open battlefield. After three days of heroic activity Bugden was killed.

The 4th Division's battalions accomplished all their missions. Every trench and several blockhouses fell to them, and finally Polygon Wood itself. They had more than 1700 casualties. The 5th Division, which had even tougher encounters, suffered nearly 5500 casualties in the three days of battles on 26–28 September.

Meanwhile, Monash and the 3rd waited for the signal to join the fray. On 22 September Haig motored thirty-two kilometres from his HQ to Boulogne to review the division in the back areas near Le Touquet. Monash, now an expert in turning on a 'good show', paraded 12,000 troops. Haig was pleased. He stayed an hour chatting to Monash and his commanders. Then came a surprise invitation, which told Monash he was still very much in favour. Haig asked him to dinner at his HQ mess. Nothing unusual in that. But it was the company and circumstances that caused Monash to pinch himself. Also present were Lieutenant-General Kidgell, Chief of the General Staff, and Major General Butler, Deputy Chief of the General Staff. They made up the key figures in the central brains trust of the entire British force. The four of them sat down at the dinner table.

After each course was served, the mess stewards left the room and the doors were locked from the inside. After earnest discussion, the C-in-C would give the signal. The doors would be opened, and the next course would be served.

The confidential chats centred on what was ahead – Passchendaele Ridge – and how the German Army, it was believed by these three top figures, were being worn down. All the British needed was good weather. In fact it was crucial to the timing of Haig's hoped-for smash through, which he was predicting would provide the impetus for winning the whole conflict.

'Nothing could have been more charming than the affability and cama-raderie of these three great soldiers,' Monash wrote, caught in the euphoria of the moment. He was being taken into the inner sanctum of the British war presidium. This triumvirate was the true prosecutor of the Allied effort, given the wobbly state of the French force, and now that the Russians were out of the war for good, after a brief revival against the Austrians and Germans in July.[6]

Why, Monash would have reflected on the drive back to his château, had he been drawn into such exclusive company? The only plausible reason was that he was being assessed, measured and weighed for a higher command. Monash was aware that there was a push for an Australian

Army and an Australian to command it. Haig and the British Government were against it. They wanted control. But they were making concessions. British officers were being replaced. Even Monash's own Colonel Farmar – the 3rd's chief administrative officer – was being removed, much to the sorrow of both men. They had fused well. Farmar called Monash 'a leader of genius. The thought he has given to detail inspires every man in the Division with confidence.'[7]

Monash felt he had a fair chance of running any consolidation of Australian forces. He was the senior Australian commander in Europe. But he was not overconfident. He knew there would be attempts to stop him taking control. It was going to be a matter of whose supporters had the most clout. Monash could not rely on any influence with Prime Minister Hughes through the tenuous connection of their wives' friendship. The PM had shown a certain expediency – and even a lack of respect for Monash – over the Ozanne incident in the April elections. But with the war peaking, the British would only hand over to their anointed one from within the Australian ranks. There was no way they would have a wayward Dominion rogue commander they didn't approve of in charge of a fair chunk of the British Army.

The C-in-C would have more say in the matter than the Australian PM, unless the government vetoed the British High Command's choice.

By 27 September, after Menin Road and Polygon Wood, the British, spearheaded by the Anzac forces, were in position to make a big attack on the main – Broodseinde – 'Ridge' (in this area referring to a small gradient), which if taken would lead on to Passchendaele (which rose to just sixty metres in height over several kilometres). I Anzac Corps – 1st and 2nd Divisions – were now moved north of Polygon Wood to a launching place. Then II Anzac Corps – Monash's 3rd Division and the New Zealand Division – were moved in beside them and in line. This caused a ripple of anticipation along the four-division front. It was the first time that three Australian divisions, along with the Kiwis, had ever lined up together. The whole sense of the Anzac legend bristled for several kilometres as men sent messages up and down the line. The energy generated by the common bond on Gallipoli was reinstated. The soldiers were itching for action.

Monash sensed the mood. There was no need to put out stories about

German atrocities here. These men would be driven by emotions unwritten, even unspoken.

In all, twelve divisions would burst over the top on a thirteen-kilometre front on the planned attack day, 4 October. The four Anzac divisions would this time form the spearhead. The 1st, 2nd and 3rd Divisions faced Broodseinde 'Ridge'. The New Zealand Division on their left was looking at Abraham Heights, which joined the main 'ridge' (not so low ground) at Broodseinde.

Monash and his fellow divisional commanders studied the weather forecasts and the skies above. They decided to speed up road and rail construction.

On 1 October, seventy-two hours before the planned attack, Monash moved his HQ to a dugout labyrinth at Menin Gate under the eastern rampart of Ypres. It was similar to a mine with tunnels and chambers. Monash had a portable generator, which meant he always had light. He had lived in a lot of stately homes and châteaux during his service, but this wasn't one of them. 'It is cold and dank and overrun by rats and mice,' Monash scribbled while waiting for equipment and files to arrive. 'It is altogether smelly and disagreeable.' It would be his home for three weeks. His staff, clerks, signallers, cooks, batmen and officers were tucked away in tunnels, chambers, little cabins and recesses.

Monash had wandered around Ypres. 'Once a marvel of medieval architectural beauty,' he noted, 'it lies all around us a stark, pitiable ruin . . . ever since the close of the second battle of Ypres in 1915, this town has lain under easy reach of the Boche guns. It has been shelled day and night.' Although the Germans had been pushed back several kilometres east of the city, they still shelled the town with 'long-range high-velocity guns'. 'Every day a few more of the gaunt, spectral pillars, which once were historic buildings, are toppled and crumpled into dust,' Monash wrote. Knowing Vic's love for racing, he attempted to describe the 'ordered chaos' in the Ypres region in terms she would grasp:

Imagine the traffic in Elizabeth Street for an hour after the last race on Cup Day, multiplied tenfold and extending in a line from Flemington to Sandringham. Imagine streams of men, vehicles, lorries, horse, mules and motors of every description moving ponderously forward in either direction all day and night in a never halting, never ending stream . . . ploughing its way painfully through the mud, men and horses plastered to the eyes in it, and a reek of smoke and petrol everywhere.[8]

Two days later, he was under pressure and only had time to write in his diary: 'Very busy harassing day. Finally see Brigadiers.'[9]

He had spent the three days since moving into Menin Gate working on the detail of a rushed battle plan. With rain falling and squalls on 3 October, he told his brigadiers that if the Germans attacked first, the soldiers were to stand fast and not go out to meet them. Monash's spies were good. The Anzac attack was set down for 6 a.m. on the 4th. At 5.20 a.m. white and yellow German flares, 'hazy in the drizzle, rose in sheaves on the Australian front'. Then came the heavy 'crump crump' of a German barrage. The flares exposed the waiting Anzacs. Ten minutes later, a heavy trench-mortar barrage hammered 'the troops lying in shell-holes along the white tapes marking the start-line'.[10]

About one man in seven was struck. But the Anzacs, disciplined and under instruction, waited an agonising thirty minutes.

At 6 a.m. the British barrage hit. The shells fell in the slush created by the night's rain and threw up smoke and steam made eerie by the flashes of artillery fire and first shafts of dawn. But they also killed more of the enemy than expected. The Germans, under General Ludendorff's direction, had changed their tactics in response to the British step-by-step strategy. Now the so-called 'counter-attack' divisions were brought forward from the rear, where they had waited before dawn to support and thicken the front line.

The Anzacs scrambled from their shell holes and straight into Germans of the 212th Regiment coming out of their trenches just twenty-five metres away. Their attack times had been identical.

Australian Lewis and machine-guns opened fire, cutting down the enemy. Those who were not struck were bayoneted or they broke and scattered. The Australians pressed forward, heading for their targets. The 3rd's 37th and 43rd Battalions had trouble with those ubiquitous pillboxes – those unforgiving small fortresses that looked like huge stone versions of Ned Kelly's helmet. Yet they still carved their way to their first target on the valley bounded by the Gravenstafel Ridge.

There was mixed success and heavy losses. The 37th Battalion fought hard, losing 152 wounded and forty-seven killed. Lance Corporal Walter Peeler, a Pioneer with the battalion, using a Lewis machine-gun, attacked several enemy posts and killed thirty-one Germans. This paved the way for the 37th to capture 420 prisoners and twenty-two machine-guns.

The 37th dug in. Then the 38th and 42nd Battalions moved through to cheering and yells of inspiration from the men with their shovels. They ran into heavy shelling but secured their objective on the Broodseinde Ridge's slopes by 7.15 a.m. En route, an inordinate number of prisoners were captured, creating a problem for the prisons at the rear.

Those first four battalions were more fortunate than the 39th, 40th and 41st, which ran into wire in the swamps. It slowed their progress and made them easier targets for gunners and snipers. The ensuing fighting was fierce, with the 40th having the toughest time. Sergeant Lewis McGee decided of his own volition to change the situation. Armed with just a revolver, he charged across sixty metres of open ground straight at a machine-gun crew that was holding his battalion down and causing scores of casualties. He shot three Germans, captured the rest, took control of the gun and waved his men forward. The effort would lead to his being recommended for the VC.

The 40th's captain, H. J. Dumaresq, and Lieutenant C. H. Cane were frustrated when stopped by Germans in two blockhouses. Dumaresq, carrying a revolver, slithered under the view of one. When an armed German emerged, the captain knocked him out with an upper cut, then captured the others inside. At the same time, Cane advanced stealthily on a second blockhouse and surprised the thirty-one Germans inside. They gave up without firing a shot.

Despite these surprise capitulations, the 40th Battalion's losses were heavy, but with performances like those of McGee, Dumaresq and Cane, all three battalions also made the final targets on Broodseinde Ridge itself.

It was now 9.15 a.m. Of the 7500 soldiers from 3rd Division who went over the top, about 6000 were digging in, their objectives reached.

Monash was in his bunker armed with his maps and aerial photos. He had cool control, although he was unhappy that some information was coming in an hour late owing to signals traffic congestion. At 11.08 a.m. he sent out a message, typical of hundreds like it, to one of his brigade leaders, W. R. McNicoll:

Artillery observers have seen some of our men in the cemetery East of the Blue Line. That is just exactly where our barrage will come down at 12.26. You have an hour and a quarter to take some steps about it. We may expect counter-attack in the next 2–3 hours. Now is our time to prepare. You are perfectly satisfied 40 Bn have got a good supply of SOS rockets? Are you in touch with [commanding officer] Lord? Has he told you where he is on the Blue Line?

Well, McNicoll, I will trust you to do your best.[11]

McNicoll fired a message to his men to clear the cemetery and get back west of the blue line.

At 11.46 a.m. Monash sounded as if he had reversed his role with Godley when he sent him a terse note about the non-appearance at his HQ of the operations staff of the relieving division: 'I think it is high time that the Division following me should send up their G Staff to begin to take hold. Will you kindly arrange that?'[12] In the heat of battle decision-making his contempt for Godley, which started on Gallipoli and festered on the Western Front, was exposed. Monash had been up since 2 a.m. and would remain on his feet commanding his own men, even after being relieved of overall command.

When the Australian artillery came into action, it belted the enemy for another two and a half hours. The effect was measurable. Only the 41st was forced to fight off two counter-attacks anticipated by Monash.

Some of the soldiers wanted to advance, but Monash was very clear in his order to one of his favourite commanders, Brigadier Cannan, whose men were shaped in his aggressive image. He was told to stay put and not be adventurous. Monash didn't want soldiers being caught by waiting German artillery. It was imperative now to consolidate and work on a broader plan for another advance.

There had been a similar success across the eight-division line. Godley and other corps commanders were barely containable, wanting to push on in the Haig tradition and reach the Bellevue Spur, which joined the Pass-chendaele Ridge at the village. Godley asked Monash for his thoughts. Monash was concerned that his leading battalions had suffered heavy losses: 1810 casualties, or twenty-seven per cent of the force engaged. He was also worried about the time it was taking to get orders through. But initial reconnaissance supported a further limited move forward. Monash reserved judgement. He wanted his brigadiers 'to think it over'. Godley took this mixed response as at least not a 'no'. He and the other corps commanders saw Plumer and put their case. But the old slow bowler was cautious. He said no. It was stumps on the day of a huge success for the British war effort.

The Anzac force had managed its biggest victory ever. Monash's 3rd Division had its second successive big win in two outings. Now 1st and 2nd Divisions could at last boast of a clear, defined domination of a battle.

Haig wrote to Monash congratulating him on his part in the 'greatest battle of the war'. The C-in-C was keen to push on to Passchendaele. His continuing propaganda, rather than reasoning based on hard intelligence, was that the enemy was demoralised, fatigued and weakened. Monash agreed, up to a point. He didn't want to attack if the weather was rotten. It had begun raining on the 4th, too late to affect the Broodseinde battle. But now it had set in.

It was still coming down on 6 October when the 3rd was relieved by a British division. But Monash's men barely had time for a bath and a change of clothes, and to repair their equipment. Haig and Plumer, recognising the 3rd's capacity, wanted it to be a big part of Passchendaele.

It kept pouring. Monash found himself the odd one out in the attitude to attacking in the bog. Plumer, Harington and Godley were carried away with the success at Broodseinde. Birdwood sided with Monash, but did not oppose his boss. Gough, surprisingly, was uncertain.

By the next day with still no relief from the wet, Plumer and Gough changed their minds. They were nervous about approaching Haig alone, so they put to him a joint proposal to end the campaign. Haig dismissed it. The push to Passchendaele had to go on. It was now an obsession.

Even a close aide remarked that it would take the impact of a travelling planet to shift him.

Godley informed Monash that the two British divisions, the 49th and 66th, would go out first on 9 October. Exposing his own uncertainty about Haig's decision, he then warned Monash that, if they failed, the 3rd would have to go in and 'do it' by the 12th. Monash spoke bluntly about the futility of attacking in a bog. Godley said it didn't matter. The C-in-C was set on the 9th as attack day, and that was that.

The rain became torrential on 8 October, making a cavalry division redundant. But it was still held in reserve. Haig and some of the other British commanders wanted the horses there as a symbol of successes in the previous century. In the swampy conditions, they were useless.

The next day, the preliminary attack began. The intense bombardments in the area over the last two years had ripped the land to shreds, breaking up the drainage system of the flat land. The effect was accentuated by the first British artillery barrage. Every ditch and waterway was dammed with clumps of the land. The rain of the past few days transformed the battlefield into a horrible slush, getting worse all the time.

The troops went over the top and into a quagmire. Even with the Australian 2nd Division backing up, the British divisions could only make small gains. The soldiers found it tough to drag their feet through the morass. One of the British commanders remarked that there would be 'no try' in these conditions. This camouflaged the inhumanity in Haig's craving to crash through. Thousands would again needlessly spill blood in the Flanders mud because of the C-in-C's impatience.

On 11 October the rain had not abated. Every dip in the land, crater or shell-hole was flooded. Guns, lorries and carts were always going to be bogged. No matter what the planning, supplies were not going to reach the infantry in the front trenches.

Monash realised that nothing could stop the campaign. He now tried a stalling tactic to bring his superiors to their senses. He pleaded with Godley that the 3rd's entry be delayed twenty-four hours. When this was rejected, Monash went over his head to Plumer, but received the same response. The British High Command was now a bunch of the deaf and the blind. They couldn't see what would happen, and they refused to listen to anyone with a contrary view to that set in train by Haig.

Monash's experience since Gallipoli with an intransigent, poorly prepared, haphazard command in difficult circumstances meant he didn't need to see a clairvoyant for a prediction of what was about to happen to his men. Anticipating carnage, he directed the best possible medical back-up and ordered more than 200 of his infantry to act as extra stretcher-bearers. He even produced an ambulance system akin to a cab rank at the rear. For the sake of speed and efficiency in the certain confusion, each vehicle would return to a 'rank' after going to the aid of a fallen soldier, where it would wait for the next assignment.

They were to come soon enough, even before the attack time. At 6 p.m. the 3rd's battalions began their march from east of Ypres into the wet night as mustard gas shells rained down on them (as it would on the troops in reserve in the rear for the next four nights, in the worst gas attack experienced by the Anzacs). They arrived at the starting point tapes at 2.45 a.m. Russell's New Zealand Division was on the left of the 3rd Division's 10th Brigade. On the 10th Brigade's right was 9th Brigade.

With nothing to do for a few hours 10,000 Anzacs pulled their water-proof sheets over their heads and slept, or attempted to sleep, with the clatter of war around them. The shelling didn't stop. More were struck as they waited. Ambulances began coming off the rank.

The British artillery began at 5.25 a.m., but it was a fraction of earlier barrages. It failed to weaken the German defences. At 6 a.m. the Aust-ralians went over the top and into the worst conditions yet faced. The machine-gun fire and the shelling were heavy. After retarding the New Zealand Division's attack, the Germans were able to turn their attention to the 3rd.

The conditions were the worst they had encountered. The ground was a mud pond. Guns and ammunitions were sinking in the slush. The artillery shells didn't explode, making it impossible for the diggers to follow a barrage, even if they could make it through the shell craters. They couldn't link up. Supplies couldn't get through.

The soldiers who managed to get somewhere were soon knee or waist deep in mud. In much of the battlefield the only way across the bog, which was now akin to quicksand, was by duckboards (slatted footways). Soldiers falling or being blown off the duckboards needed aid to climb back on. Wounded soldiers, who under dry conditions could have been saved, had little hope. They would sink and drown. There was no hope of even a vaguely uniform or quick straight-line attack. Even those who managed to stay on the duckboards or find their way through the mud were slow-motion targets. Entire platoons, waist high in slime, were wiped out by machine-gun fire. Those who struggled on encountered the enemy in bayonet fighting.

The 10th Brigade on the left of the advancing Australians was closest to the extra barrage and fared worst.

Those ambulances were working harder than in any previous conflict.

Monash, in his bunker under the eastern ramparts, was again frustrated by communications, his lifeline to command. Observation planes were less effective in the wet. When two of them were shot down, the others were grounded. Runners were not only slower than normal in the con-ditions, they were also mostly ineffective. Monash had to wait until 9.30 a.m. to tell Godley that both brigades engaged to start – the 9th and 10th – had begun to advance on the blue line, which was the second of three objectives. It was at the Crest Farm, just a few hundred metres from Passchendaele village.

At 9.55 a.m. a confused picture was coming from the battlefield. Some reports said the 10th Brigade was in trouble. Others suggested that the 9th Brigade, under Monash's friend Major General Rosenthal, had reached Crest Farm and the second objective, the blue line.

At 10.05 a.m. Monash realised that only sections of the 9th had reached Crest Farm when he received a message from McNicoll saying that the 9th Brigade was too weak to go beyond the blue line. It was the first inkling that the 3rd would not be able to reach Passchendaele village.

At 10.50 a.m. Monash learned that the New Zealand Division on the left of 10th Brigade had been hit hard and would not reach the first objective on the red line short of Crest Farm from the left. The New Zealanders had encountered trouble crossing the wide, flooding Ravebeek River. It had been wired on the northern (enemy) bank. The New Zealand Division therefore could not get a foothold on the Bellevue Spur, which led to Crest Farm. This meant that the left flank of the 10th Brigade's advance was exposed to fire from many concrete forts scattered over the spur.

That explained how the 10th was impeded. Monash asked the New Zealand Division to use their artillery barrage at the red line. Then he ordered McNicoll to bring up his reserve battalion to secure the ground already won.

Ninety minutes later the scene was clearer. McNicoll confirmed that he had not taken the second objective at the blue line. But reports from 9th Brigade confirmed that some groups had pushed as far as Passchendaele church. Monash ordered Rosenthal to secure his gains at Crest Farm.

But at 1.15 p.m. Godley called off the New Zealand attack. Monash was forced to do the same. The mass withdrawal of the two divisions was nearly as tough as the attack.

By 2 p.m. no ambulances were to be seen at the rank.

By 3 p.m. the 3rd Division, depleted in numbers and morale, had mostly withdrawn to within a hundred metres of the start line. Passchendaele – the mission that should never have been started in such atrocious conditions – was over.

The 3rd Division suffered 3200 casualties out of 5000 soldiers who went over the top. Among those to lose his life was Lewis McGee, attempting another smash-through act. He would never know he had been awarded the VC for his courage at Broodseinde.

The New Zealanders had 3500 casualties.

Monash wrote his battle report, critical of many aspects of the campaign. He was adamant that a longer preparation for the conflict – forty-eight hours instead of twenty-four hours – and good weather would have seen it successful. He recommended saturation artillery fire at the German defences. He mentioned that old bugbear communications, and reckoned he needed much more time for better reconnaissance. Then he got down to his specialty, analysis of the fine detail. Taping of the approach routes had been inadequate; the duckboards (for vehicles) had not been laid properly; and bridging, platforming of guns and ammunition supply had not been up to standard. This was partly an indictment of his own division, but mainly a criticism of the British High Command. Rushing things in bad conditions wouldn't allow time for any of the above and was always a recipe for disaster.

In private, he was more pointed. He thought that the High Command was wrong to have started the campaign on 9 October in the bog. In the end the New Zealand and the 3rd Divisions had to take on the failed objectives of the two British divisions. 'It amounted to this,' Monash wrote, 'Russell [New Zealand] and I were asked to make a total advance of 1.75 miles [nearly three kilometres] – in a day.'[13]

So much for the limited objective. Three kilometres in the mud would have been twelve kilometres in the dry. It was an impossible task. But once the battle began on 9 October, Godley, Plumer, Harington and Haig would not quit until 12 October – after four days of fighting in which several thousand British and Anzac soldiers were killed or injured advancing less than a net 100 metres.

After the heady success at Broodseinde on 4 October, Passchendaele was a bitter blow. It was a microcosm of the entire British Flanders offensive. Since July it had advanced eight kilometres at a cost of 250,000 casualties. It was also a turning point in the eyes of Monash and other senior Australian military personnel.

'Our men are being put into the hottest fighting,' Monash wrote, 'and are being sacrificed in hare-brained schemes, like Bullecourt and Passchendaele, and there is no one in the War Cabinet to lift a voice in protest

. . . Australian interests are suffering badly. Australia is not getting anything like the recognition it deserves.'[14]

The fiasco put him in a disgruntled and reflective mood as he and the 3rd Division prepared to move back for rest at Fauquembergues, near Boulogne. They were to be replaced by the Canadian Corps, and in the short change-over period II Anzac Corps came under the command of Lieutenant General Sir Arthur Currie, who impressed Monash 'as a very able man' – a description that he reserved for very few in the British forces. Haig had mixed up Currie and his background as an auctioneer from Victoria, Vancouver, with Monash, an engineer from Melbourne, Victoria. The confusion was understandable if the starting point was ignorance and contempt for militiamen from the Dominions. The performances of these two, both now unofficial honorary members of the club, had done much to erase Haig's attitude. (A month later Currie and the Canadians were to learn from the mistakes of Passchendaele, which they attacked and took from the Germans – in dry conditions.)

Currie's liaison man sent to smooth the changeover with Monash was Prince Arthur of Connaught, first cousin of the King, who had shown Monash around Vimy in France on an earlier visit there.

The brief experience with Currie and the Canadians caused Monash, when back at the Château Hervarre again, to urge that his division join the rest of the Australian Corps. Seeing the way the Canadians were set up, and after the taste of unity at Broodseinde, it was time for all the Australian divisions to be linked into one fighting force. He had also had enough of being answerable to Godley and wanted to come under AIF command in training and fighting.

Many Australian minds at the end of 1917 were thinking along the same lines. It was time for an Australian army, or at least more autonomy of organisation and control. In October after Passchendaele the Australian Government made an urgent request to Haig that the five Australian divisions be brought together under Birdwood's control. Haig again stalled, saying that five divisions together would be unwieldy. Pressure mounted. Murdoch, acting for Hughes, lobbied Lloyd George, who was looking for ways of curbing Haig's omnipotence and continual high-casualty follies on the Western Front. One way was not to let him have more reserves of men. This further devolution of power – by letting the Australians form their own quasi-independent force – could help. The AIF would still come under Haig's control while he was C-in-C. But it would want an Australian Government–approved commander. Birdwood was acceptable. An Australian would be better.

Haig still resisted. But since the performances of all Australian divisions in combat was second to none, he couldn't argue any more about British regular commanders being better or more experienced.

Birdwood and White came up with a suggestion that demonstrated lateral thinking. The Australian Corps should be just four divisions, with one held temporarily as a depot division to supply reinforcements for the others. With the high battle attrition rate, Haig accepted the proposal and capitulated.

On 1 November 1917 the Australian Corps was born. Fifteen days later 3rd Division transferred to it. Monash was elated and relieved to be free of the Godley yoke, which he had endured since arriving in Egypt early in 1915. 'So at last I have parted from Godley,' Monash wrote. 'I have not much to be grateful to him for. I served him loyally and faithfully for nearly three years and he has done nothing for me that he could not help doing.' Yet Godley was 'nice and amicable' towards the end, and he sent Monash off with a 'quite splendid farewell banquet'.[15] His act of largesse was too late. Yet it was not surprising. Monash had proved himself and had boosted Godley's own reputation. The English veteran was also aware that Monash's star was in the ascendant. He knew that in the future he might well be on the way down, passing his former subordinate on the way up.

On 20 November Haig launched the last British offensive of 1917 when General Byng's Third Army, led by 381 tanks, broke the German line at Cambrai and penetrated eight kilometres, losing 4000 men in one day. The Germans counter-attacked ten days later and forced the British back to where they had begun. Both sides were now near exhaustion. Manpower shortage was going to be a physical and political problem from now on. Lloyd George was determined to restrict Haig by not allowing him reinforcements. This brought a reduction in division size from twelve to nine battalions. To win the war, the British would have to think and strategise differently from any other previous era in military history. Manpower would not be enough. The conditions were right for a commander like Monash to come to the fore. His entire military career

had been directed towards this opportunity. He was in accord with the thinking of Prime Ministers Lloyd George and Hughes, who were appalled, on behalf of their worried electorates, about the shocking loss of life over the four years of war so far.

'I had formed the theory that the true role of the infantry was not to expend itself upon heroic physical effort, nor to whither away under merciless machine-gun fire, nor to impale itself on hostile bayonets, nor to tear itself to pieces in hostile entanglements,' Monash wrote. Instead, he wanted his force 'to advance under the maximum possible protection of the maximum possible array of mechanical resources, in the form of guns, mortars, aeroplanes (also tanks); to advance with as little impediment as possible; to be relieved as far as is possible of the obligation to fight their way forward'. Monash wanted his soldiers to march on to the appointed goal or line. Then they would be important in holding and defending territory gained – 'and there to gather the fruits of victory in the form of prisoners, guns and stores'.[16]

It remained to be seen whether he could show that this was possible. Although he was the favourite, there were no guarantees that he would take control of the new combined Australian force. But whoever took up the position at the head of it would have a position of both enormous responsibility and opportunity. The Dominion troops, for reasons of sacrifice and superiority, would be the spearhead of the British effort. The Australians, as the biggest corps, would be the most prominent.

Monash was told to go on leave in December. His small Collins Paragon diary had almost shorthand notes on romantic weeks of dining, theatre-going, shopping, strolling and carousing with Lizette. His previous experience when a youth and a young man, when first his parents, then his wife read his diaries, made his entries concerning his lover sketchy and furtive. Lizette was either 'L' or 'Liz'. The pocket diary's size too was an indication of his desire to keep his experience inconspicuous. Yet still he had the compulsive diarist's need to record them, for himself and posterity.

He managed to squeeze in a night with Walter and Louise and his nieces, but spent most time with Lizette.

It was important for him to relax. Monash's notes suggest he had more than an instinct that 1918 was going to be the most challenging year of his life.[17]

15
1918: LUDENDORFF'S LUNGE

Monash received a boost on New Year's Day 1918 when Birdwood rang to congratulate him on being made a Knight Commander of the Bath. Someone other than Hughes had probably recommended him. The nod could have come from the Australian Federal Government, the states or even, in special circumstances, the British Government. In war the conditions for handing out the honour often reverted to their original intention. It was a reward for defending the British Empire on the battlefield.

Monash's 'K' would most likely have come from Haig after the successes at Messines and Broodseinde, with the King only too willing to endorse the award. The monarch, like an airline frequent flyer manager, could still reward or reject someone at a whim or with wilful intent. Monash, as Haig and the King's relatives all knew from being recommended to him, was his number-one Dominion subject, especially now that he was winning battles.

Monash speculated that Plumer too would have had a say, but he was never told. The kudos was big, useful and welcome. In the arcane world of titles and position, being known as Major General Sir John would see even more heel-clicking, salutes, deference and grovelling than ever before. Monash the pragmatist saw it as a prestigious label but didn't feel he had 'something to live up to'. He rated his divisional commandership far higher. It challenged him.

He let loose his feelings in a letter to Vic, saying that commanding one of the 'crack' divisions of the British Army, not a government award, had caused him to 'acquire a feeling of complete confidence and mental poise'.

'Now this is a monstrously egotistical letter,' Monash said, perhaps after a glass or two of his favourite Scotch, 'but I suppose – like the male peacock before the pea-hen – one may be permitted to do a little strutting before one's own wife, once in a while.'

He paraded his ambitions. Perhaps he would be vice chancellor of Melbourne University, 'or later on, chancellor'. There probably would be 'a high honorary degree'. The government was bound, he believed, to offer 'some very high post in the military', although he was not set on any permanent post. Dreaming on, he reached his ultimate fantasy. 'Don't be amused,' he told Vic, 'I merely write of it, but because I am in frank humour [there was always the possibility of] a [state] Governorship . . . The day when State Governors will be chosen from Australian citizens is rapidly approaching . . . Now, please don't laugh, but regard with equanimity the prospect of your, one day, becoming an Excellency!'[1]

It allowed some reverie for Vic, who had had a tough time with loneliness and life-threatening illness. She often wondered in her private moments if she would ever see her husband again. Monash's words were more than comforting and an attempt at compensation for the empty years without him. Vic's world was a social one. She was thrilled to be told that only the wives of the Governor-General and State Governors ranked higher than her in Australia. She was to be called Victoria Lady Monash.

The orphaned daughter of an English immigrant merchant and pubowner never felt the pressures of being an outsider as her ambitious husband did when he strove for recognition through his achievements. Yet for Melbourne's parochial, stiff social set, dominated by Toorak matrons, gongs and titles were helium to their social balloons. She could float high with this honorific. How should she sign her cheques, she wondered. 'My darling,' she cabled him, 'Best love wonderful man. What a genius you are. Jewish community gone mad, off their heads. KCB!!! I don't think I have anything left to wish for as a title and to dine at Government House were both my greatest ambitions.'[2]

Monash would love to have seen her place being a devoted, supportive wife and mother higher than a nice dinner with regal trappings and status. But at least he had her full respect, which he hadn't felt for many years. This was satisfying enough, but not the stuff of true love and affection, which he was now receiving elsewhere. His excuses for keeping her from visiting him were not entirely to do with any fears for Vic's safety. They were rooted more in a desire to keep his freedom and affair with Lizette Bentwitch going, and to evade the restrictions of a marriage with limited rewards.

The war had provided a chance for him, unwittingly at first, to move on, if he really wanted to. Monash was leaving that to time. Apart from these indulgent moments of reflection and hopeful looking forward, he was consumed by events on the battlefield.

Lenin, Trotsky and a further handful of Bolshevik revolutionaries had changed the dynamic of the war by taking over Russia in October 1917 and a month later by decreeing that they would not be taking part in the current 'capitalist' conflict. Once the Russians' opting out of the war was accepted as genuine, the German High Command began the task of marching and transporting about a million soldiers from the Russian to the Western Front from early in 1918. At some stage in the first half of the year, the Allied High Command expected a massive attack from the bolstered German Army over the Somme. Everything done now by Haig would be with that in mind.

During the winter of 1917–18, two of the three ablest members of the AIF, Monash and White (the other being Chauvel) came into contact more often than ever before. When Birdwood was on leave, Monash, as the senior commander, took charge of the corps, and White was second in command. They disagreed on several issues, including tactics. It didn't seem to disturb the basic equilibrium between the two, which augured well for the corps if it were ever to be an ensemble.

One major issue of tactics in dispute was use of the machine-gun. Monash thought it should be used as an offensive weapon. White thought it was purely defensive. Monash went on a brief course at machine-gun school at Camiers, and then wrote a paper for his officers on its status and how it should be used both offensively and defensively. He concluded that it was the most effective weapon in the Allied armoury next to artillery.

Monash and White had a long conference on the issue on 10 January. The latter conceded that machine-guns should be used 'offensively and deny the initiative to the Germans'. Monash spoke of 'scoring heavily' over the issue, but it was not just to beat White in an argument. When he ran 4th Brigade with 5000 soldiers, he wanted absolute consistency of thought and policy. At 3rd Division he was doing the same with 20,000 soldiers. If

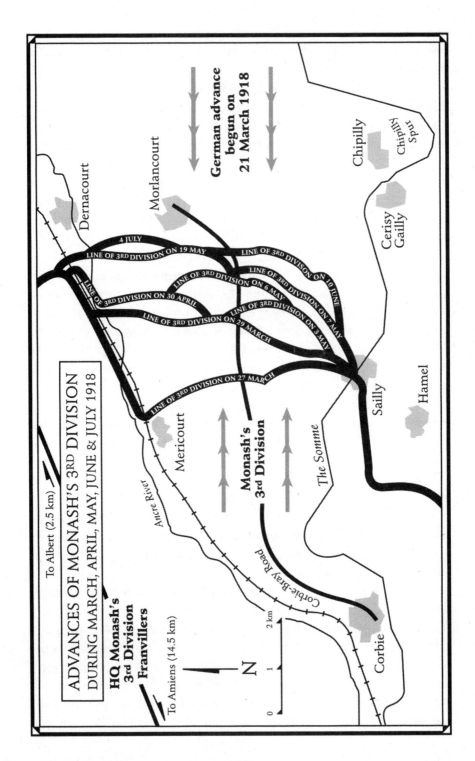

ADVANCES OF MONASH'S 3RD DIVISION
DURING MARCH, APRIL, MAY, JUNE & JULY 1918

German advance begun on 21 March 1918

Monash's 3rd Division

HQ Monash's 3rd Division Franvillers

To Albert (2.5 km)

To Amiens (14.5 km)

N

0 1 2 km

Dernacourt

Morlancourt

Chipilly

Chipilly Spur

Cerisy Gailly

4 JULY

LINE OF 3RD DIVISION ON 19 MAY

LINE OF 3RD DIVISION ON 10 JUNE

LINE OF 3RD DIVISION ON 6 MAY

LINE OF 3RD DIVISION ON 7 MAY

LINE OF 3RD DIVISION ON 30 APRIL

LINE OF 3RD DIVISION ON 3 MAY

LINE OF 3RD DIVISION ON 29 MARCH

LINE OF 3RD DIVISION ON 27 MARCH

Mericourt

Ancre River

Corbie-Bray Road

The Somme

Sailly

Hamel

Corbie

he took over the Australian Corps, which promised to be the biggest of the twenty corps in the entire Allied army, he wanted perfect harmony of thought and policy from the commander down to the lowliest private. He wanted no arguments about who said what and how things should be done. Differences had to be thrashed out – as he had done with White on many points – before policy and decisions were set in stone. It was always too late to be guessing about any tactic, strategy or policy once a battle had begun.[3]

Monash 'won' all such debates between the two, often because he had commanded in battle, where theory was tested in practice, and White had not. White had acted as acting Corps Commander before the Australian Corps formed. But he had never been in charge of a battle. Monash's painstaking post-mortems of conflicts in his thorough, detailed reports, and his capacity to communicate them, gave him advantages over White or anyone else in dispute over military issues. Monash believed in not making the same mistake twice. He advocated clear, concise analysis of how a battle was won and lost. No one in the AIF, and probably the entire allied Army, could match him in turning theory and plans into practice and in learning from the experience, whether it was in training or actual war.

Despite Monash's domination, he and White got on well without being close. There was strong mutual respect between them. But White was developing a feeling of inferiority, which could influence his judgement on who was best suited to run the Australian Corps.

The corps still had yet to act as force in itself. The divisions for the moment were hived off to where Haig needed them. Over the 1917–18 winter Monash and the 3rd were back in the action, first in raids into no man's land around Messines, then in the familiar Armentières area to take over from a failed Portuguese division. Late in January it was once more in the mudflats around Messines.

Monash took an aggressive stance with his raids, hitting the Germans at Warneton, eight kilometres east of Messines, so hard on 10 February that they thought the 3rd Division was trying to take it. More than 200 soldiers of the 37th and 38th Battalions attacked in the middle of the night. It was emphatic. The battalions had ten casualties, inflicted forty and took thirty-three prisoners. On 3 March the 9th Brigade sent 235 men to the same area with a similar result. They had just six casualties, inflicted thirty and took eleven prisoners. The Germans hit back but without the same force. Their raiding parties numbered about a hundred in strength and did not penetrate the lines effectively. Monash ordered immediate counter-punches, making the point that his division was not to be trifled with.

When prisoners came in, German-speaking officers would interrogate them and then report to Monash. If there were a prisoner of interest, he would come in and take over the probing, in German. Officers spoke of a noticeable concern from the captured men with him in the cell. He was never brutal or bullying, but always direct. Monash's eyes stayed on them. It was unnerving. He was the master of the pregnant pause. Prisoners seemed anxious to fill it.

Monash wanted to know when the expected big German push was coming. The prisoners, even the officers, claimed they didn't know the date, which was acceptable. Ludendorff and only a handful of his closest commanders would know. The prisoners were also adamant that they didn't know where the attack would be. Yet there was accord from every one of them questioned on where it would not be. 'The Boche . . .' Monash wrote, 'certainly has no intention of doing so [attacking] on the front of the Australian Corps.'[4]

The German High Command would take on the opposition where it was weakest, not strongest.

The 3rd Division took a break on Saturday 9 March, and Monash began three weeks leave, again opting for a week in Paris followed by a lazy beach time at Menton on the French Riviera. He ate as usual at his favourite restaurant, Café de la Paix, and saw the Folies Bergère revue. He drove down with an aide (nephew Paul Simonson), taking with him a pile of papers and magazines (*The Times*, *Punch*, *La Vie Parisienne*) and a stack of books, including O. Henry's short stories and Bernard Shaw's tome on Wagner's Ring cycle. Monash stayed once more at the Hotel Regina Palace and Balmoral. He enjoyed a night at the opera at Monte Carlo and lunched with the visiting Rosenthal at the Regina on 22 March.[5]

As the two friends were relaxing over a convivial meal, the Germans were embarking on their spectacular surprise attack. Forty-seven German divisions hit the British Third and Fifth Armies across an eighty-kilometre front, from Cambrai (eighty kilometres south-southeast of Ypres) to La Fère. The Germans smashed through Gough's Fifth Army and pushed the right (southern) part of the Third Army back. On 22 March, the Fifth was forced to retreat to the Somme. On 23 March, when Monash received a recall order, the Fifth Army's soldiers had to slip back over the river. The Germans were right on top of them. There was resistance for the next few days, but the Germans had picked their attack line brilliantly. The Fifth Army crumbled.

After a confusion of orders, the Australian 3rd Division was told to move from Boulogne south to Doullens and the HQ of the British X Corps. On the night of 25 March, Monash was driving around trying to find X Corps' HQ. The force of the German assault had changed the game of the last three years, which had been built on trench warfare and fixed HQs. Commanders and officers had to decamp with haste to safer areas. Monash eventually found the HQ at Doullens. Defeated British soldiers were straggling into the town with stories of the 'Boche Cavalry' close behind them. To Monash's relief, minutes after arriving Rosenthal and a battalion of his 9th Brigade came in by train. Monash detailed them to guard the eastern advance to Doullens, until the rest of the brigade arrived.

Monash then drove on to Mondicourt, again train-spotting, this time welcoming in McNicoll and the 1st Battalion of the 10th Brigade. He too began to defend the station and its surrounds, pulling up any soldiers from the British force and ordering them to stop and assist. Next, Monash took over a château with a good telephone exchange at Couturelle. Its grateful owner provided him with 'a much needed meal'.[6]

On 26 March Monash hit the road again, and ran into people retreating, with all their worldly belongings. Among the throng on the run were British soldiers from Gough's Fifth Army with their equipment. In effect the Fifth was no more. It had disintegrated.

Monash watched them with mixed feelings. He would like to have forced them back into a line as McNicoll had done. But Monash at that moment didn't have a line. He was a battle commander in search of official directives and without all his troops.

He made contact with Sinclair-MacLagan and his 4th Division at 4 p.m. They arranged for a string of outposts in a line towards the southeast and the advancing German divisions. The enemy had taken Albert – a major military town throughout the war – and opened a breach of sixty kilometres through the British lines. They were only thirty kilometres from Amiens – the biggest centre of the entire Western Front – and its railway junction, a major strategic target. The French had garrisoned Amiens until 1916 when the British took over. They based their hospitals there. Most of their supplies from the UK came to Amiens via the coastal French city of Le Havre. It was even the army's recreational centre.

From the German perspective, retaking Amiens (it had been theirs temporarily in 1914) was the key to the war's outcome. This would have the dual result of cutting off the British while making Paris – just 120 kilometres south – the next target. The Germans had hit Amiens with air attacks for three and a half years, but it wasn't until this March offensive that the city came under a major attack. It had to endure almost continuous artillery bombardment. Most citizens were evacuated, and the Pope was asked by the local bishop to intercede with Kaiser Wilhelm to save the mighty Notre Dame Cathedral from the shelling.

At 9 p.m. on 26 March, Monash learned that he had been switched to the 7th Corps at Montigny, not Corbie, where its HQ had been just an hour earlier. Such was the German push that Monash was checking every order before he got into his car again. This time he took with him four of his staff in two cars and two despatch riders on motorbikes. There was no moonlight. They made slow progress in the dark, weaving through the mass of refugee traffic.

Like many of the Australian troops heading south against the tide, they were told they were going the wrong way. 'You won't hold them,' was now a cry familiar.

They arrived at Montigny at midnight. Monash found the leaders of the shattered 7th Corps in a darkened château. Only its commander, General Congreve, and an officer, Alexander Hore-Ruthven (later the Earl of Gowrie), seemed to have their wits about them. 'Thank heavens,' Congreve said, greeting Monash, 'the Australians at last.'[7]

Congreve got straight to the point. The Germans from Albert to Bray had shattered his corps' line of defence. 'The enemy is now pushing westwards,' Congreve said, 'and if not stopped tomorrow will certainly secure all the heights overlooking Amiens.'[8] He wanted Monash to deploy his division across the German path. The valleys of the Ancre and the Somme offered good points on which the division's flanks could 'rest'. Congreve wanted the Australians to move as far east as they could. But if stopped they should occupy a good line of old trenches running from Méricourt-l'Abbé towards Sailly-le-Sec.

Monash snatched some sleep in the early hours. At dawn, he, Paul Simonson and a staff officer drove to an elevated position above the town of Franvillers. They got out of their car. Monash used his binoculars. Looking east over the Ancre River he could see the German cavalry and advance guard near Malancourt. They were forcing back scattered British troops. Monash noticed that the cavalry was moving about slowly. He thought they seemed puzzled at their success in getting so far and finding no one to challenge them. Monash judged that he had to send in his troops to cut them off as fast as possible. 'It was really a question of an hour or two,' a worried Monash thought, 'whether we could intercept the enemy or not.'[9] He and his two officers could see several German armoured cars in advance of the enemy troops coming quickly in their direction. They had to leave. If not, they could be captured. They jumped in their car and sped back to Franvillers. At that moment, Monash and his two staff officers were the only ones standing between Amiens and the German advance.

Monash sent out his orders from his HQ. Much to his relief soon afterwards – at 8 a.m. – sixty double-decker buses, seconded from London, began arriving with two battalions from Cannan's 11th Brigade. They were followed by troops from McNicoll's 10th and finally Rosenthal's 9th. Monash's anxiety subsided. He judged now that they had a fair chance of blocking the German advance.

None of the 3rd Division's battalions had slept properly for two nights, but on a sunny spring morning the soldiers lined up in a determined spirit. Company by company, Monash sent them down the road to the little village of Heilly and across the Ancre River.

> The spectacle of that infantry will be memorable to me [Monash wrote] as one of the most inspiring sights of the whole war. Here was the Third Division – the 'new chum' Division, which in spite of its great successes in Belgium and Flanders, had never been able to boast, like its sister Divisions, that it had been 'down to the Somme.' It had come into its own at last, and was called upon to prove its mettle.[10]

It shouldn't take much imagination to think of what Monash said to them in his continued use of psychology to inspire the troops. The 'Boche' had superior artillery and gas shells. But what sort of fighters would they be without the support of heavy firepower from fixed positions? How would they fare on a more level battlefield before their artillery was in position to strike?

Where the British were shattered, the Australians were full of the necessary bravado that might or might not be maintained depending on how they fared. Monash wrote: 'They were going to measure themselves, man to man, against an enemy, who, skulking behind his field works, had for so long pounded them to pieces in their trenches, poisoned them with gas, and bombed them as they slept in their billets.'[11] The Australians were ready and willing, despite the negative, although friendly calls from British soldiers going the other way. Comments were pithy. 'Gerry will have your bloody guts for garters,' was a common cry.

The French villagers had a different attitude. The men shook their hands; the women kissed them and threw flowers. Their homes, their way of life, their lives were at stake. The diggers could see the fear, hope and affection in the faces of the locals. This fired them up further. It was one strong reason of many for coming from Australia. '*Fini retreat, Madame* [or *Monsieur*],' was a French phrase every digger knew, as well as: '*Fini retreat, beaucoup Australiens ici.*'[12]

But were there enough?

At 11 a.m. on 27 March, two battalions of the 3rd had relieved the spent British infantry of the depleted 35th Division and sections of the 9th Scottish Division, who had defended stoutly in the triangle between the Ancre and Somme rivers. Some of the Scots had to be persuaded to go. They wanted to help, especially when it was learnt that the British 1st Cavalry Division on the front line was in part being shifted to help fragments of the Fifth Army south of the Somme.

Similarly, north of the Ancre, two battalions of the 4th Division relieved more of the beleaguered Scottish 9th who were at the foot of a hill on the vital Amiens to Albert railway. The four Australian battalions were in the front line alongside the cavalry and some of the more stubborn Scots, who were adamant that they could hold the Germans now.

By the night of 27 March, the nucleus of a good, mainly Australian defence stretched from Hébuterne to the Somme. For the first time since 21 March, the German advance was halted. But the halt promised to be only temporary if something was not done about the situation south of the Somme where the north flank of the French was being pushed southwest. Elements of the British 1st Cavalry along with a ragbag of other British and Scots units were stretched thin in the ever-widening gap between the new Australian position and the French.

Monash conferred with Congreve on the night of 27 March, and suggested he send his 9th Brigade under Rosenthal along the Somme from Sailly-le-Sec west as far Aubigny (three kilometres west of Corbie). It was a thin, extended line, but enough to give the Germans now flowing into the gap something to reckon with. The Australian front now blocked the enemy sweep towards Amiens.

Monash was proving to be a dynamic commander in the fluid conditions. He believed always in attack rather than defence wherever it was possible with minimum risk to his troops. Instead of digging in on the night of 29 March, he advanced the left of his line 1800 metres from south of Heilly along the Ancre to east of Buire. The right of his line pivoted south and cut off the Germans from 'valuable vantage ground' along the main road from Corbie to Bray. It ran equidistant between the Ancre to its north and the Somme to its south. The road split the apex of the triangle formed by the rivers.

The Australians met the German opposition, captured prisoners and took up positions on the new line.

Further south between the Somme and Villers-Bretonneux, the situation had deteriorated for the Allies. Monash was ordered, very much against his will, to give up control of the 9th Brigade. It was needed to reinforce the British 61st Division's losing battle.

Monash, who was moving all day between planning conferences and visits to his brigade commanders, had to maintain his hold on the small but strategically important section of the Ancre. He asked for and received Pompey Elliott's 15th Brigade (of the 5th Australian Division) to plug this gap as fast as possible. The interchange was complete by 30 March.

On the same day, two German divisions moved up their considerable artillery. They bombarded Monash's line (from Buire to the Corbie–Bray road) and over it, hitting Monash's Franvillers HQ two kilometres away so hard that Congreve ordered him to take his staff to a new HQ location at St Gratien. Monash, who by now had a good eye for a nice sleepover place with a good telephone system, found a fine Louis XI château. It belonged to the Comte de Theilloye, who was only too happy to make the Australians comfortable. Already their presence was giving French civilians confidence that the invaders from the east might not have it all their own way.

The Germans had other ideas. Thinking that their artillery had softened up the Australians, they made a full frontal attack. 'My artillery [and British] were firing over open sights,' Monash noted, 'and had never in their previous experience had such tempting targets.'[13] The result was 3000 dead Germans. The attack was repulsed. The line north of the Somme was now secure. The British 35th Division was withdrawn. The 3rd Division extended its line left (north) and connected with the Australian 4th Division.

The British 1st Cavalry Division, busy stretching itself between the Somme and the French left flank, was grateful for the Australian stand. Its commander, Major General Mullens, wrote to Monash thanking him and his artillery commander.

> It was a very real relief to know that I had your stout-hearted fellows on my left flank [he said], and that all worry was therefore eliminated . . . the placing of your heavy guns and batteries so as to cover my front was of very real assistance, and incidentally they killed a lot of Huns . . . it was a pleasure and an honour to be fighting alongside troops who displayed such magnificent morale.[14]

The rumours among British troops about the Australian corps of volunteers, who were said to be rough and undisciplined, were evaporating in the heat of battles. The 3rd and 4th Divisions had formed a front overnight and were defending it. No other division on either side could have achieved this with greater speed, efficiency, professionalism or courage.

Although the enemy had been halted in this part of the Somme by the end of March 1918, the artillery shelling of all ranges continued, and put everyone in danger. Monash, who moved about more than at Flanders and Gallipoli because the changing battlefronts demanded it, continued to cheat death. Just as in his early life on engineering sites and bridges, and then on Gallipoli and in Flanders, he continued to reach or leave a location within a short time of its being obliterated or someone being killed. On 1 April he arrived at 11th Brigade minutes after shelling had killed three officers. It had happened so many times that it was either extremely good luck or providence. By chance his fetish about punctuality – never being more than fifteen seconds late for an appointment – kept him alive.

Monash, it seemed, never set up a meeting with the grim reaper.

In the comparative lull in the first few days of April, Monash organised 'town majors' to gather up goods, produce and livestock, such as wool, wheat, oats, bran, cattle, sheep, wine and furniture, which would otherwise rot in the war zone. He totted up its value with typical exactitude – £94,472 13s 6d – and had it passed over to the French. He also allowed his men to relax when off the front line with the best of what the French countryside could offer. They could carouse in the green fields of abandoned farms. They enjoyed the local champagne or wines, along with any pork, chicken or crops that they could turn into meals.

Sporadic fighting continued until 4 April, when the Germans hit with force south of the Somme at the village of Hamel, defended by a fatigued British division, which had been sent the night before. The Germans took Hamel and ended up on the eastern outskirts of Villers-Bretonneux to the southwest. On the same day, a British division on Monash's right (south) was beaten into a retreat, leaving the flank exposed. He was annoyed.

He kept his thoughts private but did tell Vic that the British divisions were the 'absolute limit'. He berated the poor troops, staff and commanders. Monash was also scathing about the collapse of the British Fifth Army. He believed it had been avoidable, and he put it down to a 'gross lack of leadership and efficiency'.[15] As on Gallipoli, he did not think the English lacked courage. On the contrary, he had respect for the fight in them, particularly the Scots. But he had no time for the inept officers and commanders, whom he had plenty of chance to assess as Australian and British brigades were rotated under his control in anticipation of further German assaults.

They came the next day. The enemy now hammered battalions of the 4th Division that were defending the high ground north of the Ancre and the railway to Amiens. The fighting was heavy as the much smaller band of Australians attempted to hold positions in what became known as the battle of Dernancourt, after the village on the Ancre. If the Germans made it through, the 3rd Division would be trapped in the river-bound triangle by the enemy to the east, north and south.

Monash monitored the battle through the day, aware that if the 4th

Division's soldiers cracked, he would have to withdraw the 3rd fast. By nightfall the Germans, using three divisions in rotation over twenty hours of intense fighting, could not break through. Enemy thrusts as strong as this, after two weeks, were over for the moment on this limited section of front.

On that same watershed day, the Australian 5th Division came into the line, at last relieving Monash's division and the British 1st Cavalry Division on a four-and-a-half-kilometre front. He was anxious to have his 9th Brigade back under his control. But it had linked up with the 5th Brigade (of the Australian 2nd Division), which had been whipped away from the trenches in Messines. They were both fully engaged taking the Germans head-on in attacks and counter-attacks between Villers-Bretonneux and Hangard, which formed the French northern flank.

These two brigades and the Australian 5th Division were under the control of the British III Corps, which had been beefed up to fill the gap between the Somme and the flanks of the sagging French Army. By now the British High Command was rushing divisions to any point where the German flood was greatest, thus splitting the Australian Corps in a way at odds with the main reason it had been formed in the first place. The emergency of the mighty German push of 21 March aside, it was as if the British High Command had little respect for the new formation.

Even the 1st Division, which was on its way to join the 2nd Division at Villers-Bretonneux, was hurriedly turned around and moved back to Flanders to combat a new enemy push that had taken it nearly to Hazebrouck (which it did successfully). But the Australians resented the news that Messines, Armentières and Ploegsteert Wood had been lost after all the work they had done to win and hold them.

After all the jibes about ill-discipline from the British, and suffering under what they saw as incompetent British officers, the Australians began circulating derogatory stories about the 'Tommies' and their commanders. Monash moved fast to stamp it out. He knew how much fighting the two nations would still have to do in combination. Yet his private correspondence shows that he agreed with the crude criticisms. Even he flagged in private moments when alone, especially when the sons of friends under his command were reported killed. But most importantly now, he had to keep up the morale of his force. He never missed a chance to inspire or use positive propaganda.

✕

On 21 April two of his Lewis gunners – relieving cooks – near the Somme held in their sights an easily recognisable red-painted German Fokker triplane. It was tailing a cumbersome British RE8 artillery spotter from 2300 metres down to fifty metres. The Fokker itself was being tailed by an RAF Sopwith Camel piloted by a Canadian ace, Captain Roy Brown. He fired at the Fokker. Seconds later, the gunners, who had waited until the Fokker was overhead, opened fire. The bullets ripped the fuselage; the plane's engine faltered, and it flipped and crashed into the next field. The elated cooks could not rush to their 'kill'. German artillery maintained fire in a circle around the plane for half an hour, while a formation of Fokkers circled overhead. When it was clear that no one was going to emerge, the German planes flew off.

The pilot in the crashed plane had to be a VIP. The cooks, who would have a story to tell in mess halls for the rest of the war, and other artillerymen, removed the dead pilot, who had been hit in the head and heart. Papers on his body confirmed that he was the legendary Red Baron Manfred von Richthofen. He had a record number of 'scores' against Allied planes of the type he had been chasing. Monash was notified. He rushed to the scene and collected 'a tiny piece of the red fabric of Richthofen's machine' and a piece of the wooden propeller. Monash sent the fabric home for a prominent place at Iona. The propeller piece went with him.[16]

Once it was known that the victim was the famous Red Baron, a debate raged over who had shot him down. Roy Brown claimed the 'kill'. The Australian gunners did, too.

The British instructed that von Richthofen be buried with full military honours. Monash had his No. 3 Australian Flying Squadron place a wreath on the grave. Later the RAF dropped the dead hero's personal effects over the German lines, with a message of condolence. The news was a boost to the 3rd Division's spirits and a dampener for the Germans, who had been quick to fable the Red Baron's exploits.

Soon after the strike, another German Fokker was hit, and it crashed not far from where the former leader went down. 'The pilot was slightly wounded but the officer observer [who had been in the plane's rear seat] was quite all right,' Monash wrote. 'He was brought to me; I gave him a glass of wine, and he talked freely. He told me that the German Flieger Corps much appreciated the placing of the wreath on the Red Baron's grave.'[17]

✕

Two days after this morale booster the 9th Brigade was retired from the front line at Villers-Bretonneux after it had kept the Germans from taking it for three solid weeks. While it was rested, the British 8th Division took over. On 24 April the Germans attacked with four divisions and took the town. It was another avenue for the enemy to Amiens.

Despite heavy gas shelling of the area around Monash's new HQ at the elegant Bertangles château, eight kilometres northwest of Amiens and two kilometres from Villers-Bretonneux, and a cut in communications, he was able to cooperate with the British III Corps. It requested from his current command the Australian 15th Brigade under Elliott and the 13th Brigade under Major General T. W. Glasgow (a Queensland grazier, who had a German wife) for an attempt to retake the vitally strategic town. Using shrewd psychology, the counter-attack was set for the early morning of the following day, 25 April. The two weary brigades were galvanised for a supreme effort on the celebration of Anzac Day's third anniversary.

The surprise element of the Australians hitting Villers-Bretonneux so soon after the rout of the relieving British regular division, and the ferocity of the attacking 13th and 15th Brigades, stunned the town's new occupiers. 'They [the Australians] advanced [in the early hours of Anzac Day] 2700 metres in the dark without artillery support,' Monash wrote, 'completely restored the situation, and captured 1000 prisoners. I can see the prisoners pouring past the château [Bertangles] as I write this letter. It was a magnificent performance.'[18]

It was also a bitter blow to the Germans. Their thrust had been going thirty-five days. Had they held this vital town, they could have regrouped, pushed up their artillery and gained breathing space for an assault on Amiens from the north and south. Instead, they were forced to pull back to no particular focal point, and many soldiers were captured.

Monash was in no doubt that the Anzac spirit had inspired his soldiers. It might have been a minor battle, but in the context of the entire war – as the German Supreme Commander Hindenburg later admitted – it was a turning point.

✕

The Australian Corps HQ was now at Bertangles, and for the first time its divisions were acting in some unison with three in line and one in reserve. Monash's 3rd still occupied the sector between the Ancre and the Somme on the front line, which was more or less the one it had won on 29 March.

But Monash kept a dynamic in his division's activities. He realised the soldiers were bored with 'stationary warfare' and weren't satisfied with raids. To keep them motivated, Monash devised a series of minor battles designed to gain ground, capture prisoners and machine-guns, and to demoralise the Germans. The 9th and 10th Brigades engineered the battles on 30 April and 3, 6 and 7 May with the desired result. They gained more than one-and-a-half kilometres and 'deprived the enemy of valuable observations, and forced back his artillery'.[19]

While Monash was exerting steady pressure to the east, he was concerned that the Australian divisions to the south remained static because Hamel had been in the Germans' hands since 5 April.

'I was in possession of much the higher ground,' Monash noted, 'and was able to look down, almost as upon a map, on the enemy in the Hamel basin' where there was concealed German artillery, which could hammer the exposed valley next to him. It would have been dangerous for the Australians if they moved into it. This annoyed Monash. The only way to eliminate the problem was to retake Hamel. He put the plan to Birdwood, not once but four times. Birdwood looked at the maps and couldn't see the problem from Monash's point of view. He vetoed the plan. So did White. He argued that Hamel had originally been thought of as a useful feint for another bigger attack elsewhere. If it was just useful as a feint then, he said, why should manpower and equipment be wasted on taking it now? This was a fair point. But Monash had a specific reason for snaring it. Hamel was a part of a much bigger scheme he had in mind. Removing the town as a problem was just a first step in a grander vision.

This approach highlighted critical differences between him and White. The latter's skills were on display in his masterful managing and planning of the Anzac withdrawal from Gallipoli. But it was a finite project and not a battle. He had sat in on plenty of battle plans but had never initiated a plan or carried any through as a commander. This restricted his vision. Monash saw Hamel as a small fragment of a vast jigsaw. Once it was in AIF hands, Monash could attempt to create the bigger scheme that was bubbling away in the back of his brain.

Both were sensitive men in dealing with day-to-day issues. People who met them knowing or not knowing their positions in the army found them kindly gentlemen. They were compassionate human beings with integrity. Both were men of moral and physical courage, although not sabre-rattlers who were built to lead a cavalry charge or behave like Jacka in the trenches.

Yet from there these two exceptional soldiers diverged. White was at heart defensive. Monash was obsessive about precautions and detail. But by nature he was offensive. He had an unfathomable self-confidence, partly born of an exceptional, hungry eclectic intellect. There was also a belief that he could take on the German Army on any scale and win.

Monash had psyched himself into handling death on a large scale, which was the inevitable consequence of war and his planning, no matter how concerned he was about preserving life and organising machines to dominate battles. Early on at Gallipoli, Monash had to deny deep feelings or sentimentality about dead soldiers, friends, fellow officers, even relatives. It was not something that came naturally. He had to write and think about it long and often. Once he found that he had mastered that emotional side, which often mentally destroyed other officers, he realised he had enough steel in his make-up to command anywhere in any situation.

Monash, characteristically a caring person, had learned to set aside compassion to succeed in the war business. Ian Hamilton had spotted this quality in him in the blistering heat at Lilydale early in 1914 when there were no thoughts about calling off the mock battle to spare his men. The King had sensed it in a telling moment at Larkhill in 1916 when Monash had the temerity to correct him. Birdwood was becoming aware of it by observing Monash's toughness at Messines and Broodseinde and in his keenness to take Hamel.

The press too, from time to time, experienced this side of Monash. Bean had been in conflict with him over his reporting, which had exacerbated his prejudices about Monash. In mid-May F. M. Cutlack, the second official war correspondent (next to Bean), called on Monash at 3rd Division's HQ to get details on some important goods salvaged in French villages, and received some of Monash's less diplomatic directness and disregard for the sensibilities of journalists.

Monash was still concerned that he and his division was not receiving enough publicity. At the end of the interview he asked Cutlack whether he had been at the review of the 3rd Division by Haig a few days earlier.

'No, Sir John,' Cutlack replied, and made his excuses about obtaining a story about some fighting by 2nd Division battalions.

'Did you cable anything about the review in Australia?'

'I did not, Sir John.'

'And may I ask why not?'

Cutlack, who had been on the 3rd's intelligence staff and knew Monash well, felt he had to maintain his independence now that he was a member of the Fourth Estate. 'Let me be frank, sir,' Cutlack replied. 'The last time Sir Douglas Haig reviewed an Australian division, only a few months ago, it was the 3rd Division, and to tell you the truth, I was mindful of what people in other divisions might say, and I thought it savoured a little of advertisement.'

'What if it is advertisement?' Monash replied. 'It is also news; but take it as advertisement. Has it occurred to you that we all have to advertise the AIF in Australia, and do you appreciate why? The conscription referendums have failed. Voluntary enlistment may be insufficient to maintain all our units in France. Have you read of the route marches in Australia – all advertisement – to attract recruits? So I say again: what if it is advertisement?'

A chastened Cutlack promised to send a cable. Monash then offered peace.

'Here, cut yourself a pipeful of this nice fresh Havelock tobacco, the real stuff,' Monash said, handing him his plug and tobacco chopper.[20]

Monash continued daily to gaze down on Hamel like a man with a nasty splinter in his foot that he wasn't allowed to remove. If he ever had the chance, he would take a scalpel to it. But for the moment the irritation remained.

After forty-six days' effort, Monash and his division were removed from the front line for a rest.

COMMANDER TO THE CORPS

The opportunity for Monash to do whatever he wished in the region came sooner than anticipated. On 12 May, Birdwood recommended him to the Australian Government for the corps command. Birdwood himself was on his way to run the Fifth Army. He had wanted to stay and had dreams of controlling a huge Dominion army of Australian, Canadian and New Zealand divisions. But it wasn't to be. Yet he hung on to a quasi-management of the Australians by retaining administrative command of the corps.

Birdwood felt there were only two real candidates for Corps Commander: his own deputy White and Monash. He adored White, who was the administrative brain behind him. But Monash was his senior. He had commanded in battle. White had not.

'Monash has commanded first a brigade then a division in this force without a day's intermission since our training days in Egypt in Jan. 1915 to the present time,' Birdwood wrote, putting his case to Hughes and Pearce much more firmly than he did when recommending Monash for a division command a year earlier.

'Of his ability, there can be no possible doubt, nor of his keenness and knowledge,' Birdwood continued. 'Also, he has had almost unvarying success in all the operations undertaken by his division, which has I know the greatest confidence in him.' Birdwood was mindful of the hysteria in some circles in Australia about Monash's German background, which had made Hughes nervous. 'This has, I think,' Birdwood added, 'been entirely lived down, as far as the AIF is concerned, by his good work.' The good work was killing Germans. Gone were the feeble fears that Monash might baulk at fighting them.

Birdwood concluded, in a firm manner for him, with: 'I do not think we can in justice overlook in any way his undoubted claims and equally undoubted ability to fill the appointment.'[1]

Not even Monash's reluctance to ride around on a horse to cheer up the troops was now held against him.

To be fair to Birdwood, he had to couch his recommendation in double negatives and caution. In theory, the Australian Prime Minister had more power than he concerning Australian troops. If any British war leader tried to be dictatorial it would not be diplomatic and could lead to a backlash. In reality, Hughes and every politician knew that the judgement on the best man to run the corps had to come from superiors inside the British High Command.

Hughes had reservations about Monash. The most influential voice in his ear, that of Keith Murdoch, was set against Monash. Hughes had happily inherited Murdoch from former Prime Minister Andrew Fisher after his commission of the journalist to assess Gallipoli. Murdoch had been Hughes' agent in pushing hard in England's power circles for the formation of the Australian Corps. Since this had succeeded too, Murdoch was now a strong, precocious political player in his own right. He had first been alerted back in March 1918 when chatting with Haig that Monash was favoured for the top spot. This annoyed Murdoch and upset Bean. The latter, it seemed, had never recovered from the ticking off he had received from Monash on Gallipoli over the journalist's lack of reporting of the gutsy efforts of his 4th Brigade. This, plus Bean's affection and enormous respect for White, caused him to oppose Monash. A third factor was Bean's anti-Semitism. Monash could have his Jewish background as long as he didn't have too much influence. But Bean would not have someone he described as a 'pushy Jew' running the most important position in the AIF.

On this one major issue in his distinguished career, Bean stepped out of his role of recording military history and decided to create it himself. His intrigues with Murdoch for the not-so-merry months of May and June 1918 were never recorded in their writing for public consumption. But for a short period they jostled centre stage with key politicians and military men in attempt to get their way.

They saw any appointment by the British High Command as the

wrong one. They suspected that the choice would have to be under its thumb and therefore someone who would not look after Australian interests. They felt compelled to support the most appropriate Australian, who had not been selected by the British. It was loose logic, and it underestimated the chance of any Australian chosen (in this case Monash, who could not have been more pro-Australian) to be in a position to look after his country's interests, if he were strong enough.

Both men ditched honesty and integrity in a near-hysterical drive to block Monash and have White take command of the AIF. Bean first heard the news from Birdwood on 16 May. Monash would be commander; White would go as chief of staff with Birdwood, who would be the British Fifth Army Commander and head of AIF administration.

Bean was stunned. At this time, he spoke about Monash to Birdwood's deputy adjutant general, Colonel Dodds. Bean's imagination and hyperbole were running wild. Monash, he said, had worked for corps commandership 'by all sorts of clever well hidden subterranean channels'.[2] Dodds was not happy with the accusation. He guarded all the plotting channels that led to his boss's desk. Monash had never appeared in any of them. He – and White for that matter – were not schemers, except against the Germans.

'You are an irresponsible pressman,' an angry Dodds told Bean.

But Bean, the correspondent-as-commander-maker, was hell-bent on making his case. In pushing aside Dodd's rebuke, he first had to convince himself by preaching to the converted – himself – in his diary. He recorded that he 'blurted out' to Will Dyson, an official war artist, and Hubert Wilkins, a photographer, the news about Monash and found there was 'immediate consternation'. This reaction was understandable from two men employed by White and attached to AIF HQ. Despite the fact that they were unqualified to judge the merits of the candidates on any level, their views formed the basis for extrapolation of the two conspirators' argument that there was strong opposition to Monash's appointment.

Bean set the agenda of the discussion with Dyson and Wilkins. 'We had been talking of the relative merits of White who does not advertise and Monash who does,' Bean informed his diary on 17 May, exposing his position. Dyson, who as a military expert made an excellent sketcher, became the lynchpin of Bean's argument. 'Dyson's tendencies are all towards White's attitude,' Bean wrote and then quoted Dyson's rendition of this: ' "Do your work well – if the world wants you it will see that it has you." '

Bean then seemed to have Dyson arguing against his case. 'Dyson thinks it (White's if the world wants you attitude) a weakness. But he [Dyson] takes it better than the advertising strength which insists on thinking or insinuating into the front rank.' This brought Bean full circle to his racist bias, which was his root objection to Monash. Here he quoted another's similar prejudice: 'Dyson says – "Yes, Monash will get there. He must get there all the time on account of the qualities of his race; the Jew will always get there."'

Bean then finished this diary entry, allegedly quoting his mouthpiece again, and reduced his own argument to absurdity: 'I'm not sure that because of that very quality Monash is not more likely to help win the war than White. But the manner of winning it makes the victory in the long run scarcely worth the winning.'[3]

The correspondent's intellectual hand-wringing (which Bean forty years later recanted by admitting that Monash had not pushed for the commandership) was not as threatening to Monash as Murdoch's manipulation. He knew more about clever, well-hidden subterranean channels than any political troglodyte. His successes behind the scenes fuelled him for more attempts to have influence over events. Dictating the choice for the first ever Australian AIF commander was as big an issue as he was likely to ever see. Whereas Bean was playing an uneasy, unusual role for him, Murdoch was right in his element, and without his co-conspirator's fever about Monash's background. Murdoch didn't care if he were a Jew or Gypsy. He had to go. White should be in the top saddle. He was thought to be a far easier character to manipulate than Monash, whose cerebral capability made him less malleable for Murdoch's purposes.

Murdoch met with Bean and Dyson in London on 18 May. Dyson was asked by Bean to repeat what he said about White and Monash. Murdoch scribbled notes, which encouraged Dyson, whose creativity had until now been restricted to art, to be bold. The AIF wanted White, not Monash. Everyone he met or painted was saying it. The would-be kingmakers were in quick accord. Monash should be offered a big desk job in London – as administrative head of the AIF. White should be commander. And Birdwood, who now was running the admin AIF job and the Fifth Army? Well, Birdie could run the Fifth Army if he wished, but he would have to give up his admin desk at AIF London.

The two plotters went into action. Bean sent a telegram to Pearce advising him not to allow White to be lost to the Australian Corps. He was 'universally considered greatest Australian soldier'. Murdoch cabled Hughes in the USA making the demands and citing his deep research, which, in actuality, was the discussion with Will Dyson the day before. The artist morphed into 'some officers'. They claimed 'that in operations strategy and understanding of Australians [White] is much superior to Monash whose genius is for organisation and administration and not akin to the true AIF genius of front line daring and dash'.[4]

The fact that White had never commanded under battle conditions and that front line derring-do was not relevant to the position, whether Monash or White had that or not, was not mentioned. To say that Monash had less comprehension of his fellow countrymen was specious and unprovable. And they were both exceptional administrators in their own way.

Hughes, who until now had enormous faith in Murdoch and his judgements, went into a flap. He was in Washington, a long way from home, and disgruntled. He cabled Pearce, whose cable machine was now jammed with demands and counter-demands. But the distance from Melbourne was proving tyrannical. Pearce had approved Birdwood's recommendation of Monash five days ago. Hughes let Murdoch know.

The journalist had plenty of subterranean avenues of attack left. The political path was blocked, so he went the press route by cabling the Sydney *Sun*. The crisp message, claiming there was a 'strong unanimous view' (those of the artist, the historian, himself and perhaps the cook who came to dinner) and then cited the demands. Murdoch's language was cute. He now referred to Monash as the 'supreme administrator', perhaps thinking that he might be flattered into taking up the position if such a title were aired in the press. But there were now more blockers than in a blood pressure pill. This time the Australian Chief Censor rejected Murdoch's cable. But the censor had a two-way bet by deciding not to announce Monash's appointment either. He would hold it back for a month to see whether it stuck.[5]

Murdoch was as resourceful as he was politically expedient. He now turned Federal Government lobbyist and persuaded businessmen and a union boss to get their mates in high places to make representations to Hughes and Pearce.

His fourth line of attack was his first real foray into the military ranks. He attempted to persuade Birdwood to give up his London AIF administrative job. His argument that Birdwood should not prevent an Australian from having the position didn't wash. Birdie was shrewder than his demeanour advertised. He didn't bother with shorthand, cryptic, overly dramatised cables. Instead he put his thoughts on paper by writing to Pearce (copying Hughes) and the Governor-General, Munro Ferguson, who hated to miss anything.[6] He summed up Murdoch as an 'Australian Northcliffe'. This reference to the just-gonged Viscount Northcliffe, who at sixty-three had developed megalomaniac tendencies recently, was pointed and perspicacious. Northcliffe owned the London *Evening News*, the *Daily Mail* and *The Times*, which gave him enormous clout in the years before television and radio. He used his papers ruthlessly to get what he thought was right for the empire without regard to fair reporting.[7]

Murdoch, at thirty-two, would have loved the comparison but not the inference. Birdwood claimed that Murdoch's efforts had stirred up anger and resentment at AIF HQ. Dodds, still simmering from Bean's accusations about Monash, also wrote to Pearce. Seeing through the plot by the artist, the correspondent and the mini-Northcliffe, Dodds told the defence minister that Murdoch was misrepresenting AIF opinion.[8]

But Murdoch kept on. He showed he had learned much by being around politicians by his fifth tactic of setting up Monash for an attempted bribe. First Murdoch wrote the softening-up letter to him offering warm congratulations. Monash replied politely, as he would have done to anyone. A day later Murdoch responded more expansively without giving anything away. Monash's instincts were alerted. He knew there was a push by Murdoch, Bean and Hughes to replace him with White, and he saw Murdoch as a danger and 'profoundly distrusted' him. Any overture from him, which would have Hughes' backing, should be received with caution.[9]

Monash consulted Birdwood, who suggested he write to Hughes urging him not change the new set-up at least until after he had visited him (Monash) and his troops.

Then came the bribe. Murdoch, writing with his address as '*The Times* office' began with what Monash regarded as red lights flashing: '. . . men . . . have in some insidious way tried to lead you to regard me with suspicion and even with hostility, just as on occasions some have whispered and lied to me about you.' Next, the flattery: 'I do want to say earnestly that I value your extraordinary ability very highly as an Australian, and I have always admired your work as a soldier. It takes two to make a friendship, of course, but please let me assure you that you have my personal esteem as one young Australian towards a much abler and wiser compatriot.'

Then Murdoch tried apparent candour by telling Monash what he already knew. Murdoch had recommended White as Commander of the Australian Corps. 'I honestly thought your genius would lie in the somewhat higher sphere of administration and general policy.' He again referred to Monash's 'genius' and how he had been telling 'high authority' in London about it.

Then Murdoch painted a black picture of the eventual alternative to him. An Australian cabinet minister might have to be placed in London with a military staff. This was an attempt by Murdoch to appeal to the army's aversion to political interference. He puffed up the London desk job as much as he could, adding that Birdwood was English. How could he possibly handle political issues on Australia's behalf? It was a worthy point, but not the main argument. Two big inducements were put to Monash, now a lieutenant general. The first was that he would be made a full general if he took the position. This would have been very fast tracking for any army. The second was meant to appeal to Monash's ego and vanity. Murdoch's articles were cabled to 250 newspapers worldwide. Murdoch offered to be the conduit for Monash's views on a grand scale.

Murdoch's case would have made Machiavelli proud. It was cunningly crafted by a young master political strategist. But there was one problem. Murdoch underestimated and misread his man.[10] Murdoch would have known about Monash's concerns for recognition, both awards and publicity, but misunderstood the motives, especially where his brigade, division and now corps were concerned. Monash had long seen publicity as a device for gaining a stronger voice and therefore position for himself and the men under him. Awards (VCs, mentions in despatches and so on) were recognition for deeds done and useful prestige. Gongs were nice for one's image. But above these accolades, for an outsider who thrived on them, Monash was driven by the need for him and his troops to have an independent powerful voice and control over their own destiny.

He was the first Australian in a position to have a real say in how the AIF conducted itself in war. It was now being manoeuvred into a critical position of impact, where it and the Canadians could be the most powerful force on the Allied side in the conflict. Monash had spent a lifetime in the militia and three years in the thick of the most important war in history. This was his time, and he knew it. There was no way he would pass up the chance to run what was to him a mighty fighting force that would – he was convinced, if properly managed and directed – play a major part in defeating the German Army.

Monash's deep sense of history also wouldn't allow him to back out. He had studied all the major wars of the last 150 years and was conscious of the current conflict's place in history and of the power of the force now in his hands. The AIF was by far the biggest corps of either side.

'My command is more than two and a half times the size of the British Army under the Duke of Wellington, or of the French Army under Napoleon Bonaparte, at the battle of Waterloo,' Monash wrote home in the middle of the Murdoch–Bean–Hughes intrigue. 'Moreover I have in the Army Corps an artillery which is more than six times as numerous and more than one hundred times more powerful as that commanded by the Duke of Wellington.'[11]

Size mattered to Monash. He salivated at the flexibility it presented him in the ability to conduct battles. For many commanders, this sort of elevation was dizzying or intimidating. But not for him. He couldn't wait to get his engineer's brain on bigger maps, resources, ideas and opportunities to win. Perhaps above all else, Monash was quietly but mightily proud that he, the outsider, had risen to be Australia's first native-born commander-in-chief. He was insulted by Murdoch's try at suborning him.

'It is a poor compliment,' Monash wrote in his diary, 'both for him to imagine that to dangle before me a prospect of promotion would induce me to change my declared views, and for him to disclose that he thinks I would be a suitable appointee to serve his ulterior ends.'

It took all his considerable diplomacy to restrain himself from telling Murdoch and Bean what he thought of their caballing, especially at this critical time in the war. At first, he wrote a neutral, friendly response to Murdoch avoiding comment on the bribes. Its passivity concerned him. He drafted the start of another response, explaining his desire to prove himself as a corps commander.

'You and your friends believe my abilities are mainly administrative,' Monash began. 'You probably think that a non-professional soldier is unlikely to be a good commander; that in the past I have been a figurehead controlled by professional soldiers . . .'[12]

But he put his pen down. He couldn't go on. It was too much from the heart; too revealing. Monash was beginning to understand his two adversaries. He was aware of Bean's unqualified admiration for White. Hero worship was something he could overcome, by his success on the battlefield. Racism, which Monash sensed from Bean, was something he had lived with and which he accepted from people who didn't know or understand him as a human being. Although Bean's judgements were distorted by this blind spot, he seemed by nature to be trustworthy and not dishonest.

But Murdoch was a far bigger problem. Whereas Bean genuflected to his ideal man, Murdoch's ego wouldn't allow him to bend the knee to anyone. Murdoch behaved as if he was on a par with Prime Ministers, heading to some place with an even greater power base. He appeared to believe that everyone had a price and could be bought in pursuit of his (Murdoch's) aims and position of ultimate potency.

Better, Monash thought, not to give the plotters anything to work on or with. The second letter was never completed or sent.

It might have been the correct move in his fight for self-preservation. The two-man undermining team kept their campaign running. They bailed up AIF officers and politicians anywhere they could find them and tried to make their case against Monash and for White. But there were none with influence among them who would put his name to their cause.

The issue reached a head in mid-June 1918, when Hughes arrived in London. Every key officer in the AIF, including Birdwood, rushed to greet him, except the new chief, Monash, who stayed at Bertangles, pointedly working on a new battle plan. The political wrangling began. Birdwood proved loyal to Monash. Where Birdwood had often been cautious in war in speaking his mind to Haig, he felt freer in front of the blunt-talking Australian politicians and conniving journalists to say what he believed.

At an official reception for Hughes, Andrew Fisher, who had been High Commissioner since 1916, was contemptuous of Monash. Birdwood told him to his face that he didn't know what he was talking about, which was accurate. Murdoch was there. 'Do you really think Monash is fit to command the corps?' he asked, which was not a thoughtful probe, given that Birdwood had made the appointment.

'Of course,' Birdwood replied. 'He can do it better than I.'

The Fifth Army Commander was working the room on Monash's behalf, or was it working him?

Hughes chatted to him about Monash, and Birdwood expressed his confidence in him. He dropped the names of two officers whom Hughes knew were heavyweights in the British Army – Generals Plumer and Rawlinson – who also supported Monash and had great faith in him.

A key player who had kept in the background and not been consulted in the Murdoch–Bean schemes was White himself. He had not wanted to contradict his boss, Birdwood. Now with Murdoch openly attempting to lobby for him, White was embarrassed. He wished to distance himself. He told Birdwood he would not accept commandership of the corps if it were offered. It would suggest, he said, 'that I've been intriguing with Murdoch'.

Maybe. But it didn't stop Murdoch and Bean. They saw these functions in the summer of 1918 as the chance to secure what they had so feverishly pursued now for months.

The movable feast of political gyrations spun on to the Ritz Hotel for another reception for Hughes by the British Government and War Council. The two journalists networked the ballroom. Murdoch kept checking who was there. If they were important enough he was in their ears. Lord Milner, Secretary of State for War, was not impressed. Rawlinson listened but didn't like what he heard. Later, he referred to Murdoch as 'a mischievous and persistent villain'.[13]

Bean, less proficient in the Byzantine ways of political lobbying, reverted to his real forte: writing. He sent Hughes a memo setting out, point by point, the case for White and against Monash (and Birdwood, who would lose his AIF position if their coup was successful). He also wrote to White. His letter was too emotional and too much like hero-worship for the recipient's liking. White dismissed the appeal to second him.

This proved a problem for the two kingmakers. Their potential king would rather remain a prince. At heart he didn't really want the job desperately enough. Certainly not as much as his wily supporters would have wished. But Murdoch and Bean knifed on, convinced of their rightness.

Their messianic approach ignored salient points. One was that Monash's popularity – from the grass roots up to the top of the AIF and with the British military and beyond – had been growing since the day he had taken charge of creating 4th Brigade in October 1914. His reputation had been established in those forty-four months. A backlash against the plotters was beginning, and Monash had powerful cards to play. Apart from Birdwood, Army Commanders Rawlinson, Plumer and Gough would support him. Then there was the Commander-in-Chief himself. Haig had the AIF commander's position earmarked for Monash almost as soon as he had taken over the 3rd Division.

Then there was King George, whom Murdoch and Bean could not hope to overcome even if they were aware of any interest he might have had in the matter of the Commander of the Australian Corps. Monash could never appeal to him. Nor could the King step in and support him. But the mere fact that Monash was a King's favourite son in his army, and that Haig and others were aware of it, weighed in Monash's favour. Haig, who said Monash could take another army corps command if the Australian cabal managed to dislodge him, had already presented a fallback position.

Yet Monash would wish only to run the AIF.

Monash's geographic distance from the politicking at the Ritz didn't stop him defending himself. He took time out to write in his own defence to Pearce, and to listen to Birdwood's report of what was said at the receptions for Hughes. The reports were unsettling and prompted Monash to see the Bean–Murdoch plot in anti-Jewish terms. He wrote home with more of a dry observation than a feeling of persecution, which he had not expressed before: 'It is a great nuisance to have to fight a pogrom of this nature in the midst of all one's anxieties.'[14]

Through all this, Monash got down to running the four divisions of the AIF at his disposal. 1st Division was still stuck in Flanders at Hazebrouck and Merris doing defensive work for British XV Corps. At first his style was seen to be far different from that of the affable Birdwood, and it caused wonderment among staff and officers. Monash was happy to ride around in the Rolls-Royce that Birdwood had used, except that he put a bigger Australian flag on it. He thought that the HQ atmosphere was too slack. He made all ranks salute, so much so that very soon everyone from the lowliest private up seemed to have an arm tic. Monash didn't mix like Birdwood, who was popular because he stopped to make small talk and remembered names easily. Monash rode or walked around with a frown, not in anger but deep in thought, and only occasionally worked on his attribute of the common touch. Days after Birdwood and White had left for London to take up their new posts on 31 May, Monash was heard barking at his aides. No one knew that they were his nephews ('Mo' and 'Half a Mo') and that they adored him anyway. He was also brusque on the phone. If the recipient didn't get the finely articulated command first time, then it was bad luck. There was less room for niceties and chat about the weather.

Monash was also running the corps with certain ambitions. Whereas Birdwood was not a planner who drew up battle schemes, Monash had the job with two aims in mind: to defeat the German Army and to prove himself a commander. When Birdwood had all the divisions under his control he was content to wait for C-in-C Haig or Fourth Army Commander Rawlinson to direct him, at least for the time being. He was happy to tread water. He knew he was going elsewhere and was in transit. Monash had no intention of going anywhere else. He had arrived at the right destination for him. He would of course accept directions and orders from Rawlinson and Haig, but he would be attempting to set his own agenda, which they would receive from him as battle proposals.

Monash was determined to sharpen the HQ atmosphere. It would be in keeping with his drive and aims. In parallel, he had to settle his command and staff, and this had to be done in collusion with Birdwood and White. His divisional commanders were a priority. Out went Walker (1st Division) and Major General N. M. Smyth (2nd Division), the last of the senior British regulars. Glasgow and Rosenthal replaced them. His old 3rd Division leadership was more problematic. McCay, who had originally bid to take over the AIF, had coveted it, but Birdwood didn't want him anywhere near the corps. He thought Monash's long-standing friend was too abrasive for a command in the revised formation. Monash might have agreed, but he had another problem with McCay.

They had been rivals since McCay had beaten him to being dux of Scotch College in 1880. McCay had headed him into the AIF and into running a division. McCay had always been his senior; someone he confided in and complained to about his apparent perpetual outsider status. But in the past year their roles had reversed. Vic had danced a little jig of victory when Monash received a higher-ranked knighthood at the beginning of the year. Monash himself did not. He had not rejoiced in the down-grading from divisional commander to depot commander of his once-illustrious rival. McCay had felt the strain of battle command as a man in his early fifties was expected to do in a young man's game. Now Monash was embarrassed at the thought of being his boss. It just wouldn't work.

Birdwood offered him McCay for 3rd Division knowing Monash wouldn't accept him, which allowed Birdwood to slip in White's choice and friend, Major General Gellibrand, who had displayed heroic leadership, notably at the second battle of Bullecourt. He was often prickly to those above and below him in rank. He also had some prejudices against Monash, which he expressed in Egypt when there were rumoured doubts about Monash's German allegiances.

Gellibrand proved true to form within days of his appointment, clashing with McNicoll, who regarded his new superior as both bombastic and overbearing. Gellibrand, for his part, thought that McNicoll's 10th Brigade was slack and undisciplined. McNicoll complained to Monash, saying he wanted either to resign or transfer. Monash attempted to smooth matters. Despite some frustrations over the years, he had a high regard for McNicoll's combat leadership and courage. He didn't want to lose him. In the end he had the two men agreeing to disagree in the uneasiest of alliances. Gellibrand remained abrasive, and McNicoll remained unhappy. McNicoll considered Monash a brilliant commander and accepted his toughness and demanding style when combat was on. He knew that Monash had firm control of the levers. He had complete faith in his fast decision-making under pressure. But he worried that Gellibrand, for whom he had no respect, would be a blustering bully in tense moments.

Although Monash was not entirely satisfied with the choices, the new-look AIF leadership was now more or less in Monash's image: Australian and with a volunteer citizen-soldier flavour. He also had only a partial say in his own staff. He was content with his chief of staff, 33-year-old Brigadier General Blamey, who had a reputation for working and playing hard. He was a former teacher from Wagga Wagga in New South Wales and an army regular since 1906. He also had a good record at Gallipoli. The administrative head was Brigadier General R. A. Carruthers, a close friend of Birdwood. Monash didn't like his laziness and wanted him replaced by the brilliant soldier and manager, Major General Bruche. But Birdwood, as head of AIF administration, had the power of appointment at least at this early stage, and he won the battle of the friends, despite putting up a weak argument. Bruche had German origins. Birdwood told Monash that he didn't want that issue being revived. Monash thought about asking Birdwood if he wished to replace the King on the same grounds, but decided to accept the 'extremely stupid' ruling.[15] Carruthers' slothful work practices in the office would not impinge on planning or combat operations. Besides, he was charming and amusing. His competent assistant, Lieutenant General G. C. Somerville, made his shortcomings tolerable. The only other senior British officer was the heavy artillery commander, Brigadier General L. D. Fraser. Monash's long association with artillery made him a critical judge of this position. He thought Fraser was the best available man.

Another capable assistant was the urbane twenty-six-year-old Australian major, R. G. Casey, who was from a new generation and young enough to be Monash's son. The AIF staff then was a blend of maturity and youth, volunteers, regulars, Australians and a handful of experienced British officers. It was an excellent pool on which the new commander could draw for ideas, inspiration, experience and intelligence.

Monash would need all of them working in harmony to achieve his aims. If Hughes could be kept at bay, Monash would have just three superiors in the British Army he had to sway to have his battle plans implemented. The top two were Rawlinson and Haig. Fifty-four-year-old Rawlinson was a veteran of the 1886–87 Myanmar Expedition, the 1898 Sudan campaign and the Second Boer War of 1899–1902. His Fourth Army chief of staff, Archibald Montgomery (later Montgomery-Massingberd) was the third party he would have to keep on side.

Monash's focus now would be on understanding them, their motives, fears and aspirations. With the characters, foibles, strengths and weaknesses of those above him clear in his mind, he now set out to impose his will – 'a moral ascendency' – over his entire staff. He wanted them to think as one, and he was number one. There was to be a single administrative and tactical policy. Yet the atmosphere at HQ was far less dictatorial than this aim would suggest.

Monash ran the army (which it was becoming in all but name) as if it were a huge engineering operation, or even the way an editor would run a newspaper. Everyone had access to his office, and the atmosphere was less disciplined and more relaxed than anything ever seen in the Australian force or any other British army. Monash refused no one and remembered everything, absorbing opinions and views like a sponge. His objective was to leave nothing to chance. This meant exhausting staff work to cover every contingency, in depth. And like a good newspaper boss, he prepared no editorials or plans without comprehending all concepts put to him. His overarching schemes would embrace what he saw as the best points.

The final act before battle while he was in charge would be the conference, which Birdwood had avoided. Monash used conferences to create a uniform tactical thought and method throughout his command. A conference would see an open and free exchange of ideas that would develop teamwork and efficiency and settle the final battle plans. Then the general would be prepared to move with confidence and allow his natural instinct for offence to run free.

✕

The first plan that Monash was ready to put to his superiors concerned that irritation he wished to remove surgically: Hamel. It sat neatly on the other side of Vaire Wood just two and a half kilometres northwest of Villers-Bretonneux. Since taking command on 31 May, Monash looked over at the area every day. It caused him to frown as if the Germans wandering about in full view of his field glasses were goading him. The Allies had not made one sizeable offensive since Passchendaele seven months ago. Monash believed that the rumours about imminent German offensives, especially from prisoners, were more bluff than reality. He wanted to take the initiative, not with the slaps of raids, nor the knockout right cross of a massive counter-attack, but with a sharp jab that would wind the opposition and lower its morale.

Monash wanted something special to start his campaigns as a corps commander. The use of tanks was very much in his thinking. Early in June he jumped in his Rolls with Blamey and drove thirty kilometres to have a long chat with the commander of the British Tank Corps attached to the Fourth Army, Major General H. J. Elles.

They were shown the latest models: the Mark V and Mark V Star. They looked like their predecessor, the tank that had so let down the Australians at Bullecourt. But there were big differences. The Mark V only needed one pair of hands to drive it instead of four pairs. The special gears, the greater power and 'the improved balance of its whole design', Monash the engineer observed, 'gave it increased mobility, facility in turning and immunity from floundering in ground even of the most broken and uneven character'.[16] The more powerful engines rarely broke down. Its reinforced armoured shell could take anything short of a direct hit from a field gun. They were quicker, too, or at least less slow, at five kilometres per hour.

Until now, the tank had been viewed as a defensive weapon, one that formed a mobile shield for infantry. But Monash wanted to know whether they could be used, like his doctrine on machine-guns, as offensive weapons. Elles was adamant that they could. He spoke effusively about tanks leading raids and causing havoc behind enemy lines. A direct artillery hit would be near-impossible if the tank rolled into an enemy camp and smashed up an HQ. That made the vehicle unstoppable. Haig would allow this next year, Elles informed them.

Was it possible now? Monash asked. Yes, was the reply.

Monash and Blamey returned to Bertangles with a daring possibility to consider.

'I proposed an operation for the recapture of Hamel,' Monash wrote. It was conditional on the use of tanks, a small increase in his artillery and an addition to the AIF's 'air resources'.[17]

Tanks dominated the first draft plan of attack in Monash's mind. But he needed to win over the allegiance of his men, who were no lovers of these oversized mechanical killers. They had only bad experiences or heard only bad stories about them. There was another pertinent factor. Tanks would usurp their role in the battle. These men hadn't come to fight on the Somme as second-stringers to armoured vehicles. Monash arranged for the likely participants to go by bus to Vaux, a village tucked away in a quiet valley northwest of Amiens, where they spent a day with Elles's corps. The show turned into a party. Groups of soldiers rode around in tanks. Their forward and reverse gear flexibility was demonstrated.

Mock machine-gun nests were constructed. The tanks were rolled and backed over them. The soldiers examined the result. It was as if a boot heel had been brought down on a beetle. The drivers and the infantrymen worked on ways to communicate and special manoeuvres between them.

They left Vaux pleased at the thought of this powerful new weapon being with them in an attack. Monash could now sit down and plan Hamel with tanks prominent. He took in comments from his battalion commanders, who nevertheless still didn't wish their infantry to play an inferior role to this new big brother weapon.

Monash thrashed out an arrangement with the flexible Brigadier-General Courage of the 5th Tank Brigade. First, he allowed the infantry commanders to be in charge of his tanks. Second, he agreed that his vehicles would advance level with the infantry. And third, he was willing to risk the tanks coming in close with the infantry behind an artillery barrage; the danger being that the taller tanks, at nearly three metres in height, could be hit by shells falling short.

Monash knew that the tanks would be the main weapon, even if only on the grounds of extreme intimidation. The infantry would back them up by attacking strong enemy positions that the tanks might find difficult to overrun. The soldiers would also 'mop up and consolidate the ground captured'. This was military jargon for destroying or capturing anything or anyone the tanks missed.

There would be three waves of about 8000 infantry – eight battalions – in total, and tanks: fifteen machines in the first, twenty-one in the second and nine with the 'mopping up' infantry.

Monash wanted to use one of his conjuring specialties, flavoured smoke. It would be fired every morning at the proposed zero hour just before dawn to accustom the enemy to it. This incorporated two Monash innovations. First, on the day of the attack, it was hoped that the smoke screen on the flanks and across the entire six-kilometre front, with the left flank on the Somme, would hide the attack. Planes would be used along with the artillery to provide noise to hide the squeal of the advancing tanks. Second, the enemy would have no idea whether the smoke were harmless or deadly gas. They would don their gas masks. 'This would obscure his vision,' Monash predicted, 'hamper his freedom of action, and reduce his powers of resistance.'[18]

Monash added battery emplacements on the Villers-Bretonneux plateau to hit German anti-tank guns (and tanks if the enemy had any).

Rawlinson received the plan on 21 June. Four days later, Monash felt a little surge of satisfaction and power when Haig approved the first major battle plan of his corps commandership.

Bertangles and the surrounding areas were swamped on 30 June with conferences for the Battle of Hamel. Monash had inculcated a culture of communication and clarity from the moment he created the 4th Brigade in 1914. Now he had control of the entire AIF, his style of environment was developing in the four divisions. Officers and commanders from brigades and battalions who might have been uncomfortable with articulating their thoughts, or lazy about putting them on paper, were rehearsing their speeches or redrafting their ideas to impress, please and fulfil the Corps Commander's demands. Soldiers and officers who had no idea about the operations of the other arms of the AIF military now had at least a superficial comprehension of all of them. Cross-fertilisation of ideas between artillery, machine-gun, infantry, tank, flying corps, ambulance corps and other officers was rife as they sought to plan their coordination in battle.

Monash held the biggest conference. It lasted four and a half hours. Two hundred and fifty officers attended and sat through the ticking off of his 133 items on the agenda. They ranged over everything from the supply of gas masks and water to reserve machine-guns. Nothing raised and unresolved before the conference was missed. Every key officer had to explain his plans. The others were encouraged to air opinions, opposing views and problems. Monash hated late changes. He wanted to walk way from the meeting with final decisions and proposals fixed and in place.

The conference marked the end of the planning stage. Monash was as happy as he could be that every major or minor issue had been ticked off and tied up.

The battle was set to commence before dawn on 4 July 1918.

✕

Early in July Monash had two VIP visitors. He was happy on the 1st to see Haig, who was impressed by the arrangements and, as ever, praised the new Corps Commander. But Monash protested to Birdwood about Hughes' plans to turn up the next day. 'The whole business is extremely awkward,' Monash said. With three days to go before Hamel, the commander's mind was immersed in the battle plans, and . . . 'Mr Hughes has chosen a time which could hardly be more inconvenient'.[19]

But Birdwood didn't need to remind Monash of the continuing plot to replace him. And earlier, Monash himself had implored Hughes to visit the front and see his AIF in action. Reluctantly, the commander had to set aside vital time for the visit.

Hughes came with the deputy Prime Minister, Sir Joseph Cook, the Navy Minister, late in the morning, along with a retinue of pressmen and photographers. They were both unaware of the secret plan for Hamel. Monash decided the only way he could handle the visit and keep abreast of the unfolding of the build-up to the battle was to let them in on the secret plan. This way Hughes became aware of the impact and power of the man whom he was thinking about unseating.

Monash told me his plans for battle [Hughes said]. He was no swashbuckler nor was his plan that of a bull at a gate. It was enterprising without being foolhardy, as was to be expected of a man who had been trained as an engineer and had given profound study to the art of war. Monash always understood thoroughly the ground he was to fight on. Maps lived for him.

Hughes asked him what the battle would cost in casualties.

He had made his plans so that they would be as low as possible [the PM commented, on reflection after the war]. His estimate was about 300, including walking cases. This stamped him, in my mind, as an outstanding figure of World War I. He was the only General with whom I came in close contact who seemed to me to give due weight to the cost of victory. He said: 'This is what we want to do; this is the way to do it with the least cost in human suffering.'

While Hughes was forming a positive impression of Monash, Bean and Murdoch were powering on behind the scenes to undermine him. Bean had primed White for taking over by lying to him about Monash being on the brink of accepting the bribe to leave the corps to become a full general. Murdoch had built his propaganda about Monash being unpopular with his key officers into a major deception for Hughes' consumption. The PM until this moment had been set to announce Monash's replacement by White. But White, honourably, had let Monash know in a letter that he wasn't supporting the move. He had washed his hands of the plotting and plotters. If Monash agreed to leave the corps, then White told him, the basis for his resisting the Bean–Murdoch scheming would be 'knocked from under' him.[20]

But Hughes had not put anything to Monash by midday on 2 July. He was too busy being thrilled by the meetings and the activity at Bertangles and in the valley beyond it. He lunched with General Hobbs and his 5th Division staff (which included Bruche) and then had a private discussion with Hobbs about Monash. Hobbs recommended him as Corps Commander.

At 2 p.m. Monash laid out the broad Hamel plan and had officers, who were coming to update him, brief Hughes and Cook as well. There was much poring over maps and viewing of the proposed battlefield with field glasses from vantage points.

In the early afternoon, Monash took them to inspect eight battalions of soldiers who were parading in full battle-gear in preparation for moving off to the assembly positions from which, on 3 July late at night, they would march into battle.

Both politicians were caught up in the electric atmosphere of anticipation. Monash invited them to address the troops. At about 5.30 p.m. with the sun throwing long shadows, Hughes mounted a gun carriage in front of a West Australian battalion in full battle dress, and began a speech. 'There was a major by my side,' Hughes recalled later. 'I found the shells flying overhead a little disturbing to the necessary flow of oratory.' He turned to the major and told him it was too noisy. 'Couldn't you let up a little?' Hughes asked him, 'I won't be long.'

'I'm sorry, sir,' the major replied, 'but I can't do anything about it. That's the other fellow.' The Germans were aiming their shells at Monash's HQ at Bertangles château a kilometre away.

'Only a little flattening of the trajectory was needed to carry me out of France and into the next world,' Hughes noted. 'I finished my sterling oratory in short order.'

'The stirring addresses,' Monash wrote, 'did much to hearten and stimulate the troops.'[21]

Hughes in particular was excited and in awe of his own power, in theory, over this impressive volunteer force, whose divisions had built reputations and which, as a unified Australian army in all but name, promised much.

Monash seized the moment. When they were alone for a few minutes at about 6 p.m., he told Hughes that he wanted to discuss the crisis over his commandership. Hughes thought it would be better to talk about it 'later'. Monash wanted to address it then. 'I am bound to tell you,' he said, eyeballing the PM, 'that the arrangement which would involve my removal from the command of this Corps would be in the highest degree distasteful to me. I would regard any removal as a degradation and a humiliation . . .'

Hughes broke in and, putting his hand on Monash's shoulder, said: 'You may thoroughly rely upon your issues in this matter receiving the greatest possible weight.'

It wasn't enough for Monash. 'I want you to know,' he said, 'I will not voluntarily forgo this command.'[22]

Hughes would have felt the full impact of Monash's intent. The commander was on his territory on the Western Front with his men. They were on the fringe of an important battle in Australia's history, set up by the man Hughes had come to confront. It was a long way from a safe politician's office in Melbourne. Even an at times brazen, expedient politician like him knew that he could not remove a commander on the brink of a battle. There would be no sacking that day.

Monash would have been aware that he had stepped right into the controversial issue that he discussed in his 1912 essay, 'The Lessons of the Wilderness Campaign – 1864': the conflict between a politician and a military commander over who should have the power over whom. Monash held the view that commanders should not be interfered with by politicians bending to 'public opinion'. In this case, Hughes seemed about to buckle to two journalists who had no claim to any opinion but their own. Monash made it clear to Australia's prime elected official that he would not accept his order to go. Was it a bluff? How far would Monash go?

Soon after the discussion that never was, Monash penned a quick note to Birdwood, telling him of the Hughes meeting. He added a postscript for White, reassuring him that he trusted him.

After Hobbs' strong endorsement of Monash at lunch, Hughes made a point of asking the other corps' divisional commanders and several brigade leaders in private for their opinions of Monash and whether White should replace him. They all favoured Monash. Only the temperamental Gellibrand didn't give him a strong endorsement, yet even he acknowledged Monash as the best commander in the AIF. Hughes realised that Murdoch had not been straight with him about the feelings of these alleged officers whom he claimed opposed Monash.

That night, Hughes confronted Murdoch and demanded to know the names of the anti-Monash faction. The journalist had no response.

'Well, I haven't met a single one of them that thinks as you do,' Hughes said. 'They [the commanders] all say the same thing. You say tell me there are men who think the other way [who want White] – where are they?'[23]

Murdoch remained mute, but was not deflected from his aims. The PM set aside any decision, unless Hamel proved a disaster.

On 3 July, Monash took a few minutes to write a more considered note to White. He repeated his trust in him, but said he thought White's recent warning letter had been cryptic. There had to be something behind it. Then Monash put aside all the distractions. The timing of Hughes's visit had proved fortuitous. Monash was relieved that he was still at Bertangles and in charge. Hamel now took his complete attention.

There was one unforeseen problem that needed his full concentration and nerve; otherwise Hamel would be called off. Monash had chosen 4 July, American Independence Day, in deference to a US contingent – 2000 soldiers in eight companies – under his command in the battle. The Americans had been drawn from two divisions of ten training with the British in the areas behind the front. Because of secrecy, it wasn't until late on 2 July that the American commander, General Pershing, was informed that his men would be in the Battle of Hamel. He objected. No American soldiers had ever fought under a foreign commander. Pershing didn't want the unusual distinction of being the first American general to allow it. He compromised with Rawlinson, saying he would allow the equivalent of one battalion – 1000 men – to fight. The other thousand had to be withdrawn. The American officers and soldiers were incensed about the decision. They had been in the reserve areas undergoing training and were ready to fight. Monash had to redraw his plans with the assault leader, Sinclair-MacLagan.

During the next twenty-four hours Pershing became unhappier with the idea of any of his troops taking part. Monash was at the HQ of the 3rd Division at Glisy, when Rawlinson notified him by phone of the new decision to pull out all the Americans. It was 4 p.m. on 3 July, barely twelve hours before the battle was set to begin.

Monash was angry. He refused at first. Rawlinson said it had to be done; otherwise there could be an 'international incident'. Monash was prepared to stand up to his superiors. He had done it to Cox on Gallipoli and in Egypt and to Godley at Passchendaele. Now he told Rawlinson that he had better come to the HQ and explain it all to Sinclair-MacLagan, who was also unhappy with this sudden troop reduction. At 5 p.m. Rawlinson arrived with chief-of-staff Montgomery.

First Rawlinson and then Montgomery insisted that the Americans had to be withdrawn. Monash stood his ground. His dealings with Rawlinson so far had found him flexible to the point of indecision, which might have been owing to his recent years of battle failures. Monash had heard one story about Rawlinson, which confirmed his own experience. At an Army Commanders' conference with Haig earlier in the war there was discussion about whether to go around a wood or through it. Rawlinson had said at once, 'Certainly I would go around it.' After a discussion, the majority thought it best to go through the wood. Rawlinson then said, 'Certainly, I should go through it.'[24]

Monash saw some softness in the Army Commander. He picked the moments to attempt to drive through it. This was one of them. He pointed out that his soldiers were already on their way to battle stations. The artillery would soon, under cover of darkness, be arriving at positions in the battle zone and setting up. 'Even if orders could still with certainty reach the battalions concerned,' Monash told them, 'the withdrawal of those Americans would result in untold confusion and in dangerous gaps in our line of battle.'[25]

Rawlinson became agitated. He spoke again of an 'international incident'. Monash responded that there could well be such an incident between the Americans en route to the battlefield and their fellow Australian combatants if they were to pull out now. The first thousand Americans taken out had been unhappy. The others could become hostile.[26]

Rawlinson and Montgomery would not accept this. Monash summed up his position. First, it was too late to pull out the Americans. Second, the battle would have to go on with or without them, or not at all. Third, unless Monash was ordered by Haig to abandon the battle, Monash intended to go on with the original plan. And fourth, unless he received a cancellation order by 6.30 p.m. the battle could not be stopped anyway. As he spoke, the preliminary stages were beginning.

Rawlinson repeated that Monash had to obey Haig's order.

'The Commander-in-Chief could not have realised that his order [to withdraw all the Americans] would mean the battle had to be abandoned,' Monash said.[27]

Rawlinson's charm and sympathy for Monash's position had evaporated. 'You cannot disobey an order,' he insisted.

'But you can,' said Monash, the lateral-thinking lawyer, putting his case with logic. 'As the Army Commander, it is open to you to disobey in light of what you know.'

Rawlinson was rattled. 'Do you want me to run the risk of being sent back to England?' he said. 'Do you mean [defying the order] is worth that?'

'Yes, I do,' Monash replied. 'It is more important to keep the confidence of the Americans and the Australians in each other than to preserve an army commander.'[28]

The comment wouldn't have endeared him to Rawlinson, who was closer to Haig and very concerned not to make any false moves. His reputation for being a competent commander had received a severe dent two years earlier when on 1 July 1916 he had ordered a disastrous charge at the Battle of the Somme. His miscalculation led to 60,000 wounded and the loss of 20,000 British soldiers killed, the greatest carnage ever in a single day of warfare. Matters did not improve much for the next 139 days of that battle. With this in mind, Rawlinson was cautious. Yet he was riding on Monash's determination to fight. If the Battle of Hamel were to be a success, Rawlinson would receive needed credit. He was also aware that

Monash was a favourite of the King and Haig. Rawlinson might have been senior in rank, yet he knew at these critical moments that Monash's power was intrinsically greater. With this in mind, Rawlinson let Monash's firmness and rationale sway him. He agreed to make a decision by 6.30 p.m. Rawlinson couldn't contact Haig until 7 p.m. Haig agreed with Monash that the Americans should not be withdrawn.

The attack, the C-in-C directed, should go ahead as planned. If it failed, Rawlinson, who had felt the pressure, would manoeuvre to help Bean, Murdoch and Hughes get rid of Monash. If it succeeded, his shaky commandership would be strengthened. Any commander who could plan even a modest victory at this stage would gain considerable prestige.

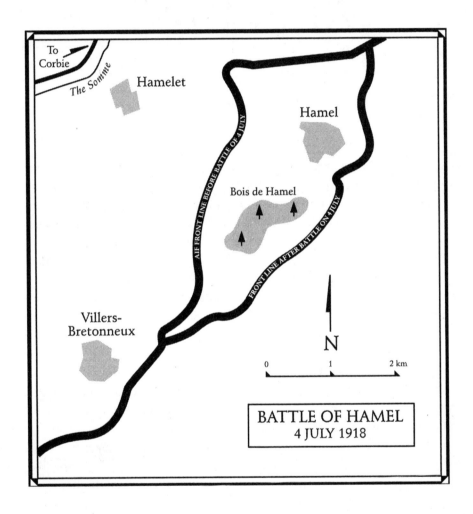

To
Corbie

The Somme

Hamelet

Hamel

AIF FRONT LINE BEFORE BATTLE OF 4 JULY

Bois de Hamel

FRONT LINE AFTER BATTLE ON 4 JULY

Villers-
Bretonneux

N

0   1   2 km

BATTLE OF HAMEL
4 JULY 1918

BREAKTHROUGH AT AMIENS

Success at Hamel depended on the start. If the Germans knew the Australians were coming they could position their artillery and machine-guns along the six-kilometre front and pick off the thin line of attackers before the tanks could wreak havoc. At 2.45 a.m. 7000 Australians and 1000 Americans were lying on the grass and crops in the fields on the start line. The RAF night-fighters began their daily swoop over the German lines ahead of the familiar pre-dawn artillery bombardment. The Germans on front line duty put on their gas masks and braced themselves for nothing more than the usual strafing, shells, smoke and interminable noise from their loud opposition across the low-gradient valley.

There was one difference on that fateful 4 July 1918. A thick fog, rare for the middle of summer, descended on the area like a huge crocheted blanket. This made it difficult for commanders and officers to make observations. Guidance was tougher. But the fog had the overriding use of making the attack more of a surprise. With the noise drowning the sound of the tank movements, by the time the Germans knew they were being invaded, the vehicles were just metres away and emerging from the fog like monsters. Those Germans who didn't freeze were flattened, chased or fought by the tanks and the supporting infantry.

There were some pockets of resistance from well-fortified machine-gun emplacements and artillery, which belatedly defended. But it was a rout. The Battle of Hamel, on which Monash had staked so much, was over in just ninety-three minutes. It was a modest encounter in the context of the war, but the rapidity of the victory, with much gain and little cost, meant an immeasurable lift in the confidence of the Australian Corps and the entire Allied command. The British Tank Corps at last had something to celebrate. This precedent would be the model for every British attack using tanks for the rest of the war.

The Australians, in their first action as a corps, had won a near-perfect victory. And Monash revelled in the sense of harmony achieved by his infantry, the Tank Corps, the Royal Artillery and the RAF. It had worked the way he planned it and always dreamt perfectly prepared battles should be. He counted 800 casualties in his force, but most were walking wounded who would see action again. Monash's aim to have the machinery protect the infantry could not have been better executed. But in this conflict even the tanks came through far better than expected and better than they ever had before. Only three were put out of action, but even they would be repaired to fight again.

The Australians were happy to collect 1500 prisoners, a huge haul for such a small battle. Monash was pleased that perhaps half of them were wearing gas masks, which was evidence that his smoke trick had worked. Another 1500 Germans were killed or made casualties. The booty – always a useful boast in war – was impressive. It included two field guns, twenty-six mortars and 171 machine-guns. Territory gained – another military measure of success – was four times that by any other force of a division or less in 1917, when the last British offences happened.

Another aspect of Hamel was the American involvement. It was the first time they had been in an offensive battle in the war, and Monash was keen to increase this link.[1] There were no negative repercussions from his decision to insist on their fighting despite their Commander-in-Chief ordering them out. In fact, Pershing revelled in the after-glow of the Hamel victory, and the men who fought had a status that other US divisions envied.

Monash's other notable inclusion, apart from strong support for the much-maligned tank, was the use of planes to drop ammunition to the machine-gunners. It required two men to carry a box holding 1000 rounds, which one gun could fire off in less than five minutes. It was heavy, dangerous work for the carriers, often under fire. Now that risk to soldiers had been reduced. Time had been saved; efficiency was increased. It was a small advance. Yet when put in the context of how it increased the proficiency of machine-gun use as an offensive weapon – another Monash edict – his faith in the technology and his capacity to incorporate it effectively were increased. Everything had worked, from the use of smoke and every latest artillery projectile to machine-guns and planes.

Monash and his force had set some sort of standard, recognised by the British Army, which sent out a staff brochure on the operation to all officers. This brought him much kudos, but he was more interested in his survival as a commander. A clue came from a long, effusive telegram from Hughes who, after visiting Bertangles and the AIF, had moved on to an Inter-Allied War Council meeting at Versailles outside Paris. The telegram included a message from Haig to Hughes: 'Will you please convey to Lieutenant-General Sir John Monash and all ranks under his command, including the Tanks and the detachment of 33rd American Division, my warm congratulations on the success which attended the operation carried out this morning, and the skill and gallantry with which it was conducted.'[2]

This was the sort of endorsement Monash wanted. He hoped Hamel had bought him time. Yet he would not rest on this achievement. Even late on the day of the victory, he ordered Sinclair-MacLagan and Hobbs to start patrolling into enemy territory. In reality it was raiding. While adhering to the doctrine of the limited objective, whereby territory was gained and held, Monash never stopped planning aggressively. Even as the tanks were bringing back the cheering, waving soldiers, including the wounded, he was stretching over his maps in the war room at the château. Some of his officers might have been opening champagne and unwrapping fat cigars, but Monash, smoking a pipe, was busy with the tireless Blamey putting down coloured paper and using a cue to move miniature infantry markers.

Monash was a realist. He sensed that the near-faultless Hamel success had been due mainly to his strategic skills. But its completeness was also partly because of the fatigue and battle-weariness of the Germans, despite the massive reinforcements that had all now arrived from the Russian Front. The enemy was stunned and defending. Now was the time to shake up their defences even more.

The next day, he asked Rawlinson to reduce his expanded front of eighteen kilometres. It was too wide for his four divisions, even on rotation, to maintain.

Some of his brigades needed a long rest. Monash began to visit his men, inspiring them to be prepared for more hard work and battles. Everywhere the Rolls-Royce with the prominent Australian flag appeared, Monash received spontaneous applause and cheering. Ever since Gallipoli his popularity had increased. There was always a good response for chatty, ebullient Birdwood, or the muscular leadership of the inspiring Pompey Elliott, or the fearless drive of Cannan. But Monash's reputation had been built on a solid foundation of training, planning, detail and performance. His attention to the little things that affected every soldier filtered down to them. His preference for control and decision-making from the expanding engine room at HQ rather than being seen at the front had developed a mystique based on solid, reliable performances from the 'old man'. The name 'Monash' was now associated not only with a strong organisation but also with winning. Nothing would please him more than for it to be equated with victory. Furthermore the way he articulated the soldiers' success and what it meant in the bigger scheme of things had also endeared him more and more to every man in the corps. The men at the front appreciated his directness. He wasn't promising girls and beer but guns and batteries that still had to be taken on and defeated.

Monash now read the mood of his men with more certitude than a latter-day politician reads electronic polling on an electorate's mindset. He wanted to fuel the AIF's huge and hungry appetite for the fight. One way was to push Rawlinson and Haig for the return of the 1st Division. The AIF spirit was on such a high that he wanted to build on its morale by having all five divisions together. Monash was confident that if he could arrange this, then he could create a huge psychological advantage and sense of invincibility in the force. This feeling was important to his leadership. He had studied the attitudes of Napoleon and Wellington to the sense of being winners. This created an aura of invincibility, which built the confidence of its members and destroyed the morale of the opposition. Hamel had been the first step. Monash's aim, like that of Wellington, was to build the feeling that no matter what the position on the battlefield, his force could always find a way to win. His own interrogation of German prisoners confirmed that the enemy was already more than wary about tackling the Australians. One of Monash's aims, indeed themes, in discussions with officers and commanders was to build on this belief, even if it meant bluffing the enemy.

After repeated requests it was agreed that the 1st would join the rest of the Australian Corps and be in reserve for the start of the next major engagement.

✕

The result at Hamel was firming up the attitudes of others, too. Monash received a letter from White that confirmed his last message was indeed enigmatic. Now White made it clear that his friends – Bean and Murdoch – were not conspiring at his 'suggestion' or with his 'approval'. This did not mean that White didn't covet the Corps Commander's job. He was just making clear to Monash that the frenetic, persistent plotting had nothing to do with him. But White still hadn't confronted his friends. He had not yet told them he was not a competitor for Monash's position.[3] Then again, he was now in London away from the action, and had not had a chance to speak to the peripatetic Murdoch and Bean since before Hamel.

White's distancing of the himself from the conspirators, along with the positive reaction from Hughes and Haig, and the news that the French Premier Clemenceau was on his way to congratulate the Australians, all buoyed Monash on 6 July when he met with Murdoch at Bertangles. His guard down and his confidence up, Monash told the journalist what he had not been able to write earlier: when he had won battle honours, he would be happy to take up the administrative role in London.

This gave the plotters hope. But Monash did not specify what battle honours would satisfy him. Would he be content with another Hamel and then leave? Or would he want to push on into 1919 and be part of the actual victory, if it were to come the Allies' way?[4]

When Murdoch told Bean what was said at the meeting, the correspondent urged the journalist to advise Hughes not to give Monash time. But the PM was not ready to oppose him straight after Hamel. White, too, was in a different mood. His refusal to lobby against Monash was justified. In a face-to-face meeting on 12 July, White attacked Murdoch for 'impropriety, ignorance and dangerous meddling'.

The journalist didn't like the rebuke, especially after Hughes' rebuff over his concocted sources. But these minor setbacks had not diminished his view of his role as a power-broker who would get his way. From that moment, Murdoch was not a White supporter any more. He now fell back on a jingoistic argument and viewed White as politically naïve and 'subservient' to England. White had been the plotters' choice because he had not been the British selection. But now that he showed no inclination to unseat Monash, Murdoch had branded him an English lackey. It was a weak argument. The Bean–Murdoch position now seemed brittle, but they were nothing if not tenacious.[5]

Bean thought differently from Murdoch, although his aims were the same. Unlike Murdoch, who saw issues in terms of politicking and how he could manipulate the main players, Bean viewed everything in terms of what was right or wrong, as interpreted by him, in historical terms. But after Hamel he became desperate and was carried away with his self-importance. He wrote to White imploring him to step forward and ask Hughes to appoint him Corps Commander. Bean saw it as perhaps 'the major job in his [Bean's] life' to ensue that Monash was made administrator in place of Birdwood and that White got the corps.[6]

Despite his change of heart over White, Murdoch knew that no one else was a suitable choice after Monash to be the Corps Commander. This caused him to persist too, trying to cajole Monash with more inducements of grandeur. But again he misjudged his man. Murdoch puffed up the London desk job more, saying that the PM was seeking someone to take over 'much of the semi-political, semi-national, economic and financial character' of the work. Yet Monash never saw himself as a politician or even an economist. The position did not challenge him. He was a soldier first, and not a politician second or third.[7]

Murdoch also thought he was teasing Monash by telling him that a most important immediate post-war position would await him. Monash knew the job to be repatriation, but it was the last thing on his mind after Hamel. There was much to do on the battlefield before any such operation. The correspondence shows that Monash for the first time was beginning to toy with his tormentors. He kept his communication with Murdoch friendly and open while still deftly closing off all options.

Victory against the two would-be commander-makers, if attained, would be as sweet as that over the Germans. At least the latter's attempts to get rid of him had not been personal.

Monash was pleased to welcome the French Premier, the cultured seventy-six-year-old Georges Clemenceau, on 7 July. He was the most important Allied political figure, and had a few months earlier managed to persuade other government heads to place Ferdinand Foch as sole military commander, ahead of Haig. Monash admired the journalist and statesman Clemenceau for his single-minded determination to defeat the Germans and his declaration that he would wage war 'to the last quarter hour, for the last quarter hour will be ours'.

Monash assembled a large contingent of the soldiers who had participated at Hamel, and who were resting at Bussy. He was looking for every means to keep his fighters buoyant and willing. He couldn't think of a better person – the top representative of the country for which AIF soldiers were primarily fighting and dying – to speak to them. Monash was aware that Old Georges, one of France's foremost political writers, and a lover of the Impressionists, especially Monet, would himself make a deep impression with his heartfelt words.

He addressed the Australian volunteers in English, speaking about the attitude to freedom in Australia, England, France and Italy.

> That is what made you come [he said]. That is what made us greet you when you came. We knew you would fight a real fight, but we did not know that from the very beginning you would astonish the whole continent with your valour . . . I shall go back [to Paris] tomorrow and say to my countrymen: 'I have seen the Australians; I have looked into their eyes. I know that they, men who have fought great battles in the cause of freedom, will fight on alongside us, till the freedom for which we are fighting is guaranteed for us and our future.'[8]

It was the right stuff, especially as the AIF was expected to be the spearhead of future battles. Every soldier understood why Clemenceau was nicknamed Le Tigre. It was just the sort of inspiration Monash was looking for as his eager troops waited for more and bigger challenges.

But Foch and Haig restrained him. Commanders who had made disastrous decisions to attack when they should have planned better were now timid when they should have been bold. Many failures, and public opinion moving against them, were having an impact on their decision-making.

For the rest of July, Monash's divisional generals had to be content with nibbling at the enemy's forward positions. Rosenthal led the way with his 2nd Division, which advanced the Australian line by one kilometre opposite the east of Villers-Bretonneux by taking Monument Wood. It had been thick with Germans. This advance rid that part of the town from the fear of being machine-gunned by the enemy, who could peer into the streets.

By early August, Foch and Haig concluded that there would be no more big German pushes into Allied-held territory in the Somme Valley.

The enemy was thought now to be purely on the defensive. The German Second Army, astride the river, was now the target and ripe for a massive attack. Monash began drafting a battle plan based on the strategies and tactics at Hamel.

He had not been satisfied with the French XXXI Corps of General Debeney's army on his right or southern flank. He was at pains to explain that it wasn't because the two forces didn't get on. A strange common vernacular – it was dubbed Francalian – had even developed between them, and they fraternised well. But Monash was worried by the real language differences, which counted in the heat of battle, the gap in the style of fighting tactics and the 'divergent temperaments'.

'The French are irresistible in attack as they are dogged in defence,' he said diplomatically, 'but whether they will attack or defend depends greatly on the temperament of the moment. In this they are unlike the British or Australian soldier, who will at any time philosophically accept either role that may be prescribed for him.'

In other words, the British and Australians were better disciplined and drilled, making them more reliable under pressure. Besides that, even if Monash applied his rusty French in an attempt to charm his hosts, he couldn't get them to push back the Germans in the French force's allotted territory. After Hamel, the front line had a nasty bump in it where the Australians had pushed forward, but the French had stayed put. This made the AIF's right flank vulnerable. Monash knew they weren't weak, but he was baffled by their intransigence. He wanted that front line bump free and straightened out. But because of a different policy, or sheer French bloody mindedness, he worried about them in forthcoming 'much more serious undertakings'. His concerns were exacerbated when he visited Field Marshal Pétain.

'If the Boche attacks,' the French leader told him, 'we'll fall back.'[9]

Now Monash feared he would be vulnerable on both flanks if the French were there. He asked Rawlinson for and received Currie's Canadians on his right instead of Pétain's French. Now he had a worry only on his left flank at the Somme with the British III Corps led by General Butler on the other side of it.

Again, Monash was nervous about the British commanders, whom he did not think were up to the difficult task north of the river. But there was nothing to be gained by airing this. Instead of complaining about Butler and his staff, he told Rawlinson he wanted his force to be 'astride' the river.

Much against his will, Monash was forced to wait until the battle to see whether the problem unfolded as predicted.

There were other problems out of Monash's control in the build-up to the AIF attack. Although the Germans were not attempting infantry retaliation, they had no compunction about drenching the AIF front with mustard gas, fired by their artillery. On many nights, the Germans would think nothing of expending 10,000 shells on the half-ruined and partly deserted Villers-Bretonneux or in the woods surrounding the town where the Australians sheltered.

The soldiers dreaded mustard gas. In its pure form this chemical weapon was colourless and odourless. But the Germans had given it a whiff by adding a mustard-smelling impurity. It increased fear. When that smell hit an area, soldiers were alarmed. Its symptoms and consequences could be horrific. It often began as an itchy skin, which in a few hours led to blisters. It made the eyes sore; the eyelids would swell. In mild cases it lead to conjunctivitis; in some it caused blindness.

Mustard gas had a rotten habit of not going away. The smell might disappear in the early morning, but when the warm August sun rose, invisible or brown-coloured pools of it, scattered over several kilometres, would form a vapour and strike unsuspecting soldiers. On hot days, concentrations were higher. Soldiers who inhaled it more often than not had bleeding and blistering in the windpipe and lungs. An end result could be pulmonary oedema, or even cancer, which could strike early or take decades. (Many an ageing digger would complain of lung problems that began with mustard gas. If it didn't get them on the battlefield it struck them down over time.)

The French, not the Germans, first used gas – in August 1914. They fired tear-gas grenades (xylyl bromide). But the Germans were first to study the development of chemical weapons and to use them in strength. They began in the capture of Neuve Chapelle in October 1914 with a formula that caused sneezing fits. The Germans often found French soldiers convulsed and clutching handkerchiefs in the trenches. It gave the Germans hope that they could win the war by making all their enemies sneeze themselves to capitulation or death. Inspired by the French experience in the early spring, they loaded up their howitzers with this gas on the Russian Front at Bolimov in the middle of winter. But there was no sign of Russian soldiers grabbing their noses or making violent head movements. The gas had failed to vapourise in the freezing conditions. Disappointed that they couldn't win the battle of the sneeze, the Germans used the first poisonous gas – chlorine – in April 1915, at the start of the Second Battle of Ypres. It choked its French and Algerian victims, destroying their respiratory systems. The British were quick to condemn the Germans while rushing to develop their own chlorine bombs, which were to be delivered in artillery shells.

The Germans stayed in front by developing something even more insidious than chlorine: phosgene. This horror was subtler. It caused less coughing and choking. But more of it was inhaled. Its effect was delayed. Apparently healthy soldiers would collapse two days later. The French used prussic acid to make nerve gas, which they introduced now and again. Mustard gas, the worst of the lot, was used first by the Germans against the Russians at Riga in September 1917.

'This form of attack,' Monash recorded, 'and the constant dread of it, made life in the forward areas anything but endurable.'[10]

In the lead-up to the Battle of Amiens, the diggers scrambled to put on their gas masks as soon as a bombardment hit to avoid being a casualty before the whispered big battle began.

Haig and Rawlinson had considered a massive counter-attack in May but were not confident about the unconvincing plans on the table. They abandoned them after the big German offensive on 27 May. The two discussed it again in June. But still no thoroughly thought-out plan was put up.

That all changed at Hamel. Monash's 'win' was based on an unprecedented harmonious use of tanks, aircraft, artillery and ground troops. Just at a moment when the Allies needed to be shown the way, Monash's solid ideas emerged out of the pack of concepts from twenty-five commanders under Haig and proved successful. From 1 July – three days before Hamel – for the next three weeks, Monash pushed hard for the instigation of his blueprint for a massive counter-attack, based on the tactics he used at Hamel. He had a meeting every day from 4 July with Rawlinson. This veteran general was now more willing to consider the 'Dominion' commander's plans. So was Montgomery. Monash discussed his work in progress and urged them to take the initiative now while the enemy was vulnerable. The day after Hamel, Monash was convinced that he could drive through the German defences eight kilometres or more if he had that promised Canadian support on his right (southern) flank. It was not then set in concrete. There was much hard work to do before Rawlinson would be confident about any huge counter-attack.

At a meeting on 13 July, Montgomery asked for some specific proposals.

'Reduce my front [to further concentrate his Australian force], return 1st Division [from Flanders in the north assisting the British at Haze-brouck] and use the Canadians [on his southern flank],' Monash responded.

He again spoke to Rawlinson and Montgomery at length about the overall scheme on 14 July. He said his position 'was analogous to an inventor who conceives a new scientific idea, and who talks it over with his colleagues and friends. They all make suggestions, which are discussed, some being adopted and others rejected, so that ultimately the new idea takes a definite form and substance.'[11]

Monash's 'friends and colleagues' were his staff, divisional commanders, Haig, Rawlinson and Montgomery. He redrafted it for several weeks, incorporating all their useful contributions (apart from a few key points that he would argue in future meetings) until his plan had 'form and substance' and broad consensus – a critical point in coordinating a military operation on this scale.

Monash fine-tuned every aspect of the battle from the use of tanks, aircraft and artillery to deception methods, such as smoke and noise screens. His request to Montgomery for the 1st Division was motivated too by his fervent desire to unite and direct all five Australian divisions in a battle for the first time. Monash was proud of the courage, fortitude, resilience, endurance and fighting abilities of his men and all the Australian force that invaded Turkey in 1915. Then he and his fellow commanders had been handicapped by poor planning from the British High Command, a very narrow beachhead on which to fight and a severe lack of resources and support. Now Monash would be given all the resources he wished. He had a much wider front on which to operate. And he had what he considered the best fighting force in the war to direct as the arrowhead for the Allies.

Monash had instigated the recognition and commemoration of Anzac Day. Now he was determined to advance the sense of nationhood an important notch beyond Gallipoli. He wanted victory. The move towards it would begin by presenting the German Army with its biggest surprise of the war.

On 15 July, Monash briefed Rawlinson in detail about his 'counter-offensive' plan, and next day presented it to Haig when he visited Bertangles. It focused on the role of the AIF, but incorporated a broad strategy for four attacking corps, running from left to right (or north–south) facing the enemy: the British, the Australians, the Canadians and the French. The Australians and the Canadians would form the point of the arrowhead. The British on their left and the French on their right were meant to guard the flanks of the main attacking corps.

Monash had not been part of any failed plan on the Western Front apart from the battle of Passchendaele. He was keener than anyone of Haig's army or corps commanders to seize the chance to smash through the German lines. His aggressive attitude, based on his confidence in his own detailed planning and intelligence, saw him emerge in these critical days of mid-1918 as the most forthright leader in Haig's pack.

Haig's position had been strengthened in March 1918 when he helped dislodge his superior, French General Robert Nivelle, Supreme Allied Commander on the Western Front, in favour of a friend, another French general, Ferdinand Foch (who became Supreme Commander of all Allied forces). Haig and Foch proved an amicable combination. The Scot got his way much more than he had under Nivelle. He could now exercise full tactical command of the British armies (including the Australian and Canadian forces), which Nivelle had never allowed.

Haig's brutal reputation had been tempered by his role in helping to stop German offensives of March and May. Monash was giving an enormous further boost to Haig's status. Mindful of the King's appreciation of Monash, and his capacities as a thorough, brilliant strategist, Haig was now paying him more attention than ever.

Monash's plans were also attractive for another reason that would enhance Haig's image and modify his reputation as a butcher. They were structured for a minimum of casualties. That was a novelty in July 1918.

Haig sat on the château's piazza and read this most recent blueprint for victory against the Germans. He pronounced it 'very good indeed' and made some other favourable remarks without any suggested changes. The British commander reminded Monash that he had to be patient. He also mentioned that he couldn't 'authorise it without consulting Generalissimo Foch'.

Monash asked how long that would take. Haig thought two weeks, and said he was going to take a break 'in Touquet to play some golf'. Haig suggested Monash also take some long overdue leave but in London rather than Paris. It would be easier to contact him. Monash thought he would go. Haig told him to 'tell Henry [Rawlinson] I recommend it'.[12]

Monash suggested they both put out press releases concerning their plans to take leave. This would deceive the Germans into thinking that no counter-attack was being contemplated.

Monash sent his written plans to Rawlinson later on 16 July. The Army Commander, who was admired more for his fluent French and skills as an artist than his capacities as a strategist, submitted formal proposals to Haig the next day. They incorporated his own ideas and an 'edit' of Monash's master-plan for an AIF thrust, with refinements for the other three corps.

Rawlinson didn't like Monash's 'artificial' boundary between the British corps and the Australians. Rawlinson put back the Somme River as the boundary. He also put the first objective 'finish line' in the attack short of the German artillery. Monash wanted to take the artillery in one hit. Past experience taught his command that not taking the artillery left the advancing force vulnerable to the enemy regrouping and using it against them.

Monash had ignored Rawlinson's plans for the cavalry, believing that horses were superfluous in the planned encounter except for 'mopping up' after the main conflict. But Rawlinson was still rooted in warfare techniques from the previous century. Besides, Haig insisted that the cavalry be in the fight. There was nothing like the odd charge on horseback to spice up a battle. Monash thought it wasteful and a nuisance to have horses and tanks attacking together. The equine speed was considerably faster than that of the crawling, creaking armoured monsters. But it didn't matter. Haig wanted them in, so they were in.

Rawlinson agreed with Monash's request to reduce his front from seventeen kilometres to less than seven kilometres. He also allowed the Australian 1st Division to join the corps from Flanders, where it had been fighting in. This was an enormous boost for Monash and the AIF.[13]

On 18 July news came through of a successful counter-attack by the French led by General Mangin ninety kilometres away to the southeast at Soissons, and supported by France's Sixth Army. They went in with 2000 guns, 1100 aircraft and 500 tanks in support of twenty-four divisions.

They took 1500 prisoners and 400 guns. Coming two weeks after Hamel, this success seemed to confirm German vulnerability, and it speeded the Allies' plans.

Haig approved them on 19 July. Two days later, Rawlinson called a meeting of all the key commanders for this new offensive – to be known as the Battle of Amiens. It was set for 8 August.

The rendezvous location was a pretty village of Flexicourt on the Somme, obscure enough for there to be little fear that an enemy spy would notice the unusual, pretentious motorcades arriving on the lawn in front of an elaborate white mansion. It had been commandeered for the beautiful, still summer's morning by Rawlinson. The black and red flag of the Fourth Army Commander hung over the mansion's entrance. Monash, punctilious as ever, was looking at his watch as he arrived in a Rolls-Royce with the Australian flag prominent. General Currie, the Canadian Commander, rolled up, his flag flying too. He was following General Butler of the British III Corps, General Kavanagh of the cavalry and then senior representatives of the Tank and Royal Flying Corps.

Rawlinson outlined the complete army plan, which was largely Monash's creation. The commanders sorted out the broad plans for the attack. Rawlinson imposed no limitations on them for what they did within their own boundaries, as along as they met their objectives and didn't let the other corps down. Monash's aim was to advance eight kilometres.

Currie was happy with his plans, which Rawlinson had refined after he had seen Monash's proposals. Tanks were an additional item in the Canadian operation. Monash didn't think he had enough of them after his unprecedented success with them at Hamel. Rawlinson increased his quota to nearly 500.

Monash was concerned about the confusion surrounding transmission of urgent messages from the front. There was no certainty about finding a phone terminal, and even then messages were transmitted too slowly for an effective response by HQ. There was also a problem with the speed of transmitting messages up the chain of command from battalions to brigades and divisions. By the time messages reached HQ – often more than twenty minutes later – the battle conditions most likely had changed. Responses would be late. Monash proposed the use of planes for reconnaissance and message transmission. He was granted nearly 800, each one carrying a pilot and observer, from the No. 3 Australian Squadron. Monash expected to cut the time he and his staff received messages and intelligence from the front to something around ten minutes.

The corps commanders were happy with their 2000 artillery pieces. Yet there was concern about the numbers held by the enemy. Monash objected that Rawlinson had not approved of German gun positions being a target in the first phase of the three-phase attack, which would cover three kilometres. The Australian troops had complained that in earlier battles, if artillery was not taken or smashed in the first phase, the Germans retreated with it in the pause before the second phase and used it against them later. Rawlinson consented to this change.

Monash was also unhappy to see that Rawlinson had made the Somme a northern boundary for the Australian Corps operations. Monash wanted at least one Australian brigade (4000 soldiers) over the Somme so that he controlled both sides of the river. He thought it was an unnecessary boundary.[14]

'It creates a divided responsibility [between him and the British commander in charge of the corps north of the river],' he told Rawlinson. Monash suggested that this would make it harder for him and the British commander to cooperate. His real worry was Chipilly Spur, a rocky ridge beyond some terrace meadows just north of the river, which was stoutly defended by Germans because of its vantage point. The Somme meandered as a boundary to those somnolent fields, then encountered the steep wood-covered slope, which ran for several kilometres. The Germans would find easy targets among the Australian troops moving forward in the meadows as well as being tough themselves to dislodge from their dominant position.

The spur offended Monash's obsessive dedication to ironing out all problems before any attack. It continued to dog him. There had already been fierce fighting there. Monash wanted to command the attack on Chipilly, fearing that his left flank would be exposed if the British couldn't take it. Butler objected.

Rawlinson supported Butler, saying that this target remained with the British III Corps. Monash was uneasy. He suggested that Butler had to take Chipilly. He had to keep attacking until he secured it. This suggestion caused some tension, but Rawlinson agreed. A disgruntled Butler was under instruction now to make Chipilly a priority.

Monash was still not happy. He had little confidence in Butler and his staff. During a break, Monash told Sinclair-MacLagan to prepare a defensive flank in case the British failed. He knew how fluid matters could become once a conflict began. He would continue to urge that he be given control of the operations north of the Somme.[15] For the moment he had to be content with his prescribed boundaries marked to the north by the river and the south by the railway. The country – the Australian Corps battleground – in between was flat, open and dotted with woods and villages.

At the end of the meeting, Monash obtained Rawlinson's approval for leave in London as long as he was 'prepared to return at very short notice'. Rawlinson also arranged that Monash would receive a coded phone message via the War Office in London when he had to return.

Monash took off from Bertangles on Tuesday 23 July, picking up a boat that took him from Boulogne to Folkestone, where a car ran him to the Prince's Hotel, London, in time for an evening with Lizette.

On 24 July they lunched at his hotel and spent the afternoon shopping. On 25 July, Monash sat for Australian painter John Longstaff. At night he and Lizette went to the theatre to see *Naughty Wife*. They went again on 26 July to see *Going Up*. It was light relief that helped him escape the hell across the Channel.[16]

Monash visited the War Office each day. He did press interviews, which he considered important in putting an Australian perspective on events. The War Office had underplayed his corps' contribution. It didn't want Dominion forces to be perceived as bearing the brunt of the fighting or, more bluntly, as cannon fodder. It was feared that Hughes might feel it necessary to pull Australia's armed forces out of the conflict if he thought they were overexposed. Nonetheless, Monash felt compelled to fly the flag for himself and his men.

Time was swallowed up fast. He accepted an invitation to attend the opening of Australia House on the Strand on 3 August, but never made it. After just five days of comparative bliss the War Office rang his hotel late on Sunday 28 July to give him the coded message. He could have done with a month's leave, but at least he had had a break from the constant grind, misery and din of war, and the interminable demand for decisions.

Monash said goodbye to Lizette in London on Sunday night. He preferred not to take the then risky option of flying. Instead, the next morning a car picked him up just before dawn. He was driven to Dover, where a destroyer was waiting for him at 7 a.m. It took him to Boulogne. A car then drove him the 130 kilometres to Bertangles, where he lunched with his staff and division commanders.

On 31 July, Monash called for a conference with his divisional commanders, and asked for their plans. They were put to the meeting for discussion, comment and questions. Monash, as usual, dominated the conference without taking it over. He encouraged criticism on even the minutiae.

Haig dropped in to Bertangles, giving words of encouragement to all the divisional commanders. He went out of his way to express how much confidence he had in Monash. At this conference, they worked out the deployment of the field and heavy artillery, the tanks and armoured cars, and the Cavalry Brigade, which Haig had repeated must be used. They also covered the use of infantry, the methods of attack and the tactics.

On 1 August, Monash summed up the meeting in memos sent to all the divisions, and they covered many of the outstanding queries. Blamey remarked later that he doubted that any commander in any major battle in history would have matched his leader for preparation. 'Elements of the meticulous, careful forethought reached every member of the AIF,' he noted, 'and gave them even greater confidence and inspiration.'[17] Bean expressed a similar sentiment, with the benefit of hindsight. '. . . the range and tireless method of his [Monash's] mind were beyond any that came within the experience of the AIF,' he wrote. 'His men went into action feeling, usually with justification, that, whatever might lie ahead, at least everything was right behind them.'[18]

The Australian 1st Division was transferred from under the command of the British Second Army to join Monash's Corps. It had been rushed down from Flanders early in April when Amiens was threatened during the first battle of Villers-Bretonneux. The 1st was then hurried back to help the hard-pressed British line near Hazebrouck. Now the division mustered for something big and still secret. As the soldiers travelled south by train, they could only make guesses based on rumours as to what it would be. They were pleased to be joining Monash and the rest of the Australians.

They had heard of the success at Hamel and were expectant about joining a far bigger campaign. These experienced soldiers were disappointed to learn as they arrived at Amiens that they would be held in reserve for whatever was about to unfold.

The movement of two Canadian divisions (about 30,000 troops and equipment) to a point south on Australia's right flank – on the other side of the Amiens–Nesle railway line – was kept as secret as possible. The reason leaked everywhere by HQ was that the Canadians were relieving the Australians so that they could have a long, well-earned rest after their years of hard work at the front. There was no hint that the Canadians were joining them for a massive attack.

Yet it was impossible early in August not to make German intelligence suspicious as brigades began intricate manoeuvres in preparation for the attack. The Germans decided on a raid in the area into which the Canadians were moving and replacing Australian brigades.

On the night of 4 August, the 4th Australian Division's 13th Brigade was spread over a five-kilometre front. If it occupied the front-line trenches the Germans would be alerted. There was no option but to defend its area with a series of small, isolated posts. One of these posts was on the road to Roye beyond the southernmost part of the area occupied by the Australians. The Germans raided it. A sergeant and four soldiers were captured. They were taken behind lines and interrogated. The Australians refused to disclose anything but their names and units, which was their right, if they could withstand the pressure.

Monash and his staff were not aware of the bravery of the captured men. The command could only hope that they had held out or that they knew nothing of the imminent plans. It decided to leave the 13th Brigade where it was and not to displace it with Canadian troops until the last minute before the Allied attack. Monash planned to replace this brigade of the 4th Division with one – the 1st Brigade – from the incoming reserve of 1st Division. It arrived at night on 6 August, just in time to be slotted into the order of battle of 4th Division under General Sinclair-MacLagan.

Also arriving after dark for the 4th and 5th Divisions were eighteen tanks stuffed to the brim with rifle ammunition, Stokes mortar bombs and petrol. They rolled and squealed into a small plantation a kilometre north of Villers-Bretonneux, from where the massive attack would be launched.

The strike was set for the morning of 8 August 1918 at 4.20 a.m.

It was a day of tension on 7 August. While it was not all quiet on this section of the Western Front, there was a definite lull. The Germans, like the Allies, had new listening devices for tapping telephones. Monash ordered the restricted use of telephones, especially in areas closest to the enemy. This meant that commanders and staff had to walk or hop in their cars or on to horses in order to make final inspections and directives.

'A strange and ominous silence pervaded the scene,' Monash noted. 'It was only when the explosion of a stray shell would cause hundreds of heads to peer out from trenches, gun-pits and underground shelters, that one became aware that the whole country was really packed thick with a teeming population carefully hidden away.'[18]

At night, Monash's artillery commander, Brigadier-General Coxen, made his last round of battery positions – a dangerous job. The Germans were firing shells at random into the area. Coxen reached the plantation where the tanks, covered with tarpaulins, were sitting. He and the soldiers protecting him went to ground as the last of a dozen shells whistled towards them. It fell into the centre of the tanks. They exploded. A cloud billowed into the area. The Germans, unaware that they had hit an important spot by chance, then turned a concentrated artillery barrage on the plantation. In twenty minutes, fifteen tanks and their valuable cargoes were destroyed.

Coxen rushed back to Bertangles to inform Monash that the fire was an accident. The enemy was unlikely to have had prior knowledge of the pending strike or the tanks that would be in the front line. Monash had the tanks and stores replaced. He would go on with the attack as planned.

On the afternoon of 7 August, he had a message sent to all of the 166,000 Australian troops in his corps. It read:

TO THE SOLDIERS OF THE AUSTRALIAN ARMY CORPS.

For the first time in the history of this Corps, all five Australian Divisions will tomorrow engage in the largest and most important battle operation ever undertaken by the Corps.

They will be supported by an exceptionally powerful Artillery, and by Tanks and Aeroplanes on a scale never previously attempted. The full resources of our sister Dominion, the Canadian Corps, will also operate on our right, while two British Divisions will guard our left flank.

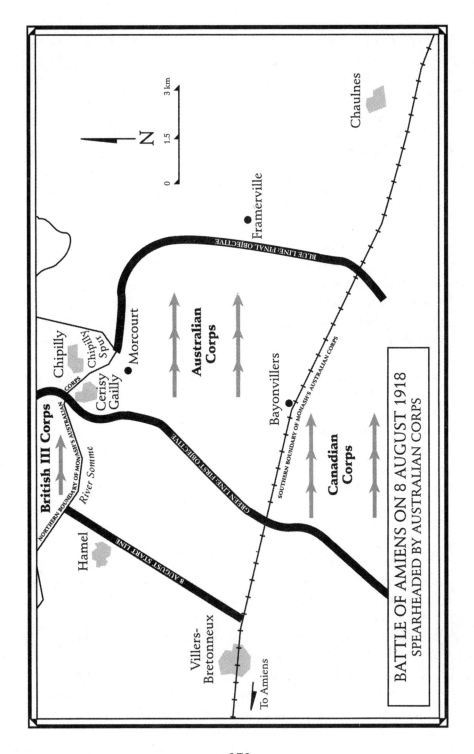

Chaulnes

Framerville

BLUE LINE: FINAL OBJECTIVE

Morcourt

Australian Corps

Chipilly

Chipilly Spur

Cerisy Gailly

CORPS

British III Corps

NORTHERN BOUNDARY OF MONASH'S AUSTRALIAN

River Somme

GREEN LINE: FIRST OBJECTIVE

Bayonvillers

SOUTHERN BOUNDARY OF MONASH'S AUSTRALIAN CORPS

Canadian Corps

Hamel

8 AUGUST START LINE

Villers-Bretonneux

To Amiens

BATTLE OF AMIENS ON 8 AUGUST 1918
SPEARHEADED BY AUSTRALIAN CORPS

N

0   1.5   3 km

The many successful offensives which the Brigades and Battalions of this Corps have so brilliantly executed during the past four months have been the prelude to, and the preparation for, this greatest culminating effort.

Because of the completeness of our plans and dispositions, of the magnitude of the operations, of the number of troops employed, and of the depth to which we intend to over-run the enemy's positions, this battle will be one of the most memorable of the whole war; and there can be no doubt that, by capturing our objectives, we shall inflict blows upon the enemy which will make him stagger, and will bring the end appreciably nearer.

I entertain no sort of doubt that every Australian soldier will worthily rise to so great an occasion, and that every man, imbued with the spirit of victory, will, in spite of every difficulty that may confront him, be animated by no other resolve than grim determination to see through to a clean finish, whatever his ask may be.

The work to be done tomorrow will perhaps make heavy demands upon his endurance and staying powers of many of you; but I am confident, in spite of excitement, fatigue, and physical strain, every man will carry on to the utmost of his powers until his goal is won; for the sake of AUSTRALIA, the Empire and our cause.

I earnestly wish every soldier of the Corps the best of good fortune, and glorious and decisive victory, the story of which will echo throughout the world, and will live forever in the history of our homeland.

JOHN MONASH,
Lieut.-General
Cmdg. Australian Corps.[19]

At 3.30 a.m. on 8 August, Australian Gunner J. R. Armitage lay in readiness for the attack. He wrote in his diary:

It was utterly still. Vehicles made no sound on the marshy ground . . . the silence played on our nerves a bit. As we got our guns into position you could hear drivers whispering to their horses and men muttering curses under their breath, and still the silence persisted, broken only by the whine of a stray bullet or a long range shell passing high overhead . . . we could feel that hundreds of groups of men were doing the same thing – preparing for the heaviest barrage ever launched.[20]

At 4.00 a.m. the only noise now came from Allied planes droning over the enemy as a cover for the menacing sound of those squealing tanks that kept inching forward. Monash was woken by one of his aides, Major Berry. He dressed, read final reports and then walked into the Bertangles grounds. At 4.20 a.m. the Battle for Amiens began. By 7 a.m. it was clear that Monash's surprises, including deceptive coloured smoke, a massive artillery barrage, and the stealthy, secret movement of 500 tanks, 800 planes and 100,000 Australian soldiers in the initial attack, meant that the Australian Corps was heading for a huge victory.

By early afternoon on 8 August, victory was confirmed.

At 2.05 p.m. Monash made the 'body-count' report, telling Rawlinson that casualties were 'under 600'. There were more than 4000 prisoners with 'many more coming in'. Soon after, he could reinforce the extent of the rout by cabling his superiors that the 5th Division had captured the LI German Corps HQ at Framerville on the final phase red line.

The 8 p.m. final communiqué to Rawlinson and Haig noted that more than 6000 prisoners had been taken. The haul was 100 guns, including the dangerous heavy and railway type, a train, and 'hundreds of vehicles and teams of regimental transport'. Then came the less palatable news that 'total casualties for the whole Corps will not exceed 1200'.[21] Given that the number engaged in the assault on day one would have exceeded 100,000, this was an attrition rate of about one per cent. It was a figure that any general could live with, especially in comparison to the hideous carnage resulting from the poor and rushed planning of previous big battles. Monash, naturally ebullient, would sleep well enough on the night of 8 August 1918. His espoused policy of supporting and preserving troops with the coordinated back-up of tanks, air power and artillery had worked in favour of the soldiers.

Overall, the attack had been too successful for Rawlinson and his staff to digest at Fourth Army HQ. Instead of ordering Monash to push his corps due east, the thrust was to be made southeast. The Canadians would take up the cudgel on its front. The Australians would swing their thrust to the right and protect the Canadian left flank along the Amiens–Nesle railway (the southern Australian boundary). Currie's troops would advance between the railway and the Amiens–Roye road, heading for Lihons. The Australians were supposed to pivot their left on the Somme to Méricourt.

Rawlinson's ultimate objective for both corps was to take the important railway centre of Roye, east of Lihons. Failing that, it was hoped that the threat to capture it would force the German Army to retreat from the great 'salient' or bulge of territory it had eaten into during a big offensive in April and May. At the least, this would stop the Germans using trains from Roye to feed their operations in this salient.

Despite not being fully aware of how brilliant the 8 August attack had been, Monash, by instinct and experience, would have pushed on east to the big bend in the Somme, where the Germans held the towns of Bray, Péronne and Brie. Reports from the front were clear. If he ordered a further drive that continued into the night of the 8th and the next day, the area around that important, almost ninety-degree bend in the river would be overrun by the Australians.

Monash was well aware that the bend territory had been fought over in 1915 and 1916. Then the French and Germans sat tight and belted each other with artillery, converting the area into a wasteland. It was seared with trenches and wire entanglements in the easternmost part on the German front. But between the bend and that devastated area there was another eleven kilometres of unharmed country. Monash wanted to ram home a further advantage across it. But he was restrained, not for the first time in the war. He might have been the thinking commander, who preferred remaining at HQ to wandering around the front line risking his neck in displays of bravado. But when it came to an instinct for forcing victory, he had a more determined streak than any of his peers or superiors.

The orders from Rawlinson stood. Monash had to resist the need to quench his thirst for territorial acquisition. Instead, he wrote new plans and directed Glasgow's 1st Australian Division to assist the Canadians along the railway.

The success of the Australian advance the day before created a problem. The last two of the 1st Division's brigades arrived later than expected from the north. When instructed to march on from Amiens railway station to the front, they found it much further than anticipated. The troops arrived late on the morning of 9 August, and missed the move out by the Canadians at 11 a.m.

This logistical problem was covered by the 5th Division ordering its right line brigade – the 15th led by 'Pompey' Elliott – which was patrolling the railway itself, to fill the breach before the troops from the 1st Division arrived. Elliott's men found stiff opposition, but hung on until the foot-weary 1st Division turned up. Then Monash ordered the swing right – southeast – of the 1st and 2nd Divisions. They sliced through the captured Framerville and ended up on 9 August at the foot of Lihons Hill. Resistance had been strong at times but sporadic along a moving front of six kilometres. The Germans had been able to regroup along a ridge at Lihons Hill. They used field and machine guns to attack the Australians, who had to dig in. The tanks were the main targets for the defending Germans. They knocked out many of them.

At night the Australians made contact with the advancing Canadians on the railway.

By the end of 9 August, Monash had most concern about his left flank over the river. The night before, as anticipated, the English 58th Division couldn't budge the Germans on Chipilly Spur. As planned, Sinclair-MacLagan had formed a defensive flank for the Australian 4th Division, yet the Germans had hit several tanks across the river. Artillery duels continued. Monash repeated his requests to Rawlinson to take command of this troublespot. Butler objected, but then suddenly he was removed. The official line was that he was taking prearranged sick leave, which was unlikely at this critical time. General Godley replaced Butler, and to say this pleased Monash is an understatement. For the first time, Monash was in a position of superiority, running the far bigger corps and acting as the spearhead of his own plan.

Monash put an urgent demand that was more like an order to Godley that he (Monash) take over Chipilly Spur. Godley dithered. Under Rawlinson's orders, he had control of the British sector, not the Commander of the Australian Corps. But Godley, like the entire British High Command, had witnessed Monash's near-complete annihilation of the enemy the previous day. This gave him an enormous immediate prestige and power. There had been nothing like this success by British forces before. It caused the forceful Godley to hesitate. Monash pressed him. Godley demurred. Monash put his case in more vociferous terms knowing that the 'elegant' (as Monash referred to him) Englishman, who lacked 'technical ability', would have to capitulate. When he did, Monash was handed 'limited jurisdiction' over the north bank of the Somme. Better late than never. He could now tackle that damned spur, which had worried him so much.

'This was merely getting in the thin end of the wedge . . .' Monash wrote. He found himself 'where I had so strongly desired to be from the first, namely, astride the Somme Valley'.[22]

The best available brigade was the 13th. Before the major 8 August attack began, it had stayed south of the railway line to deceive the Germans about the arrival of the Canadian Corps. It was now ordered to take Chipilly. But since Monash's urgent requests, Godley had appraised the situation and decided to take action before the Australians could march there. He had directed the experienced 131st American Regiment to attempt to take it. The Americans began their task at about 4.30 p.m. Two hours later, after heavy fighting, they controlled nearly the entire ridge.

At this time, the 13th Brigade arrived and sent a battalion across the river at Cerisy. 'They joined the Americans,' Monash noted with satisfaction, 'and helped clear up the whole situation. This made my left flank more secure. It enabled MacLagan to withdraw the defensive flank, which he deployed along the river from Cerisy to Morcourt.' That night of 9 August, Monash took over the 131st American Regiment from the British III Corps and attached it to his 4th Division. Sinclair-MacLagan was put in charge of the newly captured front, which extended several kilometres north of the river to the Crobie–Bray road.

Monash's organised mind was well satisfied at the end of 9 August with the Australians' relentless advance. His 1st, 2nd and 4th Divisions ran south to north in the line of the new front.

By contrast, General Ludendorff, the joint dictator of Germany with Field Marshal von Hindenburg, was distressed to the point where his staff wondered whether he would have a nervous breakdown. That would come later in the autumn, when he would receive psychiatric counselling. Now he could only attempt to absorb and counter the horrific events of the past forty-eight hours. He wrote in his memoirs: 'August 8th was the black day of the German Army in the history of the war. This was the worst experience I had to go through . . .'[23]

The Prussian-born Ludendorff (who, at fifty-three, was the same age as Monash and George V) had been mainly responsible for Germany's military policy and strategy from August 1916. He had devised the big 21 March offensive on the Western Front. Ludendorff's plan was to force a decision favourable to the Germans in secret negotiations between the two sides before the Americans joined the war in Europe. Another million German soldiers at the Western Front had boosted his troop numbers after the 1917 Russian Revolution and Russia's withdrawal from the war. But he underestimated the resistance of the French in their own homeland and the British forces, especially the Australians and Canadians.

Ludendorff would never have dreamed that a general with a Prussian–German background born at the same time and with roots in a town close to his own birthplace of Kruszewnia, near Poznan, would be his key opponent and nemesis in war. Given Ludendorff's support for Adolf Hitler in a 1923 *coup d'état*, and the general's fascist links and paranoia about Jewish conspiracy theories, he would have been driven to his psychiatrist's couch a lot quicker if he ever learned later that Monash was a Jew.

In his memoirs, writing of the shock of the 8 August attack, Ludendorff described with some feeling how the Australians and Canadians attacked in thick fog 'that had been rendered still thicker by artificial means' (Monash's smoke-screen) with 'strong squadrons of tanks, but for the rest with no great superiority. The [German] Divisions in line allowed themselves to be overwhelmed.' To add to the confusion he mentioned how tanks had run through divisional HQ. This might have been a deliberate error on the HQ staff's behalf. In fact, they had been terrorised by sixteen armoured cars, commanded by one of Monash's staff officers, Lieutenant Colonel Carter, which would not have sounded so frightening. Ludendorff recalled:

> The exhausted [German] Divisions that had been relieved a few days earlier and were lying in the region south-west of Péronne [near the Somme's big bend] were alarmed and set in motion by the Commander in Chief of the Second Army. At the same time he brought forward towards the breach all available troops. The Rupprecht Army Group dispatched reserves thither by train. The 18th Army threw its own reserves into the battle from the southeast.

The desperate Ludendorff ordered the German Ninth Army, 'itself in danger', to help out. Such was the attack's surprise that it was days before troops could reach the troubled area.

'It was a very gloomy situation,' the depressed General noted. 'Six or seven Divisions that were quite fairly to be described as effective had been completely battered . . . The situation was uncommonly serious.' Ludendorff emphasised that if the Australians and the Canadians continued to attack 'with even comparative vigour' the Germans would not be able to resist 'West of the Somme . . . The wastage of the Second Army had been very great. Heavy toll had also been taken of the reserve which had been thrown in . . . Owing to the deficit created, our losses had reached such proportions that the [German] Supreme Command [essentially the overworked Ludendorff himself] was faced with the need to disband a series of Divisions, in order to furnish drafts . . .'

The picture of Germany's reduced capacity to resist confirmed Monash's instinct to push east to capitalise on the enormous blow of 8 August. It wasn't to be. Yet the physical and psychological impact would remain and influence peace negotiations, which were dictated for the Germans by Ludendorff and von Hindenburg.

The 'deeply confounded' general saw the writing on the wall for the Germans in the entire conflict when he concluded: '8 August made things clear for both [opposing] Army Commands.'[24]

The Allies now had the upper hand on and off the battlefield.

The Australians had advanced the predicted eight kilometres and taken seven villages, 8000 prisoners, 173 guns and a great deal of extra booty. The Canadians had moved forward nine and a half kilometres, secured twelve villages and taken 5000 prisoners. In all, the British Fourth Army had pushed forward with seven divisions and three in support, against six German front-line divisions. The French on the right had taken a further 3500 prisoners. It was the biggest breakthrough for the Allies in the war so far, and it created a massive bulge in the front line.

Monash pushed his troops on to support the Canadians with diminishing results over the next few days. But the damage was done. Germany had been heaved backwards, and was reeling from a technical knock-out. It would recover and fight on, but now there was no hope of the German Army being other than on the defensive.

Ludendorff was realistic amidst the gloom. 'We cannot win this war any more,' he told a colleague, 'but we must not lose it.'[25]

Fighting continued through 10 August, intensely in some areas, as the Allies advanced sixteen kilometres east. The smooth running of Monash's grand plan removed any danger that Amiens, the last bastion before Paris

– 120 kilometres south – would be captured. German resistance increased as Ludendorff shored up defences after the irreparable damage of the previous two days.

By 11 August the Allied leaders had fully appreciated Monash's success and what it could mean for the future. In the early morning, when he was preparing plans for a further advance, Winston Churchill, now British Minister of Munitions, called in to congratulate him and discuss the 'state of play'. Churchill was interested in Monash's views about German morale.

At 11 a.m. Haig was driven to Bertangles to 'formally thank me for the work done'. He brought his Chief of the General Staff, Sir Henry Lawrence. General Sir Julian Byng, the Commander of the British Third Army, arrived while Haig and Lawrence were there. Haig thought it opportune for him to discuss operations with Byng and Lawrence. Monash made as if to leave them in a room near his office, but the others insisted he stay for the entire conference. Monash was pleased that he was 'frequently asked for my opinions'. He had been so immersed in his command that he hadn't yet fully comprehended the ramifications of his breakthrough in such a decisive and sweeping victory. The Allied leaders were relieved at last to have a commander with the brilliance and courage to plan victories, particularly without massive carnage of its troops.

Monash's star was in the ascendant. Everyone wanted to make contact.

At noon, Rawlinson phoned to tell him that Marshal Foch himself was also coming to Bertangles – at 3 p.m. Fresh orders about tactical policy would be given. Monash told Rawlinson that Haig was meeting the five Australian divisional commanders at 2.30 p.m. in Villers-Bretonneux. Rawlinson then changed plans and arranged for Foch to be at an army conference in the fields just west of the village.

In this heady, spontaneous atmosphere of felicitations, Monash realised that his battle planning would be interrupted for the rest of the day when he was informed that Sir Henry Wilson, Chief of the Imperial General Staff, was also in France and wished to call on him at Bertangles. Wilson, normally someone a general would have to drop everything for, was told that he could find Monash in the village between 2.30 and 3.30 p.m. Wilson would have to join the line of VIP well-wishers.

Monash was driven in the Rolls to a shady spot under trees in a field on the outskirts of the village, which was a hive of activity. Australian and Canadian railway specialists were relaying the track in time for the first train since 7 August to come through from Amiens. A large, wired-in prisoners' cage was in view across the main road. Small groups of Germans were being herded in to join thousands of inmates.

'An immense stream of traffic was pouring up the road towards the front,' Monash noted. 'Guns, troops, strings of horses and mules, hundreds of motor lorries, ambulance wagons, and the usually motley traffic of war.'[26]

At 2.30 p.m. Haig met Monash's divisional commanders – Major Generals Hobbs, Sinclair-MacLagan, Rosenthal, Gellibrand and Glasgow. Haig made a complimentary speech. He became emotional. 'You do not know what the Australians and Canadians have done for the British Empire in these days,' he said. Haig tried to go on, but could not. He began to cry. The Australian commanders were embarrassed. They moved away. Yet the moment had its impact. Haig was strong and ruthless. Such a display of his feelings was unprecedented and pertinent.

At this moment Rawlinson arrived with Montgomery. Then Lawrence, Wilson, Currie, Godley and commanders from the cavalry, tanks and Royal Flying Corps turned up.

At 3 p.m. Rawlinson, surrounded by huge maps, began the army conference as planned. He didn't get very far before more cars appeared carrying Foch, Clemenceau and the French Finance Minister, Klotz. 'Villers-Bretonneux, only three days before reeking with gas and unapproachable, and now delivered from bondage,' Monash wrote, 'was the lodestone which had attracted the individual members of this remarkable assemblage.'[27]

Rawlinson rolled up his maps. There was no chance of meetings now as the VIPs praised Monash and Currie in heartfelt speeches. The relief in the congratulations was palpable. Uncertainty and hope had been replaced by a true sense now that the enemy would be repulsed thanks to the Australian and Canadian drive.

The deference to Monash exhibited by all the key members of the Allied command surprised him but sank into his psyche. He had stood up to, if not over, the indecisive Rawlinson before the Battles of Hamel and Amiens. Monash would now be even bolder and more inclined to take calculated risks. Like the AIF fighting machine he had built and controlled, he would take some stopping.

Monash's war planning was again interrupted the next day, 12 August, when he prepared for the arrival of George V at Bertangles. It was an appropriate moment for the King to invest him with a knighthood bestowed months earlier. Monash, aware of his detractors and the political capital that could be made from the occasion, made sure that photographers and film cameramen were there to catch the ceremony.

The King too was keen to make a point by making a public acknowledgement of his own good judgement.

Monash, who had a sense that the King had had some influence in his rise, arranged a guard of honour of 600 men at Bertangles. They lined the driveway under tall chestnut trees. Monash also made sure that an impressive line-up of war trophies was placed in the leafy château's grounds. The booty included several hundred guns, howitzers, heavy-machine guns, light machine guns, anti-tank guns, field searchlights, transport vehicles, range finders and hundreds of other minor trophies. Monash included 'a representative selection of a dozen enemy vehicles, both horse-drawn and motor drawn, with teams of horses and harness complete, just as captured'.

Monash organised the 600-strong troop formation. It was made up of 100 men from each of the Australian divisions and another hundred from the Royal Garrison Artillery. They lined both sides of the drive from outside the front gates, with their heraldic figures and coats of arms, to the steps of the piazza in the middle of the château's 100-metre-long facade.

When the King's car came into view in brilliant sunshine along a kilometre-long avenue leading up to the château's gates, Monash called his men to attention. He, Blamey and the Australian Corps chief administrative officer, Brigadier-General Carruthers, greeted the King, who was accompanied only by two aides.

The King took the royal salute from the guard at the gate, inspected it with Monash and then walked with him along the drive. The King inspected the troops, stopping for small talk with several of the men. They then walked up the steps from the piazza to the reception room. Inside, Monash presented the King to the château's owner, the Marquis de Clermont-Tonnerre, 'a very old man with a long white beard'.

Monash then introduced his five divisional commanders with whom the King chatted. After ten minutes, they moved down to the piazza for the investiture. A sword, a small table and a footstool were arranged on a carpet on steps. With about a hundred of Monash's staff looking on, his name was called. He stepped up and stood to attention in front of the King.

'Kneel, please,' the King said.

Monash went down on his right knee.

The King then began to knight him by tapping him on the right shoulder. Monash began to rise before the King had swung the sword on to his left shoulder, but stayed down when he saw the King's movement. The investiture ended with the King saying: 'Arise, Sir John.'

He handed Monash the insignia of a Knight Commander of the Bath. The King smiled, pumped his hand and made a little speech 'commending my work and that of the Australian troops'.[28]

Onlookers applauded. The King then walked with Monash around the château's grounds inspecting the battle trophies.

The whole ceremony had been going just thirty minutes before the King's car pulled up at the steps and he left. Monash called for three cheers from the troops lining the drive. They didn't respond with much voice, especially those at the other end of the drive. Monash tried again, but the dispersed guard responded sporadically as before. It was a minor hiccup in an otherwise glittering occasion, captured for posterity on film.

Monash entry in his small diary for 12 August 1918, which he would list later as one of the three or four greatest days of his life, reflected its hectic mix of war and ceremony:

Indoors forenoon.

10 brigade captures Proyant.

Prepare for King's visit being made in front of château.

About 50 field guns, many trench mortars, machine-guns and other trophies.

Attend Army conference at Villers-Bretonneux.

12.30 Divisional Commanders attend.

Return to Corps 2.25 p.m.

The King due 2.30 arrives at about 3.00 p.m. Inspects guard walks to château steps. Am decorated with Star and Order of KCB. O'Keefe DMS Army KCMG. Later watches Boche transport and field ambulance being driven past and then departs.

Successful attack by 13 bge N of Somme. Capture 183 prisoners.[29]

The King noted in his diary on the same day:

Proceeding to Bertangles was received [by] General Monash, GOC

Australian Corps & his Generals & representatives from all the Australian divisions who are now fighting in this battle. I gave General Monash & General O'Keeff [sic] the KCB & knighted them. They showed me some of the many Guns and machine-guns & horses & carts & ambulances which they have just captured from the Germans, they got over 300 horses . . .[30]

After the tap on each shoulder, when he arose as KCB, Monash had received his battlefield honours. But there was still no thought about striding off to become a desk-bound, paper-shuffling general. The war had not yet been won. He was right in the middle of further attack plans. The well-wishers, and even the King's visit, would have been a distraction, no matter how much the visits were appreciated. Nobody was thinking that the war would not go into 1919. But Monash and other commanders were keen to drive home their advantage, now.

Murdoch kept pushing Hughes about the position of AIF GOC – General Officer Commanding, but was having no effect. The PM had seen the preparations for Hamel and had been impressed by Monash and his command. As a VIP visitor he experienced the usual deference from those he met and who recognised him as the King's first minister in Australia. Yet Hughes had also witnessed the reaction of the soldiers and officers to their commander. Two hundred thousand men and thousands of killing machines under the control of one man on a battlefield, with everyone formally acknowledging his power by speech, action and body language, was something else. It was tangible, raw potency. And if politicians understood one thing, it was power.

Hughes first received the news about Amiens from Munro Ferguson, who had cabled him on 8 August: 'Lieutenant-General Sir John Monash wishes me to convey to you on behalf of the Australian Corps that the Australian Flag was hoisted over Harbonnières today at noon.' These words would stay with Hughes for life. There was no chance of his now relieving Monash against his will. For the moment, he had become his favourite soldier. There were votes in battle wins like Hamel and Amiens. The PM saw the press reaction.

Murdoch and Bean were now left impotent. The best they could hope for was that Monash would sooner or later want the GOC. Murdoch had lost patience with White and indulged in a little less self-delusion when he wrote to Bean: 'I doubt very much if he [Hughes] will give White the Corps. That will follow ultimately, if White stops fooling about. He is every day proving himself to be less sound in his judgment than he should be.'[31] In fact, White had been serious and consistent. He remained in support of Monash.

Bean, in contrast to Murdoch, now developed doubts about his own judgement. He continued to intrigue with Murdoch but with far less fervour. Thirty-eight years later, he would write about the Bean–Murdoch 'high-intentioned but ill-judged intervention. That it resulted in no harm whatever was probably due to the magnanimity of both White and Monash.'[32]

After Amiens, Hughes could see the need for a strong politician, who had everyone's respect in London, as GOC. The war was reaching a critical stage, and he wanted to be in a position to make sure he could get his way. If the number of Australian casualties became unacceptable to the electorate, Hughes would be desperate to start pulling out the AIF. It was one thing to order it, and another to have it carried through in communication and directives from the British High Command in London to the Western Front. Hughes now told his cabinet that Birdwood should be replaced as GOC, but not by Monash, unless he wanted it, and everyone knew he would not. Hughes was saying Monash could have his choice. If he wished to stay Corps Commander, he could.

It seemed that Pearce would have to move to London to take up the GOC job. Out of courtesy to the much-respected Birdwood, Hughes on 12 August offered him the GOC position full time, which meant he would have to stop running the British Fifth Army. No one expected him to accept, but he did. Birdwood enjoyed Dominion troops and officers more than his own British soldiers. He sensed, too, that the AIF was going to continue at the forefront of the conflict. It would be more exciting, even rewarding. Some thought the offer a slight to Monash, but he could not be a politician and command the corps, especially in the current heated battles. Besides, Birdwood would not take up the full-time job until 30 November. The war was too preoccupying for such an important change at the moment.

Murdoch tried to stir the issue in an article in the Melbourne *Herald* that made the future juggling seem like a down-grade for Monash. But it had little impact. Too many eyes were now on the military struggle to worry about the shuffling of administrative chairs a long way from the front.

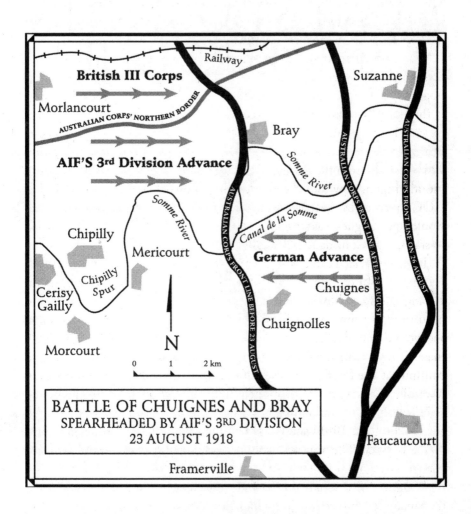

British III Corps

Railway

Suzanne

Morlancourt

AUSTRALIAN CORPS' NORTHERN BORDER

Bray

AIF'S 3rd Division Advance

Somme River

Somme River

Chipilly

Mericourt

Canal de la Somme

German Advance

Chipilly
Spur

Chuignes

Cerisy
Gailly

Chuignolles

N

Morcourt

0   1   2 km

AUSTRALIAN CORPS FRONT LINE BEFORE 23 AUGUST

AUSTRALIAN CORPS FRONT LINE AFTER 23 AUGUST

AUSTRALIAN CORPS FRONT LINE ON 26 AUGUST

BATTLE OF CHUIGNES AND BRAY
SPEARHEADED BY AIF'S 3RD DIVISION
23 AUGUST 1918

Faucaucourt

Framerville

18

JUGULAR DAYS: MONT ST QUENTIN AND PÉRONNE

The Australian Corps had a fourteen-and-a-half-kilometre front from north of the Somme to the Amiens railway line in the south on 12 August 1918. It was too long if Monash was to rotate his divisions and rest them. Rawlinson gave him another British division in reserve, which Monash preferred rather than shortening the front. He took on two extra Canadian divisions temporarily and an American regiment. This increased his command to more than eight divisions and 208,000 soldiers, which was equivalent to an army.

In a letter home, he spoke of the taxing time he was having, running the expanded corps and preparing battle plans. His weight was now down to just under seventy-one kilograms, one less than he had been a month earlier and a drop of six kilograms from a year ago. The intensity of Monash's work and his increased responsibilities were taking their toll. 'Along with his men,' Blamey wrote of his boss, 'he suffered severely from the strain of these last months. He became very thin, the skin hung loosely on his face. His characteristic attitude was one of deep thought.'[1] Monash was still using his dumbbells to keep his body toned, but he was more and more desk-bound as he worked longer and longer hours.

Monash's battle strategies and tactics were now a blueprint for the British Army. He explained them to Haig and the Third Army's General Byng as they planned another attack on 21 August. The long delay after the shattering events of 8–10 August was caused by Ludendorff scrambling together all his available reserves, drawn from all over the Western Front, to stop the push by the Australians and Canadians and, on their flanks, the

British and French. Byng had to bring in supplies of troops, transport and munitions, which delayed the next push. But when Byng's army did attack, it did well and facilitated a move up by III Corps, which had made next to no progress since 8 August, much to Monash's disappointment.

Meanwhile, he took time on 21 August to hold a prolonged battle conference for the British III Corps' 32nd Division and the Australian 1st Division. They were both expected to engage in the next operation, known as the Battle of Chuignes and Bray. It would be twice the size of Hamel. Both divisions were unfamiliar with Monash's special style, strategies and tactics. He had to explain his approach and preference for tanks, full artillery and air support. He now had two fine examples of small and large battles on which to base his lectures: Hamel and Amiens.

On 22 August, the 47th Division at last advanced past Albert and Meaulte.

The left flank of the Australian 3rd Division north of the Somme had moved up to bring Monash's corps square on to the river. It was positioned nicely on the forward slopes of the high plateau overlooking Bray and La Neuville, which were now targets for acquisition. The 3rd Division's 3rd Pioneer Battalion was busy rebuilding bridges over the Somme south of Bray and creating advanced posts on the north bank of the river.

While the engineers were doing their necessary work to prepare for Monash's corps to take control, the 3rd Division's extreme left flank – 9th Brigade – was having a tight battle in its push towards Bray. III Corps' 47th Division had faltered, which made the 9th Brigade's left flank vulnerable.

The 9th Brigade found refuge in a chalk pit and stood firm. They held the territory gained during the day, but Monash did not ask his soldiers to attempt to take Bray. He ordered them to wait until he had replanned the next moves, given the stiff German resistance, counter-attacks and the blocking of the 47th Division. Monash called up III Corps' 32nd Division. Then he considered this part of the Somme valley, which consisted of smaller broad, wooded valleys running north and south for up to eight kilometres. Clustered in them were several villages, such as Proyart, which Lieutenant Colonel Carter and his armoured vehicles had terrorised on 8 August, Chignolles, Herleville and Chuignes.

On 23 August, Monash ordered two brigades of Glasgow's 1st Division to attack along the Somme in a three-phase operation. In parallel, the 32nd Division was asked to capture the village of Herleville. 3rd Division's 9th Brigade was to take Bray.

Monash's intelligence was that the woods were heavily defended by German machine-gunners. He now called up mobile artillery and tanks, which, in the space of six weeks, were having an enormous impact on the war. Australian spies had managed to secure Ludendorff's plan of defence, which suited Monash. The German general had outposts and hidden machine-gun nests as the first line of defence. But, in contrast to earlier tactics, he had his soldiers form the main line of resistance forward rather than in the rear. It didn't prevent Monash's corps making a powerful thrust, which had a demoralising effect on the enemy.

The battle began at 4.45 a.m. with an artillery barrage, followed by a swift, hard attack by Monash's hybrid force. The tanks moved in line with the soldiers, who were ordered to fix bayonets in anticipation of meeting the bulk of soldiers early in the battle.

The tanks found that many of the German machine-gunners fought with courage. Some even stood their ground, firing until flattened. This proved an obstacle to the tank's juggernaut menace. The infantry was vital here. The most notable instance occurred when the 16th and 13th Battalions, with the 16th Lancashire Fusiliers, were ordered to advance across a kilometre of open ground just west of Vermandovillers and to remove Germans from the area. It was criss-crossed with German trenches (known collectively as Courtine Trench). The 16th moved into position, but the Fusiliers failed to link up. It was important that the Australians moved forward. Lieutenant Lawrence McCarthy, commanding D Company, decided to act without the Fusiliers. He led a platoon straight at the trenches, bombing them as they went. They were held up by two machine-guns nestled on an earth block, which were firing into the trench held by the 16th.

McCarthy called for Sergeant F. J. Robbins. They edged in front of the block and dropped into a trench. Seconds later, McCarthy shot a sentry, then set his sights on the machine-gunners who were causing his 16th Battalion distress. He ran forward, shot them, then moved on. He was now on a rollercoaster. McCarthy almost bumped into a German officer giving orders to about forty of his men. He shot the officer, whose men panicked and ran for a trench. Without a pause, McCarthy and Robbins attacked the trench with grenades. Within minutes, forty Germans, their hands held high or behind their heads, filed out of the trench in surrender.

In about seventeen minutes, McCarthy, supported by Robbins, had killed twenty Germans, captured fifty and seized all five of the troublesome machine-guns that had been blocking the 16th's advance. The effort earned McCarthy a VC, and rivalled the performances of Jacka in front of Windmill Ridge two years earlier and on Gallipoli.

Once this German defiance was overcome, the Australian soldiers, using their bayonets freely, were able to advance without fear of being mowed down by hidden assailants. There was much close combat, which gave the Australians more than an edge. They revelled in using the bayonet. Ever since Monash had taken over 4th Brigade, he had drilled his men in its use. It had proved an integral part of the Australian armoury on Gallipoli and the Western Front. In the Battle of Chuignes it was used to great advantage.

'The slaughter of the enemy in the tangled valleys was considerable,' Monash said, with less than delicate understatement, 'for our infantry are always vigorous bayonet fighters.'[2]

Apart from the usual booty of guns, Monash noted that the 3100 prisoners taken came from ten different regiments, which indicated Ludendorff's disorganised scramble to bolster the front in this area. The Germans were just as fierce fighters as the Allies. The 1st Division, suffering most with a thousand casualties, could attest to that. But the Germans were at a disadvantage without unified divisions and strong leadership. Monash read such signs as indicators that the Allies had to strike hard, often and without delay.

The British 32nd Division, inspired by Monash's order to use tanks, full artillery and air support, was successful too. Together the British and Australian forces seized 2.4 kilometres of country in a line from Herleville to the west of the town of Cappy. The Germans had been shoved back into barren, uninhabitable territory between the British–Australian line and the Somme, which had been laid waste by previous encounters.

Monash's sometimes unique, detailed strategies and tactics succeeded for the third battle in succession in fifty days.

He was mightily pleased with one acquisition: a huge 15-inch naval gun that had been pounding Amiens for a long time. The 1st Division's 3rd Battalion reached the monster first after clearing Arcy Wood with a bayonet charge. Its carriage, platform and concrete foundations weighed more than 500 tonnes. Its barrel, at just under twenty-two metres, was longer than a cricket pitch. Monash called it 'the largest single trophy of the war'. It was a fair claim when put in the perspective of the thousands of deaths it had caused in the vital city and its surrounds, not to mention the destruction of buildings and monuments. This thumper had a range of forty kilometres and fired one-tonne projectiles.[3]

Monash's appreciation of German engineering skills came to the fore as he examined the massive weapon. He judged it was similar to the type 'used in German Dreadnoughts and never intended by its original designers for use on land'. This is where the innovation came in. It had come from the giant German steel-maker Krupp.

'It had been installed with the elaborate completeness of German methods,' Monash wrote with undisguised admiration, wearing his engineer's hard hat and some ancestral pride. 'A double rail track, several miles long, had been built to the site, for the transport of the gun and its parts. It was electrically trained and elevated. Its ammunition was handled and loaded by mechanical means. The adjacent hillside had been tunnelled to receive the operating machinery, and the supplies of shells, cartridges and fuses.'[4]

The monster gun had first started firing on 2 June, with its maximum capacity of twenty-eight rounds a day. Like the despondent prisoners, it would never fire in anger again. The silencing of it, in Monash's mind, was symbolic of far more than the considerable salvation of Amiens. He interrogated some of the captured officers and found them more defeated than any others he had ever questioned. It made him contemplate for the first time that the war might not stretch into 1919 after all.

The thought made him even more determined to pursue the enemy. Monash had been thwarted after 8–10 August when he wanted to continue east and drive the Germans out of the bend in the Somme. Instead, Rawlinson had been cautious. The weight of failure in the collective mind of the British High Command since 1916 had not been balanced yet by the concept of success. He couldn't further countenance that the Germans were vulnerable and perhaps broken. Instead he had ordered the Fourth Army to push southeast. Haig supported Rawlinson, saying that his Fourth Army should ease up after its successes.

There was no immediate need, Haig and Rawlinson reckoned, to push the Germans from the Somme near Péronne, the old turreted, ramparted and moated city at the foot of Mont St Quentin.

Monash disagreed. On the surface, his position seemed to have been swapped with that of his superiors. In the past, Monash had been appalled by Haig's desire to push on in adverse ill-planned conditions. Passchendaele was the prime example in Monash's experience. But there had been many just as ill-conceived plans through 1916 involving the AIF, the other Dominion forces, the British and the French. Now, Monash was the bold one. Haig and Rawlinson, faced with real success for the first time in the war, were cautious.

The timing was the difference. Monash chose the moment based on in-depth assessments of the enemy's capacities instead of attacking blindly as his superiors had done, with disastrous consequences for tens of thousands of soldiers. It was better, he thought, to strike hard and demoralise the Germans now while they were relatively vulnerable. He knew that future battles would not be as decisive as Hamel or Amiens. The further German backs were pushed against the wall, the harder they would fight and defend.

Monash was relying here on his adage of better to have a plan than no plan at all. There was one other factor, which distinguished his thinking now from that of his superiors. He had absolute, unbending faith in the fighting skills of his AIF machine. Despite its being depleted, overworked and suffering from battle fatigue, he had no equivocation in now not just propagandising but also believing that his soldiers were invincible. With the lack of tanks, artillery, machine-guns and other weapons, in the end the raw courage and fighting skills of his men would be, in his mind, the key to ultimate success. He had seen them on Gallipoli defending the indefensible: 12,500 Anzacs against 40,000 Turks on the high ground. He had directed them in Flanders and on the Somme, as they took everything before them, except in the morass of Passchendaele, which presented even tougher conditions than at Anzac Cove and Sari Bair.

Monash knew the enormous fortitude of his diggers. He was aware of a sense of daring that saw them discussing the gaining of VCs as if it were a competition. It all helped his grand plan to give the AIF a solid sense of identity independent of the British, something that Monash was fostering.

In every battalion there were men like Jacka, who, when an advance was stopped or the enemy was set to make a breakthrough, would risk life and limb to reverse the position and put the Australians back on the offensive. These deeds, tumbling on top of each other, would inspire squads of ordinary men to achieve extraordinary deeds against the odds.

Monash was aware that they wished to deliver the *coup de grâce* to the Germans. They had volunteered to come 20,000 kilometres to do it. They had suffered and endured in the trenches from the head of Monash Valley, the Nek and Sari Bair, to Bullecourt, Broodseinde, Messines and Pass-chendaele. They had seen their mates killed every hour in battle. Every survivor from 1915 until now had waited, fought and struggled in the hope of being in the position to be part of decisive a win.

The Australians were standing taller now that they were having an impact as a national entity. They were aware they would be spearheading the push for a knockout victory. The diggers were the most hardened of soldiers. They had experienced – in varying degrees depending on the individual – the contra-dictory, inhumane feelings that killing, individually or *en masse*, produces. Fear, hate, horror, seduction, pleasure and the simple, often detached and remote sense of 'scoring' a hit on the enemy were high on the list.

Even those like Monash himself with a secret aversion to the business of war had developed a desensitised attitude, even an addiction, to killing. In a private letter to Vic a year earlier he had expressed his deeper thoughts, which, if known by the regulars in the British and Australian forces, would have confirmed their attitudes about militiamen, even though he was so well proven in battle.

> I hate the business of war – the horror of it, the waste, the destruc-tion, the inefficiency [he wrote]. My only consolation is the sense of doing my duty to my country, which has placed a grave responsibil-ity upon me. I owe something to the men whose lives and honour are in my hand to do as I will. But once my duty is done and honourably discharged, I shall with a sigh of relief turn my back once and for all on the possibility of ever again having to go through such an awful time.[5]

Now eighteen months on and plenty of battles later, Monash had buried himself deeper in the business that at heart he detested. So much so that he now believed it was time to let his soldiers fulfil the desires that he had much do to with creating and refining.

He kept urging a harder thrust due east. On 24 August Rawlinson at last gave in and approved the move. Monash was elated, but then was disap-pointed the next day when Rawlinson changed his mind. His excuse was that the appearance of a new German division, the 41st, was evidence that the enemy was reinforcing, not withdrawing. Monash protested that they had already taken hundreds of them prisoner. His corps could drive them back to the Hindenburg Line – the last and strongest German line of defence. Rawlinson didn't see it that way. Monash corrected his chief. Yes, the Germans had reinforced, but they were a hotchpotch of uncoordinated groups and nationalities: Prussians, Bavarians, Saxons and Württembergers. They were not well led. They could be smashed. He pointed out that there were more signs of running than withdrawal when the enemy was challenged. In the past withdrawal signified an ordered pulling back and a policy of destruction. The Battle of Chuignes had shown that the enemy did not have an organised plan for retreat. The German force in the area had an almost impassable river behind them – with crossings at three points: Brie, Eterpigny and Péronne. Once pushed over the river east to Mont St Quentin and the city of Péronne, the next fall-back position after that would be the last one: the highly fortified Hindenburg Line.

Monash added: 'He [Rawlinson] has got a Corps flushed with recent victories, while he [the enemy] has been suffering a succession of defeats and heavy losses.'[6]

Rawlinson wouldn't budge. His Fourth Army had done its job in drawing enemy reserves to its front. Rawlinson didn't have any tanks left. They had been destroyed, broken down or given to other forces, and would take a month to replace. Monash didn't care. He had other tactics and strategies to overcome their loss. Rawlinson would not agree. It was time for another army to take up the 'burden'. 'The Fourth Army would now mark time,' he said, 'and await events elsewhere.'[7]

But Monash squeezed concessions out of his chief. He could shorten his front and let the French take over some of it. This would allow Monash to concentrate his interest east. There was also a little out clause in Fourth Army policy, which was not expressed in the discussion of 25 August, but nevertheless was there for everyone to adhere to: 'Touch must be kept with the enemy.'

It was all Monash needed. The lawyer in him was prepared to manipulate the directive and help the aggressive military commander out so that he could carry on with his and the AIF's war. He was tired of waiting for Rawlinson to do something. The Fourth Army Commander's intransigence was mainly because of the grand schemes of Haig and Foch right along the front. Rawlinson was restrained and was under orders to hold Monash and his like-minded commanders back.

Yet staying in touch justified making more than incursions in the area Monash had been denied for nearly three weeks. He didn't have tanks, but he did have eight brigades of field artillery. On 27 August he ordered 'vigorous patrolling'. It was a precursor for his taking further calculated risks.

To overcome the absence of tanks, which had helped protect the infantry on the three major battles of Hamel, Amiens and Chuignes–Bray, Monash had two innovations. The first was to let infantry commanders control mobile battery guns. They would help counter machine-guns. The second was to insist that all batteries should carry twenty per cent smoke shells. The gunners didn't like this. They wanted all the destructive power they could get. But smoke shells blinded the German machine-gunners. 'A few rounds judiciously placed screened the approach of our entry,' Monash noted, 'and many a machine-gun post thereby rushed by us from the flanks or even from the rear.'

Hobbs (1st Division) and Rosenthal (2nd Division) had both been gunners. They backed Monash on this brilliant tactic. Again, his pain-staking effort to protect advancing infantry was foremost in his thinking. He used technology and ideas in detailed tactics that no other corps commander would find the time or the inclination to concern himself with, let alone comprehend at the battle face.[8]

Now the infantry could move forward knowing that the Australian battery gunners would either blast or blind the machine-gunners. Yet still special acts of bravery were needed to push the advantage.

The 41st battalion was having trouble on the Somme's banks trying to make Curlu. They were held up by machine-guns hidden in Fargny Wood. Lance Corporal Bernard Gordon, emulating Jacka and McCarthy, decided to attempt a breakthrough. Working alone and showing uncommon cool, he moved forward, looking for German officers. He came across two, bailed them up and caused the capture of sixty-one of their men, along with the six machine-guns that had been so hazardous. Gordon would also receive the VC.

The road to Curlu was now less troublesome, although the Germans provided continued tough opposition.[9]

By the night of 27 August, the Australian Corps had pushed its line another kilometre or so east past the villages of Fontaine, Vermandovillers and Foucaucourt on the main road. The latter had to be bombarded with

A wee sense of ennui: Monash (seated) with the Prince of Wales (later King Edward VIII) at a London function in October 1918, days after Monash's AIF had smashed the great German defence fortifications, the Hindenburg Line. The Prince, here looking bored, was Monash's least favourite royal.

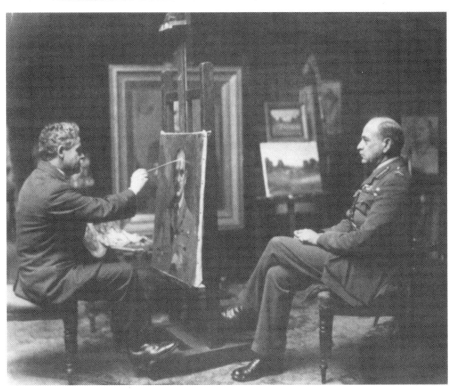

Portrait of an artist and subject: Monash being painted by James Quinn in 1919. He was in demand for preserving on canvas in 1918 and 1919.

The re-run: Monash and daughter, Bertha, at a French war cemetery in May 1919, while on a four-day tour of the battlefields of Flanders and France. Bertha kept a succinct diary of their travels.

Victory march: Monash leading the Australian troops in a London victory march on 19 July 1919. The saluting base had been erected for the King in front of Buckingham Palace. (Australian War Memorial Negative No. D00829)

Return of the conqueror: Monash and Vic return home from England on Boxing Day 1919. Vic, who was gravely ill, put on a brave face to be with her husband. She died of cancer two months later.

Let there be light: Monash (second from right) in 1921, aged 55 and now chairman of the State Electricity Commission (SEC), at the turning of the first sod on the site for the Yallourn Power House. On Monash's left is Commissioner Sir Robert Gibson. On Monash's right is Commissioner George Swinburne.

The lovers: Monash and Lizette Bentwitch at the 1925 Melbourne Cup. They were partners during the war and then from 1920 to 1931, after Vic's death.

The force and the source: Monash in 1926, aged 60, holds a lump of brown coal at the Yallourn site, two years after electricity began to flow. Only someone with Monash's vision, political skills and drive could have built such a successful industry from scratch.

Good public relations: Monash (second from right) in 1926 shows a group of State parliamentarians around Yallourn. He never failed to show off the town and its works, knowing that he would have to lobby the government for funds that would expand SEC operations.

Highly decorated: John Monash, with medals and sword on 25 April 1927. He led 30,000 diggers in an Anzac Day March reviewed by his favourite royal, the Duke of York (the future King George VI).

Father of the Anzac Day march: Monash speaks at Anzac Day, 1927, aged 61. He did more than anyone to commemorate 25 April and honour the men that had fought and died for Australia in World War I.

The academic: Monash as vice-chancellor of the University of Melbourne, at the conferring of degrees in 1930. On his left is the chancellor, Sir John MacFarland. Monash held the position from 1923 until his death in 1931. Education ranked high with his other interests, which included engineering, law, music, literature and most other areas of the arts.

Doting grandfather: Monash in late 1929, aged 64, with his grandchildren: Colin Bennett (cradled), Betty aged three, and David aged five. He enjoyed their company in his latter years.

Elder statesman: Monash, in early 1931, when he represented Australia at the opening of the city of New Delhi, India.

Last portrait: Aged 66 in mid-1931, a few months before his death.
(Australian War Memorial Negative No. H15650)

In state: Monash's body lying in state on 9 October 1931 at Queen's Hall, Parliament House, Melbourne, a day after his death. It remained there until Sunday 11 October, when more than 300,000 people lined the route of his funeral procession.

artillery before it was captured, and only then after a hard fight by 5th Division, demonstrating that pockets of Germans were prepared to stay and fight. The 2nd Division also found obstacles in Tivoli Wood.

The corps' move extended north about two and a half kilometres to the Cappy bend in the river, and included the crossing at Eclusier.

On 28 August the corps advanced more than a kilometre again, reaching the line Genermont–Berry-en-Santerre–Estrees–Frise. The next day all four divisions in the action had moved further east. The 3rd Division north of the Somme had seized the villages of Suzanne, Vaux, Curlu, Hem and Cléry. The corps' three divisions south of the river were in line with the 3rd and 'stood upon the high ground sloping down to the Somme, with the river in sight from opposite Cléry, past Péronne and as far south as St Christ'.[10]

The Australians set the pace of the conflict, and the Germans were again forced into a disorganised withdrawal. Guns, ammunition and stores were left in their wake. HQs, hospitals and dressing stations were abandoned like ghost sites, with equipment intact and missing one factor: someone to operate them. Monash now had control of the whole of the Somme Valley from Cléry (on the horseshoe river bend) westward, and was having bridges repaired.

The rapidity of events was causing him to consider a plan he had held ever since 9 August when he took control of Chipilly Spur. He was in place north and south of the Somme. His aim was to take control of the line of the river from the east. If resistance was strong, his fallback plan was to make an assault from the north. He wanted to make the Somme useless to the enemy as a defence line, and force that final retreat to the Hindenburg Line. Monash wished to do it without reliance or assistance from any other corps. It had to be 'an exclusively Australian achievement'.[11]

Monash's obscure object of desire was Mont St Quentin. It had to be taken, along with Péronne, a river town fortress, which lay one and a half kilometres south. From a high point at the bend in the river, the Mont looked harmless and did not stand out in the landscape. It reached about 110 metres at its apogee, and protected the northern way into Péronne. Possession of it meant control of approaches from all points of the compass. The hill was riddled with underground galleries and huge, well-furnished shelters. Domination of the hill – it was hardly a mount – also allowed command of both stretches of the river.

There were problems in tackling the Mont. The Germans had put off and defeated previous attempts. They sited their heaving artillery there. It was ringed with wire entanglements. Its forward slopes were flat and bare, making attacking troops easy targets.

Many of Monash's officers and soldiers studied it. Those who had been on Gallipoli were uneasy. It reminded some of Hill 60. Others shuddered at the memory of Chunuk Bair and the Nek. Not only was its disposition forbidding from an attacking point of view but also Ludendorff had put one of the German Army's finest divisions, the 2nd Prussian Guards, on the Mont to hold it. Unlike some of their disorganised, demoralised countrymen, they would not run. They would fight. This division included the Kaiserin Augusta and Kaiser Alexander Regiments, which had a fame and tradition similar to those of British regiments like the Grenadier and Coldstream Guards.

Monash calculated that if he could take this hill and Péronne, then the Germans would have nowhere to run but east.

He called a meeting on the late afternoon of 29 August to elucidate the plan that didn't include tanks or artillery. Present were Hobbs (5th Division), Rosenthal (2nd Division) and Gellibrand (3rd Division), along with General Lambert of the British 32nd Division.

Monash would use the 32nd Division as a decoy and defence. His 3rd, 5th and 2nd Divisions were to engage in a three-pronged attack. The 3rd would go for the high ground northeast of Cléry, a village right on the top of a horseshoe bend in the river about four kilometres east of Mont St Quentin. The 3rd's ultimate objective, Bouchavesnes village on the Bapaume road, was two kilometres north of the Mont.

The 5th had to strike over the river at Péronne, which was situated about five kilometres down the river southeast of Cléry. It aimed to cross the Somme Canal and marshland and take the high ground south of Péronne. The ultimate goal was the wooded spur east of Péronne.

Rosenthal's 2nd Division had mission impossible. It was to cross the river and take Mont St Quentin head-on.

This battle was too big to be called 'vigorous patrolling'. It was an attempt to take two key strategic points with a complex plan involving parts of four divisions. It would be different from anything Monash had attempted. It would be less of a set-piece project and more fluid in operation. A crude comparison could be made with the movable battle on Gallipoli at Sari Bair. But he had not been in charge there. In addition, he had strong mobile artillery back-up this time. And there was the considerable advantage of leading troops, no matter how fatigued, who had a recent history of winning.

Monash's concern was not the certain fickleness of the conflict. He only worried about communications. As long as his left division knew what his right was doing, and he could direct all of them, then he was ready. Perhaps his finest skills were his speed of decision-making and adaptability. They had been tested many times in the heat of battles and skirmishes. As long as Monash had his forensically designed blueprint plans to begin with, he was confident of being able to change direction and tactics. Commanding four different divisions that all had different objectives did not faze him.

Before he could begin, Monash had to show Rawlinson his plan. Would the Army Commander throw up his hands and say it was too big an assignment in view of Haig's current policy about the Fourth Army marking time? Or was it just too big a risk? No one had been able to dislodge these two fortified positions before.

Rawlinson came to visit him and Blamey on the afternoon before the battle was set to commence. Maps were laid for the chief and Montgomery to peruse. There was much puffing of smoke and some diffident coughing. Rawlinson asked a lot of questions and was sceptical.

'And so you think you're going to take Mont St Quentin with three battalions!' Rawlinson remarked. 'What presumption! However, I don't think I ought to stop you! So go ahead and try – and I wish you luck!'[12]

Monash was unconcerned that Rawlinson didn't think he could do it. The chief was letting him have a go. Unlike Monash's superiors – Haig and Rawlinson in particular – he had yet to have total command over a major setback. Rawlinson's decision to defy Haig's directives and let Monash loose was almost as if he was inviting him to take a fall and join the ranks of every member of the British High Command.

Monash's first flexibility test came on the first day, 30 August. The bridges he had in mind for crossing by the 2nd and 5th Divisions were either under attack or destroyed. That meant their direct assaults – the 2nd on Mont St Quentin and the 5th, in effect, on Péronne – were impossible. Monash then applied Plan B, the assault from the north. Both these divisions were sent to cross the Somme on the top of the horseshoe bend. The revised aim was to move through Cléry and behind the 3rd Division front, which would bring them to Mont St Quentin from the north. He ordered the British 32nd Division to start a clamour on the river for seven kilometres as if it were attempting to cross. This not so faint feint – another Monash illusion – distracted the Germans on the Mont.

But the 32nd found they had to make a lot of noise. The 5th Brigade of Rosenthal's 2nd Division was now down to just 1320 men, not much above battalion size. It had a hard, long trek through the night. First the diggers were blocked at one bridge because the 3rd Division had not yet taken Cléry on the river, let alone the Bouchavesnes Spur, a rugged two kilometres northeast. Rosenthal pushed the 5th Brigade three kilometres further west on the top of the now-popular horseshoe bend to a crossing that Monash had had repaired at Feuillères.

The 33rd Battalion (of Gellibrand's 3rd Division) moved from Cléry east with the objective of taking a wood (Bois Madame) one kilometre south of Bouchavesnes. They were not quite prepared for the garrison of Germans and hundreds of machine-guns. An hour into the attack on 30 August, the 33rd was held up by incessant heavy fire from the southeast edge of the wood. Its leader, Lieutenant Colonel L. J. Morshead, was beginning to think the mission to take the wood was impossible without another 500 men when he was distracted by one of his soldiers, Private George Cartwright, who stood up in the heavy fire.

Cartwright, his rifle at his shoulder, ran forward firing. He killed three Germans in a machine-gun crew at the post that was pinning down the 33rd. In the pandemonium he kept advancing and hurled a grenade at the post. It exploded on target. Cartwright kept coming. He jumped into the post, took control of the machine-gun and aimed it at the eight Germans still alive. They surrendered.

All this had occurred in full view of the rest of the battalion. Morshead and every Australian got to his feet and cheered Cartwright. It was as if they were watching a footballer making a brilliant, baulking run. Seconds later, they jumped down again. Inspired, the battalion kept attacking.

The intrepid private's bold move and the lift it gave the rest of the force was the type of act that Monash gambled on in his ambitious plan without his previous reliance on tanks. It was outside the rules, and would be regarded by British and enemy officers as 'undisciplined'. Technically this was true. Cartwright had broken ranks, and he had run, but not away. If such crazed but heroic actions gained ground and won encounters that lead to battle victories, Monash was happy to let it go on. He would even encourage it.

While the 33rd Battalion's advance to clear the wood (and so help destroy the German protection north of Mont St Quentin) looked promising, a lot depended on McNicoll and his 38th Battalion (of the 3rd Division), now down to fewer than 400 able soldiers, a third its full strength. They had been fighting for seventy hours when they reached the outskirts of Cléry.

At 9 p.m. on 30 August, Gellibrand ordered the long-suffering McNicoll to attack Cléry and so take the spur to its north the next morning, beginning at 3 a.m. McNicoll was disgruntled by this shock directive from a man for whom he had little time. He told Gellibrand that his men were fatigued and in need of rest. Gellibrand was not sympathetic, but nor was he bullying. Monash had told him to avoid confronting McNicoll. Instead, Gellibrand said that the 'old man' had ordered that Cléry had to be taken before Rosenthal's attack on the Mont. It was vital to corps plans. That was enough for McNicoll. He would do anything Monash wanted.

Next morning Rosenthal's 5th Brigade was stalled on the bridge at Feuillères. Artillery fire from Cléry was preventing them from reaching the north bank. Gellibrand ordered McNicoll to get rid of the problem.

It was then 11 a.m. on 31 August, six hours later than Monash wanted. Events were happening in slow motion rather than at a speed to test a commander. McNicoll, demonstrating his longevity and reliability as a fighting commander, took fifty men into Cléry. After a brief fight they captured fifty-nine Germans, then fought off a counter-attack. In the process, the artillery fire was silenced. Rosenthal's brigade could go over the bridge at Feuillères. It battled to control the region east of the crossing (at Ommiécourt) that had been smashed before. The bridge was repaired. Now there was an easy access route to the north of the horseshoe.

The delays caused Monash to postpone the assault on Mont St Quentin until 5 a.m. the next morning, 1 September. He saw the advantage of bringing up artillery to Cléry and strategic points on the south bank of the river overlooking the prospective target of the Mont.

The extra time also allowed some rest for the diggers. Rosenthal decided to keep 330 men of the 18th Battalion – all that was left of it – in reserve. The brigade was left with just 890 men – less than a battalion in size – for the attack. One bizarre tactic was that the men would charge the Mont yelling to make it seem as if it were a normal-sized brigade of 4000 men attacking.

There was no softening up by the artillery. Monash wanted a complete surprise with the attack by first Rosenthal's 5th Brigade (of 2nd Division) on the Mont at 5 a.m. and by 14th Brigade (of Hobbs' 5th Division) on Péronne, set for 6 a.m.

The tired troops were issued with an extra shot of rum just before attack time – 5 a.m. On an overcast morning, 5th Brigade made its rush like demented Banshees along three lines. One 'battalion' went left and hit the ruined village of Feuillaucort. Another went straight for the Mont. The third went right, hoping to move on the inside of the village of St Denis. The diggers used rifle grenades and were backed by Lewis guns. Each section alternatively gave its neighbour covering fire. They overwhelmed a brickworks harbouring seven machine-guns and a small sugar refinery. The Australians continued up the slopes.

5th Brigade's centre battalion passed through the ruins of the actual town of Mont St Quentin by 7 a.m. It was pushed back by the defenders, and had to take refuge in an old line of trenches. The right battalion also had a tough battle, encountering heavy machine-gun fire from another ruined sugar refinery. Both these battalions had trouble for the next hour in close fighting where flashing bayonets dominated. At 8 a.m. the 5th pushed the Australian flag into the dirt more than halfway up the Mont.

But it was premature.

Monash hurried in the 6th Brigade and then the 7th to assist.

It became a long make-or-break day of further fierce fighting. There several individual acts of inspiration similar to that by Cartwright just north of the Mont that lifted the entire 2nd Division and made Monash's objectives look possible. Sergeant Albert Lowerson led a company through the right of Mont St Quentin village, taking out German positions in the town. They came to an abrupt halt on the edge of town. There, in a huge crater, was a stronghold of Germans manning a dozen machine-guns. Lowerson went into action. He spread his soldiers around the crater. On

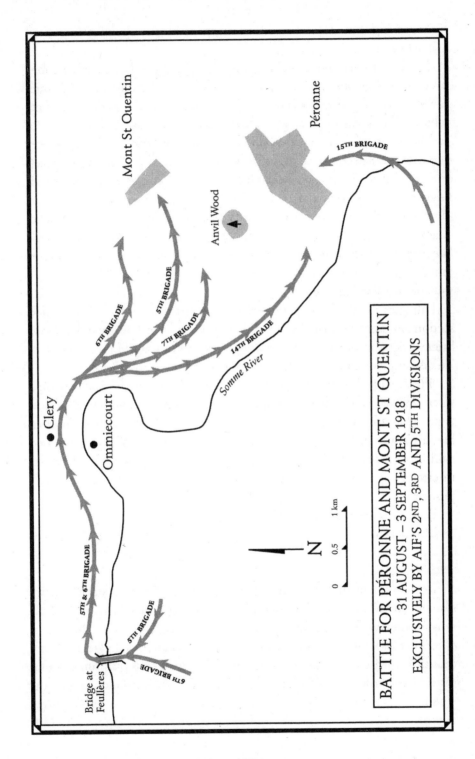

BATTLE FOR PÉRONNE AND MONT ST QUENTIN
31 AUGUST – 3 SEPTEMBER 1918
EXCLUSIVELY BY AIF'S 2ND, 3RD AND 5TH DIVISIONS

his command, he led the charge. The company took the guns and captured thirty prisoners.

Further around and down the Mont, a company's advance was blocked by barbed wire. Private Robert Mactier was sent forward to investigate. Armed with a revolver and grenades, he dashed to the wire in front of his fellow soldiers. He hurled a grenade that seemed to make a direct hit on a machine-gun nest in a trench. Without hesitation, Mactier climbed over the wire, dashed to the trench and shot the stunned gun grew. He tossed the gun out to cheers from his onlooking mates. His adrenalin pumping, Mactier then dashed to two other trenches and repeated his acts. Now on fierce autopilot, Mactier headed for a fourth German gun crew. But its members had seen the mayhem he had created. They had just enough seconds to aim their weapons at him and fire. Mactier was hit by a dozen bullets and fell dead metres short of his objective. He had lost the digger's version of Russian roulette.

No one knew what motivated this laconic soldier, who reminded people of Jacka, to do what he did. No one recalled him talking about other similar exploits. But his performance had not been in vain. The rest of his company found another level of courage and took the position.

Further up the Mont, Lieutenant Edgar Towner, of the 2nd Machine Gun Battalion, attached to the infantry, showed his ingenuity and guts in equal measure when he single-handedly captured a German gun. He then used his experience to turn the weapon on other enemy positions exposed to him. This inflicted a score of casualties. In the process he captured twenty-five prisoners and called for his battalion to advance up the Mont. Towner, in a prime position, gave support to the assaulting infantry.

These three instances of heroics earned each man the VC. Their efforts and tactical skills energised the 2nd Division at a time when Rosenthal, like all the commanders, was concerned about the fitness of his men for such demands.

By late afternoon, thousands of corpses littered the slopes and marshy flats. In the early evening brigadiers began reporting in that Mont St Quentin was Australia's. This time the flag was thumped in right on top of the hill.

Monash's instincts about his men and confidence in them was justified. But if the 5th Division couldn't take Péronne, his grand plan for a wholly Australian battle victory in the toughest and challenging conditions might end in futility.

✕

The night before the Mont was taken, Monash pushed the 5th Division's 14th Brigade into the action, ordering them to take Péronne. But it was easier said than done. The brigade had to march up the south side of the river to the repaired bridge at Ommiécourt and then down the north bank. It took them ten hours, until late evening, to hike the eleven kilometres. Monash was not happy. He told Hobbs that they should have moved faster. Hobbs objected. His men were struggling before the march even began.

'I was compelled to harden my heart,' Monash said. 'It was imperative to recognize a great opportunity and to seize it unflinchingly.'[13]

Monash could almost smell a double victory. He was pushing harder than ever. His preoccupation, obsession and *raison d'être* during the war was to win it. In these moments, as at Messines, his compassion and pity temporarily went out the window of his HQ dugout. He was squeezing the last smidgen of effort from his fatigued diggers. In this respect, he was like every other outstanding commander in history. But Monash, with command of almost a modern army, with all the technical accoutrements, which needed his exceptional skills to utilise, had far more raw fighting power at his disposal than any commander before this war. Add to this his use of engineers to rebuild bridges, viaducts, culverts, railways and roads, and his force had an unprecedented adaptability, especially in battles of relentless attack and pursuit. He had built a formidable machine that could not be blocked or stopped from coming at the enemy.

Yet still there was the human element. The soldiers were cogs in Monash's machine but not robots. Victory against such a mighty foe, even when it might have been buckling, still needed almost a superhuman effort. His soldiers still had to be pushed to topple the German giant. There was no room for mercy for the enemy or, at the crunch, his own men.

Bean, realising the futility of continuing his attempt to oust Monash, studied him with surprising, if belated, objectivity. 'In this decisive fighting,' he reflected (much later) in his official history of the war, 'he was right to work his troops to the extreme limit of their endurance.' Bean had seen enough conflict since 1915 to appreciate and comprehend that mental and physical strength counted as much as brute force in critical moments. 'At such times victory often goes to the troops that hold out the longest, withstanding strains, toil or exhaustion in perhaps unbelievable degree for an unbelievable time.'[14]

'Casualties no longer matter,' Monash said, uttering his only (recorded) insensitive or tyrannical remark of the entire war.[15] He had to resign himself to the fact that his soldiers were fighting the kind of battle that he had tried to minimise, even avoid, more than any other commander of either side. Now that they were in the middle of the thrust, stab and parry of close combat there was no other attitude for a leader to take. Anything short of ruthlessness against the crack Prussian Guards and specially selected volunteers would have led to defeat. Monash was compelled to keep the pressure on more than at any point in the war.

The Germans had turned Péronne into a fort. A moat and strong ramparts where a hundred machine-guns had been posted surrounded the ancient town. It had been a fortified town since the Roman invasion, and the massive ramparts were built in the ninth century. It was besieged and heavily damaged in 1870 during the Franco-Prussian War. The Germans invaded Péronne in 1914. It became to them what Amiens was to the British. The town was pushed and pulled by the opposing forces from then on. In August 1916 the Germans held it and prevented the Allies getting closer than Biaches, one and a half kilometres west of the Somme. In March 1917 the Allies regained it, but the Germans destroyed much of the town before falling back to the Hindenburg Line. In the March 1918 offensive, they regained Péronne and had to rebuild the results of their own destruction. But they did it with a will. Péronne was the last major stronghold before the Hindenburg Line.

The German High Command called for volunteers to defend the town. These would include the most willing, capable fighters in the still strong remnants of the German Army. The Péronne garrison commander hand-picked those who put their hand up from many different regiments. The men knew they would be making a last stand against the Australians, who had developed a reputation in the line opposite them for being relentless, uncompromising killers. The selections were tested too by being told to expect tank attacks. Those who didn't blink at the prospect of these two foes coming at them received the nod.

Another obstacle for the Australians was barbed wire. It ran all over the river's marshy flats from Cléry southeast across to the Mont and Péronne. The trick was finding the way through it. In 1917 both the Germans and French had cut or blasted paths in their efforts to occupy the area. The terrain itself created another barrier to the Australian force. Isolated sugar refineries and brick works afforded the only cover. But they were a dangerous mirage. All of them were manned as forward posts. They would not be easy to negotiate.

Monash called for a supreme effort by Hobbs' 14th Brigade against the volunteers at Péronne. It responded. The 54th battalion had to take the ground between the town and the river. While its Lewis gunner engaged the German machine-gunners, infantry rushed forward, ripped out pickets and scrambled under the wire. Many of them reached open territory but became easy prey for the machine-gunners at the ramparts. The situation demanded desperate action.

Two corporals – Alex Buckley and Arthur Hall – rose to the occasion. Slithering beyond the wire, they crept up on two separate machine-gun posts. They rushed and surprised their targets, capturing thirty German volunteers and eight machine-guns. This opened the way for the battalion to cross the swamp and waterway. They reached the centre of the town, where Buckley was killed attempting a repeat of his stalking of a machine-gun post.

Meanwhile the 14th Brigade's 53rd Battalion had to clear Anvil Wood in the approach to Péronne. The Germans turned their guns on the wood. A 77-millimetre field gun did most damage to the Australians. Private William Currey saw some of his mates killed. He snapped, and attempted to break the impasse by charging the field gun, which could not be manoeuvred quickly enough to stop him. He killed the crew and took control of the weapon. In a controlled rage, he then rushed a machine-gun post and broke it up. After these heroics, he was unstoppable. He volunteered to his commander to enter the wood and retrieve a company before the Australians began firing artillery. Currey succeeded.

He, Hall and Buckley were all awarded VCs. Their efforts were again typical of those Monash had come to rely on to lift all those who witnessed them while at the same time destroying German morale.

These uncommon acts and their resultant stimuli to the battered battalions seemed to give the 5th Division the fortress town by the evening of 1 September, but a powerful German counter-attack didn't allow the diggers to seal it. The German volunteers, like their counterparts on the Mont, would not capitulate unless every man sensed their position was hopeless.

The close, intense, continuous fighting, which Monash had always tried to spare his men, had taken its toll in casualties and on morale. A few cracks began to appear. The 59th Battalion, which seemed to have done the job at Péronne, was out of the line, resting. Most of the exhausted men were sleeping when roused to go back into action after an enemy counter-attack. A handful of the men rebelled and refused to go. It was only when reminded of the consequences of refusing to fight (court martial) that they went back into the fray. Almost out on their feet, many of the men were fighting on memory, and struggling.

The pressure from the commanders continued. Monash urged them to push for a win. This was passed down to the battalion commanders, who called on their men for one last supreme effort. By mid-morning on 2 September, Péronne, which had been battled over by other armies in other wars for centuries, was also under Australian control.

The two main objectives of the Mont and Péronne had been achieved. But there was still some heavy mopping up to do. On 2 September most Germans were on the retreat to the Hindenburg Line. Yet some fell back to the twin villages of Allaines and Haut-Allaines on the Canal du Nord. It lay two kilometres south of Bouchavesnes and two kilometres northeast of Mont St Quentin – too close for comfort for Monash. He asked Gelli-brand and his 3rd Division to get rid of them. He gave the assignment to the 43rd Battalion. It had to clear a triangle of ground between the 2nd Division advancing northeast and a British division Monash had brought in to move east.

'Mopping up' was a euphemism for what ensued. The Germans, aware that they could not now retreat, made a last stand in a network of trenches in the target triangle. They engaged with heavy machine-gun fire. The 43rd found itself bogged down. This time another corporal – Lawrence Weathers – decided to attempt to break through. He ran at two trenches hurling grenades. The German commander was killed. Weathers hurried back for more grenades, calling for mates to help him. Three stepped forward to go with him back into the heavy fire. They had a quick conference. The plan was simple. One of them – Lance Corporal H. H. Thompson – would keep the enemy well down in the trenches by firing a Lewis gun, which would be cover for Weathers. He dashed to a trench, jumped on a parapet and hurled grenades into the trench. The stunned enemy capitulated at what they saw as madness they could not defend against. A hundred and eighty of them filed out of the trenches as prisoners.

Weathers' performance earned him a VC. It also ended all resistance in the battles for Mont St Quentin and Péronne.

✕

Easier mopping up over the whole area took another few hours. Three thousand prisoners were taken, mainly from the crack Prussian regiments. Many more of them were killed. Australian casualties – those that mattered – amounted to just over 3000. About 600 died in some of the toughest, bloodiest fighting of the war. The stakes were high. Ludendorff's force had defended accordingly.

Monash contacted Rawlinson on the afternoon of 2 September. He already had an inkling from Montgomery that the Australian Corps was going to be successful. But he was still excited when told by Monash: 'By the way, we are on top of Mont St Quentin.'

'I don't believe it,' Rawlinson responded.

'Come and see,' Monash offered.

'You have altered the course of the war.'[16]

To be more accurate, the Fourth Army chief could have added 'much earlier than anticipated'. But still this comment, reflecting the High Command's surprise, was not exaggerated. The Germans, who had fought much harder than in any of Monash's three recent major victories, were retreating to the Hindenburg Line. Now Foch, Haig and all the Allied army commanders realised that Monash had been right in his instinct and judgement. The Germans were at breaking point. They had been pushed there by daring, brilliantly planned strategies and courageous soldiering.

'By this bold and successful action,' Rawlinson wrote to other British generals, 'the heart was knocked out of the Boche.' He gave high praise to Monash's tactics and strategies. 'It broke the [natural, well-engineered] Somme line of defence . . . defended by troops second to none in the German Army.'[17]

Historians agreed that the Battle of Mont St Quentin and Péronne distinguished Monash even further as a battle commander. Bean recognised it as the only important battle by Australians on the Western Front in which quick, free manoeuvre played 'a decisive part. It furnished a complete answer to the comment that Monash was merely a composer of set pieces.'[18]

English writer A. K. Smithers, steeped in the traditional battle concepts and reflecting the prevailing British attitude to war, reckoned Mont St

Quentin and Péronne were the 'true measure of the greatness of John Monash as a General . . . it meant throwing to the winds all those articles of faith about "advancing under the greatest possible protection" and not exposing the soft bodies of men to the lead and steel of defenders . . . Monash faced this knowledge (that the battle would be costly in casualties) and accepted the inevitable with the fortitude of Ulysses Grant.'[19]

In other words, Monash could stand comparison with the best generals of the last two centuries when the situation reverted to old-fashioned battle conditions. On one level, such comment would have pleased him, given his penchant for military history and the American Civil War in particular. He even suggested that the capture of the Mont was a bit like the surprise tactics employed by one of his heroes, Stonewall Jackson. But the Battle of Mont St Quentin and Péronne had been a necessity at a key turning point in the war. It produced an anomaly in his style, which was light years from the British way. That change, and the increased number of casualties, was adding to the strain on him, which was exacerbated by the many sleepless days and nights and the need for never-ending decision-making. Every one of them would mean death and injury for Australians or the enemy. As the battles and casualties mounted, no matter how rational, logical and ingenious Monash was, there was nowhere to escape from the insanity of war.

On 7 September he asked Rawlinson for three days off in Paris. The request was refused. Monash knew how his men felt.

The refusal caused Monash to turn all his attention to another dimension of his generalship that made him stand out from others. This was his attitude to the less glamorous but important matters of repair and reconstruction. To support his battle corps, Monash wanted the Péronne railway up and running towards the Hindenburg Line twenty-four kilometres east. The station and a great lattice bridge had been smashed by the Germans. They had to be fixed, no matter how long it took. Trains were vital for transporting troops, weapons, other heavy equipment, food and water supplies. Roads and bridges had to be built from scratch or reconstructed if Monash was to have his big guns come across the river.

Before, during and after battles, Monash put on his engineer's hard hat again, stood ankle deep in mud if necessary and drew on his enormous experience from his early days, which began with constructing Princes

Bridge and the white elephant Outer Circle Railway in Melbourne. He was just as much in his element as the engineer as he was commanding a battle. Once there was a break in the conflict he escaped his war room HQ to stand in the middle of a site, overseeing or just watching his engineers and pioneers at work. This transported him back in time to the West Australian outback creating a railway, or a Victorian country town forming mine infrastructure, or Elwood in Melbourne constructing a bridge.

Yet there was one salient difference from those early days. All those jobs had been disparate enterprises necessary to survive in his profession. Now his skills were all directed at one singular purpose: the chase and final defeat of the German Army.

If the Germans could hold back the Allied force in France and Belgium for another forty days, that would take them to the beginning of colder weather in mid-October. Winter would give them another three months respite and a chance to reorganise.

The enemy in the overall conflict still had factors keeping it strong militarily. Its submarine campaign might have fallen short of its aims, but it was still potent. The Allied blockade of all goods heading for Germany – from motor fuel to food – had been tough, but the Germans were hardy and resilient. They had survived it so far.

There was an urgency in Monash's reconstruction, re-equipping and preparation for a relentless pursuit. He saw a real chance of a complete victory on the Hindenburg Line, much earlier than anticipated by anyone. If he could do it quickly, he might just save him and his men a rotten winter, or even another year of combat.

It put him under extreme pressure to meet a tight deadline.

OPERATION
HINDENBURG
LINE

Monash now had other distracting problems that were nearly as pressing as his battle plans to win the war. Since all the five divisions had begun to fight as one corps under his command there had been a shift in the motive for fighting and being on the Western Front. The success of the AIF in five weeks since 8 August had meant that a powerful bond had developed between all its divisions. It had become a military state within a state. When the divisions had been used to fill gaps and plug holes for the British armies, they had cried out to be identified as Australians. Now they were together, they wanted to be viewed as the Australian Corps.

As ever, Monash articulated and set the mood with his preaching to the troops. His sermon in speeches and news sheets had until 8 August been focused on telling the soldiers to fight for Australia. Now it was fight for the AIF. He was no longer appealing to their patriotism. He was beating a drum for the powerful, lean fighting machine he had developed. It was a subtle change in propaganda. The AIF had gained a reputation not just generally but also, more importantly, among its own members. It was a formidable entity. The soldiers also now believed they were unbeatable. In the psychology, motivation and philosophy of any competition, let alone war, this was the most powerful force of all.

Part of this switch in emphasis was motivated by the lack of recognition the AIF was receiving in the press, which was the fault of the British High Command. News reports given to journalists for consumption worldwide never mentioned other than British successes. Few were aware that the battles of Amiens, Chuignes, Bray, Mont St Quentin, Péronne and even comparatively modest Hamel had been led and largely won by Australians. It peeved Monash, his staff commanders and soldiers. Their mail and press cuttings from Australia reflected the ignorance of AIF achievements. Monash lobbied hard for more recognition, using as his line that the Australians were sporting and competitive by nature. They liked to see their winning scores on the board. He could have added that the 'scores' – battle victories – could be recorded with a little more flourish, a fraction more sense of occasion. He thought Bean's writings about Péronne were bland. Perhaps the correspondent's effort was all a consequence of battle fatigue. This was his fourth year on the job. Maybe it was a case of Bean there, done that.

Monash yearned for an Australian Ashmead-Bartlett who would inject life into the reports. It was all part of his effort to boost the Australians' sense that they were in a powerful 'team' that could beat any other force. Newspaper reports that included a sense of drama would build that feeling of invincibility.

Many AIF leaders, including Monash, were doing what they could to circulate the stories of heroics and victories in internal bulletins and here and there in the Australian press. Such names as Jacka, McCarthy, Gordon, Cartwright, Lowerson, Mactier, Towner, Weathers, Currey, Hall and Buckley were already mini-legends. Many heroic acts were being reported as the AIF continued on its winning way.

Monash's expectation was that once the diggers received clippings from home, and read about their exploits and 'importance' in battles, it would help motivate them further. It was the same with reports of heroism, which were to be read and seen the same way as a 'best-on-ground' story on a football match. The only difference was that on the Somme, awards for heroism were for best on battleground.

Monash was now using his prestige within the British Army as its most successful corps commander. He told Rawlinson and others in the British High Command that he did not accept their argument that it was better not to publicise Australian successes since German propaganda was saying that the British were climbing to victory over Australian and Canadian corpses. Nor did he buy the further High Command argument that political opposition to the war in the Dominions would use any publicity about their successes as evidence

THE AUSTRALIAN CORPS CAMPAIGN IN FRANCE
4 JULY – 5 OCTOBER 1918

N

0   5   10 km

FURTHEST POINT WEST REACHED BY GERMAN ARMY IN MARCH 1918

● Bertangles

● Albert

Bray
●

Chipilly
●

Amiens
⚡ To Paris

Hamel
●

Morcourt
●

Area Taken By
Monash's AIF
4 July – 5 Octobe

● Villers-
Bretonneux

Harbonnières
●

Railway

Chaulnes
●

FRANCE

Roye
●

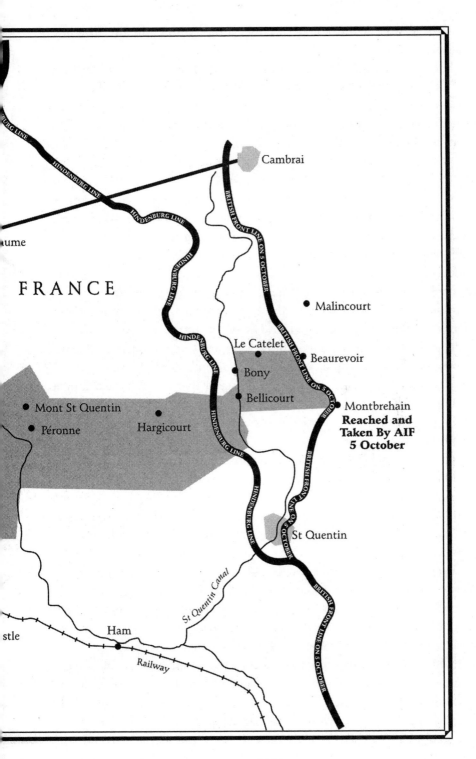

FRANCE

Cambrai

Malincourt

Le Catelet

Beaurevoir

Bony

Bellicourt

Mont St Quentin

Hargicourt

Montbrehain
**Reached and
Taken By AIF
5 October**

Péronne

HINDENBURG LINE

BRITISH FRONT LINE ON 5 OCTOBER

St Quentin

St Quentin Canal

Ham

Railway

stle

ume

that the troops were being used as cannon fodder in the toughest fighting zones.

For once Monash, Hughes, Murdoch and Bean were as one in their drive for due recognition being given to the AIF for its victories. Each had his own motive. The journalists wanted their bylines on big Australian victory stories. Hughes wished to strut the world stage with influence. The AIF had taken more than its fair share of the burden of the conflict. Hughes and his government wanted the prestige to flow from that to his having a say at the expected peace settlement.

Hughes showed perspicacity about how important recognition of Australia's contribution to the war effort might be to its future security. He knew that the British ruling elite from the King down appreciated the AIF's efforts. But after recent trips to the USA he was aware of the ignorance about them in Washington DC. He couldn't find anyone who realised that Australians and Americans had fought together, under an Australian commander. Hughes, the pragmatist's pragmatist among politicians, saw the USA, not England, as its insurance for survival as an independent nation of four million Europeans at the bottom of Asia. Americans, Hughes, appreciated, were strong on loyalty and 'paying dues'. He believed that the USA had to understand that Australia had fought hard and made huge sacrifices for the Alliance's cause. Publicity was one way – perhaps the main way – for this to be communicated to the powers in Washington.

Hughes and Murdoch arranged for three press parties to be taken to the Australian front from 12 September. A journalist for the London *Weekly Despatch*, Arthur O'Connor, then described Monash as 'somewhat rugged with alert yet kindly eyes'. He spoke 'quietly, deliberately, unhesitatingly'. He was 'a strong man', and summed him up as 'intellectual, original, democratic, ruthless'.[1]

Every visitor was impressed by Monash, including Arthur Conan Doyle, who was acting as a journalist. Monash didn't have aggressive body language. There was no bellicose message about smashing the Boche. That would be reserved for his staff and commanders, in private. Nor was he other than matter-of-fact about AIF victories. Instead visitors were taken with his sheer presence. He had an undemonstrative charm. His well-chosen, precise words inspired. Doyle found him the greatest of all the generals he met on the front. He had 'an attractive aura' and 'a rare compelling personality, whose dark flashing eyes and swarthy face might have seemed more in keeping with some Asiatic conqueror than with the prosaic associations of the British Army'.[2]

Monash had charisma in an era when the term was not a hackneyed, meaningless description associated with limp-wristed film stars or script-driven, semi-literate political candidates.

His opening up to the press did much to redress the problem of Australia's record being absorbed under the heading 'British Victories'. But it also created another situation of conflict for him and Hughes. Monash's public prestige would now lift even further after his profile had jumped to something approaching what it should be, just when Hughes was under increasing pressure at home from some quarters to reduce the size and effort of the AIF in the hoped-for final stages of the war. The diggers had done more than enough and the status was theirs, the argument went. Time to bring the boys home.

Hughes had been based in London since June and monitoring the politics behind the war, especially the conflict between Lloyd George and Haig and his High Command. Lloyd George had been withholding British manpower from Haig in the hope of limiting his capacity for mass offensives. They led to huge casualties, which caused even the anaesthetised British public to protest through the press. Apart from offending Lloyd George's sensibilities, high body counts threatened his chances of re-election. He was gambling on the Americans taking over the war early in 1919. This would spare thousands of British troops, his election hopes and his chance of history seeing him in a favourable light.

Hughes now fell into a similar feud over numbers at the front with his C-in-C, Monash, which the Australian PM also knew was about electability and his place in the history books. He had been told by someone high in the British High Command that the war could even stretch into 1920. Hughes didn't see how the AIF could go on at such frenetic pace and end up with any of its divisions intact.

Hughes had long been urging that he be given power of veto over how, when and where the AIF was used. During the big battles from 8 August on, Haig had ignored him, and the Australian PM had been forced to remain quiet. But in the lull after the Battle of Mont St Quentin and Péronne, Hughes began making his demands again. Instead of going through Haig, who was blocking him with lack of responses and 'too busy to talk' signals, Hughes turned up with the first contingent of journalists on 12 September with his trusty supporters, Murdoch and Bean, in tow and ready with notebooks in hand. They had both been urging the PM to confront Monash.

Monash accommodated them and the other writers and journalists at Amiens, not at his hut HQ at Belloy-en-Santerre. This way they would not interfere with his planning for the Hindenburg Line offensive. Unlike Hamel, the proposed attack this time would be kept secret, even from Hughes.

At lunch, Hughes took the time to chat with Monash. Blamey characterised the meeting as a confrontation between an 'Alsatian [Monash] and a Bantam Cock [Hughes]'.[3]

The PM had been cautious with Monash on the battlefront just before Hamel in early July. The general's stature since then had grown exponentially. But this time Hughes believed there wouldn't be a battle for some time (The plans were kept from everyone but the High Command and senior commanders.) The apparent lull between conflicts was the moment for the Bantam Cock to strike. Hughes told Monash that the AIF must cease all fighting by early in October, less than three weeks away.

This was not quite the blow to Monash that the 'pogrom' he endured courtesy of Bean and Murdoch in June and July had been. But he could do without the interference. He had come to the conclusion for different reasons than Hughes that the AIF couldn't go on longer than early October anyway. It would be a relief if he could get them out by then. He felt near breaking point himself and was well aware that his fighting infantry felt the same way. The Australians had been used, willingly, as shock troops. They were always at the pointy end of the action – the arrowhead in thrust after thrust. There was a limit no matter how he rotated his troops. He and they were fast approaching it. The near-mutiny of a handful of the 59th Battalion was one of a few similar incidents among men who had been straining to join the hot spots after the Australian Corps took shape in May 1918. Now there was a growing feeling within the ranks that they had done far more than their fair share. Monash was watching the feeling. But he was determined not to let go or stop. Not yet. Not until he considered he had done his job. Monash had told others, Bean and Murdoch among them, that he wanted control of the corps to prove himself as a commander. But he was well beyond that.

When Hughes sprang his surprise 'order', Monash remained composed. He tried to explain to Hughes that he too wanted them out of the line by early October, but in war, it would irresponsible to withdraw men on an appointed day so far ahead. What if they were in the middle of action? How would other corps react seeing the Australians marching off? Also, once winter set in, it could be difficult to withdraw his troops. They were an integral part of the fighting force needed to win the war. Taking them out without regard to the conditions at the time would be tantamount to handing the German defence a huge advantage.

Hughes would have none of it. He now warned Monash that the corps had to be out of the line by that date. Monash's job depended on it. Instead of acceding to the demands, Monash held his reserve. He would have thought again of his prize-winning essay in 1912, in which he made clear his view that politicians must not interfere in the way commanders conduct war. He felt alienated from the PM, who was using his rightful power as a democratically elected national leader. Monash, the commander of the AIF, would attempt to defy the elected leader by using his own influence within the British military structure as he had contemplated when Hughes was about to remove him from his command just before Hamel. Monash could not, would not walk away from his position now; not when the aim he had programmed himself for – winning the war – might be only months away.

Hughes told Murdoch after the meeting he thought 'the General' had something up his sleeve. Would Monash dare to cable Pearce and other members of the cabinet and protest with his exceptional powers of persuasion, Hughes wondered. Monash's prestige at that instant was so high that Hughes thought his cabinet might well overrule him.[4] In effect, he feared a long-distance coup. But Monash was subtler than that. The lawyer in him noted a loophole in the PM's order if he needed it. Hughes had not specified by which day 'early in October' troops had to be pulled out.

Haig agreed that the Australians should be away from the front line by the same time. So, despite his caution, Monash remained more or less in accord with Hughes. The difference was that the PM might well call it quits for good and disband the volunteer corps. Monash believed the war would stumble on through the 1918–19 winter (although he was working hard to make the enemy fall apart before then). To think otherwise would cause complacency, which he thought irresponsible. Hughes' dictum had bought him time. He would worry about the consequences of it later. The situation was so fluid and unpredictable that it was best not to worry too far ahead.

✕

Hughes told Murdoch: 'He [Monash] sees only one thing. He wants to fight on. He wants to be there at the finish.'[5] The PM was being critical where many would see Monash's conduct as praiseworthy and be more damning of a commander who wished to drop out before his mission was accomplished.

Murdoch urged the PM to take action to show Monash who was boss. Why not direct Birdwood, who was head of the AIF's administration, to order Monash to send 800 original Anzacs to Australia, immediately, for two months leave? It was a clever ploy. This way the PM didn't have to face Monash or any of his generals, and no one in the British High Command. The PM followed the suggestion. Then he accompanied Bean and Murdoch to Bray, where the likely chosen ones were, and told them of his decision. The two journalists then rushed to report the story to pre-empt any move by Monash to cable the cabinet back in Australia to stop it.

Hughes' action in undermining his chief military commander with his troops was a desperate show of strength, and something always dreaded in army circles. Monash's earlier action just before Hamel in telling Hughes he would not go lightly if sacked as Corps Commander had forewarned the PM and his co-conspirators that they had better think through any attempts to weaken his command. They now were getting some retribution by stepping into Monash's military state, geographically outside Australia and under British control, but bound to Australian governmental rules.

Hughes went further in his disruption by telling the troops that he himself would make sure they all saw out the winter of 1918–19 in good weather and conditions in Italy and France. This vote-garnering exercise was as thoughtless as it was counter-productive. If the AIF was still in the conflict, it could never be promised three months sunny vacation.[6]

Monash was furious and worried. He agreed with the idea and the principle behind relieving the Anzacs, but not with the timing. Most of the men would come from Glasgow's 1st Division and Sinclair-MacLagan's 4th Division only days before they were preparing to go into action in the first battle for the Hindenburg Line.

Monash didn't think the soldiers chosen would be happy to leave at such short notice. Birdwood, who had to do Hughes' bidding, didn't agree. He did his usual pressing of the flesh with the soldiers concerned and found the prospective furlough-makers 'happy . . . with smiles on their faces'.[7]

Yet all Monash's commanders agreed with him. How would the privileged 800 be selected from 6000 eligible Anzacs? Pompey Elliott was bitter that his brigade would be broken up and rendered inoperable for 1919. 'If Mr Hughes had been in the pay of the Germans,' he commented, 'he could not have dealt us a more paralyzing stroke.'[8]

Monash protested to Hughes. Murdoch, on the PM's behalf, had delight in telling the general he had better comply with the order of rest for the 800 or else Hughes would take further action, presumably to sack him. Monash consulted his commanders. With further battle plans being drawn up, the suggestion was that Monash should comply but slowly and with only about half the 800 men Hughes had ordered out of the war. That way the 1st and 4th Divisions could go in the next battle, almost intact. Two hundred or so soldiers from each would drop their numbers by about seven per cent, which would be just manageable for one more battle.

Monash, however, was well aware that this sort of threat to his force was intolerable for future encounters. He could not call back any of the exhausted 2nd, 3rd or 5th Divisions from their more than well-earned rest. They had only been resting for a week after the bruising Mont St Quentin and Péronne battles. Better, he believed, to ask the British High Command for two American divisions. Just two months earlier he had been officially denied absorbing even one American soldier under his command (although he was able to keep a thousand). Now his influence was such that his request was granted without question or argument. He would now control 50,000 Americans. Monash was thrilled. The total force under his command was close to 200,000. The additional men from another country increased his independence and confirmed his power over his own military state. The force was now international and confirmed the British High Command's faith in him. Even if Hughes sacked him, Haig would ensure that he had a fighting corps for these late thrusts at the enemy. Monash was most likely now to have a chance to achieve his messianic, driving goal to be there at the death of the war and see final victory.

That problem solved, Monash was ready for the final assault a week after he had won the Battle of Mont St Quentin. Rawlinson, Montgomery and the other Fourth Army corps commanders (Butler, now over his health problems, and Braithwaite, who had served under Ian Hamilton) met him at AIF HQ at Belloy-en-Santerre, close to the Somme, which had been occupied by the Germans. 'There, quite informally, over a cup of afternoon tea,' Monash recorded, 'the great series of operations took birth which [he hoped] would so directly help to win the war.'[9]

Despite his run-in with Hughes and the perennial plotters, he was at the peak of his military powers. Rawlinson was giving him everything he wanted to continue to lead the fight. Blamey recalled the days less than a year earlier when the AIF would have to beg for equipment. Tanks had been out of the question. Big artillery had not been forthcoming. Even machine-guns had been handed over grudgingly. Now it was a case of 'The equipment should be with us in a few days, John' or 'Another division, John? I'll see what can be arranged.'

Haig, Rawlinson and Montgomery were only too willing to give assistance. They knew Monash had the skills and determination and the right, willing force. Until August, these British commanders were men destined for the forgotten or detested file in history. Now, with victory a distinct possibility, their reputations were being salvaged. Haig was no longer 'that butcher'. For the moment, Rawlinson's disastrous charge at the Somme in 1916 was not mentioned in newspaper reports. He and Montgomery were no longer 'the butcher's assistants'. If Monash and the other forces he was taking with him could drive on, then the three of them might just emerge with winners' epithets, which would be for life. Winning this conflict – allegedly the war to end all wars – would not just be talked about at the Officers' Club. It would be recorded for posterity.

All three were fox-hunters in the British tradition. They loved to ride to hounds. Now they could do it on the battlefield. The hounds were Monash and his soldiers, and the foxes were the Germans.

In September, the scent was strong.

Monash surveyed the country where the chase would continue. For fourteen kilometres east, the country was beautiful, composed of woods and valleys, with deserted villages here and there – good fox territory, although they were nowhere to be seen. Beyond this was another area similar to the one on the Somme, which had just been won. It was ten kilometres long and became more and more devastated the closer it was to the Hindenburg Line. This was the result of trench warfare by the British Fifth Army from September 1917 until the great German offensive of 21 March 1918.

Reconnaissance in this belt showed unusual signs of life, not of the former French inhabitants but the Germans burning villages, stores and ammunition as they retreated. Those unforgiving foxes had teeth. Their destination – the Hindenburg Line (the Siegfried Line to the Germans) – was an eighty-kilometre long, nine-kilometre wide system of trenches and fortifications. Perhaps only the Germans, with their industrious capacity for unaesthetic but efficient construction, could have conceived and created it. They had built it over three months until the early spring of 1917. It was a solid barrier that could be manned by a minimum of soldiers so that a maximum number could go forward and attack the Allies. It had formed an impregnable wall to British and French assaults.

On 16 September Monash brought his divisional commanders, Glasgow (1st) and Sinclair-MacLagan (4th) to a meeting along with Courage (tanks), Chamier (Australian Flying Corps), Fraser (heavy artillery) and the four generals on his own staff. Glasgow and Sinclair-MacLagan were fresh and had been resting while Rosenthal, Gellibrand and Hobbs exhausted themselves and their men winning at the Mont and Péronne.

Monash had requested that the Australian Corps would have a shortened front of six and a half kilometres, and this was also acceded to. That was just feasible for the limited number of Australians – around 6900 soldiers and officers – left available for this new thrust, once Hughes' requested Anzacs had been subtracted (they numbered 450 in the end, not 800). The British III Corps would be on their left; the British IX Corps and First French Army would be on the right. The entire attacking line would run for twenty-seven kilometres. Its aim would be to smash the Hindenburg Line but not in one hit. It was too vast. The nine-kilometre-thick fortifications were composed of four barriers or targets, which would have to be taken in separate attacks.

The first was the Hindenburg Outpost Line (also called the Hargicourt Line). Second was the Hindenburg Main Line, consisting of a long canal and tunnel system. The third target was the Le Catelet Line. The final enemy defence was the Beauvoir Line.

Monash received a huge boost when an innocent-looking lorry was captured on another front. It contained vital maps and documents concerning the whole Hindenburg system. His appetite for minutiae was whetted and then satisfied when he sat down to peruse the many detailed maps and descriptions of every tactical feature of the defences. The position of every gun emplacement, searchlight, machine-gun pit, observation post, telephone exchange, command station and mortar emplacement was well marked.

Monash spent many days hovering over the maps, which showed the topographical and tactical features of the ground, while the documents laid out action plans for every garrison unit. They formed a fine starting point for planning how to take target number one: the Hargicourt Line. The French and the British armies would make a synchronised attack with Monash's force.

His main worry was the lack of tanks. He had missed them at Mont St Quentin and Péronne and, after his earlier experiences from Hamel on, he would be uncomfortable without them again. He requested several hundred, but the repair shops and those coming off England's production lines would not be there in time. Monash was appalled when told that only eight would be ready for his use on 18 September. Yet he was to have his tanks, even if he produced them by one of his conjuring tricks. He ordered the manufacture of dummy tanks to make up the shortfall. That directive produced raids on dumps and stores as pioneers and engineers competed to produce some odd-looking monsters. Each dummy was hauled forward just before dawn on attack day. When the sun came up the enemy would see a frightening line of tanks on the horizon.

This extra Monash illusion played a big part in the outcome when the 1st and 4th Divisions (each on a frontage of one brigade), fortified with a shot of rum, attacked in heavy rain after an artillery bombardment. The enemy this time did not include any Prussian guardsmen. They mainly surrendered or ran, with some opposition coming at hamlet of Le Verguier. Monash's old brigade, the 4th, was given the demanding task of taking it. Three battalions – the 13th, 15th and 16th – combined in an assault. The 13th's Sergeant Gerald Buckley (alias Sexton) led the way in the dawn attack as the fog and smoke cleared.

Perhaps he had read about his namesake Alex Buckley at Péronne, or maybe he had had an extra shot of rum. Whatever, the reason his actions were extraordinary. Sexton rushed a field gun and a mortar on the bank straight ahead. Firing his Lewis gun from the hip, he blasted the field gun crew, then turned his attention to the mortar crew. Sexton urged his section to follow him. Impatient to take out the mortar and its crew, he sprinted a hundred metres under heavy machine-gun fire and achieved his

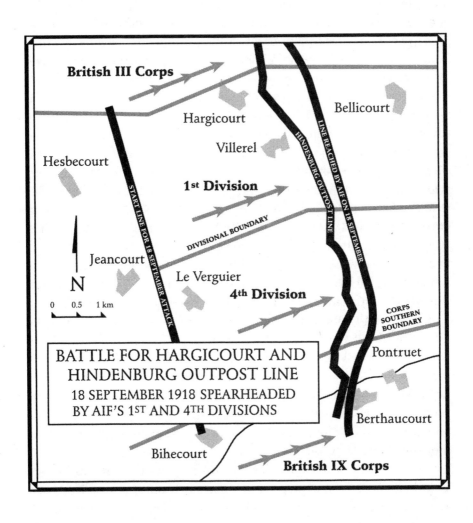

British III Corps

Hargicourt

Bellicourt

Villerel

Hesbecourt

1st Division

HINDENBURG OUTPOST LINE

LINE REACHED BY AIF ON 18 SEPTEMBER

START LINE FOR 18 SEPTEMBER ATTACK

DIVISIONAL BOUNDARY

N

0   0.5   1 km

Jeancourt

Le Verguier

4th Division

CORPS
SOUTHERN
BOUNDARY

Pontruet

BATTLE FOR HARGICOURT AND
HINDENBURG OUTPOST LINE
18 SEPTEMBER 1918 SPEARHEADED
BY AIF'S 1ST AND 4TH DIVISIONS

Berthaucourt

Bihecourt

British IX Corps

objective, without help. Sexton then returned to the bank and fired into four entrances to dugouts. Thirty prisoners emerged. It was then he realised he had flushed out the HQ of the German 58th Infantry Regiment.

Sexton could have been forgiven for taking a rest behind the lines but, in keeping with his fierce dedication, he continued with the 13th Battalion, leading attacks with assistance now on five other machine-gun posts.

He would deservedly also receive a VC, despite their now being much tougher to attain, such was the fury and intestinal fortitude being shown by so many in the final push by the AIF east of Péronne.

Acts of outrageous daring were coming faster now as if the men sensed they really were approaching some sort of climax. It was being hastened by all sorts of rumours, some of them conflicting, about going on leave to an exotic place or even home. They were also now reading about Australian victories in newspapers being circulated among the troops. The soldiers had been inspired by the stories they had heard or read in bulletins. But reading them in clippings from the major city papers, or just the local town journal, had more impact. They presented more credibility than word of mouth or official army propaganda.

One of many soldiers impressed by what he was reading was Private James Wood of the 48th Battalion (positioned on the right or southern side of the Australian front at Le Verguier). Leading a four-man patrol, he stumbled on a strong entrenchment of Germans on a ridge behind the 12th Brigade. If the enemy advanced or the 12th fell back, the entire battalion could have been wiped out. Wood asked one of his patrol to dash for assistance. When the runner didn't come back with help after half an hour, Woods consulted his two mates. They could see activity at the enemy position. They were preparing for something, maybe an advance from the rear. If Wood didn't act now, he reckoned the Germans might make their move on the 12th Brigade.

The three intrepid soldiers hit the two trenches of Germans as they were donning their kit in preparation for a march and attack, as Wood had guessed. The Australians killed one of the enemy. Thirty others decamped, leaving six machine-guns. Wood and his mates settled in the trenches.

It took the Germans only minutes to realise that just three men had jumped them. The enemy decided to counter-attack. Wood and Co. could have stayed in the trenches and fired outwards with their rifles, but they would have been overwhelmed by the opposition. Wood decided they had to defend with grenades and hope that the runner had got help in time to save them. He crawled on to a trench parapet and hurled grenade after grenade as the other two handed them up to him. The blasts created such disorganisation that the thirty Germans could not reach the trenches. When they regrouped, they found themselves surrounded by Australian reinforcements. The runner had done his job, just in time to save Wood and the others.

The position was secured. Le Verguier belonged to the Australians. Private Wood would soon be reading about his own exploits and citations.

By 10 a.m. on 18 September Monash had control of the old British front line of 21 March. It had taken three days short of a half a year to restore the status quo.

The day's objective, the Hargicourt Line, was still 1700 metres away. Both divisions pushed on now with the expectation that there would be fierce opposition from the trench system that had defied the Fifth Army for years. Glasgow's 1st Division encountered some resistance, which led to tragedy and more heroics. Many men would be considered unlucky after fighting from Gallipoli through Flanders and on the Somme for four years inclusive only to be cut down at the final hurdle. One high-profile instance was the popular captain Wally Hallahan, a machine-gunner of the 11th Battalion. Forty-eight hours before he was to be married to an English woman while on leave in London, he was called back to fight in the battle for Hargicourt. The veteran Anzac and his future bride were planning to return to Australia on home leave. Hallahan would never be married or make it back. He was killed during the battle on the outskirts of the town.

Despite the Australian onslaught and the confidence that they would prevail against still fierce opposition, the weakened troops still needed inspiration to meet their objectives. A mate of Hallahan's in the 11th Battalion, Captain E. W. Tulloch, provided it. Tulloch refused to be bogged down by two machine-guns at the entrance to the town. He selected two fighters and rushed the Germans. They killed fifteen of the enemy, captured as many and knocked out the guns. This would have earned the captain a VC before the battles of Mont St Quentin and Péronne. Instead he was awarded the MC and a promotion to lieutenant colonel.

By dark on 18 September this kind of endeavour ensured that Glasgow's men had overwhelmed the Hindenburg outpost garrison along its front.

✕

Sinclair-MacLagan's soldiers of the 4th Division had a tougher assignment. They were advancing in full view of the Germans and on more difficult terrain. They were exhausted 450 metres short of the objective. Monash conferred with Sinclair-MacLagan. They decided the troops should be rested, while the artillery was brought up for a drenching of the enemy before a final assault.

The 4th Division attacked at 11 p.m. and encountered a determined enemy. Not long after midnight, Sinclair-MacLagan's men speared the Australian flag into the ground to signal another quick, decisive victory, this time in the Battle of Hargicourt.

The numbers were satisfying to Monash. Thanks to Hughes' subterfuge, he had gone into the battle with what he perceived as the bare minimum of men. The 1st Division's strength was 2854 infantry. They suffered 490 casualties but killed four times that number while capturing 1700 Germans. The 4th Division (with 3048 soldiers) had 532 casualties. It killed more than 2000 and captured 2543. After the anomalous hand-to-hand brutal encounters of Mont St Quentin and Péronne, Monash was relieved to produce figures more in keeping with his doctrine of using the machines to do damage and of protecting his foot soldiers.

'There is no record in this war,' Monash noted, 'of any previous success on such a scale, won with so little loss.'[10]

The British Corps left and right had not been quite as quick or as successful. The IX Corps on the Australians right (south) would take another day to reach their target. But the III Corps on the left (north) had no hope of bringing their line up level with the Australians by 19 September.

✕

Just when Monash was pleased with the first-up victory in the multi-staged attack on the Hindenburg defences, he was confronted by another problem with rebellious troops, this time because they wanted to fight, not avoid it.

It began with one of the most inanely timed orders from the British High Command in the entire war. It had decided to reduce the number of battalions in each brigade from four to three. Monash was happy with the theory this move seemed to support: that more weapons could compensate for fewer soldiers. He thought an extra thirty Lewis guns in a battalion would be adequate. But the order came just before the climatic battles in the war. Command wanted the AIF to disband eight battalions.

Monash had to sit down with his divisional commanders and work out who would go. It was a painful process. When informed by their officers, only one of the eight battalions said it would comply with the order. Seven went on strike. They ignored all directives from the AIF, generals, staff and commanders. Then they sacked their officers, installed their own and demanded that Monash negotiate with them.

It was in effect a mutiny, but perhaps the strangest in the annals of war. Some of their members – the Anzacs – had been happy to take up Hughes' recent offer to go on leave to Australia, or Italy and France, for the rest of the war. But that was a different proposition from being broken up and informed they were no longer needed. The psychology of being told they could no longer fight with their mates and the corps itself, before the job they had come to Europe to do was completed, was bad enough. But it was too much to take when coupled with the added blow that they had been selected while three other battalions in each brigade had not. It was an insult to their pride. It shattered the very sense of the lives these diggers had experienced over four years.

Monash's building of such a 'winning' entity, which was now generating publicity commensurate with its progress on the battlefield, along with reports of amazing individual exploits, had been too successful. Nobody wanted to be dropped from the 'team'.

The High Command had never really understood the mentality of the Australian soldier. Monash did. He secretly sympathised with the men and was touched by their courage. He went against all protocol and army rules and met with the mutineers' representatives from the 37th Battalion, who spoke for all the rebels.

Monash had a dilemma. He understood their grievances and was furious with the timing of the disbanding order. On the one hand, he couldn't officially allow these battalions to survive. It defied everything he had preached about obeying orders. On the other hand, if the order was enforced and the mutineers resisted, the situation could be dangerous. Not only that. All the other battalions, who hated one of their number being dissolved like this, might go on strike too. This was just when Monash was drawing up his grand plan for what could be the AIF's biggest battle of the war.

He first tried to appeal to their common sense and see if they would respond. 'I have done a thing unprecedented in military annals in holding an informal conference such as this,' Monash told them, 'but I realize that the AIF is different from any other army in the world.'[11] There would be no charges or arrests if they went quietly, he informed them. Did they want their battalions to go out of existence with a bad reputation, especially after the wonderful, professional way they had build their names? Monash didn't talk about 'breaking up' or 'disbandment'. He used softer language, emphasising 'dispersal' and an 'honourable end'. But the new rebel leaders were stubborn. The meeting ended with no resolution.

The mutinous action had immediate ramifications for events on the front line. On 20 September, the day after the conference, the British III Corps still had not managed to fight its way to level with the line the Australians had secured. Butler, the III Corps leader, asked for help. Could Monash spare a battalion to take over 450 metres of the front allotted to III Corps? Monash agreed. 1st Battalion of 1st Division was asked to oblige, just as they were leaving the line for a break after doing their job with fierce professionalism. Already aware of the stalemate at the rebel–Monash conference the day before, the 1st Battalion's diggers protested at this sudden order. They had been called on to fill the gaps and do the work that the English troops had failed to do many times before. This was a demand too much.

A hundred and nineteen men refused the order to move to the unoccupied front. This was the second crack in the AIF edifice in twenty-four hours, and the third since the night of 1 September at Péronne.

The rest of the 1st Battalion obeyed orders and took up the slack on the 450-metre front as requested. The 1st Division Commander, Glasgow, a strict disciplinarian, went into a rage. He had the men charged with 'mutiny', which carried the death penalty. Glasgow disagreed with Monash's not putting down the battalion rebellion at the conference of the day before. Glasgow thought a stand had to be taken before mutinous acts became endemic. Monash had to mollify his divisional general, but also realised he couldn't let this situation hang in the air, as he had done with the rebels at the conference.

Monash suggested the charge on the 1st Battalion men should be changed to 'desertion'. The result was still ugly, with the men facing up to ten years imprisonment in the notorious Dartmoor prison in England.

And it was a tragic possibility, given the incredible work these soldiers had done, many of them for up to four years since Gallipoli. But it avoided the horrific prospect of 118 diggers (one charge was dismissed) being executed by firing squad, as Glasgow had urged (although there was some debate over whether this was possible legally during the war). Monash refused to contemplate that or where such action would have headed.

The 118 new rebels were to be kept under 'close arrest', which meant that they were confined to camp. The Corps Commander had to confirm the sentences. The paperwork for that sat on Monash's desk and was ignored. He wanted their sentences dropped, but it was too early to do so. Had he used his power then to veto the sentences, it might have encouraged others wavering in the ranks to desert. He decided to wait until a more appropriate moment to act.

With that problem suspended, Monash, playing judge, advocate, witness and negotiator, held a crisis conference over the seven 'disbanding' battalion rebels with Birdwood and the five divisional commanders. It was 25 September. The next major battle was due to begin on the 27th, and the Australians would come in on the 29th. If the AIF now enforced the disbanding, the other battalions would strike in sympathy. This would destroy the final massive assault on the Hindenburg fortifications, at least before the winter weather set in. The conference agreed that the last battle should be over inside two weeks (i.e. by 9 October). Could the order to break up the battalions be stalled until then? The Corps Commander now turned problem-solver by asking Rawlinson and Haig if they would agree to this postponement. When warned by both Birdwood and Monash that the consequences could be dire if they did not allow it, Haig conceded.

Monash could now concentrate on his schemes to breach the German defences, with his entire force available, including the 118 charged rebels if necessary. His plans for the five divisions under his command were adopted, except for the Beaurevoir Line, the last German stronghold that had to be taken. Monash had it marked down for taking on day one. Rawlinson suggested that he should wait to see the result of the prior stages: the taking of the canal and tunnel system that made up the Hindenburg main line and the Le Catelet Line.

The earlier captured documents showed that the canal would be the toughest to take without a huge number of casualties. Whereas both

British and French forces on his flanks were prepared to attack it directly, Monash was not. He decided to drive over the tunnel to his north. After that, the troops would storm the section of the canal on his part of the front, from behind and in front. The concept was to envelop it, then strangle its German defenders.

✕

Before any attack could be made he attempted to educate the Americans – the 27th and 30th Divisions commanded by Major General G. W. Read as a corps – in his methods and tactics. Read was happy, at Rawlinson's polite request, to act as 'an interested spectator' while Monash commanded his men. The American was sensible. His 50,000 troops (the divisions were twice the size of the British divisions) were inexperienced. They had not, like the Australians, learnt from experience – both mistakes and successes – on the battlefield over four years.

Monash organised what he called an Australian Mission under Sinclair-MacLagan, which had the task of teaching the Americans. Two hundred and seventeen officers were chosen from the resting 1st and 4th Divisions to instruct their American cousins. The Americans lacked experience and training in all areas of warfare, from discipline, 'quick initiative and capacity to anticipate the next action', to understanding of weapons and explosives. The old chestnut that had agonised Monash from his early days in the militia – communicating clear orders – was a problem. American officers underrated the need for a good system of supply of food and water to the troops. They didn't seem to understand how to attack and then protect themselves from unnecessary losses. None had even heard of the term 'mopping up'.

Monash became concerned at his final conference with his own generals and the American generals and their staff. He explained the 'set-piece' plans. 'It was to be a straightforward trench to trench attack,' he noted, 'from a perfectly straight "jumping off" line to a perfectly straight objective line, under a dense artillery and machine-gun barrage, and with the assistance of tanks.'[12]

It was a yawn for his commanders and staff, who had heard much of it before at Messines, Broodseinde, Hamel and the first stage of the Amiens battle on 8 August. But it left the Americans frowning. They asked so many questions that Monash was forced to give a three-hour lecture, complete with chalk, blackboard and diagrams. At the end of it, he was certain the generals knew and understood what was happening. The problem was whether they could pass it all on down the chain of command to 50,000 neophytes.

Big sections of the two American divisions attacked on 27 September with the task of taking the section of the line that the British III Corps had still not managed to reach. They had fallen 900 metres short, causing a dangerous situation on Monash's left (north). It had to be taken before the Australians and the rest of the Americans entered the battle on 29 September.

Monash's battle plan was the best he had ever prepared. It drew on all his experience now of attacking since the difficult days on Gallipoli.

Everything began well, but then went awry. The Americans swept over and past trenches, not realising that many Germans, warned of the coming attack by the artillery barrage, had ducked into shellproof dugouts. The Americans had left their mops at the start line. They did not allow for the Germans bobbing up out of the trenches behind them. The concept hammered into the generals did not seem to have filtered down the chain of command. The result was many unnecessary casualties. To make matters worse, Monash lost contact with the divisions. Not even his planes could find them. The Americans did not use their flares to alert the Australian Air Corps of their locations.

The problem flowed on into 28 September when Monash wanted to move his artillery up to allow further barrage cover for the troops. This wasn't possible if the Americans were fighting or lying wounded in areas that could not be pinpointed.

Monash wanted a day's delay to get the mopping up done, but Rawlinson refused. The other armies were attacking their sections of the canal. He didn't want Monash's corps behind and not pressuring the Germans in front of him. Monash then asked for more tanks. They were granted.

Monash told Haig he was 'in a state of despair' over the situation. The American failure had offended his tidy mentality. Haig told him not to worry, but to attack the next day – the 29th – as planned. This forced Monash to gamble, not knowing whether his left flank was even partially cleared up. He had trouble sleeping before the 5.55 a.m. assault by 200,000 men, the largest number he would ever command in one battle.

The thousand-gun artillery force hammered the target. Special fused shells that could cut through the wire emplacements were catapulted at the enemy. Mustard gas was sent out for the first and only time by the AIF. It causing the Germans in targeted living quarters and the defences to scramble to put on their masks.

The Americans moved out first, two sections of the two divisions side by side, followed by Australia's 3rd and 5th Divisions. The right attacking US division did well. It and Hobbs' 5th pushed forward nearly two kilometres ahead of the left division.

The star of the 5th's advance was Major Blair Wark of the 32nd Battalion (8th Brigade). At 9 a.m. the 32nd followed the American division into the battle near Bellicourt. Wark showed ingenuity by commandeering one of the few tanks in the battle and directing it to overrun two nests of troublesome machine-guns. Mid-morning the 32nd came across 200 Americans from the division that had gone out in advance of them. Their officers had been killed, and the soldiers were wandering aimlessly. Wark, a forceful leader, encouraged the Americans to join his battalion, telling them it was safer to do so. The Australians knew where they were going. Together, they could tackle the enemy better. The Americans, eager for direction and success rather than failure from meandering without purpose, fell in with Wark's men.

Within minutes they were glad to have done so. Wark grabbed another tank. He believed the shock value of even one such machine was valuable. Relishing his enlarged force, he organised an attack on the village of Nauroy. It was theirs after a twenty-minute encounter.

Wark's men commandeered machine-guns and artillery and took prisoners. His expanding force was now encouraged to push on. The first target was Etricourt, a base for a dangerous battery of seventy-seven-millimetre guns. Wark selected his six best fighters, then struck out for the battery. He soon captured it and those manning the guns.

By just afternoon, he and his force reached the outskirts of the hamlet of Joncourt. He organised a solid defence. It was challenged by an onslaught from 400 Germans in the town, which was repulsed.

The American division on the left and Gellibrand's 3rd were not so fortunate or successful. They were caught in a powerful German counter-attack. Late afternoon the situation was obscure. The right attacking force of Americans and Hobb's 5th Division had launched itself over the Bellicourt tunnel, while the left had not made it.

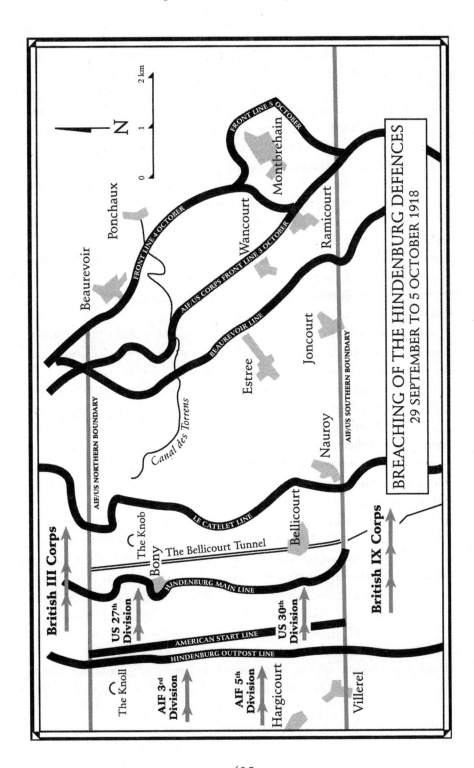

BREACHING OF THE HINDENBURG DEFENCES
29 SEPTEMBER TO 5 OCTOBER 1918

FRONT LINE 5 OCTOBER

Montbrehain

FRONT LINE 4 OCTOBER

Ponchaux

Beaurevoir

Wancourt

AIF/US CORPS FRONT LINE 3 OCTOBER

Ramicourt

BEAUREVOIR LINE

Estree

Joncourt

AIF/US SOUTHERN BOUNDARY

Nauroy

Canal des Torrens

AIF/US NORTHERN BOUNDARY

LE CATELET LINE

Bellicourt

The Knob

The Bellicourt Tunnel

Bony

HINDENBURG MAIN LINE

British IX Corps

British III Corps

US 27th Division

AMERICAN START LINE

US 30th Division

HINDENBURG OUTPOST LINE

The Knoll

AIF 3rd Division

AIF 5th Division

Hargicourt

Villerel

The problem, as on 27 August, had been the inexperience of the Americans, who couldn't achieve their objectives. Monash's plan had been based on what was attainable by his battle-hardened, precision-disciplined and drilled troops. The Americans, courageous, cheerful and willing, were not up to a battle on this scale. Blamey, a bullyboy on occasions, tongue-lashed an American divisional commander. But it was well after the event. Monash was angered that the American generals had exaggerated the capacities of their commanders well beyond reality.

Instead of lamenting the situation, he, Rawlinson, Montgomery and Sinclair-MacLagan held a hurried meeting late on the afternoon of 29 September. Monash had no compunction about throwing away his best-ever plan. He faced the fact that he had not allowed for the human factor. Every other scheme he had created since Hamel, when he was first in charge, had more or less followed his blueprint.

The rewrite called for AIF reserve brigades to attack north and take the town of Bony and the left (northern) end of the tunnel.

Minutes after the meeting, Monash rang Gellibrand to explain elements of the revised plans. His 3rd Division had borne the brunt of the fighting after the American debacle. Monash told him that the British corps to the north and south, along with the French, had done well. He thought that the British successes would reduce the amount of opposition. Some of the Americans would be withdrawn. The XIII British Corps would be 'pushed up' to take over from them, while the Australian front would be shortened to just 3600 metres.

The onus was now on Gellibrand and Hobbs' 5th Division to take complete control of the troublesome tunnel. Monash expected 5th Division to push hard from the right (south), and make its way along the 'railway ridge' to the third line of resistance, the Le Catelet Line. Gellibrand was ordered to call up as many tanks as he could in one group. Hobbs would do the same.

Gellibrand broke in: 'My real trouble is artillery action in view of the possibility that Americans were in the line [in front of 3rd Division].'

'Exactly so,' Monash replied. "The question is whether you cannot do without artillery action. We cannot tell where the Americans are.'

Monash thought Hobbs could safely bombard the German stronghold of Bony, which the Americans were not near. He said he would leave some of the Americans in the action as long as they were doing well. When the Australians could do without them, he would order all the Americans to be withdrawn. 'Work it out,' Monash told him, '. . . in view of the success in other parts, things will be better tomorrow than today.'[13]

The new plan was implemented on 30 September. The German resistance was reminiscent of Mont St Quentin and Péronne. They knew it was their last stand. If this section of the mighty Hindenburg fortifications collapsed, then Germany would lose the war. The defending soldiers faced capitulation or death, and many bravely chose the latter.

With fighting often hand-to-hand in the 'perfect tangle' of trenches, no one could really judge whether the new plan had worked by early afternoon. Tension mounted.[14] Just after 5 p.m. Monash upbraided Gellibrand on several points, including the fact that he had not reported tank losses and for attacking on such a narrow front.

Gellibrand tried to explain that he only had 200 men. There was no other option but to maintain a smaller front. Monash refused to accept that the battalion had shrunk to that size. But Gellibrand knew the situation. Monash was bullying him. He was desperate not to lose the battle after the Americans had let him down.[14]

Monash knew how strong his old division was. But that was the problem. He was thinking of it with battalions at something like full strength, not half-strength. Still Monash would accept no excuses for their not performing. If they were slow or bogged down, Gellibrand had to call the bluff of his commanders. This exasperated him. He had been to the front. It had to be a slow, hard fight. Gellibrand's diaries at the time conceded that it was his job to push his men, as it was Monash's to push his divisional heads.

In the next three hours, Gellibrand found the right message, or perhaps the right battalion leaders. Cannan and McNicoll led the way in concentrated, fierce encounters. By nightfall the 3rd, struggling all day at the troublesome north end of the tunnel, had advanced 900 metres.

Monash was in contact with Hobbs, too. But his division was progressing. Wark began a pre-dawn assault on Joncourt and took it by midday after heavy fighting. He would later be rewarded with a VC. It took another winner, Private John Ryan, to keep the 5th's momentum going over the tunnel. Armed with bayonet and grenades, he led the repulsion of a determined German counter-attack at Bellicourt.

By late afternoon the division was clearing the tunnel like a shark in a fish school.

✕

Satisfied that his second plan (it was a complete rewrite, not just a revision) was working, Monash snatched two hours sleep before ordering a set-piece frontal attack – a replica of the start two days earlier – by 3rd Division early on the morning of 1 October. Gellibrand protested. The problem was still more on his left flank. Monash revised the intelligence coming in, agreed without hesitation and apologised. His anxiety not to lose, along with the strain of six months in charge, was beginning to show. Yet he remained in control of himself and the mission.

The flank attack proved correct, and the Germans at last cracked owing to the pressure from all directions. The British IX Corps on the Australians' right had done well, outflanking the enemy. By mid-day the tunnel, which seemed to have been defended more strongly than at any point along the long, beleaguered fortifications, was won. The reserve brigades of 3rd and 5th Divisions had taken Bony as directed. These divisions then pushed on, as Monash had originally planned, to soften up the Beaurevoir Line, the very last objective, which was still outstanding.

At night on 1 October, a weary but cheered Monash congratulated all the divisional commanders, reserving special praise for his old 3rd Division and Gellibrand, with whom he had argued several times during the battle.

Early on 2 October, Rawlinson visited Monash and told him his job had been brilliantly done. He should go on leave. Monash was grateful and definitely in need of rest. Tremors in his right hand that had been begun less than two months earlier had returned with a vengeance. He could hide them by putting his hand in his pocket. It was a warning. He managed, with his supreme self-discipline and will, to carry on. He would not leave the conflict before it was over.

He wrote to a friend on that day: 'At times, when I feel very tired, I am tempted to hope that it will be the last serious work I shall ever do in my life.'[15]

He decided to stay in charge another two days and depart on 5 October. In the meantime, he sent the 3rd and 5th Divisions out of the line to join their comrades in the 1st and 4th. The 2nd Division, which had been resting for a month, now was ordered in for a last push on 3 October.

The night before, the Germans seemed to let go the biggest gas bombardment of the conflict. But it didn't stop Rosenthal and his men. The 2nd Division's 5th and 7th Brigades, making a spine-chilling noise after an artillery barrage, surged out over a 5400-metre front with a full-on attack on the Beaurevoir Line. The enemy would normally repulse such a thinly dispersed force, but they were shell-shocked. The Australians were on them before the Germans organised their defences. Their engagement was still tough, but by midday the last German line collapsed.

Rosenthal, daring as ever, thought he could go on to the heights that looked down from the German side on the fortifications. But the ten hours of brutal fighting was enough. He settled for a strong footing on Beaurevoir Spur.

Rawlinson was thrilled by the result. Monash wanted 2nd Division out of the line now that the Hindenburg fortifications had been smashed. But his chief had two last demands. The Americans were meant to relieve 2nd Division, but they needed twenty-four hours to get organised and into the new front line. Could Monash ask Rosenthal to stay put for just one more day – 4 October? And while his division was there, could it advance the line further east? Rawlinson was responding to Haig's obsession with using the cavalry, which could ride in and exploit what the infantry, tanks and artillery had softened up for them. Monash's men needed to secure a bit more of the area to make it easier for the men on horseback.

Haig might well have been looking ahead to days at the Officers' Club when he could reminisce about charges in the grand tradition in his war to match the reverie of those wallowing in their wars of the previous century. Monash had regarded the cavalry as superfluous. When Haig had wanted them in a battle, Monash had obliged. But they had been pushed to the rear in any attack plans. Now that the main conflict was all but over, the cavalry were going in as window dressing to please the C-in-C and a few of his mates.

The Haig–Rawlinson demand was unreasonable, given the effort put in already. Monash and Rosenthal conferred. It could be done with fresh troops. All divisions in the AIF had been pushed beyond the limits they imagined they could endure. But Monash had fed them on victory. When battalions were flagging, he urged his commanders on. They in turn were able to squeeze that little extra out of men who had gone beyond expected and acceptable limits. The spur always was 'the win'; the aim of flying the Australian flag in a position once held by the enemy was enough. The fact that they had never failed to do it since being a unified corps lifted them at critical moments.

With whiffs of mutiny in the air in recent days, it would have been a different story if Monash's AIF had a mixed record of victory and defeat. But with a string of momentous victories behind them, beating the some-times formidable opposition was the motivation.

'I selected as a suitable objective the village of Montbrehain,' Monash wrote. 'It stood on a plateau that dominated any further advances.'[16] It was a few kilometres east of the Hindenburg Line. The village itself featured steep streets and blind corners. Its elevation and natural internal defences – rises and tight alleys – promised some tough house-to-house fighting.

Rosenthal drew up his 6th Brigade, which, similarly to the 5th and 7th Brigades, had not seen action for a month. They had some tank support, but the battle for Montbrehain was a tough project.

The 6th Brigade began its attack at 6.05 a.m. on 5 October. Again the adventurism of one man, Lieutenant George Ingram, lifted the entire force. He led a thrust against a German strongpoint on the ridge, captur-ing nine machine-guns and forty-two prisoners. But it was just an appetiser for the main achievement when he led a rush on a quarry defended by forty-two machine-guns and a hundred of the enemy. Appar-ently not sated, Ingram left his men to clear up the area while he went into Montbrehain in search of a sniper who had caused havoc among the British 139th Brigade when it failed to take the town – or the ruins of it – the previous day.

Ingram had heard from the British that a sniper, or snipers, had picked off about twenty unsuspecting targets when a battalion had advanced on the ruins. The Australian deliberately went alone. He wanted the element of surprise in his favour, rather than the sniper's. Ingram stalked his way into the town's narrow streets around sharp, blind corners, waiting for fire that was aiming in the direction of his brigade. One location began to betray itself. The shots were not coming from an elevated position, which was where the unlucky British forces had been looking.

After an hour of stealthy movement among the ruins, Ingram spotted the source. A machine-gun was aimed out of a house's cellar ventilator. Ingram crawled from the side of the cellar while firing was coming from it. When within a metre of it, he stood up and fired his revolver into the ventilator, killing the sniper. Hearing other shocked German voices in the cellar, he dashed around to the back of the house, booted down the back door and bailed up thirty of the enemy. Ingram then waited coolly until his men entered the town.

His bravery was rewarded with the last VC for an Australian in the war.

One other soldier who should have won one at Montbrehain, but who unaccountably missed out, was Lieutenant N. F. Wilkinson, of the 6th Machine Gun Company. He was attached to the 2nd Division's 2nd Pioneer Battalion. They had been thwarted at the southern entrance to the village by heavy machine-gun fire. Wilkinson, knowing everything there was to know about the weapon, was surprised by the intensity of the defence. Instead of blindly rushing in, he selected a soldier to accompany him on a quick reconnoitre. They took a roundabout route to a railway cutting. They eased along it, keeping their heads down. The firing became louder as they reached an embankment. For a moment Wilkinson was stunned. He could see, from a side-on position, an estimated hundred Germans with their machine-guns pointing in the direction of his battalion. Wilkinson sent his companion back to his men with the order to bring up two gun teams.

He had a nervous wait. The gunners he had ordered were waylaid fighting two German machine-gun crews who had positioned themselves along the cutting minutes after the runner passed through the area on his way back to the battalion.

The Australians arrived after twenty-five minutes, set up and began firing from the side-on position. This caused mayhem among the German gunners, who did not have time to reposition their weapons. The result was thirty Germans dead and fifty more wounded. The other twenty or so scattered.

One of the captured Germans said that if they had known the Australians were their opponents, they would not have attempted to defend Montbrehain. It was one of scores of such comments recorded by the end of this frantic period of annihilation for the Germans. They thought that the Australian style of fighting, whereby one rogue soldier, for reasons of bravado, courage, showmanship, competitiveness or just plain insanity after so long in combat, was nigh-impossible to counter. Man for man, the enemy was just as courageous as the Australians. But this element of apparent craziness, or even near-suicidal intent, defied the tenets of rigid German discipline and usually caught them off guard. These reckless acts could cause a small encounter to change its direction. If the Germans had the upper hand, it would often be lost after a gutsy initiative from left-field – or madness, depending on the perpetrator or the beholder. Added up, these moments of inspiration in search of glory or an end turned a battle and again cumulatively finished the war.

Montbrehain was the last in an amazing string of battles beginning at Hamel on 4 July and ending three months later. As always when the Americans arrived to take over, they found the Australian flag fluttering from a pole over the skeleton of the town's post office. It was the symbol that kept the AIF going far beyond accepted limits of endurance in war.

There was always a cost. At Montbrehain it was a price too high for indulging Haig's whim. The 2nd Division suffered 430 casualties, performing to the highest standard seen in the entire war.

Monash ordered the 2nd Division out of the front line, leaving no Australians in the war. Their job was done. Over the past six months, they had taken 29,144 prisoners and liberated 116 towns and villages over an area of 660 square kilometres. No one knows precisely how many enemy were killed, but 60,000 would be a conservative figure. In the same period Australia lost 5500 dead and had 24,000 casualties. They had taken on thirty-nine enemy divisions and beaten every one of them, from the crack Prussian Guards who fought to the last to cobbled-together forces that ran when attacked.

Long before the great German offensive of 21 March, the enemy knew where the strength in the Allied armies lay. They were careful not to attack where Dominion forces were in the front line. After 8 August captured German commanders were admitting that the combination of tanks and Australians coming through the dawn mist was overwhelming.

Monash pointed out that the period of the last thrust from 8 August to 5 October was the least 'costly' period for the AIF, despite it providing the shock troops and spearhead of an attack. The key reason was Monash's emphasis on machine and weapons protection for the infantry without lessening its role. It was his greatest conjuring trick.

His strategies delineated the Australians from the rest of the Allies. They marked a change in the way war was conducted from a nineteenth-century mentality whereby men were cannon fodder. Monash's detailed command of the equipment, the weaponry and all the technological accoutrements of war put his thinking perhaps a half-century ahead of his contemporaries. The other important difference was that he could put the theory into practice, and he did it to devastating effect.

On 5 October, Prince Max von Baden, on behalf of the German Government, asked for an immediate Armistice on land, water and in the air. It was the beginning of the end of the war. Fighting would go on, but the enemy had no line of defence left in France. He would have to retreat at an increased pace.

With this news, a spent Monash later in the day departed for London and saw a congratulatory Birdwood and White en route. Arriving early on the 6th, he told Major General Dodds at AIF London to provide him with a car. He was to keep people – press, politicians, friends, relatives, anyone – away. Even PM Hughes was not to disturb him.

Monash, exhausted and relieved, just wanted a quiet day or two to himself and Lizette. He didn't feel like ever returning to the front.

AFTERGLOW

Monash needed much more than the day he had with Lizette in the country to recover from a kind of post-commandership depression. He felt ill and dispirited after the concentrated work in the killing fields. Once back at the Prince's Hotel on Tuesday 8 October, not even visits to the West End theatre could lift him. The next day, Monash agreed to see Hughes. They discussed the last campaigns. Hughes seemed better disposed towards him, which wasn't surprising. He was already basking in the reflected glory of Monash's corps having played such a big part in the lead up to and the smashing of a chunk of the Hindenburg fortifications. The PM asked for an account of the corps' achievements. Monash began writing, and this boosted him, as he began to articulate what he had been through.

On 10 October he had a sitting for Longstaff, lunched at Scott's and called for Lizette at 5.30 p.m. They later had dinner at a West End Jewish restaurant they were making their own. He began accepting invitations and realised that he was a celebrity. Probably only Sir Donald Bradman, thirty years later, stood with him among Australians in the twentieth century, so much in demand in England. Monash's reputation as the finest corps commander on either side spread fast. The war was almost over. The British wanted to celebrate war heroes, the men who had saved them from the enemy.[1]

The event he appreciated most was a dinner put on at the Dominions Club by the New Zealand shipping magnate Sir James Mills. Monash and the Foreign Secretary Arthur Balfour were the guests of honour. The war was the topic. Balfour spoke solemnly for an hour on the 'retention of the German colonies' in a style that, according to Monash, was 'impressive but somewhat ponderous'. The audience listened with 'polite indifference'. Monash was then invited to speak. He had been surprised to find 'gloom and pessimism' in London in the week of his return. Rigid censorship had not allowed news of his success on the Hindenburg Line to filter through. 'I asked Sir James Mills' guests what on earth was the matter with them all,' Monash said. 'I assured them that the war would be over before Christmas. Just as we had captured the Hindenburg Line, the Line of the Meuse and the Line of the Rhine would most certainly be broken in the next few weeks.' He drew thunderous applause. Balfour and other guests congratulated him.[2]

He was swamped with lunch and dinner invitations. He had a laugh when his old superior, Major General John Stanley, who had lent his name to the weapon that Monash had invented, invited him to dine. The elderly soldier was still arrogant and selfish, and fighting the wars of the previous century. He still behaved as if Monash was his subordinate. He had no idea of the number of battles Monash had just been through and won.

More pleasing was a phone call from the first girl Monash had ever taken out, Clara Stockfeld. He had been eighteen. She had been sixteen. She reminded him that they had taken the train from Elsternwick Station into Melbourne at night. He remembered with a little regret that his sister Mat had been with them. Clara had been smitten by him then and seemed more so now. She recalled something inspiring and poetic he had told her, for which she had 'blessed him ever since'. They lunched. There were nostalgic reminders of Melbourne and a life he had been away from now for four years.

In a letter to Vic, he also mentioned visiting a 'beautiful Elizabethan home', which was used by forty convalescing Australian officers. The Earl of Darnley – the Honourable Ivo Bligh – owned it. His wife, Lady Darnley, was formerly Florence Morphy of Benalla. Bligh had led an English cricket team to Australia. When it was beaten, Florence was among some lovely young women who had given him a small urn containing ashes of burnt bails. It was a symbol of English cricket. Bligh had fallen in love with Florence. He sailed her back to England to marry.

'The Earl showed me, on his writing table,' Monash noted, 'a tiny little urn under a glass cover . . . which is supposed to contain the Ashes.'[3]

Monash enjoyed the limelight, but never became carried away. The fortune he had in staying alive and the brutal experiences he had been through wouldn't allow it. He was well centred in his own personality and character and did not need continual affirmation of his greatness. He was happy to go unrecognised, and revelled in the anonymity of wearing civilian clothes.

Paul Simonson recalled an incident at the theatre in October. He was in uniform; Monash was in civvies. At the interval Simonson was engaged in conversation with a Light Horse officer, who had just arrived from Egypt, when Monash joined them. The officer was in full flow explaining an action during the Middle East campaign. Monash interrupted, and remarked something to the effect: 'Oh, yes, that was when Chauvel moved a brigade round the right flank.' The Light Horse officer was surprised, but carried on. A few minutes later, Monash broke in again with a pertinent comment. The officer was confused.

'Weren't you in Egypt with us?' he asked.

'No,' Monash replied.

'I do know you from somewhere,' the officer said, with a puzzled look. 'Weren't you the quartermaster at . . . ?'

'No.'

The conversation about the Light Horse continued. Then Monash made a penetrating remark, showing insider knowledge of the campaign.

'Look, I do know you,' the frustrated officer said. 'Who are you?'

'Monash,' was the quiet reply just as the warning bell announced the interval was over.

The shocked officer, on instinct, stepped back to give a hurried salute. He was close to a wall and crashed into it. Monash and Simonson left the officer standing to attention, his AIF hat of flowing feathers askew.[4]

Monash was also kept level-headed by the nagging knowledge that there might still be a job to be done on the front. The war was not quite done, even though the honours had begun to pour in as if it was over. The French gave him the Croix de Guerre with Palm Leaf; the Belgians made him a Grand Officer of the Order of the Crown and gave him their Croix de Guerre. The Americans, more modestly, offered the Distinguished Service Medal.

After the break, Monash was ready for more conflict if ordered to return to the fighting. But slowly diminishing hand tremors were a private reminder that he was really one of the 24,000 Australia casualties.

A week after Monash's meeting with Hughes, Blamey, who was at the front with the five divisions, reported that Rawlinson had asked how long before the AIF would be ready to go again. Two months, he replied. Two days later, on 20 October Rawlinson rang to say that the AIF would be needed in one week.

Blamey and Hobbs were alarmed. They wrote to Monash, asking him to prevent it. Hughes had told the men they would be on leave from early October. That had yet to be granted. If they were forced back into action with at least two divisions unfit (the 1st and 4th), there could be problems.

Monash was now speaking for himself as much as for his men. He and they had had enough. His judgement that a good break was needed – two months and more if possible – from early October seemed appropriate. But the British High Command wanted to throw its spearhead back into the fighting. Monash wrote to Hughes asking him to intervene. They met and decided to see Sir Henry Wilson, Chief of the General Staff and Lloyd George's principal military adviser, independently.

Hughes told Wilson the AIF had done enough, but Wilson was frosty. He was unhappy that Hughes had promised the AIF that it would be out of the action for the winter. Monash told Wilson that Hughes had instructed him not to allow his corps to fight any more. Monash put his case that it at least needed months to recuperate. He was gambling that if he could stall the High Command, the war would be finished before the Australians were called on again.

Wilson promised to refer the matter to cabinet, but he couldn't have done so with much force. Rawlinson was still demanding that the Australians prepare for more combat. On 27 October, the day they were supposed to resume at the front, Monash and Birdwood went to see Haig at High Command HQ in France. The C-in-C wouldn't budge. Monash explained the poor condition of his 1st and 4th Divisions. Haig conceded that they could be spared unless matters became urgent. The other three divisions, which were fit, would have to go.

Monash's dilemma of serving two masters, the British High Command and his PM, was never more conflicted. But in the end his duty was to his men, who were bound to the British Fourth Army. After three weeks off he felt far better and ready, if need be, for battle command once more. He wrote to Hughes to explain that he tried to prevent the AIF being used again. He was surprised to learn that the PM had been persuaded by someone in the British cabinet, probably Lloyd George, that the

Australians' presence on the battlefield was important to the final victory, if only to put further pressure on the Germany Army and government to capitulate. Having read Monash's account of the corps' efforts, Hughes saw the value of flying the flag to the very end of hostilities and then on to peace negotiations, in which he wanted a say. (For instance, what would happen to former German possessions in the Pacific?)

Monash used his report to Hughes as the basis of his account for Pearce and the government in Australia. He wrote of the decisive part his corps had played in the Allied campaign of 1918, splitting it into five stages. First, there was the arrest of the German offensive of 21 March. Second, there was the turning of that enemy campaign into a defensive one. 'Next followed the great, initial and irredeemable defeat of 8 August,' he said. 'According to the enemy's own admissions, it was the beginning of the end.' Fourth was the stopping of the Germans' respite on the Somme, which might have allowed it to recover for another year of war. And fifth was the overthrow of the 'great defensive system' – the Hindenburg fortifications. It was Germany's 'last bulwark' for safeguarding its hold on French soil, 'a hold that would have enabled him [the enemy] to bargain terms'.

Monash was adamant that whatever contrary claims were made, Germany's surrender on 5 October was caused by its defeat on the battlefield. It followed so closely after his force had smashed the Hindenburg defences that Monash believed it was a 'final, determining cause' of the capitulation. Despite evidence that Hindenburg and Ludendorff had been seeking an armistice in late September, Monash would not be shaken from his claim that the corps played an important part, sometimes a predominant part, in each stage of operations that led to Germany's overthrow. He later wrote that there was no better testimony for such a conclusion than the admissions of Ludendorff himself. Monash also asserted that the AIF's performance was better than that of 'any similar body of troops on the Western Front'.[5]

The same day, 5 November, the corps was ordered to the front once more. Since they had last been in the line, the fighting and pursuit had gone on. The German retreat had seen it give up Lens, Armentières and the Aubers Ridge without a struggle. This enabled the British Second and Fifth Armies to occupy Lille and the industrial centres adjacent to it. Germany's tactic was to delay the inevitable by destroying bridges, ripping up railways and bombing every important road intersection. The pursuing

British and American troops were exhausted as the armistice negotiations dragged on.

On 10 November, Monash began moving to HQ at Le Cateau, while Glasgow and Sinclair-MacLagan and their divisions were on their way to the front, with the other three soon to follow after the corps had rested along the banks of the Somme between Amiens and Abbeville.

Monash felt a surge of satisfaction as he drove on 11 November towards his new château, which had been the base of General van der Marwitz, Commander of Germany's Second Army. Monash's corps had been pitted against his troops for several months. But Monash's feelings became numbed as his Rolls with the Aussie flag at full mast hurried the 200 kilometres from Eu to Le Cateau. The journey took him over the entire length of his battlefields from Villers-Bretonneux. If he felt like a conquering hero, he never expressed it. He was more saddened than anything as he drove past 'the formidable and forbidding desert of eighty odd miles devastated by war'.

The spacious château was set in country with hedgerows and woods like rural England. It was untouched by the holocaust of the previous four years. The departing Germans had stolen its paintings and used its many grand mirrors and windows for target practice, leaving the place 'cold and cheerless'.[5]

He had just settled in when the order arrived for the cessation of hostilities. After the intensity of the AIF operations until 5 October, it was an anti-climax, but a welcome one. Monash would never again have to give or receive orders in war.

There was a new kind of mopping up to complete. Soon after the real Armistice on 11 November Monash was summoned to see Hughes in London on 18 November. There was no way to keep the Bantam Cock at bay now. Without a war to fight, the politicians could step in and take charge again.

Monash had no idea of the backbiting going on over preparations for getting the troops back home. He had assumed that the AIF's administration – the GOC – would handle it. But Hughes had other ideas. He wanted total control. This could be achieved by putting demobilisation and repatriation under political, not military, management.

Monash let it be known that he would like to take over GOC, if and when Birdwood stepped down. But he didn't really care. It would be nothing like being a fighting commander. As usual, Murdoch and Bean were pushing for White. Bean still idolised him, although with a little less passion than before. Murdoch still saw him as someone he could manipulate, and that was important because the big stories now would be in 'getting the boys back home'. But Hughes, as was his habit, remained a contrary kind of bird. He had never been as convinced about White as Bean was.

Bean alleged in his diary that Hughes had reservations about Monash because he was a 'Jew' and 'showy', but this would have been his interpretation of the PM's attitude, which was nowhere expressed this way in his own writing. Hughes had become a Monash supporter, up to a point.[6] There was no doubting his stature. The British in high places were referring to him with great deference as the best man in France. Monash now carried enormous clout. That would be useful in getting things done over repatriation. Hughes both admired and feared him. He would like to see Monash do the job – and out of Australia for as long as possible, just in case he had any latent political ambitions. Hughes' political antennae were sensitive. If Monash, the popular, mighty warlord, came home during the euphoric immediate post-war period, he and others might get ideas about leadership in another sphere. A couple of hundred thousand war veteran votes spread all over the nation would be the general's, for a start.

Monash was surprised to be offered the position of Director-General of Repatriation and Demobilisation. It pleased him. He didn't fancy sitting on the Rhine with nothing to do in a cold winter. Birdwood loved his job. He would stay where he was for the moment. That left White as the bridesmaid again. He was keen to stay and assist Monash. But Monash wanted his own staff. He had great respect for White, yet he had become used to harmony, and the two had never quite clicked. Monash recommended to White that he go home and run the army. After the initial shock, White was not unhappy about the idea. There would be nothing for him to do under Birdwood now, given that Monash had once more been given the number-one prestige and power job in the AIF.

Refreshed by a new challenge, Monash summoned all his senior commanders and officers to Le Cateau. He announced that Hobbs would take over as Corps Commander. No Australian divisions would be going to Germany as part of the occupying force. Instead, he would be steering them home, but it would be a massive and complex operation that would take time, perhaps up to a year. Monash was already bubbling with plans for helping every soldier prepare for his new civilian life.

An item on Monash's agenda concerned the 118 soldiers from 1st Brigade who had 'deserted'. Monash and Hobbs thought it would a good idea if Glasgow, as their divisional head, pardoned them. He wouldn't do it.

After the meeting Monash took Hobbs aside for a chat about the 'deserters'. It might be a fine first act as Corps Commander, he told him, if every one of them was pardoned. Besides, he didn't want any Australians spending Christmas on Dartmoor. Hobbs was concerned about Glasgow's reaction. Monash knew he would be ropeable. But he told Hobbs not to concern himself. He was Corps Commander now, and all divisional leaders took orders from him.

Thus fortified, Hobbs' first directive as head of the peacetime Australian war machine was a humane one. The soldiers were pardoned.

Corps staff arranged a banquet to farewell Monash. On the way back to London with his aide and nephew Paul, he saw the sights in Brussels and squeezed in a trip to Waterloo to go over the battleground he knew so well but had never seen.

Now that the war was truly over, there was no excuse for not inviting Vic and Bertha to join him. But he put them off until the early spring of 1919 when the weather would be better and the journey safer. This was all legitimate and honest as far as it went. But at heart, he would rather be free, and spend time with Lizette. In the weeks he had returned from the front since 6 October she had become more like a partner than a lover. They were 'an item' on the London social scene. His married life with Vic had stopped by circumstance, not design or misadventure, at the end of 1914. That was fours ago. He had loyally kept in touch, having written correspondence that would fill several volumes. But that was not the same as being living, breathing partners physically together. He had moved on in ways he would never have dreamt of or expected. Lizette had been the woman in the right place at the right time. But he wasn't worrying about the consequences. There was too much happening at work and at play. He would face any problem when it arose in the spring.

The social whirl continued. Although his affair with Lizette was obvious, every other invitation was for him only; some were for all-male functions, usually to do with the military. Monash had set up in a West End service flat, lunching or dining out at least once a day. If it were a brisk two-kilometre walk, he would do it. If further, or if he were in a hurry, he would use the Rolls-Royce and driver he had hijacked from the AIF, much to Hobbs' irritation. He was 'clubbing' in London even more than he did in Melbourne, and responding to select invitations from the high and the mighty. He didn't discriminate against friends and associates, but if he was not familiar with the individual, they had to be stimulating, well known or famous in their field. Lord Northcliffe was an example. Viscount Bryce, the historian and statesman, was another. He made notes on all of them, notching up famous contacts on his belt like Hugh Hefner did with play-bunnies. It was as if he was always conscious that this rarefied post-war afterglow period would leave him like Cinderella at midnight.

Those who didn't wish a selfish one-on-one with the great General Sir John invited him to share his brilliance, charm, wit and experience in vanquishing the Hun in speeches at lunches and dinners. He had to be selective here, too; otherwise he would be spending too much time writing and rehearsing his speeches, with Lizette often his practice audience. There was the Eccentrics Club, where he tried to live up to its name by explaining some of his own off-centre idiosyncrasies. His penchant for souvenirs – especially items that nearly killed him – brought laughs. The Smeaton-ian Society of Engineers gave him a long-standing ovation for his explanation of the importance of engineers in everything, especially winning wars. He narrowed down this speech for the 'Dynamicables' (more engineers), calling it 'Engineering in War'. The members gave him their undivided attention as he described how professionals had been used to reorganise his fighting machine after Mont St Quentin and Péronne (with bridge-building and railway reconstruction) for the relentless pursuit of the Germans after they fled the Somme.

By contrast, he wrote a poignant speech for the Ladies' Victory Festival about the importance of nursing and ambulance work in war, and enjoyed the flirtations afterwards. Lizette was not always his companion, and Monash, for an unlikely period in his maturity, reverted to the life he had led as a university undergraduate, where he enjoyed the company of females as much as, if not more than, that of men. Women responded to his charm, and those extra dimensions of power and fame, which even surpassed the attraction of the dark good looks and bristling intelligence of his youth.

The Jewish community couldn't get enough of him. He was a curio, this Australian-Jewish general. Not since Old Testament days had one of their own distinguished himself in war as much. They wanted to probe, interview and dissect him. Was he Orthodox? Was he a Zionist? Would he be the first Governor of Palestine? Or maybe its military governor? Would he put money into worthy Jewish causes? Was he married? Was he wealthy? Monash let it be known that he had no interest in military governorship. Yet he felt an obligation to respond and used the forum of the Maccabean Society to make some very generous remarks, which might have made Birdwood and White in the audience feel a fraction uncomfortable.

Monash painted a glowing picture of Australia as free of discrimination. He spoke of the equality of opportunity for everyone of both sexes 'regardless of social or religious considerations'. He 'gratefully' acknowledged that since his school days he had never experienced disfavour on 'any question of race or religion'. He went further. 'In Australia we have no Jewish question,' he said.[7]

These comments were more true than not, when comparing it to discrimination and anti-Semitism in Russia and Germany. But knowing that his every utterance would be picked up in the general and Jewish press in Australia, he would have been attempting a pre-emptive strike against racism in his home country.

After the initial sittings for artists in October, when the Corps Commander's mind was still planning the destruction of the enemy, he accepted more offers to be painted. Now with his mind cleared, he had an eye on posterity. He wanted to be preserved on canvas and film and, in turn, was thinking hard about writing his own account of the war. All those speeches he was making, and the paucity of good press coverage in Australia on the AIF's effort, were nagging him.

Luncheon clubs were in vogue, but Monash, although enjoying himself, was watching his food intake. He added a few kilos, which looked better on than off. He kept up daily exercise so that he maintained a hardness of muscle that he had since Salisbury Plains, when he made up his mind that if he were going be a divisional commander then he would look like one. Since then they had called him 'the old man'. He was living up to that now with thinning hair and enough wrinkles to make plastic surgeons salivate. But no one mentioned Tweedledee or Tweedledum again.

Monash had a most memorable time at the Australian and New Zealand Luncheon Club and was pleased to see Sir Ian Hamilton, for whom he never lost an affinity. Hamilton congratulated him warmly, and reminded him yet again of that hellish day in Lilydale. He, with good humour, would forever claim to have picked Monash as General material long before anyone else.

Churchill, Hughes, Birdwood and Hamilton all spoke. Hughes and Birdwood referred to him, just. But remarks by Hamilton and Churchill were more than dipped in praise. The mention of his name would have been enough to make him feel good. But the fact that every time it was mentioned there was spontaneous applause was more than gratifying. He was now well aware that he was more than flavour of the month. Monash was happy for the recognition for him and those who had fought under him. But he was not a twenty-year-old film star. He was fifty-three and had had a life without fame. Now that it touched him, there would be no life changes or swollen ego. Monash simply revelled in the moment. He accepted that the way he was being fêted in England would not last. It made it easier to enjoy.

Hughes was not so thrilled on such occasions. The PM had sensed Monash's palpable strength in his own force field at Hamel in July and again in September when he undermined him. Yet he didn't expect the Corps Commander to be the focus of attention away from the battlefield and in a civilian atmosphere dominated by politicians and businessmen. No one wanted the PM's autograph on a menu. The conga line of people wanting to press Monash's flesh curled out the door. Hughes' nose might or might not have been out of joint. But this occasion would have impressed on him the importance of this figure he would claim to have appointed. The PM had never experienced such respect and admiration bordering on hero worship for anyone, let alone himself. The London-born Welshman and the first minister of the Crown in Australia was downgraded in Monash's presence. He might as well have been the rock-breaker and swagman of his youth for all it was worth at such gatherings in the presence of this quasi-rogue warlord. Hughes regarded Monash as driven and ambitious. Could the momentum of his war effort and his influence in England propel him into politics in Australia? Could he be a political threat? Hughes was planning a federal election in 1919. He would make sure Monash wasn't there for it.

Monash noticed Hughes' reaction and sensed an enmity. Their rapprochement, which had seen him secure the repatriation job, was short-lived. The negative feelings between them would grow. Yet in those heady days, Monash had few enemies. The British elite of the military, society, academia, the press, business and the Jewish community embraced him. The royals, particularly, continued to be enamoured of him.

In December 1918 Monash attended the British Empire Boxing Tournament and was supporting the Australian contestants when he received an invitation from the King's second son, Prince Albert (the future King George VI, who was just short of his twenty-third birthday) to join the royal box. Present also was the Marquis of Milfordhaven (formerly Prince Louis of Battenberg).

'Prince Albert is a real jolly boy,' Monash recalled, 'full of fun.'[8]

Monash was surprised when asked to spend the rest of the evening with him, but he should not have been. So far, apart from being a royal, the military had been the Prince's life. He had served in the navy for four years until 1917, and was now in the air arm of the navy and was heading in the next year for the Flying Corps. Albert, like his father, appreciated men like Monash, who had saved them from fates unknown. He had plenty of questions, and Monash went away far more impressed by him than he had been with the moody, self-absorbed Prince of Wales, who often seemed under sufferance (in Egypt, early in 1916, and on Monash's staff in late 1918). He couldn't recall one question emanating from the Prince of Wales' insouciant lips.

The pinnacle of those early post-war celebrations for Monash came on 27 December 1918 when he attended a state banquet at Buckingham Palace held by the King and Queen for President Wilson. Monash was one of about sixty guests. He spoke to the President and the King for about five minutes each, but with Queen Mary for closer to fifteen minutes. One of the subjects discussed was how her son was faring on Monash's staff after he had been attached to it at the King's specific request.[9] Monash would have been at his diplomatic best. He had little time for the playboy Prince.

Whoever prepared seating plans for state banquets knew what they were doing. Monash couldn't have found the company more stimulating.

He was placed over dinner between the author Rudyard Kipling and Lord Burnham (owner of the *Daily Telegraph*). Monash had read plenty of Kipling, who had been born in the same year as him. Monash even kept a scrapbook for more than twenty years, in which he cut and pasted Kipling poems and short-story extracts from Melbourne newspapers.[10]

The author, who had won the Nobel Prize for Literature, was an imperialist, who believed anyone born beyond the English Channel was a 'lesser breed', which was not a good basis for a rapport with Monash. But the Australian had read a fair swathe of his works, enjoying his tales about British soldiers in India and Burma as well as his novel *Kim* and *The Jungle Book*, which he had read to Bertha when she was six. It wouldn't have bridged the gap, yet it would have helped.

Monash had met Kipling at a lunch when the author had visited Melbourne just before the war. 'Kipling amused us by recounting apocryphal stories about me,' Monash wrote. 'He had heard them from diggers on leave.'

Monash reminded the author that he (Kipling) had used a fountain pen (then a novelty) to scrawl his name several times across a menu card at the Melbourne lunch. Monash had cut up the menu and distributed the autograph to several other interested guests while keeping one for his own collection. He told Kipling about a book he had that contained the signatures of 'my friends and acquaintances in Egypt, England, France and Australia, before, during and after my days of war service'. He even collected the King's signature on one of his visits to Monash's HQ in France. (The King had insisted on taking the book from him. It was returned a month later containing the autographs of the King, the Queen, the Prince of Wales, Princess Mary, Prince Albert, the Duke of Connaught and Prince Arthur of Connaught.) Kipling insisted on adding his scrawl to the signature book.[11]

Opposite Monash at the banquet were the British-born American portrait painter J. S. Sargent and Churchill. Monash found Sargent a little too serious and reserved, but they had something in common in their appreciation of the Spanish painter Velazquez. Churchill was at his anecdotal best. Even his stutter had an eloquent resonance.

Monash, without tongue in cheek, ranked the occasion up there with being in the company of a humble, notorious bushranger he had met at Jerilderie forty-one years earlier. It's probable that, in the unrestrained atmosphere of the victors' banquet, Monash would have regaled his dinner companions with the story of that meeting one hot summer's day in the Australian bush.

Five days after the banquet, Monash was appointed Knight Grand Cross of the Order of St Michael and St George (GCMG) in the New Year honours list of 1919. In Australia only Munro Ferguson and Deputy Prime Minister Sir Joseph Cook had such an honour. Hughes would not have recommended it. The most likely explanation is that the King put down his name for the enhancement. It was so rare that few people reacted or knew anything about it.

Monash delighted in designing the coat of arms that went with the decoration. He chose the Southern Cross, symbolising his country; a bridge recognising engineering, his first great love and occupation; a sword enclosed in a laurel wreath that depicted his finest achievement; the Lion of Judah and the compasses of Solomon, which at once embraced the symbols of his heritage: war, wisdom and engineering. He chose a prosaic Latin motto, 'For War and the Arts'. Perhaps, in keeping with his struggle in that language, he left out a negative. 'For the Arts, not War' might have been more appropriate. Then again, fighting had been on his mind. It had consumed his whole being for four years.

The results of four years' fighting would continue to occupy him as he rolled up his civilian sleeves, dropped the military formalities and applied himself to the big challenge of repatriation. He wanted the return of 180,000 diggers to be achieved with dignity and promise for every one of them.

Monash felt an unfathomable sense of debt to his men, which was bound up with honour, guilt and admiration. He had created the fighting machine and had pushed, urged and cajoled it from Amiens to Montbre-hain. Now was the time to practice more of what he had preached to his officers and serve it.

The diggers couldn't all be sent home at once. Monash organised each division into groups of a thousand soldiers – a number suitable for travel by train and then ship. The longest-serving diggers were to be sent home first.

Those waiting would be offered 'Extra Military Employment'. Monash had to persuade Hughes to drop the idea of setting up national workshops useful for Australian industrial development. They would take too long to

set up, and it represented too narrow a spectrum of training and education. Monash overcame the PM's dislike for formal education and instead
contacted established institutions, mainly in England but also in several
other countries. They were urged to open their doors to the diggers. A
variety from Oxford and Cambridge universities to farms, factories and
even trade unions invited them in. There were a few odd requests. One
Tasmanian wanted to be a lion-tamer. By the time a circus was found that
was willing to help, he was on his way home. A Queenslander thought it
would be useful to have a qualification in deep-sea diving. Only the navy
had such a school in England.

There was a big rush to Yorkshire to learn about the wool manufac-
turing industry. But diggers were welcomed all over Europe. Some
studied for exams in a special school set up at the mouth of the Somme
that would allow them to enter Australian universities, the civil service or
professions.

Monash weaved his creative administrative magic to turn the corps of
trained belligerents into a huge educational enterprise, in which 40,000
took part. It was hoped that the result would be a pool of qualified men
who could slip back into civilian life with less difficulty than if they had
done nothing while waiting in camps of boredom and potential trouble in
France and England.

Monash and Hughes had several meetings over repatriation in the first
months. Hughes' attitude to him had deteriorated ever since the day at the
Australian and New Zealand Luncheon Club. Monash realised over the
weeks that Hughes had a complex about being overshadowed by him in
London. It led to the PM being discourteous and treating him shabbily.
Monash, in response, had trouble in being polite.[12] He had the feeling that
the PM was intent on slowing up the repatriation process.

Monash might have mentioned this in a roundabout way to Murdoch,
who now focused in a positive way on Monash. He was the key to big news
stories, and there was nothing bigger for Australians in the last months of
1918 and most of 1919 than how and when the diggers were coming
home.

Murdoch had an eye to the headlines with the papers at home. The
pressure from the public was for their return to be speedy. Aware that
Hughes was against this, Murdoch saw Monash as a useful conduit. After

some natural initial caution, Monash began to see the newspaperman the same way.

Murdoch, in an apparent break with Hughes, began sending back despatches that suggested the government was slowing down the return of the diggers. It put pressure on the federal cabinet in Melbourne. Hughes, virtually an expatriate PM in London, was forced to tell the press that everything was being done to hasten the diggers' return. A Murdoch cable early in 1919 was stark. He wrote that the government had capitulated over the issue and called Monash the 'driving force'. He even warned that if politicians got in his way, Monash would go home. Sounding like an enthusiastic Dr Frankenstein, Murdoch wrote glowingly: '. . . Never can there be any questions about Monash's brain. It is there, a living, searching, strong intelligence, breeding ideas, and judging them shrewdly. His motto is Action, and his energy already pulsates through the demobilisation scheme.'[13]

Encouraged by Murdoch's line, Monash responded more to his request for interviews and put his case. 'If we can concert,' Murdoch quoted him as saying, 'the means and machinery to enable our men to equip themselves for their future industrial life, then we are going to render a service to our nation that cannot be measured.'[14] Such a patriotic appeal and sentiment helped Monash to fight Hughes' surreptitious filibustering.

The only signs of unrest surfaced in the 3rd Division's artillery early in January 1919. The soldiers went on strike. Monash urged Gellibrand to go easy on his men, and he blamed the problem on officers being too strict. Monash sent a message to the gunners, urging them to be patient. The repat scheme would take effect soon. His message helped, along with a contribution from Hobbs, to smooth matters.

It was a small distraction compared to Monash's problem with the British Shipping Controller. Australia was producing troops faster than he could supply ships. Monash treated the situation as a battle. The controller was the enemy, and he soon realised what German Army commanders had faced when tackling the Australian.

'I have now got the Shipping Controller absolutely beaten,' Monash wrote in combat language. '[I] have created such a pool of troops in England, and have secured such a rapid rate of delivery from France . . . that by no possibility can the Shipping Controller catch up to me.'

Monash was back on the Somme, attacking the Mont and Péronne: 'I am not giving him any rest. Scarcely a day passes that I do not deliver an attack upon him from a new angle.'[15]

Monash loved the new position's challenge, and the stretch. It was just the right therapy for him in 1919, as his men launched into their own rehabilitation with study and training. The more problems that arose, the more he relished the role. It was accurate to blame the Shipping Controller, but he had a tough job. Carriers were needed for several countries, including South Africa, India, the USA and Canada, as governments struggled with bureaucracy and shipping companies to get troops home.

Monash also had to face administrative bungles. The British High Command changed its mind several times on whether or not it needed Australian troops to occupy Germany. This affected tens of thousands, and helped to cause the unrest among the 3rd Division's artillerymen, who were given five different directives in three months over whether or not they would be needed. It was infuriating for him and them to be pushed and pulled as if they were still on the front line. Monash began to use his weight here and there, and more than a few British bureaucrats in the military and government felt both his wrath and the subtle use of his now intrinsic, intangible power. In the heady first year after the war, his name carried weight, and he used it.

One of many examples occurred when the British War Office attempted to veto a farewell Anzac Day march through London. The excuse was that there would a parade of overseas troops eight days later on 3 May.

Monash insisted on the Anzac Day parade. He had become father to this memorial. He was not going to have his child disappear on its fourth birthday. He would make one call to Haig. If he didn't fix it, Monash would contact the King. The monarch had often told him to be in touch if he wanted anything. So far he had only taken him up on leather vests for the 3rd Division in 1916 when the King had said the lads would freeze in France in the winter without warm clothing. Yet he didn't have to use his ultimate contact in the British system. The War Office, on the threat of Haig being approached, capitulated.

Before the parade Monash reminded his troops: 'You represent the great and immortal Australian Army Corps. Every man should try and look as he ought to feel, proud of his division and the Australian Army.'[16] Monash and Hobbs rode at the head of the 5000 diggers on the five-kilometre march. It wound from Hyde Park along the Mall across Trafalgar Square, then down the Strand to Australia House, where the cheering crowd was twenty deep. Monash took the salute from the Prince of Wales, Haig and Chauvel. Hughes, again in an inferior role, was on the saluting stand, too. It was another reminder of Monash's capacity for the poignant ceremonial occasion, something that politicians aped and envied, but for which they never quite had the skills. Overhead Australian pilots did some spectacular, if not overadventurous diving and loop-the-loops.

Monash's fetish for precision and strong performances was satisfied by the event that he was determined to immortalise.

BACK TO THE
FUTURE

Monash faced his dilemma over Lizette Bentwitch late in April after some serious soul-searching. In January he had made up his mind not to divorce Vic. His heart might well have been with Lizette, but the responsibility associated with Monash's public image, fame and reputation, as well as his sense of loyalty to his wife, would always mean that his head would rule. But after doing the right thing and informing his lover that his wife would take precedence, he had continued to see Lizette, which gave her hope. They continued to be an item, turning up at functions where the press was present. On 4 April they were at a well-publicised dinner dance to mark the closing of the Officers' Club at 138 Piccadilly. It was their last function together before Vic arrived.

On 26 April – three days before Vic and Bertha were due to arrive in England – he had another serious discussion with Lizette, who tried to change his mind about his future. He refused her again, but was torn. Time and circumstance had caused him to love two women at once for different reasons. It was a situation that was contrary to his nature and placed him in an emotional tangle, although he believed he had sorted out the problem before he went down to Plymouth to meet Vic and Bertha on their boat from Australia. It was 29 April 1919, four days after his triumphant march through London.[1]

He was in an ebullient, expectant mood, having announced their arrival in *The Times*, which was protocol for a knight and military commander of his standing. The gap of fifty-two months since husband and wife had been together saw all the angst that had at times marred their marriage slip away. Both had been encouraging in letters, where it was easy, with a little effort, to be affectionate. Neither mentioned the dangers in their lives. Monash told amusing anecdotes about everything as if he was at Queens-cliff on Easter camp with the old North Melbourne Battery. He had to report deaths of friends and acquaintances, yet he did it as if it were bad luck, rather than explaining that it was amazing good fortune for anyone to survive all the war zones and fronts unscathed. Few of the letters to Vic and Bertha articulated his daily loathing and horror of war, which his diaries often did. This calmed his family's fears; although Vic and Bertha daily lived in trepidation that they would receive official notification from the government that General Monash was dead. Many times since Gallipoli such rumours had surfaced.

Vic had put just as brave a gloss on her life. Despite his being in the war zone with bullets and artillery shell hitting within millimetres of him and killing scores of other soldiers, cervical cancer had brought her closer to death. Vic was frail, thin and easily fatigued. She had the constant fear that the cancer would return.

After a separation that would have strained any marriage, they embraced on board ship, brushing away the lost years in an instant.

There would be no mention of Lizette, except when Vic inquired about her London-based friend and wanted to see her. She knew her husband had seen her occasionally, but she assumed they were friends and nothing more. He had managed to keep the affair secret from his family. Monash told Vic that Lizette would meet them when they docked at Tilbury. (In a romantic touch, he didn't bring Vic and Bertha back to London by train but instead accompanied them on the boat to Tilbury.)

He was particularly keen to see Bertha, now twenty-six years old. They had always been close. She had also been a loyal correspondent and a loving, constant supporter.

Bertha was astonished to see the change in her father's physical appearance. Gone was the middle-age girth that prosperous men wore with pride. She was amazed at his fitness, but this joy was sobered by his looks. Those four years of unmatched war responsibility were sculpted into his face and greying hairline. Yet the warmth in those crinkled eyes was even deeper, if that were possible. He had aged, but seemed far from broken by what he had been through.

At Tilbury, Lizette went through with the charade of meeting her old friend. The Rosenhains were at the dockside, too.

The Rolls took Monash, Vic and Bertha and their considerable luggage to an apartment in Queen Anne Mansions, Marylebone, not far from Regent Street, and walking distance from his own apartment.

Vic and Bertha hardly had time to settle in when they and Monash entered a dimension of social activity that had been denied him without a wife. Lizette had accompanied him to the theatre, restaurants and the country. But he could not parade her in front of royalty or the military hierarchy, or at official functions. With Vic by his side, he could now accept invitations to dine with the Hamiltons, the Rawlinsons among others. Vic had kept a friendship with Mrs Hughes, and the three went out to dinner, then a show – notably without the PM, who made sure he was unavoidably detained elsewhere. The Monash–Hughes relationship had soured to a point where they could not stand each other's company unless it was necessary at an official function.

Vic picked up her long-term friendship with Lizette, and the four often went out together. Monash was uncomfortable. It would have been painful for Lizette, too. Yet he would have been in a position to compare his feelings about the two women. The rows he had resumed with Vic might have made him think that Lizette was better suited to him temperamentally. The intelligent Bertha, who was sensitive to every nuance of her father's emotions and body language, sensed some tensions between him and Lizette.

But the charade continued. Unsuspecting Vic saw Lizette as a valued friend in the dizzying, unreal scene of never-ending social rounds. She was someone she could gossip with and confide in. Perhaps her attitude to a famous, not always easy-to-deal-with husband, would have encouraged Lizette. No doubt Monash expressed his ambivalence about Vic, especially when their verbal wars resumed with all their old vehemence. The fact that Monash was keeping a separate abode was making it easier for Lizette to see him when he needed succour after his fighting with Vic. Whatever it was, something made Lizette cling to hopes and dreams that Monash would be hers, even after he had been straight with her about their not having a future together.

On 3 May, Vic and Bertha watched with pride as he rode behind Chauvel with a thousand diggers in the parade through London for Dominion troops. Vic was in her element on the London scene, which made her Melbourne socialising seem like a billabong campfire by comparison. The heady atmosphere of Lord Mayors' balls, dinners, parties, art exhibitions and events lifted her as spring rolled on. She thrilled at being in the Royal Enclosure at Ascot, where she met the King and Queen. Vic thought it surreal to see the King lean across to her husband and invite them to lunch privately at Buckingham Palace. When the monarch asked if it would be all right if Prince Albert came along, because he would like to see Monash again, she was speechless.

She met the King and Queen several times more. Vic would have pinched herself when she and Monash were singled out for attention at a Royal Academy private viewing of a painting of the Corps Commander by the AIF's official portraitist, John Longstaff.

Vic was not well enough to join Monash and Bertha on a four-day tour of the battlefields of Flanders and France.

They took off on 16 May from Folkestone by boat for Boulogne on a whirlwind five-day tour. Monash relived the whole vivid experience of his war in Flanders and France. They took photos everywhere, especially of friends' graves, which would be given to grateful families. Bertha recorded the entire event in a tight, fourteen-page document, *My Trip with Dad to France – May 1919*.[2] Monash-style precision was evident. Every visit was timed to the minute as they followed in fast-forward the vivid path of struggle, conquer and destruction taken by Monash from 1916 to 1918. Bertha absorbed it all visually and verbally:

> Took 4 photos, including dad on steps at spot where he received his knighthood [she noted at Bertangles] . . . Dad explained the importance of the high ground at Villers-Bretonneux, which overlooked Amiens . . . reached Albert. Town is absolutely destroyed . . . long look at ruins of Cathedral . . . proceeded over the high plateau between Ancre and the Somme intro Bray village . . . area completely devastated . . . saw the blown up bridges over the Somme, which had been repaired by 3rd Div. Engineers . . . see the ruins of the great gun of Chuignes . . . took photograph . . . reached Méricourt Château . . . was HQ occupied by Dad in September . . . crossed the Cerisy Chipilly Bridge, built by the 3rd Pioneers, of which Dad has a model . . . saw ruins of Hamel village . . . reached Amiens, called on the town mayor . . .

Along the way, they kept coming across gangs of German prisoners. Bertha's raw notes highlighted the ruins in every centre and painted a picture of a flattened war zone. Yet at every opportunity she recorded where her father, the engineer and battle commander, had ordered the rebuilding of bridges in the pursuit of the enemy. This began the resuscitation of towns, where life was beginning to re-emerge: '... a few people back in Péronne, a few wooden huts being erected, and a little restaurant open ...'

The Monashes were moved by the memorials to the fallen. 'Reached the summit of Mont St Quentin,' Bertha wrote. 'Saw the wire entanglements all over the western and southern approaches to it. Saw site of the Second Division Memorial, the foundations already laid. The design is an Australian soldier crushing German eagle underfoot.'[3]

While Monash relived the horrors and triumphs he had been through, he remained in civvies. Apart from a few instances, he did not announce himself. He wished to see it all from the fresh perspective of his new life, and remember it all.

Vic was present when Monash on 29 May was invested with his GCMG at Buckingham Palace. Then at the same venue on different occasions there was a garden party and that promised private lunch with the King, Queen and Prince Albert.

In June and July Vic and Bertha also attended Oxford and Cambridge Universities, where Monash was given honorary degrees. But the pace caught up with Vic, who was fatigued. The resumption of their less than blissful marital state would not have helped. She happily missed farewells for Hughes (which Monash had to attend), White, McCay and Chauvel. Monash would have to stay for the rest of the year. The quick, successive departures by the PM and such prominent AIF personnel early in August were reminders that the elongated great party of his life had to end.

Monash used the most significant date in his military career, 8 August, as a motivating force for him to get down to some serious writing. He had a contract with London publishers Hutchinson for a book with a pertinent title that would raise eyebrows: *The Australian Victories in France in 1918*. The advance was £1100 (equivalent to $100,000 in 2004). Hutchinson offset that money by selling the serial rights to Lord Burnham and the *Daily Telegraph*. He had been impressed by Monash at the state banquet in the previous December. Murdoch had proved handy by competing with Lord Burnham for the serial rights on behalf of the Melbourne *Herald* and the Sydney *Sun*.

The King, in a thoughtful gesture, remembered the anniversary of Monash's battlefield knighting of 12 August 1918. 'General & Lady Monash came to luncheon, he commanded [the] Australian Corps . . .' the King wrote in his diary of 12 August 1919.[4]

Lunch engagements continued as did his repatriation work, but the nights were now disciplined. He cut his socialising and worked most nights from 7 p.m. to midnight to produce 115,000 words in about sixty days, which meant writing around 2000 words a day – a more than productive rate, given the constant need for map references and accurate research. The manuscript with '9 folding maps in colour and 31 (photographic) illustrations' was due for publication in 1920, and would follow a plethora of war books. Monash saw only some of the galleys. He left Walter Rosenhain with the job of proofing the balance and making sure it was returned to the publisher on time.[5]

Monash had been interrupted once during his writing. He was asked by two key members of the newly commissioned State Electricity Commission of Victoria – geologist Edgeworth David and chief engineer H. R. Harper – if he could assist them in a little industrial espionage. They wanted him to 'acquire' information from Germany about how to use brown coal to produce cheap electricity.

Monash knew the new Victorian Premier, Harry Lawson, and two senior members of the SEC, engineer and politician George Swinburne and Robert Gibson, brother of John, who was running Monash's reinforced concrete operation. He was happy to oblige. He put together a crack squad of intelligence officers and soldiers under mining engineer Major E. N. Mulligan to carry out the operation. The target city was Cologne. The mission was to invade the Fortuna mine and other installations to demand, borrow or steal everything that would unlock the secret of how the Germans lit up their cities.

Even with the Allies occupying Germany, it was never going to be an easy task. Monash's order was to carry out the mission by any means possible. Mulligan could use bluff with papers and orders from an occupying power, if that would work. He could even use force, if necessary. And as a last resort he could buy the intelligence. It was irregular, but Mulligan and his squad, waiting at an army camp for the signal to go home, were only too pleased to have a quasi-raiding role, perhaps for the last time in the soldiers' careers.

They succeeded in their mission, even 'acquiring' a working model of a machine that made briquettes (small bricks of compressed coal used for fuel). Monash took time off from his book to write a comprehensive report for the SEC. In early November it used the report in a submission to the government suggesting that Victoria should exploit its brown coal deposits at Morwell to produce electricity. The government accepted the submission.

Monash's exercise in espionage and the resultant report were instrumental in Victoria taking serious steps towards producing cheap electricity.

✕

Monash's last days in London in mid-November 1919 were fraught with emotion as he said his farewell to Lizette. He had hated the subterfuge, but had played the game to avoid any family confrontation while trying and failing to appease her. He admitted in his diary to being very sad at leaving England. He was thinking of Lizette more than anything else. He promised to phone her on the morning of Saturday 15 November when he, Vic and Bertha were to sail on the *Osmonde* to Australia.

The final phone conversation was distressing.[5] He had been firm about his decision to stay with Vic, yet his misgivings were painful as he faced the severing of the most satisfying relationship of his life. Annie Gabriel had been his most passionate affair, but it was never really tested beyond youthful, sexual assignations. Lizette had been calming and warm, and she rarely argued with Monash. Again, the relationship had been superficial and illicit and not really a test of a true marriage. Yet Monash felt she was the woman most temperamentally suited to him as he waded through his mature years.

While she had been within walking distance in London, he felt better even knowing it was over. When the boat sailed and he couldn't see her, he was depressed.

The tiffs with Vic continued. His mood would have exacerbated the squabbling. He wrote that the situation left him feeling very much alone.[6] Then, halfway through the voyage, Vic complained of feeling ill. Monash arranged for her to see the ship's doctor. His examination was not helpful. He suggested she see a specialist when she returned to Melbourne. Vic remained sick.

Being forced into the company of Birdwood on the trip did not help Monash's demeanour. The chirpy Englishman had treated him fairly, but the accumulation of honours for Monash had changed his attitude. It was hard for Birdwood to accept that a non-professional soldier about whom he had early doubts and had been slow to promote would climb over him in a short time and achieve so much on the battlefield. It had been tough for Birdwood in May 1918 when Haig pushed him aside to allow Monash the prime, prestige position in the AIF as Corps Commander. It had been even harder in November 1918 when Birdwood was once more over-looked for both command of the Australian Corps and the top job of repatriation. Under normal circumstances, a competent, courageous regular army man such as him would hold his place and be promoted on the basis of seniority. In the crush and pressure of war, hidden skills of subordinates of genius like Monash and Currie were given full expression, and relegated less gifted professionals such as Birdwood to lesser positions.

The genial, popular Englishman let his guard slip when writing to Munro Ferguson. They both used the expression 'extremely able' in refer-ence to Monash, which was a coded preface for their unfavourable feelings for him. His 'ways and methods' put Birdwood on edge. The Governor-General was put off by Monash's 'offensive' tone. They agreed he had 'the faults of his race', and they did not intend to refer to Australia, although in essence they were. In that era it was impossible for an Englishman of the ruling class, especially one with Munro Ferguson's influence in and over Australia, to countenance that a home-grown product could be so superior on every level – in intellect, articulation, education, leadership, military skills and strength of character. The G-G was 'offended' because Monash wouldn't jump when he demanded it. He had been put offside by Monash eyeballing him and treating him like any other individual. It was a then very British ruling-class thing to put someone different in their place by slapping on a label – 'Jew' was good enough to superficially explain away this upstart. 'Irish' was another such label. 'Black' would need no other exposition either. But not even labels, it seemed, could stop Monash. In his time in Australia, Munro Ferguson had never met another of influence like him. Hughes, despite his feisty nature, by comparison was manageable. His class background would always give the G-G an advantage.[7]

Monash had to be some sort of threat. Hughes had nightmares about a military coup or Monash running against him for high office and made sure that his return to Australia was after the federal election of November 1919. Monash would have been open to running for federal parliament. Throughout 1919 there had been many calls for him to enter politics. But missing the election thwarted any chances of doing so for several years. Munro Ferguson worried that he might lose his job to Monash. Birdwood had already done that twice. What infuriated the Governor-General was that Monash seemed to be favoured by the palace. It was unbearable that he had been given the same knighthood ranking as him.

The only way to put Monash in his place would be to give him precisely nothing on his return. Whether the PM and G-G conspired directly or not was incidental. Their common attitude would intertwine to stop any rise Monash might contemplate in Australia's power circles.

Hughes, aware of Birdwood's disgruntlement, had invited him to tour Australia, not always in the same places but simultaneously. It was a way of taking the limelight from Monash, especially when the PM failed to turn up to greet him in Melbourne when the *Osmonde* docked on a sunny Boxing Day. Yet his absence didn't spoil the moment as family, the press, regular army and local political dignitaries, along with big crowds, turned out to greet him in St Kilda and the city.

The next day, 27 December, he was swamped with visitors at the Menzies Hotel where he would stay for two weeks. But after the first day, he couldn't enjoy it. He was most concerned for Vic. At the height of the holiday season, there was a struggle to find a specialist, but he tracked down three. They saw them all. Examinations were still inconclusive. Vic was ordered to rest. She stayed in bed at the Menzies, but showed her usual fortitude to get up on New Year's Eve for a night at the theatre.

The invitations poured in from clubs, societies, the Jewish community, the press and civic receptions. Fame, with all its superficialities, was beginning to stalk him. Attention had somehow been exhilarating in London, but in provincial Melbourne it was suffocating. Monash responded, with Bertha accompanying him everywhere. It reached absurd proportions by mid-January when the interminable syrupy praise and speeches became too much. He decided he had endured enough. He would attend a civic reception for Birdwood on 18 January, for appearances sake, judging that not going would be seen as a snub. He would also attend a dinner for him at Government House on 20 January. But that for now would be it.

Vic's condition declined by early February. Monash became consumed with anxiety. Then the specialists told him what they didn't tell his wife. The cervical cancer had returned. It might have spread elsewhere. In the middle of the hot month, he was told there was no hope for her. She had weeks to live.

Vic died on 27 February 1920. The homecoming that had promised to be the happiest of moments turned to grief.

Monash was not allowed time for bereavement. He turned down plenty of invitations, but for every one he rejected, twenty more poured in to open schools, charities, carnivals, fêtes, sporting events and art exhibitions. Offers to be president of this or vice-president of that, guest of honour, to write, to speak and just be in attendance seemed never ending.

There were some events that he would attend as long as he was physically able. They were the unveiling of war memorials or honour boards for veterans. No matter what the pain, Monash would turn up and have to say something in an attempt to comfort those who had lost friends and family at Gallipoli, or in France, Belgium and the Middle East.

He joined the Prahran Branch of the RSL, which was the nearest to Iona, and was the prime mover or supporter of anything that involved the Anzac spirit. Within weeks of Vic's death he was laying the foundation stone of Anzac House in Collins Street and lecturing at Australian War Memorial functions. While he made clear his abhorrence of war, he did not run from any responsibility connected with what he had been through. Monash could have been forgiven for not wanting constant reminders of his battles to save France and Belgium. But he responded without hesitation when asked to be president for Australian movements to help towns and cities in those countries devastated by the events 1914–18, such as Amiens and Villers-Bretonneux. Nor did he hide from other connected responsibilities, such as giving aid to unmarried British mothers, whose children had digger dads.

The press made no concession for personal suffering. His phone rang all day and into the night. Monash was wanted for a comment on everything. He would give it, if he felt he could enhance or clarify a debate. But he refused any words about politicians or most politics. Monash gave what journalists called 'great copy'. His quotes were always articulate, to the point, original, thought-provoking, intelligent and sometimes controversial. They recognised him as something rare: a strong man of obvious integrity with definite views that he could express with precision.

He supported a move for a League of Nations, saying that soldiers knew of the horrors of war. Anything that would go someway to restricting conflict should be encouraged. Monash was also loyal to his old school, which made demands for fund-raising and support. But his attitude was not restricted to the old school tie. He was a supporter of education and helping the young. Any institution that approached him received help. Monash was a great believer that an educated nation was a stronger and more democratic one.

Long before his grieving ended and the constant public demands on his time, energy and intellect settled down, Monash had to make decisions about his future. His hopes for some grand gesture or offer from the Federal Government faded fast. He realised within months of returning that while Hughes was in power, he would be offered nothing. The PM was on his home territory now, which was a long way from Monash's bastions on battlefields and in London. Hughes did everything in his power not to give Monash any platform, at least on a federal level, that would allow the military strongman to capitalise on his enormous popularity and capacities for a launch into politics. But Monash never entertained any ambition other than being Australia's first native-born Governor-General or perhaps a State Governor. Unless the Prime Minister supported him here, he had no chance. Hughes would never countenance even the thought of the talented Monash moving around the country or the state making speeches or pontificating on issues, even if they were politically neutral.

Monash was stung, too, when he became aware that the military, which he had so recently dominated, had been persuaded to ignore him. He was not recommended for a full generalship. There was never any official mention of his mighty effort and management of the diggers coming home. Others, such as Pearce, influenced by political need for public recognition, took the bows, although they had had little or nothing to do with an enterprise that Monash had masterminded. Even the Governor-General's speech at the opening of parliament mentioned Birdwood's visit but ignored Monash's return.

The press, aware of the persistent snub, rallied in support of Monash. The RSL gave voice here and there, and some parliamentarians complained with vehemence. But Hughes was prepared to follow a policy of no support. His political instincts were that as war slipped away in time, support for Monash would diminish, especially if he had a reduced public profile.

The former Corps Commander had no hope of being offered the position of Commander-in-Chief, or any position in the regular armed services. He was not honoured with any payment, either. The British Government gave Haig £100,000 and an earldom. Rawlinson received £30,000 and a barony; Birdwood £10,000 and a baronetcy. In Canada, Currie grumbled a lot and received some recognition. Monash was allowed to keep his sword, and that was it.

The publication of his book in April 1920 (it had come out in London in February) lifted – or at least gave substance to – his profile, but there seemed very little objective reading of it. Reviews were mixed and not perceptive. Its high price of 27s 6d, which Monash had protested against, restricted its appeal, although sales of almost 5000 were good. It failed in England, chalking up only a thousand sales. The English general market was not prepared to accept that a Dominion militiaman had risen to a point where he exerted a strong influence on the outcome of the war. The despatches about Australian soldiers had been acceptable; they had the image of good fighters. But suggestions that a lieutenant-general Corps Commander had dominated plans for deciding battles needed confirmation from more than a few reviewers.

A cheaper edition of the book was promised but would be some time coming.

The government cold shoulder continued. When the Prince of Wales visited in May for a four-month stay, which would include the laying of a foundation stone for the new federal capital, Canberra, Monash was not officially invited to greet him. The *Bulletin*, the most read political journal of the day, and the most nationalistic of the respected papers, had long been a supporter. It editorialised about the government's mean-spirited attitude. The Governor-General, the government and the military hierarchy pretended there had been errors of omission. It is probable that the Prince let it be known that he expected Monash at other functions. The invitations for royal occasions arrived, but the damage had been done, or at least exposed. The Prince, although not Monash's favourite royal, went out of his way to shake hands on arriving and when leaving at the lunches, garden parties and at the theatre. He was making a point, but it would not change anyone's mind, least of all the PM's. Hughes was ostracising his perceived rival, and would do so until Monash was not believed to be a threat.

X

Monash was further miffed that the anniversaries of Hamel on 4 July and Amiens on 8 August slipped by in 1920 without any public recognition. He organised a private dinner with key commanders to commemorate 8 August, which would become a quiet tradition until the end of his life. He was moving on, facing his mature years as a widower and with concerns about what he should do for work, but there were some events, such as 25 April and 8 August, that he would never abandon, even though the war itself had drained him.

The unexpected loss of Vic had shattered him. But he proved resilient. He felt fit for big challenges and was searching for the next one. In his private life, companionship could be fulfilled if he wished. He was writing to Lizette again. After twenty years based in London, she was willing to return to Melbourne, if he was prepared to commit himself to her. His relationship with her during the war years was fresh in his mind and desires. Lizette had provided the understanding, warmth and friendship he craved. On top of that, she was simply fun to be with. She was bright. Her sophisticated tastes and social skills were just right. He didn't want a queen, but a scrubber wouldn't do for dinners at Government House, either.

Monash would have reflected on life's ironies. His loyalty to a shaky, accidentally broken marriage had seen him choose Vic when he preferred Lizette. A twist of fate had presented a chance to resume a relationship with the latter. She wasn't his only choice. Others with the pretensions and qualifications to be the wife of General Sir John presented themselves. There was a theatre actress, who had appeared in a silent movie; an unconventional but gifted sculptor whom Monash liked for her art but not necessarily her artfulness; an heiress looking to increase her fortune; a widower who wrote poetry to him; and even a stunning university graduate more than thirty years his junior. He was flattered yet not too distracted by these overtures. His mind was on the proven woman he knew. It didn't take him long to decide to invite Lizette to be with him. But her arrival had to be discrete, even secretive, although, given his profile, secrecy would now be impossible.

She slipped into Melbourne on the *Naldera* late in September 1920. Monash set her up for the time being in the city's Grand Hotel. There was no announcement in any of the papers this time. Walter and Louise in London were against her, claiming that she was scruple-free and fast and lose with the truth. They cited her age. She said she was around forty; they reckoned she was nearer fifty. Monash ran a check at the Registry of Births, Deaths and Marriages, just to settle a moneyless bet with Walter. She was forty-six. No one won. Monash thought it a woman's prerogative to lie about her age, especially if her excellent figure and wrinkle-free features seemed to support her claim.

'A designing woman [like Lizette] may be more difficult to deal with,' Walter warned Monash, 'than . . . a Hindenburg system.'[8]

Monash was unperturbed and not swayed. He appreciated that anyone who showed interest in him would run the gauntlet of the family, especially Bertha, so soon after Vic's death. When his daughter learned of Lizette's installation in Melbourne she was furious. Iona, which could comfortably accommodate eight people, was not big enough for her and that woman. She and her husband-to-be Gershon Bennett were sharing the family home with Monash. But she said she would move out and have nothing to do with her father if that woman moved in. It was emotional blackmail, given that it was his life, and he felt he had earned the right to do just about anything he liked in his declining years.

Bertha would have had his deception of her mother in London as a weapon of guilt with which to beat him. Monash capitulated. Lizette would not live with him. Instead he would set her up in an apartment. But he reserved the right to have a relationship with her.

Not too long afterwards, the *Bulletin* hinted that he would marry Lizette. He wrote to the magazine a not-for-publication letter of protest in which he denied the story. The whole business stressed him so much that he thought he was ill. Doctors examined him, but their diagnosis was inconclusive, except that he was stressed and in need of rest. He could have told them that. He ignored their advice, happy not to have anything life-threatening.[9]

Perhaps brother-in-law Walter was not far off the mark. His fighting with Bertha over Lizette caused exceptional strain, like handling the Hindenburg system. Yet he had yet to see Lizette as a designing woman.

✕

Change was preferable in his working life, too. After toying with the idea of returning to the Reinforced Concrete Co., Monash decided he wished to move on from it and its South Australian set-up. He sold his shares in the company he had created to Gibson for £6000 to be paid over six years. When that was all in the bank, Monash's assets would total more than £62,500. He could juggle that and a few directorships and live well in retirement. But he was not yet ready for reminiscing over long lunches at his various clubs. He had just turned fifty-five and, although slowed up physically, still had prodigious mental energy.

Monash preferred to tackle a new venture that taxed his skills and stretched him. Successes in engineering, business, war and repatriation were hard acts to follow. Since his return a few months earlier there had been no overtures from political parties for him to run for office. Such a call would certainly not be forthcoming from Hughes, especially since Monash's popularity had not diminished in his first year back in Australia. Monash was forced to explore other avenues of suitable employment. A few, such as in state railway expansion and overhaul, were examined and found wanting, despite attractive salaries. Others that seemed promising, such as heading a royal commission into taxation, fell through. The director-generalship of a new Institute of Science and Industry seemed ideal at the juicy salary of £4000. But it took too long for legislation to be passed and was uncertain to be enacted. That job also fell through.

Then came an offer to manage the Victorian State Electricity Commission. It was just a name, a shell that had to be developed from scratch. Monash looked at it. He was familiar with the SEC after having written up the industrial espionage report for it in November 1918. He knew its key people well. The more he reflected on the position, the more it attracted him. He would have to create a huge industry to bring electricity to Melbourne and the rest of the state. He would have to build a new town. The job blended his refined skills in engineering, business and managing thousands of people from various trades and professions. On top of all that, he would need to use his power, name and political skills to achieve everything he envisaged. It wasn't an attractive job on the surface. *Smith's Weekly*, a strong supporter like the *Bulletin*, had been pushing for his employment as a national director to tackle the drought problem that threatened survival in rural Australia. It billed the job as the nation's 'Western Front'. It didn't think much of Monash being fobbed off with running a mere state instrumentality. But no one else could even imagine his ambitious vision for the SEC, let alone be confident about creating it.[10]

He said he would go along with the job at £3000 a year, if there were the promise of £5000 annually when successful. There was just one catch. 'Success' was measured by the SEC causing lights to go on in Melbourne. Monash's first trick would be to turn huge light coal deposits in Victoria's La Trobe Valley into cheap electricity that would overcome a hurdle for the development of local industry. He already knew the technology required. The key would be getting the right German equipment and know-how. That meant German engineers would have to come to Victoria with their technology. He had great respect for them after seeing the results of their operations during the war.

Before accepting the position Monash showed his considerable talent as a businessman and lawyer by setting out certain conditions. He asked for legislation to be passed that made him not simply a manager but Chairman of Commissioners. It meant that he was answerable to no one, not even the Premier. He could be sacked only by an act of parliament. Next he wanted a loan appropriation of £1.43 million. It was effectively his budget, which he could use the way he saw fit in constructing the town of Yallourn and an eight-storey head office building in Melbourne's William Street.

Monash knew a little of the value of reduced competition after his early experience with exclusive reinforced concrete patents in Victoria. He demanded that the SEC be made a monopoly. It had to have control over the generation, sale and distribution of power in Victoria. In other words, there was to be no competition if the 'economies of scale' – cheap power for all – scheme was to work. Monash the capitalist wanted state socialism from a conservative State Government.

Such were his prestige and powers of persuasion that every demand was granted.

But even before he was appointed the SEC's chairman, there was some stiff opposition to his ideas. Some didn't buy his argument that the SEC would first use both brown coal electricity and hydroelectricity, then phase out the latter. One naysayer was a top engineer and friend, A. G. M. Mitchell, who challenged Monash's costings. Mitchell was having a two-way bet as a consultant to both the SEC and the Victorian Hydro-Electric Co. If the latter were to fade to nothing, he would lose a consultancy. He 'debated' Monash before a government select committee. Mitchell had not done his homework on two counts: the figures to back his case that using Morwell's brown coal would not be cheaper, and on Monash's unbeaten record as an advocate (except in the case where the judge was corrupt).

According to F. W. Eggleston, a member of the select committee and witness to the 'debate', Monash dissected Mitchell and demolished his case in half an hour.

That done, he began his new job on 10 January 1921. Monash identified his main hurdle. The coal was too sodden. The best technology and engineers, as his espionage report pointed out, needed to overcome this on the massive scale he wanted were sitting in Germany. But Germanophobia was very much a problem so soon after the bloodiest war in history. Monash had been partly responsible for it in his fervent desire to call the Germans during the conflict the despicable Boche, Hun and other assorted names in order to drive terror and hatred into the minds of the Australian public and soldiers. Now he had to undo some of that earlier hypocrisy and sing the praises of certain engineers who would have to be employed in Victoria to install plant and equipment.

Monash managed to sneak through an order for the plant from the Zeitz Co. of Halle, Germany. It arrived during 1921 without incident. But when the engineers tried to obtain temporary work permits there were howls of protests from the RSL and trade unions, who were odd bedfellows. Once Hughes realised that Monash was behind the work permit request, the Federal Government backed the protestors. Monash counterattacked by lobbying supporters in the federal and state parliaments. He ridiculed the xenophobic, myopic outlook that would stop such necessary work in peacetime. His bold tactics won through. In March, the Federal Government relented.

Six Germans soon after arrived to supervise the installation.

In April 1921 Rabbi Jacob Danglow married Bertha and Gershon Bennett, a Melbourne dentist with a likeness to the young Monash. 'Gersh' had been a long-time friend to Bertha, and Monash had helped him get a commission in the AIF after he had studied in the USA. The two men had become good friends, which facilitated the development of Bertha's relationship with the young man. It blossomed during Bertha's visit to England in 1919.

About eighty guests, including Lieutenant-General Chauvel, attended a reception at Iona. The *Argus* reported the event in detail and called it 'the wedding of the week'.[11] But the union didn't change any living arrangements. The couple remained at Iona. Lizette was at her hotel, forever in exile from the family.

The SEC's equipment was being installed and the technicians were in place when another major hurdle presented itself in 1922. Although Monash had made sure that legislation ensured the SEC would have a monopoly, opposition emerged from three sources: rural interests, many local government bodies and private power companies. They were willing to accept that the SEC could control the wholesale production of power. But they were going to fight it on retailing.

Monash asked the government for amending legislation to tighten up the SEC's overall monopoly. He argued that provincial bodies – private and local government councils – were all making a loss, despite selling electricity at too high a price, because they were inefficient. They provided poor service and didn't maintain equipment. Their construction and engineering methods were questionable. By contrast, Monash hammered the positive points about monopoly. They centred on the argument that one monolithic body (the SEC) supplying everything at wholesale and retail levels offered much cheaper electricity for the home consumer and industry. It would be far more efficient, too.

The State Government hesitated. Public opinion, and therefore votes, favoured leaving provincial bodies – and the Melbourne Electricity Supply Co. – in place. Monash countered by saying there would be a lot more votes if the cost to homes and businesses was kept down. Electricity would be for the masses and not just those who could afford it.

The government, which had supported him, compromised in an attempt to please everyone and not lose support. If the local councils asked the SEC to take over retail, then it could. This would slow the process, but Monash had to accept it. He still didn't have the power flowing. His argument would not have the required impact until he had a product to sell.

Yet one by one municipalities in country areas began to come across. Rural interests lobbied the State Government for a flat statewide price to the consumer, their argument being that this would attract business to regions outside the big cities. Monash checked the numbers and rejected this argument. He insisted on extra charges (tariffs) to cover the cost of sending electricity long distances. The state was prepared to carry the losses that this would incur, but Monash was not. It would offend his business sensibilities to run at a loss and drain the public purse. There was no logic to him in running any enterprise that way.

The autonomous chairman of the SEC got his way. Monash's strategy followed the methods he used in attacking the enemy at the Hindenburg fortifications. Instead of taking on the biggest block to his SEC – the Melbourne City Council (MCC) – head-on, he decided to attack and defeat the weaker obstacles and then surround the main opposition. With local councils around the state capitulating monthly in 1923, Monash began to concentrate on the MCC. It was supplying Melbourne efficiently enough. Its main weakness was the high prices it was charging customers through its retail operations. This generated big revenue, which it claimed it could use to keep those same consumers' rates down. Monash argued that this favoured those wealthy enough to buy electricity, and stopped the product reaching the entire Melbourne populous. The lower rates argument, he suggested, was weak. It only favoured property owners, who had to pay rates.

As the SEC captured other councils, Monash seemed to be setting up a win in the main battle for Melbourne. He learned that the Essendon Council had long felt neglected by the MCC in its power supply. Monash reached an agreement with it to take over the small North Melbourne Electric Tramways and Lighting Co., which would supply Essendon and North Melbourne.

The coup caused a reaction at the MCC. Its councillors could see the fat revenues from electricity retailing disappearing. Although it did help cut some property rates, much of that money was not passed on directly to ratepayers. It went into expanding but questionable MCC operations and plenty of free lunches for councillors.

The MCC's town clerk, T. G. Ellery, and the Lord Mayor, J. W. Swanson, decided to play rough. They formed the honourable-sounding Electrical Defence Committee for the launch of its dishonourable activity. The main target was Monash. Journalists were paid on the side to investigate him and find dirt, if possible. That failed. Ellery and Swanson then concentrated on accusing the SEC of failing to fulfil its charter in some areas and overextending it others. They forced the State Government, with some (paid) press support, to investigate the SEC through the ubiquitous answer to all problems: a select committee.

Ellery and Swanson put their case to the committee. Monash was in his element confronting his underhand tormentors. He destroyed every argument presented. Like the engineer Mitchell and just about every antagonist Monash ever faced in any kind of court forum, they were humiliated and made to look like profligate fools. Monash even ran through a list of embarrassing extravagances by the councillors, from the use of cars and junkets to street parties and those never-ending fat cat meals.

Just when the select committee retired to consider its verdict on the SEC, a crisis occurred in Melbourne. The MCC, which had been trying to destroy Monash's credibility, was in desperate need of his services. A long-running dispute between the Victoria Police and the State Government concerning the need for far better pay and pensions for retired officers reached a head. It had been exacerbated by the government's decision to appoint 'supervisors' to watch the performances of police officers at stations around the city. The police regarded the watchers as spies and wanted them stopped.

Police at Melbourne's Russell Street Barracks went on strike on the evening of Thursday, 1 November 1923. By noon the next day, 600 metropolitan police – half the entire force – were out. The City of Melbourne was in its worst ever crisis. The strikers were dismissed. But the government and MCC now had the problem of how to keep order. Swanson, who was retiring as Lord Mayor, called in sick and stepped aside to allow the Lord Mayor-elect, W. Brunton, to handle the problem, just as gangs began looting in city streets. The first thing he did was something Swanson could not. He picked up the phone and called Monash. Would he be part of the Citizens' Protection Committee?

The general said he would. Monash suggested that he enlist Brigadiers-General Pompey Elliott and Johnson (who had both served under Monash) and his old mate James Whiteside McCay. Within minutes he was thinking like a corps commander again. But this time it was much closer to the real thing than strategies to overcome difficult city councils. An armed force would be needed to replace the sacked police, put down the riots and keep law and order.

The Citizens' Committee, with Robert Gibson of the SEC as its vice-chairman, was to meet the next morning, Saturday 3 November.

During Friday night, mobs hit Melbourne and spread into the suburbs. Looting and brawling increased. About 200 people were injured. Two were killed.

At the emergency committee meeting Premier Lawson, the state's Attorney-General, Sir Arthur Robinson, and the Chief Commissioner of Police, Alexander Nicholson, let Monash dominate proceedings. He directed Elliott, then a federal senator, and Johnson to go to the Melbourne Town Hall and start recruiting 'special constables', who would be mainly former AIF diggers. The instruction to Elliott was to form the 'specials' into squads under 'competent' former officers.

Looting began again on Saturday afternoon. Monash drove into the city to see for himself. The violence and theft had abated by the time he was on the scene, but he realised 'the paralysis of the police'. 'I decided there and then,' Monash said, 'to create an organisation independent of the Police.' At midnight on Saturday, he contacted Elliott and told him to set up an HQ and a 'fighting and feeding staff, on military lines'.[12]

Melbourne shut down. Monash was designated 'Commander' of the special force set up at the town hall. The word spread fast through Melbourne suburbs. Diggers heard about the call to arms on the phone, in pubs, on playing fields and at work. General Monash wanted them. In response to the call, a thousand men, mostly ex-soldiers, dropped what they were doing and within hours were sworn in. They had seen or heard what was happening with the mobs in the city and suburbs and were thrilled to hear the bugle call once more. Whether their lives were empty or full, the response was the same. Within twenty-four hours they were operating in parts of Melbourne.

McCay, who had been in Sydney, contacted Monash early on Sunday morning. Monash put him in charge over Elliott, who was designated 'outside commander'. Monash and McCay were able to contact a further group of ex-officers. They rallied at the town hall, where they found Monash in complete control hovering over maps of Melbourne and the suburbs with coloured pins marking the depots.

By late Sunday, the volunteer force had risen to the brigade size of 5000. He and McCay organised the ex-diggers into five battalions. The public was ordered off the streets by day and by night as the 'specials' marched around keeping order. Many thought law and order had never been better.

Monash put out a press statement: 'We are now in great strength. Efficient bodies of experienced men are in reserve in thirty depots in the city and suburbs, ready with horse and motor squad for any emergency.'[13]

On Sunday night there were pockets of riots in the suburbs. The city was quiet. On Monday, the looting was all but mopped up. Monash eased the street curfew. By Tuesday – Melbourne Cup Day, 6 November – the crisis was over after just four days. More than 125,000 people attended the Cup at Flemington to watch the favourite, Bitalli, win, which no doubt helped the demeanour of punters and perhaps some would-be rioters. The police situation stabilised. Not a man had refused duty all day.

Six days later, Monash began demobilising the special force, which was replaced by an interim auxiliary police force run by McCay.

Monash had commanded another mini-battle, and he loved it. While others panicked and dithered Monash's calm and quick reaction had averted a disaster. Handling marauding, disorganised mobs was a doddle after the brutal attacks of the Turks inspired by the fearless Mustafa Kemal or the last-man-standing effort of the Prussian Guards on Mont St Quentin.

With the irritating distractions over his work with the SEC, the police strike invigorated him. Five years after his last war engagement Monash was able in a flash to organise a formidable armed force. This capacity was unique in the nation. Its power-brokers, political aspirants, would-be revolutionaries and anti-communists alike were alerted to power of the strongest man in Australia. The 'White Army', a right-wing clandestine group with strong bases in Victoria and New South Wales, was encouraged. Its members were believed to include prominent army and former AIF names, such as White and Blamey.

The moment in early December 1923 seemed right to announce the winner of an architectural competition for the design of a Shrine of Remembrance. The site on St Kilda Road had been chosen a year earlier. Monash had been acting for the State Government as chairman of assessors. The winners were two ex-soldiers, architects P. B. Hudson and J. H. Wardrop. The inspiration for their effort was the Mausoleum of the city of Bodrum (formerly Halicarnassus) in southwest Turkey, completed in 350 BC for King Muassollos of Caria.

It seemed that now the government would fund the Shrine's building. But Keith Murdoch at the Melbourne *Herald* began a negative campaign to prevent its construction. After days of attacking the design, Murdoch shrewdly created another distracting campaign to search for other concepts to replace the winning entry. The paper's line was that the Shrine should have some positive use connected with war. Hospitals and war widows' homes, both established and new designs, were the most popular choices, but Monash and the various committees that had been involved with the project had decided on a non-utilitarian construction.

The *Herald's* campaign had impact. The government was frightened off supporting the winning design, and the project was shelved. Murdoch seemed to have won a small victory against Monash's interests. But Monash would not abandon such an important concept. It was a big part of his sense of duty, honour and obligation.

Timing was everything. He would wait.

Despite this setback, the frantic interlude of the police strike had put the State Government and MCC in Monash's debt for saving the city. It was no surprise in mid-December that the Select Committee investigating claims by the MCC against the SEC and Monash reported almost 100 per cent in Monash's favour. Hours after the verdict, the State Government passed five new Acts, which expanded the SEC's powers, gave Monash a boosted budget, and again increased his independence.

The MCC was now all but under SEC control concerning electricity retailing, and there was just one major target to conquer now: the Melbourne Electric Supply Co., the biggest surviving distributor.

In the meantime, the SEC's main technical problem continued to be the moisture content of the coal, which hovered around two-thirds of the weight. This was much more than original surveys by the Mines Department. It had first done work on the seam in the cut at North Yallourn. The new cut at Yallourn, which was to produce most of the brown coal, had a different seam and contained the troublesome higher moisture content. Monash was so concerned that he took coal home for a private experiment, weighing it each day.

Late in 1923, comment about the problem was made in parliament. The press contacted Monash. The *Age* waded in against the SEC, while the *Argus* and Melbourne *Herald* stayed supportive. Monash denied that the project was in jeopardy. Brushing aside criticism, he repeated an earlier prediction that the SEC would produce electricity in 1924.

Early in that year, he began working on a strategy to win over the Melbourne Electric Supply Co. First he offered its manager a job as an SEC commissioner. He took the bait. Then Monash lobbied for legislation to enable the takeover. But to see it through parliament he had to pretend that he supported an enabling provision in the Act to set another separate commission: a Melbourne Electricity Commission (MEC), which would be a sister set-up to the SEC. The illusion was that the MEC would create special deals for the city. This appeased the opposition, although there was never any chance of the MEC coming into existence. The SEC would control everything.

Now nothing would stand in Monash's way, if the technology would work.

In parallel with these long-running political battles, Monash set up the new city of Yallourn as a garden town. He gave the architect, A. R. Le Gerche, and the engineer, W. E. Gower, free reign. All housing – at least at the beginning – was to be publicly owned, with the SEC acting as the landlord. Monash's love of the country made him a conservationist and early environmentalist. He wanted the town's structures and aesthetics to be right, but not at the expense of unnecessary disturbance of the national habitat.

By mid-year 1924 the emerging Yallourn began pumping out electricity. The generators worked. Power flowed along the main transmissions lines to Melbourne on 16 June.

Monash had kept his promise. He made another one: the SEC would be profitable in three years.

MANY CAUSES;
ENOUGH TIME

Monash's post-war life was not just a matter of scoring victories for the SEC. It took up about half of his precious time, which was often allocated by the minute. He made space for all those people and institutions that had been part of his life or loyal to him, and countless others who had not. He had one motto among several: there was always space for one more cause, one more person to be helped, encouraged or inspired. Few other prominent Australians in history put in so much for so many, when, like many old soldiers, he could have simply shut down and faded away.

It was for many of those old soldiers, too, that he always made an effort. The letters from them never stopped. The saddest were from diggers who couldn't get work; some who were bitter that they had done so much and received nothing in return. There were times when Monash could help by a call to the tramways or railways to find a job. But often he could not, and it hurt him to write and say so. As the 1920s rolled on, those requests grew and were harder to fulfil. Australia was running from a recession to a depression. Those ex-diggers would be around thirty when it hit. Many would join the long queues in the big cities looking for any kind of labour to give them money for food and a little dignity.

Monash heard or read all their cries. They served to increase his obligation to them.

Monash was generous with more than his time. In desperate cases, such as an incapacitated soldier who had been injured at Messines, Monash paid off his outstanding loans. He gave to charities designed to help diggers in need. There was always someone among his family and friends who needed financial help. He continued his pre-war act as a kind of benevolent godfather, but one who never needed, or asked for, favours in return.

He had his pet worthy causes. He became Melbourne University's vice-chancellor in 1923 and helped it raise funds. His duties for his alma mater were equivalent to full time. Long before the US Republican Party of the twenty-first century had $10,000-a-plate dinners to raise money, Monash and seventy-nine fellow graduates at the Menzies Hotel were hosting eighty prominent businessmen to provide a library fund of £20,000. Monash looked at the university's accounts and asked why it should pay £5000 for maintaining its grounds when it could be done by the Melbourne City Council and the money saved used to create a new professorial chair.

Monash cared, too, for his old civil profession of engineering and sat on various councils. The mere presence of his name on a letterhead was enough to stir interest, commitment, donations and deals. He was for two years the country's spokesman for science: president of the Australasian Association for the Advancement of Science from 1924 to 1926. When offered the position he corrected those who approached him with a response that would make a pedant proud, saying he was an applied scientist, not a scientist in the accepted sense. They didn't care. They wanted him, not a label. He rarely just made up the numbers or acted as a figurehead. It was not in his nature. Monash had to achieve something for the cause. In this case, he lobbied the Federal Government to set up the Council for Science and Industrial Research. When he succeeded, he went further and secured fair funding for the new body.

Monash, as his army veteran friend McGlinn observed, was a national possession, to be used, it seemed, by any person or group who approached him. He didn't mind being consumed by the arts in their different guises. He devoured them with equal voracity. Music was his premier sensual pleasure. He didn't miss one night of 1924's seventeen-day opera season with Lizette by his side. That was his record for attendances, but he was a regular every year. He was one of the prime movers in establishing a permanent Melbourne orchestra. If he wasn't at music concerts he found time almost daily to listen to his growing library of classical gramophone records. He ranged across the great composers from Mozart, Beethoven, Mendelssohn and Haydn, and would sit for hours absorbing them. His favourites for inspiration were Chopin and Wagner.

The latter was the nearest he felt any composer could get to the symphonic power of war. Wagner, the dominant musician of the second half of the nineteenth century, inspired Monash. Listening to the musical translation of the composer's ruthless, megalomaniacal genius would refresh Monash to the point where he could take on anything. Even the most disagreeable characteristics of Wagner – his belief that the Germans were the super-race and his virulent racism – didn't upset Monash. He had conquered both, and would do so again, if ever the need arose.

Monash loved art and was a collector. He liked to sketch and paint. Lizette Bentwitch, who was herself a competent miniature portraitist, was knowledgeable and encouraged his interest, especially in Australian art. Post-war he began patronising Australians, accumulating etchings and paintings by Longstaff, Arthur Streeton, Tom Roberts, George Bell, Walter Withers, A. E. Newbury, Dora Meeson, Esther Paterson, Thea Proctor, Jessie Traill and Norman Lindsay. Iona was cluttered with their pictures and his war memorabilia.

Monash collected books, too, with the urgency of a man concerned that there were too many of them and not enough time left for imbibing the best. He had a library of 5000 books. Like all his other collections – from souvenirs to records – it was catalogued. Post-war he went through a hungry reading period that took him back to his first years at university when he consumed books the way a person with a sweet tooth consumes chocolate. By 1924 Monash's sleep patterns had settled down to an uninterrupted seven hours a night. He often read until the early hours, the only time he could escape the demands on him and his time.

A post-war, post-Europe pattern emerged that complemented his early reading and filled in gaps in the considerable book and play library of his mind. Having helped save France, a country he loved more than any other after Australia, he wanted to read the fruits of that salvation. Down went Voltaire, Balzac and Anatole France. Having done much to defeat the Germans, he pillaged only their finest literature, starting with Emil Ludwig's biographies, Thomas Mann and Robert Musil. His correspondence with others in England demonstrated that he still respected the breadth of English literature more than any other. He paid special attention in this late period to Samuel Pepys, Robert Louis Stevenson and Oscar Wilde.

A special shelf or two was filled with reminiscences and histories of the war. Among them were books by people he now knew, including Churchill and Hamilton. The writings of Liddell Hart and General J. F. C. Fuller also captured his attention. They both recommended Monash's kind of mechanised warfare, the tanks and air force being important in their thinking. Liddell Hart (along with Montgomery, Churchill and many others) regarded him as the best commander of the war. But that was not why Monash read him. He wanted to see how the young man (Liddell Hart was just thirty years old in 1925) expounded on his advocacy of machines and his emphasis on two Monash specialities: mobility and surprise.

Monash stuck, too, with his tried and trusted literary companions, such as Charles Dickens. He was setting aside a couple of nights a week for reading with Gershon and Bertha. In several years they consumed the best passages of English greats and some popular fiction, such as Conan Doyle's Sherlock Holmes. There were also some poetry readings with Lizette, who was settled in at East Melbourne's Cliveden Mansions (now the site of the Hilton Hotel) opposite the MCG. She enjoyed her reading and drama. Her photographic memory, which astonished her lover, allowed her to recite poems and sections of plays after little preparation.

By 1924, most of Monash's leisure and pleasure time was spent with his family and Lizette, separately. Gershon and Bertha had produced two sons, John in 1922 and David in 1924. (Elizabeth was born in 1926.) His grandchildren gave Monash great joy, and he grew attached to young John.

The relationship with Lizette was by now open and established. There were problems with invitations every so often, but Monash refused them if she was not included. They lunched at the Menzies Hotel and were inseparable at the theatre and concerts. Their relationship had been going seven years, with the ten-month interruption from November 1919 to September 1920, and it was the most satisfactory of his life.

Strait-laced Melbourne at first reacted to her fashion tastes at the races, especially the Melbourne Cup. But this reflected the negative Anglo attitude to more vivid colours. Lizette preferred more variety and tone in her dresses and hats in keeping with French and Italian styles. Photos taken with and without Monash show her in bright summer dresses that accentuated rather than hid her bosom, derrière, good hips and shapely ankles. This would have appealed to the young peacock in Monash, who had a taste for more sensual – even exotic – fashion.

Lizette's influences over him were varied. Her extended family were Zionists – part of the nationalist movement that aimed to create a Jewish state in Palestine, the ancient homeland of the Jews. Lizette's cousin was the Englishman, Professor Sir Norman Bentwitch, then Attorney-General in the mandatory government in Palestine. Russian Jews had been immigrating there since the failure of the 1905 Russian Revolution. By 1924 there were about 100,000 settlers in urban and rural settlements. Two Russian Zionists living in England, Chaim Weizmann and Nahum Zokolow, had obtained the Balfour Declaration from the British in 1917. This was after the Allies, with the brilliant Chauvel leading the Anzacs, had won the battle in Palestine against the Turks and Germans. The declaration promised British support for the homeland. The League of Nations approved a British mandate, which was meant to push the movement forward.

Lizette had turned Monash into a moderate Zionist after he seemed to be aligned with anti-Zionists in England. In 1922 he avoided presiding over a Zionist recruitment meeting in Melbourne by saying he was too busy. Given Monash's motto that he could always add one more commitment to his hectic schedule, this could only mean he was a reluctant starter. But Lizette's active interest in the issue had changed him by 1924. Then he chaired a meeting of the Palestine Welfare League of Victoria. It aimed to buy 250 acres for £5000 to settle fifty families.

This increased involvement with a controversial issue eased Monash into a more prominent position in the Jewish community. Until now he had referred to himself as a 'cultural Jew', which was a way of saying that he had drifted from orthodoxy – because of his background and agnosticism – yet not from his heritage. His fame and his loyalty to his roots were causing the community to claim him more and more.

From the mid-1920s, much of Monash's time and influence was given over to re-establishing solid remembrances of the diggers who died in the war.

After the euphoric welcome home in 1919, there had been few, small marches on Anzac Day. It was almost as if the sacrifices of the 170,000 who came back and the 60,000 who were killed had faded from the memories of the public. This would have been impossible, given that just about every Australian family was connected to someone who had volunteered and served. In reality many diggers were suffering aftershocks (later to be known as post-traumatic stress disorder) of their horrific war experiences. This was the ugly downside of the AIF's huge success as a fighting machine. It might have been invincible, but it was not how the diggers felt now about themselves. They tried to forget. They fell silent about the death and destruction they had seen. Few mentioned how they felt or how it affected them. It was not done. But as the years slipped away, a need evolved for the diggers to gather and reminisce. They could not and would not forget their fallen mates. Yet this could not be done with anyone who had not been through the war. They could never really understand. They weren't part of that unbeatable team, the brethren who had fought on Gallipoli, in Palestine or the Western Front.

The revival of the Anzac tradition occurred in November 1923 when Monash organised those 5000 diggers to cope with the police strike. The other tens of thousands of AIF men around the country who heard or read about it were stirred and inspired. It triggered a flood of memories and pride, and a qualified sense of invincibility when considering the Australian Corps and what it had achieved and could again, if ever required.

Monash had been chased for the national presidency of the RSL, but he would not put himself up for an election. After being the most senior man in the corps, he thought he should either be handed the job or not. This only increased the need for Monash to be acknowledged. The entire ex-AIF was conscious that its greatest son and spokesman had been neglected. They didn't know why this had happened, but it irritated everyone from the rank and file to the senior officers. It was taken as a rejection of all of them.

In Sydney and Melbourne, clubs sprang up to support him, although he was not seeking endorsement or recognition for anything. Monash was just as popular in Sydney. The RSL was trying to persuade him to go there to be honoured and to help them organise Anzac Day as he had in Melbourne.

One unofficial support group – called the KK Club – met each month at Melbourne's Scott's Hotel to dine. Monash attended. The non-denominational group of thirty-five was brought together partly because he was not elected to the Melbourne Club, an elite institution in all but its intellectual scope. When asked about his non-election, he laughed and said he would not be 'bloody fool enough' to put his name forward in the first place.[1] But others did, and it was rejected.

He thought that Jews were banned or, in the subtle language of the club in that era, 'not invited to attend'. The Melbourne Club claimed this had never been true and that it did have Jewish members. After all Monash had achieved, it bothered him less than it would have earlier in his more ambitious days when such a snub might have played on his sensitivities as a classic outsider. It was the club's loss. It certainly didn't stop him accepting dinners and lunches as a guest in the antiquated and quaint all-male preserve. (A more classic rejection occurred after Sir Isaac Isaacs had been an honorary member while Australia's first native-born Governor-General. When his term was up he wished to remain a club member, but it would not have him.)[2]

✕

On Anzac Day 1924, half a decade after demobilisation, there was a remarkable banquet for Monash at the Melbourne Town Hall organised by the RSL. One observer claimed that a complete microcosm of Australia was present in the packed hall.[3] Every profession, trades union, religion and political party was represented.

Albert Jacka had proposed earlier, on 23 February, that diggers speak about Monash at the function. 'As a soldier,' the VC winner told an *Age* reporter, 'he's like one of ourselves, and doesn't like swank. I think he'd like an address from us better than anything else.'

Jacka's utterance created anticipation. Monash would receive the diggers' direct acclamation. On the night, he sat quietly to one side of the hall. An ex-soldier, calling himself a 'digger spokesman', took the floor.

'The standard by which they judged him was personal efficiency, character and integrity,' he began, but was drowned out by clapping and cheering. 'Mass opinion was almost always an infallible index of a man's true worth.' There was more interruption. 'The secret of his popularity lay in the fact that he possessed that rare and indefinable quality which entitled the man to be regarded in the digger's eyes as "dinkum."'

The town hall erupted. It was the finest tribute the ordinary digger could give someone of his esteem and rank. He is one of us. He could be trusted like a mate going over the top.

Monash was touched more than he had been on any other public occasion. He was called up to the stage. Applause and cheering was sustained.

Monash held up both hands. The room fell silent. They could see he

492

was moved. He was dinkum all right. Monash gathered his thoughts. He said he didn't care about non-recognition. He was just like everyone in the hall. He never hoped for more than esteem from his comrades on active service. He had a regret or two. One was not spending more time on the front line. He apologised. His humility was palpable, but the diggers saw it as a strength.

The reception was humbling, especially for a former commander who had often 'hardened his heart' and given orders that would cause increased casualties and deaths of the mates of the men in front of him.

He drew more applause when he said that all his honours had been given to him as a servant of the AIF. All the glory was theirs. Then he launched into the kind of speech that the diggers wanted to hear. Tens of thousands of them had suffered after the war. There was no counselling, little or no financial support and no understanding of their private mental suffering, regardless of physical injuries. Many had found life tougher out of the service than in it. Some had turned – hard – to alcohol to drown their sorrow, bad memories, nightmares and desperation. They were angry about the government's non-recognition of and support for them. Monash's experience of being ostracised had struck a chord. That's why he was the focus that night. It was as if his every word would mean something, and he knew it.

Monash began with the meaning of Anzac Day, which touched every listener. The cheering and clapping now was replaced with silence. The 'boss', the 'old man', the 'top cocky' was bringing some clarity to the mist and voids. He spoke of the importance of the Gallipoli campaign and what it meant to Australia as a nation. The finest traditions of a potentially great nation had been created in the fire of that uninviting terrain. He articulated the importance of the AIF in a way that none of them had heard said with such honesty and passion.

When he paused there was a standing ovation. Monash put up those big hands again. Having said how important the diggers were and had been, he gave a broad hint that they would be needed in the future.

Monash had been appalled at the running down of the country's defences and the cutting of funding to the armed forces since the end of the war. The Federal Government had done this after negotiating a strong mutual defence treaty with the USA. They didn't see the reason for wasting money on the services when Big Brother was looking after Australia. Monash said the decision to cut funds was 'like deciding that we will have no more burglaries and then dismissing the police force'.

'It is difficult for a former soldier to talk about defence,' he said, getting a knowing ear from everyone there. It laid him open to a charge that he was a militarist, a fire-eater and a jingo. This comment brought cheers. The diggers understood. They had all been there.

Monash said that war was rotten; no one in the hall wanted another. For that reason, he said, he was 'anxious'. His comments were open to interpretation, but one thing was clear. He wanted a strong defence force. Anything less would make Australia vulnerable.

Having made his grand statements eloquently, he admonished his patrons for the night, the RSL. It had to dampen down its internal strife. Its challenging job was to teach the traditions of the AIF.

The applause that followed was deafening. Every ex-soldier there felt lifted and alive. He had told them they were important, articulated why and made sense of what they had been through. He had given them hope. Every single one of the 700 diggers in attendance filed past Monash to shake his hand and look into those warm, weathered eyes. Those who had suffered since coming home from war might have found their private hell a little more bearable that night.

✕

Anzac Day 1925, a Saturday, saw a modest 5000 ex-soldiers march through Melbourne. Monash led the parade, dressed in civvies and carrying an umbrella, not a sword. It was symbolic of his attempts to put the war behind him, which in some ways his mental strength and resilience allowed him to do. But the Anzac spirit clung to him.

After the march he joined the diggers, the Prime Minister (now Stanley Melbourne Bruce), the Governor-General and the public at the Exhibition Building for the commemorative service. As soon as Monash entered the hall, there was spontaneous, sustained applause and cheering. He looked embarrassed. It was a solemn occasion. He didn't wish to be a distraction from it. His popularity on returning to Australia had been high. Now he was the most respected national hero. Many spoke or wrote about him being 'the greatest living Australian'.

The number of requests to attend and usually speak at RSL functions began to multiply. They kept wanting him in Sydney, too. And, belatedly, in federal politics.

Soon after the 1925 march, an impressed Bruce approached Monash about joining his Senate team to contest the 1925 elections. Two years earlier Bruce had broken from Hughes and, with other 'free traders', had joined the Country Party to form the National–Country coalition. The forty-two-year-old Bruce drove a Rolls-Royce and wore spats and plus-fours, aping the British aristocracy. He was more British in experience, aloof demeanour and speech than Australian. He had fought at Gallipoli in the British Army, was wounded and won the Military Cross. He was also at the Western Front until 1917. Bruce had been born in St Kilda, educated at Melbourne Grammar School and Cambridge University, where he did more playing on and off the river (he was in the crew) than studying for a modest BA. Bruce thought he could harness Monash's incredible appeal across the board in the Australian electorate. But it was too late.

'The decision [to go into politics],' Monash wrote, 'really had to be made four and a half years ago on my return from war service. There was then a clear call for me to enter federal parliament, but the Prime Minister of the day [Hughes] placed very definite obstacles in the way of my return in time for the election of 1919.' Several members of the Federal Government, he said, had suggested that Monash's abilities could be used in one of many spheres. 'But after I had been kept in suspense for nine months,' he added, 'nothing whatever eventuated . . . Since 1920 I have consistently shaped my course in the belief that my services are not wanted in the federal sphere.' It was too late to go back on his 'tracks'.[4]

Perhaps he could have added that he would not be a good subordinate to Bruce, who had a similar background to him in their education, work in law (Bruce worked for the London branch of the family law firm, Paterson, Laing & Bruce while practising at the English Bar) and military service. Monash would have foreseen clashes. The sheer weight of his industry, popularity and political skills would have seen him a rival to the PM.

Henry Rawlinson, who became a peer after the war, died in India in 1925, after five years running the British forces there. He was sixty-one. As with Haig, the verdict on his capacity as a military commander was mixed but had been salvaged by Monash's commandership from August to October 1918. British historians and reviewers, who preferred to ignore the AIF and Canadian contribution to the end of the conflict, seemed confused by Rawlinson's (and Haig's) sudden success after years of disastrous battles.

Writers decades later attempting revisionism, which began in earnest in the 1990s, played up Haig and Rawlinson at a safe distance from the emotions and consequences of bad leadership.

✕

Early in 1926, the design for the St Kilda Road Shrine of Remembrance was abandoned at a conference between representatives of the war memorial committee and the State cabinet. Against Monash's wishes, it was replaced by the concept of a city square with a cenotaph at the top of Bourke Street. The RSL and the MCC came in behind the new plan.

Murdoch at the *Herald* was pleased. His win over Monash seemed complete.

✕

About 12,000 veterans in Melbourne marched on Anzac Day 1926. Inclement weather didn't stop them or the crowded who turned out to clap and cheer them. This time Monash sensed the groundswell of feeling in support of the diggers. He decided to lead the parade in full uniform. Weighed down with medals, sword, orders and decorations, he strode with Blamey at the front and received a huge cheer at every corner. The crowds were big, despite having been down in recent years. The diggers jutted out their chins and swung their arms with a little more vigour. They were reluctant heroes, who didn't crave adulation. But they did want to be respected and remembered for everything they had done.

The day was becoming a lifeline for many diggers. The disaffected, the alcoholic, those injured mentally and physically, and the rest looked forward to this occasion more than any other on the calendar.

Anzac Day now had all the signs of a ritual. The 'Old Man', now sixty, was exhausted by it, but pleased. His hope ever since the first commemoration among the heat, files and choking dust of Tel el Kebir in Egypt in 1916 had been that it would last. After a decade it had a chance.

✕

The year 1927 saw the breakthrough. Monash's favourite royal, the Duke of York (Prince Albert), was the catalyst. He was visiting Australia for Canberra's official opening. Monash decided it was time for another big royal show. He and all the key AIF soldiers, including Birdwood, made every effort for the largest turn-out yet. Diggers, some of them from remote parts of the nation, came to Melbourne for the occasion. Monash looked at the numbers, and suggested 25,000 would march, which was just short of the figure he had organised for George V on that fateful day 27 August 1916, when he presented his 3rd Division. In the end, 30,000 soldiers poured into Melbourne in the days before the march.

It was the second time in less than four years that Monash had shown how he could rally his loyal diggers, for a big parade like this or for duty, as in the police strike. This physical force, coupled with his personal popularity, maintained his reputation as the most powerful individual in Australia. At a time when the professional armed forces were being run down, the ex-volunteer soldiers as a group outnumbered the army and all the state's police services put together. The diggers had enormous experience, and they were still young. Many were disaffected after the war. They would not have second thoughts about answering another call. But they could be so aroused only by one man, Monash. Such was the trust they had in him that, if he made a case, they would respond. The fact that Monash's creation – the most effective force of the 1914–18 war – was lying dormant but still ready to emerge, if Monash wished it, was not lost on many interested parties as Australia faced growing economic problems in the late 1920s.

But the main thing on his mind in April 1927 was the coming Anzac Day march and organising the diggers for a special effort.

On 24 April – march eve – at the RSL dinner, Monash spoke and built his theme around the need for the Shrine as the best memorial to the diggers. He was firm that it should be for that alone, not as a tourist attraction or to beautify the city, as the square proposal would do. He considered the Shrine design was magnificent, dignified, noble and appealing. It was 'eminently suited as a memorial of great service and sacrifice, without the ridiculous note of victory and conquest which characterised the memorials of the barbarian past'.[5] He thought the Shrine would be similar in its impression to the tombs of Napoleon in Paris and General Grant on the Hudson River in New York.

By prearrangement, supporters at tables scattered around the hall jumped up to applaud his argument. The euphoria generated by the knowledge that this would be a great march, and Monash's well-articulated passion, saw a groundswell of support for the Shrine. A vote was called for. A big majority of hands backed it.

The next day the crowd was the biggest ever seen in Australian streets for any event. The newspapers put it at about 600,000, ten times the number of people who attended the most recent big sporting event, a grand final between two big rivals in the Aussie Rules code, Melbourne and Collingwood. It was long joked that Melbourne spectators would turn up in numbers to the opening of an envelope. The fact that almost half the city's population was in the streets to see the war veterans was evidence enough of the attitude to them. The occasion would have boosted the self-esteem of every participant.

Monash marched alone at the head of the force, with Birdwood, White and McGlinn in the line behind him. These exertions were now tough for Monash. He had troublesome blood pressure, and his condition had slipped in the last few years. But no one knew except Lizette, the family and his doctor. Monash was still a hardy old man to the nation, his diggers and his indirect employers, the State Government.

When Monash reached the temporary cenotaph in front of Parliament House, he broke away and joined the Duke of York to take the salute as the 30,000 diggers, all of them proudly displaying their decorations and medals, pumped by, an army reborn.

Many memories would have flooded Monash's mind, particularly of that special parade of the 3rd Division on Salisbury Plain. But this occasion would have meant more. These men were representative of all five divisions, and they were six times the numbers of those in the 1919 victory march in London.

There was another crucial difference. The 3rd Division in August 1916 was still a bunch of untried, if well-drilled tyros. They looked good, but had yet to be tested. This 1927 squad was of hardened, experienced fighters, who had proven themselves in the toughest of situations.

At the service in the Exhibition Building after the parade, only he and the Duke spoke. When Monash took the podium a big cheer went up. He checked it with a firmly raised hand, silently reminding everyone present that this was a commemoration service, not a rally. His speech was sharp, and simple, yet inspirational. He thought always about how a good tradition could be built into another to lift the fledgling nation. Monash was mindful of the growing economic malaise that threatened Australia, and caused his mail to be stacked with letters from diggers and others down on their luck. His message was that the Australians who fought in France were 'spurred on to finer effort' by the slogan 'Remember Gallipoli!' Now that slogan should be used in the 'titanic task of nation building'.

Monash would forever see that Gallipoli and Western Front experience as the true examination for the young nation when the spirit of its manhood was tested against incredible odds. He wanted it to be the base for the next century at least in Australia's development, especially when times were tough.

With his interests in so many areas, Monash was aware quicker and more than most of the problems confronting the nation.[6]

✕

The appeal of Monash, now sixty-two, had grown since he first found he had hero status in 1919. He had not joined a political party or shown any inclination to capitalise on his fame, popularity or power. He had only ever shown a dedication to his old corps. His paternal instincts towards it were sustained almost a decade after the war had ended. His influence when supporting a cause was substantial. The Anzac Day march might never again reach the peak of 1927, but his efforts had institutionalised it.

The success of the march also gave the Shrine project new momentum, along with the RSL's change of mind and endorsement the night before at the dinner. The day after the march, Monash put out a strong press statement on the Shrine supported by several of the key officers, including Grimwade, Coxen and Elliott. The *Age* and the *Argus* for the first time swung behind the idea of the Shrine. But the *Herald* stayed in support of the city square.

Murdoch was caught off balance. He thought his paper's long-running campaign for the city square had won the day. He went on the attack, calling the Shrine 'a tomb of gloom'.[7] It was a nice headline, not much more. Murdoch's overworked spin was that the 'people had spoken'. But the people had never been consulted. It was a power play between the State Government, the MCC, the RSL, Melbourne Legacy (the organisation that supported veterans' families), the Institute of Architects (which had put held the design competition) and the newspapers.

Monash saw a chance to get his way. He had lobbied for several years but not with the intensity he now applied. State cabinet would make the final decision, but there was an election coming up on 20 May 1927. Monash had to work on key ministers and shadow ministers, telling them that Murdoch's attack was immature, unsubstantial and missing the key point about a non-utilitarian structure.[8]

Monash joined a subcommittee of the war memorial executive

committee, which would now decide which proposal would be put to the State Government. This time he worked on showing that the cost of the city square would be prohibitive. This argument worked with a cost-conscious new Labor Government, which took office on 20 May 1927.

The *Herald* and Murdoch gave up their campaign. Monash, in keeping with his career policy, was careful not to gloat, writing the newspaperman a complimentary reply to his conceding defeat.[9] Yet it gave him pleasure to know he had again overcome one of his main former antagonists, who post-war, especially over repatriation in 1919, had been supportive.

At the same time he was celebrating success over the Shrine and its positioning, Monash was making a modest but public celebration of his decade-long relationship with Lizette. They sat for a miniature portrait by artist Agnes Paterson at Lizette's apartment at the Windsor Hotel, to which she had moved. The Victorian Artists Society exhibited the eighty-seven millimetre by 106 millimetre watercolour on ivory.

It was hardly a coming out. They had been photographed as an item on the social and culture circuit in Melbourne since she returned. But the portrait was a statement confirming the strength of their relationship, which the rest of family, led by Bertha, had failed to acknowledge. Monash had also made sure that Lizette accompanied him wherever possible at the many functions for the Duke of York in Melbourne. She made it to about half of them. She was with Monash at the Grand Ball on 27 April, but not the official reception – to which he took his daughter – the next day. He had challenged the rigid protocol in the puritanical city regarding his paramour and had won and lost some invitations for her.[10]

ZENITH AND END

Monash's power and influence was reaching a peak. In 1928 he was still fighting for the growing SEC when he put a proposal to the McPherson Nationalist State Government for an extra allocation of a million pounds in funding. It was rejected.

'Sir John arrived at the outer doors of the cabinet room,' recalled Robert Menzies, then a thirty-four-year-old junior honorary minister in the State Government. '[He] demanded admittance [to the Cabinet room].'

The 'amiable' Premier Sir William McPherson asked for Monash to be brought in. When he entered the room every cabinet member stood up 'instinctively'.

'We were in the presence of a man we knew was a greater man than we would ever be,' Menzies said.

'Well, Premier,' Monash began, 'I gather that the Cabinet has rejected my proposal.'

'Well, yes,' the Premier replied. 'I think that's right, Sir John.'

'That can only be because you've utterly failed to understand it,' Monash said. 'I will now explain it.'

Menzies recalled standing 'rock-like' as Monash took half an hour over an exposition of the proposal.

'One by one we became convinced, or, at any rate, felt we were convinced of the error of our ways,' Menzies said. 'We were left silent.'

No one objected. Monash looked at McPherson and remarked: 'Well, sir, I take it that your decision is reversed. Indeed, anticipating your approval of my proposal, and so that there will be no delay, I have brought with me the Order-in-Council that will be necessary for this purpose.'

Monash pulled it out of his breast pocket.

'He passed it around,' Menzies said. 'It was signed, and he went out.'[1]

This kind of awe and respect was common from people who knew his work habits and style. Others with power bases, who did not know him, saw him as an empty vessel into which they could pour their sometimes wild political ambitions. They had noted that Monash had said he 'only had to lift his finger and the AIF would spring to life'. It was no idle boast.

As Australia slipped further towards the abyss of depression, some right-wingers, such as the 'White Army', saw him as the ideal dictator to take over the government by force.

There had been precedents in other countries. Ludendorff had been installed as front man for the unsuccessful *coups d'état* of Wolfgang Kapp in 1920 and of a former 1914–18 war corporal, Adolf Hitler, in 1923. These dangerous dalliances did the German war hero leader no harm. In fact, they sustained his already huge profile. Ludendorff was a member of the National Socialist Party (Nazis) from 1924 to 1928. He made a legitimate bid for power in 1925 by running against his former commander-in-chief, Hindenburg, whom he now hated. Another fascist hero for Australian extremists was Italy's Benito Mussolini. Wounded while serving with the Bersaglieri, a corps of sharpshooters, he returned to his homeland after the war a convinced anti-socialist. Like Ludendorff and Hitler, he was egocentric and had a sense of destiny that matched his hunger for power. They were all driven by a hatred of communism that had been gaining ground in Europe since the Russian Revolution. This same drive was causing extremists in Australia to get excited by the thought of Monash being in charge of the Federal Government.

Some ex-AIF officers linked to right-wing groups (such as the White Army and the New Guard) were members of the same organisations that Monash had attended, such as the Naval and Military Club. His absence now – he was spending more time with the family and Lizette – only expanded the mystique and myths about him. They saw potential saw in him as a key player in their dreaming and plotting.

There would have been plenty of stories – apocryphal, exaggerated and based on fact – about Monash facing down former PM Hughes while working on repatriation. There would have been other tales about how Monash handled Hughes when he attempted to undermine his military commander at the critical end of the war. Some conspirators wanting justifications for their clandestine endeavours would have read Monash's prize-winning essay in 1912. They would have construed from it that he was against politicians interfering in military matters during wartime. This thinking would have been extrapolated into guessing Monash's attitude in an economic crisis.

Their moustaches were twitching with excitement over the possibilities of his leadership, especially with the Depression about to bite. Two Sydney groups – the Imperial Patriots and the Warringah Constitutional Club – had already made overtures.[2] Monash had ignored them, which highlighted one major problem with the scenarios being discussed in Sydney and Melbourne from 1927: few of the conspirators understood Monash well.

Douglas Haig died early in 1928. Although Haig's earlier failures would not be forgotten or forgiven by the British people (except the odd unconvincing revisionist more than seven decades after the war), attitudes to him were mixed. Haig travelled through the British Empire raising funds for impoverished servicemen from 1920 to the year before his death. At least the former 'Butcher of the Somme' (like Rawlinson) remained obligated to his former charges and the memory of those whom he sent to their deaths en masse after poor battle planning and execution.

If the would-be coup-makers in Australia had known Monash's mentality and circumstances in early 1929, their hopes would have received a setback. He was shattered by the death of his elder grandson, John Monash Bennett, after he contracted a rare influenza virus. The 'talented and lovable' six-year-old had been just a few days at Scotch College's junior school. His grandfather had spent a great deal of time with him and had proudly taken him down to his old school to meet the principal, William Littlejohn.[3]

When Tante Ulrike died two years earlier, Monash had been sad. Her death had been the end of an era in the family. But to lose someone as young and promising as John made no sense. He wanted to write a short memoir of little John's life. He collected everything he could on him, but the moment he sat down to write, he was too grief-stricken to start.

Monash tried to give some meaning to the family tragedy by endowing a drinking fountain and a school prize to Scotch so that the boy's name would live on. He turned his attention to the other two grandchildren, David and Elizabeth. He put his spare-time energy into building a doll's house over several months for Elizabeth (Betty), who was then just two years old. He created a two-storeyed, four-roomed edifice. Everything was designed to the ultimate, including the stairs and the furniture.[4]

He taught five-year-old David arithmetic, writing and basic world geography. But the shock of John's loss drained him. He had planned a trip to England and France but would not leave the family, except for a trip to Sydney for the dedication of the Cenotaph at Martin Place.

Monash would never be consoled, yet he found joy in the birth of a third grandson, (John) Colin Monash Bennett in August.

The Depression took hold. Nobody was immune. The poor became poorer, were out of work or had their wages cut. The rich saw their businesses slump or fail, and their investments dwindle as the stock market crashed. Monash saw his SEC salary slashed by twenty-seven per cent. Investments netted him less. He didn't wish to eat into capital he had put into property and preferred to cut his expenses. He dropped out of several clubs and societies, and gave away wine and tobacco, much to his doctor's delight. He had been warned that his blood pressure was too high – a problem that beset his father Louis late in his life. Monash was overweight, but by six kilograms, not the twenty-six kilograms extra he was at the beginning of the war. He was spending more time at Iona, indulging a new hobby, astronomy, and an older one, carpentry, in his well-equipped workshop. He was also turning more to the solitary satisfaction of painting, an extension of his youthful skill as a portrait cartoonist. The Iona garden was more and more another form of relaxation, so much so that some visitors thought he was the hired help.

His chauffeur, Patrick Dwyer, recalled an incident one Sunday morning when Monash was working on a pergola. A man delivering a load of lime, thinking he was a gardener, asked him how long he had been doing the job.

'Oh, some time,' Monash replied.

'What kind of man is Monny to work for?' the man asked.

'Oh,' Monash said, 'all right, when you get to know him. Of course, you can't please everybody.'

The man with the lime walked to the back and commented on the new man working on the pergola.

'That's Sir John,' Dyer told him.

After a few seconds pause the man asked, 'Is there a back way out?'

Dwyer recalled car trips that helped Monash get away from the pressures of work. On one trip to Anglesea, a surf beach 120 kilometres southwest of Melbourne, they stopped at Geelong for a cup of tea. A drunk approached them.

'Excuse me, Guv, guv'nor,' the drunk said to Monash, 'could you give me a shilling for a drink?'

Monash obliged. As he got back in the car he turned to Dwyer and said: 'That's an honest man, Dwyer.'[5]

More people than ever turned to Monash for help. Cutbacks in expenditure at the SEC saw some staff being laid off. Monash had to deal with the aggrieved reaction of employees. Diggers in increased numbers wrote or approached him. Monash started an RSL committee in an attempt to deal with the problem. He didn't have the energy to chair it, but did act as treasurer. The State and Federal Governments sought his advice and wanted him to be on secret committees. Monash had answers to every problem the Germans presented in the war. In the first depression he faced in the 1890s, he had been a driven, hard-working, young businessman. He would fight his way out of all problems by taking on every scrap of work he could. But four decades on, Monash, like everyone else in countries affected, didn't have answers. He expressed only the conventional 'wisdom' that the basic wage and pensions should be lowered to match the fall in the cost of living. The theories of John Maynard Keynes, sitting in an ivory tower at Cambridge University, who advocated increased government spending in such times, were years from being fashionable.

James Scullin's Labor easily beat Bruce's Nationalists at the October 1929 election. Monash was considered above politics except by right-wing extremists, and it was no surprise when the new Prime Minister allowed him to keep his place on the Council of Defence with White. They were not happy when he abolished compulsory military training. But Labor had been elected – as usual in crises – by a nation wanting basic services to be maintained at the expense of others. The military seemed expendable as the 1914–18 war slipped into history.

Scullin became the first Prime Minister to write to Monash and acknowledge his record by making him and Chauvel full generals on 11 November – Armistice Day – 1929. It was a decade late, but both men were grateful for the honour. A month later the Institution of Engineers, Australia gave him its highest award, the Peter Nicol Russell Memorial Medal. These recognitions and the ups and downs of the year caused Monash to consider it was time to write his memoirs. The deaths of his grandson and his long-time business partner and friend John Gibson made him reflect on his own mortality.

He began making notes and outlines during the Christmas holidays.

Apart from cutting down on late nights out, Monash's life in 1930 remained full, active and hectic as it had been since he left school approaching half a century ago. Yet he was honest with himself. He faced the truth about his slowing up. He told others that he didn't have the 'elasticity of mind' for new responsibilities, such as presidency of the RSL. Monash modified his will to account for his shrinking assets. He totted up the value of his properties, investments and securities against debts and was not happy to see that his net value had slipped to £33,773, down about twelve per cent on the previous year, because of the Depression.[6] Monash was haunted by the impecunious ends of both his grandfather and father, and had worked hard to avoid such pressures in his later years. He was a little alarmed that his net wealth had shrunk about 40 per cent over the last decade, and this caused him to stay in his SEC job.

Monash's will represented his charitable nature and responsibilities as a family patriarch. Bertha and Gershon would be left Iona, worth about £8000. His son-in-law would receive £1000 cash. His three nieces, Mona, Nancy and Peggy Rosenhain, were left £500 each. He bequeathed annuities of £200 a year to Lizette and £50 – to be paid quarterly – to sisters Mathilde and Louise, brother-in-law Walter and cousins Mathilde and Sophie Roth. Showing his appreciation for the way Iona and his precious garden had been maintained, Joseph Dyer, his gardener, would also receive £25 a year for life. A hundred pounds was to be paid out to 'Jewish and other charities' annually for ten years as 'my trustees see fit'. He gave annually to about twenty charities, with hospitals, Jewish organisations and diggers prominent among them.

Bertha would receive the rest – the balance of his assets and returns from investments. This amounted to about £26,000, if the value of Iona was split between her and Gershon.[7]

Despite Monash's concern about the erosion of his assets, he was still relatively well off. His capacity to generate wealth was seen in a strongly developing SEC. It had assets of £20 million and was generating £3 million a year. The press was now a supporter of the project.

The *Age* reported on 'Yallourn, a Model Town': 'Yallourn is the only town in the southern hemisphere in which all details confirm to a definite plan.' It cost £500,000 to build 400 dwellings, a shopping centre, public buildings, churches and tree-lined streets. It was, the newspaper reported, 'an excellent example of applied town-planning ideals'.[8]

After hesitating, he decided to march one last time on Anzac Day 1930. A surprise highlight was a goodwill statement to mark the occasion made by Mustafa Kemal, who from 1922 had been president of Turkey. He referred to 'those glorious men of Anzac who came out of the sea to grapple with unknown foes in the spirit of gladiators of old'.[9]

Some of those gladiators and others were becoming restless. The deepening Depression brought the extremists out. Monash's appearance at this critical moment made him once more the focus for them overcoming their increased feelings of alienation. Officers and diggers wrote to him, urging him to act. Some said they were ready to take up arms whenever he gave the command.[10] There were mixed motives and perceptions. Most of the pleas were to counter communism. A Hobart Catholic priest saw a threat from the non-believers following Stalin, Trotsky and the Moscow line. He telegraphed: 'Assume dictatorship do not fear save Australia as Mussolini saved Italy.'[11] The Empire Loyalty League wasn't so worried about the 'commies'. Its members wished to put down the 'Irish Catholics' – like the Hobart priest – who were pushing for an Australian Governor-General. Presumably the League was referring at least to Scullin, whose motives were connected with his country's independence from the 'mother country'.[12]

These extremes demonstrated again how little the public knew about Monash and his beliefs. He was conservative, with qualifications. His true political equilibrium could be gauged by his attitude to events brewing in Germany and Russia. Both had dangerous elements that were anti-Jewish. He recognised in 1930 that fascism represented a bigger immediate threat to democracy than communism.

He was not anti-British but, like Scullin, he wanted Australia to follow its own path. A first step would be a local product – like him – being made Governor-General. At the time the Empire Loyalty League was approaching him to beat off the Catholics, Scullin was battling George V over who should take the position. The King wanted Birdwood, whose affiliation and love for the AIF had made him an honorary Aussie despite his background. 'Birdie' would be a soft choice. He would take the British line in any conflict, just as Munro Ferguson had.

Scullin was considering Monash and Isaac Isaacs. If the King was forced to have an Australian there was no question his choice would have been Monash, but for one factor. He was a single man with a lover, unless he married Lizette. His family, led by Bertha, would not let him take that step even though his relationship with Lizette was strong and had lasted twelve years. Once Vic died in 1920 he could never be G-G. Only a married man could fill such a position. It just wouldn't do for such a prominent job.

One writer to the *Bulletin* wanted Australia under semi-military rule with Monash as the nation's saviour.[13] An ex-AIF man at an Adelaide Rotary meeting received a fine reception when he said that he had dreamt Monash and the diggers were in control of the government for a five-year term. He cursed when he woke up and realised he had been dreaming.[14] Monash usually filed communications like this. But every so often he received a more serious approach from military officers and businessmen he had had contact with. He was then forced to reply like a lawyer, spelling out his position in uncharacteristic language, making it clear he would never be involved in a coup.

The need to be 'like Mussolini' came up more often in 1930. But the proposers missed a vital point. Monash's doctrine was the complete antithesis of that espoused by Ludendorff, with his born-to-rule mien, or the strutting Hitler and the posturing Mussolini. If someone like one of them had emerged in Australia, then that might have sparked Monash into action in opposition to them. Yet regardless of his politics, he was not an egomaniac hell-bent on power and the desire to foist his vision on a vulnerable nation.

The issue became critical late in the year, but only in the minds of the extremists. The one Australian who could have raised an army and led a coup was never going to do it. In December, perhaps because of concern that there would be unrest, Scullin shrewdly chose Monash to represent Australia for the opening of New Delhi, India. This would see him out of the country for the first three months of 1931. Scullin had complete trust in Monash, but he would have realised that removing him would ease the nation's political pressure cooker.

The conspirators sniffed a conspiracy. 'My friends,' Major General Grimwade wrote to Monash, 'view your selection very gravely and think there are sinister motives behind it.' Monash seemed bemused, if not amused by the contradictions in the approaches to him. He wrote back to Grimwade saying that different groups with different motives wanted him to stay in Australia and not go to India. One wanted him to stay put to lead a revolution. The other wished he remained to suppress a revolution. He was confident that any change, such as ousting the Governor-General and forming a republic, would come about by constitutional means.[15]

Monash himself was the least worried of anyone about upheaval. But the efforts to enlist him became an irritation. In response to a Sydney businessman claiming that he was in a group that deplored his taking up the Indian offer, Monash felt compelled to drop his masquerade behind legalese to make his position plain.

In just about the best of his 75,000 letters left to the nation, he wrote:

> What do you and your friends want me to do? To lead a movement to upset the Constitution, oust the jurisdiction of Parliament, and usurp the Governmental power? If so, I have no ambition to embark on High Treason, which any such action would amount to.
>
> What would you say if a similar proposal were made by the Communists and Socialists to seize political power for the benefit of the proletariat and the extinction of the bourgeoisie, as they have done in Russia? Would you not call that Revolution and Treason to the Crown and Constitution?
>
> Depend upon it, the only hope for Australia is the ballot box, and an educated electorate. You and your people should get busy and form an organisation as efficient, as widespread, and as powerful as that of the Labour Party.

He ended the letter with a line of pure Monash power, brilliance and logic: 'If it be true that many people in Sydney are prepared to trust to my leadership, they should be prepared also to trust my judgement.'[16]

It was still not quite game, set and match in the debate. Overtures would keep coming in. But Monash's position was steadfast and along clear, unambiguous lines, just the way he had communicated as a battle commander. He supported the democratic system in Australia as it stood. He admired the British institutions of government, parliament and law, which he compared favourably to less fortunate former European colonies in South America, such as unstable Argentina. The tone of his letter indicated that any attempted coup would be opposed by him, no matter what the background or inspiration. That left any would-be coup masters with a 'Catch-22 situation'. An overthrow of the government could be led only by him. Without him it would never happen. Yet the pressures continued.

The year 1930 proved to be one of agitation and sadness. His close mate McCay died, ending a lifelong rivalry that brought out mainly the best in them.

Monash still had many friends. His enemies were dwindling. The McInerney clique had been silenced by Monash's success. McInerney himself appeared to have modified his stance after the war. The two men more than once lunched with each other. Murdoch and Monash would never be close, but there was a mutual respect that kept their relationship civil. Murdoch's attitude had changed, especially after he witnessed Monash's military success at the end of 1918 and his handling of repatriation in 1919. Their battle over the Shrine was tough at times but ended sportingly and without recriminations.

Bean remained confused over his revision of what made an ideal commander, and was taking a long time to acknowledge that he had been unfair in his analysis of Monash. He had a lot of soul-searching to do yet over his assessment. For his part, Monash had long ago forgiven Bean, believing charitably that he had been sometimes misguided. He even went to the trouble of recommending him for an Honorary Doctorate at Melbourne University.

Perhaps only Monash's longstanding feud with Hughes would never be reconciled. The former PM never stopped niggling. After the twenty-one-year-old cricketer Don Bradman had toured England in 1930 and established himself as the best batsman ever, Hughes called him the greatest Australian ever born. Sports fans, who made up a fair majority of the nation, endorsed this line. But Hughes had been irked by many commentators putting that daunting mantle on Monash since the war. He wanted to make sure it was placed on someone else. Bradman was a worthy contender. But in 1930 (or ever), he could not be compared with Monash.

✕

Monash managed to arrange for Lizette to tour India with him. It turned out to be a wonderful break during which he had plenty of time to slow down and reflect. The endless requests for his time, money and endorsement went blissfully quiet. He had a listless interlude on the boat across the Indian Ocean where he read one of the thirty books that he hoped to plough through. He did little exercise. He and Lizette began their Indian visit with two days at Government House in Bombay, then three at Agra where they strolled by the Taj Mahal at night. Next was the unprepossessing holy city of Benares, followed by New Delhi, where they stayed six days at the Viceroy's palace.

Currie was there representing Canada. He and Monash had much in common as successful former corps commanders and businessmen, who had experienced the English way of war, which they didn't always adhere to and made efforts to change.

There had been plenty of Indians at the celebrations, but both men were surprised at the paucity of the country's own VIPs at the vice-regal functions. Had the English snubbed them, or had they rejected invitations?

Monash was also fascinated to be on the spot when the sixty-one-year-old leader of the Indian nationalist movement, Mahatma Gandhi, was released from gaol. He had been imprisoned after leading a peaceful march to the sea to protest the tax on salt, which hit the poor hardest. But this and private conversations with Currie were the extent of Monash's immersion in local politics. He relaxed and enjoyed the ceremony marking New Delhi's beginning. This was followed by a long trip to the Khyber Pass, where he and others in the party were warned about rebel snipers. After his close calls from Turkish marksmen above Monash Valley on Gallipoli, such a threat did not perturb him. They went over the Afghan border, where he didn't approve of the army's display of force and had to restrain himself from reprimanding the local commander.[17]

The British rulers of India wanted him to extend his tour, which he did with two more weeks in the south. Mysore intrigued him. He saw it as proof that the Indians could govern themselves. Monash fell in love with 'a thousand Indias', finding culture, art and refinement everywhere. It was stimulating, aesthetically pleasing and invigorating. He had planned to attack his memoirs on the trip, but was so taken with the country that he didn't stop writing to others about it.

The exotic atmosphere drew him closer than ever to Lizette. They were in no hurry to get home. They went via Madras to Ceylon and spent five days in the hills.[18] After three months of an idyllic break they arrived back in Australia on 21 March 1931. Harsh reality was waiting.

The day he returned he learned that Annie Gabriel had died in February. He regretted he had not been able to say goodbye to the woman who had first loved him in every sense. They had remained firm friends and had been regular correspondents before, during and after the war. Monash, she always said, was the one true love of her life.

Just when he was reeling from that news, he received a call from an old army officer late at night on 22 March. Pompey Elliott had committed suicide by stabbing himself in the arm and bleeding to death. He had tried to gas himself in February.

Elliott had suffered from post-traumatic stress disorder. He was just one of countless ex-soldiers who, for reasons then unexplained, had gone 'mad'. During the war this fine and most courageous of commanders, one of Monash's favourite's in the entire AIF, had been a depressive. Elliott, who would never send his men on a mission he would not undertake himself, suffered every time his directives led to death or casualties. Now the hero and survivor of the Gallipoli landing, Lone Pine, Fromelles, Polygon Wood and Villers-Bretonneux himself had become a casualty of war, twelve years after it finished.

Monash was deeply upset. But as usual he was never allowed time for grieving. He had a huge backlog of SEC work to plough through. On top of that he had to contend with the renewed push for him to 'save the nation'.

While he was away the undeveloped, disparate movement had grown. In early March rumours had swept through rural Victoria and New South Wales that there had been a communist takeover of the Federal Government. The *Bulletin* and the Melbourne *Herald* were urging the creation of an emergency governing body to run the country, with no one but Monash mentioned as the leader. A prominent radio commentator touted him as a benevolent dictator. Calls came from all over the country.

The points he was making to individuals in letters throughout 1930 now had to be explained to audiences at dinners and civic receptions. His theme emphasised that he had 'no desire whatever to upset the constitution of Australia'. He continued to make it clear that he was no Hindenburg or Mussolini. His inaction defused the issue.[19]

But the nation continued to be reminded of his unmatched power. At 1931's Anzac Day parade, he just couldn't bring himself to march again. His body was not up to it. He didn't want to make an effort and drop out in front of his men or the spectators. Instead, he did what Blamey had suggested a year earlier. He got on a horse and took the salute as the soldiers swung by with more pump and pageant than ever before. The sight of Monash sitting tall in the saddle of a big white stallion, in full general's uniform, lifted them. The sunken jowls, the grim, even critical look, as if he was searching for imperfections that could still improve their presentation, made him appear as resolute as he proved on Gallipoli or the Somme.

But away from the public gaze he was deteriorating physically. In May he was still walking a couple of kilometres a day, yet after it he was out of breath. Even climbing the stairs at Iona had him puffing. He saw his doctor. The diagnosis was disturbing. He had an irregular heartbeat, dilation of the heart, some valvular leakage and the suspicion of a cancerous growth in the abdomen. He was prescribed digitalis, the main drug then for irregular heartbeat. But there was nothing to be done with the growth. The specialist feared his heart would not stand an operation.

It was enough for Monash, who said he felt 'rather downcast'. He began to prepare for the worst by first putting his affairs and papers in order in a way that pleased him. If he was going to die soon, he wanted to be in control at the end. Monash kept up his SEC work, but most nights he returned home, usually after dining with Lizette at the Windsor, to sift through his files. He listed papers to be burned. These included some miscellaneous erotica – mainly artwork he had picked up in France, all Annie Gabriel's letters and most of his correspondence from Lizette.

In September 1931, only a few people, including family, Lizette and close friends, knew that he was ill. Apart from his SEC duties, he continued as if nothing was amiss, except that he feared each event might be the last of its kind for him. Meetings for the University Council, the Shrine Committee and the odd dinner were attended, with his diggers taking precedence.

He was at the 6th Battalion reunion on 23 September. In a brief speech he told them he didn't expect to be at another one. He regretted 'that political and government authorities offer so little stimulus to the young men of today to follow the example of those of the past generation'.[20] Monash was still thinking about the welfare of his country and putting others first. He began cancelling engagements for October and writing final letters. He thought he was slipping mentally as well.

On 29 September he had a slight heart attack at Iona. On 3 October he had a massive attack, then others in quick succession. He contracted pneumonia, which did what falling bridges, innumerable snipers, bombs, shrapnel and stray bullets could not.

John Monash died at 10.55 a.m. on 8 October 1931. He was sixty-six, a reasonable age for that time. But his doctor made it clear the strain of the war had been the main cause, robbing him of perhaps twenty years.

The 1914–18 conflict had claimed another Australian.[21]

At Iona, Bertha, who had been closest in the family to Monash, was strong as she and government officials began to make arrangements for a state funeral. At the Windsor, Lizette was inconsolable. Because the family had ostracised her, she could not go to her partner. Not yet.

The country went into shock. It had happened so quickly and unexpectedly. Monash's sharp mind and spirit were still evident everywhere he went until a fortnight before his death. After all, he had been 'the old man' ever since the war and that was his image and fatherly reputation. Yet this sobriquet was earned during the war because he was one of the oldest senior commanders in the AIF. It was hard for the Australian populous and his diggers in particular to accept that their leader, and Australia's national leader in waiting, was no longer with them.

The nation reacted as if it had lost its greatest hero in his prime. A big part of his appeal was seen in the tributes from the whole spectrum of Australians. They emphasised his humane qualities, not his achievements in war, engineering, law and academia.

There was a strong move to have him buried at the Shrine, but the people with whom he had worked on the project stopped it. They brought out documents that had him saying: 'The Shrine should be no man's tomb.'

The day after he died, his body lay in state with a military guard in

Queen's Hall, Parliament House, from 5 p.m. A stream of people of all ages and from all walks of life moved falteringly around the bier. Thousands of diggers, most wearing their medals, paid their respects. They didn't stop coming until the early hours of Saturday. Lizette was among them.

The state was in mourning over the weekend in synagogues and churches. It was the beginning of the cricket season, but many district and club matches were abandoned. At the MCG, where Monash had been enticed twice in 1928–29 to watch Bradman begin his Test career, it was the Aussie Rules grand final between Geelong and Richmond. Both teams wore black armbands. The crowd of 60,000 included many diggers, who had seen Monash the night before. Jack Dyer, then a raw-boned seventeen-year-old footballer in his first season for Richmond, recalled an eerily silent crowd that didn't cheer until well after the minute's silence in Monash's honour.

Sunday 11 October 1931, the day of the funeral, began overcast and cold and remained that way. At 12.30 p.m. Rabbi Danglow conducted a private service for family, friends and military heads in Queen's Hall. Chauvel read the address. Then Monash was given over to the diggers and the public for the last time. A radio broadcast brought proceedings to the nation.

His coffin, draped in a Union Jack that annoyed some, was carried down the steps of Parliament House by a military guard in front of a sea of people. They flooded Spring and Bourke Streets beyond barriers put up to allow a march past. The coffin was placed on a gun carriage.

A chill south wind greeted 15,000 diggers, sailors, airmen and nurses, who marched by Monash. Sixty-five minutes later they were followed by the military escort, the Scotch College Cadet Corps, the Melbourne University Rifles, the gun-carriage, and that symbol of military poignancy: Monash's white charger, with boots reversed in the stirrups. Bringing up the rear and on foot were chief mourners, rabbis, officers of the general staff, representatives of the Governor-General, State Governor and Federal and State Governments.

The procession moved down Spring Street past Lizette, still forced to stay away by cruel protocol, as she stood outside the Windsor, crying, a friend's arm around her shoulder. It moved right down Collins Street, then left down Swanston Street, and over Princes Bridge, which he had help engineer and construct forty-five years earlier. The route was lined with countless fluttering flags on buildings and in the massive, crushing crowd of 300,000. Overhead planes buzzed and droned their escort. The slow march was marked by the sound of feet in unison. In the distance, a drum beat set the tardy pace.

The procession slogged along St Kilda Road. It was transformed into a monster snake by cars and tens of thousands of spectators following. It stopped for a moment opposite the Shrine, under construction. Then it coiled its way through St Kilda junction and on towards suburbia and Brighton Cemetery in North Road – a gruelling fifteen kilometres from the steps of Parliament House. About 60,000 had gathered around the cemetery.

After the Jewish service Monash's body was lowered into the grave, next to Vic's, and not far from that of their grandson, John. The Last Post sounded. It was followed by a seventeen-gun salute and the reveille. The biggest funeral in Australia's history and services around the country were finished.[22]

Perhaps Rabbi Danglow's final words quoting Scottish historian Thomas Carlyle on Napoleon were most apt: 'He had a certain instinctive and ineradicable feeling for reality and did base himself upon fact. He saw through all entanglements the practical heart of the matter. He drove straight towards that. He had an eye to see and a soul to dare and do.'[23]

John Monash was Australia's Napoleon, and much more.

POSTSCRIPT

The Memory

John Monash was never going to be forgotten. From the year of his death until the twenty-first century, lectures, memorials, portraits, statues, streets, avenues, scout troops, schools, universities, institutions, libraries, books, films, horse races, a horse, a cavern and a valley commemorated his exceptional life. There is also now the Sir John Monash Foundation Scholarships where annually up to eight awards will go to outstanding graduates from Australian universities. The aim is for the award winners to study abroad at the best and most appropriate universities for the applicable field. The Foundation was able to commence with a $4,000,000 contribution from the Federal Government in 2002. The desire is for the Monash Awards to have the status of the Rhodes Scholarship or Fulbright Award.

Thomas Blamey, who would become the second most important Australian soldier in the twentieth century, began the long-running commemoration with a speech on the second anniversary of Monash's death in October 1933. More than seven decades later the tradition continues with several speakers at a function in parliament and an oration at his most frequented club, the Naval and Military.

The Family

Bertha, who died in 1979 aged eighty-six, was a loyal supporter of her father. She more than any other was aware of his huge achievements in vanquishing a formidable foe (after the personal European battlefield tour in May 1919). Bertha followed his example with a life of public service and duty, beginning with the 1914–18 war when she was a volunteer nurse. She did fund-raising and other voluntary work for the Dental and Alfred Hospitals for the rest of her life.

Gershon Bennett had worked on the front line as a dental surgeon at Passchendaele. He carried on his successful dental practice between the wars, but let it be interrupted again when he served mainly at Darwin in the army in World War II as Deputy Director of Dental Service.

Gershon was very much the son that Monash never had. They became close, living under the same roof at Iona for eleven years. Gershon admired his father-in-law. After Monash's death, he often made glowing speeches about him. Because he was not a Monash, there were none of the expectations of greatness that always follow the son of a famous, outstanding achiever.

Gershon died aged sixty-two in 1955.

Monash's grandchildren, despite the camouflage of the surname Bennett, were burdened with living up to an unmatchable life. There were ramifications, especially in the 1930s after Monash's death when he was regarded as the most famous Australian of the era, and in the light of the early demise of the first-born male, John, in 1929. Because Monash did not have a son, much was invested emotionally in John, then in David and, to a lesser extent, in Colin.

In a Fabian Society pamphlet memoir by former politician Race Mathews, David Bennett is drawn as burdened by his heritage. At Scotch, the junior school headmaster made much of the importance of David and his family. David was almost always made form captain. This made him increasingly apologetic towards his classmates.

'He knew that he was not popular enough to have been elected,' Mathews wrote, 'nor would he have been appointed on the basis of sporting prowess or "qualities of leadership".'

David's sister Betty (married name Durre) remembered an incident when the Monash Gates in Glenferrie Road, Hawthorn, were opened early in 1936. David was 11 and Colin six. School parents and friends lined up along the long avenue.

'An announcement was made over the loudspeaker that the entire school would now march through the gates,' Betty recalled, 'with, at their head, the grandson of Sir John Monash, John Colin Monash Bennett.' Poor little Colin had been named wrongly. He 'burst into howls of fear and dismay'.

The band struck. The boys began to move.

'Undeterred by the blunderous announcement, the real David Monash Bennett advanced down the drive, quite alone, several yards ahead of the advancing phalanxes of boys.

'Such a misuse of children was something on which, in later years, David would look back in horror,' Betty said. 'It was experiences such as this one which helped him to form his thinking of the nature of schools, their morals and their mores, which became the major theme of his working life.'[1]

David Bennett at eighteen followed his father and grandfather's example by joining the army soon after leaving Scotch. He was concerned when enlisting that the recruiting officer would notice that he had 'Monash' as a middle name. He never wrote it out and mumbled over it when asked to state his full name.

David might have been able to avoid recognition about his famous relative, but couldn't evade inherited genes. He served in 2/23rd Battalion AIF as a private and saw action against the Japanese in New Guinea and Borneo. David refused opportunities for commissions.

It wasn't enough for his father, Gershon, himself a colonel.

'Your grandfather commanded 208,000 men in battle, and I command a few myself,' Gershon wrote to David while serving in northern Australia, when David expressed interest in school teaching after the war. 'You were born to command and lead men, not boys. I have never, by the way, understood your lack of ambition in the army. You belong to the officer class – a rare species. It is a much bigger ambition to command men and to lead and teach them than it is to teach boys.'[2]

David was determined to be his own man and not live in the shadow of another life, however close and brilliant. He saw his life in education or politics, and experienced a taste of each. After World War II he earned an honours degree in history at Melbourne University and a diploma in education in London. He was a member of the socialist Fabian Society, and lost an election as a federal Labor Party candidate. He later became headmaster of Era, a progressive school, in which he wished to avoid the traditions of the typical Anglo-Celtic private school. It was in part a reaction to David's own schooling, its old-world disciplines and what he viewed as the rigidity that went with it.

The career ultimate for David Bennett occurred in 1972 with a merging of his left-wing politics and radical concepts on education. He took part in one of Gough Whitlam's innovations that attempted to improve education, especially in Aboriginal communities, by becoming an education commissioner in 1972. David died in 1984, aged sixty.

✕

Betty Durre, also a member of the Fabian Society, graduated in science and (later) education at Melbourne University. She taught chemistry at tertiary level. Her longest appointment was with the (then) Swinburne College of Advanced Education as a chemistry lecturer and demonstrator from 1966 to 1986.

✕

Colin Bennett was a journalist on the *Age* for thirty years between 1950 and 1980. He had a break on a London weekly in the early 1950s, where he became interested in film, theatre and opera criticism. This led to him becoming the longest serving film critic – twenty-five years – on an Australian paper. Colin's incisive writing and comment on TV and radio in the 1960s and early 1970s did much to support Australia's fledgling film industry. When others were caught in a time warp and sense of cringe that suggested that local filmmakers could never achieve anything, Colin was constructive in his criticism. He encouraged an Australian sense of identity. He was also committed to a long-running anti-censorship campaign.

Colin had a second career running a trail-riding operation for fifteen years. In the mid-1990s he took up a third working life as a portrait painter.

Monash had been specific in his will concerning items received by the grandchildren.

'His piano was left to me,' Colin said. 'David received the war medals and Betty, the family jewels.'

They were also left paintings by Arthur Streeton, who was on Monash's staff. 'He [Monash] would say to Streeton "Paint me that scene,"' Colin noted, 'and the artist would do it.' Colin has a watercolour of a French farmhouse. David had one of Mont St Quentin and Betty one of Péronne.

Colin was two years old when Monash died, but his earliest memory is of his grandfather near the end. 'I recall him sitting up in bed,' he said, 'and me holding one of his fingers. I felt his power, his strength of character.'[3]

There are six surviving Monash great-grandchildren and six great-great-grandchildren.

The Lover

Lizette Bentwitch was loyal to the memory of her lover. Every year on the anniversary of Monash's death she placed an 'In Memoriam' notice in the *Argus* and flowers on his grave at Brighton. Her strong character helped her overcome the unjustified stigma of being the 'other woman'. Lizette was the person closest to him during the war years, and her friendship was an important factor in his stability in testing times. She and Monash were close for fourteen years. Lizette split her time between London, where she had family, and Melbourne. She remained prominent in Melbourne social circles until her death in 1954 aged eighty-one. She is buried at Brighton Cemetery, not far from Monash and Vic.

The Key Influences

George V

George V was a key influence on Monash's military career from the moment they met on Salisbury Plain in 1916. He reckoned he knew a battle commander when he met one. In 1916 the Germans held sway in the war, and George V needed all the help he could get to save his empire, his country and his own neck.

After the conflict, the King maintained the contact and his support for Monash with gongs and social invitations. His sons visited Australia in the 1920s and continued to show special deference to Monash.

In 1931 the collapse of the pound and the consequent financial crisis split the UK Labour administration. It created another moment when the

King's judgement of character and capacity would be important in a situation nearly as critical as war. To secure strong government, he persuaded Ramsay MacDonald and a part of his cabinet to remain in office and join Conservative and Liberal ministers in the formation of a national coalition government. George V's influence and selection helped stabilise his nation. In May 1935 he celebrated his Silver Jubilee. The positive public reaction demonstrated that his quarter-century reign had been appreciated.

George V died less than a year later in January 1936, aged seventy.

Ian Hamilton

Sir Ian Hamilton's report on Monash after viewing military exercises at Lilydale in 1914 carried great weight in making his name prominent in the struggle for recognition in the AIF when it was under British High Command control. He more than once reminded Monash of this after the war. Hamilton's judgement caused Kitchener to reserve his position on Monash in 1915 when others were trying to destroy his reputation.

The *Encyclopaedia Britannica*'s entry on Ian Hamilton is typical of the imprint on history of his exceptional career. It devoted all except a few lines to his failure as leader of the Dardanelles expedition. But it occupied less than a year of a distinguished career of nearly eight decades as an accomplished soldier and author.

Ian Hamilton did not fade away as an old soldier was entitled to do after the Gallipoli disaster. When the 1914–18 war was over he did what Haig, Monash and other commanders felt obligated to do regarding the men who had passed under his command. He was seen after the war in all parts of the UK opening war memorials and offering comfort to the bereaved.

Hamilton's depth of character and sensitive intellect did not allow him to ignore the plight of the defeated Germans, either. He urged others not to humiliate the former enemy with excessively harsh reparation demands. Few listened. One result was the ferment of revenge and hate in some Germans and, in particular, that Austrian-born failed painter and corporal, Adolf Hitler, who had seen both victory and crushing defeat at Messines and elsewhere.

Hitler did what Hamilton feared would happen if the Allies rubbed German noses in the detritus of war. He used the harsh terms imposed on Germany at Versailles in 1919 and his country's long-running depression as vehicles for his otherwise unlikely rise to power.

Hamilton was so concerned in 1938 that he made a point of meeting Chancellor Hitler at his mountain retreat at Berchtesgaden. Hitler loved the long line of the British elite, including the Duke of Windsor (the former Edward VIII), who came cap in hand for an audience with the swaggering dictator.

In a one-and-a-half-hour chat in German with Hamilton, the two-faced Hitler strained to charm a British aristocrat and soldier for whom he had high regard. Hamilton, like Chamberlain and the Duke, took Hitler at his word and believed he had good intentions. Perhaps at the age of eighty-five the old soldier turned pacifist was more gullible than he would have been in his prime.

A year later Hitler started his rampage across Europe, and World War II broke out. Hamilton stayed in his home at 1 Hyde Park Gardens, defied the bombs dropped on London and went on into his nineties, writing another book. He lived long enough to see the enemy defeated a second time.

He died in 1947 aged ninety-four.

The Leading Combatants

Mustafa Kemal Atatürk
Mustafa Kemal became a Turkish hero after repelling the British invaders from the Dardanelles in 1915. The next year he was promoted to general at thirty-five. He liberated two major provinces in eastern Turkey. In the next two years Kemal served as commander of several Ottoman armies in Palestine, Aleppo and elsewhere. He resigned from the army in 1919 and was chosen president of a National Congress. In 1920, when the British formally occupied Turkey and dissolved the Chamber of Deputies, Kemal opened the first Grand National Assembly of Turkey. This body then assumed national sovereignty.

Kemal consolidated his power and in 1922 proclaimed a republic. He was elected its first President and Prime Minister. The peace treaty with Britain, France, Greece and Italy signed at Lausanne in the following year established Turkey's independence. Kemal introduced a broad range of swift and sweeping reforms in the political, social, legal, economic and cultural spheres at an unparalleled speed.

Monash had been aware in the 1920s that he had faced not just the fiercest of foes at Gallipoli but also a Turkish nationalist of great stature.

In 1933 Kemal was given the name Atatürk – 'father of Turks' – by the national parliament. He died in 1938, aged fifty-seven.

Charles Bean

If Monash was the originator of the Melbourne Shrine and the man who did most to institutionalise Anzac Day, Charles Bean was the father of the history section of the Australian War Memorial. It began with him and a small staff sorting and cataloguing a huge pile of records at Tuggeranong Homestead near Canberra. It took them five-and-a-half years until 1924.

Bean wrote the first two volumes of the official history, *The Story of Anzac*. They appeared in 1921 and 1924. He then sat down and produced the next four tomes – on the AIF in France. Bean edited the remaining five volumes. He then annotated a photographic volume. The last volume of the history was published in 1942. Still not done, Bean, in the hope of reaching a wider audience, created a condensed history for the Memorial: *Anzac to Amiens* in 1946.

Even here, twenty-eight years after the end of the 1914–18 war, he struggled to come to terms with Monash, the outsider, becoming first Australian Commander of the AIF. He couldn't resist the racial qualification, referring to the elderly general as Jewish-Australian when Monash had proved as Australian in his expressed views and actions as anyone else on record.

'For the new commander, Birdwood hesitated between White and Monash,' Bean wrote disingenuously. 'Each had a brilliant record, marked with great successes.' He added the misleading and weak corollary: 'But Monash being the senior, the recommendation favoured him.'

Bean's blind spot over Monash was the only major detraction from an otherwise monumental writing output for which he was recognised by the government. It offered him a well-deserved knighthood, which he declined several times. Twenty-eight years after Monash had engineered an honorary Doctor of Letters from Melbourne University for Bean, the Australian National University in 1959 made him an Honorary Doctor of Laws.

Bean died in 1968, aged ninety.

William Morris Hughes

Billy Hughes, thanks in large part to Monash's successes, championed British and Australian interests on the Reparations Commission as a delegate to the Versailles Peace Conference in 1919 and at the 1921 Imperial Conference in London.

He changed his seat to North Sydney (from Bendigo, Victoria) in 1922 but was beaten in a party ballot by Bruce in 1923. He was then sixty-one, but his rollicking political career was far from done. Hughes, who would have had Machiavelli's approval, had his revenge when he helped to overthrow the Bruce–Page coalition. But there was a price. His party, the Nationalists, expelled him.

He continued to blitz Australian federal politics in the 1930s, first by helping Joe Lyons form the United Australia Party in 1931. From 1934, Hughes held portfolios for five years in the Lyons Government. He thought this experience, at the mature age of seventy-seven, would allow him to be Prime Minister again, but in 1939 he was pipped by R. G. Menzies.

Yet he still held the important job of Attorney-General from 1939 to 1941. Later he was also briefly Minister for the Navy and for Industry. The kind of political subterfuge that had seen him undermine Monash's AIF leadership in 1918 was evident once again in politics in 1944, but his party was wise to his ways, having seen them in operation for decades. He was expelled once more. Undeterred, he slid sideways into the Liberal Party.

Hughes died at ninety in 1952.

Erich Ludendorff

After Monash had demoralised General Ludendorff in the Battle of Amiens, the German lived another twenty years in which his pseudo-intellectual views fluctuated between the bizarre and the potty. He attempted to justify his support for a half-baked *coups d'état* that failed by insisting that he had been betrayed and misunderstood as a commander. Continuing the life of a classic 'loser', he ran for President in 1925 against his former commander in chief Hindenburg and lost. From 1924 to 1928 he was a National Socialist member of parliament.

Ludendorff created the theory of total war. At heart his belief was that a nation should be geared for and at war most of the time. 'Peace' was simply a time between conflicts. Such a belief was at once lunatic, primitive and warmongering. But in a sensitive, angry Germany, he was taken seriously. Once in power, Hitler, always in many ways the deferential corporal, wanted to make Ludendorff a field marshal, but his former commander refused the promotion.

Ludendorff's second marriage, in 1926, was to the neurologist and popular philosopher Mathilde von Kemnitz. She presented him with an eccentric theory about the evil axis of Jewry, Christianity and Freemasonry. Mathilde tried to persuade her husband that he was the true 'commander in chief' of the German people and that his energies should be directed at ridding his nation of these enemies.

Others, such as Hitler, and the old officer corps were basing their positions and grabs for power on equally dubious theories. There was little accord. In the gutter fighting that followed, the biggest thug of the competing forces, Hitler, won through. Ludendorff began criticising Hitler and his tyranny, but had no supporters.

Ludendorff died a confused man aged seventy-two in 1937, leaving behind many soldiers who supported him but who were befuddled by his weird beliefs. In essence, he had been unhinged by, and never recovered from, the decisive defeat inflicted by Monash at Amiens on 8 August 1918. The mental depression that followed the continued capitulation of the German army over the next two months until October of that year drove Ludendorff to the verge of insanity.

Keith Murdoch

Keith Murdoch returned to Melbourne as editor of Theodore Fink's *Herald*. Knighted, and appointed trustee of the National Gallery of Victoria at forty-eight in 1933, he worked hard to create a media empire. By the mid-1930s he controlled the *West Australian*, the Brisbane *Courier-Mail*, a monopoly of Adelaide's daily press and several commercial radio stations. His determination to spread his power and influence upset some politicians, especially on the left. Many of them, like Monash, felt the pressure of a strong Murdoch campaign against them or their policies.

Journalism was his main interest, but he and his wife Elisabeth had a passion for art and the arts. Keith Murdoch died in 1952 aged sixty-seven. His son Rupert replicated his father's Australian media empire on a global scale.

Superiors, Peers and Subordinates

William Riddell Birdwood

After Hughes caused Birdwood to upstage Monash's return to Australia in late 1919, Birdwood returned to the India Army, where he remained until

1930. He was hopeful of being appointed Governor-General in Australia in 1931, especially as the King supported his appointment. But the then Prime Minister, Scullin, supported Australian-born Isaac Isaacs. It was a bitter rebuff for a man who had formerly been passed over for the top job of directing repatriation in 1919. Unfortunately for the popular 'Birdie', he was English at a time when Australia was experiencing a wave of nationalism.

Birdwood was made a baronet in 1938. He died aged seventy-two at Hampton Court Palace in 1951. The South Australian town of Blumberg was renamed in his honour.

Thomas Blamey

Blamey, Monash's chief of staff, returned to Melbourne in 1919 and rose through the military ranks to become Second Chief of the General Staff by 1925. In that year he left the regular army to become Chief Commissioner of the Victoria Police, while he still had a role in the militia.

At this time a secret organisation called the White Army or White Guard was formed. Some thought it was named after the recently retired Major General Sir C. C. Brudenell White, a principal organiser. Given its anti-communist motivations, the name was more likely to have been derived from the anti-Bolshevik White Army in Russia. The Russian Revolution and its ramifications were still fresh in the minds of those who feared overthrow of the government in Australia.

Blamey was thought to be a commander of the White Army, while ruling the police force autocratically, as if he were still chief of staff in the AIF. The White Army was clandestinely held in reserve to support the police should the communist movement cause unrest and violence in a feared takeover of the state.

When war broke out again in Europe in 1939, Blamey returned to the regular army. In 1942 he was Commander-in-Chief of all Australian forces, the position Monash acquired in the 1914–18 war. Blamey proved to be a strong, tough leader who would not be pushed around by the American and British commands.[4] Yet he tended to play the bully and did not endear himself to Australian troops the way Monash had done.

After leaving his command in December 1945, when World War II had been over a few months, Blamey pursued his business interests. But he was never far from some sort of force of arms. With the rise of communist influence in Australia post-World War II, Blamey linked with 'the Association', which had similar goals to the White Army. If communism ever became a serious threat, he would have been in a position to attempt countering it by extra-constitutional means. Unlike Monash, Blamey would have been prepared to act outside the system.

The Menzies Government made him a field marshal in 1950. Blamey died the next year in Melbourne, aged sixty-seven.

Arthur Currie

General Sir Arthur Currie was Canada's Monash. He had been an insurance broker and real estate agent before the war. Currie, like Monash, began as a brigade commander and was promoted to division commander. When Sir Julian Byng was elevated to lead the Third Army in June 1917, Currie was promoted to run the Canadian Corps. Like Monash, he had pushed hard for the creation and retention of his nation's force as a coherent unit, which should not be broken up to suit the British High Command's tendency to use its Dominion forces in stop-gap operations. Again like Monash, he had Haig's strong support.

Currie was successful at Third Ypres when able to attack in fair conditions and this, along with his victory at Vimy Ridge, made his military reputation. His corps, alongside the AIF, had a similar run of successes in the last hundred days of the war, beginning at the Battle of Amiens on 8 August 1918.

Currie's differences from Monash were in character. His reputation suffered from his foul-mouthed, overbearing manner. This and his aloof style did not endear him to his men.

After the war Currie was inspector general of the Canadian militia. He was principal and vice-chancellor of McGill University from 1920 until his death in 1933, aged sixty-eight.[4]

John Gellibrand

After Major General Sir John Gellibrand commanded the 3rd Division under Monash at the end of 1918, he wanted to lead the Royal Military College, Duntroon. When passed over he returned to Tasmania but not to his apple orchard. He became commissioner of the Tasmanian public service where he stayed two years (1919–20). He was elected a Tasmanian National Party member of the House of Representatives (1925–28). Gellibrand, with Stanley Savige, founded the Legacy movement to support families of servicemen killed in war.

Gellibrand moved to a property at Murrindindi, Victoria, in 1937. He died there in 1945, aged seventy-three.

Thomas Glasgow

After leading the 1st Division of the AIF under Monash through the final battles east of the Somme, Major General Sir William Glasgow returned to Queensland and from 1920 to 1932 represented Queensland in the Senate for the Nationalist Party. He was Minister of Home and Territories (1926–27) and Defence (1927–29). During World War II he was Australia's first High Commissioner to Canada.

Glasgow died in Brisbane in 1955, aged seventy-nine.

Alexander John Godley

Sir Alexander Godley relinquished his command of the New Zealand Expeditionary Force in November 1919. He served in the post-war occupation of the Rhine. In 1920 he was appointed Military Secretary to the Secretary of State for War. Godley returned to the Rhine in 1922 as commanding officer of the British forces and became a full general the following year, which would have been galling to Monash. Godley had ended the war as a corps commander officially on a par with Monash but, in reality, in the final push for victory, he was in an inferior role. If anything, Monash learned from or avoided the major mistakes that Godley made, especially on Gallipoli where Godley's brutal, thoughtless and cavalier attitude to sending men into battle was disastrous for the Anzacs.

Godley was appointed Governor of Gibraltar and its commander-in-chief in 1928. He held those posts for four years.

Godley died at Oxford in 1957 aged ninety.

Talbot Hobbs

Lieutenant General Sir Talbot Hobbs migrated from London to Perth at the age of twenty-two and became an architect. This background, and his humane attitude to those under him while serving with the AIF as a divisional commander, led him to take special interest in the erection of memorials. Five of the six divisional memorials were designed in his simple, uncluttered style. He chose Polygon Wood as the site of his 5th

Division's memorial and Villers-Bretonneux for the outstanding national monument. Later he designed the Western Australian War Memorial. He again commanded the 5th Division from 1921 to 1927.

In April 1938, Hobbs left for France to attend the unveiling of the Australian War Memorial at Villers-Bretonneux. He died of a heart attack on the way, aged seventy-three.

Albert Jacka

After his amazing exploits at Gallipoli and in France, the much-decorated Albert Jacka returned with the 14th Battalion to Australia in 1919 and was greeted as a hero. Jacka rode at the head of the convoy to the Melbourne Town Hall where the battalion was welcomed home.

At twenty-six, he started an electrical appliance business in St Kilda. His popularity in the bayside suburb saw him elected mayor for 1930–31. The Depression ruined his business. He worked as a travelling soap salesman around the state, but contracted chronic nephritis. He died at the Caulfield Military Hospital, aged thirty-eight, in 1932. Jacka Boulevard on the St Kilda foreshore is named in his honour.

Charles Rosenthal

Major General Sir Charles Rosenthal, who commanded the AIF's Second Division under Monash in the vital final months of 1918, returned to his profession of architecture after the war and served as the Nationalist MLA for Bathurst (1922–25). The much-wounded, courageous front-line commander of Gallipoli, Belgium and France was also a cultured man, especially when it came to his musical pursuits. He had been a singer and a choirmaster in his early years. Rosenthal was also an accomplished pianist, organist and violinist.[5]

This might have made him attractive to D. H. Lawrence, the only notable foreign novelist to write about Australia. He stayed six months in Sydney in 1922 and wrote the book *Kangaroo*. This novel – not the writer's best – tuned into the mood and unrest among diggers. Rosenthal was claimed by some to be the model for the character Benjamin Cooley, a cultured, extreme right-winger. If so, it was a crude model. Rosenthal was never an extremist. Nor did he contemplate taking government by force.

He was administrator of Norfolk Island from 1937 to 1945. He returned to Sydney after this appointment and died there in 1954, aged seventy-nine.

Ewen Sinclair-MacLagan

The Edinburgh-born Major General Ewen Sinclair-MacLagan was one of only five seconded British officers to remain with the Australian Army throughout the 1914–18 war. He had two tours of Australia, first in 1901 when on secondment as adjutant of the New South Wales Rifles and deputy assistant Adjutant General of the 1st Military District (New South Wales). He was called back to Australia by his good friend (General) William Bridges in 1910 to become director of drill at the new Royal Military College, Duntroon. He was still at Duntroon when war broke out and ended up in the AIF.

After the war he returned to the UK to command the British 51st (Highland) Division from 1919 to 1923. He retired in 1925 and died in Dundee, Scotland, in 1948, aged seventy-nine.

Cyril B. Brudenell White

A week after Cyril White was ordered by Monash to return to Australia in late November 1918, he was promoted to the temporary rank of lieutenant general. He was made a KCMG in the 1919 New Year honours list. Later in 1920 he became a Knight Commander of the Victorian Order (KCVO) and a KCB in 1927.

In January 1920, White, along with Monash, McCay, Hobbs and Legge, was appointed to a committee chaired by Chauvel to examine the future structure of the army. White became Chief of the General Staff in June of that year, and it was his job to implement the committee's recommendations. Defence cuts in the following years made the task nearly impossible and led to White resigning from the army in 1923 to become the first chairman of the Public Service Board. He retired in 1928.

On 15 March 1940 White was recalled to active duty, promoted to full general – the third after Monash and Chauvel – and reappointed Chief of the General Staff. His term of office was short. On 13 August 1940 he and nine others were killed in a plane crash near Canberra Airport. He was sixty-four.

ACKNOWLEDGEMENTS

Early in 2002 I placed a newspaper item on the refrigerator door at my home about (Major) Warren Perry, then ninety-three, who had just become the oldest person in Australia to gain a Doctorate of Letters. He had attained earlier an MA with first-class honours in Germanic languages. We are not related. We had never met. The cutting was meant to be an inspiration to my son, then fourteen, who remarked that it would have to be more of an inspiration for me, because I was closer to Warren's age. It was pleasing to know such a brilliant man was a member of the clan (the Irish Perrys, as it turned out). Soon afterwards, I began the research on the Monash biography and was told that Warren Perry was the living expert on the general. He proved to be so. At the age of twenty, Perry witnessed Monash speaking at the opening of the Cenotaph in Martin Place, Sydney, in February 1929. One of Monash's divisional generals, Sir Charles Rosenthal, also gave an address on that occasion. But Perry wasn't just a witness. He is an outstanding historian specialising in the military, the two world wars and Monash.

Perry was an encouraging start to my research. I thank him for his insights, which delved into personalities and characters of the time from Billy Hughes to all the key military personalities of the era in question.

The manuscript section of the National Library of Australia in Canberra, run by librarian Graeme Powell, was essential. He and his staff were helpful in pointing me in the right direction. Monash wrote about 75,000 letters. Most of them, together with a wealth of other correspondence and material, form one of the biggest archives in the NLA.

The Australian War Memorial was another vital stop. It has a comprehensive archive on Monash's wartime correspondence and activity, along with files on other key participants in the 1914–18 war. Chris Coulthard-Clark and Ashley Ekins assisted in useful areas and with my research at Gallipoli. This led me to Kenan Celik, the expert guide on Gallipoli, whose on-the-spot thoughts on the Anzac battle against the defending Turks were helpful, especially from a Turkish perspective.

Melbourne University's Baillieu Library was a further centre for information on Monash, particularly his lengthy business correspondence, which gives an indication of his enormous industry and success as an engineer over three decades. The Scotch College archive and Dr Jim Mitchell, the school historian, provided essential assistance, as did the La Trobe Library.

Other biographies on Monash were required reading, namely those by Geoffrey Serle, who assisted the family in transferring the archive to the NLA, A. J. Smithers, P. A. Pedersen, who examined Monash's military career, and Cecil Edwards. Monash's own book, *The Australian Victories in France in 1918*, was mandatory, as was the prodigious work of the official war historian, Charles Bean. Many papers by Rabbi Brasch and Warren Perry, who both at different times considered writing biographies on the subject, were helpful. Les Carlyon's *Gallipoli* was an inspiration.

I am grateful to Betty Durre and Colin Bennett, Monash's grandchildren, who were generous with their time, thoughts and perspectives. Conversations with them revealed insights into their grandfather and family not recorded previously.

I would like to thank also Federal Government ministers David and Rod Kemp for making available the illuminating diaries of their grandfather, Lieutenant Colonel Arthur Wilson.

I must thank Her Majesty Queen Elizabeth II for permitting me to quote from the unpublished private diary of her grandfather George V and the assistance given by the deputy registrar, Mrs Jill Kelsey, at Windsor Castle. George V's support for Monash during the 1914–18 war was a key factor in his being fast-tracked to commandership of the Australian Imperial Force.

A special word for Thos Hodgson and his son Jamie who accompanied me on most of the locational research in France, Flanders and Gallipoli. Their efforts as navigators and photographers made my work much easier. I am most grateful for the ingenuity and driving skills of Jamie in extricating us from the mud at a farm next to the Commonwealth Cemetery at Montbrehain, France.

A special word, too, for the mayor of Villers-Bretonneux. When we arrived at the town to see the local school, which had been rebuilt with Australian support after the war, it was closed. The mayor, Dr Hubert Lelieur, just happened to be there. Because we were Australians, he decided to give us a tour of the museum commemorating the war and Australia's liberation of the town. At the end, we were buying souvenirs. I just missed getting a T-shirt with the impression of a small kangaroo on the right breast with the insignia 'Villers-Bretonneux' under it. Hubert began shedding clothes, and gave me the same shirt off his back. I appreciated the gesture. It was symbolic of the deep appreciation that people of the region have for the diggers' defeat of the Germans nearly nine decades ago.

My thanks also to Jane Palfreyman, publisher, at Random House, who supported this project from the beginning, project editor Jo Butler and my editor Cathryn Game.

Roland Perry
July 2004

NOTES

An important source for this work has been Monash's own papers: his letters, diaries and other papers held in the National Library of Australia and in the Australian War Memorial. Papers in the National Library are grouped in series numbered 1 to 14. These papers are referred to in the Notes below as S1, S2, etc. For full details see the Bibliography.

Engineer of Victory: 8 August 1918

1 Monash, *The Australian Victories in France in 1918* [hereafter *Australian Victories*], pp. 115–25.
2 Armitage, J. R., diary, 'Battle of Amiens', AWM, www.awm.gov.au.
3 Wilson, diary, supplied by Arthur Wilson's grandsons David and Rod Kemp. See diary and Ambulance Corps records at AWM.
4 Monash, *Australian Victories*, p. 121.
5 Ibid.
6 Ibid., p. 123.
7 Wilson, diary.

8 Monash, *Australian Victories*, p. 123.
9 Ibid.
10 Liddell Hart, *Through the Fog of War*, p. 149; also his Monash obituary in *Daily Telegraph* (UK), October 1931.
11 Lloyd George, *War Memoirs*, Vol. 6, pp. 3368, 3382, 3424.
12 Taylor, *The First World War*, p. 232.
13 Liddell Hart, *Through the Fog of War*, p. 149.

1: Going for Gold

1 The journal was called *Die Monatsschrift fur Geschichte und Wissenschaft des Judentums*.
2 Monasch, *The Life, Labours, Joys and Sorrows of B. L. Monasch*. Also S10, NLA.
3 Monasch, *The Life, Labours, Joys and Sorrows*.
4 Ibid.
5 Xanthippe: wife of the Greek philosopher Socrates. Her bad-tempered behaviour towards her husband has made her proverbial as a shrew.
6 Monash Papers, S2.
7 Ibid.
8 Ibid.
9 Monasch, *The Life, Labours, Joys and Sorrows*.
10 Ibid.

2: School of Soft Knocks

1 Mitchell, *A Deepening Roar*, p. 192, quoting Ewing, *Unsearchable Riches of Christ*, p. 7.
2 Ibid.; Scotch College archive.
3 Article on Sergeant-Major Whitehead, *Age*, 28 July 1887, Mitchell, *A Deepening Roar*, p. 29.
4 Article on Whitehead, *Age*, 28 July 1887.
5 Monash mentioned his Kelly encounter in letters (JM, letter to N. Campbell, 19 April 1929, S1, NLA), newspaper articles (Melbourne *Sun*, 2 December 1926, *Melbourne Punch* and *Table Talk*, 18 April 1929) and speeches, although not until the mid-1920s, mainly because anything other than negative comment about Kelly was frowned on until the first book about the gang was published in the late 1920s. A second source was his father Louis, who spoke independently about his purchase of a horse from Kelly. William Elliott verified Monash's story, after Monash's death in 1931. General Blamey mentioned the 'Monash meets Kelly' incident in a Monash Memorial speech in 1948.
6 JM, letter to his father, 18 July 1878, S2.

7 JM, diary, 20 July 1879, S5.
8 Jones, *Ned Kelly*, chapter 14. Also, Elliott, 'The Kelly Raid on Jerilderie'. The *Jerilderie Herald* was the successor to the *Jerilderie Gazette*. Elliott was the *Herald*'s owner and editor.
9 Mitchell, *A Deepening Roar*.
10 JM notebook, 1880, S5.
11 JM notebook, 1881, S5.
12 JM diary, 5 August 1882, S5.
13 JM to Leo Monash, 9 May 1883, S1.
14 JM diary, 3 October 1883, S5. My italics.
15 JM diary, 18 June 1884, S5.
16 JM diary, 10 August 1884, S5.
17 JM diary, 5 February 1885, S5.
18 JM diary, 1 September 1885, S5.
19 Letter to Eva Blashki, 7 October 1885 (see also letter to Rose Blashki, 14 February 1886), S2.
20 JM diary, 1 September 1885, S5.
21 JM letter to Rose Blashki, 7 December 1885. S2.

3: The Engineer's Language

1 (Sir) Archibald Glenn, who won the mathematics prize. He went on to be a successful engineer and industrialist.
2 JM diary, 6 March 1887, S5.
3 JM diary, 3 July, 21 August 1887, S5.
4 JM diary, 17 March 1888, S5.
5 JM diary, May 1888, S5.
6 Ibid.
7 JM diary, 18 June 1888, S5.
8 JM diary, August–September 1888, S5.
9 JM diary, July 1888, S5.
10 Ibid.
11 Ibid.
12 Ibid.
13 JM diary, various entries, August 1889, S5.
14 Author interview with Warren Perry, May 2003.
15 JM diary, 22 July 1889, S5.
16 JM diary, 21 August 1889, S5.
17 JM diary, 23 August 1889, S5.
18 JM diary, 25 August 1889, S5.
19 Letter to W. Steele, 26 August 1889, S1.
20 JM, letter to Annie, 2 September 1889, S1.
21 JM diary, 6 September 1889, S5.
22 JM diary, 16 September 1889, S5.

4: Battle Engagement

1 Boxes 137, 138 folders 1018–1022; 1023–1029, S5.
2 JM diary, October 1889, S5.
3 JM letter to Vic, October 1889, S5.
4 Boxes 137, 138 folders 1018–1022; 1023–1029, S5.
5 Ibid.
6 JM diary, 6, 7 September 1890, S5.
7 JM diary, 1 January 1891, S5.
8 JM diary, 8 April 1891, S5.
9 JM, diary, 10 April 1891, S5.
10 JM letter to Jim Lewis, 10 January 1892, S1.
11 JM letters, April 1894, S1.

5: Rebirth

1 JM diary, September 1894, S5.
2 JM diary, July 1895, S5.
3 Ibid.
4 JM, Commonplace Book, 29 July 1895, S14.
5 JM diary, December 1897, S5.
6 JM to Vic, 2 October 1897, S5.
7 JM, letter to Vic, 28 September, 1897, S5.
8 See Holgate and Taplin, 'John Monash's engineering to 1914',
   http://home.vicnet.net.au/~aholgate/jm/mainpages/projects.html.
9 JM, letter to Vic, 3 November 1897, S5.
10 Diaries December 1898; January 1899, S5.
11 JM, letter to Anderson, May 1898, S1.
12 From Monash's tax returns. He and Anderson each cleared £298 in 1897
   and £208 in 1898. Monash–Anderson business correspondence, S1.

6: A Bridge Too Far

1 JM letter to Dave Bevan, 25 September 1899, S1.
2 Sources include Holgate and Taplin, 'John Monash's engineering to 1914',
   http://home.vicnet.net.au/~aholgate/jm/mainpages/projects.html.; JM letter
   to Mathilde Monash, S2.
3 JM letter to Mathilde Monash, S2.
4 Anderson letter to Monash, August 1902, S1.
5 Monash letters to Anderson, Saddler, Mathilde and others, May–October
   1902, S1.
6 Comment by Cussen to Sir Robert Menzies, cited Serle, *John Monash*,
   p. 151.
7 Monash took notes on his discussions and put them in his 'Souvenirs Book',

which marked special occasions, and meeting impressive people. Records A–N; Also souvenir programs and invitations, S10.

7: Pipe Dreams Realised

1 George Farlow, speech at an Old Scotch Collegians function, 1923, S14.
2 Monash gave this advice in a letter to cousin Karl Roth, 28 June 1900, S1.
3 Unbylined journalist in *Smith's Weekly*, 10 June 1933.
4 Monash letter to Mathilde Monash, 29 June 1907, S2.
5 Monash's Notes on Qualifications, 2 May 1908, S8, Military.
6 Pedersen, *Monash as Military Commander*, p. 23.
7 Monash Paper—'Staff Duties in Operations', 18 June 1911, S8, Military.
8 Notes on Draft Exam Paper, 16 February 1910, S8.
9 Pedersen, *Monash as Military Commander*, p. 28. Monash's solutions and notes, course syllabi for 1909, 1911, War Courses, Monash Papers, AWM.
10 Vic letter to Monash, 13 January 1910, S2.
11 Magnus, *Kitchener*, p. 10.
12 Priestley, *Margin Released*, p. 84.
13 Doyle, *The British Campaigns in Europe: 1914–1918*.
14 Priestley, *Margin Released*, p. 85.
15 Northcliffe, 'Kitchener Unmoved', *Daily Mail*, 21 May 1915.
16 Monash letter to Rosenhain, 2 January 1911. S1.
17 The archives section of the Baillieu Library at Melbourne University houses these thick bound 'letter-press' books.
18 Vic letter Monash, 26 May 1913, S1.
19 Charteris, *Field Marshal Earl Haig*, p. 68, quoted in Pedersen, *Monash as Military Commander*, p. 38.
20 Monash letter to McCay, 12 November 1912, S1. White was still just White at this time; he began calling himself Brudenell White later.
21 Bean, *Official History of Australia in the War*, Vol. 1, pp. 66–7.
22 Hamilton letter to Monash, 14 February 1929, S1.
23 Serle, *John Monash*, p. 198. The issue is covered in the *Argus* of 20 March, 6, 8, 9 May and 4 July 1914.

8: 1914: The Enemy Within

1 Gilbert, *First World War*, p. 26.
2 JM, letter to Karl Roth, S1.
3 *Sydney Morning Herald*, 11, 13 and 14 August 1914; Williams, *German Anzacs and the First World War*, p. 36.
4 *Sydney Morning Herald* editorial, 11 August 1914.
5 Pedersen, *Monash as Military Commander*, p. 47.
6 'People We Know' column, *Punch*, 9 March 1911.

7 Bean, *Pamphlets on World Affairs, The Old AIF and the New.*

8 Pearce, *Carpenter to Cabinet*, pp. 224–5.

9 Letter to JM, 3 October 1915, S1.

10 Williams, *German Anzacs and the First World War*, p. 244.

11 Smith, C.P. (war correspondent), *Argus*, 4 February 1915.

12 JM, S4,

13 Ibid.

14 Godley, letter to Pearce, 30 March 1915, Godley correspondence, 3DRL/2233, AWM.

15 JM to Vic, 13 February 1915, S2. See also S 4.

16 JM, S4.

17 Birdwood, comments to Munro Ferguson (Lord Novar), 25 February 1915, Novar Papers, MS 696.

18 JM to Vic, 16 March 1915, S4.

19 JM to Vic, 25 March 1915, S4.

20 Ibid (17)

21 JM to Vic, 18 February 1915, S4.

22 From Gellibrand's annotations to Monash's *Australian Victories*, Gellibrand Papers, AWM.

23 Bean on White in Diary 2, 20 January 1915; 5 March 1915; Diary 3, 23 April 1915, AWM; Pedersen, *Monash as Military Commander*, pp. 53, 54.

24 Bean's diary, 'McGlynn' and other remarks, 20 January, 5 March, 23 April 1915, AWM. Pedersen, *Monash as Military Commander*, p. 54.

25 Bean, *Official History of Australia in the War 1914–18*, Vol. 1, pp. 46–7.

26 Hamilton, *Gallipoli Diary*, Vol. 1, p. 2.

27 Monash War Letters, 30 March 1915, S4.

28 Smithers, *Sir John Monash*, p. 65.

29 Notes for Speeches to men on battalion inspections, 11 March 1915, John Monash Collection, AWM.

30 JM War Letters, 21 April, S4.

31 Ibid., 23 April.

32 Ibid., 24 April.

33 Ibid.

34 Ibid., 25 April

35 Diary, S5.

9: Thirty Days in Hell

1 Birdwood's message, quoted in Hamilton, *Gallipoli Diary*, vol. 1, p. 143.

2 JM diary, 25 April 1915, S1.

3 Hamilton, *Gallipoli Diary*, vol. 1, p. 143.

4 JM to Bertha, 7 June 1915, S1.

5 JM to Vic, 16 May 1915, S1.

6 Hamilton, *From Gallipoli to Gaza*, p. 93.

7 Bean, *Official History of Australia in the War*, Vol. 1, p. 521.

8 JM, letter to Vic, 18 July 1915. S1.

9 Report in Melbourne *Sun*, 22 August 1925.

10 JM letter to Vic, 20 May 1915, S1.

11 Ibid.

12 Lt E. M. Little to Bean, 8 February 1924, in Bean's Historical Notes, AWM.

13 Bean, diary, 3 May 1915, AWM.

14 JM, letter to Vic, 18 July 1915, S1.

15 Bean, diary, 3 May 1915, AWM.

16 Godley, letter to Pearce, 7 May 1915, Monash Papers, AWM.

17 Pedersen, *Monash as Military Commander*, pp. 77–8.

18 Ibid.

19 JM, diary, S5.

20 JM, letter to Vic, 20 May 1915, S1.

21 Rule, *Jacka's Mob*; Grant, *Jacka VC*; Bean, *Official History of Australia in the War*, Vol. II, pp. 149–50.

22 Carlyon, *Gallipoli*, p. 280.

23 JM, diary, S5.

24 Lt N. T. Svenson to Bean, 24 July 1922, in Bean, Historical Notes, AWM.

25 Hamilton, *From Gallipoli to Gaza*, p. 79.

26 JM, Notes to Commanding Officers, Monash Papers, AWM.

27 JM, letter to Vic, 7 June 1915, S1. See also S 4.

28 JM, letter to Vic, 27 May 1915 and other war letters, S1.

10: Gallipoli Breakout

1 Bean diary, 2 June 1915, 3DRL606, AWM.

2 James, *Gallipoli*, p. 237.

3 JM, war letters, August 1915, S1.

4 Bean, obituary for JM, Sydney *Sunday Sun*, 11 October 1931.

5 JM, diary, August 1915, S5.

6 JM, war letters, August 1915, S1.

7 Ibid.

8 Ibid.

9 Ibid.

10 James, *Gallipoli*, p. 271; Pedersen, *Monash as Military Commander*, p. 103; JM, War Letters, August 1915, S1, Serle, *Monash*, p. 237; and other accounts. Allanson, described by Field Marshal Lord Slim as an unreliable type given to embroidering (which was a discreet way of saying he was a liar), hated Australians, whom he found undisciplined and with

'disgusting habits'. Allanson made up a story about Monash saying 'I thought I could command men' and that he had 'lost his head' after the strenuous 6/7 August 1915 offensive. From all research, it seems certain that Monash never spoke the words. I have not included the Allanson quote because it was a fabrication, which digresses from, and distorts, the actual events. It is also uncollaborated and was written more than thirty years after Monash's death. Furthermore, it contradicts Allanson's own testimony to the post-war UK Dardanelles Commission. James admitted to Pedersen that he would introduce 'substantial qualification' into his writing about the alleged Monash–Allanson incident if he ever rewrote his book.

11 JM, war letters, August 1915. S1.
12 Birdwood, letter, 11 August 1915 in Birdwood Papers, AWM.
13 Monash, war letters, August 1915, S1.
14 JM, war letters, August 1915, S1.
15 JM, lecture to officers, Salisbury, October 1916, Monash Papers, AWM; correspondence with Godley 21, 24 August 1915. Monash Papers, AWM.
16 Godley's vitriolic remarks reported by Bean in papers of John North, AWM; Pederson, *Monash as Military Commander*, p. 114.
17 James, *Gallipoli*, p. 308.
18 JM, war letters, October 1915. S1.
19 JM, war letters, August 1915, S1.
20 James, *Gallipoli*, p. 308.
21 JM, war letters, August 1915, S1.
22 JM, letter to Vic, September 1915, S1.
23 Ibid.
24 JM, war diary, November 1915, S5.
25 JM, war diary, December 1915, S5.
26 Ibid.
27 Ibid.
28 Ibid.
29 Ibid.
30 Ibid.
31 Ibid.

11: Goodbye to 4th Brigade

1 JM to Billie Card, 16 January 1916, S1.
2 JM, letter to Vic, 18 December 1915, S1.
3 Smithers, *Sir John Monash*, p. 32.
4 JM, war letters, December 1915, S4.
5 JM, letter to Vic, 16 January 1916, S1.

6 Birdwood, letters to Munro Ferguson, 11 February, 24 March 1916. Bean's papers, AWM.

7 Smithers, *Sir John Monash*, p. 137.

8 JM, war letters, January and February 1916, S4.

9 JM, war letters, 26 April 1916, S4.

10 Ibid.

11 Pedersen, *Monash as Military Commander*, p. 137. Quoted in Durrant to *Reveille*, 16 April 1937, Birdwood Collection, AWM.

12 Monash, *Australian Victories*, pp. 293–5. See also *Smith's Weekly*, 12 April 1929; *Everylady's Journal*, 6 February 1920; *Argus*, 15 November 1919.

13 Cox to Birdwood, 3 May 1916, Birdwood Papers, AWM.

14 Godley's comments, 20 May 1916, Godley Papers, AWM.

15 Birdwood, letter to Pearce and Munro Ferguson, 6 June 1916, Birdwood Papers, AWM.

16 JM, war letters, 6 June 1916, S4.

17 JM, war letters, 11 June 1916, S4.

18 JM, war letters, 24 June 1916, S4.

12: The King and I

1 JM, war Letters, August 1916, S4.

2 Warren Perry, interview, Melbourne, July 2003.

3 JM, war letters, 30 September 1916.

4 JM, war letters, 23 October 1916.

5. JM, lectures to officers, 24 September 1916, Monash Collection, AWM.

6 JM, war letters, 21 December 1916, S4.

13: Western Front 1917: Messines

1 JM, war Letters, 30 December 1916, S4.

2 JM, war letters, 16 March 1917, S4.

3 Huntley Gordon, 112th Bde RFA. Reed, *Battleground Europe*, p. 30.

4 JM, war letters, 4 March 1917, S4.

5 JM, war letters, 14 March 1917, S4.

6 Bean, *Anzac to Amiens*, p. 349.

7 Serle, *John Monash*, p. 289.

8 JM, letter to Felix Meyer, March 1917, S1.

9 JM, war letters, 24 September 1917, S4.

10 Godley, letter, 12 June 1917, Godley Papers, AWM.

11 JM, war letters, 7 June 1917, S4.

12 JM, letter to Felix Meyer, March 1917, S1.

13 JM and Godley exchange of letters, 20 June 1917, S1 and S4.

14: Broodseinde Up; Passchendaele Down

1 JM, war letters, 10 July 1917, S4.
2 JM, letter to Walter Rosenhain, 14 June 1917, S2.
3 JM, war letters, 19 July 1917, S2.
4 Serle, *John Monash*, footnote, p. 293.
5 Smithers, *Sir John Monash*, p. 169.
6 JM, war letters, 24 September 1917, S4.
7 Vic, letter to JM, 7 August 1917, S1.
8 Vic, letter to JM, October 1917, S4.
9 JM diary, 3 October 1917, S5.
10 Bean, *Anzac to Amiens*, p. 370.
11 JM to McNicoll, 4 October 1917. Operations Records, Monash Papers, AWM.
12 JM to Godley, war letters; 22 June 1917, S4, NLA; Godley to JM, 22 June 1917, Godley Papers, AWM.
13 JM, war letters, 15 October 1917, S4.
14 JM, war letters, 18 October 1917, S4.
15 Ibid.
16 MacDougall, *War Letters*, pp. 160, 161.
17 JM, 'small' diary, 1917, S5.

15: 1918: Ludendorff's Lunge

1 JM, war letters, 13 January 1918, S4.
2 JM, war letters, 4 January 1918, S4.
3 The difference on machine-guns is in a 3rd Division circular, G8A, 17 February 1918, Monash collection, AWM. Also correspondence in the collection, 18 February 1918. See Monash Papers, letter White to JM, 18 January.
4 JM, war letters, 15 March 1918, S4.
5 JM, diary, 1917 (one of ten small diaries 1917–19), S5.
6 Monash, *Australian Victories*, pp. 26–8.
7 JM, war letters, 2 April 1918, S4.
8 Monash, *Australian Victories*, p. 26.
9 JM, letter to Vic, 2 April 1918, S4.
10 Monash, *Australian Victories*, p. 28.
11 JM, war letters, 2 April 1918, S4.
12 Bean and other historians refer to these phrases.
13 Monash, *Australian Victories*, p. 33.
14 Ibid., p. 32.
15 JM, war letters, 4 April 1918, S4.
16 JM, war letters, 23 April 1918, S4.

17 JM, war letters, 2 May 1918, S4.
18 JM, war letters, 26 April 1918, S4.
19 Monash, *Australian Victories*, pp. 37, 38.
20 Cutlack, *War Letters*, pp. xii, xiii, foreword.

16: Commander to the Corps

1 Birdwood to Pearce, 13 May 1918, Birdwood Papers, AWM.
2 Dodds to Pearce, 15 May 1918, Monash Papers. AWM.
3 Bean's diary, 17 May 1918, 3DRL606, AWM.
4 Murdoch's cables, 20, 21 May, Monash Papers, AWM. Also see Bean's diary, 18–25 May 1918, 3DRL606, AWM.
5 Murdoch's cables, 20, 21 May, Monash Papers, AWM.
6 Birdwood Papers, AWM; Murdoch's letters, 21, 25 May, 3 June 1918, AWM.
7 Birdwood to Munro Ferguson (Lord Novar), 27 May 1918, Novar Papers.
8 Dodds to Pearce, 28 May 1918, Monash Papers, AWM.
9 JM, war letters, 31 May 1918, S4.
10 Murdoch's letter to JM, 6 June 1918, Murdoch Papers; Monash Papers, AWM.
11 JM, war letters, 31 May 1918, S4.
12 JM's unsent letter to Murdoch, Box 92, Monash Papers, AWM.
13 21 June, 15 June 1918, Birdwood Papers, AWM.
14 JM, war letters, 25 June 1918. S4.
15 JM, JM, war letters, to Walter Rosenhain, 12 July 1918., S4.
16 Monash, *Australian Victories*, p. 48.
17 Ibid., p. 44.
18 Ibid., pp. 44–50.
19 JM to Birdwood, 29 June 1918, Birdwood Papers, AWM.
20 Hughes' remarks in Thompson, *On Lips of Living Men*, pp. 140, 141. JM to Birdwood, 29 June 1918, AWM.
21 Thompson, *On Lips of Living Men*, pp. 140, 141; also letters between White and Monash, Monash Papers, box 92, AWM.
22 JM to Birdwood, 2 July 1918, Monash Papers, AWM.
23 Bean, diary, D116, 14 July 1918, 3DRL606 AWM.
24 Anecdote from Lord Wavell, Wavell Papers, Imperial War Museum, London.
25 Monash, *Australian Victories*, pp. 53–5; Bean, *Official History*, Vol. 6, *The AIF in France, 1918*, p. 274.
26 Monash, *Australian Victories*, pp. 55–60.
27 Ibid.
28 Ibid.

17: Breakthrough at Amiens

1 Monash's risk in involving the Americans began an association between the two nations, which have fought together in another six wars.
2 Monash, *Australian Victories*, p. 62.
3 JM, letters to White, Monash Papers, Box 92, AWM.
4 Bean, Diary, 14 July 1918, 116, 3DRL606, AWM.
5 Murdoch letter, 12 July 1918, Murdoch Papers, AWM.
6 Bean to White, 10 July 1918, Bean Papers, folder 195, AWM.
7 JM–Murdoch letters, 12 & 17 July 1918, Monash Papers, AWM. See also S4.
8 Monash, *Australian Victories*, pp. 62, 63.
9 Interview, Warren Perry, August 2003.
10 Monash, *Australian Victories*, p. 73.
11 JM, letter to Major General Bruche, 10 October 1919; Monash war letters, S4.
12 JM, letter to Bertha, 2 August 1918, S4.
13 Ibid.
14 Ibid.
15 Ibid.
16 JM, small diary, 1918. S5.
17 Blamey, Monash Memorial Lecture, *Age*, 9 October 1948.
18 Monash, *Australian Victories*, pp. 115–25.
19 Ibid.
20 Armitage, J. R., diary, 'Battle of Amiens', AWM, www.awm.gov.au.
21 Monash, *Australian Victories*, p. 124.
22 Ibid., p. 136.
23 Ludendorff, *My War Memoirs*, published *The Times*, 22 August 1919.
24 Ibid.
25 Ibid.
26 JM, 11 August 1918, war letters, S4.
27 Ibid.
28 Ibid., 14 August 1918, S4.
29 JM, small diary, 12 August 1918, S5.
30 George V's unpublished diary, 12 August 1918, Royal Archives, Windsor Castle.
31 Murdoch, letter to Bean, 21 July 1918, Bean Papers, AWM.
32 Bean, *Two Men I Knew*, p. 173.

18: Jugular Days: Mont St Quentin and Péronne

1 Blamey wrote this in an obituary for Monash, which appeared in *Reveille*, p. 10, 31 October 1931, Monash Papers, AWM; also S16.

2 Monash, *Australian Victories*, p. 58.

3 Ibid., pp. 161, 162.

4 Ibid.

5 JM, letter to Vic, 16 March 1917, S4.

6 Monash, *Australian Victories*, p. 168.

7 Ibid., p. 167.

8 Ibid., p. 169.

9 Ibid.; also Laffin, *Australian Battlefields*; Bean, *Anzac to Amiens*.

10 Monash, *Australian Victories*, p. 170.

11 Ibid., p. 176.

12 Ibid., p. 181.

13 Ibid., chapter 11; see also S4.

14 Bean, *Official History*, Vol. 6, pp. 487–8.

15 Ibid., p. 822.

16 Serle, *John Monash*, p. 355.

17 Rawlinson to Allenby, 14 November 1918, in Essame, *The Battle for Europe*, p. 149.

18 Bean, *Official History*, Vol. 6, p. 873.

19 Smithers, *Sir John Monash*, p. 247.

19: Operation Hindenburg Line

1 *Weekly Despatch*, London, 18 June 1948.

2 Doyle, *The British Campaign in Europe*, p. 104.

3 Blamey's response to questions after his Monash Memorial Address, 1948. Report from Dr R. Kerr, who attended.

4 Bean, *Official History*, Vol. 6, p. 879.

5 Pedersen, *Monash as Military Commander*, p. 278.

6 Ibid.

7 Letters between JM and Birdwood, 15 and 16 September 1918, Monash Papers, AWM; September 1918, Birdwood Papers, AWM.

8 McMullin, *Pompey Elliott*, p. 488.

9 Monash, *Australian Victories*, p. 221.

10 Ibid., p. 232.

11 Monash's notes of the meeting with the rebels in Monash Papers, box 89, AWM.

12 Monash, *Australian Victories*, pp. 246–50.

13 Phone transcripts, box 190a, Gellibrand Papers, AWM.

14 Ibid (13).

15 JM, letter to Dr J. Springthorpe, 2 October 1918, S4.

16 Monash, *Australian Victories*, pp. 278–81.

20: Afterglow

1 JM, entries throughout October, small diary, 1918, S5.
2 Monash article, *Memories of an Autograph book*, Argus 9 November. 1929.
3 JM, letter to Vic, 3 November 1918, S4.
4 Thompson, *On Lips of Living Men*, pp. 139, 140.
5 Monash, *Australian Victories*, pp. 286–7. Much the same material went into JM's script for White, his letter to Pearce and in his book. See Pearce, 5 November 1918, Monash papers, AWM.
6 Bean, Diary, 116, 3DRL606, AWM. Bean's entry on this was consistent with his own habit of using others to express his views. A classic example is his attitude to Jews, and Monash in particular. There is no recorded comment by Hughes that was directly unfavourable to Monash's background, although a mutual loathing developed between the two men.
7 Monash's speech, 2 March 1919. S11.
8 JM, 13 December 1918, war letters, S4.
9 JM, letter to Vic, 28 December 1918, S4.
10 JM, posted items, S13, S14.
11 Ibid., (2).
12 Letter to friend (Beardsmore) 20 September 1920, S1
13 Murdoch, 28 February 1919, Melbourne *Herald*.
14 Sydney *Sun*, 27 February 1919.
15 JM to Murdoch, 15 April 1919, S4.
16 Item in *Evening News* (London), 26 April 1919, Monash Papers.

21: Back to the Future

1 JM, small diary, April–September 1919, S5.
2 Bertha's record, S4.
3 Not surprisingly, the Germans tore this memorial down and removed it during World War II.
4 George V's unpublished diary, 12 August 1918, Royal Archive, Windsor Castle.
5 JM, small diary, 1919, S5.
6 Ibid.
7 Birdwood made several criticisms of Monash in letters throughout the war, but especially from May 1918 to the middle of 1919 and later. Note especially 6 December 1918, Birdwood Papers; 8 July 1919, AWM; Munro Ferguson, letter to Birdwood, 2 May 1919, Lord Novar Papers, NLA; also Birdwood Papers, AWM. JM diary, October 1919 to February 1920, S5; also JM letters to Walter Rosenhain, several at this time, S1.
8 Rosenhain, letter to JM, 2 September 1920; also see 18, 23 February 1921, S1.
9 *Bulletin*, 2, 25 December 1920. JM wrote private protest to *Bulletin*'s claim that he would marry Lizette, 14 December 1920.

10 *Smith's Weekly*, 7 August 1919.

11 S10, Souvenir programs and invitations.

12 JM, letter to A. Robinson (State Attorney-General), 9 November 1923, S1.

13 Perry, 'The Police Strike in Melbourne 1923'.

22: Many Causes; Enough Time

1 The KK Club has about 20 members and still meets regularly.

2 Information supplied to the author by current members of the Melbourne Club and KK Club.

3 Reports, *Age*, *Argus*, 26 April 1924.

4 Edwards, *John Monash*, p. 45.

5 RSL Victoria dinner, 24 April 1927, reported *Age*, 25 April 1927.

6 *Argus*, 26 April 1927.

7 *Herald* campaign, January to April 1927.

8 Correspondence between JM and former State Premier Harry Lawson: 30 July 1927; 1 August 1927, S 1.

9 JM, letter to Murdoch, 23 March 1927, S1.

10 Diaries, appointment books, S5; souvenir albums and invitations, S10; visits of famous people, S10.

23: Zenith and End

1 Menzies Monash Memorial address, 1965, S16.

2 Representative of Imperial Patriots to JM, 27 April 1927; representative of Warringah Constitutional Club to JM, 7 May 1927, both S1.

3 JM, letter to Walter Rosenhain, 3 March 1929, and letters to Littlejohn, 13 March, 22 October 1929, both S1.

4 Interview with Elizabeth Durre, February 2004; JM files (in Iona files) have plans for the dolls' house, S10.

5 Thompson, *On Lips of Living Men*, p. 148.

6 'Personal Documents', S10.

7 Ibid.

8 *Age*, 27 April 1930.

9 *Argus*, 24 April 1930.

10 JM, letter to businessman Robert Knox, 12 November 1930, S1.

11 Father Graham, telegram, 17 March 1931, S1.

12 Empire Loyalty representative (Johnson) to JM, 30 April 1930, S1.

13 *Bulletin*, 3 December 1930.

14 Adelaide *Advertiser*, 6 December 1930.

15 Grimwade letter, 16 December 1930; JM, letter to Grimwade, 17 December 1930, both S1.

16 JM, letter, 23 December 1930, S1.

17 'Trip to India', S13.
18 JM notes on India. S13. Also JM, letter to Rosenhain, 9 September 1931, S1.
19 *Age*, 1 April, 11 August 1931. Speech to Beefsteak Club, S10.
20 Melbourne *Sun*, 24 September 1931.
21 Dr Sewell in Melbourne *Herald*, 8 October 1931.
22 Accounts of his funeral in *Age*, *Herald* and *Sun*, 9, 10, 12 October 1931. Also see cuttings book on funeral, Monash Papers, AWM. For Lizette Bentwitch's reaction, see Serle, *John Monash*, notes, pp. 526–7.
23 Rabbi Danglow's Memorial Address, S16.

24: Postscript

1 Mathews, *David Bennett*, pp. 24, 25.
2 Ibid.
3 Author interviews with Elizabeth (Bennett) Durre and Colin Bennett, February 2004.
4 Hyatt, 'Sir Arthur Currie at Passchendaele', p. 3.
5 Perry, 'Major General Sir Charles Rosenthal', p. 5.

BIBLIOGRAPHY

Unpublished papers
Monash's papers, NLA
Most of Monash's papers are held at the National Library of Australia in the Manuscript Section: MS 1884. They are grouped into the following series:

1. General correspondence: A (letters received), 1879–1931; general correspondence: B (outward letters), 1883–1931
   Correspondence with particular individuals, 1860–1931
3. Correspondence: special categories, 1918–20
4. Correspondence: World War I, 1915–20
5. Diaries and notebooks, 1879–1931
6. School and university
7. Engineering, 1886–1932
8. Military, 1908–16
   Arbitration and royal commissions, 1896–1929
10. Subject files, A–Z and souvenir albums
11. Manuscripts, 1881–1928
12. Scientific matters, 1914–30
13. Travels, 1907–31
14. Press cuttings, pamphlets and other printed items, 1894–1929
15. Photographs and glass slides
16. Death and memorials

Addition 20 January 1983; addition 15 June; addition 28 June 1994.

Other Collections, NLA, Canberra

Hughes, W. M. Papers

Murdoch, Sir Keith, Papers

Novar, Viscount (Sir Ronald Munro Ferguson), Papers 1914–18

Australian War Memorial

Many of C. E. W. Bean's diaries and notebooks had entries concerning Monash in Egypt, at Gallipoli, in Flanders and on the Western Front, and these are held at the Australian War Memorial.

Other Papers, AWM

Birdwood, Field Marshal Lord, Collection, 1914–19
Blamey, Field Marshal Sir Thomas, Papers, 1914–18
Cox, General Sir H. V., Papers and Dairies, 1915–17
Elliott, Major General H. E., Papers
Gellibrand, Major General Sir J., Papers, including diary 1914–18 and 3rd
    Division operational reports and battle messages, 1918
Godley, General Sir A. J., Correspondence, 1914–17
Pearce, Sir George, Papers relating to war of 1914–18
White, General Sir C. B. Brudenell, Papers

Imperial War Museum, London
Allanson, Colonel C. J. L., Papers
Birdwood, Field Marshal Lord, Papers

Liddell Hart Centre for Military Archives, London
Hamilton, Ian, Papers
Liddell Hart, Captain Sir B. H., Papers
North, J., Papers
Wavell, Lord, Papers

Royal Archives, Windsor Castle
King George V's diary, 1916–18

Mitchell Library, Sydney

Rosenthal, Major General Sir Charles, diary, 1914–18

Books

Bean, C. E. W, *Anzac to Amiens*, Penguin Books, Melbourne, 1993.
—— (ed.), *Official History of Australia in the War of 1914–1918*, Angus & Robertson, Sydney: Vol. 1, *The Story of Anzac*, 1921; Vol. 2, *The Story of Anzac*, 1937; Vol. 3, *The AIF in France*, 1937; Vol. 4, *The AIF in France*, 1933; Vol. 5, *The AIF in France During the Main German Offensive, 1918*, 1937; Vol. 6, *The AIF in France During the Allied Offensive, 1918*, 1942.
—— *Pamphlets on World Affairs: The Old AIF and the New*, Angus & Robertson, Sydney, 1940.
—— *Two Men I Knew: William Bridges and Brudenell White*, Angus & Robertson, Sydney, 1957.
Birdwood, Field Marshal W. R., *Khaki and Gown*, Ward Lock & Co., London, 1941.
Cameron, James, *1914*, Cassell, London, 1959.
Carlyon, Les, *Gallipoli*, Pan Macmillan, Sydney, 2001.
Charteris, John, *Field Marshal Lord Haig*, Charles Scribner's Sons, New York, 1929.
Coulthard-Clark, C.D., *The Citizen General Staff: The Australian Intelligence Corps 1907–1914*, AWM, Canberra, 1976.
Cutlack, F. M. (ed.), *War Letters of General Monash*, Angus & Robertson, Sydney, 1935.
Doyle, Sir Arthur Conan, *The British Campaign in Europe, 1914–1918*, Geoffrey Bles, London, 1928.
Edwards, Cecil, *Brown Power: A Jubilee History of the State Electricity Commission of Victoria*, SEC, Melbourne, 1969.
—— *John Monash*, SEC, Melbourne, 1970.
Essame, H., *The Battle for Europe 1918*, B. T. Batsford, London, 1972.
Gilbert, M., *First World War*, HarperCollins, London, 1995.
Grant, Ian, *Jacka VC: Australia's Finest Fighting Soldier*, Macmillan, Sydney, 1990.
Hamilton, Sir Ian, *Gallipoli Diary*, 2 volumes, George H. Doran, London, 1920.
Hamilton, Jill, *From Gallipoli to Gaza*, Simon & Schuster, Sydney, 2003.
Holt, Major & Mrs, *Battlefield: Ypres Salient*, Leo Cooper, London, 2000.
Horner, David, *Blamey*, Allen & Unwin, Sydney, 1998.

James, Robert Rhodes, *Gallipoli*, Pan Books, London, 1974.

Jones, Ian, *Ned Kelly: A Short Life*, Lothian Books, Melbourne, 1996.

Joynt, W. D., *Saving the Channel Ports*, Wren Publishing, London, 1975.

Kingston, Beverley, *The Oxford History of Australia*, Vol. 3, 1860–1890, *Glad, Confident Morning*, Oxford University Press, Melbourne, 2001.

Laffin, John, *Guide to Australian Battlefields of the Western Front 1916–18*, Simon & Schuster, Sydney, 1994.

Liddell Hart, B., *Through the Fog of War*, Hodder & Stoughton, London, 1938.

—— *History of the First World War*, Pan Books, 1972.

Lindsay, Patrick, *The Spirit of the Digger, Then and Now*, Macmillan, Sydney, 2003.

Lloyd George, David, *War Memories*, six volumes, Odhams Press, London, 1933–36.

Ludendorff, General Erich, *My War Memoirs, 1914–18*, two vols, E. P. Dutton, New York, 1920.

Magnus, Philip, *Kitchener: Portrait of an Imperialist*, John Murray, London, 1958.

Macdougall, A. K. (ed.), *War Letters of General Monash*, Duffy & Snellgrove, Sydney, 2002.

Macintyre, Stuart, *The Oxford History of Australia*, Vol. 4, 1901–42, *The Succeeding Age*, Oxford University Press, Melbourne, 2001.

McMullin, Ross, *Pompey Elliott*, Scribe, Melbourne, 2002.

McNicol, N. G., *The Thirty Seventh: History of the Thirty Seventh Battalion, AIF*, Melbourne, 1936.

Magnus, Philip, *Kitchener: Portrait of an Imperialist*, E. P. Dutton, New York, 1959.

Middlebrook, Martin, *The Kaiser's Battle*, Book Club Associates, London, 1978.

Mitchell, James, *A Deepening Roar: Scotch College, Melbourne 1851–2001*, Allen & Unwin, Melbourne, 2001.

Monash, J., *The Australian Victories in France in 1918*, Hutchinson & Co., London 1920.

Moorehead, Alan, *Gallipoli*, Macmillan, London, 1975.

Nicholson, G. Harvey, *First Hundred Years of Scotch College Melbourne, 1851–1951*, Scotch College, Melbourne, 1952.

Palazzo, Albert, *Defenders of Australia: The Third Australian Division*, University of NSW, Sydney, 2002.

Pedersen, P. A., *Monash as Military Commander*, Melbourne University Press, 1985.

Pollock, J., *Kitchener*, Constable, London, 1996.

Portus, G. V. (ed.), *Fifty Famous Australians*, Colourgravure Publications, Melbourne, 1938.

Priestley, J.B., *Margin Released*, William Heinemann, London, 1962.

Reed, Paul, *Battleground Europe: Walking the Salient*, Leo Cooper, London, 2001.

Rose, Kenneth, *King George V*, Phoenix Press, London, 1983.

Rule, Edgar John, *Jacka's Mob: A Narrative of the Great War*, Military Melbourne, 1999.

Serle, Geoffrey, *John Monash*, Melbourne University Press, 1982.

Smithers, A. J., *Sir John Monash*, Leo Cooper, London, 1973.

Taylor, A. J. P, *The First World War: An Illustrated History*, Penguin, London, 1972.

Taylor, Phil, and Pam Cupper, *Gallipoli: A Battlefield Guide*, Kangaroo Press, Sydney, 1989.

Terraine, John, *Douglas Haig: The Educated Soldier*, Leo Cooper, London, 1990.

Thompson, John (ed.), *On Lips of Living Men*, Lansdowne Press, Melbourne, 1962.

Urquhart, H. M., *Arthur Currie*, Macmillan, London, 1950.

Wantiss, N. F., *The History of the Fourteenth Battalion, AIF*, AWM, Melbourne, 1929.

Warner, Denis & Peggy, *The Tide at Sunrise*, Angus & Robertson, Sydney, 1975.

Wavell, Field Marshal Lord, *Generals and Generalship*, Penguin, London, 1941.

Williams, John F., *German Anzacs and the First World War*, UNSW Press, 2003.

Zwar, Desmond, *The Soul of a School*, Macmillan, Melbourne, 1982.

Articles and Pamphlets

Bennett, Colin, Australia's Tribute to a Great Leader, *Age*, 11 November, 1950.

Bennett, G., 'To the Service of His Country', First Monash Oration, *Australian Jewish Herald*, 15 October 1936; also in S16.

Brasch, Rabbi Dr R., 'John Monash', *Royal Australian Historical Society*, Vol. 45, Part 4, 1959.

Callinan, B., 'Sir John Monash', Daniel Mannix Memorial Lecture, 17 June 1980, Melbourne 1981.

Celik, Kenan, & Cehan Koc, *The Gallipoli Campaign: International Perspectives 85 Years On*, Canakkale, Turkey, 2002.

Dumble, Sandra, 'Edmund Augustus Samson, Teacher', (Scotch College Archive), unpublished paper, 2003.

Elliott, William, 'The Kelly Raid on Jerilderie', *Jerilderie Herald*, 1913.

Forestry Ministry, Office of National Parks and Wild Life, *Gallipoli Peninsula, Historical National Park*, Istanbul, 2001.

Holgate, Alan & Taplin, Geoff, *The Contribution of Sir John Monash to 20th Century Engineering*, Monash University Engineering Department, October 2001.

Hyatt, A. M. J., 'Sir Arthur Currie at Passchendaele', *Stand-To*, Vol. 10, No. 1, Jan–Feb 1965, pp. 16–20.

Mathews, Race, *David Bennett: A Memoir*. Australian Fabian Society Pamphlet Number 44.

McQueen, Humphrey, 'Gallipoli's Shadow', *Age*, 26 April 2003.

Menzies, Sir Robert, 'Sir John Monash', Address at Monash Centenary Memorial Service, 11 April 1965, Australian Jewish Historical Society, vol. 1, 1966, pp. 81–4.

Meredith, Helen, 'Coming of Age', *Weekend Australian*, 7–8 August 1983.

Monasch, B. L., *The Life, Labours, Joys and Sorrows of B. B. Monasch*, Jewish Historical Society Magazine, 1986.

Monash, John, Memories of an Autograph Book, *Argus*, 9 November 1929.

Northcliffe, Lord, *Daily Mail*, 21 May 1915.

Northwood, Vernon R., 'Monash', *SEC Magazine*, December 1950.

Perry, Major E. W. O., 'The Military Life of General Sir John Monash', *Victorian Historical Magazine*, 109th issue, Vol. XXVIII, No. 1, December 1957.

—— 'General Sir John Monash: Scholar, Engineer and Soldier', *Australian Jewish Historical Society*, Vol. IV, Part VI, 1957.

—— 'Monash: The Biographer's Dilemma', *Australian Quarterly*, March 1961.

—— 'The Police Strike in Melbourne 1923', address to the Royal Historical Society of Victoria, 28 October 1969.

—— 'Major General Sir Charles Rosenthal: Soldier, Architect and Musician', *Victorian Historical Magazine*, Vol. 40, No. 3, August 1969.

Rosenthal, Major General C., 'A Great Soldier and a Great Scholar', *Reveille* (Monash Memorial Issue), 31 October 1931, p. 4.

Steele, Major Alan B., *The Western Front: A General Outline*, Arrow Printery Pty Ltd, Melbourne, 1930.

Internet

http://au.geocities.com/fortysecond battalion/level2/leaders/general-monash.htm General Sir John Monash.

www.chez.com/hamel/results.htm: The Battle of Hamel.

Holgate, A., and Taplin, G., 'John Monash's engineering to 1914', http://home.vicnet.net.au/~aholgate/jm/mainpages/projects.html.

www.macknortshs.qld.edu.au/ANZAC.htm Amiens, Mont St Quentin, Montbrehain.

Documentary Film

SEC documentary film in conjunction with Australian Commonwealth Film Production and Zanthus Films, *1918 Remembered*, ABC TV, 1999.

INDEX

A

a'Beckett, Justice 107
Aboriginal Australians 5, 9, 520
Afghan War (1878–80) 145
Age 65–66, 69, 114, 144, 145,
   264, 484, 499, 520
AIF (Australian Imperial Force)
  Australian Mission 432–33
   British High Command 447
   conscription 265–66
   expansion 238–39
   furlough 417–19
   General Officer Commanding
    331, 333–34, 385–87,
    449–50
   Haig 308
   historical treatment 495–96
   repatriation and demobilisation
    449–50, 457–60
   typhoid 157
   venereal disease 165, 171
   see also Australian Army Corps
AIF 1st Australian Tunnelling
  Company 278
AIF 1st Division
  Armistice 449

Australian Corps 357, 364,
  370–71
Australian Mission 432–33
Battle of Amiens 366
Battle of Chuignes and Bray
  389–91
Bridges commands 149,
  153–54, 162, 164–65, 171
Broodseinde 302, 339
Egypt 154, 161, 171
formation 153, 239
furlough 420–21
Gallipoli 174, 176–78, 183,
  190, 207
Glasgow commands 340
Godley 164–65
Hargicourt Line 427–28
Hindenburg Line 424
Middle East 148–49
Somme 376, 377
Walker commands 241, 340
White 153, 155
AIF 1st Division 1st Battalion
  430–31
AIF 1st Division 1st Brigade 153,
  189–90, 212, 227, 371, 451

AIF 1st Division 2nd Brigade 153, 196, 227

AIF 1st Division 3rd Battalion 391–92

AIF 1st Division 3rd Brigade 153

AIF 1st Division 11th Battalion 427

AIF 2nd (Anzac) Division
Birdwood commands 162, 173, 178–81
Hamilton commands 167
original 239
Walter commands 241

AIF 2nd (Anzac) Division 4th Brigade
Anzac Cove 172, 174–75, 179, 181–83, *182*, 190, 393–94
Battle of Sari Bair 212–13, 393–94
Bean 206–7
condition of troops 210–11
first attack plan Anzac Cove 193
Gallipoli evacuation 234–35
Hill 60 attack 222–26
Ismailia 237
JM 150–58, 161–62, 164–65, 253, 364
Lemnos (Greece) 227
new 4th and 12th Brigades 239
use of bayonets 391

AIF 2nd (Anzac) Division 4th Brigade 13th Battalion
Anzac Cove 181, 184, 189, 191–92, 214, 223
Egypt 244

AIF 2nd (Anzac) Division 4th Brigade 14th Battalion
Anzac Cove 181–84, 191, 197–98, 214, 219–20, 223
Egypt 244
Western Front 250, 251, 295

AIF 2nd (Anzac) Division 4th Brigade 15th Battalion
Anzac Cove 179, 181, 184, 185, 197, 214–15, 218–20
Egypt 244

AIF 2nd (Anzac) Division 4th Brigade 16th Battalion
Anzac Cove 179, 190–92, 194, 214–15, 218–19

AIF 2nd (Anzac) Division 18th Battalion 224–25

AIF 2nd Division 271, 302, 340, 360, 397, 399–400, 420–21, 438–39, 442, 466

AIF 2nd Division 2nd Machine Gun Battalion 404

AIF 2nd Division 2nd Pioneer Battalion 441

AIF 2nd Division 5th Brigade 323, 400, 401, *403*, 438–39

AIF 2nd Division 5th Brigade 18th Battalion 402

AIF 2nd Division 6th Brigade 402, *403*, 440–42

AIF 2nd Division 7th Brigade 402, *403*, 438–39

AIF 3rd Division
advances during 1918 *313*
Battle of Chuignes and Bray 389
Boulogne 293–94
British War Office 266
Broodseinde 294, 297, 302
Doullens 316
Fauguembergues 307

formation 239, 498
Gellibrand commands 340–41
Haig 327–28
Hindenburg Line 421, 434–37
JM 247, 250
Messines Ridge 274, 282–83
Mont St Quentin 400, *403*
Passchendaele 304–6
raids 271–72, 314–15
reputation 274–75
Somme 318–21, 323, 325, 397
strike by 459–60
AIF 3rd Division 3rd Pioneer
    Battalion 389
AIF 3rd Division 9th Brigade 255,
    303–5, 314–16, 318, 320, 323,
    325, 326, 389
AIF 3rd Division 10th Brigade
    255, 303–5, 316, 318, 326, 341
AIF 3rd Division 11th Brigade
    255, 292, 318, 321
AIF 3rd Division 33rd Battalion
    282, 400–401
AIF 3rd Division 37th Battalion
    282–83, 284, 299–300, 314
AIF 3rd Division 38th Battalion
    300, 314, 401
AIF 3rd Division 39th Battalion
    300
AIF 3rd Division 40th Battalion
    300–301
AIF 3rd Division 41st Battalion
    300–301
AIF 3rd Division 42nd Battalion
    300
AIF 3rd Division 43rd Battalion
    299, 408
AIF 3rd Field Ambulance 196

AIF 4th Division
    Armistice 449
    Australian Mission 432–33
    Battle of Dernancourt 322–23
    Battle of Hargincourt 428
    Chipilly Spur 377–78
    Egypt 243–44
    furlough 420–21
    German offensive 316, 319, 321
    Godley commands 239–40, 243
    Holmes commands 271
    Le Verguier 424
    Polygon Wood 295–96
    Sinclair-MacLagan commands
        293
    Ypres 282
AIF 4th Division new 4th Brigade
    239
AIF 4th Division 12th Brigade
    239
AIF 4th Division 13th Brigade
    239, 371, 378
AIF 4th Division 31st Battalion
    295
AIF 5th Division 239, 241, 243,
    244, 295, 296, 323, 397,
    399–400, 404, 421, 434–36,
    529
AIF 5th Division 8th Brigade
    32nd Battalion 434–36
AIF 5th Division 13th Brigade
    325
AIF 5th Division 14th Brigade
    402, *403*, 405–8
AIF 5th Division 14th Brigade
    53rd Battalion 407
AIF 5th Division 14th Brigade
    54th Battalion 407

AIF 5th Division 14th Brigade 59th Battalion 408
AIF 5th Division 15th Brigade 320, 325, 357, 377, *403*, 421
AIF 6th Battalion 514
AIF 13th Battalion 390, 424–26
AIF 15th Battalion 424
AIF 16th Battalion 424
AIF 16th Battalion D Company 390–91
AIF 37th Battalion 429
AIF 41st Battalion 396
AIF 48th Battalion 426–27
AIF 59th Battalion 418
AIF Field Ambulance xiii, 303–5
AIF I Anzac Corps 243, 278–79, 286, 295, 297
AIF II Anzac Corps 245, 278, 286, 289, 290, 297, 307
AIF Light Horse Brigade 153, 154, 195, 216–17, 271
Aitken, Lieutenant Colonel John 25
Albert (France) 316, 389
Albert, Prince (Duke of York) 261, 455, 465, 496, 498, 500
Albert Victor, Prince 262
Alexander, Rebecca 47
Alexander the Great 173
Alexandra, Queen 269
Allaines (France) 408
Allanson, Major Cecil 215–16, 221
Allenby, General Sir Edmund 270
American Civil War 134–37, 140, 348–49, 410
American Independence Day 349
Amiens (France) 317, 368, 377–78, 391–92 *see also* Battle of Amiens
Ancre (France) *313*, 317, 320, 325
Anderson, Ellen 68
Anderson, Joshua T. Noble
    engineering projects 83, 92, 94, 103, 107
    JM 61, 66, 85, 89, 93
    Monash & Anderson 68–71, 79, 82, 107
Andrew, Captain (Professor) Henry Martyn 24, 25, 27
Annandale (NSW) 81
Antoine, General 293
Anvil Wood (France) *403*, 407
Anzac (Australian and New Zealand Army Corps) *see* AIF 2nd (Anzac) Division
Anzac Day xi, 245, 325, 364, 460–61, 474, 490–94, 496–99, 507, 513
Anzac House (Melbourne) 471
Anzac to Amiens (Bean) 524
Arbitration Court 62
Arcadian (ship) 201, 203, 204
Argus 58, 65–66, 114, 145, 146, 153, 157, 484, 499
Armentières (Flanders) 267, 314, 323
Armitage, Gunner J. R. xiii, 374–75
Arras (France) 278–79
Arthur, Prince of Connaught 307
Ashmead-Bartlett, Ellis 180, 204–5, 228–29, 413
Asia–Pacific region 14, 35, 98–99, 118, 448
Aspinall, Captain Cecil 233

Asquith, Herbert 127, 226, 229
Association 527 *see also* White
　Army (clandestine army)
Aucher, A. C. 18
Austral Otis Engineering Co.
　79–80
Australasian Association for the
　Advancement of Science 150,
　487
Australian Air Corps 433
Australian Army Corps
　1st Division joins 357
　British High Command 323
　campaign in France *414–15*
　commander's position 329–52
　Haig 296–97, 307–8, 314
　Hobbs commands 450–51
　JM commands xi, xv–xvii,
　　372–73
　mutiny 429–31, 451
　recognition for 412–13
　style of fighting 441–42
　see also AIF (Australian Imperial
　　Force)
Australian Chief Censor 333
Australian Flying Corps 423
Australian Garrison Artillery 100
Australian Imperial Force *see* AIF
Australian Intelligence Corps
　(AIC) 117–21, 128, 137–40,
　141
Australian Labor Party (ALP)
　145–46, 276, 505–6, 509
*Australian Victories in France in
　1918* (Monash) 466–67, 473
Australian War Memorial 471,
　523–24
Austria 130, 147

B
Baden, Prince Max von 443
Baer-Loebel (paternal grandfather)
　1, 3–7, 9–10, 72, 131 *see also*
　Wiener, Mathilde (paternal
　grandmother)
Balfour, Arthur 444–45
Balfour Declaration 490
Balkans 154, 158
Baltzer, W. J. 81–82, 93, 101, 103
Bannockburn Shire Council (Vic)
　105, 107–8, 110
Barry, Mr Justice Sir Redmond 2
Barton, Edmund 98–99
Battenberg, Prince Louis of 455
Battle of Amiens xi–xix, 363–69,
　373, 375–80, 382, 412–13,
　471, 474, 525, 528 *see also*
　Amiens
Battle of Broodseinde *285*, 294,
　297–302
Battle of Chuignes and Bray *387*,
　389–91, 395, 412–13
Battle of Dernancourt *313*,
　322–23
Battle of Hamel xvi, xvii, 345,
　347, *353*, 354–56, 363, 367,
　371, 382, 413, 474 *see also*
　Hamel (France)
Battle of Hargicourt *415*, *425*,
　428
Battle of Krithia 204
Battle of Messines Ridge *see*
　Messines Ridge
Battle of Mont St Quentin 392,
　395, 397, 399–403, *403*,
　409–10, 412–13, 421, 428,
　466, 483, 520

Battle of Péronne 392, 395, 397, 400, 402–12, *403*, 421, 428, 520

Battle of Sari Bair 205, 209, 211–21, *217*, 283, 393–94, 399

Battle of Sarikamish 158–59

Battle of the Somme 351 *see also* Somme Valley

Baumgarten, William 15

Bavarian Divisions 284

Baxter & Saddler 80, 82, 84, 86–88, 90–91 *see also* Saddler (investor)

Bean, Charles
  AIF 417–18, 420
  anti-Semitism 151–52, 330, 337, 339, 450, 524
  Australian Corps 330, 334, 347, 352, 358–59, 386
  Australian War Memorial 523–24
  background 166, 228
  Battle of Mont St Quentin 409
  Bridges 138
  Gallipoli 188, 192–93, 212
  Honorary Doctorate 510, 524
  JM 166–67, 206–7, 277–78, 284, 327, 370, 405
  Péronne 413
  White 165–66, 330, 450, 524

Beaurevoir Line *see* Hindenburg Line

Behrend, Albert (cousin) 3, 5, 7, 16, 108

Belgians, King of the 291

Belgium 128, 267–69

Bell, George 488

Belloy-en-Santerre (France) 422

Bendigo City Council (Vic) 95–97, 103, 105–6

Benjamin, Charlotte (maternal grandmother) *see* Manesse

Bennett, Bertha (née Monash) *see* Monash, Bertha (daughter)

Bennett, (John) Colin Monash 504, 519–20

Bennett, David Monash (grandson) 489, 504, 519–20

Bennett, Elizabeth 'Betty' (granddaughter) 489, 504, 518–20

Bennett, Gershon 475, 478–79, 506–7, 518, 519

Bennett, John Monash (grandson) 489, 503–4, 506, 518

Bentwitch, Lizette 129–30, 206, 254, 264, 267, 288, 309, 312, 369, 444, 451, 462–65, 468, 474–75, 479, 487–89, 500, 506, 508, 511–14, 521

Bentwitch, Professor Sir Norman 490

Berry, Major Walter xiii–xiv, 375

Bertangles (France) xi, 325, 337, 345, 348, 356, 370, 381, 383

Bevan, Dave 94

Binyon, Laurence 273

Birdwood, Lieutenant General Sir William
  AIF 2nd (Anzac) Division command 162, 173, 178–81
  AIF General Officer Commanding 331, 333–34, 341, 359, 386, 420, 431, 447, 450
  Anzac Day 1927 496, 498

appearance and background
162–64
Australian Corps 307–8,
329–30, 334, 337, 339, 340,
346
Battle of Sari Bair 205, 209,
216, 218, 222
British Fifth Army command
329, 386
Gallipoli 189–90, 195, 223,
225–26, 231, 233
Governor Generalship 508
Hamel 326–27
Hughes 265
India Army 526
JM 192–93, 230, 238, 240–42,
248–50, 254, 270, 286, 454,
469–70
Passchendaele 302
reward 473
style of command 357
Western Front Army Corps
command 243, 312
Blackwood v. McCaughey 86–87
Blamey, Field Marshal Thomas
AIF 422, 447
Anzac Day 1926 496–99
character 436
chief of staff xiv, 341, 343, 356,
383, 399
JM 165, 370, 388, 418, 513
White Army 483
World War II 527
Blashki sisters 29–30, 51, 53
Bligh, Hon. Ivo 445
Bodrum (Turkey) 483
Boer War 148, 161, 342
Bois Madame (France) 400–401

Boldt, A. E. 102–3
Bolshevik revolution 289, 312,
379, 502, 527 *see also*
communism
Bony (France) *415*, 436, 438
Bosnia 147
Bouchavesnes (France) 400–401
Boulogne (France) 293, 296
Bouly, Princess 270
Bradman, Don 510, 515
Braithwaite (corps commander)
421–22
Bray (France) *see* Battle of
Chuignes and Bray
Bridges, Colonel W. T.
AIF 1st Division command *see*
AIF 1st Division
Australian Intelligence Corps
117
character 138
Gallipoli 174, 178, 179, 181,
186, 189–90, 193, 195–96,
202
British 6th King's Own Royal
Lancasters 219
British 8th Division 325
British 9th Scottish Division 319
British 16th Lancashire Fusiliers
390
British 25th Division 280, 282
British 29th Division 167, 172,
174, 178–79, 181, 184, 188,
196
British 29th Indian Brigade 211,
213, 215, 216, 221
British 32nd Division 389, 391,
398, 400
British 35th Division 319, 321

British 47th Division 389

British 49th Division 302

British 58th Division xvii, 377

British 61st Division 320

British 62nd Division 278

British 66th Division 302

British 139th Brigade 440

British Second Army 278, 448

British Third Army 315–16, 528

British Fourth Army xv, 394–95, 421–22, 447

British Fifth Army 315–16, 319, 322, 329, 386, 422, 427, 448

British Army amphibious landings 173, 179

British Army cavalry xvii, 319–21, 323, 366

British Army Cavalry 370

British Army Lancashire Territorials 171

British Army leadership mentality 191–94, 239–40, 290

British Army Royal Welsh Fusiliers 218

British III Corps xvii, 323, 325, 361, 368–69, 378, 389, 423–24, 428, 430, 433

British IX Corps 219, 221–23, 282–83, 287, 423–24, 428, 438

British VIII Corps 212, 317

British X Corps 282–83, 316

British XIII Corps 436

British XV Corps 339

British Expeditionary Force 269

British High Command xii, 283, 290, 296, 303, 306, 323, 330–31, 364, 377, 386, 392–93, 399, 412–13, 421,

428–31, 447, 460, 528

British marines 173, 189–92, 195

British New Army 223, 227

British Royal Flying Corps 367, 382

British Shipping Controller 459–60

British Tank Corps 343–44, 355, 367

British War Cabinet 159, 306

British War Council 158, 168, 204–5, 231, 256, 263, 266

British War Office 149–50, 238, 369, 460

Broodseinde (Flanders) *see* Battle of Broodseinde

Brown, Captain Roy 324

Bruce, Stanley Melbourne 494–95, 505, 524

Bruche, Major General Sir Julius 13, 46, 121, 125, 138, 144, 151, 153, 257, 341, 347

Brunton, W. 481

Bryce, Viscount 452

Buckingham Palace (London) 455–57

Buckley VC, Corporal Alex 407, 413, 424

Buckley VC, Sergeant Gerald 424–26

Bugden, Private Patrick 295

Building, Engineering and Mining Journal 103

Bulgaria 154, 158, 230

Bullecourt (France) 278, 281, 287, 340, 343

Bulletin 98, 473, 475, 476, 512

Burnham, Lord 456, 467

Burston, Colonel James 145–46
Burt, Septimus 91
Butler, Major General 296, 361, 367–69, 377, 421, 430
Byng, General Sir Julian 308, 381, 388–89, 528

C
Cambrai (France) 308
Canadian Corps 307, 361, 364, 365, 371, *373*, 375–76, 528
Cane, Lieutenant C. H. 300
Cannan, Brigadier James 215, 219, 239, 246, 255, 292, 301, 318, 357, 437
Canterbury Battalion (NZ) 190–91
Carlyle, Thomas 516
Caroline Islands 149
Carruthers, Brigadier General R. A. 341, 383
Carter Gummow & Co. 81–82 *see also* Gummow, Frank
Carter, Lieutenant Colonel 379, 389
Cartwright, Private George 400–401, 413
Casey, R. G. 341
casualties
    Australian 413, 442
    Battle of Amiens 375
    Battle of Chuignes and Bray 391
    Battle of Hamel 355
    Battle of Hargincourt 428
    Battle of Mont St Quentin 409
    British offensive in Flanders 306
    Canadian 413

Gallipoli 181–85, 191–94, 196, 198–99, 233
Haig's offensives 290, 303, 417, 422, 503
Menin Road (Ypres) 295
Messines Ridge (Ypres) 284
Montbrehain 442
Somme 269, 351
Cenotaph (Martin Place, Sydney) 504
Château Hervarre (Blequin) 294, 307
Chauvel, Lieutenant General Harry 154, 195, 197, 198, 216–17, 240, 248, 271, 312, 446, 461, 464, 466, 478, 490, 506, 515, 531
Chichester, Major General 270
China 27
Chuignes (France) *see* Battle of Chuignes and Bray
Churchill, Winston 158–59, 167–68, 180, 203–5, 381, 454, 456, 489
Clemenceau, Premier 358–60, 382
Clermont-Tonnerre, Marquis de 384
Cléry (France) 398, 400, 401, *403*
Coal Creek Pty Co. 69
Coastal Artillery 75
Cologne Fortuna mine 467–68
Colombo (Ceylon) 159
Commonwealth Defence Department 98–99, 111, 493–94, 505
communism 507–10, 512, 527
Communist Manifesto (Marx) 43
Congreve, General 317, 320

Connaught, Duke of 265, 291–92
conscription 125–26, 143, 256, 265–66, 328
Cook, Sir Joseph 346–47, 457
Corio (federal seat) 276
Corio Shire Council (Vic) 95, 105, 107–8, 110
Council for Science and Industrial Research 487
Council of Defence 505
Courage, Brigadier-General 344, 423
Courtine Trench (Vermandovillers) 390
Cowan, Lieutenant General Sir John 264–65
Cox, Major General H. V. 211–20, 223–26, 243, 246–48, 271, 350
Coxen, Brigadier-General 372, 499
Crabbe, Lieutenant K. G. W. 198
Crimean War (1853–56) 27, 98–99
Croy-Lobu, Prince de 270
Currey VC, Private William 407, 413
Currie, General Sir Arthur 307, 361, 367, 375–76, 382, 469, 473, 511, 527–28
Cussen, Leo 107–9
Cutlack, F. M. 327–28

D
Daily Telegraph (London) 467
Danglow, Rabbi Jacob 478–79, 516
Dardanelles 167–69, 173, 174, 204

Dardanelles Commission 216
d'Armaille, Marquise 294
Darnley, Lady Florence 445
Das Kapital (Marx) 43
David, Edgeworth 467
Dawson, Geoffrey 229
Deakin, Alfred 20, 61, 64–66, 98, 100–101, 114, 126, 136
Dean-Pitt, Colonel 67
Debeney, General 361
Depression 1890s 59–60, 63–64, 86, 113
Depression 1930s 486–87, 502, 503–7
diggers
    1930s Depression 486–87, 505
    Anzac Day and 490–94
    at JM's funeral 515
    volunteer force ('specials') 482–83, 491, 497
Djemal Pasha 160, 163
Dodds, Major General 331, 334, 443
Doll's House (Ibsen) 54
Doyle, Sir Arthur Conan 127, 416
Dumaresq, Captain H. J. 300
Durrant, Major J. M. A. 244, 249
Durre, Betty *see* Bennett, Elizabeth 'Betty'
Dwyer, Patrick 504–5
Dyer, Joseph 506
dysentery 199–200
Dyson, Will 331–32

E
Eastwood, Captain 214
Eden, Sir Anthony xviii
Edward, Prince of Wales 243–45,

262, 455, 461, 473 *see also*
Edward VIII, King
Edward VII, King 100, 129, 261
Edward VIII, King 243, 522
Eggleston, F. W. 478
Egypt 154, 155, 158, 161, 163,
170, 171, 237, 243–45, 446,
496
Ellery, T. G. 480–81
Elliott, Brigadier-General Pompey
320, 325, 357, 377, 421,
481–83, 499, 512
Elliott, William 8–10, 16–17, 21,
82
Elles, Major General H. J. 343–44
Empire Loyalty League 507–8
Engineering Association of New
South Wales 82
Engineering Students' Society 58
Enver Pasha 158–59, 169
Essendon Council (Melbourne)
480
Etricourt (France) 434
Ewing, Rev. John 11
Eydon, General J. 270

F
Fabian Society 519, 520
Farlow, George 17, 38, 66, 77, 90,
113
Farmar, Lieutenant Colonel H.
Mynors 255, 258, 259, 297
fascism 502, 507, 508, 525
Federation 98–101, 107
Fink, Theodore 526
Fisher, Andrew 330, 337
Foch, Marshal Ferdinand 359–60,
365, 381, 382, 395

Foster, Colonel H. J. 124–25, 134,
135, 138, 140, 141
Foucaucourt (France) 396–97
Franco–Prussian War (1870–71)
124, 406
Franz Ferdinand, Archduke 147
Franz, Prince 284
Fraser, Brigadier General L. D.
341, 423
French Army
Battle of Amiens 365
Gallipoli 167, 173, 188, 233
Germany 128, 147
Hindenburg Line 279
Soissons 366–67
Western Front 278, 289, 293,
296, 319–20, 323, 423–24
XXXI Corps 361
French, Field Marshal Lord 259
Freud, Sigmund 280–81
Fuller, General J. F. C. 489

G
Gaba Tepe (Gallipoli) 178
Gabriel, Annie 39–45, 47–52, 55,
59, 72, 116–17, 155, 206, 512,
513
Gabriel, Fred 39–44, 50–52, 55,
59, 155
Gabriel, Gordon 39, 44, 51–52,
155
Gail, Baron de 294
Gallipoli Diary (Hamilton) 204–5
Gallipoli Peninsula (Turkey) xi–xii,
158–59, 167–69, 172, *177*,
211–21, 231–35, 283
Abdel Rahman Spur 218–19
Achi Baba 174, *177*, 188

armistice at Anzac Cove 200
Baby 700 184, 189–93
Bloody Angle 184
Cape Helles 172, 174, *177*,
    178–79, 181, 194–96, 204,
    211
Chessboard 184
Chunuk Bair 176–78, 211, *217*,
    218
Courtney's Post 188, 189, 197,
    198
Dead Man's Ridge 184
Hill 60 *217*, 222–26, 398
Hill 971 211, *217*
Lone Pine 211, 212, 216, 222
Monash Valley 183, 184, 190,
    295
Nek 184, 191, 216–17
Pope's Hill 184, 188, 189, 194
Russell's Top 183, 186, 188
Sari Bair *see* Battle of Sari Bair
Scimitar Hill 226
Steele's Post 186, 188, 195–96,
    202
Suvla Bay *177*, 211, 221–22
Walker's Ridge 183, 207
Gandhi, Mahatma 511
gas (use of) xiii, 271, 282, 284,
    303, 318, 345, 354–55,
    362–63, 434, 438
Geelong Advertiser 97
Gellert, Leon 185
Gellibrand, Major General Sir J.
    G. 165, 340–41, 349, 382, 398,
    401, 408, 423, 434–37, 528
George V, King
    AIF 3rd Division 259–64, 283,
    288

Anzac Day 460
Australian Corps 338–39, 352
Dawson 229
Earl Kitchener 231
Governor Generalship 508
Haig 268–69, 274, 310, 365
Hamilton 226
JM 274, 291, 327, 341, 465,
    521
Knight Commander of the Bath
    xviii, 383–85, 467
marriage to Princess Mary of
    Teck 147
Prince of Wales 245
succession 129
George VI, King 261, 455, 465
German Army
    41st division 394–95
    58th Infantry Regiment 426
    in 1910 130
    Armistice 443, 449
    Australia 119–20, 128, 441–42
    Battle of Amiens xiv, xvi, 380
    Battle of Hamel 354–56
    Britain 126, 141, 143
    Broodseinde 299
    Bullecourt 281
    cavalry 318
    defeat 411
    engineers 477–78
    Gallipoli 233
    German High Command 406
    Hindenburg Line *see*
        Hindenburg Line
    Ludendorff *see* Ludendorff,
        General Erich
    occupation of 460
    Péronne 406

Prussian Guards 398, 406, 409
Russian Front 312, 356, 362
Second Army 361
Turkey 168–69
Western Front 286, 289, 292, 296, 308, *313*, 315–16
withdrawal 397, 408
Germans in Australia 3, 36, 147–50
Gibraltar 529
Gibson, John 115–16, 128, 238, 272, 467, 476, 506
Gibson, Robert 467, 481
Glasgow, Major General Sir T. W. 325, 376, 382, 389, 420–21, 423, 427, 430–31, 451, 528
Glenn, Archibald 32
Godley, General Sir Alexander
  AIF 3rd Division 275, 283
  Anzac Day 245
  background 161–62
  Battle of Amiens 377, 382
  Battle of Sari Bair 211–12
  Gallipoli 172, 189–91, 194–95, 200, 209–12, 216–19, 222–26, 529
  II Anzac Corps 239–40, 243, 268, 273, 294
  JM 164–65, 238, 241, 248, 270, 274, 286, 288–89, 301, 307, 308
  New Zealand Expeditionary Force 529
  Passchendaele 302, 303, 305, 306
  style of command 174, 176–80, 280, 290, 294–95
Godley, Lady 208

gold rushes in Victoria 1, 98
Goldstein, Major Jacob 33, 34
Gordon VC, Lance Corporal Bernard 396, 413
Gordon, General Charles 27
Gough, General Sir Hubert 268, 278, 290, 293, 302, 316, 338
Gower, W. E. 485
Gowrie, Earl of 317
Graetz (uncle) 16
Graham & Wadick 39, 43–44, 62, 66
Grange, Baronne de la 270
Grant, General Ulysses S. 134, 136
Greece 154
Grieve, Captain R. C. 283
Grimwade, Major General H. W. 255, 499, 509
Gummow, Forest & Co 101
Gummow, Frank 81–83, 92, 94, 101, 103, 112, 132

H
Haig, Field Marshal Douglas
  AIF 1st Division 357, 431
  AIF 3rd Division 257, 268–69, 279, 283–84, 296, 447
  Anzac Day 460, 461
  Australian Corps 297, 307–8, 314, 330, 338–39, 342, 358
  Battle of Amiens xv–xviii, 363–67, 370, 381, 382
  Battle of Hamel 345, 346, 350–52, 356
  Birdwood 340, 469
  British Fourth Army 392–93
  Broodseinde 302

cavalry 439, 442
Currie 307, 528
Foch 359–60
George V 262, 383
Hindenburg Line 433
historical treatment 495–96, 503
Hughes 417
JM 274, 291, 310, 388
Lloyd George 417
Passchendaele 292, 294, 301–3, 306, 393
Plumer 279, 284, 289
Rawlinson 395, 399
reward 473
Somme 250, 312
style of command 135–36, 290, 422
use of tanks 343
Western Front 278–80, 307–9, 447
Ypres 289, 293, 294
Hall, Lieutenant Colonel 75, 90
Hall VC, Corporal Arthur 407, 413
Hallahan, Captain Wally 427
Hamel (France) 322, 326–28, 343–44 *see also* Battle of Hamel
Hamilton, General Sir Ian
    AIF 2nd (Anzac) Division command 167
    author 489
    Battle of Krithia 188
    Battle of Sari Bair 204–5, 209, 211, 216, 222
    dismissal 228–30, 231
    Gallipoli 173–74, 178–83, 189–90, 192, 226

Gallipoli command 167–68, 170, 172
    JM 140–44, 150–52, 201–3, 327, 454, 521–23
Hanby, Gordon 185
Harbour Trust 60, 62, 64–67
Haret el Wasser (Egypt) 171
Hargicourt Line *see* Hindenburg Line
Harington, Major General C. H. 'Tim' 268, 273, 275, 277, 279, 280, 302, 306
Harper, H. R. 467
Hawthorn City Council (Vic) 109–10
Hawthorn (Melbourne) 23–24
Heliopolis (Egypt) 161
Henderson, G. F. R. 134, 135
Herald (Melbourne) 483–84
Herald (Melbourne) 496, 499–500, 512, 526
Herbert, A. P. 199
Herleville (France) 389, 391
High Court of Australia 98, 111
Hindenburg, Field Marshal von 279, 325, 378, 380, 502, 525
Hindenburg Line 279, 395, 397, 406, 408–11, 445, 448
    attack on 418, 420, 421, 423
    Beaurevoir Line 423, 431, *435*, 438–39
    Bellicourt tunnel 434–37, *435*
    Hargicourt Line 423–24, *425*, 427–28
    Hindenburg Main Line 423, 431–32, 433–34, *435*
    Hindenburg Outpost Line 423–24

Le Catelet Line 423, 431, *435*, 436

Line of the Meuse and Rhine 445

Hitler, Adolf 274, 379, 502, 508, 522–23, 525

HMS *Hampshire* 249

Hobbs, Lieutenant General Sir Talbot xvii, 271, 347, 349, 356, 382, 396, 398, 402, 405, 407, 423, 434–36, 447, 450–51, 460, 529

Hodges, Justice 107

Hodgson family (Melbourne) 20

Hoggart, Captain 185

Holmes, Brigadier General W. 240, 271

Holroyd, Justice 107

'Home Rule' in Ireland 144–46

Hooker, General Joseph 134

Hore-Ruthven, Alexander 317

Hudson, P. B. 483

Hughes, Colonel F. G. 145

Hughes, W. M. (Billy)
   AIF 417–19, 447–48
   Australian Corps 329–30, 333–34, 337–39, 342, 352, 358–59, 385–87
   Battle of Hamel 346–47, 356
   British War Council 256
   British War Office 369
   conscription 265–66
   demobilisation and repatriation 449–50, 457–60, 502–3
   Haig 309, 417
   JM 240–41, 243, 250, 297, 444
   Murdoch 229, 307
   Nationalist Party 276–77

political career 524–25

political rivalry with JM 454–55, 457, 464, 466, 469–70, 472–74, 476, 478, 494–95, 510

USA 416

Vic Monash 170, 241, 297

100 Hints for Company Commanders (pamphlet, Monash) 139

Hunter-Weston, General 178, 180–81

Huntsman family (Melbourne) 20

Hutchinson (publishers) 466–67

I

Ibsen, Henrik 54

Imperial Patriots (NSW) 503

India 125, 268, 508, 511–12

Ingram VC, Lieutenant George 440

Institute of Architects 499

Institute of Engineers 506

'Iona', Toorak (Melbourne) 133

Ireland 144–46

Irvine, Major F. D. 186, 195

Irving, Brigadier General G. G. H. 244

Isaacs, Sir Isaac 107–11, 114, 492, 508, 526

J

Jacka VC, Lieutenant Albert 197–98, 202, 203, 211, 250, 291, 295, 391, 393, 413, 492, 529–30

Jackson, General Andrew 173

Jackson, Lieutenant Colonel G. H.

F. 250, 254, 255, 259

Jackson, Stonewall 125, 134, 410

James, Walter 91

Japan 119–20, 141, 149

Jerilderie Herald 21–23, 82

Jerilderie (NSW) 7–8, 14–16, 82–85, 87, 456–57

Jess, Captain C. H. 151, 153

Jobson, Brigadier A. 255

Joffre, General Joseph Jacques Césaire 230

Johnston, Brigadier General Francis E. 154, 180, 190–92, 216, 481–82

Joncourt (France) 434, 437

Julius Caesar 121, 125

K

Kalgoorlie (WA) 89

Kangaroo (Lawrence) 530

Kannaluik v. City of Hawthorn 109–10

Kapp, Wolfgang 502

Kavanagh, General 367

Kelly, Ned 14–17, 82, 456–57

Kemal, Lieutenant Mustafa 178, 184, 188, 206, 210, 221–23, 226, 233, 237, 242, 483, 507, 523

Kemnitz, Mathilde von 525

Kerensky, Alexander 289

Kernot, Professor W. C. 27, 57–58, 60, 82, 83, 103–4, 140

Keynes, John Maynard 505

Kidgell, Lieutenant-General 296

Kipling, Rudyard 456

Kirkpatrick, John 196–97, 202, 295

Kitchener, Field-Marshall Earl 231

Kitchener, Lord Horatio 125–28, 140–41, 143, 152, 158–59, 163, 164, 167–68, 180, 204–5, 208, 211, 226, 229, 230, 237, 243–44, 249, 262, 522

KK Club 491

Kressenstein, Kress von 160, 163

Krotoszyn (formerly Krotoschin, Poland) 1, 3, 5, 130–31

Kruger, Paul 93

Krupp (firm) 392

L

La Houssoie (France) 250–51

LaTrobe Valley (Vic) 477, 484–85, 507

Lambert, General 398

Lands Board of New South Wales 83, 85

Landys Dream Gold Mining Co. 75–76

Larkhill (UK) 254, 288, 327

Lawrence, D. H. 530

Lawrence, Sir Henry 381, 382

Lawson, Harry 467, 482

Le Cateau (France) 449, 450

Le Catelet Line *see* Hindenburg Line

Le Gerche, A. R. 485

Le Verguier (France) 424–26

League of Nations 472, 490

Lee, General Robert E. 134

Legacy movement 499, 528

Legge, Colonel J. G. 149, 150, 152, 156, 241–42, 249, 271, 272

Lemnos (Greece) 172

Lenin, Vladimir 312
'Lessons of the Wilderness
    Campaign – 1864' (essay,
    Monash) 134–37, 348–49
Lewis, Jim 26, 33, 38, 58, 64, 66
Liberal Party of Australia 525
Liddell Hart, Sir Basil xviii–xix,
    489
Lille (France) 290, 448
Lilydale (Vic) 140–44, 454
Lindsay, Norman 488
Littlejohn, William 503
Lloyd George, David xviii, 158,
    229, 269, 307–9, 417, 447
Locke, Lieutenant 214
London (UK) 129–30, 288, 369,
    452
Longstaff, John 369, 444, 465,
    488
Lowerson VC, Sergeant Albert
    402–3, 413
Ludendorff, General Erich xvii,
    299, 315, 378–80, 388, 390,
    391, 398, 409, 448, 502, 508,
    525–26
Lyons, Joe 524–25

M
McCarthy VC, Lieutenant
    Lawrence 390–91, 413
McCaughey, David and Samuel
    82–87
McCay, Colonel James Whiteside
    8th Infantry Regiment
        command 117
    AIF 2nd Brigade command
        148–49, 153
    AIF 3rd Division 340

AIF 5th Division command
    241, 244–45, 271
Australian Intelligence Corps
    120, 134, 137, 138
Bridges 162
character 117
Citizens' Protection Committee
    481–83
Companion of the Order of the
    Bath 230
death 510
farewell dinner 466
Gallipoli 181, 196
influence 150, 152, 243
JM 340
Scotch College 17, 340
MacDonald, Ramsay 521
McFarland, J. H. 153
McGee VC, Sergeant Lewis 300,
    305–6
McGlinn, Lieutenant Colonel J. P.
    151, 155, 166, 167, 170,
    181–82, 208, 234, 244, 245,
    487, 498
McInerney, Major 145–46,
    152–53, 164, 208, 243, 510
MacLaurin, Colonel H. N. 153,
    181, 184, 186, 189–90, 195,
    378
McNicoll, Brigadier W. R. 255,
    300–301, 305, 316, 318, 341,
    401, 437
McPherson, Sir William 501–2
Mactier VC, Private Robert 404,
    413
Majestic (ship) 203
Maloney, Dr William 146, 277
Manesse, Bertha see Monash,

Bertha (née Manesse, mother)
Manesse, Jacob and Charlotte
  (maternal grandparents) 4–5,
  130
Mangin, General 366–67
Mariana and Marshall Islands 149
Martin & Monash (firm) 2, 3, 6
Martin, Louis 2, 5–6
Marwitz, General van der 449
Marx, Karl 43, 114
Mary, Queen 455
Meeson, Dora 488
Melba, Dame Nellie 93
Melbourne City Council (MCC)
  480–81, 484, 487, 496, 499
Melbourne Club 132, 491–92
Melbourne Cricket Ground
  (MCG) 515
Melbourne Cup 84, 483, 489
Melbourne Electricity
  Commission (MEC) 485
Melbourne Electricity Supply Co.
  479, 484–85
Melbourne Symphony Orchestra
  487
Melbourne Town Hall (banquet)
  492–94
Melbourne University 487, 515
Melbourne University Review
  26–27, 30
Melbourne (Vic) 2, 32–33, 59–60,
  63–64, 86, 113, 132, 470,
  481–83
Menin Road (Ypres) 295, 298–99
Menzies, Robert 501–2, 525, 527
Messines Ridge (Ypres) 274,
  277–79, 282–86, *285*, 290,
  314, 323

Milfordhaven, Marquis of 455
Military Board (Commonwealth)
  117, 119, 137–38, 144, 150,
  152, 153
Militia Garrison Artillery (Coastal)
  75 *see also* North Melbourne
  Battery
Mill, John Stuart 34, 64
Millen, E. D. 150
Mills, Sir James 444–45
Milner, Lord 338
Mitchell, A. G. M. 477–78, 481
Mitchell, David 93, 97, 106, 108,
  109, 112, 115–16
Mitchell, Edward 107
Moltke, Helmuth von 134
Monasch (becomes Monash) 2
Monash & Anderson
  Anderson *see* Anderson, Joshua
    T. Noble
  Anderson Street bridge
    (Melbourne) 83, 92
  Fyansford bridge (near Geelong,
    Vic) 92, 94–95, 105–10
  JM 68–70, 75–76, 79, 85,
    94–95
  King's Bridge (Bendigo, Vic) 96,
    97, 101–4, 106
  Kyneton, Ballarat, Mansfield,
    Upper Coliban bridges 109
  Monier bridges in Bendigo
    95–97, 101, 103, 105–6
  Monier Pipe Company 93, 106,
    109, 111
  Monier process rights 101–4, 107
  RCMPCC *see* RCMPCC
  Tambo River bridge (Bruthen)
    96

Wheeler's Creek bridge (near Creswick, Vic) 92–93, 95, 96

Monash, Bertha (daughter)
correspondence with JM 174, 208–9, 451
early life 63, 70, 71, 73, 76, 85, 89, 116, 128–30, 133, 155, 170–71
inheritance 506–7
later life 518
Lizette Bentwich 475, 500, 508
marriage to Gershon Bennett 478–79
My Trip with Dad to France – May 1919 465–66
organises state funeral 514
Osmonde 468
reunion with JM 462–65

Monash, Bertha (née Manesse, mother) 4–5, 7–12, 20, 23, 28, 31

Monash, Julius (uncle) 4, 6, 7

Monash, Leo (cousin) 21

Monash, Lieutenant General Sir John: characteristics
ambition 137, 311, 507–10
appearance 12, 113–14, 133, 151, 253–54, 259, 416–17
attributes and skills 36, 46, 78, 163–64, 196–97, 202–3, 267, 321–22, 326–27, 357
aversion to war 394, 463, 471
background (German and Jewish) xix, 150–53, 164, 208–9, 241, 242, 248, 261, 269, 277, 281, 329, 330, 339, 340, 379, 392, 453, 490, 491–92

coup makers 502–3, 507–10, 512–13
desire for recognition 286–87, 335, 454
faith in the Anzacs 393–94
interests 8, 26, 38, 65, 133, 166–67, 183, 210–11, 456, 487–89
military historian 134–35, 140, 335–36
patriotism 22, 94
politics 114, 490
ruthless streak 137, 144, 197, 211, 266, 283, 405–6, 493
vanity 227–28

Monash, Lieutenant General Sir John: education
Argus scholarship 58
engineering degree 57–58
exams 17, 18, 22–23, 24, 26–27, 32, 36–37, 57–58, 61, 63, 66
law 61–63, 66
mathematics 8, 17, 18, 27, 32
Melbourne University 19–20, 24–28, 34, 36–37, 39
Scotch College 10–12, 15, 17–18
South Yarra College 9–10

Monash, Lieutenant General Sir John: engineering career
engineering degree 57–58
engineering projects 32–33, 35–38, 55, 58, 60
Fairfield viaduct 47
Harbour Trust 60, 62, 64–67
lectures 140
Monash & Anderson *see* Monash & Anderson

Outer Circle Railway 38–41,
43–44, 58, 65, 88, 102
patents 68, 109
Péronne railway station 410–11
Peter Nicol Russell Memorial
Medal 506
Princes Bridge (Melbourne)
33–37, 58, 64, 102, 116, 515
Queen's Bridge (Melbourne) 38
Monash, Lieutenant General Sir
John: legal career
Age case 65–66, 69
Austral Otis Engineering Co.
79–80
Baxter & Saddler 80, 82, 84,
86–88, 90–91
Blackwood V. McCaughey 86–87
Fyansford case 106–10
Graham & Wadick 62, 66
Haret el Wasser court of enquiry
171
Kannaluik v. City of Hawthorn
110
law degree 61–63, 66
mine lift accident 70
patents 68, 109
Western Australia 87–90
Monash, Lieutenant General Sir
John: military career
AIF 2nd (Anzac) Division 4th
Brigade command *see* AIF
2nd (Anzac) Division 4th
Brigade
AIF 4th Division new 4th
Brigade command 239
army cadet training 13–14
Australian Intelligence Corps
117–21

Battle of Amiens *see* Battle of
Amiens
Battle of Chuignes and Bray *see*
Battle of Chuignes and Bray
Battle of Dernancourt *see* Battle
of Dernancourt
Battle of Hamel *see* Battle of
Hamel
Battle of Hargincourt *see* Battle
of Hargicourt
Battle of Mont St Quentin *see*
Battle of Mont St Quentin
Battle of Péronne *see* Battle of
Péronne
Battle of Sari Bair *see* Battle of
Sari Bair
commands xi, 239, 243, 271,
289, 294, 296–97, 388
Companion of the Order of the
Bath 230, 260, 265
Croix de Guerre (Belgian) 446
Croix de Guerre with Palm Leaf
(French) 446
Deputy Chief Censor 148–50
Director-General of
Repatriation and
Demobilisation 450, 457–60
Distinguished Service Medal
(USA) 446
Grand Officer of the Order of
the Crown (Belgian) 446
Knight Commander of the Bath
xviii, 310, 383–85, 467
Knight Grand Cross of the Order
of St Michael and St George
(GCMG) 457, 466, 470
Langwarrin and Seymour
exercises 1908–1911 123,

125, 127–28, 134
Messines Ridge (Ypres) *see*
  Messines Ridge
North Melbourne Battery *see*
  North Melbourne Battery
Oxford and Cambridge
  honorary degrees 466
Passchendaele *see* Passchendaele
  (Flanders)
rank 37–38, 45, 48–49, 75–79,
  118, 138, 208, 347
Scullin honour 506
Stanley–Monash gun invention
  45–46, 54, 62, 291
13th Infantry Brigade 138–44,
  148–49
Victorian Rifles (4th Battalion)
  25, 27–28, 30–31, 33
War Course at Sydney
  University 123–25, 134
Monash, Lieutenant General Sir
  John: military science
airpower 249–50, 257, 292–93,
  344, 355, 363, 367–68, 433
applications to warfare 25, 45,
  60, 70–71, 90, 127–28
bayonets 391
communications 127, 139–40,
  304, 399
infantry protection 124,
  191–92, 193–94, 309
machine guns 312–13
mapping 119–21, 125, 127,
  168, 173, 205, 209, 423–24
mobile battery guns 396
planning, tactics and strategy
  xii–xiii, 121–23, 142–44,
  156–57, 164, 295, 388

psychology 280–81, 318
raids 271–72, 280–81, 356
role of politicians 348–49, 419,
  503
slouch hat brim 267, 281
smoke screens 291, 345, 375,
  396
style of command 63, 157, 172,
  201–2, 266–67, 339–40,
  342, 372–73
tanks xvi, 257, 263, 287, 293,
  343–44, 354–55, 363, 367,
  424
use of conferences 188–89, 342,
  345–46, 370, 389, 430
views 114, 135–37
war games 121–23, 127, 134
Monash, Lieutenant General Sir
  John: relationships
after Vic's death 474
Annie Gabriel *see* Gabriel
girls 23, 29–30, 40, 445
Lizette Bentwich *see* Bentwich
Vic Moss *see* Monash
Monash, Lieutenant General Sir
  John: rites of passage
bar mitzvah 15–16
birth 6
early life 7
first car 132–33
fiftieth birthday at Gallipoli
  207–8
illness and death 504, 513–16
Monash, Louis (father)
early life and immigration to
  Australia 1–6
illness and death 58, 60–61,
  72–73

influence on JM 29, 44, 70, 114
Jerilderie 7–8, 14–16
money-lending business 22–23, 32
Narrandera 19, 22
Monash, Louise (sister) *see* Rosenhain
Monash, Mathilde (sister) 7, 8, 19, 28, 32, 48, 49, 51, 55, 59, 60, 70, 74, 85, 108, 506
Monash, Max (uncle) 3, 5, 7, 16, 19
Monash, Ulrike *see* Roth
Monash, Lady Victoria 'Vic' (née Moss)
  Andersons 68
  Argus 153
  correspondence with JM 174, 189, 208–9, 230, 310–11, 451
  courtship and wedding 47–51, 53–59
  death 468–71
  East Melbourne 108
  farewells JM 155
  gives birth to Bertha 63
  health 133, 238
  Hughes 241
  Kitchener 126
  marriage 70–71, 73–76, 85, 95, 116–17
  Purple Cross Service 170
  reunion with JM 462–65
  travel 128–29, 130
  Western Australia 88–90
Monier, Joseph 80–82
Monier Pipe Company 93, 106, 109, 111 *see also* RCMPCC

Monier process 83, 85, 92–93, 97, 101–4, 106, 107, 132
Mont St Quentin (France) *see* Battle of Mont St Quentin
Montbrehain (France) *415*, 440–42
Montenegro 154
Montgomery, Field Marshal Bernard Law xviii
Montgomery-Massingberd, Archibald 342, 350–51, 363–64, 382, 399, 409, 421–22, 436, 489
Monument Wood (Villers-Bretonneux) 360
Moran, J. B. 13, 258
Morrison, Dr Alexander 11–14, 18, 20, 23, 258
Morrison, Robert 13, 20, 23, 258
Morshead, Lieutenant Colonel L. J. 400
Moses Moses 12, 18, 20
Moss, Aubrey (nephew) 255, 339
Moss, Belle 49, 71
Moss, David 71
Moss, Moton 47
Moss, Victoria 'Vic' *see* Monash
Mueller, Otto 13, 18, 20
Mullens, Major General 321
Mulligan, Major E. N. 467–68
Munro, Sir Charles 230
Munro, David 33, 37–39
Munro Ferguson, Sir Ronald 142–43, 151, 248, 250, 265–66, 334, 385–86, 457, 469–70, 472, 473, 508
Murdoch, Keith
  AIF 416, 417–18, 420–21

AJA 165
Australian Corps 330–39, 347, 349, 352, 358–59, 385–87
Australian Victories in France in 1918 (Monash) 467
career 526
conscription 265
demobilisation and repatriation 458–59, 510
Gallipoli 228–29, 231
Hughes 229, 307
Ozanne 276–77
Shrine of Remembrance 483–84, 496, 499–500
White 450
Murdoch, Rupert 526
Murdoch, Will 22
Murray, General Sir Archibald 243, 245
Murrumbidgee River 87
Mussolini, Benito 502, 508
My Trip with Dad to France – May 1919 (Bertha Monash) 465–66
Myanmar Expedition (1886–1902) 342
Myers, Morris 12
Myers, Reverend Isadore 12

N
Nanson, E. J. 27
Napoleon Bonaparte 121, 125, 134, 336, 357, 516
Narrandera (NSW) 8, 19, 22
National Socialist Party (Nazis) 502, 525
National–Country coalition 495
Nationalist Party 276, 505, 524
Nauroy (France) 434

Naval and Military Club (Melbourne) 145–46, 502
Nelson, John 13
Neuve Chapelle (France) 362
New Delhi (India) 508, 511–12
New Guard 502
New Zealand Division 277, 280, 282, 294–95, 297–98, 303–6
New Zealand Infantry Brigade 154, 172, 178–80, 190–91, 211, 218, 224, 227
New Zealand Mounted Rifles 154, 211, 223, 227
Newbury, A. E. 488
Nicholas II, Tsar 158, 168, 289
Nicholson, Alexander 482
Nieppe (France) 286
Nivelle, General Robert 279, 365
Norfolk Island 530
North Melbourne Battery (Militia Garrison Artillery): JM
activities 46, 60, 62, 77
commands 63, 79, 100, 117
coronial investigation 37–38
Easter Camps 67
joins 33, 34
official leave 90
Pfalz (ship) 149
North Melbourne Electric Tramways and Lighting Co. 480
Northcliffe, Lord 127, 334, 452
nurses 157, 294

O
O'Connor, Arthur 416
O'Connor, C. Y. 91
O'Keefe, General 385
Osmonde (ship) 468, 470

Otago Battalion (NZ) 190–91
Otranto (ship) 129
Ottoman Empire 99, 154, 158, 172
Outtrim, Major F. L. 75, 76
Overton, Major Percy 213–15
Ozanne, A. T. 276, 281, 297

P
Palestine Welfare League 490
Papua New Guinea 98, 120, 149
Paris (France) 249, 275, 315
Passchendaele (Flanders) *285*, 292, 294, 296, 297, 301–7, 365, 393
Paterson, Agnes 500
Paterson, Esther 488
Paterson, Laing & Bruce 495
Pearce, George F. 150, 152–53, 193, 208, 241, 248, 250, 286, 329, 332–34, 339, 386, 419, 448, 472
Peeler, Lance Corporal Walter 299–300
Péronne (France) *see* Battle of Péronne
Perry, Captain B. H. 185
Pershing, General 349–50, 355
Pétain, Field Marshal 279, 361
Pfalz (ship) 149
Ploegsteert Wood 323
Plumer, Field Marshal
  AIF 3rd Division 283, 294
  British Second Army 282, 283, 295
  Broodseinde 301
  JM 310, 337–38
  limited objective strategy 289, 290

Passchendaele 301, 303, 306
  Western Front 268, 270, 273–75, 278–80
  Ypres 293
Polygon Wood (Ypres) 295–96, 529
Pope, Colonel 215, 219–20, 225, 239, 245, 246
Port Fairy (Vic) 46
Portland Freezing Co. 79–80
Preston Reservoir (Vic) 115
Priestley, J. B. 126
Privy Council (UK) 108, 110, 111
Proctor, Thea 488
Prussian revolution (1848) 114
Prussian wars 134
Punch 151
Purple Cross Service 170

Q
Queen Elizabeth (ship) 178, 180
Quinn, Captain 188
Quinn's Post (Anzac Cove) 184–85, 187–89, 194, 195

R
racism 152, 337, 453, 469
RAF 354
Rankine, W. J. M. 104
Rawlinson, Sir Henry
  AIF 350–52, 357, 375–77, 447
  Australian Corps 388
  background 342
  Battle of Amiens xv–xvii, 361, 363–69, 382
  Battle of Hamel 345
  Battle of Mont St Quentin 399
  British Fourth Army 392–95

Foch 381
Haig 439
Hindenburg Line 421–22, 433, 436, 438–39
historical treatment 495–96, 503
JM 337–38, 410
Mont St Quentin 409
Murdoch 338
mutiny charges 431
reward 473
Somme 250, 351, 422
RCMPCC (Reinforced Concrete and Monier Pipe Construction Company) 111–12, 115, 118, 128, 132, 467, 475–76 *see also* Monier Pipe Company
Read, Major General G. W. 432
Red Baron (von Richthofen) 324
Richardson, J. R. 95–97, 101–4
Richhill Terrace (West Melbourne) 6
Richmond Hill (Melbourne) 7
Richmond (Melbourne) 60
Richthofen, Manfred von (Red Baron) 324
Riviera (France) 275–76, 315
Robbins, Sergeant F. J. 390–91
Roberts, 1st Earl 145
Roberts, Tom 488
Robinson, Sir Arthur 482
Rosenhain, Louise (sister) 7, 8, 28, 32, 70, 74, 85, 108, 129, 264, 288, 475, 506
Rosenhain, Mona, Nancy and Peggy 506
Rosenhain, Walter 129, 131, 253–54, 267, 467, 475, 506

Rosenthal, Major General Sir C.
  AIF 2nd Division command 340, 530
  AIF 9th Brigade command 305, 316, 318, 320
  background 151–53
  Battle of Amiens 382
  Battle of Mont St Quentin 398, 401–2, 423
  Hindenburg Line 438–42
  JM 315, 396
  Monument Wood (Villers-Bretonneux) 360
Roth, Herman (cousin) 108
Roth, Karl (cousin) 108
Roth, Louis (cousin) 108
Roth, Mathilde (cousin) 506
Roth, Max 22, 32
Roth, Sophie (cousin) 506
Roth, Ulrike (née Monash, aunt) 4, 6, 7, 16, 18, 22, 108, 150, 503
Royal Australian Navy 156
Royal Military College, Duntroon 530
Royal Navy 167
Roye (France) 371, 376
RSL (Returned Soldiers League) 471, 472, 478, 491, 492, 494, 496, 499, 505, 506
Russell, Brigadier General Andrew 223, 225, 230, 249, 270, 294–95, 303, 306
Russia 128, 147, 158–59, 168, 230, 296, 490 *see also* Bolshevik revolution
Russo–Japanese War (1904–05) 119, 134, 141, 180, 204

Rutledge, Sir Arthur 84
Ryan, Private John 437

S
Saddler (investor) 93, 108, 109 *see also* Baxter & Saddler
Salomons, Sir Julian 86
Samson, Edmund Augustus 13, 258
Sanders, Otto Liman von 169, 173, 197, 210, 212, 221, 237, 242
Sargent, J. S. 456
Sari Bair (Gallipoli) *see* Battle of Sari Bair
Savige, Stanley 528
Sclater, Lieutenant General Sir Henry 258, 259, 267
Scotch College (Melbourne) 10–12, 15, 17–18, 23, 26, 117, 258, 340, 503–4, 515
Scots Church Literary Society 20
Scottish Presbyterian Free Church 11
Scullin, James 505–9, 526
Seangchoon (ship) 178, 179
SEC *see* State Electricity Commission of Victoria
Semmens, Major J. M. 119
Serbia 147, 154
Shaw, W. B. 88–89
Shew, Frank 13, 258
Shrine of Remembrance (Melbourne) 483–84, 496, 497, 499–500, 510, 514, 516
Siegfried Line *see* Hindenburg Line
Simonson, Paul (nephew) 255, 315, 318, 339, 446, 451

Simpson, John 196–97, 202, 295
Sinclair-MacLagan, Major General E. G. 153, 186, 293, 316, 350, 356, 369, 371, 377, 382, 420–21, 423, 428, 432–33, 436, 530
Smith, Adam 34, 43
Smith, C. P. 157
Smithers, A. K. 409–10
Smith's Weekly 476
Smyth VC, Brigadier General N. M. 271, 340
Somerville, Lieutenant General G. C. 341
Somme Valley (France) xv, xvii, 250, 251, 269, 312, 317–21, 323, 325, 351, 360, 376, 377, 397, 422
South African War (1899–1902) 93–94, 125, 145–46, 163, 268
South Australia 112, 115
Speight, Richard 65
Spencer, Herbert 34
Spofforth, Fred 22
Staff Officer's Scrap Book During the Russo–Japanese War (Hamilton) 141
Stanley, Major General John 37, 45, 138, 445
Stanley–Monash gun 45–46, 54, 62, 291, 445
State Electricity Commission of Victoria 467, 476–81, 484–85, 501–2, 504, 505, 507, 512
Steele, Will 66
Steen, Countess van der 270
Steenwerck (Belgium) 267–69
Stockfeld, Clara 445

Stopford, Lieutenant Sir Frederick 221–22

Story of Anzac (Bean) 523–24

Streeton, Arthur 488, 520

Sudan 27–28, 94, 125, 148, 231, 268, 342

Suez Canal 160, 237

Sullivan, Sergeant 25

Swanson, J. W. 480–81

Swinburne, George 467

Sydney Morning Herald 150, 165–66

Syme, David 65–66, 69

T

Tasmania 106

Tel el Kebir (Egypt) 243, 245, 496

Temperley, Major 224

Theilloye, Comte de 320

Thompson, Lance Corporal H. H. 408

Thomson, James S. 18

Tilney, Lieutenant Colonel 214, 246, 247

Times (London) 229

Towner VC, Lieutenant Edgar 404, 413

Traill, Jessie 488

Triumph (ship) 201

Trotsky, Leon 312

Tulloch, Major General Sir A. B. 67, 71

Tulloch MC, Lieutenant Colonel E. W. 427

Turkey xii, 99, 147, 154, 158–60, 163, 167–69, 176–78, 181–83, 188, 197–99, 233, 237 *see also* Kemal, Lieutenant Mustafa

U

Ulster (Northern Ireland) 144–46

Ulysses (ship) 156

United Australia Party 524–25

USA 110, 131, 135, 289, 349–52, 355, 378, 379, 416, 417, 421, 432–36, *435*, 493

V

Varley, Lieutenant A. S. 291

Vermandovillers (France) 390

Versailles Treaty 522, 524

Victoria Police 481–83, 527

Victoria, Queen 99–100, 261

Victorian District Military Command 137

Victorian Institute of Engineers 133

Victorian Rifles (militia force) 25, 27–28, 33

Victorian State Government 484, 499

Villers-Bretonneux (France) 322, 323, 325, 343, *353*, 360, 362, 370, 382, 449, 471, 529

Vimy Ridge (France) 528

W

Wagner, Richard 487–88

Walhalla (Vic) 75–76

Walker, Brigadier General Harold 180, 186, 189–90, 193, 194, 230, 241, 271, 340

Wanganella (NSW) 8

Want, J. H. 86–87

Wardrop, J. H. 483

Wark VC, Major Blair 434, 437

Warringah Constitutional Club (NSW) 503
Wealth of Nations (Smith) 43
Weathers VC, Corporal Lawrence 408, 413
Weizmann, Chaim 490
Wellington, Duke of 336, 357
Wesley Church Improvement Society 20, 24
Western Australia 87–90, 112, 529
Western District Brigade 75
Westminster, Duchess of 294
White Army (clandestine army) 483, 502, 527
'white Australia' Immigration Restriction Act 99
White, Major Cyril *see* White, Major General Sir C. C. Brudenell
White, Major General Sir C. C. Brudenell
  AIF 1st Division 153, 155
  AIF General Officer Commanding 329–31, 335, 347, 349, 358–59, 386
  Anzac Day 1927 498
  Australian Corps 308
  background 137–38
  Battle of Hamel 326–27
  Bean 165–66, 193
  Birdwood 240, 249, 254, 270, 286, 308
  Council of Defence 505
  farewell dinner 466
  Gallipoli 233, 240
  honours 531
  JM 137–38, 151, 312–13

Public Service Board 531
White Army 483, 527
Whitehead, Sergeant-Major 13–14
Whitlam, Gough 519–20
Wiener, Mathilde (paternal grandmother) 1, 5, 6, 131 *see also* Baer-Loebel
Wilhelm II, Kaiser 129, 147, 317
Wilkins, Hubert 331
Wilkinson, Lieutenant N. F. 441
Williams, Rabbi 58
Williamstown Rifle Range (Vic) 37–38, 102
Wilson, Lieutenant Colonel Arthur xii, xiv, xvi
Wilson, Sir Henry 381, 382, 447
Wilson, President Woodrow 455
Windmill Ridge (France) 291, 292, 391
Windsor, Duke of 522
Withers, Walter 488
Wood, Private James 426–27
Wootten, Major George 254–55
World War II 527
Wyass, G. A. 81
Wylly, Major G. G. E. 255

X
Xerxes 173

Y
Yallourn (Vic) 477, 484–85, 507
York, Duke of *see* Albert, Prince
Ypres (Flanders) 273–74, 277–79, 282–86, *285*, 289, 290, 292–96, 298–99, 314, 323, 363, 528

Z

Zeitz Co. (Germany) 478

Zichy-Woinarski, C. J. 26–27

Zionism 490

Zokolow, Nahum 490

Zox, E. L. 66